ESSAYS
on
HAITIAN
LITERATURE

ESSAYS
on
HAITIAN
LITERATURE

Léon-François Hoffmann

An Original by Three Continents

© Léon-François Hoffmann 1984

First Edition

ISBN: 0-89410-344-X
ISBN: 0-89410-345-8 (pbk)
LC No: 82-50882

Cover Art by Nick Clapp

Three Continents Press
1346 Connecticut Avenue, N.W.
Washington, D.C. 20036

ACKNOWLEDGMENTS

Parts of the following essays have already appeared, either in French or in English, in reviews whose editors have kindly permitted their inclusion. My gratitude goes to the *Caribbean Review,* for permission to include material from "The Originality of the Haitian Novel" and "Slavery and Race in Haitian Letters"; to *Études littéraires* for permission to include material translated from "Les États-Unis et les Américains dans les lettres haïtiennes"; to *Présence africaine* for permission to include material translated from "L'image de la femme dans la poésie haïtienne" and to *Conjonction,* for permission to include material translated from "En marge de *Stella.*"

Grants from the National Endowment for the Humanities and from Princeton University's Program in Latin American Studies have enabled me to make several trips to Haiti, where I have worked mostly in the Collège Saint Louis de Gonzague Collection. I am grateful to its curator, frère Constant, for his unstinting assistance and suggestions. Maureen Johnson has labored long and hard to rid my English prose of infestations of Gallicisms.

BOOKS BY LÉON-FRANÇOIS HOFFMANN:

Romantique Espagne. Paris: Presses Universitaires de France, 1961.

La Peste à Barcelone. Paris: Presses Universitaires de France, 1964.

L'Essentiel de la grammaire française. New York: Charles Scribner's Sons, 1964.

Répertoire géographique de "La Comédie humaine." Vol. I: L'Étranger. Paris: J. Corti, 1965.

Travaux pratiques. Munich: Max Hueber, 1968.

Répertoire géographique de "La Comédie humaine." Vol. II: La Province. Paris: J. Corti, 1968.

Le Nègre romantique, personnage littéraire et obsession collective. Paris: Payot, 1973.

La Pratique du français parlé. New York: Charles Scribner's Sons, 1973.

Le Roman haïtien: Idéologie et structure. Sherbrooke: Naaman, 1982.

TABLE OF CONTENTS

Introduction 3
Haitian Literature: An Overview 11
The Linguistic Situation in Haiti 29
Slavery and Race in Haitian Letters 49
The U.S. and Americans in Haitian Letters 67
The Image of Woman in Haitian Poetry 87
The First Haitian Novel: Émeric Bergeaud's "Stella" 109

Bibliography of Critical Studies
on Haitian Literature 123
Bibliography of Works
Mentioned in Text 169

Index 181

INTRODUCTION

The Republic of Haiti is somewhat smaller than Belgium and somewhat larger than New Hampshire; three quarters of her territory is steeply mountainous. Practically all of the six million inhabitants live in the lowlands, making these narrow plains among the most densely populated areas of the world.

The all but deserted Western third of Hispaniola was ceded by Spain to France in 1697, and, during the 17th and 18th centuries, a relatively large number of Frenchmen settled in the colony, which they called Saint-Domingue. From about 1740 on, Saint-Domingue's economy boomed, the prosperity of the colony resting on tropical cash crops, coffee, and sugar in particular. By 1789, it accounted for as much as 50% of France's foreign trade.

As did the other New World "sugar colonies," Saint-Domingue drew its work force from Africa. It is difficult to estimate how many millions of slaves were deported to the colony: they were so brutally exploited that, on the average, they survived no more than seven years after reaching the plantations. Probably as many as half of the 400,000 slaves in Saint-Domingue at the eve of the revolution had been born in Africa.

Saint-Domingue was organized on the same model as the other West Indies. The 40,000 Whites (who either came from the métropole or had been born on the island) provided the cadres, the planters, the majority of the skilled workers, merchants, and artisans. The Black slaves provided the work force. Most of the 28,000 Mulattos formed an intermediate class which, theoretically, enjoyed all the rights of free men, but which came to be subjected to all sorts of humiliating discriminatory measures. The original Arawak population had succumbed to mistreatment and disease within one generation after having been "discovered" by the Europeans.

Yet the destiny of Haiti was to be radically different from that of "Anglo-Saxon" or "Iberian" America. Inspired by the French Revolutionary ideal of the "Rights of Man," a general slave uprising broke out in 1791. For the next twelve years, intermittent violence reigned in the colony. Free men were pitted against slaves, Whites against Blacks, partisans of accommodation with France against proponents of Independence, French troops first against local insurgents, later against Spanish, then English invaders, finally against the Haitian army. In 1802, Bonaparte tried to reestablish French rule and the institution of slavery—which had officially been abolished by decree on 16 Pluviôse II (February 4th, 1794). The 40,000 man expeditionary corps he sent to Saint-Domingue under the command of his brother-in-law, General Leclerc, was wiped out by the Haitians and their ally, yellow fever. This was the first time a Napoleonic army had ever been defeated, a fact still carefully kept out of French history school books. Jean-Jacques Dessalines proclaimed the Independence of Haiti on January 1, 1804. Haiti was consequently the first New World land—after the United States—to achieve nationhood. It was also the first, and, for a long time, was to remain the only Black republic in the world.*

The situation of the new state was far from auspicious. The country had been devastated by twelve years of savage fighting and by the scorched-earth policy of the insurgents. Those Europeans who had not perished or managed to flee were eliminated by Dessalines right after Independence. As a result, the country was left practically without trained administrators and technicians. Until its independence was recognized by the French (in 1825), and later by other major powers, the Haitians feared a return of their former masters; they were forced to earmark for national defence energies and resources badly needed for reconstruction and organization, the Haitian armed forces retaining its privileged position up to present times. Further, the major powers (France, of course, but also England, Spain and the United States) continued to collaborate in isolating Haiti, fearing that she would "export the revolution" and inspire their own slaves to rise.

Haitian history since Independence has been characterized—as has that of most of Latin America—by dependence upon and exploitation by, imperial powers: Germany and England as well as France and the United States—and by periods of political instability and irresponsibility. Government and civil service positions were and remain a means for members of the ruling class to enrich themselves. While repression has in general been relatively mild, it has occasionally been brutal. Haitian governments have done little to better the lives of the masses; it is calculated that about 80% of the population lives off the land . . . a land, however, which can no longer feed the population.

Up until about a generation ago, most Westerners did not even have a clear idea of where Haiti was. In the introduction to his *Black Democracy— The Story of Haiti,* first published in 1928, the American historian H.P. Davis wrote:

> When the average American hears of Haiti, if he does not confuse it with the island of Tahiti—thousands of miles away in the Pacific—he thinks of a small, unimportant West Indian country. (. . .) Of the Haitians themselves, their background, or present condition, the American people generally have no conception. (2nd rev. ed., New York, 1967, p. 3.)

In 1939, an English lady-traveler, Mabel Steedman, entitled her book *Unknown to the World: Haiti;* and, as late as 1955, Pierre Massoni, a

---

*The best overall treatment of the War of Independence remains C.L.R. James' *The Black Jacobins,* New York, 1963.

French essayist, also begins a mediocre book, *Haïti, reine des Antilles,* by reminding his readers that:

> Contrary to what many people, who confuse it with Tahiti, think, Haiti is not in Africa and even less in the South Pacific. (p. 11.)*

But today, if the word "Haiti" were to be used as a cue in a word-association test, most non-Haitians would in all probability be able to respond and, in their response, would mention poverty, political repression or frenzied pagan ritual. The media has dramatized the flight of desperate Haitians who sail flimsy boats to the Bahamas or to Florida. To specialists, this comes as no surprise. Already in 1949, the *Report of the United Nations Mission to Haiti* stated that:

> Haitian agriculture is faced with the grave problem of sustaining an expanding population on shrinking land resources. It is high time to arrest the dissipation of the basic wealth of the country and to reverse the trend. (. . .) The general standard of living is so low as not to permit of further compression. (pp. 3 & 6.)

A generation later, the trend has not been reversed, and the standard of living has been dramatically "further compressed."

When François Duvalier came to power in 1957, he organized the *Milice civile* (later to become the *Volontaires de la sécurité nationale).* With their jaunty hats and dark glasses, these impassive men—immediately baptised *tonton makout* ("bogeymen") by the population—captured the imagination of the Western public, always fascinated by all forms of ominous exoticism. The media did not fail to cater to this fascination. Graham Greene's novel about Duvalier's Haiti, *The Comedians* (London, 1966) was an international bestseller, and millions saw some of the most prestigious actors of the time starring in the film version, directed by Peter Glenville. The Créole terms *Papa Dok* and *Tonton Makout* became, if not household words, then close to it.

That there was a racialist dimension to this publicity seems to me evident. In no way do I wish to suggest that reprehensible actions of the Third World—and particulary Black—governments should not be exposed and denounced to world public opinion. But I am suggesting that Westerners have an unfortunate tendency to find them picturesque as well as sinister. Just as, when their rulers dilapidate vast sums on gaudy displays of luxury, Westerners are quick to wax indignant, but slow to remember that Western governments—and Eastern Bloc ones also, for that matter—have generally found reasons to supply them with the means to indulge in these displays.

The exotic aspect of Haitian culture which has most enthralled

*Except where otherwise indicated, all translations are mine, and strive for exactitude rather than elegance.

Westerners has been Vodùn,* the folk religion of Haiti, traditionally tolerated at best, and at worst forcibly suppressed by various Haitian regimes. The ruling Westernized élite has, until very recently, generally felt that vodùn contributes towards giving Haiti a pejorative image abroad. They fear that foreigners will advance it as a proof of African savagery, as evidence that Black men left to their own devices cannot reach true civilization. By and large, the Westernized élite's fears are well justified, for ever since foreigners have chosen to write about Haiti, whether in travel books or in works of fiction,they have associated vodùn with blood (the blood of sacrificed animals and human beings, preferably of children and pretty women), with loss of consciousness during "possession" trances, and—last but certainly not least—with lascivious dancing leading to unbridled sexual excesses. As early as 1793, in his otherwise admirable *Description (. . .) de la partie française de l'île Saint-Domingue,* M. Moreau de Saint-Méry describes what purports to be a vodùn ceremony, where some of the adepts

> in this Bacchanalia, tear up their clothes and even bite their own flesh; others who have only fallen unconscious are carried by the dancers into a nearby room, where a disgusting prostitution sometimes holds sway in the dark. Finally, exhaustion puts a stop to this spectacle, which is an insult to reason. (New rev. ed., 3 vols., Paris, 1958, Vol. I, p. 67-68.)

In his 1826 novel *Bug Jargal,* which takes place in Haiti during the revolution, Victor Hugo drew from such melodramatic nonsense to describe a vodùn dance. And a century and a half later, in Gérard de Villier's *Requiem pour tontons macoutes* (Paris, 1971), a young girl is raped and hacked to pieces in a Port-au-Prince cemetery, where her killers had gone to unearth bits and pieces of a political opponent's body for use in the preparation of magic charms.

English language authors have done no better. Sir Spencer St. John, erstwhile representative of Her Majesty's Government in Haiti, published his *Hayti or the Black Republic* in 1884. The book, which appeared in French translation two years later, did much to spread the myth that human sacrifices, and even cannibalism, were intrinsic elements of vodùn ritual. The titles of several later "eyewitness reports" on Haiti are revealing: William B. Seabrook's *Magic Island* (New York, 1929), for example, or John Houston Craige's *Cannibal Cousins* (New York, 1934), or Edna Taft's *A Puritan in Voodooland* (Philadelphia, 1938). Novelists also took advantage of—and perpetuated—their readers' tendency to identify Haiti

---

*The word *voodoo* connotes sorcery and mumbo-jumbo. I shall use *vodùn,* which most anthropologists use when referring to the form of Afro-American religion practiced in Haiti.

with primitive rites: Beale Davis in *The Goat Without Horns** (New York, 1925), Henry Bedford-Jones in *Drums of Dambala*** (New York, 1932) and Richard Dohrman in *The Cross of Baron Samedi*** (Boston, 1958) explicitly refer to vodùn in their title, but it is safe to say that few English-language novels which take place in Haiti fail to treat their reader to a vodùn ceremony or, at the very least, to the brewing of potions and the sticking of pins in rag dolls. In Don Smith's *Haitian Vendetta* (New York, 1973), CIA agent Phil Sherman is sent on a mission to Haiti, where he makes frenetic love to Michèle Delorme, a beautiful Mulatto girl who of course turns out to be a *mambo*, or vodùn priestess.

The association of Haiti with vodùn and of vodùn with erotic frenzy has—needless to say—been amply illustrated by the Hollywood movie industry. One can imagine the discouraged indignation with which Haitians must have watched Baron Samedi's dance, as performed by Geoffrey Holder in *Live and Let Die,* one of the latest James Bond epics. In one of the first serious books on vodùn, *Voodoo in Haiti* (Fr. ed., Paris, 1958; Engl. trans. by Hugo Charteris, New York, 1972), the anthropologist Alfred Métraux has ample reason to begin by reminding us that

> certain exotic words are charged with evocative power. Voodoo is one. It usually conjures up visions of mysterious deaths, secret rites—or dark saturnalia celebrated by "blood-maddened, sex-maddened, god-maddened" negroes. (p. 15.)

And one can certainly sympathize with the Haitian essayist Louis Élie who laments in his *Remarques sur le vaudoux* (typescript, n.d. ca. 1945):

> What crimes are the inhabitants of our unfortunate country expiating, to have provoked the disgusting outpourings of these vile scribblers? It seems as if an evil genie had forced travellers to see Haiti not as she is, but as a nightmare, a "Magic Island" fit only to serve as Satan's stamping grounds. (p. 15.)

Haitians rightly complain that even today—or perhaps one should say today more than ever—only rarely do foreigners mention the gentleness, dignity and courtliness of Haitians, rich and poor; only rarely do they know or care about the glory of the Haitian Revolution, surely one of the noblest episodes in the history of mankind; only rarely are they acquainted with the considerable Haitian contribution in the realms of music, of painting, of sculpture and of literature.

This is not the place to show what the pejorative image of Haiti abroad owes to the phantasms that haunt the Western subconscious. My hope is, rather, to contribute to a better knowledge of Haitian literature,

---

*This title is the translation of Créole *Kabwit san kòn,* which superstitious Haitians call a person whose death has presumably been arranged in exchange for a god's favors.

**Dambala and Baron Samedi are gods in the vodùn pantheon.

which is a venerable and illustrious literature.

The independence that Haitians won by the sword, they exalted and nurtured with the pen. From the very beginning, the written word in Haiti has served to affirm national and racial pride, and to scourge internal deleterious tendencies. Explicitly, of course, but also implicitly, as we shall see: every lyric poem, humorous short story, well-constructed drama or novel was one more proof that Haitians are neither "blood–," nor "sex–," nor "god–maddened," but rational, cultivated people, masters of that most rational creation of civilized humanity, the French language.

No wonder, then, that young Haitians have always received an essentially literary education, and studied the same classical texts chosen for the edification of French youths. The country has formed generations of good hellenists and excellent latinists, who were taught that literature is the noblest product of the human mind, and literature in French the noblest one of all. As much as, and sometimes more than money or power, to have had a poem, an article or a novel published is a source of great prestige—and not only among the intellectuals, as Dantès Bellegarde somewhat acidly remarked in an article for *La Ronde* on October 5th, 1898:

> You cannot imagine the prestige enjoyed here by the printed word in the eyes of the crowd. It is enough to have written just about anything for you to appear as a superior being.

Until quite recently, a number of fine literary reviews were published not only in Port-au-Prince but also in several provincial cities and, as Edmund Wilson wrote in *Red, Black, Blond and Olive* (New York, 1956):

> (. . .) this island, since the revolution of 1804, has produced a greater number of books in proportion to the population than any other American country, with the exception of the United States. (p. 110.)

Haitian literature is remarkable not only for its abundance but also for its quality. Thanks to anthologies and to the re-issue of titles long out of print, it is at last becoming better known abroad. A few Haitian novelists, such as Jacques Roumain, Jacques-Stéphen Alexis, and the Marcelin brothers, have been widely translated. Haitian writers have also benefitted from the recent interest in Caribbean and Black literatures.

Perhaps this discovery and appreciation of Haiti's literature will—if not counteract—at least counterbalance somewhat the negative image foreigners have of the country. Just as the starving Haitian child or the humiliated Haitian adult brings shame on all men, much of Haitian literature's dignity and strength is, for all men, a source of elation and pride.

HAITIAN LITERATURE: AN OVERVIEW

Since Independence, Haitian writers have been troubled by a fundamental question: is Haitian literature condemned to imitate French models, or is it destined to attain a specific originality? And if the latter, what can the characteristics of such originality be? With very few exceptions, Haitian writers have realized that, since their country is in no way a province of France, their literature ought of necessity to become something other than a regional variation of that of the linguistic "mother country." They have accepted and pursued their collective vocation: to define and cultivate authenticity and originality. This already difficult task has been made even more laborious by a series of objective factors which have always influenced Haitian literary production.

The Haitian writer can hope to reach directly only a fraction of the small literate minority of his countrymen. Haitian publishing houses are little better than printing establishments, and there are no bookstores in provincial cities. After bearing the entire cost of manufacturing the book, the author must organize its distribution as best he can. Printings seldom reach 500 copies; a writer is fortunate to recover a significant fraction of the sum he has invested. If at least the public supported and encouraged its writers! But it is seldom the case. For the Haitian public has been educated to admire the French authors exclusively; only in the last few years have schools, with much hesitation and caution, begun to introduce students to their national literary heritage. Intellectual snobbery proclaims that only foreign authors count, and considers Haitian writers as estimable at best, but essentially second-rate. In short, as Yvon Valcin put it, perhaps too categorically, in "Pour une promotion . . ." *(Rond-point,* juillet 1962): "The contempt of our community towards its national literature is a fact."

Since he writes in French, the Haitian writer can hope to reach a wide international public, but only if his work is published and distributed by a Parisian or, as is becoming increasingly frequent, a Québecois publisher. For this to be possible, he must compose a manuscript that is directly comprehensible to the publisher and to the foreign reader, both of whom are more likely than not completely ignorant of Haitian realities.

Some Haitian poets have followed the doctrine of "art for art's sake"; some novelists have written historical romances, like Demesvar Delorme, whose *Francesca* (Paris, 1873) takes place in Renaissance Italy, or science fiction, like René Philoctète in *The Eighth Day (Le Huitième jour,* Port-au-Prince, 1971). Whatever their literary qualities, nothing in such works gives a hint of their author's nationality. But these are rare exceptions, and serve to confirm the rule: Haiti and her problems are the obsessive theme of novelists and poets, of essayists and playwrights. Their self-imposed mission is two-fold: on the one hand, to denounce injustices and abuses in

Haitian society; on the other, to celebrate their country and defend her against the vicious sarcasm, often racist in character, which foreigners have all too often directed at the Black Republic. From a practical point of view, this poses difficulties: if the writer is categorical in denouncing the abuses found in Haitian society, he will be accused of providing grist for the mill of those foreigners who disparage Haiti and her people. If, in the name of patriotic expediency, he denies or plays down these abuses, he will be accused of complacency or even of complicity. Each writer comes to terms as best he can with these contradictory purposes: at any rate, it is fair to say that Haitian literature is, and has always been, *engagée.*

A Haitian writer's obligation, according to Jean-Baptiste Cinéas in the preface of his novel *The Backlash (Le Choc en retour,* Port-au-Prince, 1948), is "to lift the curtain on a dreary stage and to scream out what the least cowardly only whisper in each other's ear" (pp. i–ii). The critic Ghislain Gouraige has rightly pointed out in *The Haitian Diaspora and Africa (La Diaspora d'Haïti et l'Afrique,* Sherbrooke, P.Q., 1974) that

> A Haitian work is not motivated initially by esthetic ambitions (. . .) The mission conferred upon literary language in Haiti is to express faith, convictions, to reach consciences (p. 169).

And most Haitian writers would agree with the novelist Armand Thoby: when accused of unpatriotic severity towards Haiti's imperfections, he declares in *Jacques Bonhomme d'Haïti* (Port-au-Prince, 1901): "If anything is more humiliating than Monsieur Gustave d'Alaux's sarcasm (d'Alaux was a French racist, author of *L'Empereur Soulouque et son empire,* Paris, 1856), it is to deserve it." (p. 56.)

Unfortunately, Haitian society has not resolved its contradictions. Novels published fifty or a hundred years ago have consequently lost little of their relevance, and remain as subversive as when they first appeared. This might in part explain why they are generally excluded from school curricula.

The fact that every Haitian literary work aims at a double public, Haitian and foreign, also poses difficult problems. Foreigners are liable to be totally uninformed about Haiti. Of course, this problem is to a certain degree common to writers from cultures that are marginal in relation to those of the North Atlantic. But it is more acute for a Haitian addressing other Francophonic readers than for an Australian addressing other English readers or for a Peruvian addressing other readers of Spanish. Haitian society, because of its history, its organization, its linguistic and religious peculiarities and its collective mentality, is profoundly *sui generis.* If, in some respects, it bears comparison with other societies— French, African, Caribbean—this comparison soon proves to be superficial if not misleading. Of this, Haitians are fully conscious. As Cinéas put it in *The Backlash:*

Our paradoxical country is the country of the unbelievable, of the impossible. (. . .) (Haiti is) where the impossible happens and the unbelievable is a fact (pp. 4, 250).

Be that as it may, for a Haitian text to be understandable to non-Haitian readers of French (and therefore acceptable for consideration by a Paris or a Montreal publisher), the author must provide a whole compendium of information and commentary concerning the history, politics, sociology, collective mentality and local customs of Haiti, as well as descriptions of her flora and fauna, topography and monuments, typical head-dress and culinary specialties. And he must do so in such a way that these didactic notations do not obscure the plot of his novel, the clarity of his essay or the coherence of his poem. The Haitian reader, on the other hand, has no need for footnotes or explanatory interpolations. He may find them obtrusive and irritating, and, perhaps rightly, suspect that the work is directed primarily at foreign readers and caters to their fancy for spicy exoticism.

Since Haitian texts speak simultaneously to two very different audiences, they can be the object of two very different readings: the foreigner will be interested in what he learns of a—for him—exotic and fascinating country. The Haitian, on the other hand, will invariably recognize a series of allusions, and focus his attention on a series of situations whose significance eludes the foreign reader.

It is interesting to note in this connection that reviews of Haitian texts published in foreign periodicals, while often laudatory, invariably betray inadequate comprehension. This should not be held against the reviewer, who can scarcely be expected to decipher a network of allusions and implications that, to be perceived or extrapolated, require long and intimate familiarity with things Haitian. An example: every reader of French sees the title of Jacques Roumain's masterpiece *Gouverneurs de la rosée* (1944, Engl. trans. by L. Hughes and M. Cook, *Masters of the Dew,* New York, 1947) as a poetic conceit: but only the author's compatriots will immediately realize that it is also the French transcription of the Créole *gouvenè larouze,* a title given in the villages to the person in charge of organizing irrigation and regulating the distribution of water. And it is significant that so cosmopolitan a critic as Edmund Wilson could totally misread *Masters of the Dew,* which he dismissed as "Marxist phantasy."

In the ongoing quest for originality, a traumatic episode in Haitian history proved momentous. Between 1915 and 1934 the country was occupied by the U.S. Marines and made a *de facto* protectorate of the United States. The worst fears of Haitian intellectuals became reality: the first independent republic of Latin America was once again under colonial tutelage. It was a brutal and deeply humiliating experience. In their most dismal times of disaggregation and anarchy, Haitians could still cling to their pride in being independent, could still see themselves as the descendants of the heroes who had defeated Napoleon's army. Now they were no longer masters in their own house. Every decision affecting the life of the country had to be cleared with the American authorities and had to conform to American economic interests. And the Marines didn't much bother to hide their contempt for both the ignorant Negro *masse* and the effete, gallicised mulatto *élite*. For the first time since the days of slavery, Haitians experienced white color prejudice in their own land. In *Scenes of Port-au-Prince Life (Scènes de la vie port-au-princienne,* Port-au-Prince, 1975), the novelist Félix Courtois remembers the shock:

> One night, we had gone to sleep (. . .) our eyes had closed on the image of an immutable Haiti, set in her mediocre pleasures, her ancient misery, her incomprehension of fundamental problems. And we awoke facing the unexpected fact of the occupation. Entire walls of the national edifice had crumbled in the catastrophe. Our way of seeing and understanding had been turned upside down, and we attempted to imagine some possible way we could adapt to the brutal reality imposed on us. (p. 143.)

During the American occupation, Haitian intellectuals embarked upon a systematic critical reappraisal of the values which had led the country to disaster. Their conclusions were articulated in Dr. Jean Price-Mars' study *Thus Spake the Elder (Ainsi parla l'oncle,* Compiègne, 1928). Price-Mars accused his *élite* compatriots of "collective bovaryism," that is, of living in a world of illusion by pretending to be dark-skinned New World Frenchmen. He pointed out the absurdity of apeing French customs, French juridical, social and political structures, and of transplanting Parisian attitudes to a country so profoundly different from France in practically every respect. He argued for a reassessment and acceptance of the Haitian personality, reminding his *élite* countrymen that 90% of all Haitians were of pure African descent, were exploited peasants, were illiterate and destitute, were practitioners of vodùn and speakers of Créole. He exhorted the *élite* to discover, avow, and sympathetically examine the values of this forgotten majority. Only then could an integrated, liberated Haitian personality emerge, and develop in dignity and pride.

Most poets and novelists set about illustrating Price-Mars' message, and the reading public was ready to answer (at least platonically) the call for national renewal and the assumption of negritude in the face of foreign occupation and racism.

Henceforth, poets exalted peasant life, which had previously inspired in them bucolic entertainments and a condescending exoticism. Leftist ideologies also contributed to acclaiming the common people as the sacred hope of the Nation, the holy soil where the tree of Freedom would (as in colonial times) take root and prosper, the pure source of authenticity and historic continuity. The poet put on the mantle of bard of the masses; he repudiated the waltz for the yanvalou, the piano for the drums, rationalism for inspired apprehension of elemental forces through vodùn trances. He had traced his roots back to the European colonizers; he will now find them in his African ancestors.

In this respect, the titles of poetry collections are significant: until about 1930, most of these titles are innocuous: *Intimate Songs, Secret Songs, Flowers and Tears, Dreams and Songs, The Petals are Falling, Tunes from the Heart,* and so forth. We now find disquieting ones: *Negro Music (Musique nègre,* Léon Laleau, 1932), *Slum Flowers (Fleurs des bouges,* Antoine Dupoux, 1941), *Ebony Wood (Bois d'ébène,** Jacques Roumain, 1945), *Spray of Blood (Gerbes de Sang,* Renè Depestre, 1946), *Black Soul (Black Soul,* Jean Brierre, 1947), and so on.

Surrealism has enabled Haitian poetry to blossom and to attain its full originality. Free from the traditional, formal, and, so to speak, academic imperatives to which they had conformed, poets were able to find their own voice and their own forms. Further, they no longer hesitated to enrich their poetic lexicon with regionalisms and créole words, the latter sometimes modified to fit the French context. The influence of the Martinican Aimé Césaire has been decisive in this respect. To compare the latest published anthology of Haitian poetry, Sivio Baridon and Raymond Philoctète's *Poésie vivante d'Haïti* (Paris, 1978), which covers the last three decades, with Renè Saint-Louis and Maurice A. Lubin's earlier *Panorama de la poésie haïtienne* (Port-au-Prince, 1950), which goes back to the origins and stops at 1950, is to understand how fruitful this new freedom has proven. After Jacques Roumain and Carl Brouard, contemporary poets such as Renè Depestre, Anthony Phelps and Jean-Claude Charles lay the foundations of an authentically Haitian poetry. Of course, that is not to say that Haitian poets ignore the work of their French colleagues. But they are no longer content to follow their lead. And their own contribution is bound, sooner or later, to exert its influence on poetry wherever it is written in the French language.

The most obvious general characteristic of the Haitian novel is that complexity of plot and subtle psychological analysis of characters are subordinated to an overriding concern with "the problem of Haiti." From the first published Haitian novel (Émeric Bergeaud's *Stella,* Paris, 1859) to the latest to appear, the basic novelistic theme is the country itself: its history, its economic and social problems, its social structure, its very viability. This characteristic in itself gives it originality within the Western novelistic tradition. Rather than being primarily a fiction in which the reader can, if he so desires, trace the implicit analysis of socio-political

---

*French slave traders euphemistically referred to their cargo as "bois d'ébène."

conditions, the Haitian novel tends to be an explicit discourse on the state of the nation. Its fictional elements appear as concessions to the novelistic genre, adopted to make the lesson proposed more palatable or more stirring for the reader. Consequently, the author, either through a character he adopts as spokesman or by direct intervention in the text, seldom hesitates to engage the reader, exhorting him to reform the abuses of Haitian society or to resist the temptation of despair. For example, in Fernand Hibbert's *Shamming (Les Simulacres,* Port-au-Prince, 1923), published during the dark years of the American occupation, the author's spokesman, Monsieur Brion, advises his compatriots:

> The present regime imposed upon us to our shame will be succeeded
> by a regime which will safeguard our national dignity. We must not
> despair. We must persevere. (p. 23.)

Nadine Magloire's *The Pain of Living (Le Mal de vivre,* Port-au-Prince, 1968) is the interior monologue of an upper-class woman who has dared to seek intellectual and erotic freedom despite the *élite's* straight-laced puritanism. The novel is peppered with such bitter denunciations of Haiti and Haitians as:

> Haiti is a pretty unlucky little island. A speck of a country no one, not
> even its inhabitants, gives a damn about. (. . .) Most of my compatriots
> are bloated with pretensions, self-centered to the point of stupidity
> and morbidly susceptible and suspicious. They lie on principle; no one
> tells the truth here. (p. 74.)

Such overt and often strident interventions are liable to baffle the non-Haitian reader, whose novelistic tradition has come to demand authorial discretion.

In surveying the principle themes treated in Haitian novels, one should distinguish between those written before and those written after the occupation.

The twenty–five novels published before 1915 fall into two main categories. First, we find historical novels, recounting the heroic times of the struggle for independence. The chief concern here is to exalt the valor of the "ancestors" and to exort their descendants to prove worthy of them. In most cases, a tenuous fictional love story is interwoven with the evocation of historical events. The second type of novel that was popular at the time is the sentimental drawing-room novel. Like its French counterpart, it fortifies the story of adultery in high society with dashes of elementary psychology. In this type of novel, the setting may indeed be Port-au-Prince, or Cape Haitian or some provincial town. There may be the odd reference to tropical fruit or to the beauty of the Haitian sunset. But the novelists are so concerned with being understood and accepted by French readers that such notations are timid and few. They systematically deny their characters anything which might indicate the existence of a peculiarly Haitian mentality, temperament, sensitivity, humor, or manner of expression. By concentrating on banal sentimental imbroglios, they avoid grounding their works in the socio-political realities of the country. Even though this kind of novel was occasionally published even after 1915, it accounts for a very small part of the Haitian novelistic production.

Three pre-1915 novelists stand head and shoulders above the rest and herald the "Indigenist" writers of the next generation. Frédéric Marcelin (who died in 1917), Fernand Hibbert (d. 1928) and Justin Lhérisson (d. 1907).

The plot of Frédéric Marcelin's *Thémistocle-Épaminondas Labasterre* (Paris, 1901) is rather simple. The eponymous hero is born into the Haitian lower–middle class. His hard–working parents make the necessary sacrifices to send him to school. He eventually becomes a follower of an ambitious, unscrupulous journalist, Télémaque, who organizes a coup-d'état, overthrows the president and is rewarded with a cabinet post in the next government. Thémistocle becomes disillusioned with his corrupt hero, mounts a press campaign against him and—having refused a bribe in exchange for his silence—is killed by the police on Télémaque's orders.

To be sure, one finds in this novel references to Haitian products, customs, landscapes, and so on. But Marcelin is careful to place them in context in such a way that no French reader would be puzzled by them. Marcelin writes in the purest academic French and his characters (be they intellectuals, petit-bourgeois or even peasants) all speak pure Parisian. Yet Marcelin is the first Haitian novelist to criticize and satirize his countrymen's love of rhetoric and their idolatry of *le français de France.*

> What anxieties we suffer because of this devilish French language! The concentration it demands makes us sweat where we already sweat enough because of the climate. In Haiti we worry much more about form than about content. We fear our verbal arrows will not pierce their target unless they are shot most grammatically. (p. 203.)

The Haitian novelists of the next generation will be very concerned with the problem of language. First, as social criticism: they will mock and reproach their *élite* compatriots for trying to ape the French, for making fluency in Parisian speech into one more barrier against social mobility, for downgrading everything Haitian, including linguistic peculiarities. And second, as an internal problem of the Haitian novel itself. On the one hand, authenticity and self-respect will demand that the novelist let his characters speak in their own idiom, pure Créole if they are uneducated, Haitian French if they belong to the *élite,* or a mixture of both, which is what is heard on city streets. The novelist has a particularly difficult problem when he must render the verbal expression of peasants and workers who speak only Créole. Academic or popular French hardly serves the purpose, because a fundamental aspect of Haitian reality is precisely that the lower classes cannot speak the official language. Not to know French, in other words, is a necessary and sufficient condition for membership in the down-trodden *masse.* As we shall see in the chapter on "The Language Situation in Haiti," the best Haitian novelists have consequently fashioned a new literary language, which seeks to give a sense of the syntactic and semantic characteristics of Créole, while remaining accessible to the French reader. The fact remains that, the more authentic a character's speech, the more difficult it will be for a French reader to understand. Every Haitian novelist has had to struggle with this problem, and each has attempted to solve it through some sort of compromise.

Another typical trait of *Thémistocle-Épaminondas Labasterre* is the Haitian penchant for ferocious self-criticism. Political mores in particular are eloquently denounced. Marcelin is quite explicit: anyone who meddles in politics in Haiti is self-serving, corrupt, criminal. Revolutions are futile: they invariably replace one tyrant with another. Political life is the business of despicable cliques, which pay lip service to the common good, but care not a whit for the welfare of the country.

Bringing the masses, and especially the peasant masses, into the mainstream of Haitian life will be an important point in the program of later *engagé* novelists. For the time being, it is still a timid, pious wish. And indeed, when Marcelin has his characters spend the day in the country, his totally idealized description of peasants show typical *élite* ignorance of the forgotten majority.

One further remark: we find in *Thémistocle-Épaminondas Labasterre* the description of what purports to be a vodùn ceremony. But the goings-on are so far removed from anything resembling a true *service* that it is very doubtful that the author ever attended one. In those years, a man of his social class who admitted having done so would have passed for eccentric. Yet Monsieur Hodelin, Marcelin's spokesman in the novel, argues that vodùn does not necessarily deserve to be feared or despised. In *Zulma's Revenge (La Vengeance de Mama,* Paris, 1902), the sequel to *Thémistocle-Épaminondas Labasterre,* the hero's fiancée avenges him by poisoning his murderer Télémaque. And the poison is supplied by a rural *hungan* (vodùn priest) who explains that, in the absence of an equitable judicial system, he puts his knowledge at the service of the persecuted; it is at least hinted that the black arts of vodùn are the last recourse of the downtrodden. Once again, the next generation of *engagé* novelists will be fascinated by, and sometimes knowledgeable about, vodùn. Descriptions of ceremonies will become practically *de rigueur.* The one in Jacques Roumain's *Masters of the Dew* in honor of the god Legba is famous and inspired many others. Roumain, who had been a student of the distinguished French anthropologist Paul Rivet, and one of the founders of the Port-au-Prince Bureau d'Ethnologie, drew from his own personal experience. On the other hand, in the foreword of her novel *Fonds des*

Nègres (Port-au-Prince, 1961), Marie Chauvet candidly admits that "the vodùn ceremonies have been taken from Dr. Louis Maximilien's *Le Vodou haïtien.*"

It should be noted here that, in most cases, vodùn is treated with very ambiguous feelings, and sometimes with open hostility. With hostility, because Western-oriented novelists are uncomfortable with its intuitive, esoteric, magical aspects. Some share the average foreigner's conviction that vodùn is a relic of African primitivism. Marxist novelists see it as one more opiate in the religious pharmacopoeia. Nationalist and populist novelists consider that vodùn fosters fatalism and that its clergy is deeply conservative. At the same time, all realize that vodùn is a basic component of the Haitian people's authentic culture and that, for better or for worse, it colors the *masse's* view of life. The ideal, of course, would be to preserve the esthetic parts of the ceremonies, the chants and dances, and forget all about their metaphysical dimensions. This Jacques Roumain's hero Manuel seems to have done:

> (...) I respect the customs of the old folks, but the blood of a rooster or a young goat can't make the seasons change, or alter the course of the clouds and fill them with water like bladders. The other night, at the Legba ceremonies, I danced and sang to my heart's content. I'm a Negro, no? And I enjoyed myself like a real Negro. When the drums beat, I feel it in the pit of my stomach. I feel an itch in my loins and an electric current in my legs, and I've got to join the dance. But that's all there is to it for me.*

All things considered, Frédéric Marcelin—who probably never attended a *service*—may have treated vodùn with more respect than Jacques Roumain, whose first-hand knowledge of the folk religion was considerable.

Fernand Hibbert's *Séna* (Port-au-Prince, 1905) tells the story of another unscrupulous politician, who leaves his wife and children and follows his mistress to France. While in Paris, he sheds some of his ignorance, vanity and egotism. He returns to Haiti determined to mend his ways and use his political position for the common good. The clique in power has only one way to deal with such trouble makers: he is thrown in jail and murdered in his cell.

Again we find a denunciation of Haitian political mores. Again we are dealing with an urban novel: the peasantry is not represented. *Séna* is particularly interesting in that it comes to grips with a fundamental preoccupation of the Haitian psyche: the problem of color. In *Thémistocle-Épaminondas Labasterre,* not once do we find mentioned that Haitians are Black or Mulatto. The physical descriptions of Marcelin's characters

---

*Jacques Roumain, *Masters of the Dew,* translated by Langston Hughes and Mercer Cook, London, 1978 (1st edition 1947), pp. 87-88.

are mute on this point. But in *Séna,* we learn that the hero is

> neither *noir* or *mulâtre,* nor *griffe.* He was *alezan.* This neutrality of
> pigmentation allowed him to belong to all the parties, or rather to all
> the factions, at the same time. (p. 13.)

What Séna most admires in his mistress is that she is light-colored enough to pass for white (at least in Paris). It is only poetic justice that she eventually cuckolds him with a blond, blue-eyed French count. Séna brings back from France a husband for his daughter, who has always, with her father's full approval, refused to marry anything less than a full-blooded Caucasian.

The exploitation of the mostly black *masse* by the mostly mulatto *élite,* and further, the subtle gradations in percentage of desirable white blood which obsess the *élite,* will be bitterly satirized by *engagé* novelists. Hibbert was the first to mention this unfortunate fixation; and he did it through comedy, knowing that sense of humor, love of satire and delight in slapstick are fundamental traits of the Haitian personality.

Marcelin, publishing in Paris and addressing a francophonic readership, has his characters speak in academic French. Hibbert, on the other hand, published in Port-au-Prince and addressed a purely Haitian public. So he does not hesitate to use a pungent Créole expression when it serves his purpose, just as *élite* Haitians have always done in everyday speech. Further, some of his characters speak only Créole: the servant Ménélas, for example, or Séna's wife Melpomène, who "had some difficulty in speaking French, for she seldom went about in high society." It is interesting to note that, in these novels, Créole words are usually printed in italics, as were slang or dialectical expressions in French novels of the time. Later novelists will usually drop this typographical distinction, as an assertion that they are not writing in two languages, French and Créole, but in Haitian, of which French, regional variations of French, and pure Créole are all components.

Justin Lhérisson's *Pitite-Caille's Family (La Famille des Pitite-Caille,* Port-au-Prince, 1905) is a classic of pure Haitian prose which all literate Haitians have read. It is so characteristically Haitian, in form as well as in content, as to be not only untranslatable but just about inaccessible to all but Haitian readers.

The plot is as simple as that of *Thémistocle-Épaminondas Labasterre* and of *Séna.* A modest Port-au-Prince jack-of-all-trades named Eliézer Pitite-Caille becomes rich thanks to his wife's hard work and shrewd business sense. He sends his son and daughter to be educated in France, as the Haitian aristocracy always did. Trouble starts when he is persuaded to run for the Senate. A professional vote-broker cheats him, the police beat him, he is falsely accused of subversive activities, thrown in jail, tortured and harassed to death. His daughter marries a ne'er-do-well who beats her, his foppish son turns into a drunken derelict and his widow becomes one of fifty concubines in the harem of General Pheuil Lamboy, the ruling strong man.

Once again we are dealing with an urban novel. Once again a lower-middle class hero comes to grief because he develops political ambitions. Once again the contemporary history of Haiti is (in Fernand Hibbert's words) "a gory operetta": Lhérisson shares the pessimism of his friends Marcelin and Hibbert.

La Famille is more original in form than in content or philosophy. Two of its characteristics are particularly instrumental in stamping the novel with the seal of authority: the first is that *La Famille* is presented in the form of an *audience*. An *audience* is hard to define. It could be compared to a French "salon," to a Spanish "tertulia," or to an American cocktail party, in that it consists of a group of friends who meet more or less regularly to chat of this and that. Topics at an *audience* include town gossip, discussions about politics, philosophy, the general state of the nation and the universe and, above all, stories and anecdotes. The idea is to make these stories and anecdotes as entertaining as possible, through mimicry, gesticulation, and, most important, the choice of picturesque, pungent language.

This choice of language is the second characteristic which gives *La Famille* its authenticity. Lhérisson has a perfect ear for Haitian speech and exploits it more skillfully and systematically than Hibbert. He unerringly knows how and when a given Haitian would use French or Créole, the lexical and syntactical peculiarities of Haitian French, the subtleties of the Haitian accent in French. His transcription of this accent is all the more remarkable in that it is individualized: he carefully varies form and intonation according to the social class, the degree of education, and the psychological make-up of each character.

The contemporary Haitian novel was born of the American occupation of Haiti, which Marcelin had feared and predicted, and which had profound effects on Haitian society. Haitian novelists writing during and after the occupation express these two basic reactions: first, shame and discouragement, and then interest in and valorization of the peasant masses.

To the first reaction we owe a number of more or less autobiographical novels, such as Jean Brierre's *Province* (part of an unfinished trilogy significantly entitled *Horizons Without Sky* [*Les Horizons sans ciel,* Port-au-Prince, 1935]), Magloire Saint-Aude's *Parias* (Port-au-Prince, 1949), and Jacques Roumain's early *Preface to a Bureaucrat's Life (Préface à la vie d'un bureaucrate,* Port-au-Prince, 1930). Their heroes suffer from frustration and from feelings of hopelessness, inadequacy and impotence. They seek escape in drink, in visits to cheap dance-halls and whorehouses, and in endless, bitter, and self-deprecating talk. They are obsessed with self-hatred and fascinated by death. Gone is the lusty gusto, the healthy laughter we find in *Thémistocle-Épaminondas Labasterre,* in *Séna* and of course in *La Famille des Pitite-Caille.* We are now dealing with writers who despair of themselves, of their class and of their country.

The second effect of the Occupation on the Haitian novel was a shifting in focus towards peasants and, somewhat later, towards the proletariat. Not that they had been entirely neglected before the occupation. But peasants and proletarians (usually represented by house-servants) were normally relegated to playing small background roles. It is true that, in passing, Marcelin, Hibbert and Lhérisson did denounce the exploitation of the masses, but what their characters' adventures illustrate is the relations within and between the different strata or factions of the upper classes. With Jean-Baptiste Cinéas, Maurice Casséus, Jacques Roumain, and the brothers Marcelin, a new type of novel, the *roman paysan,* appears on the literary scene. These novels attempt to describe rural life "from within." They seek to give literary dignity to the Haitian peasant, to make him known to the *élite* reader and to make the upper classes conscious of their duty towards the downtrodden minority.

Most of these novels were published between 1930 and 1960, during the end of the American protectorate, succeeded by the uninspired presidencies of Sténio Vincent and Élie Lescot, then the somewhat progressive rule of Dumarsais Estimé, followed by the less enlightened presidency of Paul Magloire. In 1957, when Magloire attempted to illegally extend his term of office, anarchy resulted. François Duvalier assumed the presidency and enthroned himself for life. Before dying in 1971, he bestowed the presidency *à vie* upon his nineteen-year-old son Jean-Claude.

Under Estimé's rule and part of Magloire's, hopes were rekindled for a peaceful revolution in Haitian life, for a reconciliation between the various power groups, and for a modicum of national unity and progress. Rodolphe Charmant put it with typical Haitian forthrightness in *Alcius' Incredible Life (La Vie incroyable d'Alcius,* Port-au-Prince, 1946):

> Our ruling class has always made a mockery of its duty to lead, direct and organize. It has consistently used the country, it has considered itself a superior race, it has isolated itself from the common people, it has claimed the privileges of an oligarchy, it has shamefully exploited public goods and revenues.
>
> The time has come to reform our slave-owner mentality, to fashion ourselves a new soul, dedicated to the public good, to feel the common bond of blood, land, flag, racial solidarity and national pride. We must come to form one united family. (pp. 292-293.)

The novelists who participated in the so-called "Indigenist" movement had the feeling that at last they were perhaps not clamoring in the desert, but were actually enlightening the *élite,* and were therefore influencing the destinies of the country. This feeling of commitment is quite noticeable in their work. As the poet Carl Brouard wrote in a manifesto entitled "Art in the People's Service" ("L'Art au service du peuple," *Les Griots,* octobre 1938): "Not one of us practices art for the sake of art. It could even be said that we practice preaching." Preaching is not a very felicitous term perhaps, but Sartre hadn't yet coined the expression *littérature engagée.*

However that may be, and insofar as it is possible to generalize about novelists as different from each other as Jacques Roumain is from Marie Chauvet, or the brothers Marcelin from Jacques-Stéphen Alexis, or Jean-Baptiste Cinéas from Maurice Casséus, the main points of the novelists' program are:

(1) Description of peasant life, and illustration of peasant mentality—and not of the idealized, bucolic, happy farmers of Marcelin, but peasant life as it really is in Haiti: precarious, marginal and brutalizing.

(2) Investigation and valorization of peasant customs and beliefs (family and village solidarity, vodùn, cooperative work in the fields, or *koumbit,* and so on). This valorization is by no means uncritical, but shows how peasant customs and beliefs are integrated into an overall life pattern of survival. They rightly point out that a peasant custom or belief can be at the same time a support in his present situation and a barrier to improving that situation.

(3) Denunciation of the peasants' exploitation by the *élite,* represented by the *chef de section,* i.e. the rural police chief, who wields immense and practically unchecked judicial power, the merchants, the usurers, the produce-brokers, who control the peasants' economic life, the land-surveyor, who tries to dispossess the peasant in favor of a rich city-dweller, and so on.

(4) Building bridges between mentalities. By this pretentious phrase, I mean that novelists try to show that a peasant is not necessarily incapable of functioning within an *élite* structure; that he may be adaptable to city ways, and may indeed triumph through peasant shrewdness and common sense. Conversely, novelists try to show that members of the *élite* may not be as different from their rural compatriots as they would like to think. City folks can, for instance, feel the same attachment to the land, or the same awe towards vodùn spirits, or the same love for Créole. The point, obviously, is to encourage the *élite* reader to recognize the downtrodden as fellow Haitians.

Despite the good intentions of the novelists, the practical effects of the *roman paysan* have proven to be negligible; the number and quality of the latest *romans paysans* lead to the conclusion that the genre is playing itself out. At the very least, however, it allowed for a considerable broadening of Haitian novelistic themes, and put the Haitian novel on the map. Jacques Roumain and the brothers Marcelin were translated into

English. Edmund Wilson wrote a long essay on them in *Red, Black, Blond and Olive* (New York, 1956) and prefaced the translation of the Marcelins' *Tous les hommes sont fous (All Men Are Mad,* Eng. trans. by Eva Thoby-Marcelin, New York, 1970). Gallimard published Jacques-Stéphen Alexis (who also has been translated into Spanish) and Marie Chauvet. Scholars began to devote articles and monographs to their works. Today, they are providing subjects for doctoral dissertations the world over.

In my opinion, the Haitian theater did not achieve originality before the second half of the twentieth century. What finally permitted this was the claim by intellectuals for full literary dignity for Créole and the public's acceptance of this claim as warranted and long overdue. For while there is a long and honorable tradition of French-language theater in Haiti, it must be admitted that it is of interest mostly to literary historians and sociologists. When all is said and done, theater is spoken literature; the Haitian theater could hardly claim authenticity before the language heard on stage was not only the perfect French spoken by a very small privileged minority but also that spoken in its regional variations, and Créole, the only means of expression for the mass of the people.

Theater in Créole seems to me progressive not only because of its generally populist and sometimes revolutionary ideology, but also its use of popular gesticulation, rhythms and choreography. The playwright looks for inspiration in vodùn ritual, rural markets, peasant wakes, and the street scene. He turns to his country's living reality. This is probably why several recent Créole dramas have played to standing-room only audiences, while it is difficult to attract, for more than two or three performances of a French-language play, a public recruited exclusively from the upper strata of the ruling classes.

The first Créole plays were adaptations; in 1954 Félix Morisseau-Leroy adapted Sophocles in *Antigone en créole,* and Nono Numa's 1975 *Jeneral Rodrig* is based on Corneille's *Le Cid,* which generations of hapless Haitian children have been forced to memorize mindlessly. Later Créole playwrights, such as Frankétienne with his *Troufoban* (1978), will begin to strike out on their own; the same year, in the sequel to his *Antigone (Roua Kreon),* Morisseau-Leroy blends classical reminiscences and allusions to contemporary Haitian politics in a play where vodùn priests and gods enact the tragedy of Haiti and the drama of the human condition. It is not impossible that this vital Créole theater will infuse new life into the traditional French-language Haitian theater, but only time will tell.

Between 1935 and 1955, an exceptional generation left its mark on Haitian letters. For political and economic reasons, the following generation, that of our contemporaries, was disclosed and scattered in a new diaspora. Jacques-Stéphen Alexis died attempting to lead an insurrection;

Francis-Joachim Roy died in exile, in Paris; Marie Chauvet died in exile, in New York; Franck Fouché died in exile, in Montreal; René Depestre has lived in exile, first in Havana, now in Paris; Jean Brierre lives in exile, in Dakar, as do Félix Morisseau-Leroy, Gérard Chenèt, and Roger Dorsinville; Anthony Phelps lives in exile in Canada, as does Gérard Étienne. The best Haitian literature today is being produced abroad, and is often not distributed in Haiti.

Judging by works such as Gérard Étienne's *The Crucified Negro* (*Le Nègre crucifié*, Montreal, 1974) and Anthony Phelps' *Memory Plays Blind* (*Mémoire en colin-maillard,* Montreal, 1976), realism and populism are still the basis of the writers' commitment. But, under the influence of fury and despair, their vision becomes apocalyptic. To express it, they have recourse to a variety of techniques: internal monologues, free association of images, dislocation of narrative time, systematic obscenity, and so on. Of course, they have not invented these techniques, but they put them to remarkably effective use, not as exercises in technical virtuosity but as organic expressions of a particular vision. This is probably what Jacques-Stéphen Alexis was hoping for when, in "Du réalisme merveilleux des Haïtiens" (*Présence africaine,* juin-nov. 1956), he encouraged his colleagues to fashion a Haitian "marvellous realism."

The concept of "marvellous realism" is due to the Cuban novelist Alejo Carpentier. And if one had to relate contemporary Haitian letters to another literary tradition one could, it seems to me, consider it as the francophonic branch of Latin American literature. In the manner of many of the best writers of Latin America, Haitian writers apply their talents to the basic historical, religious and ethnic myths of their peoples. Through the medium of literature, fabulous and monstrous episodes of the history of Haiti, the nobility and mystery of vodùn, the aspirations and contradictions of negritude, engage our common humanity.

THE LINGUISTIC SITUATION IN HAITI

In Belgium, Canada, and Switzerland, French is one of two or more official languages and is foreign to large segments of the citizenry. No one in the "Francophonic" countries of Africa has French for his mother tongue; it is the official language to which national ethnic groups, each speaking its own vernacular, must resort in order to communicate with one another. In France itself, regional languages still survive; many Frenchmen are bilingual, in French and Alsatian, French and Breton, French and Basque, French and Provençal, or, in the West Indian "Départements d'Outre-mer," French and Créole. While many Martinicans and Guadeloupeans are more at ease in Créole, all are able to use French without difficulty.

The linguistic situation in Haiti is unique, in that all citizens are perfectly fluent in Créole, while no more than 10% have a working knowledge of French. Yet French is—and always has been—the only accepted language for use in government, and legal and educational activities. It is also the language of the media and of commercial advertising (although lately Créole has challenged its supremacy in these areas). Manipulation of access to the learning of the official language has effectively kept 90% of the Haitian people illiterate, and has made it virtually impossible for them to express their wishes, and to participate in the management of the country. Créole has no official status, and is still widely held to be, at best, a dialect, and, at worst, a corrupted, infantile form of French. He who speaks only Créole in Haiti belongs to the mute majority.

Linguists are not in complete agreement about the origins of Haitian Créole.* It is widely believed that Créole evolved from a *lingua franca* spoken on board French ships during the sixteenth, seventeenth, and eighteenth centuries, a mixture of various French dialects which allowed illiterate French sailors to communicate. To this *lingua franca* African, Portuguese, Spanish and English expressions were incorporated, since much of the French navy was engaged in the slave trade, and sailors often had to deal with speakers of these languages (or were themselves of non-

---

*Much has been written about creole languages in general and Haitian Créole in particular. Among the most important works are:
Robert Chaudenson, *Les Créoles français,* Paris, 1979; Suzanne Comhaire-Sylvain, *Le Créole haïtien,* Wetteren & Port-au-Prince, 1936; Yves Dejean, *Dilemme en Haïti: français en péril ou péril français,* New York, 1975; Jules Faine, *Philologie créole,* Port-au-Prince, 1937; Robert A. Hall, *Haitian Creole,* Philadelphia, 1953; Frantz Lofficial, *Créole-français: une fausse querelle?,* La Salle, P.Q., 1979; and Albert Valdman, *Le Créole,* Paris, 1978.

31

French origin). The first settlers of Saint-Domingue were seamen whose common idiom was this pre-Créole *lingua franca*. This theory of the origins of Haitian Créole is not entirely speculative; a Créole very similar to those spoken in Haiti and in the French West Indies developed on the other side of the world, in the Indian Ocean island of Mauritius, which was also settled by French sailors, at roughly the same time. As the French developed Saint-Domingue, it is very probable that Créole was used not only to communicate with slaves, but among the native-born settlers themselves. We know, for example, that Créole-language poems and songs were composed by French planters in the eighteenth century. Still today, a Créole very similar to that of Haiti is spoken on Saintes Island (off Guadeloupe), where only descendants of Breton settlers live.

This theory implies that Créole is a "white man's language," which the Black slaves were forced to adopt and to the elaboration of which they contributed little. To quote Alfred Métraux: "it is the last to date of the Romance languages, descended from French, just as French is derived from Latin." (*Haïti,* Neuchâtel, 1957, p. 9.) The Haitian linguist Michelson Paul Hyppolite subtitled his *Phonétique historique haïtienne* (Port-au-Prince, 1978): "L'haïtien, nouvelle langue romane."

In recent times, Haitian essayists have countered that Créole is a "Black" language; Charles Fernand Pressoir, for example, in *Débats sur le créole et le folklore* (Port-au-Prince, 1947), calls it "a language of Blacks, that can clearly be tied to the Sudanese linguistic group" (p. 9). This claim for the "Africanity" of Créole rests on the fact that—even though its lexicon is overwhelmingly of French or regional French origin—many Créole words, especially in the vocabularies of cooking and religion, come from West African languages. More significantly, some syntactic traits of Créole, which occur neither in French nor in any of the other Romance languages, are found in many West African ones. The main traits are: (1) the post-position of the article:

FRENCH	CRÉOLE
la table	tab la
la femme	fam nan
les tables	tab yo
les femmes	fam yo

and (2) the indication of the tense of the verb by prefixation:

CRÉOLE	FRENCH	ENGLISH
m-ap domi	je dors	I (am) sleep(ing)
ou ap domi	tu dors	you sleep
li te domi	il (elle) dormait	he (she) slept
	il (elle) a dormi	he (she) was sleeping
l-a domi	il (elle) dormira	he (she) will sleep
medam yo ta domi	elles dormiraient	they would sleep
etc.		

But the arguments about the origin and nature of Créole are more often ideological than scientific. It used to be that the defenders of Créole stressed its links with French, while its opponents submitted Créole's African traits as proof of its inferiority. With time the reverse became true: "Africanity" became a quality and "Frenchness" an unfortunate detail to be glossed over. The defenders of Créole now argue that the Black slaves "stole" the language of the masters by altering it phonetically and syntactically, and used it to forge their unity; Michel R. Trouillot explains— in Créole—that even though the planters generally separated those newly arrived slaves who spoke the same African language,

> (. . .) èsklav yo bay kolon yo payèt. Yo pran lang kolon yo, yo plòtonnin-l nan youn pakèt lang afrikin èpi yo mètè krèyòl kanpè.
> (the slaves got the best of the planters. They took their language, mixed it in with a lot of African languages and elaborated Créole.)
> (M.R. Trouillot, *Ti difè boulè sou istoua Ayiti,* Brooklyn, N.Y., 1977, p. 26.)

Soon, the argument goes, the planters themselves were forced to adopt Créole. Not only to communicate with their Black slaves, but because this new linguistic creation was so much better adapted to the particularities of life in the Caribbean. So that Créole, having been imposed upon the White settlers, at the very origins of the culture of the future Republic, is in fact the first operation in the long fight for its political and national identity. To the question: "What is Créole?," Michelson P. Hyppolite answers, in *The Future of Haitian Créole (Le Devenir du créole haïtien,* Port-au-Prince, 1952):

> You might as well ask: What is the Haitian nation? (. . .) In other words, Haiti could be born only because Créole existed. (p. 5.)

And three years later, Odnell David, in the August 1955 issue of *Panorama,* begins an article entitled "Créole, the National Language of the Haitian People" by asserting that: "The history of the Créole language is at the same time the history of the Haitian people's formation and evolution." (p. 221.)

Be that as it may, Haitian Créole is in 'no way an inferior, simplified or bastardized form of French, as the ruling class has long claimed. It is, and has long been, an original, complex, and expressive language, which no speaker of French can hope to understand and speak without much study and practice. And the reverse is also true: the Haitian peasant will have as much difficulty as any foreigner in mastering his country's official language.

In colonial times, successive waves of immigrants from France probably used French (or learned it) if they settled in the towns. Again probably, those who landed knowing only a metropolitan dialect and went to settle in the countryside adopted Créole. Of course, fluency in French sooner or later became indispensable to economic success and social integration and upward mobility within the ruling *élite*. At the top of this *élite* were the colonial administrators sent from Paris, who had nothing but amused contempt for the Créole language and the Créole way of life. Racialism played a part in the negative attitude towards Créole, since it was *also* the language of the Black slaves who were not only not taught French but explicitly forbidden to learn it; it was obvious to everyone that ignorance of French effectively disqualified one from the exercise of power.

It is no wonder, then, that French was highly prized not only by the Whites and Free Men of Color, but by the slaves. For a few slaves did learn French, or at least some French; those, for instance, who had been trained as bookkeepers or accountants, those whom their masters had taught a trade and allowed to work for pay (the master retaining most of the earnings, needless to say), and who had dealings with metropolitan civil servants, travellers, or newly-arrived settlers still unfamiliar with Créole. These "house slaves" and *nègres à talents,* as they were called, enjoyed more freedom and better treatment than the field hands. Knowledge of French was—for slaves also and for slaves especially—a factor and a proof of superiority.

The leaders of the Haitian War of Independence wanted to eliminate the French and institute liberty and dignity for all Haitians. But they never intended to abandon the French language in favor of Créole. They wanted the Republic to take its place in the concert of nations; even if it had been possible to adopt Créole, the result would have been to isolate Haiti intellectually, just as she was already isolated politically and economically. Also, since Créole was only a spoken language, making it into a language of learning and of transmission of learning would have required efforts the young nation was in no way able to undertake. Finally, many of the Haitian leaders were literate in French, trained in French, and sincerely admiring of the French (among whom many counted a father or a grandfather). It cannot then be argued that the War of Independence was fought in the name of an oppressed culture, or for the right to use a language suppressed by the ruling power (as was later the case in the Austro-Hungarian empire, or, more recently, in Canada). Probably by choice, surely by necessity, the revolutionaries used French to write their proclamations (including that of Independence), to correspond with each other, and to carry out administrative duties. On the other hand, they could only use Créole to harrangue their troops.

Once slavery had been abolished and national independence won, the power wrested from the French passed into the hands of a new *élite*, made up of military leaders and "enlightened" (i.e. literate) men. Just as under the colonial regime, knowledge of French remained a necessary condition of access to positions of leadership. Administration and commerce became the exclusive preserves of the new *élite*, who did not go so far as to forbid the teaching of French to the common people, but arranged matters so that practically the same result was achieved. On the one hand, only a minimal part of the national budget was earmarked for education, and on the other, French was imposed at all levels, in towns as well as in the countryside, as the only language allowed in schools organized on the metropolitan model. To this day, even though most children from peasant families or from city slums have literally never heard French spoken, they are assumed to be as fluent as their contemporaries from the Loire valley in the language of Racine and Voltaire. Instruction and testing are carried out in bad French; most teachers use good Créole only to berate their charges for stupidity and laziness.

Since all systems of education reflect the ideology of those who hold power, and since the main concern of those who hold power in Haiti has always been to keep from sharing it with those who don't, the use of French as the language of education is perfectly logical. In the first place, it ensures the failure of the overwhelming majority of that small minority of lower-class children who reach school. In the second place, it convinces these children that they are indeed inferior, since they systematically fail where *élite* children, whose parents allow only French to be spoken in the home, generally succeed. In the third place, it guarantees that those exceptional have-nots who do obtain some education despite tremendous odds, will join the haves and perpetuate the system; so that, as Charles Pierre-Jacques put it in "La Question scolaire en Haïti" (*Collectif Paroles,* 8, sept.-nov. 1980, pp. 18-19):

> (. . .) from 1804 to now, we don't believe that there has been any change in the goals of education. The situation today is the prolongation of the situation in colonial times: an education available to a privileged minority.

And in fact—while we do not have any reliable statistics—it is obvious that today's estimated level of more than 90% illiteracy cannot be much lower than it was in the 18th century.

It should be noted that, in 1979, a "reform" of education was decreed, calling for the use of Créole in the first grades of primary school, and the concommitant teaching of French as a foreign language. While this is obviously a sound decision in principle, it remains to be seen how widely the reform will be enforced, and what practical effects it will have.

While French has always functioned as a very effective bar to upward social mobility, it has also served less objectionable ideologies. French-speaking Haitians have always felt that Francophony is an important component of their national identity and originality. As the poet Normil G. Sylvain put it, in the manifesto of *La Revue indigène,* in July 1927:

In this Spanish and English America, we share with Canada and the French West Indies the glorious destiny of defending the French language and traditions.

It is worth remarking that, for Haitian intellectuals at that time, fidelity to the French language was part and parcel of being "indigène." The poet Georges Sylvain, Normil Sylvain's father, had already written in 1906 that, should his compatriots give up their French heritage,

> What would become of us, lost in the mass of enslaved New World Blacks? A pinch of Anglo-Saxon dust! (. . .) The more we hold on to our French culture, the more likely we are to keep our Haitian personality. (Quoted by A. Magloire, *Étude sur le tempérament haïtien,* Port-au-Prince, 1908, p. 187.)

And, in 1929, Dantès Bellegarde said roughly the same thing in *For a Happy Haiti (Pour une Haïti heureuse,* Vol. II, Port-au-Prince, 1929):

> We belong to Africa by our blood, to France by our minds. *It is this allegience that has fashioned our national personality.* To give up our French heritage would be to amputate half of our self. (p. 428; italics in the text.)

Haitians were proud of having been the first in Latin America and, for about a century, the only people in the Caribbean, to have attained independence; they also felt that they were heirs to a culture and language superior to that of their neighbors. The French are masters at convincing those they conquer, and the world at large, that theirs is a paragon among languages, but in the case of the young Haitian nation this was more than Gallic brainwashing.

Haiti was not only an independent country, it was also the first Black Republic. White racists and European colonialists systematically presented its political instability, technical backwardness, and religious peculiarities as proof of the Black man's innate inferiority and congenital incapacity for self-government. First the expelled French planters and the publicists they commissioned, then journalists such as Adolphe Granier de Cassagnac, with his *Voyage aux Antilles* (Paris, 1842) and diplomats such as Sir Spencer St. John, with his *Haiti, The Black Republic* (London, 1884)—to name the most vicious—did much to etch in the collective foreign imagination a picture of Haiti as a primitive and grotesque land of African savagery, superstition and inefficiency.

Haitians were understandably indignant, but they accepted the challenge. From the very beginning, Haitians declared themselves to be the spokesmen of Blacks everywhere, and as the inspirers of future African independence. On June 22, 1861, for example, Camille Borno wrote in *La Feuille du commerce:*

> Our origins make it our duty to prove, by incontrovertible acts, that Blacks, just like Whites, have been created intelligent. The vindication

of the Black race is the purpose we have adopted; is it not worthy of Haitian society?

In a more lyrical vein, Pierre Lafleur, in the July 23rd, 1885 issue of *L'Oeil,* imagines Haiti as an allegorical virgin who declares:

> I am Haiti! (. . .) I am the North Star of an entire race of men, to whom I am linked, whose destiny I represent. I am the affirmation of the Black race's existence. Through me it thinks, through me it grows, through me it lives, through me it hopes!

And an anonymous editorialist reminds the world, in the December 5th, 1903 issue of *Le Justicier,* that "Haiti is the vanguard of Africa (. . .) it is destined to become one of the hinges of civilization."

What Haitians were arguing is not that African cultures were worthy of respect (Negritude's hour had not yet struck), but that, given a chance, all Blacks could contribute to Western culture and equal the White man's intellectual achievements. And Haitians considered themselves the living proof of this fact, since they had mastered the crowning glory of European civilization, the language of France. Semextan Rouzier proudly writes, in his *Dictionnaire géographique d'Haïti* (Paris, 1892): "The French language is dominant in social relations and official documents (. . .) There are Haitian writers that France would not disown." (p. 104.) One of these writers was the novelist Demesvar Delorme, who was praised by his compatriots for

> (. . .)showing that the qualities of purity and elegance characteristic to the French language (. . .) can be found in the felicitous style of a writer belonging to our own supposedly inferior race. (N. Hector, "Demesvar Delorme," *Le Petit Haïtien,* août-nov. 1907.)

Fluency in French being incompatible with intellectual inferiority, Louis-Joseph Janvier does not hesitate to write, in an essay significantly entitled *The Republic of Haiti and the Defamers of the Black Race (La République d'Haïti et les détracteurs de la race noire,* Paris, 1882), that: "The French language is the common one, the only one, and all peasants understand it." (p. 27.) Only the desire to counter the outrageous arguments of anti-Haitian racists can justify this bare-faced lie. Still, Janvier did endow the French language with amazing properties: in a lecture on "The Influence of the French Language on the Black Race," which unfortunately does not seem to have been published, he is reported by *Le Courrier d'Haïti* for March 31, 1888 to have declared that: "The French language will destroy color prejudice, as it has already destroyed numerous other prejudices."

This vision of French as the palladium of Haitian originality and the justification of the Black people's claim to potential equality was exacerbated during the U.S. occupation, which lasted from 1915 to 1934. To reaffirm one's appurtenance to French culture meant, for the *élite,* to resist American influence and to proclaim its own superiority to the barbarian invaders. Reviewing one more sensationalistic and comtemptuous report on Haiti, W.B. Seabrook's *Magic Island,* an anonymous journalist writes in the July 1, 1930 issue of *La Petite revue:*

> (. . .)by her legislation, by her customs, by her education, Haiti has a civilization, French, to be sure, but perhaps superior to whatever the U.S. could offer her.

As a protest against the occupation of his country, the poet Edmond Laforest committed suicide and was reportedly found clasping a Larousse dictionary to his chest. This was a symbolic act of fidelity to French and, at the same time, a protest against Americanization. Speaking in 1962, Jean Fouchard attributes to Black blood and to French speech Haiti's successful resistance to cultural assimilation by the occupiers: "To organize our Resistance, we used our origins and our language for barricades." *(Trois discours,* Port-au-Prince, 1962, p. 64.) "Our origins and our language . . ." These are *mutatis mutandis,* the same weapons Puerto Rican intellectuals have been using to defend their people from absorption into American Anglophony since the annexation of the island by the U.S.—with, of course, one fundamental difference: all Puerto Ricans are Spanish speakers. Only a small minority of Haitians speak French— and, to boot, most of them speak it as a second language.

Fidelity to French and, through French, to Greco-Roman Classicism, was no doubt a commendable act of resistance, but less hazardous than those of the peasants who took up arms and fought the U.S. Marines. Those who died with Charlemagne Péralte or fell before American machine guns at Marchaterre were not defending classical antiquity, of which they had never heard, nor the beauties of French, which no one had taught them.

Most of today's Haitian intellectuals are torn between their love of French and their feeling that it is the badge and weapon of the privileged minority. Neither Jacques Roumain, nor Jean Price-Mars, nor the brothers Marcelin, nor Jacques-Stéphen Alexis, nor René Depestre, to name Haitian writers whose reputation is well established at home and abroad, has written in Créole. Nor, to be sure, should they have felt obliged to do so. But it is a fact that their readership is mainly found beyond Haiti's borders and that the common folk whose spokesmen they aspire to be would not understand a word they wrote, even if someone could be found to read aloud from their works.

Créole used to have a populist and even subversive aura. It was thought, somewhat naively, that every "advance" of Créole (in social acceptability, as a literary medium, in the school system . . .) would be an important victory for true democracy. This was not only believed by many potential revolutionaries, but feared by the power *élite.* In the last few decades it has become apparent that in Haiti the medium is not necessarily the message, and that Créole can be as effective a tool of alienation and deception as French ever was. Consequently, most of today's intellectuals are much less peremptory about the supposed merits and dangers of Créole. Its partisans realize that, while acceptance of Créole as a legitimate means of expression is a necessary condition of structural reform, it is far, very far, from being a sufficient condition. And those who feared that the acceptance of Créole would be a threat to their privileges now feel secure that, if it is a threat at all, it is a very, very long-range one. Spirited (but, one fears, rather academic) debates, pro and con, on the use of Créole now take place both in Haiti, among supporters of the régime, and in New York, Montreal, or Paris, among its exiled enemies. As the "Créole question" is being defused, the study, use, and celebration of Créole is meeting with far less opposition.

Until quite recently, Créole was strictly a spoken language. For written communication, Haitians would use French, the language in which they were literate. Even today, Haitians who normally speak Créole to each other (close friends, family members), exchange letters in French. This is for two often complementary reasons. First, because they have been taught at home and in school that Créole is the language of the unwashed and that while it is permissible to use it in informal and intimate conversation, it should not be dignified by adoption for formal speech or, *a fortiori,* for writing. And second, it is only recently that a systematic effort to transcribe it has been made. Haitians are not being coy when they claim to have difficulty in reading Créole. As a matter of fact, the question of how to transcribe Créole and of which variation of Créole to adopt as standard was the object of decades of debate. "Purists" still argue that rural Créole has been less "corrupted" by borrowings from French and other foreign languages, but it seems that, for reasons of logic and expediency, the Port-au-Prince variety will ultimately be chosen to provide the norm. On the question of transcription, there were two schools of thought. The so-called "etymologists" argued that the French transcription of phonemes should be used, while the "phoneticists" argued for a strictly phonetic transcription. Thus, they would transcribe the Créole word for "where" *kibò,* while the etymologists would spell it *qui bor,* since it comes from the agglutination of two French words: *qui* and *bord.* This was no idle quarrel, but reflected conflicting ideologies as to the nature of Créole and different strategies for the fight against illiteracy. The etymologists saw Créole as essentially related to French, a fact they wanted to symbolize through French spelling. And they argued that making someone literate in Créole is half the job, since only literacy in French opens the doors to advanced education and to upward social mobility; learning the idiosyncracies of French spelling from the onset would make the transition infinitely easier. For the phoneticists, on the other hand, Créole is as different from French as French is from Latin, and should have its own system of transcription. They further argue that the gratuitous intricacies of French spelling would make the already staggering task of educating the people even more difficult. Phoneticists have all but carried the day; in the majority of newspapers, plays and poems now appearing, the phonetic transcription is preferred. In fact, a governmental decree dated 18 September 1979 standardized the transcription of Créole for use in connection with the educational reform according to strict phonetic principles. It is interesting to note that Article One of the decree reads:

> L'usage du créole, en tant que langue parlée par les 90% de la Population Haïtienne, est permis dans les écoles comme langue instrument et objet d'Enseignement.
>
> (The use of Créole, as the language spoken by 90% of the Haitian population, is permitted in the schools as a language of instruction and as a subject for study.)

What effect a decree which "permits"—rather than imposes—will have is a question. It is also significant to note that Créole is defined as "the language spoken by 90% of the Haitian population." This is of course a disingenuous formulation; the truth is that Créole is the language spoken by 100% of the Haitian population, and the only language spoken by 80% of the citizenry.

Slowly but surely a corpus of Créole language Haitian literary works is being constituted. Already in 1901, under the title *Cric? Crac!*, Georges Sylvain had published Créole adaptations of La Fontaine's fables. Several poets, such as Massillon Coicou (1867-1906), Frédéric Doret (1866-1935), and Oswald Durand (1840-1906), occasionally composed in the vernacular. One of these Créole poems, Durand's *Choucoune*, set to music by Mauléar-Monton, is still played by most West Indian musical groups; its English title is *Yellow Bird*. Edmond Chenèt collected about fifteen hundred items in his *Proverbes créoles*.

But it wasn't until 1950 that poets systematically started to write not only in French but also in Créole—and sometimes exclusively in Créole. Morisseau-Leroy adapted Sophocles in *Antigone en créole* (which would be spelled *Antigòn an kreyòl* today) in 1953, and Franck Fouché did the same for *Oedipe-Roi* in 1958. Both plays were produced in Port-au-Prince and were received by some with enthusiasm, by others with indignation. In 1975, the first full-length Créole novel was published: Franketienne's remarkable *Dezafi*.

The development of Haitian Créole literature has been slow, for obvious reasons: as long as a goodly number of Haitian readers claim not to be able to, and not interested in, reading Créole, printings of Créole works will remain miniscule, and do little for an author's reputation. For a long time, the fact that an author used the vernacular made him suspect of having populist sympathies and possibly revolutionary aspirations, so that to write in Créole was, if not politically inadvisable, at least socially frowned upon. And lastly, Créole was supposed to be fit only for quaint folk wisdom or for humorous—and usually salacious—double-entendres, not for serious literature.

These anti-Créole prejudices are fading, but slowly. More and more Créole plays are being written and more and more brochures of Créole verse are being printed both in Haiti and in the "diaspora." If these plays were performed before monolingual Créole speakers in the slums and in the hills, and if that poetry were recited to them directly or through the radio, Créole literature might indeed be on the way to being truly the people's literature. But after *Dezafi,* the only Créole novel published was Emile Célestin-Mégie's very conventional *Love Knows No Barriers (Lanmou pa gin bariè)* in 1976. There is still no history of Haitian Créole literature. And we are still waiting for a good anthology of Haitian Créole poetry.*

The recent standardization of Créole transcription, and the reform of primary education, will probably favor the development of Créole letters. But, once again, all will depend on whether or not significant numbers of Haitians will ever become able and willing to read their national language.

While we can only speculate about the future of Créole letters, we cannot fail to observe that the originality of Haitian literature written in French rests to a considerable degree on Créole. This apparent paradox is due to two related factors: on the one hand, the presence of Créole within French texts, and, on the other hand, the influence of Créole on French texts.

Most Haitian writers have at one time or another included Créole words within their texts, some with hesitant parsimony, some with joyous abandon. Obviously, most of these words are Haitianisms without exact equivalents in French. Some refer to cooking, like *tassau (taso),* or *coui (kwi),* some to vodùn, like *papa-loi (papalwa), caplata (kaplata), assotor (assotò),* or *garde-corps (gadkò); tokaille (tokay,* from the Spanish *tocayo)* is what a person who has the same first name as one is called; proverbs are likely to appear, such as *Grangou for passé maladi (gwangou fò pase maladi).* All of the above examples are taken from what is probably the first Haitian short story: Ignace Nau's *Isalina,* published in 1836 by the Paris *Revue des Colonies.***

---

*For more details about Haitian writers in Créole, see Duraciné Vaval, *Histoire de la littérature haïtienne,* Port-au-Prince, 1933, pp. 463-474; and Maximilien Laroche, "Panorama de la littérature créole" in Yves Dubé (ed.), *L'Haïtien,* Montreal, 1968, pp. 84-95.

**I have given the words in their original spelling and, in parentheses, in the newly prescribed transcription. A *taso* is a strip of dried and marinated meat; a *kwi* is a

The frequency of occurences of Créole words and expressions in a given text will not be simply a factor of the author's preference in the matter. It will also depend on whether the author is being published in Haiti (and therefore addresses only his compatriots, since for all intents and purposes Haitian publications are not exported), or whether he is being published in Paris, and is aiming at the general Francophone readership. In the first case, he will not hesitate to sprinkle his prose with Créole, knowing that all allusions will be understood. Thus, to take a rather extreme case, most of the dialogues in Clément Magloire St. Aude's novel *Parias* (Port-au-Prince, 1949) are in pungent Créole, while the expository passages are in elegantly polished French. On the other hand, in those works aimed at Francophones in general, when the meaning of Créole words and expressions is not evident from the context, they are translated in parentheses, or foot-noted. To give an example, when in *Masters of the Dew* Jacques Roumain uses the Créole word *avalasse* *(avalas)*, which means a monsoon-like tropical storm, he prefaces it with two French words: *averse* ("downpour") and *avalanche;* the clause reads: *le ciel noir s'ouvrait pour l'averse, l'avalanche, l'avalasse torrentielle.* When, in the same novel, a Créole song is being sung:

> *Femme-la dit, mouché, pinga (Fam la di, mouche penga)*
> *ou touché mouin, pinga-eh (ou touche mwen, penga-e)**

Roumain provides the reader with a French translation in a footnote.

Now, this is not extremely different from what happens in regionalist French novels, where the odd Breton, Provençal, or Auvergnat expression is used to give "local color." And indeed, several Haitian critics have voiced disapproval of this technique; Edgard Fanfant, for example, when he reviewed Justin Lhérisson's novel *Zoune At Her Godmother's (Zoune chez sa ninnaine,* Port-au-Prince, 1906) for the December 1906 issue of *Le Petit Haïtien:*

> We understand that (. . .) in a Haitian novel where our everyday life is depicted, Créole words will be found. There are occasions when they are necessary (. . .) But to lavish them here and there under the pretext of local color, of making "national" literature, is inadmissible. No, to have a national literature does not mean to pepper the French text with Créole idioms. That would be too easy; and besides, it makes for grotesque style.

The poet and essayist Frédéric Burr-Reynaud (who didn't hesitate to

---

half calabash used to carry water or food; a *papalwa* or *kaplata* is a vodùn priest; the *asotò* is a large drum, a *gadkò* is a protective charm. *Gwangou fò pase maladi* means "disease is nothing compared to hunger."

*The song, rendered directly in English in the translation by Langston Hughes and Mercer Cook (New York, 1947), reads: "The woman said, man!/ Behave yourself!/ And don't touch me!/ Behave yourself!

"créolize" his own newspaper articles), in a review of Jean-Baptiste Cinéas' *The Tragedy of the Land* (*Le Drame de la Terre,* Cap-Haïtien, 1933), in the September 9, 1933 issue of *Le Temps,* wrote:

> I deplore the excessive use of Créole, which adds nothing to local color. And besides, a Haitian book is not written for Haiti only. If it is good enough, it must cross our borders and reach a world-wide public.

It seems to me that these critics are right when they argue that a dash of Créole does not make a piece of writing authentically Haitian. But I also suspect that what really bothered them is something else: the fact that Haitian novelists and short story writers, like their colleagues in other countries, tried to render the speech peculiarities that mark a given character's class membership. Thus, in Fernand Hibbert's novel *Séna* (Port-au-Prince, 1905), Senator Rorrotte speaks only French to his daughter, only Créole to his servants, and a mixture of both to his wife and cronies. About the speech of the urban middle and lower-middle classes, Nadine Magloire writes, in *The Pain of Living* (*Le Mal de vivre,* Port-au-Prince, 1968):

> Everyday language is Créole or, for many, a French-Créole mixture (. . .) when you can't think of the French word immediately, you replace it with its Créole equivalent. (p. 76.)

Obviously, this mixing of languages makes for sure-fire comic effects and that is probably what worried the critics, who feared that foreign readers would get the impression that Haitians were gibbering buffoons.

It should in fact be noted that much of Haitian upper and middle class humor is based on improper use of French. More precisely, what those Haitians find irresistibly funny is the misunderstanding that results when a French word is mistaken for its Créole cognate; when, for instance, children sing the national anthem with only the vaguest notion of what the French words mean, and instead of singing the refrain *Marchons unis! Marchons unis!* ("Let us march united"), sing *Machàn diri! machàn diri!* ("Rice merchant!"). Or, conversely, barbarisms can result from misguided efforts to speak correct French. (A lower-middle class man marries an impoverished aristocrat. When the wife comes home she cries out: *"Chéri, je suis là!,"* to which the husband replies: *"Et moi, je suis le!"*)

Hesitant or incorrect French is not only the butt of the literate minority's sarcasm. It is also an important factor in determining how low the speaker is placed on the social scale. At the very top of the pyramid, the bourgeoisie speaks remarkably correct French, with just enough West Indian intonation not to be accused of speaking like a *blan franse.* Members of the bourgeoisie attend the prestigious congregational schools in Port-au-Prince, where the majority of the teachers are French priests or nuns. Many perfect their French during vacation trips to Europe, or while pursuing their higher education at a French university. Along with the very top layer of the *classes moyennes,* these are the Haitians who are truly bilingual. As one goes down the social scale, facility in speaking and writing French decreases, doubts about the correctness of one's French increase, as does one's Créole accent and the number of vernacular words, expressions, and cognates used. It would not be an exaggeration to state that, more than riches and phenotype, virtuosity in handling the official language is the main source of social prestige—although, as could be expected, most virtuosi are *Mulâtres* and, if not necessarily very rich, at least well-to-do.

Haitians who know that they speak impeccable French will take every opportunity to show off this proficiency by speaking—long, loud, and clear—in social gatherings, in political meetings, into the microphones of radio stations. Since a syntactical error or a word misused or mispronounced exposes the perpetrator to merciless ridicule, those not among the bilingual happy few will constantly be hampered by their linguistic inferiority complex. They will hesitate to express themselves, lest they become the object of the same sarcasm directed on January 20th, 1831, to the editors of *La Feuille du commerce* by their competitors of *Le Phare:*

> *La Feuille du commerce* is making good progress in French; we are astonished to note that its last issue contained not more than seventeen solecisms.

Almost exactly a century later, the pro-government *Le Temps* of October 7th, 1932, claims to have received a letter criticizing President Vincent's policies from

> (. . .) two feeble-minded Haitians who reside in Cuba and (. . .) express their indignation with a hundred mistakes in French grammar and a thousand mistakes in spelling.

Despite the Créole proverb that cautions: *Bon franse pa lespri* ("Good French does not necessarily imply good sense"), the linguistic repressive mechanism does function at all levels of society: speech, denied to peasants and workers, parsimoniously doled out to the lower-middle class, and granted at their own risk to the middle-middle class, remains the privilege and the badge of the aristocracy.

Besides becoming proficient in academic French, there has always been another way to gain entry into Haitian society: to be on the winning side in a coup d'état or a civil war. Of course, once a lower or lower-middle class person reaches power and its financial rewards, he will make absolutely certain that his children learn to speak with the correctness and intonation of the *élite,* into which they will probably marry, thus consolidating the family's new social position.

The presence of the odd Créole word, and the occasional mixing of

French and Créole, certainly contribute to the originality of Haitian literature, and especially of Haitian fiction. But what is just as important, and certainly more subtle, is the influence of Créole on French language texts. By this I mean that some of the best Haitian novelists have created new words that the Haitian reader will recognize as derived from Créole, yet that will easily be deciphered by the Francophone reader, either by analogy with an existing word or because the Créole word is in fact a French archaism or regional expression. For example, Jacques Roumain uses *malédictionné* ("accursed"), which exists in neither French or Créole. But the Haitian reader will recognize it as coming from Créole *madichonen*, and the Francophone reader, who knows that a *malédiction* is a "curse" will, by analogy with *condition/conditionné* or *position/ positionné*, immediately understand the newly minted adjective. A more interesting example is the use of the word *nègre* throughout the novel; the characters as well as the narrator use it, to refer to themselves and to others. Old Delira, the hero's mother, calls her husband *O, Bienaimé, nègre à moué.* The hard life of the Haitian peasant leads Bienaimé to conclude that *en vérité, le nègre est une pauvre créature.* The French reader, aware only of the ethnic connotation of the word, would take the sentence to mean that Black peasants suffer in a world dominated by Mulattos and Whites. But all Haitian readers know that *nèg* is the Créole word for "man," or "human being," and they therefore interpret the sentence as a home-spun comment on the human condition.* One last example: Jacques Roumain consistently uses the word *mitan,* which all Frenchmen would recognize as the archaic word for—and all Haitians as the only Créole word for—*milieu* ("middle").

Further, the best Haitian authors have succeeded in imposing what Pradel Pompilus calls "the staccato rhythms of the Créole sentence" on French.** How Roumain or J.-S. Alexis or F.-J. Roy manage this would make a fascinating study, but it cannot be attempted here, and should be left to the phoneticians. Perhaps the English language reader can extrapolate from speech patterns which give a peculiar rhythm to the English spoken by some of the characters in V.S. Naipaul's *A House for Mr. Biswas,* or to the Barbadian English of some of the characters in George Lamming's *In the Castle of My Skin.* At any rate, this hard-to-define linguistic resonance gives Haitian prose its most striking originality. It allows the Haitian writer to feel that, although he writes in the language of European Whites, he can inflect it in such a way that his New World

---

*In their translation of the novel, Langston Hughes and Mercer Cook render the first sentence as "Bienaimé! Oh, honey!" and the second as "Yes (. . .) a black man's really bad off."

**Pradel Pompilus, *La Langue française en Haïti,* Paris, 1961, p. 116.

Black and Mulatto compatriots can claim it for their own. As René Depestre argued, about Jacques-Stéphen Alexis' novel *My Mate, General the Sun (Compère Général Soleil,* Paris, 1955), in *Pour la révolution, pour la poésie* (Montreal, 1974):

> *Compère Général Soleil,* written in French, belonging to the general movement of literatures of French expression, nevertheless remains, with every metaphor, with every shimmering of feeling and thought, a fundamentally Haitian phenomenon. (p. 193.)

Little by little, the Paris literary establishment is coming to accept Francophone writings as more than amusing curiosities. So far, it is mostly the Québecois writers and the odd Martinican who have been extensively read and taken seriously by the critics. But one can hope that some day both African and West Indian Francophone writers will be given full membership in the club; perhaps then the Haitian contribution to the literary treasure will be recognized, and the originality of Haitian letters admired rather than tolerated.

Créole has been gaining acceptance and respectability during the last twenty-five years, but not only for ideological reasons. A very large number of Haitians no longer have faith in the possibility of attaining economic and personal security within the country's borders. Emigration to the English-speaking islands, to the French West Indies, to Latin America, to Canada and especially to the United States has reached epidemic proportions. Since much of this emigration is illegal, statistics are approximate at best, but it is estimated that as many as one million Haitians are living abroad, half of them in the United States. If emigration, preferably to an English-speaking country, is one's ultimate goal, the motivation to perfect and refine one's French—or even simply to learn it—is weakened if not eliminated altogether. Learning English will ultimately prove much more advantageous, and to speak Créole will no longer be an obstacle to success. Lower class émigrés who return to Haiti for the holidays, having forgotten most of what French they used to know, are living illustrations that speaking the national rather than the official language is not proof of backwardness or inferiority. In the country itself, large numbers of missionaries (mostly American Protestants) bypass French altogether: they evangelize and educate directly in Créole and, if they teach another language at all, they teach English. It is almost certain that, today, more natives of Haiti are competent in English than in the official language of their country. This new development is already beginning to make itself felt in literature, as will be illustrated below, in the essay entitled "The United States and Americans in Haitian Letters."

The linguistic situation in Haiti is fascinating to the linguist and the sociologist. It may appear quaintly picturesque to some, but I am afraid it reflects the fundamental contradictions of Haitian society. Just as these contradictions seem further away than ever from some sort of resolution, so does the chaotic linguistic situation appear to become more and more complex and unmanageable.

What does the future hold? The most varied and contradictory predictions have been advanced: gradual spreading of literacy in French to the whole population; parity of French and Créole as official languages; replacement of the former by the latter; gradual replacement of French by English and eventual English-Créole bilingualism . . . I for one would not dare to speculate, and will conclude with an obvious truism: the evolution of the linguistic situation in Haiti will be organically linked to the social, political and economic evolution of the country. When, if ever, a movement of national reform, national solidarity and national progress develops, there is no doubt whatsoever that it will choose or fashion its functional means of expression from the component parts of Haiti's present multilingual incoherence.

SLAVERY AND RACE
IN HAITIAN LETTERS

Haiti is the only Caribbean land where the aspiration to independence was born of the struggle against slavery; the two became inextricably linked as the conviction grew that the former was the only way to ensure once and for all the elimination of the latter. Haiti is also the only Caribbean land in which both emancipation and nationhood were achieved at the same time, and were not granted by the European métropole but conquered by force of arms, at the cost of untold sacrifices.

Of the four Founding Fathers of Haiti, whose statues give its name to the central Place des Héros de l'Indépendance in Port-au-Prince, three were born in slavery: Toussaint Louverture, Henry-Christophe and Jean-Jacques Dessalines; only Alexandre Pétion was born a "free man of color." Haitians are rightly proud of their slave ancestors; they revere them as national heroes and also for having provided all Blacks, whether in bondage in the New World or under colonial rule in the African homeland, with models to follow. The Martinican poet Aimé Césaire, in a striking and often quoted line from *Notebook of a Return to the Native Land* (*Cahier d'un retour au pays natal,* New York, 1947), celebrates Haiti "where, for the first time, negritude rose and stated that it believed in its humanity."

Haitian writers have never hesitated to evoke the time of slavery and the inhumanity to which their forefathers were subjected: tortures and humiliations, whippings and insults are here no cause for embarrassment and foster no self-deprecating image, for they were never borne passively, but avenged to the full. An insult avenged brings pride, not dishonor. As the baron de Vastey, a remarkable polemicist who was born a slave and became King Henry-Christophe's secretary, put it in his *Political Remarks . . . Concerning Hayti* (1817; Engl. trans., London, 1818): "Our swords have conquered again our native rights; we have wiped away in their detested blood the spots of slavery." (p. 74.) The very same sentiments are expressed by Pierre Faubert (1806-1868) in his poem "Aux Haïtiens" (in *Ogé*, Paris, 1856, p. 143):

> Brothers, we have broken the infamous yoke
> Which too long kept our heads bowed;
> Blacks and Mulattos with heroic flames
> We have avenged our humiliations.

And Hérard Dumesle (1784-1858) is the first of many Haitian poets to have sung the exploits of *Macanda* (or, more commonly, Makandal), the runaway slave and precursor of the revolution who led a bloody uprising and was burned at the stake in 1758.

The first Haitian novel, Émeric Bergeaud's *Stella* (Paris, 1859), is an allegorical account of the war of independence. Its first chapters detail the horrors of colonial life and tell how its two heroes (who bear the symbolic names of Romulus and Rémus) avenge their mother, who died under the lash: they burn the plantation and kill their former master. Amédée Brun's *Two Loves (Deux amours,* Paris, 1895), celebrates the friendship of the slave Jean-Louis and the liberal Frenchman Henry Lermant, who rise to high ranks in the revolutionary army. Massillon Coicou's *La Noire* (unfinished, published in installments in the Port-au-Prince daily *Le Soir* in 1905) also opens with a detailed description of the horrors of slave life, as does a modern historical novel, Marie Chauvet's *The Dance on the Volcano (La Danse sur le volcan,* Paris, 1957). Even in novels or stories which do not deal specifically with the days of slavery, one finds frequent references to the suffering and the heroism of the "Ancestors." Indeed, the "Ancestors" are remembered in the refrain of *La Dessalinienne,* the Haitian national anthem composed by the novelist Justin Lhérisson:

> For the Fatherland, for the Ancestors,
> Let us, let us be united.

In short, far from being a source of shame or feeling of unworthiness, the "peculiar institution" is at the very roots of Haitian patriotic self-exaltation. Further evidence that slavery has left no traumatic memory in the Haitian collective imagination is the fact that writers feel no compunction at describing instances of relations between slaves and masters based on friendship and mutual respect. In *Between Masters and Slaves (Entre maîtres et esclaves),* a collection of short stories published in 1943, Jean-Joseph Vilaire tells of an old slave woman who protects the planter's humane wife during the revolution, while a slave girl hides her young master, with whom she is in love. In another story, a strapping young slave rescues his master's daughter from a house on fire; the girl's fiancé will give him an accolade, and freedom. Elsewhere, Vilaire narrates one of the early colonial settlers' long and happy life with the Black woman he loves and the many children she bears him.

It is possible for Haitian writers to treat the theme of slavery with the detachment accorded to ancient, and therefore exotic, matters. However, even today, writers also use colonial slavery as a metaphor for the oppression of the country's destitute, illiterate rural masses by its urban, Western-oriented upper class. With deep-felt indignation, Haitian intellectuals accuse this self-styled *élite* of having taken the place and adopted the mentality of the former slave owners, thus betraying the ideals of the country's founders. As the Marcelin brothers write in *The Beast of the Haitian Hills (La Bête de Musseau,* 1946, English trans. by Peter C. Rhodes, New York, 1946):

> (. . .) although their ancestors had abolished colonial slavery at the price of their blood, these poor people were still held down by the ruling class in chains of servitude, ignorance and misery. (p. 17.)

In *Zulma's Revenge (La Vengeance de Mama,* Paris, 1902), Frédéric Marcelin bemoans the succession of bloody tyrants who periodically seize power in Haiti:

> (. . .)the barbarous planter has all too often, alas! been succeeded by the sanguinary despot issued from our ranks, from our own midst. (p. 206.)

In an article published in the August 29th, 1936 issue of *Le Temps,* Louis Mercier attacks the Haitian *élite:*

> We have overthrown the colonial system but not the colonial soul. It makes of us either overseers or slaves: overseers when we hold the least bit of power (. . .) vile, crawling slaves with no spirit or dignity when we are not in power (. . .) It makes us accept as something perfectly natural the fate of our brothers steeped in vice and destitution.

What is significant here is that the writers do not accuse their compatriots of having a "slave mentality," but rather denounce the upper classes for having a "planter mentality," for apeing the erstwhile masters; in a word, for having adopted an essentially un-Haitian ideology. Jean-Baptiste Chenèt is addressing his own class when he writes in "Une Chartre" (*Études poétiques,* Port-au-Prince, 1846):

> When the colons were forced to submit
> To our efforts, they had their revenge:
> We inherited their obsession of hate
> And also their absurd prejudice.

What is shameful, then, is not being descended from slaves but forgetting this fact by perpetuating the very injustices the Ancestors died to eradicate, and thus betraying what is most admirable in the national tradition.

It may seem paradoxical that the writers of Haiti should accuse the descendents of slaves of committing the sins of the masters. But the accusation is in fact perfectly understandable: those Whites who were still in Haiti in 1804 were eliminated by Dessalines. In most of the other Antilles, White immigrants have continued to arrive through the years. In some, Asian laborers have been brought in from China or the Indian sub-continent. This has not been the case in Haiti, where the ruling class is not made up of descendents of White planters or Asian shop-keepers and entrepreneurs, but of Mulattos and Blacks. It is true that a small number of impoverished Near-Eastern immigrants arrived in Haiti at the end of the nineteenth century, and that their descendents have by now almost monopolized wholesale trade. When the Haitians realized that commerce was rapidly passing into the hands of the "Syriens," they unleashed a virulent press campaign against them. In 1905, the weekly *Anti-Syrien* (which changed its name to *L'Agriculteur* the following year) used the kind of ranting invective that Julius Streicher would adopt, thirty years later, for his infamous *Der Sturmer*. An expulsion decree against the "Syriens" does not seem to have been very effective, and the hate campaign eventually abated. Yet in 1938, Edna Taft, a somewhat gushing but not unperceptive American tourist, observed in *A Puritan in Voodoo-land* (Philadelphia, 1938) that:

> A good many retail shops are run by Syrians. These Syrians are not liked too well in Haiti. The élite regards them somewhat as the Park Avenue dowager on the Social Register who looks down upon the Jewish peddler with his pushcart. (p. 76.)

Writing in 1974, Alix Mathon points out that, then as now, "the Haitians have always refused to consider them as belonging to the white race." (*The Flag at Half Mast* [*Le Drapeau en berne*, Port-au-Prince, 1974, p. 17.]) Be that as it may, very few "Syrien" characters appear in Haitian fiction.

Since the ethnic composition of Haitian society is comparable to no other in the world, it is not surprising that the theme of race receives a distinctive and unique treatment in Haitian letters.

While the founders of Haiti were forced to organize the country according to European models, they loudly proclaimed it a *Black* republic. Legend has it that, when a flag was to be designed for the Black Republic, Dessalines ripped the white band off a French tricolor, thus symbolically rejecting any European participation in the destiny of the nation. Haiti's first consititution forbade the acquisition of land by Whites and granted the rights of asylum and naturalization to all persons of African extraction. Haitians have always been aware that the victory which made them free was not only one of slaves over masters but one of Blacks over Whites, and that it therefore had an exemplary value for all Africans and their descendents. Again to quote the baron de Vastey: "Does (our independence) not supply undoubted proof that Africa is capable of civilization?" (*op. cit.,* p. 74.) Vastey makes it clear, in a footnote to the sentence just quoted, that this is not Negritude *avant la lettre:*

> Africa, we are of opinion, can be civilized only by a conquest, of which the object is civilization (. . .) To influence men who are buried in profound ignorance, they must be enlightened (. . .) The Romans themselves owed their civilization to the Greeks alone, and the Greeks to the Egyptians.

Since it would take the West a century or more to become aware that there was such a thing as African cultural life, one can hardly fault the Haitians for not having celebrated it. But in another of Vastey's works, *An Essay on the Causes of the Revolution and Civil Wars in Hayti* (1819; English trans. by W.H.M.B., Exeter, 1823), we find a very interesting passage: Vastey has just noted that the palace of Sans Souci and its chapel (both badly damaged in the 1842 earthquake, but still tourist attractions today) were completed in 1813, and he comments:

> These two structures, erected by the descendents of Africans, show that we have not lost the architectural taste and genius of our ancestors who covered Ethiopia, Egypt, Carthage and Old Spain with their superb monuments. (p. 137.)

Vastey is not making any claims for his African contemporaries, but he is asserting that their—and his—ancestors were present at the dawn of Western civilization. I believe he is the first New World Black to have claimed ethnic identity with the builders of the Pyramids, whom he sees as having handed the torch of civilization to the Greeks. He is arguing that Haitians are on the way to fulfilling a manifest destiny that he had identified two years before in his *Political Remarks . . .* while exhorting his countrymen:

> Blacks as we are, and yellow in complexion, bowed as we have been for centuries under the yoke of slavery and ignorance, assimilated to the condition of the brute; how resolutely ought we to exert ourselves; how much of perseverance, wisdom and virtue is necessary for reanimating our race, to this. moment enchained, and in darkness! (p. 9.)

In a very long essay entitled *On the Vindication of the Black Race by the Republic of Haiti (De la réhabilitation de la race noire par la république d'Haïti,* Paris, 1900), Hannibal Price elaborates Vastey's argument. Price is well satisfied that his country's achievements have given, and will continue to give the lie to the hoary arguments advanced by Whites as proof of the congenital inferiority of Negroes, and that

> (. . .) this Black Republic (. . .) is the glory of all Negroes, for it is the noblest, strongest achievement of our common mother, the Black Race. (p. 101.)

Conversely, writers have often pointed out with sorrow that the sins of Haiti bring disgrace not only upon the nation but also on the race. A journalist who signs "Sentinelle" writes, in *L'Opinion nationale* of February 4th, 1893:

> What must others think of our Republic? If our history as a nation were known abroad, wouldn't the friends of our race shrug their shoulders and sigh with discouragement?

From the first productions of Haitian letters to contemporary works, Haitians have assumed the role of spokesmen for their exploited brothers wherever they might be. It would be easy to put together an anthology of Haitian prose and poetry consisting solely of texts that denounce White racism and protest against its more repulsive manifestations. The lynching of Negroes in the American South, the rape of Ethiopia by Mussolini, forced labor in the French African colonies, apartheid in South Africa, the hysterical fear of White women confronted by Black men, the callous exploitation of Black workers, artists, and athletes—all have been duly noted and exposed by Haitian authors. In his marvellous poem *Ebony Wood (Bois d'ébène*, Port-au-Prince, 1945), Jacques Roumain sings of Black brotherhood and sorrow:

> Negro peddler of revolt
> You know all the highways of the world
> From the time you were sold in Guinea (. . .)
> But I also know a silence
> Of twenty-five thousand dead Negroes
> Of twenty-five thousand ebony cross-ties
> Of the Congo-Ocean railway line
> But I know
> Shrouds of silence on cypress trees
> Petals of Black blood-clots on the thorns
> Of that wooded grove where my Georgia brother was lynched
> And, Ethiopian shepherd,
> What terror gave you, Ethiopian shepherd,
> This mask of mineral silence?

As with other committed Black writers, whatever their nationality and language of expression, this angry detailing of abuses suffered is coupled with affirmations of Black beauty and pride, and with visions of a fraternal world born of revolution. René Depestre's *Crossroads (Croisée des routes*, Port-au-Prince, 1946) sums up this ideological position:

> . . . I am a nigger
> I am murdered at every street corner
> I am mistreated, debased, prostituted
> My mug inspires painters of grotesques
> I remain face to the winds at the doors of temples
> When I rest sewers are palaces
> Compared to the black holes where
> Certain men of my race sink down
> When night comes (. . .)
> My life is a horrible penitentiary
> A prison without bars
> An ageless despair (. . .)
> In their own language I sing my own beauty
> I sing my own love (. . .)
> I know that pain is preparing a dreadful message
> Which will set on fire
> The frontage of wooden houses and of brick homes (. . .)
> And there will I be the liberated Negro
> My chains will serve children as toys
> And will be made into broaches
> For the glittering busts of wives.

Long before the Harlem Renaissance, the Afro-Cuban school and the

Paris-based Négritude writers, Haitian authors were articulating what Jacques Roumain called the *Black Man's Grievances (Griefs de l'homme noir,* Paris, 1939) as well as what Jean Brierre called (in English) *Black Soul* (La Habana, 1947). This ideological quality of Haitian literature is, of course, essential and permeates some of its most inspired works. It would be interesting to compare this corpus with the writings of other Black writers from Africa, the United States and the rest of the Caribbean to determine whether—and if so, in what measure—Haitians have contributed a distinctive note to the expression of the common concern. But this project would demand a long and detailed study which cannot be attempted here. Let us instead consider the theme as it reflects the peculiar, indeed the unique, aspects of race relations in Haitian society.

Unlike other Caribbean Blacks, Haitians have never experienced racial discrimination at the hands of their White compatriots since, for all intents and purposes, there are no White Haitians. The word *blan* in Créole means "foreigner"; a Black American visiting Port-au-Prince would be referred to as a *blan nwa.* Caucasians in Haiti are foreign merchants, missionaries, teachers, development technicians, and simple tourists. Many do appear as characters in Haitian novels and stories; some as open-minded, well-intentioned observers of Haitian reality. These include Phillips Benfield, the American anthropologist patterned after Melville Herskovits (the author of *Life in a Haitian Valley),* in Jean-Baptiste Cinéas' novel *The Sacred Legacy (L'Héritage sacré,* Port-au-Prince, 1945), and the sensitive Frenchman Jean Luze, in Marie Chauvet's *Love, Anger and Madness (Amour, Colère et Folie,* Paris, 1968). Others are brutal, prejudiced exploiters; as could be expected, most American characters found in fiction dealing with the U.S. occupation of Haiti are of this type. In short, the image of foreign Whites in Haitian letters is neither systematically favorable nor consistently pejorative.

More to the point, Haitian writers use White characters to expose the color prejudice they find rampant among the nation's ruling classes. Despite loudly proclaimed racial pride, this *élite* all too often interiorizes White racism and—albeit tacitly—equates intellectual distinction and physical attractiveness with Caucasian features. Foreigners (White foreigners, that is) are therefore considered by them as desirable mates, because they can produce offspring of a more "attractive" physical type. This far from admirable quest on the part of many Haitian parents for White sons-in-law (White daughters-in-law are much less frequently mentioned, possibly because few unattached White women come to settle in Haiti) has inspired Haitian satirists such as André Chevallier in *He's White! (Li blanc!,* Port-au-Prince, 1916):

> Good old Madame Busybody loved everything white, to distraction. Despite her years, she dressed in white. When a chicken was served, she would only eat its white meat.

> She used so much powder that, even though she was really sepia,
> she became almost white. She had sworn to marry her two daughters
> to no one but Whites, but to authentic Whites, to full-blooded Whites—
> for the improvement of "the race." (p. 10.)

Other writers are less amused. Maurice Casséus' comments in his novel *Viejo* (Port-au-Prince, 1935) read like a bitter indictment:

> You, all of you here, dream of finding for your daughter any White
> man just off the ship (. . .) It is enough that he be White for you and
> your daughters and your wives to fall into a swoon. It is enough that
> he be White for you to endow him with universal learning, to bestow
> upon him all titles and diplomas. It is enough that he be White for all
> obstacles to fade in his path as if by magic. (. . .) And with all that you
> claim to be at the forefront of Blacks in the whole world! (pp. 114-
> 115.)

And, more recently, Nadine Magliore testifies to the persistence of the preference for White husbands; the heroine of her novel *The Pain of Living (Le Mal de vivre,* Port-au-Prince, 1968) declares:

> A White man is a much appreciated game for our girls to bag. First,
> because he is generally not broke; also, because marrying White gives
> you a lot of prestige, and above all because you thereby "improve the
> race." (p. 73.)

The theme of race in Haitian letters must not be viewed exclusively in the context of Black struggle against White oppression; it also reflects the tensions that have existed, and continue to exist, in Haiti between Blacks and Mulattos. In the absence of other ethnic groups, these tensions take on a pervasiveness and intensity unique in the Caribbean.

In colonial times, many French settlers emancipated the children they had had by Black women. These *gens de couleur,* whose human rights and privileges were—theoretically at least—guaranteed by the 1685 *Code noir,* eventually formed an intermediate class which, by the time of the Revolution, had considerable economic power. It is estimated that they owned as much as a third of the land and a fourth of the slaves in the colony. While they came to be feared and despised by the Whites, who subjected them to all sorts of of discriminatory measures (denial of representation in the local assemblies, non-eligibility for officers commissions in the militia, segregation in public places, and so on), their wealth and status were also based on the exploitation of Black slaves. Some left the country along with the Whites; those who remained, since they were generally educated and skilled, quite naturally filled the positions of leadership vacated by the French. In the new Republic, they soon established themselves as the ruling class and jealously defended their power and privileges against the illiterate, unskilled mass of Black slaves. The self-perpetuating Haitian ruling class was not, however, composed exclusively of *gens de couleur;* it included Black military leaders, who also established themselves as important land-owners and public officials. As was to be expected, members of the ruling class henceforth tended to intermarry and to consolidate their position by making upward social mobility as difficult as possible. With time, this small self-contained *élite* saw its absolute supremacy challenged by a growing class of mostly Black professionals, technicians, and shop-keepers, which Haitian sociologists identify as the *classes moyennes*. Since most of the *élite* were Mulatto and most of the *classes moyennes* were Black (as well, of course, as the downtrodden *masse* which was, and is, exploited by both), specification of race came to denote social class, and vice-versa. Jacques Roumain's party line statement on color prejudice in *Analyse schématique du Parti communiste haïtien* (Port-au-Prince, 1934) seems to me somewhat simplistic:

> The Haitian Communist Party considers the problem of color prejudice as extremely important, because it provides the cloak under which Black and Mulatto politicians would like to conjure away the class struggle. (p. 3.)

This could fit every instance of color prejudice (or possibly of any kind of prejudice) in the world, and—as happens in Communist analysis—refuses to consider that psychological complexities may be more than economic epiphenomena. René A. Saint-Louis is, to my mind, more convincing when he writes, in *Haitian Pre-sociology (La Présociologie haïtienne,* Montreal, 1970):

> Haiti is a typical example of racial characteristics having influenced, and continuing to influence, the formation of social classes (. . .) so much that they are at the origins of what might today be called Haitian ideology. (p. 12.)

A Créole proverb, attributed to the leader of the peasant revolt of 1843, Jean-Jacques Acaau, puts it more succinctly: *Nèg rich se milat, milat pòv se nèg* ("A rich Negro is a Mulatto, a poor Mulatto is a Negro").

Complementing and refining the French adjectives *noir* and *mulâtre*, the Haitian obsession with appearance has led to the creation of a whole set of other terms to indicate all possible combinations of pigmentation (from very dark to lightly tanned), hair characteristics (from fuzzy to silky), and facial traits (from negroid to caucasian); we thus find, among many others: *marabout, chabin, griffe, grimaud, caïmite, rouge, kribich chodé, takté kodind,* all of which are mysterious for non-Haitian readers of French, and sources of practically unsurmountable difficulties for translators of Haitian works.

In the Haitian context, then, the terms *noir* and *mulâtre* do not refer to ethnic type exclusively. They also carry social and political connotations. Social, because while the illegitimate child of a Black working woman and a White sailor on shore leave might be described as *mulâtre* in appearance, he would certainly not be considered as belonging to the *mulâtre* (i.e. upper) class. Conversely, a Black high government official or successful businessman would be—and would in all likelihood make certain he was by marrying into a *mulâtre* family. Haitian political factions traditionally form along class—and therefore color—lines. However, to maintain the illusion that politics and not color determines party affiliation, the *mulâtre* group makes it a point to include some ethnic Blacks in the government when it is in power, while the *noir* group does the same for Mulattos when its turn comes.*

Thus understood, "race" must be taken into account in any discussion of Haitian class tensions and social behavior. The theme is present in Haitian letters from the very start. The reader may have noticed that the quotation from Pierre Faubert's poem "Aux Haïtiens" addresses both Blacks and Mulattos; stanzas which follow call upon them to desist from their fraternal contentions in the name of national unity and of God "who, in man, values / only the soul, and not the color." The same appeal is found in Bergeaud's *Stella,* where Romulus is *noir* and his brother Rémus *mulâtre;* only when they put aside their mutual distrust can they unite to overthrow the colonial oppressor, and only if they remember the nation's motto, *L'Union fait la force,* will Haiti prosper.

By acknowledging the existence of an internal racial problem in Haiti, the first generation of writers were already refusing to participate in a conspiracy of silence. An understandable conspiracy: admitting that color prejudice survived the elimination of the White planters would undermine the Haitians' claim to legitimacy as illustrators and glorifiers of negritude. And we have seen that this claim is essential to the image Haitians want to present to the world, essentially, in fact, to their collective and personal self-respect. The persistence of color prejudice was—and continues to be—a source of constant embarrassment, all the more so since foreign observers of Haitian reality seldom fail to expound upon it. Be that as it may, the fact, again according to René A. Saint-Louis, is that

> (. . .) the question of color prejudice (. . .) has never been raised openly
> and objectively (. . .) It remains a taboo subject, discussed in the
> privacy of the home or with intimate friends, never with strangers, be
> they White or Black (. . .) (Haitians) deny the existence of this problem
> in their country. *(op. cit.,* p. 114.)

But successive generations of Haitian writers will refuse to keep silent and will tirelessly identify color prejudice as a fundamental cause of the nation's stagnation if not degradation. Without going back to baron de

---

*Systematic discussions of the concepts of race and class as they pertain to Haiti can be found in Leslie F. Manigat, *Ethnicité, nationalisme et politique. Le cas d'Haïti,* New York, 1975, and David Nicholls, *From Dessalines to Duvalier, Race, Colour and National Independence in Haiti,* Cambridge, 1979.

Vastey, who accused the Port-au-Prince Mulattos of having inherited color prejudice from their *colon* fathers or grandfathers, one could quote Cadet Jérémie, who wrote in *L'Effort* (Port-au-Prince, 1905):

> (. . .) color prejudice is a sequel of colonial domesticity. If it weren't a social reality, it would not be used so often as a political weapon. (p. 194.)

Most of Jérémie's contemporaries would probably rather not have been reminded of the gap between the official "Black pride" ideology of the Republic and the reality of its everyday life. Just as Roger Dorsinville's readers, forty years later, would probably have liked to forget, as he points out in *Letter to the Light-colored (Letter aux hommes clairs,* Port-au-Prince, 1946), that while

> (. . .)it has recently been written that the color question has now become irrelevant. In fact, it has never ceased to exist in Haiti, (. . .) under the veil of courteous urbanity, it is a secret unrelenting war. (p. 1.)

Everyone regrets, but hardly anyone denies, that the question of color today still hangs over Haitian social and political life. Writing about François Duvalier's accession to power, one of his exiled opponents, Jacquelin M. Despeignes, writes in *New Glance (Nouveau regard,* Sherbrooke, Quebec, 1975):

> The question of color, which blinded the masses, and the false interpretation of Estimism* as the denial of mulatto power made things easier for the reactionary *noirisme.* (p. 27.)

Obviously, all Haitian authors do not adopt the same tone when exposing their countrymen's prejudices. Some do it in a gently sarcastic way: in *The Pitite-Caille Family (La Famille des Pitite-Caille,* Port-au-Prince, 1905), for example, Justin Lhérisson makes fun of one of his characters, a local Casanova whose taste in women is so eclectic that the seventy-nine children he fathers run the gamut of possible Haitian phenotypes:

> These children were of all hues: *nègres francs, nègres rouges, chabins, tacté-codinde, griffes, mulâtres, sacatras, marabouts, tchiam-pourras,* etc. (p. 17.)

Others, like Stéphen Alexis in *The Masked Negro (Le Nègre masqué,* Port-au-Prince, 1933), are more explicit and do not mince words:

> Despite White prejudice, which lumps us all together, from the lightest octoroon to the darkest Negro, as objects of contempt, you still establish wretched epidermic differences among yourselves: Don't

---

*From the name of president Dumarsais Estimé, who came to power in 1946 and was overthrown by General Magloire in 1950. Under Estimé, an effort was made to give more power to the masses and to the Black middle-classes.

complain about American prejudices *(Alexis was writing at the time of the American occupation)*: the attitude of many among you justifies it. (p. 13.)

The question might legitimately be raised of whether the physical type of individual influences Haitian authors' views about, and treatment of, the theme of race. I do not believe the question is relevant in the case of writers from the origins to quite recently (World War II). Whether light or dark-skinned, they all belonged to the *élite* and had generally been born into it. None defended the color prejudice; almost all of them deplored it vehemently, and set themselves up as spokesmen for its victims: the peasant *masse,* of course, and also the emerging *classes moyennes.* But, during and after the "Revolution of 1946" and the *noiriste* presidency of Dumarsais Estimé, many young writers from the Black *classes moyennes* entered the literary scene. While it is dangerous to generalize, I think it can be argued, first, that they were even less hesitant than their predecessors to attack color prejudice and, second, that their ideological position was more radical. Until then, writers deplored the *élite*'s successful efforts to keep a monopoly on education and power, but did not seriously question its conception of what Haitian culture was. And this conception was fundamentally French, or European (White at any rate), in its orientation. The French language was considered infinitely superior to Créole, Catholicism to vodùn, imported waltzes to domestic yanvalous. The African (i.e. popular) contributions to Haitian culture were systematically downgraded and, whether they admitted it or not, Haitian writers were anxious to fashion their country into "a little Black corner of France" (as the French historian Michelet once called it).

This unabashed francophilia may explain why so many admirable French characters appear in Haitian novels of two or three generations back. These Frenchmen are usually either priests or teachers, and do not hesitate to criticize Haiti and Haitians. In Frédéric Marcelin's *Thémistocle-Épaminondas Labasterre* (Paris, 1901), for example, Monsieur Hodelin has come from France to teach not only academic subjects but civic virtue; he declares:

> The country folk are those in whom you must have confidence, for whom you must struggle. When I finally see a man of your middle class leave the towns and go to the mountains to wage the fight against ignorance under all its forms, then I'll say: "There is a citizen, and the nation needs many like him." (p. 121.)

Monsieur Hodelin takes his charges on excursions to show them the beauties of their country. He even takes them to a vodùn ceremony, and preaches tolerance for the people's religion. In Léon Laleau's *Le Choc* (Port-au-Prince, 1932), Father Le Ganet, a handsome Breton priest,

(. . .)wore his knowledge as he did his cassock, with humility but with dignity. (. . .) Even though he was a favorite of high society (. . .) he gave it nothing he wouldn't give the poor and—if he showed any favoritism—it was towards his peasant flock. (pp. 12-13.)

In Delorme Lafontant's *Célie* (Port-au-Prince, 1939), Edard, a French doctor who practices in the town of Jacmel, accuses his Haitian hosts:

You like routine, easy work, good food. The least effort exhausts you. The 1804 epic has left you drained. And when, by some chance, one of you stands out for his talents or his virtues, you grind him down with calumny. (p. 136.)

These virtuous, learned, and eloquent French authority figures serve of course as the authors' spokesmen, and a Parisian or Breton accent seems to give Truth a clearer ring than that of Port-au-Prince or Cap-haïtien. One could wonder whether this is simply a proof of admiration for the intellectual mother-country, or a typically colonial lack of self-confidence, or even perhaps internalized prejudice. Are Professor Hodelin, Father Le Ganet and Doctor Edard so admirable because of their professions? Their nationality? Or their race? Obviously, it is hard to say but, as could be expected, even those Haitians who bemoan it, show themselves to be not entirely immune to prevalent color prejudice. The most revealing examples are usually esthetic judgments which show conscious or unconscious dislike of the Black phenotype. In *Idalina* (Paris, 1836), for example, Ignace Nau describes the vodùn priest Galba, whose

(. . .) broad and wooly head has absolutely no resemblance to the truly African type which improves considerably *(s'améliore considér-ablement)* in our country.

Fifty years later, Louis-Joseph Janvier, in *L'Egalité des races* (Paris, 1884) and Anténor Firmin, in *De l'égalité des races* (Paris, 1885) argued that the Haitian physical type proves that "a race's beauty . . . develops in direct proportion to its degree of civilization" (Firmin, p. 277), and that among Haitian Blacks "an amelioration, then a true intellectual and physical transformation took place" (Janvier, p. 24). (Quoted by Ulrich Fleischmann, *Ideologie und Wirklichkeit in der Literatur Haitis,* Berlin, 1969, p. 52.)

In his novel *L'Amant idéal* (Port-au-Prince, 1926), Aimard Le Sage, a furious opponent of vodùn, describes the priestess Agathe thus:

She has lips like a thirsty she-camel's; with a single kiss she copiously sprays your face. O, what an adorable Congolese! (p. 51.)

Still today, one very occasionally finds rather shocking descriptions, such as the one Mercédès Guillard makes of an ugly woman in *The Desperate Ones (Les Désespérés,* Port-au-Prince, 1964):

Hélène was ugly: an expressionless face, underlined by a square chin, dull eyes, a blurry skin pigmented by splotches and pimples, a broad mouth and a flat nose (. . .) this unattractive face was crowned with scanty fuzzy hair. (p. 26.)

Taking their clue from the Haitian sociologist Jean Price-Mars who, in *Thus Spake the Elder (Ainsi parla l'oncle*, Compiègne, 1928) and other works, had accused his countrymen of suffering from "collective Bovarysm" in refusing to accept and respect the African component of their cultural heritage, most writers would henceforth celebrate it. They exalt the beauty of vodùn, the courage of peasants, the tenacity of poor Black students of the *classes moyennes*. Créole words and expressions are introduced into French-language texts—no longer to amuse or provide an exotic note, but with the same respect given to the official language. Indeed, some poets and dramatists chose to compose entirely in Créole; novelists eventually followed their lead.

It might be, and has been, argued that this is populist writing, to be viewed in the same light as Zola's proletarian novels or Mistral's Provençal poems. That Haitian writers are once again looking to Paris for inspiration and, in typically neo-colonial fashion, lag fifty years behind the times in their choice of literary models. The point is, in fact, that the term "popular" in Haiti is just about synonymous with "Black," in contrast with the term *élite* which, as we have seen, is practically synonymous with "Mulatto." So that by celebrating the poor, writers are, implicitly at the very least, taking a position not only on the class but also on the color issue. Further, to return to the question of the writer's pigmentation, we should note that the new ideology cut across color lines; its most vocal proponents were as likely to be light *mulâtres*, like Jacques Roumain, as Blacks of the *classes moyennes*, like Jean-Baptiste Cinéas.

When dealing with the race issue, most Haitian essayists side with their Black compatriots and, as could be expected, most novelists dramatize their unfair treatment at the hands of those of lighter pigmentation. The rejection of a young *noir* by a *mulâtre* girl who wishes to "improve the race," or of a dark girl by a socially ambitious young man are stereotypic. In Hénock Trouillot's *Flesh, Blood and Treason (Chair, sang et trahison*, Port-au-Prince, 1947), Georges Larue, a *mulâtre*, is driven by financial necessity to marry a *noire*, Germaine Charles, *la douce brunette:*

> Georges felt ashamed, but of one thing only: of having had to show himself, during the dazzling wedding celebrations, with his bride, a Black, to the assembled guests, whom he took to be flabbergasted by his loss of caste. (p. 17.)

Although Germaine is an exemplary wife, she will be driven to an early grave by her husband's obsessive contempt and cruelty.

Yet the defense of *Noirs* against *Mulâtres* is by no means a reflex reaction on the part of Haitian writers. They also speak up when Mulattos are unjustly persecuted. Their plight during the *noiriste* agitation of 1946

is remembered by Philippe Thoby-Marcelin in a poem, *Without Security*
(*A Fonds perdu*, Paris, 1953), whose onomatopoetic title "Ta lala hope"
evokes the beat of "savage" drums:

. . . Conical rutting of jungle drums
Black, screaming anarchy
Of gesticulation
Kill the mulatto, the son of a dog
(Ta lala hope!
     hope!
          hope!)
Misfit Jew of Haiti
Give us the land
You pogrom-fodder
Your place is not here
(Ta lala hope!
     hope!
          hope!)
We'll take your woman
The honey of your blood
Your subtle guts!. . .

In two of her novels, Marie Chauvet evokes the persecutions to which
the Mulattos were subjected, in 1946 (in *Daughter of Haiti* [*Fille d'Haïti*],
Paris, 1954), and—although it is not specified in so many words—during
the Duvalier regime (in *Anger* [*Colère*], Paris, 1968). Both Marcelin and
Marie Chauvet were *mulâtre* in phenotype and social status, but Black
authors do not hesitate either to denounce the opportunistic or even racist
foundations of some *noiristes'* political stances. In 1937, for example, E.L.
Vernet wrote in *Haiti's Worst Enemies (Les Pires ennemis d'Haiti*, Port-
au-Prince, 1937):

In our country, most of our dark brothers who speak or write about
race and color prejudice are themselves full of those prejudices. Their
defense of *la race* (. . .) is tainted with feelings of jealousy and arrogant
individualism. And several, taken individually, would immediately
cease being concerned with these matters if only Whites and the
pretentious Mulattos agreed to tell them this: "The Black race to which
you all belong is in fact inferior; but *you personally* constitute an
exception and are our equal." (p. 14.)

In his fine novel *The Music of Trees (Les Arbres musiciens,* Paris,
1957), Jacques-Stéphen Alexis, who was Black phenotypically and who
died fighting the Duvalier régime, shows how one form of racism
engenders another. He argues that the pro-Mulatto government of Élie
Lescot (1941-1946) exacerbated tensions and gave rise to color
ideologies which would, ten years later, result in revengeful persecution of
the *élite:*

(. . .) odd and dangerous pararacist theories were evolving in the petty bourgeoisie, and pseudo-revolutionary "colorism" was wreaking havoc. (. . .) Under the ashes of the stupid "lescotian" policy, the old traditional struggles between liberals (i.e. *élite*) and nationalists (i.e. *classes moyennes*) of the preceding century were being stirred up. (pp. 155-156.)

To sum up, Haitian authors have always been willing to admit the existence of color prejudice in their country. Their lucidity and courage are all the more praiseworthy in that by doing so they risk being accused of providing grist for the mill of malevolent foreign analysts. Haitian authors have not limited themselves to platonic expressions of dismay and pious appeals for universal brotherhood; they have instead underscored the peculiar economic, social and political dimensions of the Haitian racial ideologies. Any open-minded foreign reader familiar with Haitian letters cannot fail to realize that, in its essence and in its manifestations, the "race problem" in Haiti resists hasty analyses, and that as far as it is concerned, seeking analogies between Haitian society and other societies, Caribbean or otherwise, would in all probability lead to erroneous conclusions.

THE U.S. AND AMERICANS
IN HAITIAN LETTERS

Until the last decades of the 19th century, relations between the United States and Haiti amounted to little more than modest commercial exchanges. Very few U.S. concerns tried to establish themselves on the island, and very few American citizens came in search of fortune or adventure. In fact, diplomatic relations between the two countries were not established until 1862. This was due in part to fierce opposition from Southern legislators who feared that granting recognition to the Black Republic would encourage their own slaves to revolt. Consequently, the U.S. took little interest in Haitian affairs and did not much influence them. Haiti conducted most of her foreign trade with Europe and, in the absence of the United States, the French, German, and English imperialists were left to compete among themselves for whatever spoils Haiti might offer.

On several occasions, even before 1862, private and public American organizations encouraged the emigration to Haiti of free Black Americans. This was at the request of the Haitian government, which was seeking to remedy the country's lack of technicians and specialized workers. Taking advantage of the automatic right of residency and almost automatic right of naturalization granted by the Haitian constitution to persons of African descent, some 13,000 Black Americans settled in Haiti between 1824 and 1828; others arrived in 1856; sixteen thousand landed five years later. And in 1863, a last contingent of 500 settlers reached Ile-à-Vache, off the southern coast. These projects were badly organized and each, in its turn, ended in failure. For instance, fourteen hundred of the sixteen hundred immigrants of 1861 demanded and obtained repatriation to the U.S.*
Hence, it is no surprise that the presence of Black American settlers seems to have left no trace in Haitian letters. Still, one does find, in Émeric Bergeaud's *Stella* (Paris, 1859), the first novel ever written by a Haitian, a reference to Miss Francis *(sic.,* for Frances) Wright. The author reminds us in a footnote that:

> Miss Francis Wright, a very rich lady of Scottish origin, came to Haiti in 1832 with about thirty slaves, intending they should enjoy the benefits of freedom. These slaves had been purchased from a Louisiana plantation. When she bought them, Miss Wright, who had preached against slavery, wanted to prove to the American *colons* that a benevolent and humane treatment was preferable to their own violent and cruel system, which was founded on the supposed congenital depravity of Africans. She had failed (. . .) Therefore, as we said, the philanthropist left this land of selfishness, and came to Haiti with her slaves, in order to set them free. (pp. 325-326.)

*See Ludwell L. Montague, *Haiti and the United States, 1714-1938,* Durham, N.C., 1940, Chapter IV, "Negro Colonization."

Bergeaud refers to the Americans as *colons,* rather than *planteurs,* as they are generally called in French. He thus identifies them with those French *colons* whom the Haitians had fought and vanquished a half-century earlier. As we shall see, it is not the last time that Americans are identified with the French oppressors of long ago. Further, Bergeaud celebrates and exalts a generous American the better to denounce her racist, slave-owning compatriots. Similarly, two of the three references to Black slavery in the U.S. that I find in Haitian poetry during this first period are panegyrics to the memory of John Brown, the White abolitionist executed in Charleston, West Virginia, in 1859. In a poem dated 1884, Tertulien Guilbaud compares John Brown to Toussaint Louverture and declares:

> What old Brown did is more divine, I find;
> The martyr's gallows conjure up the Cross! (. . .)
> To privilege born, to have chosen duty;
> Being free to hate fetters; being White to die for Blacks;
> Love alone could this wonder achieve.

And the poem ends with a denunciation of the Virginians who have executed the hero:

> Happy Virginians, dizzy with
> Victory's wine, hurl your mocking jibes
> At this woeful gallows-tree. Boast, and boast again
> Of your victory, tacking on to this pure, noble name
> The bitter insult—the only bounty granted the just
> Here below! You do well. As for us,
> At the foot of this gibbet we fall to our knees.
> (T. Guilbaud, "John Brown," in Saint-Louis, C. & Lubin, M.A.,
> *Panorama de la poésie haïtienne,* Port-au-Prince, 1950, pp. 86-88.)

In the tercets of his sonnet *John Brown,* Edmond Laforest also compares the abolitionist to the Messiah:

> Redeemer of Blacks, Brown dies for their freedom
> Like the Divine Christ, full of humanity
> He soars on the gallows, transfigured, sublime!
> From his seed will some day the righteous tree sprout
> Right will have might and slaves will be men;
> A great people will drown in its blood a great crime.
> (E. Laforest, "John Brown," in *ibid.,* pp. 183-184.)

When in 1865 Pierre Faubert exhorts his Black and Mulatto compatriots to stop their fratricidal struggles, he reminds them of the heroic times of the War of Independence:

> For us then, ah! What glorious days!
> Old Europe applauded our heroes' great deeds
> And that nation, oppressor of millions of slaves
> Trembled to hear the fall of their fetters.

This is a rather telling example of the Haitian *élite's* systematic Eurocentrism: to claim that old Europe had, in contradistinction to the young U.S., applauded the insurgent slaves is singularly to ignore history. At any rate, times had changed and this "nation, oppressor of millions of slaves" hardly trembled anymore. If any trembling were henceforth to be done, it would be done by Haitians:

> What! divided, when so near to your shores
> Mulattos and Blacks are oppressed!
> When those northern supporters of slavery's ways
> Avidly stare at your bountiful land?
>
> Hatreds? Dissensions? And while in your skies
> This vulture rapaciously glides
> And the better to further your race's misfortune
> Makes ready to pounce on the island of Cuba.
> (P. Faubert, "Aux Haïtiens," in *Ogé*, Paris, 1856, pp. 143-146.)

Faubert's poem is, to my knowledge, the first denunciation of U.S. imperialism found in Haitian letters, and the first warning against American expansionist policies. In the second period we shall deal with, which goes from about 1880 to the landing of the U.S. Marines in 1915, these warnings will become numerous and urgent.

There was ample reason to worry; in 1868, President Andrew Johnson proposed, purely and simply, the annexation of Haiti and Santo Domingo. Fortunately, Congress refused to approve the plan. In 1890, taking advantage of Haitian political instability, the U.S. Navy tried to establish a naval base at Môle Saint Nicholas, on the north coast. The Haitian government refused to cooperate, and the project was finally abandoned. Seven years later, the U.S. occupied Cuba and Puerto Rico; Haiti had had a narrow escape. It was, nonetheless, quite clear that, on the pretext of protecting the Panama Canal, the U.S. had become a Caribbean power. And coincidentally, it had carved out for itself the lion's share in the economy of the West Indies. By 1903, 73% of the goods imported by Haiti came from the U.S. The formerly negligible U.S. investments in Haiti were steadily increasing; Haiti was being drawn into the U.S. sphere of influence. As Anténor Firmin wrote, in *Monsieur Roosevelt . . . et la République d'Haïti* (Paris, 1905):

> Evidence can not be denied: the U.S. has acquired a practically undisputed preponderance in the international relations of the New World. (p. 480.)

Direct U.S. intervention in Haitian affairs—indeed, the imposition of a U.S. protectorate—had become not only possible, but likely. In his *Réflexions diverses sur Haïti* (Paris, 1873), Demesvar Delorme addressed those among his compatriots so discouraged by Haitian anarchy that they had come to consider U.S. trusteeship as a possible solution:

Haitians, if ever, may God forbid it, you were to lose your nationality, you would not have the right to speak as men in your own country. You would be reduced to bowing your heads before foreigners. (. . .) You would be kept in a servitude as vile as slavery. You would be despised and mistreated in the U.S. This danger is no longer remote (. . .) it is here, present, pressing, in our island, at our door. (pp. 123; 133.)

In *Bric-à-brac* (Paris, 1910), Frédéric Marcelin cautions those of his compatriots who put their hopes in a fifty-million dollar loan that the U.S. might grant Haiti. For the novelist, who had been Finance Minister and therefore knew whereof he spoke, this development aid would be no boon but, on the contrary, a grave danger. Some speculators would profit from the loan

(. . .) but, poor little Haiti, poor little simple and naive Negroes that we are, what is to become of us in ten years, in five, perhaps tomorrow? Our awesome neighbors have a keen appetite: the more they eat, the hungrier they become. They hardly take the time to digest. Who knows whether they don't think this is an excellent time to unleash the falcon? Too bad for you if your President, your Cabinet, your Congress are turned into decorative vassals of the Honorable Resident-General of the United States! They have already been paid off. (pp. 90-91.)

Half a century later, in his créole-language poem "Diacoute" (Montreal, n.d.), Félix Morisseau-Leroy would bitterly state:

The more the government takes American money
The poorer the Haitian people get.
You'd think American money is bad luck
The more our leaders gobble up American money,
The poorer the Haitian people get. (p. 24.)

In 1905, Anténor Firmin was less pessimistic. The proximity of the U.S. is, in his opinion, an opportunity for Haiti, since:

The U.S. can supply everything we need to propel us on the road to active, hard-working civilization. Americans possess all kinds of assets: capital, technology, work experience and the energy to overcome difficulties.

Firmin does not believe in the possibility of a military intervention:

What responsible U.S. statesman would wish to acquire by force the territory of Haiti, or even a part of her territory? (. . .) No one can doubt that Haiti, to safeguard her independence, has the resolve to fight to the last breath of her last citizen. After all the horrors of a savage war, an invader could only rule over ruins heaped on a sterile battlefield. For so practical a nation as the U.S. to embark willingly upon such an adventure, it would need a motive, the prospect of advantages immense enough to over-rule thoughtful reflection. I can not see how this could come to pass. *(op. cit.,* p. 476.)

Unfortunately, history would not justify Firmin's optimism. Ten years later, on July 28, 1915, Admiral Caperton's Marines landed without encountering resistance.

During the decades which preceded the catastrophe, Haiti's *élite* worried about the U.S.'s might. But what in fact did Haitians know about the U.S.? Very little. And it is precisely for that reason that Anténor Firmin had composed *Monsieur Roosevelt (. . .) et la République d'Haïti,* the first part of which is a long essay on the history of the U.S., on the character of its citizens and on the peculiarities of American civilization. As he points out in the preface:

> Haitians know too little about Americans. To neglect to study the history, life and institutions of a great people with whom we have so many tangible and intangible points of contact constitutes a failing and even a danger that must be eliminated as soon as possible. *(op. cit.,* iv.)

Politicians, journalists, and essayists endeavor to guess the U.S. government's intentions, and to warn and advise Haitian leaders. But in *belles-lettres* as such, the U.S. and its citizens hardly appear at all. We could mention Massillon Coicou's poem "Yankisme," where the poet accuses the American people of having sacrificed the ideals of Benjamin Franklin and George Washington to the pursuit of gold. This declamatory poem incorporates several English expressions (printed here in italics):

> You need gold – or nothing – to be – or not to be.
> *Time is money.* So is crime
> And money always! Always important sums!
> A lot of gold for us Americans!
> *All right!* Straight on to whatever goal
> To which we are drawn by hope of gain.
> *Cotton is king!*
> (M. Coicou, "Yankisme," *Poésies nationales,* Paris, 1892.)

We might also mention, from Frédéric Marcelin's novel *Thémistocle-Épaminondas Labasterre* (Paris, 1901), an ironic reference to an American sea-captain who

> (. . .)belonged to that admirable North American breed which has enrolled the Lord Himself under its commercial banner, without of course sharing the profits with Him. Every time the sea-captain succeeded in evading the coast guard he kneeled and raised his arms to Heaven: "O Everlasting! who art the true, the only God, Thy name be hallowed! Thou hast allowed me to slip my cargo through customs! May thy name be glorified for ever and ever!" (p. 298.)

Haitians, of course, are not the first to have accused Protestants in general and Anglo-Saxons in particular of taking the Deity for a commercial partner. But is is amusing to note that, as late as 1972, Roger

Gaillard still harps on the theme in his *Charades haïtiennes* (Port-au-Prince):

> As far as I know, only the Atlantes *(i.e. the Americans)* have succeeded in uniting love for the Almighty and the grossest appetite for material goods. (p. 158.)

In Fernand Hibbert's *Le Manuscrit de mon ami* (Port-au-Prince, 1923), a Haitian writes his impressions of the U.S. to his friend: "Today, money over-rides everything: New York is the living proof of this." Even the behavior of American women seems to him to reflect an obsession for cash:

> I never tire of observing American women. Above all, I look in their eyes from which dreams are absent. The only word they speak with a tender inflection is DOLLAR. (p. 100.)

What characterizes Americans above all, in Haitian eyes, is materialism, profit pursued by every means and with a clear conscience. And also, of course, color prejudice. The few Haitians to have visited the U.S. bore witness to the abuses inflicted upon their Black brothers. Thus Demesvar Delorme reports, in 1858, that he saw "a light-skinned colored man" slapped in the face by a thief he had caught picking his pocket. Far from condemning the aggressor, the crowd laughed at the victim. Frédéric Marcelin points out in *As Memory Dictates (Au gré du souvenir,* Paris, 1913), that, while

> The Haitian Black looks straight ahead, straight at you; his glance is neither vascilating nor furtive, the American Black keeps his head lowered, and his eyes always seem to look at the ground. (. . .) This is, no doubt, a result of the terrible servitude in which he was kept and from which he never managed to free himself by his own means, and as a result also of the harsh conditions under which he suffers today. (p. 82.)

After mentioning that in New York "race prejudice is still very strong," Fernand Hibbert points out that "the term Black also applies to light-skinned Browns: in the U.S. a Negro and a Mulatto are both called 'colored man.'" Once the American protectorate was established, the Haitian Mulatto *élite* was to receive bitter verification of Hibbert's remark. Meanwhile, the racist abominations perpetrated upon Black Americans provoked the indignation of Haitian intellectuals, to be sure, but it is doubtful that they really identified with the victims. In Fernand Hibbert's novel *Les Thazar* (Port-au-Prince, 1907), the eponymous comic character, who is systematically ridiculed by the author, exclaims at a soirée:

> "Another Negro has been lynched in Georgia (. . .) And time and again our brothers are hanged, crushed, exterminated on the faith of unproven accusations (. . .) In a country which claims to be civilized!

When will Divine Providence inspire a North American Dessalines to conquer true freedom for the martyrs of the American South! (. . .)
Monsieur Thazar's tirade was greeted by rather ironic smiles. (p. 94.)

Doctor Remo, who serves as the author's spokesman, retorts: "Personally (. . .) I think we would be better advised, rather than to worry about the fate of American Negroes, to worry about that of our own Negroes," and Dr. Remo goes on to detail the injustices and abuses suffered by the peasant masses. To want to reform one's own country before criticizing someone else's is of course commendable, but Dr. Remo and his friends receive the horrible news of the lynching in Georgia with surprising equanimity.

Haitian analysts expressed great admiration for American dynamism, enterprise and organizational skill in everything concerned with material life. But as for esthetic sensitivity, courtesy, and plain human decency, Americans were considered as barbarians, especially when compared to the French, who were seen as models of reason and tolerance, as the creators of a civilized way of life which Haitians claimed as their own. Luce Archin-Lay declares, in "France et Haïti" *(Haïti littéraire et scientifique,* 20 avril 1905):

> (In the U.S., colored people are told): *Yellow and Blacks go away, go away to France!* Thank you, for us and for France, the universal motherland, the source of true civilization, of enlightenment, of sublime generosity.

In point of fact, few indeed were those Haitians who had visited the U.S. Haitians rather went to France, to study at the Sorbonne, to drink at the source of savoir-faire and civilized living. And Haitians at home had little occasion to meet American citizens: tourism was for all intents and purposes non-existent, and a census of foreign residents in Port-au-Prince, prepared by the U.S. legation in 1914, shows only thirty-two American citizens. Further, we have no proof that Haitian intellectuals had significant knowledge of American cultural life. Once again, it is in Europe, and especially in France, that they found models. Yvette Gindine is quite right in pointing out that:

> Before 1900, the United States barely existed in the consciousness of the Haitian intellectual élite, a miniscule oligarchy taking its cultural clues and styles from France and totally uninformed on American matters. (Y. Gindine, "Images of the American in Haitian Literature during the Occupation," *Caribbean Studies,* Oct. 1974, p. 38.)

The situation will change, and will change dramatically, with the occupation of Haiti. Numerous American civilians, mostly technicians and administrators, often accompanied by their families, land in the wake of the Marines. In Port-au-Prince as in the back country, Americans are everywhere, in government departments and ministries, on building sites and in custom houses, in army and police barracks, and in technical education centers. American firms obtain concessions. Journalists come in search of stories, businessmen in search of orders. Like it or not, Haitians constantly deal with Americans, who rent houses, take out membership in social clubs, and become part of the scene in general. It becomes useful, if not downright indispensable, to know English. Such American expressions as *shine, boss, payroll, freeze,* etc, become naturalized in Créole. All manners of consumer goods, food products, textiles, and machinery are introduced by the occupants. In nightclubs and social affairs people learn to dance to American jazz. The U.S. and its citizens, once remote and exotic, are now all too at hand and familiar. They are present not only in everyday life but, as could have been expected, in literature.

Gindine's above-quoted article is an excellent overview. Through careful analysis of relevant novels, short stories, and plays, she shows that the image—or, rather, the images—of Americans in Haitian literature at the time of the occupation were diverse and subtle. Side by side with sadistic psychopaths like major Smedley Seaton, in Stéphen Alexis' *The Masked Negro (Le Nègre masqué,* 1933), one finds colonel Harry Murray, who deplores his countrymen's prejudices and admires the refinement of his Port-au-Prince high-society friends (in Annie Desroy's *The Yoke* [*Le Joug,* Port-au-Prince, 1934]). Systematic denigrations of the U.S., as well as balanced and sympathetic analyses, were put forward. Of course, censorship saw to it—especially during the first years of the occupation— that attacks against the U.S. remained within what were considered acceptable bounds. But also, writers were perfectly aware that their criticism would be all the more convincing were they to keep at least the appearance of objectivity. And, needless to say, the condemnation of a given policy becomes particularly eloquent when it emanates from one who is forced to enforce it; Gindine gives several instances of American officials who criticize, explicitly or implicitly, the actions of the occupation authorities.

Without summarizing Gindine's findings, I will offer some complementary remarks. It must be remembered that the trauma of the occupation forced the Haitian *élite* to search its collective soul, to try to understand how it had managed to lead the country to disaster. Writers didn't hesitate to stigmatize, sometimes very violently, the selfishness and lack of civil spirit of the ruling classes. They saw the occupation as an act of aggression, of course, but also and perhaps especially, as a well-deserved punishment meted out by God or by history. In this context, the American citizen and his country function as reactives which make it possible to illustrate the whole spectrum of possible conducts adopted by Haitians during those somber times.

Some collaborate with the Americans, and prosper from them; others learn to live in silent indignation, or attempt to resist by legal means, by writing articles and attending public meetings; still others opt for direct action and join the peasant guerrillas. Peasants did not hesitate to take arms when their property, their freedom, or their dignity was threatened by the Marines. The urban *élite,* on the other hand, resisted vocally, if at all, and without spilling its blood. Certain of its members followed Dr. Jean Price-Mars in his search for a new national self-image based on the proud acceptance of the African heritage, and appreciative respect for the up-to-then despised peasant masses. Price-Mars' ideas had more important applications in Haitian arts and letters, which have been thoroughly studied and do not directly concern us. But other Haitian intellectuals chose instead to affirm and celebrate more than ever the nation's roots in Latin and more precisely French culture, a culture, as they tirelessly pointed out, far superior to that of the "American Anglo-Saxons." To be French in manners, in taste, and especially in language, became a proof of patriotism, a form of resistance. Writing in *Le Temps* for June 12, 1937, G. L. argues:

> It is said that Haiti imitates France. That is how it should be (. . .) Hence that strong personality which impressed the occupiers. Without that suit of armor, without all those French traits that are inborn in us or that we have assimilated, we would have remained primitive Africans, and the U.S. would have swallowed us up in one gulp.

Americans are systematically and, needless to say, unfavorably compared to Frenchmen. The French are tolerant, the Americans racists; the French dislike violence, the Americans exercise it blindly; the French are cultured, the Americans ignorant. Even the large cities of the U.S. do not bear comparison with the Spiritual Metropolis. In Mrs. Virginie Valcin's novel *La Blanche Négresse* (Port-au-Prince, 1934), Anna Ménard protests when her father claims to find New York beautiful:

> Paris is far prettier, Father. Here we have houses, in New York they have colossal lumps, mass-produced objects stupidly trying to impress visitors. (p. 9.)

And she then tells, sparing no gruesome detail, how she once saw a Black man being lynched in the deep South.

In addition to the buildings, the women of France are incomparably superior to those of the U.S. As Fernande Vernon explains to her husband in Annie Desroy's *Le Joug:*

> If you observed them, as I do, you would notice that the very way American women dress reveals, if not downright lack of education, at least a totally plebian laisseraller. They lack what is characteristic of French women: elegance, taste, breeding, class. (pp. 37-38.)

And over thirty years after the end of the occupation, Marie Chauvet creates, in her novel *Amour* (Paris, 1968), an American businessman, Mr.

Long, a cynical and dishonest brute who is in total contrast with the French hero, Jean Luze, a handsome, virtuous, courageous, and flawless human being.

There is, however, one context in which Americans are identified with Frenchmen. Not with contemporary Frenchmen, but with those of long ago, with the racist *colons* expelled from the island by the heroic Fathers of the Country. The comparison is obvious and the lesson is clear: only with the departure of the Americans could Haiti recover its freedom and dignity. In a 1928 article entitled "Le Peuple et l'élite," published in *Le Petit impartial* (and quoted by C. Fowler in *The Knot and the Thread*, Washington, D.C., 1980, p. 45), Jacques Roumain writes: "Today we are facing the Americans, just as our forebears faced Bonaparte's armies." Three years later, in his novel *The Bewitched Mountain (La Montagne ensorcelée*, Port-au-Prince, 1931), Roumain creates a peasant hero, Désilus, who has never studied history, but knows instinctively that

> One hundred years ago we kicked their asses out into the sea, but they
> have come back again, those White American dogs. (p. 103.)

In Maurice Casséus' *Viejo* (Port-au-Prince, 1935), the hero returns to Haiti after many years as a cane-cutter in Cuba, to see a Marine officer strutting under the porch of the Presidential Palace. A compatriot explains:

> "Oh, yes, a colon, again a colon, and this one didn't even have to fight
> for the land (. . .) He too is your enemy, just like those who were here
> before 1804. (p. 7.)

In *Jésus ou Legba?* (Poitiers, 1933), Milo Rigaud claims that

> It is said that, following the example of Caradeux (*a Saint-Domingue
> colon famous for his cruelty*), certain American lieutenants have
> already trained attack dogs to be used against any Haitian who steps
> out of line. (pp. 104-105.)

And, again in *Viejo*, André David, who is planning a demonstration against the occupation, exhorts his followers:

> You all know the old song *Desalinn pa vle ouè blan (Dessalines can't
> stand Whites)*, don't you? Well tonight, on the Champ de Mars, we are
> going to show these pigs that we are still men of 1804. (pp. 96-97.)

It is no coincidence that, during the occupation years, Haitian poetry is characterized by formal refinement (scrupulous syntactic correction and lexical mannerism) and, thematically, by the frequent celebration of the War of Independence saga. In other words, the allegience to Francophony is re-affirmed, while the celebration of past heroic deeds is an indirect call for resistance in the present.

One last remark: as we have seen, there are very few American characters in Haitian letters before the occupation. Reference is generally made to the many vices and few virtues of the "yankee nation": the

Virginians who hang John Brown or the sea captain who thanks Divinity after evading Customs have an emblematic value. But from 1915 on, we shall begin to find individuals whose physical appearance and psychological complexity are carefully delineated. Insofar as it makes any sense to try to draw a "composite picture" of these later American characters, two peculiarities stand out: ruddy skin and green eyes.

Smedley Seaton is "a young green-eyed officer" while his compatriot Walter Kelsey, a torture specialist in the Port-au-Prince penitentiary, has "a bestial carrot-colored face, lit up by two horrible tiny green eyes" (S. Alexis, *Le Nègre masqué*, pp. 107, 123); Americans are "as red as ripe tomatoes" (Alix Mathon, *The Flag at Half Mast* [*Le Drapeau en berne*], Port-au-Prince, 1974, p. 18); Mr. Long, the business agent, is "red as a lobster (. . .) he looks like a boiled lobster" (M. Chauvet, *Amour*, p. 59); Dr. McLeslie was known as "favorably disposed towards Black people, despite his blond mop of hair and his green eyes" (M. Casséus, *Viejo*, p. 100); Colonel Little is "the Mason-Dixon line incarnate, with his ruddy skin which seems lit up by lynching flames" (Jean Brierre, *Province*, Port-au-Prince, 1935, p. 192); Jacques-Stéphen Alexis' Lieutenant Wheelbarrow has "light green eyes" (*Songbook for the Stars* [*Romancero aux étoiles*], Paris, 1960, p. 183); the U.S. financial advisor has "a sharp face illuminated by green eyes" (Félix Courtois, *Scènes de la vie port-au-princienne*, Port-au-Prince, 1975, p. 222); and so forth.

Since Americans are invariably supposed to be blond or red-headed Nordics whose pale skins are very sensitive to the tropical sun, a ruddy complexion is understandable. A reddish tint also has symbolic value, being associated with anger, vanity, and bestial appetites. Finally, the American occupiers guzzle rum all day long, a further proof of hypocrisy (since they have instituted Prohibition in their own country). This excessive drinking also contributes to their flushed appearance. Jacques Roumain shows them "flushed with liquor and arrogance, parading around in their shiny sedans" (*The Buffoons* [*Les Fantoches*], Port-au-Prince, 1931, p. 76).

As for eye color, it is surprising to note that in all cases where an American character's eye color is indicated, that color is green. The one exception is little Hélène, daughter of Mrs. Gaby in Maurice Casséus' *Mambo* (Port-au-Prince, 1950); her eyes are blue. It seems highly unlikely that this uniformity is simply a coincidence. To be sure, Créole speakers generally refer to light-colored eyes (whether blue, green, gray, or hazel) as *je vèt* (green eyes) or *je chat* (cat's eyes). But the Haitian writers are writing in French, not in Créole. A more plausible explanation might be that in Haitian folklore, green eyes (which are rare but not non-existant among Blacks and Mulattoes) are associated with malefic powers; perhaps Haitian writers have, consciously or unconsiously, endowed their American characters with a physical trait considered alarming by popular superstition. Perhaps it is because she is still young enough to be innocent that little Hélène has blue eyes. Her mother, of course, has "eyes of a green that gleamed in a strange way" (op. cit., p. 103).

To summarize: between independence in 1804 and the end of the occupation in 1934, the United States and its citizens constituted for the Haitians at first an unknown entity, then a danger, and finally a humiliating and detested presence. The image of a powerful, materialistic, and expansionist U.S., and of greedy, racist, and brutal Americans, is of course perpetuated in Haitian letters even after the occupation. To document this would be easy but quite tedious. Rather, I prefer to examine new elements which appear in the two succeeding periods of Haitian letters. The first begins with the end of the occupation in 1935 and extends until 1960; the second, from 1960 to the present.

In Haiti, the first of these periods is marked by an ideological shift away from integral nationalism towards Negritude or Black Solidarity. This shift was promoted by the writings of Price-Mars and his followers. Henceforth, Haitians began to show interest in Africa, and to express their solidarity with colonized Africans and their New World brothers, with U.S. Blacks in particular. This was only fair, since many Black American intellectuals had protested the American occupation. In 1920, in a series of influential articles in The Nation, James Weldon Johnson cogently argued that intervention had been decided not to re-establish order in Haiti, but to further American banking interests. Johnson further denounced the atrocities being committed by the Marines (which eventually led to Congressional investigations). Langston Hughes, who was to co-author the translation into English of Jacques Roumain's Masters of the Dew with Mercer Cook, had visited Haiti; in 1932, he composed (in collaboration with Arna Bontemps) a wonderful children's book, Popo and Fifina, which, while it does not gloss over the poverty of Haitian peasants, also illustrates their civility and sense of personal worth. The first respectful treatment of vodùn, Tell My Horse, was published in 1939 by a Black American woman, Zora Neale Hurston.

Of course, Haitian writers had always denounced American color prejudice, segregation, and lynchings. But, as we have seen, they did so with a somewhat disdainful compassion for Black brothers who had not managed to gain their freedom, not to mention their independence. After having undergone in their own country a mild version of the treatment American Blacks knew only too well, Haitian writers changed their tone somewhat. Also, as far as literature—which enjoys such high prestige in Haiti—is concerned, several Harlem Renaissance writers had attained world-wide reputation, and young Haitian intellectuals "had memorized Langston Hughes' poems, which René Piquion had translated" (Félix Morisseau-Leroy, Crop [Récolte, Port-au-Prince, 1946]). In Haitian eyes, the U.S. was becoming the land where Blacks, supported by White progressives, were fighting for dignity and attaining equality in the realm of thought.

More and more analyses of the U.S. made by Haitian intellectuals came to be influenced by left-wing ideologies, to which many of them subscribed. Americans, even racist Americans, were no longer seen simply as evil by essence, but rather as cogs in the huge capitalist machine. Already in 1933, the hero of Stéphen Alexis' *Le Nègre masqué*, René Sinclair, had saved an American soldier from execution at the hands of his guerrilla captors by arguing

> This poor child is innocent. He is also a slave. He has been sent here by Wall Street to protect its depredations. (p. 144.)

And Jacques Roumain, who founded the Communist Party of Haiti, writes in *The Black Man's Grievances (Griefs de l'homme noir,* Port-au-Prince, 1939) that

> Racial prejudice, manipulated as an instrument of division, diversion and distraction simultaneously, renders possible the subjection of important segments of the White population in the U.S.

At the same time, Black French writers such as René Maran, Guy Tirolien, Léon Damas, Paul Niger and Aimé Césaire were showing Haitians that their idealized conception of France hardly corresponded to reality. In his novel *The Music of Trees (Les Arbres musiciens,* Paris, 1957), Jacques-Stéphen Alexis shows the U.S. Ambassador receiving the French archbishop of Port-au-Prince for dinner. The diplomat wants to enlist the priest's support for an American sisal exploitation project. The two men get along like thieves at a country fair because:

> (. . .) the one spoke only of freedom, of democracy, of aid to development and of Western civilization, the other of Heavenly rewards, of virtue, of charity and love, but they had one thing in common: they were bent on imposing their presence and their domination on others. (p. 77.)

Young Haitian intellectuals now realize that the manichean conception according to which the U.S. represented absolute Evil and France embodied pure Virtue was a bit simplistic. This realization was helped by the fact that the U.S. had fought alongside France (and the Soviet Union) against the overtly and aggressively racist Axis powers. Needless to say, this less intransigent vision is manifested in literature also. In *The Blink of an Eye (L'Espace d'un cillement,* Paris, 1959), for instance, Jacques-Stéphen Alexis writes of Marines out on the town during the occupation:

> Marines may be drunkards, bullies and racists, but their fits of insanity, their brutal lechery, their cruelty and violence are intermixed with flashes of kindness, with childlike candor and with idealistic impulses.

> That is one of the peculiarities of Uncle Sam's easy-going, happy-go-lucky and generous nephews. (p. 134.)

And, while condemning racist aberrations, Jacques Roumain pays tribute to the American people and their President:

> How can this admirable nation, whose generosity and courage are embodied in President Roosevelt, how can it mix light and darkness, democracy and the Ku-Klux-Klan, freedom and lynching, intellectual activity and color prejudice? *(op. cit.,* p. 4.)

It is also during this period that American scholars observed Haitian society and analyzed it objectively and responsibly. The work of Herskovits *(Life in a Haitian Valley,* 1937), Leyburn *(The Haitian People,* 1941) and Katherine Dunham *(The Dances of Haiti,* 1947) was a welcome change from such malicious trash as Seabrook's all too famous *Magic Island* (1929), or John Houston Craige's *Black Bagdad* (1933). In the 1940s, an American painter, De Witt Peters, and the American Anglican Bishop of Port-au-Prince, Alfred Voegeli, encouraged young Haitian painting. In 1956, Dr. Mellon founded the Schweitzer Hospital for the peasants of the Artibonite Valley. Haitians paid hommage to those Americans, who had come in order to understand and help, rather than to denigrate. Herskovits even appears in Jean-Baptiste Cinéas' novel *The Sacred Legacy (L'Héritage sacré,* Port-au-Prince, 1945) as Phillips Benfield, an American anthropologist.

In the Haitian literary works of this period we also find evidence that English is beginning to influence Haitian speech. Thus, in *Les Arbres musiciens,* Jacques-Stéphen Alexis pokes fun at the Haitian Army's Chief of Staff, whose affectation it is to speak like a West Point graduate:

> Ainsi, avant les parades militaires, parlant à son "boy," il disait toujours:
> -Hé, petit boy! faites seller mon "horse"!
> Aux "meetings" de l'état-major, mâchant inlassablement sa chique, il jetait invariablement aux rapporteurs:
> -Well! OK? . . . Faites donc faire un "survey"! . . . Pour dire bonjour, c'était:
> -Hello, guys! . . . (p. 159.)
> (Before parades, he always says to his *boy:*
> -Hey, little *boy!* Have my *horse* saddled!
> At the staff *meetings,* where he ceaselessly chewed gum, he invariably told the section heads:
> -*Well! O.K.!* Let's have a *survey* made! When greeting his fellow officers, he said:
> -*Hello, guys!)*

But the military are not alone in learning English. Students usually do as well, since it is now to the U.S. rather than France that most of them will go for their university education, as Alexis notes:

The foremost "Master of" mills were Columbia, Fisk and Yale. Inside
dope could be had for the asking:
-"At Columbia, you can get an MA in two and a half months!"
-"Big deal! I got an MS at Fisk in sixty-five days!"
-"And I got a Master in Arts and a Bachelor of Technology at Yale,
both in exactly two months." (*idem,* p. 168.)

This brings us to the last period, which goes from around 1960 to
today. It is what Haitians call the Second Diaspora. The political climate
has forced a large number of writers to become exiles: Francis-Joachim
Roy and Jean Brierre; Roger Dorsinville and Marie Chauvet; Anthony
Phelps and René Belance; Franck Fouché and Félix Morisseau-Leroy;
Francis Séjour-Magloire and Gérard Etienne . . . and many others. At the
same time, worsening economic conditions compel Haitians of all social
classes to leave the country. This massive emigration has been directed
primarily towards the U.S. As a result, important Haitian colonies have
developed in New York, in Miami, in Boston, and in Chicago. At present,
the number of Haitians legally or illegally residing in the U.S. is
conservatively estimated at 400,000.

From our viewpoint, this massive emigration has had two consequences: the first is that Haitians have a better knowledge of American
reality, no longer acquired from readings but directly and, so to speak, *in
situ.* Today, Haitian families who do not receive letters or visits from their
émigré members are rare indeed.

In the immigrant's America, God knows all is not perfect; far from it.
But at least free schools and social services are available, and the Haitian,
like the Irish, the Italian, the Jew or the Puerto Rican before him, can hope
for economic survival and social integration. The U.S. may not be
Eldorado, but it is at least a possible option. In Franketienne's *A Wall to
Burst Through (Mur à crever,* Port-au-Prince, 1968), a Haitian lady who
has sent her son to the U.S. explains:

> The important thing is to have someone over there. It makes things
> much easier. He'll open the gate to the big cities for us. Soon the
> whole family will settle in New York. That's all I ask. Here, life has
> become im-pos-sible. (p. 143.)

In the same novel, one of the male characters is willing to marry a girl who
is carrying another man's child because:

> The girl is leaving for New York soon, and Roland had been waiting to
> go to the States for a long time. This marriage is a wonderful
> opportunity: It is the surest way for him to get a resident's visa. *(idem,*
> p. 78.)

The American consulate's waiting-room becomes a hallowed place,
where Haitians anxiously await a decision as to their future. There, as
everywhere else, inequality is rampant, as Liliane Devieux-Dehoux shows

in *Love, Yes! Death, No! (L'Amour oui, la mort, non,* Sherbrooke, Quebec, 1976):

> A distinguished gentleman rises, takes his leather briefcase, straightens his tie, nods to the secretary and follows her into the consul's office. Monsieur Bardier has been called. He will probably be admitted, thanks to his impeccable curriculum, to his diplomas, to the material and moral guarantees he can offer. He will go, he will find a good job—unless color prejudice prevents it—he will adapt to the *American way of life,* he will pile up dollars, he will take root in foreign soil. But how about the man and the woman who yawn and sigh in the corner? Poorly dressed, poorly shod, with their naked hands as their only asset, when will they be called? (p. 49.)

The U.S. now exerts pressure on Haitians in a new way: in order to prevent the expression of opposition to their policy, Roger Gaillard explains in *Charades haïtiennes* that Americans can always threaten to withhold the precious visas:

> If you are against us, say these trembling gentlemen from the U.S. Embassy, you will not treat the soil of the New Atlantis; the gates of Paradise will be slammed in your face (. . .) Because, without a visa, all is lost: You can't go for sophisticated medical treatment, nor to find a better job. You can't even send your children to college. (pp. 206-207.)

Life in the U.S. used to be imagined as inhuman and—for a Haitian—hardly bearable. And this pejorative image persists, particularly among writers in exile. But, for many other Haitian authors, the U.S. has its beauty, and to find happiness there is not out of the question. As early as 1935, in *Viejo,* Maurice Casséus had celebrated Harlem, where his hero

> (. . .) had known a marvelous life. He thought of Harlem, Harlem and its bars, where jazz bleeds its blues in the night, and of the little burnt sepia American girl he had loved there, for a whole season! A desperate nostalgia engulfed him. (p. 63.)

And in Jacques-Stéphen Alexis' *My Mate, General the Sun (Compère Général Soleil,* Paris, 1955), a Haitian tells his friends about New York: "There's a city for you! Dollars, like stars in the sky. And lights! It rumbles, it roars, a wonderful city!" (p. 207.)

In this context, a work recently published in Port-au-Prince is worth mentioning. It is a collection of six short stories by Marie-Thérèse Colimon, entitled *The Song of the Sirens (Le Chant des sirènes,* Port-au-Prince, 1979). They all deal with emigration, seen at times as a last resort, more often as an ardently pursued ideal. A woman is abandoned by her husband, who has gone to seek his fortune "in New York, in this blessed land where unemployment is unknown" (p. 54) and who will never send her either a visa or even a money order. An old lady dies alone, far from her children, who have long ago gone to New York, to Chicago, to Boston and to Los Angeles. A poor little girl, humiliated by her richer school-mates, dreams of the day when her parents, who have sailed illegally for Miami, will call her to the land of refrigerators and supermarkets. All of Mme. Deltour's daughters are abroad: Marie-Odile, who was born retarded, has been institutionalized somewhere in France; Claudia, the liberated woman, has left for the U.S. "where permissiveness is accepted"; she has become rich "somewhere in California," and is on her third marriage. Michelle, after receiving her MD from one of the best medical schools in the U.S., is a respected cardiologist in a Toronto hospital. As for Alexandra, she has fallen in love with the scion of one of the richest families of Port-au-Prince Lebanese merchants. Both families having decided that the marriage would be a misalliance, the lovers "had simply left for the great, welcoming, liberal land where the right to love is freely granted." (p. 117.) And Mme. Delcour realizes that:

> We have become a sort of people in transit, always ready, like swallows, to fly off to more hospitable skies (p. 107).

While Marie-Thérèse Colimon's first concern is to condemn a society which forces its members to seek fulfillment abroad, what interests us here is the idyllic vision she gives of the U.S. Since many Haitians have come to share this vision, it is not surprising to find the U.S. called, in Colimon's work: a "great and altruistic country," "a Promised land," "a Paradise," an "advanced country which allows intelligence to flourish," a "blessed country," and so forth.

Colimon underscores a second consequence of massive emigration: the "popularity of English." This is a popularity indeed understandable, since it goes along with the dream of settling in New York or Chicago. And just as understandable is the fact that English words and expressions slip into the speech of those who have left long ago, like Claudia Deltour, who now speaks:

> (. . .) with quite a pronounced American accent and many English expressions: *je vais faire un call . . . je vais cancel ma réservation . . . je suis très busy, anyway, je viendrai te voir* (p. 98).

Or like Adrienne Sarty, whose letters to her friend Silotte are peppered with words like *overtime, subway, lunch* at the *snack-bar, market, drug store,* etc . . . And there is more: English filters down even into the speech of those who have remained in Haiti, such as old Maman Ya, all of whose children have emigrated:

> (. . .) her lexicon had become enriched by new terms redolent with mysterious promises. She delighted in bizarre sounding words like *traveller check, transfer, long distance, collect,* and others (p. 77).

The significant thing is that Colimon has not felt the need to translate or even to explain these "bizarre sounding" English words for her Haitian readers. Neither does Jean-Claude Charles who, in *Holy Pigs' Drifting*

(*Sainte dérive des cochons,* Montreal, 1977), doesn't hesitate to use English, as in the following passage:

> (. . .) et moi avec plein de petites cartes dans les poches zeu social security card zeu green card zeu I.D. card zeu credit card avec plein de bills pour l'électricité le gaz le téléphone la tivi zeu feurnitoure la bagnole ford pinto runabout ford maverick ford galaxie 500 le frigo le vacuum avec plein de tokens so many factories you know n'ayant nul répit nulle window nulle fuite. (p. 32.)

And English is also present in works written in Créole. For example, we find it in Frankétienne's *Pélin-tèt* (Port-au-Prince, 1978), which takes place in a New York basement and has Haitian émigrés as characters. The contamination of Créole by English is the theme of a monologue entitled *You lòt lang (Another language)* by the Haitian humorist Maurice Sixto, on his record *Choses et gens d'Haïti.* The play as well as the record were huge successes in Haiti, even though in order to understand them it is essential to know English . . . or at least to know *some* English.

Again, this is not to say that the pejorative image of the U.S. and of Americans has disappeared; far from it. For ideological reasons, or simply because of affective incompatibilities, Haitian writers in French and Créole continue to denounce American economic and cultural imperialism. But it can hardly be denied that, at the same time, the U.S. is often seen as a land where one can find well-being and freedom and even spiritual and esthetic satisfactions.

A consequence of the American way of life which Haitians adopt not only in exile but in Haiti itself (since the island is rapidly becoming "Americanized") is the increasing importance of English in everyday life. This evolution has already begun to manifest itself in literature. Up to now, at least acquaintance with Créole was necessary for the thorough understanding of French-language Haitian literature. Will it soon be necessary to be familiar with English in order to read Haitian writers? So far the language situation in Haiti is characterized by di-glossia: will it soon become tri-glossic? Time will tell, but it is not necessarily an absurd hypothesis.

THE IMAGE OF WOMAN
IN HAITIAN POETRY

Ce n'est pas sans raison qu'on a toujours vanté
des femmes d'Haïti la grâce et la beauté
Qu'elles aient la couleur de l'or ou de l'ébène.

A. Fleury-Battier (1841-1883)

The evolution of Haitian poetry, as one might expect, closely follows that of French poetry, though Haitian Pre-romanticism, Romanticism, Surrealism, and Symbolism developed some years after their French counterparts and were profoundly influenced by them. At the same time, Haitian poetry has come to search for, and to find, its own voice. The lexical, syntactical and rhythmical emancipation of the French poetic idiom in the twentieth century has facilitated the process. Thus freed from academic conventions, Haitian poetry is fast developing its own originality.

Examining the image of woman as a theme allows us to highlight certain peculiarities of Haitian poetry. It is evident, and has often been pointed out, that much Haitian poetry is essentially "committed" poetry. While Haitian poets are concerned with questions of form and esthetics, they are even more concerned with political, social and moral problems. And of these problems, that of ethnic identity and color antagonism has been a constant preoccupation. Explicitly or implicitly, it influences how and why Haitian poets celebrate Woman.

During the early 19th century, Haitian poets looked to French models, with a marked preference for neo-classical and pre-romantic ones. In the serious mode, ringing patriotic dithyrambs alternate with long philosophical and didactic disquisitions. Lighter genres do not evidence much originality either. However, in lyric poetry, a distinctive note begins to be heard. To celebrate the fatherland and its liberators, lofty abstractions couched in stately alexandrine verse did very well. But as soon as surrounding reality is to be described, a specifically Haitian vision imposes itself. Just as Haitian *mornes* and royal palms are different from French Alps and apple trees, Haitian woman is different from her French sisters. But, if she is Black rather than Mulatto, the Haitian poet does not have at his disposal a traditional poetic vocabulary with which to praise her appearance. Frenchmen who happened to have celebrated Black beauty perceived it as exotic; Haitian woman might be exotic in the eyes of a Parisian, not in the eyes of her compatriots.

As a matter of fact, to sing the beauty of women of color seemed, in the 19th century, to indulge in paradox. Many Haitian poets simply abstained. Most of the time, the very real linguistic difficulties stymied them; we shall see that there were other reasons for their reticence. These poets chose to remain secure under the wing of abstraction: it would be impossible to guess that Jules Solime Milscent (1778-1842) addresses the following madrigal to one of his compatriots:

Dawn on you freely bestowed
Pearls to ornament

Your eyes and your mouth as well.
When your modesty is alarmed
The roses of your complexion
Betray Flora's generosity.
(from A. Viatte, *Histoire littéraire de l'Amérique française*, Paris, 1954,
p. 348.)

Pierre Faubert (1806-1868) does no better:

Alas, far from my Delphine,
I can no longer sleep,
And in my humble cottage
Only my wails are heard.
(idem., p. 357.)

Damoclès Vieux (1876-1936), in "Badinage," compares his lady love
to the graceful women immortalized by 18th century painters:

Tell me, are you a sprite?
Have you escaped from
A Watteau painting? (. . .)
O, lovely one, truly
Your profile is like
A pastel by Latour.
(from N. Garret, *The Renaissance of Haitian Poetry,* Paris, 1963,
pp. 39-40.)

And, as late as 1913, Léon Liset celebrates, in "Intoxication"
(published in *L'Éclaireur* on March 26th, 1913), his beloved's "dainty little
white breasts."

These poets do not turn to Haitian reality for inspiration, but rather
to Parisian anthologies such as the annual *Almanach des Muses.* Their
protestations of love follow French patterns, and not always the latest or
most admirable ones at that. But poets could not long continue to produce
artificial sighs for rococo shepherdesses. Haitian women began to appear
in Haitian poetry, though quite timidly at first; poets simply identify them,
without describing their physical appearance. Thus the ancestral African
woman sailing on a slave ship to the New World, as imagined by Coriolan
Ardouin (1812-1835):

She was at the prow; you would swear you were seeing
So beautiful, with tears flowing on her cheek,
The angel that comes in our even-time dreams.
("The Slaver's Departure" ["Le Départ du négrier"], from C. St.-
Louis and M.A. Lubin, *Panorama de la poésie haïtienne,* Port-au-
Prince, 1950, p. 16.)

Or Louis Duplessis Louverture (1887-1961), when he evokes the Haitian
peasant's traditional hospitality:

Your place will be set at the head of the table
And perhaps the maiden who sighed in the shadows

> Recognizing in you the one she awaited
> Will bring you the gift of her soul and her body.
> ("Hospitalité," in *Panorama . . .,* p. 290.)

Succeeding generations of Haitian poets strove to establish a national tradition, and made it a point to celebrate all that is characteristically Haitian, including, of course, the women of Haiti. Yet it would be quite possible to compose an anthology of poems written from Independence to the present, which give no indication that the women they describe are Haitian, or, for that matter, that the poet was born in the New World. No one would argue that a poet, whatever his nationality or language, is required to give detailed physical descriptions of the women who inspire him. Yet, as we shall see, a Haitian's choice of how to describe a woman— or whether to describe her at all—is invariably problematic.

A Haitian writing in French (rather than in Créole) writes in a language fashioned on the other side of the Atlantic, by people for whom his country is unknown or irrelevant. French, his learned official language, is hardly designed to express the rhythms of tropical life, or the sensitivity of the Black man. As Léon Laleau (1892–1979) complains:

> (. . .) can you imagine this pain
> And this despair, to none akin:
> To tame with words from France this heart
> Which came to me from Senegal?
> ("Treason" ["Trahison"], in *Musique nègre,* Port-au-Prince, 1931.)

Some poets, trying to stifle "this heart which came from Senegal," meekly avoided any regional allusions, especially in love poetry, and all typically Haitian words and expressions that might puzzle a Parisian reader. Many, seeking inspiration in Parnassian or Symbolist models, affected vagueness and melancholy allusions. Edmond Laforest (1876-1915)'s "Shadows in the Dark" ("Ombres dans l'ombre") is a good example:

> Where do these slow-floating
> Forms of women go,
> These vaporous forms,
> Scattered flakes of shadow,
> Dark mists caressed by breezes
> Wafting from graveyards?
> They flow in their sorrow
> To the river of death.
> *(Panorama . . .,* p. 10.)

And explicit Haitian notations are also absent from the excellent Surrealist poems of Magloire Saint Aude (1912-1971):

> No more voice, no more fingers
> At the pleading, at the gong of laces
> Chaste on the flank of my latent sweat.

On my chalk without substance or depth
The Chinaman weaves my death.

Sleep at last, scrap-iron mine
Which would have loved me
At the gates, at the cities of my image.
("Peace" ["Paix"], idem, p. 463.)

Beside these works which can only be called Haitian because of their authors' nationality, another and, from our point of view, a much more interesting poetry developed. It incorporates local terms and idioms into academic French. Tropical plants appear with their Haitian names, as does the vocabulary of vodùn; from time to time, a particularly apposite Créole expression will be admitted. Of course, this may make the poem somewhat obscure for the non-Haitian reader: the following stanza, from Liautaud Ethéart (1826-1888)'s "To the Zombis" can hardly be understood without some familiarity with the terminology of vodùn:

(. . .) the houngan, hiding in his houmfort
Says Azibloguidi, calls on the assotor
And filled with the power of a fantastic houanga
Invites his followers to a mangé-marrassa
O, Zombis!*
(idem., p. 37.)

Such poetry, no longer purely French and yet not written in Créole, might be considered truly Haitian. It will also serve to celebrate Haitian women, and their beauty.

But, once again, how was one, without seeming paradoxical, to sing of wooly hair, flat noses, and thick lips? Many poets did not take the risk, and not only because of lexical difficulties. In general, the poets were Mulattos and, for most of them, true feminine beauty demanded long hair, European features and skin no darker than deep tan. As late as 1930, Dominique Hippolyte (1889-1967) regrets that:

Brown poets find it difficult
O Black woman, to sing your Haitian litheness.
("To the Poet Carl Brouard," from N. Garret, op. cit., p. 48.)

It goes without saying that, in real life, these poets didn't scorn Black women; but when they had affairs with them, it was usually as a pastime, and entailed no sentimental commitment. The Black woman would generally be a peasant, a maid, a street vendor, a factory worker, a prostitute, sometimes a passing fancy, but rarely a great love. Alcibiade Fleury-Battier (1841–1883)'s "The True Amulet" ("Le Vrai Ouanga") is a

---

*A houngan is a vodùn priest, the head of a houmfort, or temple. Azibloguidi is an African incantatory word, an assotor is a seven-foot-tall ritual drum; a houanga is a charm, either evil or protective, and a mangé-marrassa is a ceremony dedicated to the Marrassas, or sacred twins.

case in point:

> What is sweeter than honey?
> What can intoxicate us so
> That we forget heaven and earth?
> –It is the kiss of a Black woman.
> What is better than the nectar
> Of the Gods? Than the wind caressing
> A flower? Than a glance of love?
> –It is the breasts of a Black woman.
> (from *La Revue Express,* 26 août 1891.)

In 1842, Pierre Faubert composed "La Négresse,"* a poem not very flattering to the Black woman who inspired it:

> I am proud to say it, O Black woman, I love you
> And I like your black color, and do you know why?
> Because Heaven endowed you with noble virtues,
> A chaste heart, beauty, even, in short, all that is charming.

The poet then proceeds to expound on the woman's "noble virtues" and "chaste heart," but nothing more is said about the fact that has "beauty, even." And Faubert, who must have been either a fool or a boor, explains:

> When White Elina, admired by one and all
> Despite all her promises took her pledge back
> When Fortune at last no more on me smiled
> Who took back an ingrate? It was you!
> (from *Ogé,* Paris, 1856, pp. 132-133.)

In other words, the down-on-his-luck poet falls back on ancillary love only after having been abandoned by the desirable Caucasian. The same note is sounded in "Black Laetitia" ("Laetitia-la-Noire") by Dominique Hyppolite; the poet has an assignation with a peasant girl:

> From afar I shall see the gleam of your teeth
> In your face, flat-nosed and the color of night;
> Under the branches of the avocado tree
> We will savor love as one does a ripe fruit.
> I want you to plunge me in raptures tonight
> O Black woman whose soul is sweetness itself!
> For a while you will make me forget all the lies
> That your less naive sisters weave to deceive me.
> (*Panorama . . .,* p. 304.)

The "less naive sisters" in question are of course light-colored sophisticated city women. In a way, Hippolyte's poem is but one more variation on a traditional and universal theme: the healthy and virtuous country life contrasted with the artificial and perverse existence of the city.

---

*In French and in "Haitian French" usage, the word *négresse* is descriptive, and generally carries no pejorative connotation.

But here the original note is that the peasant maiden is no blond milkmaid or rosy-cheeked shepherd girl, but a Black woman, with a flat-nosed (*camuse**) and night-colored face. In 1842, Faubert simply said "I like your Black color"; in 1927, Hippolyte gives at least the beginnings of a physical description. A few years later, Luc Grimard (1886-1954) is less hesitant in his "Flower of the Fields" ("Fleur des champs"):

> In a blue denim skirt, while her ebony breast
> Peeks out from a white working-shirt,
> She offers to all her robust and naive
> And charming and almost perturbing graces.
> On the luxuriant pile of her oily tresses
> A madras head-dress is tied "tignon-fashion."
> She is like the flower of a cold-fearing plant
> Whose buds are bursting open all over.
> With her hands on her hips she's daydreaming
> In the morning air which shivers at times.
> A very sweet smile shows off her white teeth
> As a nest is revealed through the leaves of a tree.
> (*Panorama* . . ., pp. 276-277.)

The same obvious metaphors which keep recurring in poems that describe Black women—"ebony skin," "color of night," "dazzling smile"— are hackneyed affectations, but at least they allow the poet to celebrate negroid physical traits which—in French as in English—are traditionally associated with ugliness. And when Haitian poets compose in the realist vein, and evoke unattractive peasants or working-class Black women, they can be as brutal as any racist. Thus Léon Louhis (1867-1935), when he describes "Black Peasant Women in Blue Denim Shirts" ("Négresses de la plaine au caraco bleu"):

> Black peasant women in blue denim shirts
> Who come down every day, driving before them
> Donkeys with loads of dry grass or of hay
> Looking as God, the Almighty, decreed,
> In their ebony bosom, with its generous dugs
> Under skulls made of bronze, with their hair short and stiff
> And their young blood a-coursing, ardent as flame,
> Through the murky darkness of flesh
> They feel hazy desires, shadowy dreams (. . .)
> And their souls, through their coarsely clad bodies
> Shivers at times calling out to
> Pleasure from up high, from the infinite blue.
> (*Panorama* . . ., pp. 138-139.)

---

*While the adjective *camus* is not complimentary, it is less graphic than "flat-nosed" in English. Edna W. Underwood avoids the problem altogether and offers as a translation: "In that mischievous face which is the hue of the night" (*The Poets of Haiti 1782-1934,* Portland, Maine, 1934, p. 124).

It seems obvious that Louhis sees his peasant compatriots as exotic, animal-like beings; the higher plane of existence to which they instinctively aspire is no doubt familiar to him, not because he is a poet, but simply because he doesn't belong to the lower classes. Victor Mangonès (1880-1949) is just as callous when he describes the *trieuses* who sort out the beans for the coffee exporters, with their "drooping breasts" and "billy-goat smell" (*idem*, p. 220). And Charles Moravia (1876-1938)'s "Kerosene vendor" 's head-rag is made even dirtier by "the lubrification of her unruly mop"; her feet are "broad and flat," she also smells "like a billy-goat," and she hawks her wares in a shrill voice, so that

My sense of esthetics was assaulted by her
Through smell, and sight, and hearing at once.
(from L. Morpeau, *Anthologie d'un siècle de poésie haïtienne*, Paris, 1925, p. 211.)

When precise negroid traits are described, it almost seems as if a pejorative view of the woman were intended, either because she is dirty, or ugly, or poor, or vulgar. When Philippe Thoby-Marcelin (1904-1975) claims "I shall sing of you now, little Black girl, your turn is long overdue," he begins:

A thick mouth, a flat nose, she is really homely,
The little Black girl, really homely,
And very Black, like all the sins together.
But you smile, and it is angels rejoicing
Softness of your white eyes
Innocence of your white teeth . . .
("Little Black Girl" ["Petite Noire"], from *Panorama . . .*, p. 369.)

We are not surprised to learn, a few lines later, that the "Little Black Girl" in question was a maid in the Marcelin household, who took care of the poet when he was a child and taught him riddles. And when our grateful bard wants to celebrate her beauty, all he can think of is white eyeballs and gleaming teeth, which Black women of course share with many women of other ethnic types. Even a "négriste" poet like Carl Brouard (1902-1965) can only find a pejorative metaphor for the wooly hair of "Iris," one of his dance-hall conquests:

Tropical Iris, shall I sing of your hair
Crimped like a false musical pitch . . .
(from N. Garret, *op. cit.*, p. 125.)

And when Brouard wants to praise a Black woman's beauty, he too must fall back on hackneyed images and metaphors, as when he addresses the object of his "Désir":

In the dark night of your face
Your teeth are a ray of light.
(*idem*, p. 124.)

Or in "Poème," when he remembers a dead lover:

Where is Rose gone
With her jet-black skin
and her teeth
white as a night of love?
(idem, p. 126.)

It would, on the other hand, have been surprising if Black woman had not been endowed by Haitian poets with a symbolic dignity. She is both a racial and a national symbol at the same time. In the expression of Haitian patriotism, exacerbated by the misfortunes of the nation, and its shabby treatment at the hands of contemptuous foreigners, racial resonances are essential. Whence the paradox: explicitly or implicitly disdained by the cultural élite, Black woman is chosen by this very élite to represent the Nation, and its African roots. Amédée Brun (1868-1896), for example, sees his "Patria" as a Black woman, crucified on a mountain top by unscrupulous politicians:

The savages, hidden in the valley below
Had riddled her divine and black body with arrows.
(Panorama . . ., p. 20.)

In "The Black Island" ("L'île noire"), Charles F. Pressoir, addressing "Women of my country, Black women with bare feet," explains "You are, my heart knows it, Africa in flesh and blood." And the poet's ironic conclusion must have been deeply shocking to his gallicized, refined, and mostly light-skinned readers:

Your island, if one looks, is revealed to be
A piece torn out from the old Black continent.
(idem, p. 443.)

Without going that far, Damoclès Vieux writes, upon hearing an old Black woman's song:

An ancestress has sung (. . .)
A song of faith
The same which soothed, under leafy domes
Our African forefathers
Dressed in loin clothes, adorned with rings, armed with spears.
And listening to your song, Grandmother,
I understood, in my soul and my blood
That the roots of your life
Still tied you to stricken Africa.
(idem, p. 178.)

In this context, a Mulatto woman can be celebrated for her blackness when she is perceived as persecuted for her race. Louis Duplessis Louverture (1887-1961) dedicates a poem "To Aphrodisia the Mulatto." This Aphrodisia is a character in Aphrodite, a mediocre historical novel by the French writer Pierre Louys. Aphrodisia, a slave, has been accused by her mistress, the courtesan Bacchis, of stealing a mirror, and she is crucified during an orgy:

> I saw them sacrifice your beautiful, fraternal body,
> I felt the tortures their rage had inflicted;
> My sorrow was great, and such my despair
> That you, on the cross, could not have suffered more.
> And you never knew that (. . .)
> I had come to denounce this odious torture
> And to weep at your feet for my race they insulted.
> (from L. Morpeau, *op. cit.*, pp. 186-197.)

From about 1930 on, many Haitian poets have embraced militant populist ideologies and placed their pen at the service of the revolution and of *la masse*. In their poems, unflattering descriptions of Black women are no longer the expression of color prejudice or snobbish fastidiousness, but rather of indignation: they are designed to shock and to shame the Haitian reader. Thus does Carl Brouard exhort the masses to revolt:

> You
> You beggars
> You who are filthy
> You who stink
> You, you peasant women who come down from our hills
> With a brat in your belly
> You whores
> You crippled whores dragging your fly-laden stinks
> All of you, the mob,
> Rise up
> And swipe the broom wide.
> ("Vous," from *Pages retrouvées*, Port-au-Prince, 1963, p. 20.)

These revolutionary poems affirm their solidarity with all the wretched of the earth. They shun the erotic, and their violent realism avoids all traces of exoticism. To them, Black woman is not a national symbol, but a victim of injustice and inequality. Their poetry, directly concerned with the struggle for a better tomorrow, leaves little place for the joys and sorrows of love. As Louis Neptune (b. 1927) aptly puts it in "Pour nous":

> for us
> the stink of prison has replaced the scent of necklines
> the cold wind of stone walls my Caribbean girl's soft breath.
> *(Panorama . . .,* p. 602.)

The theme of prison is taken up by Auguste Thénor (b. 1933), who is separated from his "Guerilla Girl" ("Ma Partisane"):

> If I could only cut some flowers
> A thousand bunches I would send you
> My hands without you have lost their power

> You will not get bouquets from me.
> Between us two there is a wall
> It can not harm our mutual faith
> To you I often sing my song
> Some day all men will happy be.
> (from S. Baridon and R. Philoctète, *Poèsie vivante d'Haïti*, Paris, 1978, p. 260.)

René Despestre (b. 1926) explains why "I shan't come by" ("Je ne viendrai pas"):

> I shall not come
> to see my insane hope
> reflected in the mirror
> of your savage eyes
> for what sense could we give our kisses
> our embraces, this fevered burning night,
> since our love remains unheeding
> human suffering's desperate pleas?
> (from N. Shapiro, *Negritude*, New York, 1970, p. 112.)

When all is said and done, it is in these revolutionary poems that Black woman finds true dignity, precisely because they present her neither as an erotic curiosity nor as a convenient national symbol.

As far as the White woman is concerned, we have seen that she inspired, at one time, many an insipid madrigal. For Louis Morpeau (1895-1929)—who, besides editing *Anthologie d'un siècle de poésie haïtienne,* also wrote verse—she seems to be some pure, ineffable, virginal ideal, cleansing the poet from the sinful memory of past affairs with

> . . . Women that I probably loved (. . .)
> You have purified my heart
> From its carnal desires.
> Your hands glide on my face
> Calm and patrician
> As palm fronds.
> ("To a White Lady" ["A une dame blanche"], L. Morpeau, *op. cit.,* p. 343.)

But, as poets became more and more conscious of their national and ethnic heritage, the presence of white women in their works became negligible. In St. Louis and Lubin's anthology, where 147 poets from Independence to 1950 are represented by nearly 500 poems, she appears in only three selections. Oswald Durand (1804-1906)'s "The Son of the Negro" ("Le Fils du Noir") is the complaint of a Mulatto in love with a White girl:

> At twenty I loved Lisa. She was white and whispy
> I, the child of the sun, alas, too brown for her

Did not get a glance from her innocent eyes! (. . .)
Left an orphan, I saw Lisa and I loved her as much
As I once did that other White woman, my mother.
But her virginal brow paled when she heard of my passion:
The son of the Negro scared the White people's daughter.
(Panorama . . ., p. 26.)

The theme was taken up again by Émile Roumer (b. 1903). In "Ten
Lines" ("Dizain"), he imagines himself in love with "a golden-haired
beauty," who "would refuse her lips to my kisses" because "the love of a
Black prince would make her a laughing stock." (from N. Garret, *op. cit.,*
p. 134.) And René Depestre paints a "Portrait of a Racist Girl" ("Portrait
d'une jeune fille raciste") (from *Poète à Cuba,* Paris, 1976, p. 93):

She looks at me and never sees me
I am in her eyes
The invisible man,
The pit into which
Her blond magic
Fears to tumble.

Oswald Durand (1840-1907) seems to have soon forgotten "The
White people's daughter" in the arms of "Our Women" ("Nos Payses"):

I shall not, leaving the New World,
Strum my lute for a White blue-eyed girl
Auburn, or red head or blonde
Pale, under cloudy skies! (. . .)
Nothing is as fine as our women,
With their skins brown in the sun
And their white teeth that look like
Pearls in a bright-red setting.
(from L. Morpeau, *op. cit.,* p. 17.)

White woman has (albeit rarely) served as a symbol of slavery. But
slavery was abolished in Haiti so long ago that Émile Roumer can evoke
"Saint Domingue, 1762" with more irony than indignation:

The planter's gentle daughter
Quite naked takes her ease
And with ingenuous grace
Stretches her tempting body.

A slave brings in the coffee.
Her older sister is scandalized:
"How can you remain undressed
Before this arrant good-for-nothing?"

But, playing with a bit of lace,
The blond virgin justifies herself:
"When you bathe, darling, do you bother
If a dog is present?" she asks.
(Panorama . . ., pp. 360-361.)

Women are, in Haitian poetry, endowed with great sensuality. From this point of view, White woman is judged to be markedly inferior to her darker-skinned sisters. According to Henri Chauvet (1836-1928), the Lord first created Eve:

> But, looking at her whom they call
> The Blonde Eve, and at her cold beauty
> Where glowed no sensual fire—even after the apple
> Was eaten—He said, depressed:
> "That is not what I wanted," and
> So that a warmer blood might flow,
> He made the Créole.
> ("The Jérémienne," from *Panorama* . . ., p. 109.)

And this supposed frigidity of White women is taken by René Depestre to symbolize their racism. In his "Voodoo Mystery Poem," entitled "A Rainbow for the Christian West," Depestre imagines that the vodùn spirit Chango comes down to earth to cure an Alabama woman and her daughters from their racist sterility. Chango sings:

> O white daughters of Alabama prostrate yourselves
> At the feet of my innocence
> And take off all your clothes
> I dip my hand in the hot oil
> And very slowly I rub your cursed breasts
> I rub the rebellious ivory of your limbs
> That emerge little by little from shadows
> I rub one by one your astonished sex
> Now you are forever as pure as my eyes
> Now you are ready to bear in your loins
> All the bursting of life in the dawn of humanity!
> (Translated by J. Dayan, *A Rainbow for the Christian West*, Amherst, 1977, p. 155.)

It is not easy for a Haitian poet to describe a White woman. If he mentions her "whiteness" he can choose not to mention his own "blackness," and thereby appear to be ashamed of his roots; his compatriots will claim that he wants to be assimilated among the poets of France. If, on the other hand, he chooses to mention his "blackness," he is forced to take a position on the problem of "race relations," and—whether he wants to or not—to "commit" his poetry. White woman simply cannot provide him with purely erotic, or even purely esthetic, inspiration.

It would seem that, for Haitian poets, Black Woman represents Africa and White Woman represents Europe, before the fusion of which Haiti was born. For them, the symbol of national reality is the "mixed blood," the Caribbean woman whose originality is—like that of the Republic—the result of amalgamation . . . and also whose appearance best conforms to their esthetic preference.*

It should be mentioned here that Créole (and Haitian French) have a considerable variety of terms to describe a person of mixed black and white ancestry. Even when some of these terms exist in "metropolitan" French, they do not necessarily mean exactly the same thing; so that, for example, *créole* does not mean a White person born in the islands, as it does in France, but any Haitian who has any Black "blood" (i.e. any authentic Haitian). A *mulâtre* is not the son of one Black and one White parent, but a straight-haired *créole;* a *jaune* is someone with a very light skin; so is a *grimeau,* except that he also has wooly hair; a *brun's* skin is darker than a *griffe's;* a *noir* is of pure African descent, but if his hair is straight, he is called a *marabout.* Some of these terms, and there are many others, go back to colonial times; but they have no meaning for the French reader of today. And since they have no exact equivalent in English, I will not translate them when they appear in quotations.

Even when Woman is seen independently of ethnic or social considerations, she is seen in a particular way, which deserves examination. It must first be remembered that to describe and celebrate Haitian woman, rather than some external, ethereal feminine image, was long considered by Haitian poets as a patriotic endeavor. It is almost defiantly that Alcibiade Fleury-Battier declared himself proud of Haiti, of her warriors, of her landscapes, and of her women:

> I come from this land, where the *brunes* are in bloom
> With their skins that resemble ripening grapes,
> Where *griffonnes* are vivacious with their big eyes of black
> Where the *négresses* have stolen the color of ebony
> And my Emma that of gold . . .
> ("My Country!" ["Mon Pays!"], from *Panorama . . .,* p. 56.)

In our generation, Franck Fouché (1915-1978) expresses the same pride:

> In December we have creole nights
> Where blues and golds play, fairy-like
> On the diamond studded dome of the sky
> While palms, made tipsy by the breeze
> Majestically nod in insolent pride
> Our country is peopled with women
> Beautiful, each with her own glow and hue,
> Yet one and all sharing the same Haitian beauty,
> For the women of our land are her poems
> And no other women look like them.
> ("Our Country" ["Notre pays"], from *Panorama . . .,* p. 535.)

---

*Micheline Labelle's research, in her fine study *Idéologie de couleur et classes sociales en Haïti* (Montreal, 1978), shows that, among Haitian men of all social classes, the ideal feminine beauty has dark (but not black) skin, long (but not silky) hair, and European (but not sharp) features.

Actually, it is rare to find a poet vaunting the beauty of Haiti without in the same breath vaunting the beauty of her women. In this vision, Nature and Woman seem to complement each other, and descriptions of the Haitian landscape are often couched in erotic terms. More to the point, Woman is usually seen as a product of Nature, as Nature herself, subject to man, created for his delight and use, yet transcending him by being—like Nature—part of a mysterious religious realm of which he has at best only fleeting intimations.

Generation after generation of Haitian poets have used "botanical" images to describe women. Of course, so have French poets, with their long-stemmed ladies with lips like ripe strawberries. But while French poets usually have recourse to similes, Haitians prefer metaphors. The Haitian woman's body becomes a veritable basket of tropical fruit. Already Fleury-Battier, when describing a young "Washerwoman" ("Blanchisseuse"), speaks of her "cherry lips" and her "two love apples" (Panorama . . ., p. 60); for Isnardin Vieux (1865-1941), "The Griffonne" has "eyes of tamarind, but shaped like almonds" (idem, p. 120); in "Evocation," Solon Ménos (1859-1918)'s beloved has "lips more appetizing than that exquisite fruit the sapodilla" (idem, p. 95); Oswald Durand is more interested in the sapodilla's shape, which reminds him of "Idalina" 's bosom:

> The wind half opens her dress
> To unveil a double globe;
> You would swear that you were seeing
> Rising above twin sapodillas
> Two black grapes, or maybe raisins;
> Her lip, by some god painted
> Is even browner than her skin:
> For it is as purple as
> Our lovely caymitos.
> (from M.A. Lubin, Poésies haïtiennes, Rio de Janeiro, 1956, p. 11.)

Émile Roumer whispers to his love:

> I hold in my arms your beautiful body
> Fragrant of flowering vines that have woven your bed;
> The pulp of your lip has a mamey apple taste.
> ("Areytos," from L. Morpeau, op. cit., p. 356.)

Elsewhere, he will tell her:

> You are black, and your odor of cloves
> Gives fire to your honeyed pineapple kisses.
> ("You Are Black" ["Tu es Noire . . ."], from Panorama . . ., p. 363.)

Carl Brouard evokes his "Muse," a toucouleur whore:

> See how beautiful she is
> With henna reddening her mouth

Which is thick, but melts like a mango.
(C. Brouard, *op. cit.,* p. 18.)

And Lorimer Denis (1904-1957) hungers for "Cecilia":

Brown girl from the banks of Momance
Never will the dawn come up
Without your kiss leaving on my lips
The taste of our green fruits.
(Panorama . . ., p. 373.)

The poet often identifies the whole woman, rather than her lips or breasts, to a fruit. Dominique Hippolyte says of "Nigra":

And her youth makes her an adorable fruit
Ready to fall from its pliant branch.
(M. Lubin, *op. cit.,* p. 58.)

Oswald Durand sings:

Round, red, sugar-sweet
Little island girl, you are an orange.
(from N. Garret, *op. cit.,* p. 99.)

René Philoctète (b. 1932), in "These Marching Islands" ("Ces îles qui marchent"), calls to the dance the "virgins with their hot citrus bodies" (S. Baridon and R. Philoctète, *op. cit.,* p. 229). And finally, Anthony Phelps (b. 1928) writes, in "Présence":

Here you stand before me
Like a well ripened fruit
Defenseless and full of sap
That I could grasp by just
Stretching out my hand.
Here you stand before me
Like a bursting full fruit
That just waits to be melted (. . .)
(idem, p. 210.)

One could find many more examples. Let us rather quote Luc Grimard (1886-1954)'s "Basket of Tropical Fruit" ("Corbeille de fruits tropicaux"), where woman is turned into a veritable pomological catalogue:

When I see you I see the fruit of my country
So juicy, so subtle and deliciously sweet;
Your teeth make me think of young corn's pearly grains
And on your breath wafts the perfume of our guavas.

I have never touched your lips, your smooth arms,
But when I see them so round, pure and firm of flesh
I hunger to taste them as a traveller bites
The mahogany apples that edge our country lanes.

I recognized in the softness of which boasts
The fine and tender velvet of your cheek

Yolk of eggs, and rose apple, and in your downy skin
The blooming honey-berry where the winds like to play.

Your bosoms are sisters of the marmalade plums
Those fruit blond and heavy of our blessed land;
Ah! If only your heart was not quite as hard
As those small nuts we call Guinea coco-nuts!

But all these delicious fruits: meaty sour sops,
Coco plums and cinnamon apples and mangos,
All these fruit, I think, I really think
Would I find if only I could taste your tongue.

And we would have delectable melting kisses
Kisses that prelude to other acts of love
And we would know the taste, in one exquisite moment
Of these fruits as divine as you, delicious custard apple.
(Panorama . . ., pp. 273-274.)

While woman is often likened to a fruit, I have been able to find only very few poems where she is likened to a flower. One is Etienne Bourand (1892–1957)'s rather insipid rondeau "L'Haïtienne":

A Haitian woman sleeps
Beside vermillion roses,
And two twin roses
Bloom on her bosom.
(idem, p. 314.)

Seymour Pradel (1876-1943) does no better in his pathetic "For Woman" ("Pour la femme"):

I seek the kiss of your lips in bloom
Knowing it causes pain, and at times even death.
(idem, p. 168.)

And Constantin Mayard evokes "Creole Women Under the Moon" ("Créoles au clair de lune"):

Beneath the white dream of a moon I like to see
Fat women who walk away indolently.

Rare flowers of flesh blooming richest with the night,
Making drunken the winds with some troubling delight. (. . .)
(Translated by E.W. Underwood, *op. cit.,* p. 90.)

To what can this peculiarity of the Haitian poetic imagination be attributed? There is one prosaic explanation: the land of Haiti produces many fruit but few flowers, and so Haitians are more familiar with the former than with the latter. This explanation is not very satisfactory, especially since flowers are grown commercially in Kinskoff, in the hills above Port-au-Prince; bougainvillia, orchids and hibiscus grace the gardens of well-to-do Haitians, and poets are either well-to-do or, by virtue of being literate, at least well-off enough to have a modest garden themselves.

If Woman is seen as a fruit rather than as a flower it is, I think, because Haitian sensuality is not satisfied with purely esthetic enjoyment. The beauty of a flower is enough to make it precious; the quality of fruit is revealed only when it is tasted. In the same way, woman is considered in Haiti as the object of an eventual possession. Of course, her physical aspect makes her more or less desirable, but does not represent a value per se. And it is well known that sexual symbolism identifies the fruit one tastes to the partner one possesses, the act of eating to the act of love. And fruit is not the only comestible that supplies erotic metaphors to the Haitian poet. Pétrus Blot (1876-1937) remembers strolling with his love along the "Boat Basin" ("Carénage"):

> The sea-spray that made your hair curly
> Gave your kisses a salty, tangy taste
> The taste of sea-food I savored
> On the nape of your brown skinned neck.
> (*Panorama . . .,* p. 196.)

Normil Sylvain (1866-1925) celebrates in "Curious Morals" (Moralités insolites"):

> The woman whose mouth I kiss,
> Whose lips taste of sour ball candy.
> (*idem,* p. 346.)

Regnor C. Bernard (1915-1980) finds a marvelous image to evoke "the woman who offered me the slow waters of her mouth" ("Fogs" ["Brumes"], *idem,* p. 526). But Émile Roumer does him one better with "The Bridegroom owns one pair of pants" ("Le Fiancé à pantalon unique") who tells his bride: "The kisses from your mouth are more gooey than turtle soup" (from S. Baridon and R. Philoctète, *op. cit.,* p. 240). Roumer is a very humorous poet, and everyone in Haiti knows his "*Marabout* of my Heart" ("Marabout de mon coeur"), in which the recipient of the poem is compared to the most appetizing specialties of Haitian cuisine:

> *Marabout* of my heart, with breasts like tangerines
> I find that you taste better than eggplant stuffed with crab.
> You are the slice of tripe within my gumbo soup,
> The dumpling in my beans, my tea of herbs and cloves,
> You are the bully beef whose rind my heart provides,
> The syrup and corn meal that trickles down my throat,
> You are a steaming dish, you are mushrooms and rice,
> Cod-fritters very crisp, fish fried to golden brown.
> I hunger for your love. Where you go I will trail
> Your buttocks, bouncing boats with bounteous vittles laden.
> (*Panorama . . .,* p. 364.)

In French poetry, feminine beauty is often defined as a formal harmony. Regular features and a well-proportioned body contain in themselves their own esthetic value. Woman is generally pictured in repose, in an attitude designed to make her resemble a work of art. In Haitian poetry, on the other hand, movement is an essential component of beauty. For a Haitian, a handsome body contains the promise of a proud bearing, of a graceful gesture or a suggestive litheness. The poet does not seek to turn a woman into a painting, even less into a statue. What he wants to translate is, on the contrary, her vitality; the harmony of form is secondary to the rhythm of movement, so that the woman reveals the true essence of her beauty by walking or, better yet, by dancing. A beauty not fixed in mineral immobility, but ever-changing part and parcel of organic life. Nerva Lataillade (1910-1931) elevates walking woman to symbolic heights, for she contains the radiance of spring, the beating of hearts, and the moans of desire:

> You carried with you a radiant spring,
> Your easy, undulating, feline walk
> Make hearts beat with dazzling dreams
> And the soul moan with yielding desire.
> ("The Old Woman" ["La Vieille"], from *Panorama . . .,* p. 167.)

For Dominique Hippolyte, "Nigra" 's gait is the proof of her association with the divine:

> My undulating walk is the dance of a God
> Who knew how to go unhurt through the flames.
> (M.A. Lubin, *op. cit.,* p. 59.)

What French poet would be so bold as to detect in a woman's steps the mysterious throb of the universe? In Haitian poetry it would almost be a commonplace. Duraciné Vaval (1879-1953) describes a "Creole Girl" whose walk, while remaining happily human, reflects Nature's fundamental vitality:

> When she passes, solemnly moving,
> Her hips twisting like frail bamboos (. . .)
> When the gracious, and soft and calm child smiles
> To the vague vibrations of the Infinite,
> To the rhythms which come from beyond herself
> Rhythms of nights, rhythms of flames, rhythms of jewels,
> Rhythms of hearts beating blessed words of love,
> Then the grace which wraps and braces her
> Holds you like the sea in its amber wake.
> (*L'Ame noire,* Port-au-Prince, 1933, p. 101.)

And René Depestre says of true women (whom he calls "garden-women"):

> They are beaches with powerful surf beats
> They are evenings sitting astride our hills
> Garden women have electrical buttocks
> Garden women have cyclones in their love play
> And in their cries the geography of volcanos

And in their movements, the geometry of she-lions
And in their blood all the seasons of the sea.
("Alleluia for Garden Women" ["Alléluia pour les femmes-jardins"],
Poète à Cuba, Paris, 1976, p. 82.)

As these examples show, when Haitian poetry is inspired by woman, it does not hesitate before frank and sensuous eroticism. But it does not seek to shock; it is neither smutty nor demeaning. Rather, I think, one could speak here of religious sexuality. For the Haitian poet's expression of sexuality often resembles a search for a higher reality. It is not unlike a metaphysical quest, a quest for the mysterious realm where harmony reigns between Nature and Humanity. Woman is supposed to be part of this realm, sharing as she does the elemental world's awesome fecundity.

And never is Haitian woman's special relation with the invisible world more apparent than when she dances at vodùn ceremonies. At that time, lucidity is set aside, instinct is liberated, and—through religious trance— another plane of existence is reached. Despite her violent, often suggestive movements, the desirability of a dancing woman's body is no longer relevant; it becomes the medium that will allow the Gods to manifest their presence.* Charles F. Pressoir understood it well:

Your panting breasts strain towards love,
I see Damballa** when your body swoons! (. . .)
I can not watch your brown nude legs
The flame in your eyes dances rhythms of vodùn.
("Black Island" ["L'île noire"], from *Panorama . . .,* p. 443.)

And Léon Laleau, in "Vodùn," reminds Carida, an old woman, of the time when she was a young priestess of the Gods:

Deep in your distressed body you felt the presence
Of an insane God who came from the unknown.
You danced, you danced as if you were on fire
With nimble loins and rapture in your eyes.
(L. Laleau, *op. cit.,* p. 248.)

Perhaps Ulysse Pierre-Louis (b. 1925) has given the best poetic expression to the mystery of the possession experience:

Tonight the lugubrious drum is calling.
It punctuates the savage play
Of undulating hips

*When in a trance state, the person loses consciousness and "becomes" the God, whose voice, mannerisms, and conduct she adopts. More details can be found in any study of vodùn; for example, Alfred Metraux's *Voodoo in Haiti* (New York, 1972), or Maya Deren's *Divine Horsemen* (New York, 1970).

**Damballa is one of the most important Gods in the vodùn pantheon. He is represented as a snake and, when "possessed" by him, the faithful dart their tongues and creep on the ground.

And the dishevelled priestess
Possessed by all the cosmic forces
Of the mysterious jungles
Rouses the entrails of the shivering night.
And the frantic priestess screams out
An oath of subjugation to the Gods
Who rule on earth, in water and in air.
("Message of Hope" ["Message d'espérance"], *Panorama . . .*, pp.
582-583.)

René Depestre puts it more succinctly:

How soon would the Gods grow old,
If Woman did not exist!
("How the Angels Would Weep" ["Comme les anges pleureraient"],
from S. Baridon and R. Philoctète, *op. cit.,* p. 115.)

When she is not used as a symbol, woman's place in the Haitian
poetic imagination is ambiguous. More often than not she is considered as
a sexual object. Her value is a function of the desire she arouses . . . or of
the desire that can be aroused in her. Like a product of nature, she has
been created for man's pleasure. That, however, in no way means that she
is considered inferior; on the contrary, she participates better than men
ever can in the harmony of nature. Her instinct is more precious than
masculine rationality, for through it she can attain an intimate knowledge
of the world of essences.

Could one say that in Haiti, as it does in Spain, "the existence of
women swings like a pendulum from adoration and semi-divine respect to
indignity and humiliation?"* Possibly, but with one important difference:
in Haiti, both adoration and indignity would be devoid of that sense of the
tragic which dominates Iberian sensitivity. Tropical sensuality and a finely-
sharpened sense of irony insure that the image of woman remain rooted
in humanity. Indignity? Adoration? Let us rather say respect tempered
with irreverence.

*Dominique Aubier & Manuel Tuñon de Lara, *Espagne,* Paris, 1956, p. 41.

THE FIRST HAITIAN NOVEL:
ÉMERIC BERGEAUD'S "STELLA"

Émeric Bergeaud was born in the provincial town of Les Cayes in 1818. In 1848 he was forced to flee the country, having been implicated in a conspircay against President Soulouque, who was soon to become Emperor Faustin the First. Bergeaud went into exile on the island of Saint Thomas, where he died ten years later. *Stella,* his only published work and the first novel ever to have been written by a Haitian, appeared in Paris in 1859, under the imprint of the famous publisher Edmond Dentu. A "second edition," which was in fact a second printing, was put out by Dentu in 1887. The text has never been reprinted since. Inasmuch as only a handful of specialists have had the opportunity to read *Stella,* I will briefly summarize the novel.

In the colony of Saint-Domingue Le Colon, a vicious planter has a slave woman (identified as L'Africaine) whipped to death—a crime all the more heinous in that he had fathered her son Rèmus. Rèmus has an older half-brother, Romulus, sired by an African war chief before L'Africaine was captured and transported to the New World. On their mother's grave, the two brothers vow to avenge her martyrdom. They become maroons; one night they attack Le Colon's plantation and set it on fire. The villain manages to escape, but in the smoking ruins of his manor-house, Romulus and Rèmus find Stella, a young woman generally—and erroneously—thought to be Le Colon's daughter. Their first impulse is to kill her; but a mysterious force stays their arms and even compels them to worship her on bended knees. Stella tells them her life story: she was born in Paris, and lived among the common people of the capital until the French Revolution degenerated into the Reign of Terror. She then fled to Saint-Domingue. Le Colon wanted her, and when she refused to be his, kept her a prisoner. It is by now becoming obvious that Stella is the incarnation of Freedom. She joins the sons of L'Africaine, and advises them as to the best strategy to achieve victory. Sometimes she moderates their reckless daring; at other times she stimulates their flagging determination. Fighting at their side, she warns that setbacks are bound to occur. She also reminds them time and time again that in unity there is strength and that final victory depends upon the harmony and trust between the two brothers.

So far, we seem to be dealing with a novel, with one of those clumsily symbolistic abolitionist novels so popular in France during the first half of the century. But Bergeaud will soon start recounting the main political events which took place in Haiti between 1789 and 1804. Fifteen years, and what astounding years! Planters and metropolitan officials, royalists and republicans, Blacks and Mulattos, freemen and slaves, an English expeditionary force, invading Spaniards . . ., and factions within each group struggle, form alliances, betray one another, make peace, wage war, burn, pillage, and issue manifestos. Toussaint Louverture appears in *Stella,* as does his Mulatto enemy Rigaud, as well as Pétion—who will be the first president of Haiti—Henry-Christophe, future king of the Northern half, and Sonthonax, the well-meaning envoy of the French Republic; also General Leclerc, who will die in Saint-Domingue, and his successor Rochambeau, and many others. They were all complex human beings, larger-than-life personalities, whose true adventures are more rousing than any fiction. Bergeaud recounts the epic in detail, presenting in chronological order the complexity and interconnections of its episodes. Even had he been content to chronicle only the most important incidents in this dizzying saga, the historical subject matter is so rich, and so dense, that it constantly overwhelms the imaginary adventures of the fictional characters. So, after the first eighty pages, Le Colon, L'Africaine, Stella, Romulus, and Rémus lose their individuality and become "episodic" characters or, more precisely, incarnations of contending forces. And it all ends with an apotheosis: on the Altar of the Nation, to the sound of drums and trumpets, Stella harangues the Haitian people, who have just conquered freedom. Then:

> The adorable virgin gave them her most tender smile and, unfolding her angel's wings, flew up towards the Heavens. All followed her flight with tears in their eyes, until she vanished in space, leaving behind her a long golden trail. (p. 308.)

Stella is a fairly long novel of over 300 pages. It is divided into thirty-nine chapters, each one with a title summarizing its subject matter: "The French Expeditionary Force," "The Defense of La Crête-à-Pierrot," "The French Army Departs," and the like. *Stella* has no foreword, no Preface or Introduction. This is a pity; it would have been interesting to know what Bergeaud's purpose was, why he chose this particular form and structure, and what models inspired him. Be that as it may, the question arises: is *Stella* really a novel and, if so, is it a historical novel?

Let us agree that (simplistic as this definition is) a text must, in order to be called a novel: (1) constitute, at least in part, a work of the imagination, a "fiction," either by describing actions which never took place, or by presenting characters who never existed; and (2) deal with both individual characters and a social organization. In other words, to chronicle the adventures of one or more souls, and those of whatever society they find themselves in.

Stella fulfills both conditions. Of course, it does contain a long series of events which actually took place in Haiti from the eve of the French Revolution to the Proclamation of Haitian Independence. If that were all, *Stella* would have to be described as a historical tale, as a mere vulgarization of information gathered from memoirs and archives. But the presence of characters (symbolic, no doubt, but surely invented) like

L'Africaine, Stella, Romulus and Rémus, and of episodes (also symbolic, but invented) such as Stella's adventures during the French Revolution, or the brothers' oath on their mother's grave, make *Stella* a novel. And the characters act out their lives in a society whose evolution between 1788 and 1804 is chronicled by Bergeaud, a society which determines their lives and which they attempt to mold according to their ideals or their interests.

Stella is also a historical novel insofar as, besides those characters invented by the author, numerous real characters appear, speak, and act. Also, in that the invented episodes are inserted among the real events which transformed Saint-Domingue into the Republic of Haiti. So that Pradel Pompilus is somewhat too severe when he writes in his *Manuel . . . de la littérature haïtienne* (Port-au-Prince, 1961):

> Because of the author's inclusion of much fictional material, we are forced to place *Stella* among the novels while, in fact, it is simply a tale of our struggle for independence, seasoned by an ingenious invention of the imagination. (p. 201.)

Bergeaud realized the danger of so closely combining history and novelistic fiction. In the third chapter, he attempts to define the characteristics of the two genres:

> History is a river of truth which flows majestically through the ages. The Novel is a deceitful lake, whose depth is hidden from sight; calm and pure on the surface, it sometimes hides in its bowels the secrets of the destiny of nations. (p. 19.)

Bergeaud is claiming a lofty role for the novel: it "sometimes hides in its bowels the secrets of the destiny of nations." Is he pleading here *pro domo sua?* Is he encouraging us to seek in *Stella* the secret of the destiny of Haiti? Later, he compares his novelist's craft to that of the historian:

> History is the echo of human storms, whose clamor and fury it faithfully reproduces. To face these storms and convey my savage heros to a safe haven, I would need more than a frail bark canoe; and besides, I, too, am a savage, with no charts, no compass, no knowledge of navigation. So, leaving the stormy sea to experienced pilots, I claim the peaceful lake: if we abandon ourselves to the breath of God, perhaps we shall reach the end of our voyage, guided by our country's star. (pp. 19-20.)

The guide in question is of course Stella, the star of Freedom. The "end of the voyage" is no doubt the discovery of the secret lying in the bowels of the novel. And, from his St. Thomas exile, Bergeaud is pleased to suggest that the inventor of fiction, because he possesses a special intuition, is a better guide for the nation than a politician armed with the practical knowledge of past and present history. We are reminded of Chatterton, the eponymous hero of Alfred de Vigny's 1835 romantic drama. Bergeaud cannot fail to have known this famous play, and remembered the discussion between the poet and the Lord Mayor, in which Chatterton compares England to a ship:

> "The King, the Lords, the Parliament are in the ship's castle, at the helm, at the compass. As for us, we must climb the masts, hoist the sails and load the cannons; we belong to the crew and no one is useless in the running of our glorious ship."

And the Lord Mayor asks:

> "What the devil can the Poet's role be?"
> "He reads in the stars," (answers Chatterton), "the road the Lord shows us." (Act III, scene 6.)

To return to *Stella:* During the civil war, Rémus (i.e., in this episode, the Mulatto leader Rigaud) put up a feeble defense against Romulus (i.e., Toussaint Louverture). Why was Rémus so ineffectual after having been so ardent? Bergeaud writes:

> History doesn't say. History can only say what she knows. Her sight is limited by the horizon of palpable reality and rarely perceives the truth shining beyond it. The world of the marvelous is not her domain. She leaves the field of mystery to the Novel. (p. 146.)

We shall return to the explanation Bergeaud offers of Rémus' conduct. Let us for now remember that Bergeaud considers the novelist as a visionary, capable of piercing the mystery of the world and explaining it through symbol and allegory. In other words, Bergeaud claims for the novelist the vision that the romantic school reserved for the poet.

Analysis of the main characters of *Stella* confirms that the novelistic elements which dominate in the first chapters will soon pale and be replaced by historic elements: the evocation of a complex and fascinating reality finally smothers an abstract symbolic fiction.

Stella, the main character, is quite different in the last pages from what she is in the first chapters. At the beginning of the book she is a typical melodrama heroine: pure, beautiful, and persecuted. We have no idea who she is: a mysterious identity is characteristic of melodrama heroes and heroines. While in Paris she is scorned by the rich and powerful and protected by the common people: melodramas are often the vehicles of populist ideology. Le Colon, who wants to possess her, locks her up in a dungeon: the cell is a privileged setting in melodramas, where the heroines suffer in body and soul, as demanded by the sadistic strain so often evident in the genre.

Once she joins the slave insurrection, Stella becomes more and more idealized. She turns into a sybil, an idol. Every time the two brothers win a battle, "they went to Stella's mountain retreat, to dedicate their triumph to her and to receive inspiration from her advice." (p. 121.) When the disagreement between Romulus and Rémus leads to civil war, Stella refuses to take sides in their quarrel. The two brothers finally come to their senses when General Leclerc's troops land to re-establish slavery and the rule of the planters. They unite their forces and do penance at Stella's feet for, as Rèmus says:

> If we have offended her, we have thereby offended the Divinity she represents. Let us not be sacrilegious. Let us go throw ourselves at the feet of the holy idol to whom we have dedicated our lives. (p. 204.)

Realism (or historical truth) and idealism (or novelistic imagination) are not manifest only in the heroine. Two other protagonists are interesting from this viewpoint. The first is L'Africaine, who can be considered as Stella's first incarnation. Until her murder by Le Colon she is a true novelistic character. We know her life story: we witness her existence on the plantation, and we see her raise her sons. The description of her horrible death is savagely realistic:

> The whip snaps. A scene of horror unfolds. Punctuated by the repeated sound of blows, piteous, high-pitched screams progressively weaken and become a death rattle. The whip falls and falls again, two hours long. The victim writhes, gnashing her teeth. She foams at the mouth, her nostrils gape, her eyes bulge out of their sockets. Life is gone, but matter still shudders and the whip keeps falling until only an inert corpse remains. (pp. 17-18.)

But the martyr's last movement is already symbolic:

> (. . .) L'Africaine's last stare, as eloquent as the spoken word, pointed to the mountains where her sons would soon flee to avenge her death. (p. 18.)

L'Africaine's tomb becomes a sacred place where the two brothers swear revenge, where they seal their reconciliation, where Le Colon will be executed. Her bloody dress is Haiti's first flag:

> Atop a mast raised in the middle of the camp, they fixed L'Africaine's dress, a somber red flag whose bloody folds rippled in the wind. Another color, the blue of our sky, was later added to the one symbolizing revenge, either to soften its sinister glow or as a testimony to the dual nature of the struggle for Haiti's independence, achieved by the common sacrifice of men of two different epidermic colorations. (pp. 212-213.)

From time to time, L'Africaine's ghost appears to her sons: she berates them for losing heart, she congratulates them when they are victorious. The symbolic value of the character is clear. As Bergeaud puts it: "Their mother will soon be reincarnated for them as independent Haiti." (p. 216.) And when Stella promises to stand by Romulus and Rèmus, she pledges to take their mother's place: "My feelings for you both will henceforth take the place of all your mother's love; you can depend on it." (p. 43.)

L'Africaine and Stella, Haiti and Liberty, are thus fused into one symbolic character who preaches the struggle against oppression and the unity which will be the mainstay of the nation.

Alongside Stella and L'Africaine we can put The Nation's Spirit (Le Génie de la Patrie), described as a giant who resembles an alabaster statue, "a venerable incarnation of wisdom and intelligence who blends authority, graciousness and strength." (p. 148.) Ghostlike, he appears in Chapter 22 to order Rémus, in the nation's interest, to cease the struggle against his brother, despite the righteousness of his cause and the prospect of victory. The function of The Nation's Spirit is, then, to explain the mystery evoked by Bergeaud at the beginning of the chapter. The mystery had baffled historians; the novelist will explain Rémus' hesitation through the symbol of the giant and his allegorical visitation.

This kind of explanation is obviously meaningless for a historian; and no one can be forced to enjoy the presence of the marvelous in literature. Bergeaud chose to give his country's history a symbolic interpretation. The reader is free to choose whether or not to accept it, whether or not to enter the novelist's universe.

Le Colon also is an emblematic character, an amalgamate of vices, a concentrate of evil. But in no way does he represent the French Nation. He stands for that small minority come to Saint-Domingue for dubious reasons, whose overriding ambition is to become rich, and who will stop at nothing to reach that goal. Lecherous, cruel, hypocritical, devious, cowardly, he doesn't hesitate to betray France in order to defend his privileges. Bergeaud is historically accurate when he shows Le Colon opening the borders of Saint-Domingue to the British and the Spanish. In the first part of the novel, Le Colon is the melodrama villian, the hateful slave master we find in many works of abolitionist inspiration. But, in the same way that Stella becomes the incarnation of Liberty, Le Colon rapidly becomes the incarnation of the planters or, more precisely, of the Saint-Domingue Whites whose prejudice undermined every effort for conciliation. Le Colon is executed on L'Africaine's grave just as Dessalines will avenge in white men's blood the crimes they committed in colonial times.

Romulus and Rémus are, with Stella, the only two fictional characters called not by a common name (L'Africaine, Le Colon, or The Nation's Spirit) but by a proper name taken from Latin. Bergeaud claims to have chosen them "less to establish some sort of analogy with the Roman twins than simply because they are brothers." (p. 20.) Nevertheless, the names Romulus and Rémus seem very fitting; true, our two heroes are not twins, and were not even sired by the same father, but this biological detail is irrelevant. Like the sons of the She-Wolf, they also create a nation, and their fratricidal struggle precedes the founding of Haiti, just as the fratricidal struggle of their ancient namesakes preceded that of Rome.

By superimposing his fiction on historical reality, Bergeaud was setting strict limits on his imagination, not only with respect to the plot, but also to the characters. This is especially true of the two brothers. Since it is fused with that of Haiti, their destiny is foreordained. So are their personalities, since Romulus and Rémus are emblematic and composite characters.

They are emblematic, because it is quite evident that, as Le Colon represents the Whites of Saint-Domingue, Romulus stands for the Blacks and Rémus for the Mulattos. In Bergeaud's work, the genesis of the Republic of Haiti comprises three movements. First, the Blacks and Mulattos rise against the Whites; Romulus and Rémus fight Le Colon and win. Then, the Whites forment dissensions between the Blacks and the Mulattos, allying themselves with the former, the better to betray them later; Le Colon uses Romulus to neutralize Rémus and then calls upon General Leclerc's expedition to re-establish the *status quo ante*. Finally, the Blacks and Mulattos unite, beat back the invaders and eliminate the Whites once and for all; the two brothers execute Le Colon.

Romulus and Rémus are composite as well as emblematic characters. When he is dealing with historic political events—revolts, battles, conspiracies, and the like—Bergeaud invents nothing. The novelist, therefore, cannot help modeling L'Africaine's sons on those Black and Mulatto leaders whose destiny they shared. But, from 1791 to 1804, the Blacks furnished not one but several leaders, and so did the Mulattos. Even though Toussaint Louverture fought against André Rigaud, we cannot identify Romulus with Toussaint only, nor Rémus solely with Rigaud, if for no other reason than that neither Toussaint nor Rigaud were present at the founding of Haiti. Hence, Romulus is not only Toussaint but also Christophe and Dessalines; Rémus is Rigaud, and Pétion and Boyer as well. That is why Bergeaud can only endow his heroes with a rudimentary individuality. Their private lives are never revealed; of their feelings, their habits and idiosyncracies we learn only what has a direct bearing on their political actions. Did they love women? Did they have children? Or friends? How did they spend the time not devoted to fighting? We shall never know. Since Romulus had to be at the same time Toussaint, Christophe and Dessalines, Bergeaud could not endow him with personality traits which would identify him with one—rather than another or the third—of these historic figures.

There is on the other hand no problem when Bergeaud directly evokes men like Commissioner Sonthonax or Generals Leclerc or Rochambeau. In their cases, the novelist could make use of what is known of their personalities. Rochambeau's cruelty, for example, is strikingly illustrated by two historic incidents: the ball to which the French general had invited the wives of his "native" officers to show them, at the end of the party, their husbands' murdered bodies, and, in Chapter 35, the horrible training of attack dogs to be used against the rebels. We reach the somewhat paradoxical conclusion that, from a literary point of view, the novel's historical characters are better drawn, more "lifelike," than the fictional ones.

The public a writer addresses influences both the form and content of his work: we must remember that Stella, a didactic novel, a propaganda novel in the best sense of the term, was aimed at Haitian readers and at French readers simultaneously. On the one hand, Bergeaud wants to redeem and justify his country in the eyes of the French, who held it in low esteem and looked upon Haiti as a comic opera republic governed by Soulouque, the blood-thirsty buffoon.* He also wants to teach them something about Haitian history, which they knew, if at all, through the biased versions of French historians or the elucubrations of hacks specializing in spine-tingling exoticism. Bergeaud wants to remind—or to teach—these readers that "many nations occupy a larger territory; none has a nobler birth." (p. 257.)

Bergeaud's purpose in addressing the Haitian reader is twofold. Like other writers of his generation, he wants to inspire in his compatriots respect and pride for their country. The persecutions of which élite Mulattos were victims since the "noiriste" government of Soulouque had come to power, and which forced Bergeaud himself into exile, reinforced the élite tendency to denigrate all things Haitian. Despairing of the future, the élite turned more and more towards France, apeing the way of life of Parisian high society, adopting its complex of superiority and its intellectual myopia. The Haitian élite was falling into the "collective Bovarysm" that Jean Price-Mars was to denounce seventy years later. It was urgent to remind the Haitian reader of his origins and of the sacrifices made by his ancestors to attain human dignity. It was urgent to combat this collective abdication, this temptation to take refuge in unauthenticity. Thus, as an enterprise of valorization, so to speak, Stella is aimed at the Haitian reader almost as much as to the French one.

Bergeaud's novel also develops an ideological argument which does not concern the French. The author seeks to convince his compatriots that the antagonism between Blacks and Mulattos, which goes back to the very origins of Haitian history, is the root cause of the nation's misfortunes, that it makes progress impossible, and that it must be done away with. Bergeaud ridicules color prejudice and argues that it was invented to justify slavery and exploitation, and used by Haiti's enemies to divide and

---

*French cartoonists and humorists never tired of depicting Emperor Faustin I as a grotesque ape. But this was not entirely racist nastiness. France was also governed at the time by an emperor, and it was of course forbidden to criticize him. On the other hand, no one could prevent readers from identifying one emperor with the other. Victor Hugo explicitly and repeatedly compared them—and the comparison was never to Louis-Napoleon's advantage.

conquer. The Machiavellian Colon advises Romulus to beware his mulatto brother:

> The color of your skin makes you different from your brother. Yours is darker than his; that is why he considers you morally inferior to him and can't accept you as his leader. (p. 133.)

Bergeaud concludes that "color prejudice is vicious stupidity" (p. 134), and that

> The combination of the two differently colored groups which make up Haitian society can only favor its prosperity. It has already produced Liberty and Independence; it will lead us to Civilization. (pp. 96-97.)

Bergeaud aims to educate the reader and to raise his consciousness rather than to amuse him. Like the novelists Hibbert, Marcelin and Lhérisson at the end of the century, like Cinéas and Brierre at the time of the U.S. occupation, like Roumain, Alexis, Chauvet and Phelps in our generation, Bergeaud wanted to be his countrymen's intellectual mentor.

Bergeaud's ideology is determined by the exigencies of his day. The march of history and the passage of time may have made this ideology obsolete, and one can understand that, half a century later, Frédéric Marcelin was impatient with *Stella*. Speaking of his own novels, he writes in *About Two Novels* (*Autour de deux romans*, Paris, 1903):

> I could have wrapped myself in the veils of fiction (. . .) and manufactured a conventional novel. Like that author who celebrated Toussaint Louverture and André Rigaud under the bizarre appellations of Romulus and Rémus, (. . .) I could have given you a pure, perfect newborn Haiti immolating Tyranny, inspired by the vengeful breath of Liberty and Justice. I wanted to do something else. (p. 27.)

In 1903, Marcelin wanted to do something else because it was no longer relevant to exalt Haiti's past. Bergeaud and his fellow writers had succeeded—succeeded too well, in fact. The exaltation of the Haitian revolution had been institutionalized, had become a new form of escape, an opiate, a dream complacently indulged in instead of confronting the problems of the present. Marcelin, like his friends Hibbert and Lhérisson, indeed wants something else: to bring his readers back down to earth, to show them the current misfortunes of the Republic, to urge them to face up to their responsibilities, to suffuse the Haitian collective mentality with concern for the national interest.

If we forget when and why Bergeaud wrote, certain characteristics of *Stella* are surprising. For example, the care he takes not to attack France, charging her at worst with errors, never with crimes, making the planters and their allies responsible for everything. For Bergeaud, Commissioner Sonthonax is a lay saint and General Leclerc a conscientious soldier stoically applying a policy he doesn't approve. Even in Rochambeau, the bloody butcher, he recognizes personal courage and the odd chivalric gesture. Time and time again, Bergeaud associates the Haitian with the French Revolution. The day the first emancipation of slaves is decreed he has the exultant crowd sing this verse of the Marseillaise, which expresses the aspirations of both peoples:

> Sacred love of the nation,
> Support and guide our avenging arms.
> Liberty, beloved Liberty,
> Fight alongside your defenders,
> Let Victory, hearing your virile call,
> Rush to our banners.
> Let the expiring foe
> See your triumph and our fame. (p. 100.)

Why this moderation? Because Bergeaud is anxious not to displease either his French readers, or his Haitian ones who were hypnotized by—and identified with—an idealized France.

Stella is a blond girl, a fact today's readers might find puzzling. Did L'Africaine's reincarnation have to have such an obviously Nordic appearance? The point is precisely that Bergeaud wanted to show the exemplary nature of the Haitian revolution, to place it within the venerable tradition of humanity's fight against oppression. Negritude's hour had not yet struck—which doesn't mean that Bergeaud didn't foresee it, or wasn't conscious of Haiti's role as redeemer of the Black race: L'Africaine is Mother Africa and the Haitians are her champions. Stella prophesizes that Romulus and Rémus

> would give back a despised race its right to humanity and would found
> for her a glorious nation on the ruins of the guilty colony. (pp. 73-76.)

One last remark: Bergeaud describes the history of Haiti as a fight among giants and supermen. The common people, the lowly foot-soldiers, the humble cannon fodder who sacrificed themselves unsparingly, are given rather short shrift. Bergeaud's purpose was to encourage the *élite* to identify with the abstact concept of Nationhood. To attempt to arouse its admiration for a mass it ignored, feared, and despised, would have been a waste of time. Marcelin, Hibbert, and Lhérisson will eventually make the Haitian middle class a literary subject. As for the peasants and workers, they will have to wait for post-occupation writers like Pétion Savain, Jacques Roumain, or Jacques-Stéphen Alexis. And yet one sentence of *Stella* shows that Bergeaud was not totally indifferent to the anonymous, powerless masses. Criticizing the agrarian policies of a Romulus manipulated by the planters (he is obviously thinking of Toussaint Louverture in 1800), Bergeaud writes:

> Evidently, for him the Nation didn't include the unhappy field hands
> who had been forced back to the plantations and who were forced to
> toil ceaselessly or be whipped, often to death. (pp. 165-166.)

The readership Bergeaud wanted to reach also determined some of the novel's formal traits. Bergeaud had to provide his French readers, who were quite ignorant about things Haitian, with some essential information: the first chapters describe the topography, the flora and fauna, the wonderful climate and the beautiful sky of Haiti. The Haitian reader, obviously, hardly needed a summary description of his homeland. With the French reader in mind, Bergeaud avoids such names of plants, animals and topographical features as might puzzle him; he speaks of lemon trees, of orange groves, of royal palms but not of *manceniliers,* of *mapous,* or of *bayahondes.* We encounter swallows but no *pipirits,* no *malfinis;* we have storms but no *avalasses,* and so on. It should however be noted that, either in the body of the text or in the notes, Bergeaud informs his French reader of what *bois de fer* is, and of what a *makoute* is used for. Still, "Haitian French" and especially Créole are used exceptionally and with extreme caution. "Haitian French" might shock Frenchmen, who, as everyone knows, are fanatical about so-called linguistic purity; it might also offend the Haitian readers of the time, who, even more than their counterparts of the Métropole, swore by Vaugelas' grammar and the Dictionary of the Académie française. Créole was of course despised by the Haitian élite. The next generation of novelists began to use Créole either in its pure form or in its frenchicized form, and the Haitian novel attained an extraordinary linguistic originality. But Bergeaud's style remains insipidly academic and all his characters declaim in the old-fashioned rhetoric of yore.

We might finally notice that many historical characters and place names are identified in notes at the end of the book. According to Note 7, for instance, "a conquered town" is Tiburon, and according to Note 8 "another English stronghold" is Léogâne; thanks to Note 14, we learn that "one of Romulus' lieutenants" is General Maurepas, and Note 17 tells us that "one of Romulus' former lieutenants" is General Henry-Christophe. Thirty-six notes of forty-eight simply indicate the name of a person or place. If these names are important, one might well ask, why not give them in the body of the text? And if they are not, why bother to give them in the notes?

For the French reader, who wants above all to read a rousing good story, it matters little whether General Capoix or General Clairvaux occupied Miragoane or Jérémie, especially since no information is given about these towns or these soldiers. Accumulating names of superior officers and provincial villages would have added nothing. In fact, it would probably have needlessly distracted the reader.

But it is more than probable that the majority of Haitian readers had only vague notions about the many episodes of the War of Independence chronicled in *Stella.* Books on Haitian history were few and superficial; they still are. For the curious, then, Bergeaud specified where given incidents took place and who was involved. By including the notes, he insured that the interested reader would not only be inspired, but also informed.

Numerous poets, novelists, and playwrites have been inspired by the Haitian War of Independence: Victor Hugo and Kleist, Lamartine and Wordsworth, Aimé Césaire and Alejo Carpentier . . . To claim that *Stella* deserves to stand among the works of those masters would be foolish. But it can be argued, I think, that *Stella* is more than a literary curiosity, more than merely the first novel written by a Haitian; it eloquently articulates the basic obsession of all Haitian writers: a passionate affirmation of Haiti's originality and dignity, and an anguished fear that the sequels of colonization, which still infect Haitian society, may prove stronger than patriotic efforts to eliminate them.

A BIBLIOGRAPHY OF CRITICAL STUDIES ON HAITIAN LITERATURE

The present bibliography updates HOFFMANN, Léon-François, "Etat présent des études littéraires haïtiennes," *The French Review,* 49, 5, April 1976, pp. 750–758, and *idem,* "Pour une bibliographie des études littéraires haïtiennes, *Conjonction,* 134, juin–juillet 1977, pp. 3–54, and its "Premier supplément," *Conjonction,* 152, janvier 1982, pp. 43–57.

The place of publication of periodicals mentioned will be found on pages 165 to 168.

I. BIBLIOGRAPHIES

AUBOURG, Gérard, *Haïti—Bibliographie des travaux publiés en France 1915–1975,* published as *Cahiers d'anthropologie* (Paris, C.N. R.S.), 2, 1976. (Literature is covered on pp. 56–61.)

BERTRAND, Wilfrid and Daniéla Devesin, "Bibliothèques haïtiennes d'aujourd'hui," *Conjonction,* 127–128, déc. 1975, pp. 9–53.

BISSAINTHE, Max, *Dictionnaire de bibliographie haïtienne,* Washington, D.C. The Scarecrow Press, 1951. (The fundamental work of Haitian bibliography; 1055 pages, over 9,000 entries; author and title indices.)

BISSAINTHE, Max, *Dictionnaire de bibliographie haïtienne, premier supplément, 1950–1970.* Metuchen, N.J.: The Scarecrow Press, 1973. (An appendix lists over 300 titles published before 1950.) Updated by MANIGAT, Max, q.v.

DEVESIN, Daniela, see BERTRAND, Wilfrid, supra.

DUVIVIER, Ulrich, *Bibliographie générale et méthodique d'Haïti,* 2 vols., Port-au-Prince: Impr. de l'Etat, 1941. (Literature is covered in Vol. II, pp. 209–239.)

FONTVIEILLE, Jean-Roger, *Guide bibliographie du monde noir,* 2 vols. Yaoundé: Université fédérale du Cameroun, 1971. (Cursory and unreliable as it pertains to Haiti.)

GROPP, Arthur E., *Guide to Libraries and Archives in Central America and the West Indies.* New Orleans: Tulane University Press, 1941. (Haiti material listed on pp. 465–482.) Updated by BERTRAND, Wilfrid, q.v.

HERDECK, Donald (ed.), *Caribbean Writers: A Bio-bibliographical-critical Encyclopedia.* Washington D.C.: Three Continents Press, 1979. (The Francophone literature from the Caribbean section, by Maurice A. Lubin, is on pp. 261–547.)

MANIGAT, Max, *Haitiana 1971–1975.* La Salle, P.Q.: Collectif Paroles, 1979. (An appendix lists 156 titles which do not appear in Bissainthe's *Premier supplément.*)

PRIMUS, Wilma, "Bibliography of Haitian Literature, 1900–1972," *Black Images,* 2, 1, Spring 1973, pp. 44–59.

The catalogues of two important Haitian collections have been published:

LOWENTHAL, Ira P. and Drexel G. Woodson, *Catalogue de la collection Mangonès.* New Haven, Conn.: Yale University Antilles Research Program Occasional Papers 2, 1974.

LUCIEN, Jean, i.c., *Catalogue de la bibliothèque haïtienne des frères de l'Instruction chrétienne,* mimeo. Port-au-Prince, 1958.

WOODSON, Drexel G., see LOWENTHAL, Ira P., supra.

II. HISTORIES OF HAITIAN LITERATURE

BERROU, frère Raphaël, see POMPILUS, Pradel, infra.

FARDIN, Dieudonné, see JADOTTE, Hérard, infra.

FOUCHÉ, Franck, *Guide pour l'étude de la littérature haïtienne.* Port-au-Prince: Panorama, 1964.

GOURAIGE, Ghislain, *Histoire de la littérature haïtienne.* Port-au-Prince, Impr. N.A. Théodore, 1960.

JADOTTE, Hérard and Dieudonné Fardin, *Panorama de la littérature haïtienne,* 4 vols. Port-au-Prince: offset, 1968. (3rd revised edition, 1969.)

LA SELVE, Edgar, *Histoire de la littérature haïtienne depuis ses origines jusqu'à nos jours.* Versailles: Impr. de Cerf, 1875.

LHÉRISSON, Lélia J., *Manuel de littérature haïtienne.* Port-au-Prince: Impr. du Collège de Vertières, 1945.

MARC, Jules A., *Regards sur la littérature haïtienne.* Port-au-Prince: offset, 1973.

NEPTUNE, Daniel, *Dissertations de littérature haïtienne.* Port-au-Prince: Panorama, 1964. (2nd edition, 1968.)

POMPILUS, Pradel and frère Raphaël Berrou, *Histoire de la littérature haïtienne,* 3 vols. Port-au-Prince: Caraïbes, 1975.

POMPILUS, Pradel and Frères de l'instruction chrétienne, *Manuel illustré d'histoire de la littérature haïtienne.* Port-au-Prince: Deschamps, 1961.

VAVAL, Duraciné, *Histoire de la littérature haïtienne, ou l'âme noire.* Port-au-Prince: Impr. A. Héraux, 1933.

VIATTE, Auguste, *Histoire littéraire de l'Amérique française.* Québec: P.U. Laval and Paris: P.U.F., 1954, pp. 329–479.

III. ANTHOLOGIES

BARIDON, Silvio F. and Raymond Philoctète, *Poésie vivante d'Haïti.* Paris: Ed. de la Quinzaine Littéraire and Sherbrooke, P.Q.: Naaman, 1977.

CHARLES, Christophe, *Rêves d'or.* Port-au-Prince, 1977.

GOURAIGE, Ghislain, *Les Meilleurs poètes et romanciers haïtiens.* Port-au-Prince: Impr. La Phalange, 1963.

JANNINI, Pascuale A., *Breve antologia della poesia haitiana*. Milano: Il Sofà letterario del Mese Sanitario, 1962.

LUBIN, Maurice A., *Poésie haïtienne*. Rio de Janeiro: Casa do estudante do Brasil, 1956.

LUBIN, Maurice A., see SAINT-LOUIS, Carlos, infra.

MÉNOS, Solon, Dantès Bellegarde, A. Duval, and Georges Sylvain, *Auteurs haitiens—Morceaux choisis précédés de notices bio-graphiques*. Port-au-Prince: Impr. de Mme F. Smith, 1904. (With minor revisions, this work appeared in 1950 as *Oeuvre des écrivains haïtiens*, 2 vols. Port-au-Prince: Deschamps, with Dantès Bellegarde as the sole author.)

MORAND, Paul, *Anthologie de la poésie haïtienne indigène*. Port-au-Prince: Impr. Modèle, 1928.

MORPEAU, Louis, *Anthologie d'un siècle de poésie haïtienne*. Paris: Bosard, 1925.

PHILOCTETE, Raymond, see BARIDON, Silvio F., supra.

POMPILUS, Pradel, *Pages de littérature haïtienne*. Port-au-Prince: Impr. de l'État, 1951.

REY, Ghislaine, *Anthologie du roman haïtien (1859–1946)*. Sherbrooke, P.Q.: Naaman, 1978.

SAINT-LOUIS, Carlos, and Marice A. Lubin, *Panorama de la poésie haïtienne*. Port-au-Prince: Deschamps, 1950.

VILAIRE, Maurice, *Poètes protestants haïtiens*. Port-au-Prince: s.ed., 1964.

VILAIRE, Maurice, *Prosateurs protestants haïtiens*. Port-au-Prince: Impr. des Antilles, 1964.

IV. GENERAL STUDIES

ALAUX, Gustave d', "La Littérature jaune," *Revue des Deux-mondes*, 1, sept. 1852, pp. 938–967; 15, déc. 1852, pp. 1048–1085.

ALAUX, Gustave d', "Les Moeurs et la littérature nègres," *Revue des Deux-mondes*, 15 mai 1852, pp. 762–795.

ALEXIS, Jacques-Stéphen, "Contribution à la table ronde sur le folklore et le nationalisme," *Optique*, 23 jan. 1956, pp. 25–34.

ALEXIS, Jacques-Stéphen, "Du réalisme merveilleux des Haïtiens," *Présence africaine*, 8, 10, juin–nov. 1956, pp. 245–271.

ALEXIS, Stéphen, "Modern Haitian Thought," *Books Abroad*, 30, Spring 1956, pp. 261–265.

ARGYLL, Pierre, "Propos de lettrès," *La Nouvelle revue*, II, 4, déc. 1908.

AUGUSTE, Yves L., "L'Amour dans la littérature haïtienne," *Le Nouvelliste,* éd. spéciale de Noël. 24 & 25 déc. 1963. Repr. in *Présence africaine,* 60, 4, 1966, pp. 159–171.

AUGUSTE, Yves L., "Littérature noire des États-Unis et d'Haïti: la couleur: appât ou barrière," *Présence africaine,* 112, 4e trim. 1979, pp. 113–120.

BERROU, frère Raphaël, *Les Pionniers.* Port-au-Prince: Impr. Ponec, 1967.

BLANCHET, Jules, *Le Destin de la jeune littérature.* Préface de F. Morisseau-Leroy. Port-au-Prince: Impr. de l'État, 1939.

BLANCHET, Jules, and René Piquion, *Essais sur la culture.* Port-au-Prince: Vve Valcin, 1938.

BONAVENTURE, frère, *La Littérature haïtienne se découvre,* M.A. Thesis, University of Ottawa, 1952.

BONNEAU, Alexandre, "Les Noirs, les Jaunes et la littérature française en Haïti," *Revue contemporaine,* 1 déc. 1856, pp. 107–155.

BOSTICK, Herman F., "Towards Literary Freedom: A Study of Contemporary Haitian Literature," *Phylon,* 17, 3, 1956, pp. 250–256.

BRUN, Gérard, "Lengua y literatura: Dos aspectos de la cultura del pueblo haitiano," *Thesaurus,* 21, 1, enero–abril 1966, pp. 194–198.

CALIXTE, Nyll F., "Les Difficultés pour l'écrivain haïtien de se faire éditer et diffuser," *Culture française,* 24, 3–4, 1975, pp. 62–68.

CHARLES, Asselin, "Voodoo Myths in Haitian Literature," *Comparative Literature Studies,* 17, 4, Dec. 1980, pp. 391–398.

CHARLES, Christophe, *Dix nouveaux poètes et écrivains haïtiens.* Port-au-Prince: UNHTI, 1974. (R. Bauduy, G. Camfort, G. Dougé, Franketienne, E. Jean-Baptiste, R. Labuchin, M. Lafontant-Médard, U. Rosarion, M. Vallès, J.A. Marc.)

CHRISTIE, Emerson B., "Haiti's Contribution to Literature," *Pan American Magazine,* 44, 3, March 1931, pp. 216–226.

CINÉAS, Jean-B., "Y–a–t–il une littérature haïtienne?," *Le Temps,* 26 juin 1940.

COOK, Mercer, "Mountains and Manuscripts," *Americas,* 3, 9, Sept. 1951, pp. 13–16.

COOK, Mercer, "Trends in Recent Haitian Literature," *Journal of Negro History,* 32, 2, April 1947, pp. 220–231.

DASH, J. Michael, "Haitian Literature—A Search for Identity," *Savacou,* 5 June 1971, pp. 81–94.

DASH, J. Michael, *Literature and Ideology in Haiti 1915–1961.* London:

McMillan, 1981.

DASH, J. Michael, "The Way Through Africa: A Study of *Les Griots*," *Bim*, 58, June 1975.

DEPESTRE, Renè, *Pour la révolution pour la poésie.* Montreal: Léméac, 1974.

DESPRADEL, Alberto, "El personaje haitiano en la época de Trujillo," *Ahora!*, 22 sept. 1975, pp. 52–56.

DOMINIK, Maks, "Vodou ak litèrati ayisyin," *Sèl*, 6, 41, août 1978, pp. 26–31.

DORVAL, Gèrald, *Etudes, romans et peintures.* Port-au-Prince: Fardin, 1976. (B. Posy, O. Vincent, N. Magloire, Frankétienne, R. Oliver, G.P. Hector.)

EFRON, Edith, "The 'New Movement' in Haiti," *Caribbean Quarterly*, 4, 5, Jan. 1955, pp. 14–15.

ÉTIENNE, Gèrard, *Le Nationalisme dans la littérature haïtienne*, Port-au-Prince: èd. du Lycée Pétion, 1964.

ÉTIENNE, Gèrard, "La Femme noire dans le discours littéraire haïtien," *Présence francophone*, 18, printemps 1979, pp. 109–126.

FABRE, Michel, "*La Revue indigène* et le mouvement Nouveau Noir," *Revue de littérature comparée*, 51, jan.–mars 1977, pp. 30–39.

FIEVRE, Justin O.: see infra JEAN, Eddy A.

FLEISCHMANN, Rose Marie, "Die haitianische Literatur: ein Uberblick," *Die Neuren Sprachen*, 3, Marz 1963, pp. 117–129.

FLEISCHMANN, Ulrich, *Ecrivain et société en Haïti.* Montreal: Centre de recherches caraïbes de l'Université, 1976.

FLEISCHMANN, Ulrich, *Ideologie und Wirklichkeit in der Literatur Haitis.* Berlin: Colloquium, 1969.

FOUCHARD, Jean, "L'Amour dans la littérature haïtienne," *La Relève*, 3, 8, février 1935, pp. 11–20, & 3, 9, mars 1935, pp. 1–6.

FOWLER, Carolyn, "La Prise de conscience dans la littérature haïtienne: la constitution d'une tradition," *Ngam*, 1–2, 1977, pp. 66–77.

GAILLARD, Roger, "Indigénisme haïtien, négritude et internationalisme," *Le Nouveau monde*, 6 mai 1979.

GAVRONSKY, Serge, "Linguistic Aspects of Francophone Literature," *The French Review*, 51, 6, May 1978, pp. 843–852.

GINDINE [TARDIEU-FELDMAN], Yvette, "Images of the American in Haitian Literature During the Occupation," *Caribbean Studies*, 14, 3, Oct. 1974, pp. 37–52.

GLÉMAUD, Marie-Josée, "Pourquoi écrire? Lettre ouverte à Jean-Claude Fignolé," *Collectif paroles*, 7, juillet–août 1980, pp. 27–29.

GORLICH, E.J., "Die französische Literatur Haitis," *Antares,* 5, 7, nov. 1967, pp. 41–43.

GOURAIGE, Ghislain, *Continuité noire.* Dakar–Abidjan: Nouvelles éditions africains, 1977.

GOURAIGE, Ghislain, *La Diaspora d'Haïti et l'Afrique.* Sherbrooke, P.Q.: Naaman, 1974.

GOURAIGE, Ghislain, "Littérature haïtienne et littérature française," *Culture française,* 26, 1, printemps 1977, pp. 5–16.

GOURAIGE, Ghislain, "Haïti, source de la négritude," in *Littératures ultramarines de langue française.* Sherbrooke, P.Q.: Naaman, 1974, pp. 58–67.

GOURMONT, Jean de, "Revue de la quinzaine: Les Revues [about *Les Griots*]," *Mercure de France,* oct. 1938, pp. 179–182.

HEURTELOU, Daniel, "La Critique littéraire," *La Relève,* 2, 11, 1 mai 1933, pp. 21–26.

HOFFMANN, Léon-François, "Coup d'oeil sur la littérature haïtienne," *Notre librairie,* 48, avril–juin 1979, pp. 41–52.

HOFFMANN, Léon-François, "Les Etats-Unis et les Américains dans les lettres haïtiennes," *Études littéraires,* 13, 2, août 1980, pp. 289-312.

HOFFMANN, Léon-François, "Slavery and Race in Haitian Letters," *Caribbean Review,* 9, 2, Spring 1980, pp. 28–32.

HURBON, Laënnec, *Culture et dictature en Haïti: L'imaginaire sous contrôle.* Paris: L'Harmattan, 1979.

HURBON, Laënnec, "Dialectique de la vie et de la mort autour de l'arbre dans les contes haïtiens," in G. Calame-Griaule (ed.), *Le Thème de l'arbre.* Paris: Klincksieck, 1969, pp. 71–92.

JADOTTE, Hérard, "Idéologie, littérature, dépendance," *Nouvelle Optique,* 1, 4, déc. 1971, pp. 71–84.

JEAN, Eddy A. & Justin O. Fievre, *Pour une littérature haïtienne nationale et militante.* Lille: Jacques Soleil, 1975. (C. Brouard E. Roumer, J. Brierre, R. Camille, J.S. Alexis, R. Depestre.)

JEANNOT, Yvan, "La Paysannerie et nos lettres," *La Relève,* 4, 6, 1 déc. 1935, pp. 7–9.

KESTELOOT, Lilyan, *Les Écrivains noirs de langue française,* 4ème édition. Bruxelles: Éd. de l'Institut de Sociologie de l'Université, libre, 1971.

KOSHLAND, Miriam, "Development of the Literary Idiom in Haiti," *Black Orpheus,* 7, June 1960, pp. 46–56.

LAFERRIÉRE, Dany, "L'Humour à *La Ronde,*" *Le Petit Samedi Soir,* 151, 26 juin–2 juillet, 1976, pp. 28–30.

LAGUERRE, Michel, SJ, "Brassages ethniques et émergence de la culture haïtienne," *Revue de l'Université Laurentienne,* 3, 2, 1970, pp. 48–65.

LARAQUE, Paul, "André Breton en Haïti," *Nouvelle Optique,* 1, 2, 3 mai 1971, pp. 126–138.

LARGE, Camille, "La Littérature haïtienne de 1896 à nos jours," *La Nouvelle Ronde,* 1, 4, sept. 1925, pp. 62–65.

LAROCHE, Maximilien, *L'Image comme écho.* Montréal: Nouvelle Optique, 1978. (Collection of essays.)

LAROCHE, Maximilien, "Image du Nègre et rhétorique dans la littérature haïtienne," *Études littéraires,* 7, 2, août 1974, pp. 291–297.

LAROCHE, Maximilien, *Le Miracle et la métamorphose.* Montréal: Éd. du jour, 1970.

LAROCHE, Maximilien, "Panorama de la littérature créole," in *L'Haïtien,* Montréal: Éd. de Ste Marie, 1968, pp. 84–94.

LAROCHE, Maximilien, "Portrait de l'Haïtien," in *L'Haïtien,* Montréal: Éd. de Ste Marie, 1968, pp. 15–98.

LAROCHE, Maximilien, "La Quête de l'identité culturelle dans la littérature haïtienne," *Notre librairie,* 48, avril–juin 1979, pp. 55–67.

LAROCHE, Maximilien, "Violence et langage dans les littératures d'Haïti et des Antilles françaises," *Présence francophone,* 16, printemps 1978, pp. 111–121.

LECHAUD, Thomas H., "Le Rire dans les lettres haïtiennes," *L'Essor,* avril 1912.

MANIGAT, Leslie, *Une date littéraire, un événement pédagogique.* Port-au-Prince: Impr. La Phalange, 1962.

MARCELIN, Émile, *Médaillons littéraires; poètes et prosateurs haïtiens.* Port-au-Prince: Impr. de l'Abeille, 1906. (M. Déjean, A. Brun, V. Sampeur, J. Dévot, T. Guilbaud, D. Delorme, Ch. S. Villevaleix, Th. Madiou, B. Ardouin, E. Nau, O. Durand, Jérémie, G. Sylvain, L. Etheard, P. Lochard, F. Marcelin.)

MARCHETTI, A., "Uno sguardo sulla letteratura di Haiti," *Francofonia,* 1, 1981.

MARINAS OTERO, Luis, "Evolución del pensamiento haitiano," *Cuadernos hispanoamericanos,* 182, feb. 1965, pp. 325–347.

MARTY, Anne, "La Littérature haïtienne en quête d'identité," *L'Afrique littéraire et artistique,* 38, 4, 1975, pp. 2–9.

MORISSEAU-LEROY, Félix, "La Littérature haïtienne d'expression créole, son avenir," *Présence africaine,* 17, déc. 1957–jan. 1958, pp. 46–57.

MORISSEAU-LEROY, Félix, "Le Mouvement littéraire," *Le Temps,* 20 oct. 1937.

MORPEAU, Louis, "Le Mouvement littéraire en Haïti," *La Vie des peuples*, 4, 53, sept. 1924, pp. 82–105.

MORPEAU, Louis, "Un dominion intellectuel français, Haïti 1789–1924," *Revue de l'Amérique latine*, 3, 8, oct. 1924, pp. 332–341.

MORPEAU, Pierre M., "Haiti," *Crisol*, 4, 7, 31 mayo 1932, pp. 290–300.

MOURALIS, Bernard, "L'Image de l'indépendance haïtienne dans la littérature des Caraïbes," *Revue de littérature comparée*, 48, 3–4, juill.–déc. 1974, pp. 504–535.

NGANGU, Pius, "Littérature négro-africaine: Jalons antillais et africains," *Congo-Afrique*, 11, 1971, pp. 447–461.

PAUL, Emmanuel C., *Culture, langue, littérature*. Port-au-Prince: Impr. de l'État, 1954.

PIERRE-LOUIS, Ulysse, *Esquisses littéraires et critiques*. Port-au-Prince: Impr. de l'État, 1959. (J. Dorismond, G. Vilaire, M. Coicou.)

PIQUION, René, *Manuel de négritude*. Port-au-Prince: H. Dechamps, 1965.

PIQUION, René: See BLANCHET, Jules, supra.

POMPILUS, Pradel, "Le Vodou dans la littérature haïtienne," *Rond-Point*, 8, juin–juillet, 1963.

PRADEL, Seymour, "Les Deux Tendances," *Haïti littéraire et scientifique*, 5 jan., 5 mars, & 5 mai 1912.

PRICE-MARS, Jean, *De St-Domingue à Haïti, essai sur la culture, les arts et la littérature*. Paris: Présence africaine, 1959.

PRICE-MARS, Jean, "L'Etat social et la production littéraire en Haïti," *Conjonction*, 34, août 1951, pp. 49–55.

RAMIRE, Alain, "Littérature engagée ou désengagement de la littérature: les tensions essentielles de la littérature haïtienne," *Maintenant* (Montreal), 96, mai 1970, pp. 161–163.

REBOULLET, André and Michel Têtu, *Guide culturel, civilisations et littératures d'expression française*. Paris: Hachette, 1977. (The chapter concerning the French–speaking West Indies is by Alain Baudot.)

RÉMY, Ernst, "Les Grands courants littéraires," *La Nouvelle Revue des Deux-mondes*, déc. 1972, pp. 608–613.

ROSE, Max, "La Jeune littérature française d'Amérique: Haïti," *Le Figaro* article, repr. in *La Relève*, 4, 8, 1 fév. 1936, 3–9.

ROSE, Max, *La Littérature haïtienne*. Bruxelles: Conférences et théâtre, 1939.

SAINT-LOUIS, Carlos, *Manifeste de l'école réaliste haïtienne*. Port-au-Prince: Deschamps, 1948.

SAMEDY, Jean-Claude, "Literatura e historia en Haití," *Revista de la Universidad nacional de Córdoba,* 12, 4–5, 1971, pp. 783–790.

SYLVAIN, Normil, "Chronique–programme," *La Revue indigène,* 1, 1, juill. 1927.

SYLVAIN, Normil, "La Jeune Littérature haïtienne," *La Revue indigène,* 1, 2, août 1927, pp. 42–53.

TARDIEU-FELDMAN GINDINE, Yvette, "The Magic of Black History: Images of Haiti," *Caribbean Review,* 6, 4, Oct.–Dec. 1974, pp. 25–30.

TÉTU, Michel, see REBOULLET, André, supra.

THOBY-MARCELIN, Philippe, *Haiti's Writers Find the People.* Washington, D.C.: Pan-American Union, 1950.

THOBY-MARCELIN, Philippe, "La Littérature d'hier et celle de demain," *La Nouvelle Ronde,* 2, juill. 1925, pp. 28–31.

THOBY-MARCELIN, Philippe, "Le Problème de la langue," *La Relève,* 6, 10 avril 1938, pp. 18–20.

TOUGAS, Gérard, *Les Écrivains d'expression française et la France.* Paris: Denoël, 1973.

TROUILLOT, Hénock, *Les Origines sociales de la littérature haïtienne.* Port-au-Prince: Impr. Théodore, 1962.

TROUILLOT, Hénock, "Deux concepts de la négritude en Haïti," *Présence francophone,* 12, printemps 1976, pp. 183–194.

VALCIN, Yvon, "Pour une promotion de la littérature nationale dans la communauté," *Rond-Point,* 1, juill. 1962, pp. 14–17.

VAVAL, Duraciné, *La Littérature haïtienne—Essais critiques.* Paris: Sansot & Cie, 1911. (O. Durand, T. Guilbaud, P. Lochard, E. Vilaire, F. Marcelin, F. Hibbert, G. Sylvain, E. Bergeaud, M. Coicou, A. Innocent, H. Chauvet, D. Delorme, A. Fleury-Battier, A. Chévry.)

VAVAL, Duraciné, "Toussaint Louverture à travers la littérature nationale," in *Conférences historiques.* Port-au-Prince: Impr. l'Abeille, 1906, pp. 29–60.

VIATTE, Auguste, "Indigénisme et culture française dans la littérature haïtienne," in *Actes du IVe Congrès de l'Association internationale de littérature comparée.* Paris–La Haye: Mouton, 1966, pp. 1169–1174.

VIATTE, Auguste, "La Littérature haïtienne vue par la revue *Présence africaine,*" *Oeuvres et critiques,* 3, 2, & 4, 1, automne 1979, pp. 53–57.

WILLIAMS, Walter, *"La Relève." Focal Point of Haitian Literature,* M.A. Thesis (Washington D.C.: Howard University, 1950).

WILSON, Edmund, "Haiti, 1949," in *Red, Black, Blond and Olive.* New

York: Oxford University Press, 1956, pp. 69–146.

WILSON, Edmund, "Voodoo in Literature," *Tomorrow*, 3, 1, Autumn 1954, pp. 95–102.

V. THE NOVEL

ALEXIS, Jacques-Stéphen, "Où va le roman?," *Présence africaine*, 13, avril–mai 1957, pp. 81–101.

CAMILLE, Roussan, "Il est trop tôt et trop tard," *La Relève*, 6, 1, juill. 1937, pp. 30–32.

CIVIL, Jean, "Le Roman haïtien après l'occupation," *Présence francophone*, 1, 1970, pp. 121–127.

CONDÉ, Franck, "La Question du roman en Haïti," *La Relève*, 5, 11, mai 1937, pp. 16–21.

CONDÉ, Maryse, *La Parole des femmes, essai sur des romancières des Antilles de langue française*. Paris: L'Harmattan, 1979.

COOK, Mercer, "The Haitian Novel," *The French Review*, 19, 6, May 1946, pp. 406–412.

DASH, J. Michael, "The Peasant Novel in Haiti," *African Literature Today*, 9, 1978, pp. 77–90.

DOLCÉ, Jacquelin, "La Problématique du roman haïtien," *Le Petit Samedi Soir*, 186, 26 fév.–3 mars 1977, pp. 28–30.

DORSINVILLE, Hénec, "L'Oeuvre de nos romanciers," *L'Essor*, juin 1913.

GOURAIGE, Ghislain, "Le Roman haïtien," in *Le Roman contemporain d'expression française*, Actes du colloque de Sherbrooke, U. de Sherbrooke, 1971, pp. 145–155.

HOFFMANN, Léon-François, "L'Étranger dans le roman haïtien," *L'Esprit Créateur*, 17, 2, Summer 1977, pp. 83–102.

HOFFMANN, Léon-François, *Le Roman haïtien—idéologie et structure*. Sherbrooke, P.Q.: Naaman, 1982.

HOFFMANN, Léon-François, "The Originality of the Haitian Novel," *Caribbean Review*, 8, 1, Jan.–Mar. 1979, pp. 44–50.

JEANNOT, Yvan, "Où sont nos romanciers?," *La Relève*, 5, 6, déc. 1936, pp. 34–35.

KNIGHT, Vere M., *The Roman Paysan in Haiti*, M.A. Thesis, The University of London—The University of the West Indies, 1965.

LALEAU, Léon, Jean-F. Brierre, F. Morisseau-Leroy, and Pétion Savain, "Table ronde: Les Problèmes du romancier en Haïti," *Optique*, 2 avril 1954, pp. 34–46.

MACLEOD, Murdo J.. "The Haitian Novel of Social Protest," *Journal of*

Inter-American Studies, 4, 2, April 1962, pp. 207–221.

MORAILLE, Yvon, "Le Roman et la gratuité de l'art en Haïti," *La Relève,* 5, 11, mai 1937, pp. 22–25.

PIERRE-LOUIS, Ulysse, "Le Roman français contemporain dans une impasse: Perspectives communes du roman d'Haïti, des peuples noirs et de l'Amérique latine," *Présence africaine,* 27–28, août–nov. 1959, pp. 51–68.

PIQUION, René, "Le Nouveau personnage de roman," *La Relève,* 5, 12, juin 1937, pp. 23–28.

ROMÉUS, Wilhem, "La Majorité silencieuse: le créolophone dans le roman haïtien," *Le Nouvelliste,* 24 janvier 1978.

ROSE, Max, "Le Roman en Haïti," *La Relève,* 6, 4, oct. 1937, pp. 10–12.

SHELTON, Marie-Denise, *L'Image de la société dans le roman haïtien,* Ann Arbor, Michigan, University Microfilms, 1979.

SHELTON, Marie-Denise, "Le Paysan dans le roman haïtien: le drame de la terre," *Présence francophone,* 22, printemps 1981.

TARDIEU-FELDMAN GINDINE, Yvette, "Satire and the Birth of Haitian Fiction 1901–1905," *Caribbean Quarterly,* 21, 3, Sept. 1975, pp. 30–37.

THOBY-MARCELIN, Philippe, "Pour la défense et illustration de la langue créole," *La Relève,* 5, 11, mai 1937, pp. 15–16.

VI. THEATER

ANON., "Du Théâtre haïtien" (about Eugène Nau's *La Fiancée de Léogâne), La Feuille du Commerce,* 20, déc. 1856.

BAUDUY, Robert, "Aux sources du théâtre populaire haïtien," *Conjonction,* 111, 3, 1969, pp. 24–29.

BAUDUY, Robert, "Un second souffle pour le théâtre haïtien," *Conjonction,* 124, août 1974, pp. 55–71.

CORNEVIN, Robert, *Le Théâtre haïtien des origines à nos jours.* Montréal: Léméac, 1973.

DENIS, Hervé, "Introduction à un manifeste pour un théâtre haïtien," *Nouvelle Optique,* 1, jan. 1971, pp. 132–141.

DUPONT, Georges, "Le Mouvement théâtral en Haïti," *Optique,* 4, juin 1954, pp. 37–40.

FOUCHARD, Jean, *Le Théâtre à St-Domingue.* Port-au-Prince: Impr. de l'Etat, 1955, *Plaisirs de St. Domingue... artistes et répertoires...* idem, ibid; *Plaisirs de St. Domingue ... notes sur la vie sociale, littéraire et artistique;* idem, ibid.

FOUCHÉ, Franck, *Vodou et théâtre: Pour un nouveau théâtre populaire.*

Montreal: Nouvelle Optique, 1976.

GRIMARD, Luc, "Existence historique du théâtre haïtien," *World Theatre,* 16, 5–6, Sept.–Dec. 1967, pp. 534–535.

KUNSTLER, "La Critique dramatique et le théâtre national," *Optique,* 17, juill. 1955, pp. 67–77.

KUNSTLER, "Le Mouvement théâtral haïtien gagne du terrain," *Optique,* 21, nov. 1955, pp. 63–71.

LAROCHE, Maximilien, "Le Théâtre haïtien et la conscience du peuple," in Alain Baudot et. al., *Identité culturelle et francophonie dans les Amériques III.* Québec: Centre international de recherche sur le bilinguisme, 1980, pp. 172–175.

MORISSEAU-LEROY, Félix, "Plaidoyer pour un théâtre en créole," *Panorama,* 4, juin 1955, pp. 129–132.

MORLAC, Jacques, "Questions de théâtre: notre drame," *La Nouvelle revue,* 1, 2, oct. 1907.

POMPILUS, Pradel, "Les Chances du théâtre haïtien contemporain," *Conjonction,* 111, 1969, pp. 14–18.

TROUILLOT, Hénock, "Les Traditions du théâtre national," *Revue d'histoire, de géographie et de géologie,* 35, 116, sept. 1972.

WATERS, Harold A., "An Aspect of African and Caribbean Theatre in French," in S. Okechukwou Mezu, ed., *Modern Black Literature.* Buffalo, N.Y.: Black Academy Press, n.d., pp. 145–155.

VII. POETRY

BARIDON, Silvio F., "Notre sulla poesia haitiana contemporanea (1945–1973)," *Annali* (Feltre: Instituto Universitario di lingue moderne), 1973.

BÉLANCE, René, "Introduction à la poésie haïtienne," *Conjonction,* 4, juill. 1946, pp. 4–12.

BRUNER, Charlotte, "Haitian Poets Cross Swords," *Gar,* 33, Feb. 1979, pp. 22–24.

CHARLES, Christophe, "Regards sur la jeune poésie haïtienne," *Conjonction,* 139, juill. 1978, pp. 59–72.

COULTHARD, G.R., "The Coloured Woman in Caribbean Poetry 1800–1960," *Race,* 2, 2, May 1961, pp. 53–61.

DEPESTRE, René, "Introduction à un art poétique haïtien," *Optique,* 24, fév. 1956, pp. 7–31.

DORET, Michel R., *Aliénation dans la poésie d'Haïti du XXe siècle,* Ann Arbor, Michigan, University Microfilms, 1982.

FOUCHARD, Jean, [Chanteclerc], "Question d'école . . .," *La Relève,* 1,

11, 1 mai 1933, pp. 16–18.

FOWLIE, Wallace, "Letter from Haiti," *Poetry*, 94, 6, Sept. 1959, pp. 398–404.

GALPERINA, Eugenia, "La Critique soviètique parle de la poésie haïtienne," *Le Matin*, 30–31 mars 1962.

GARRET, Naomi M., *The Renaissance of Haitian Poetry*. Paris: Présence africaine, 1963.

GOURAIGE, Ghislain, "D'une jeune poésie à une autre," *Rond-Point*, 12, dèc. 1963, pp. 14–18.

HOFFMANN, Lèon-François, "L'image de la femme dans la poésie haïtienne," *Présence africaine*, 34–35, oct. 1960–jan. 1961, pp. 183–206.

HOFFMANN, Lèon-François, "The Climate of Haitian Poetry," *Phylon*, 22, 1, Spring 1961, pp. 59–67.

KENNEDY, Ellen Conroy, *The Negritude Poets*. New York: Viking, 1975.

LAFOREST, Edmond, *L'Oeuvre des poètes*. Port-au-Prince: L'Abeille, 1908.

LALEAU, Lèon, "D'une poésie non versifièe," *Rond-Point*, 12, dèc. 1963, pp. 3–13.

LALEAU, Lèon, "La Poèsie haïtienne: Tentative de synthèse," *Conjonction* ‚115, 1, 1971, pp. 62–66.

LENOIR, Jacques, and Paul Laraque, "A propos des problèmes de la poésie nationale," *Optique*, 20, oct. 1955, pp. 21–27.

LIZAIRE, Paul, "Le Sceau de la poésie nègre," *Projection* (revue de l'Institut haïtiano-américain), II, 1, mai 1952, pp. 45–50.

LUBIN, Maurice A., *L'Afrique dans la poésie haïtienne*. Port-au-Prince: Éd. Panorama, 1965.

LUBIN, Maurice A., "Quelques poètes haïtiens de la jeune gènèration," *Conjonction*, 103, dèc. 1966, pp. 35–57.

MORPEAU, Louis, "Un siècle de poésie haïtienne," *Revue de l'Amérique latine*, juill. 1922, pp. 196–203; août 1922, pp. 303–312.

MORISSEAU-LEROY, Fèlix, "Les Poètes du dernier tiers du siècle," *Le Temps*, 30 mai 1934.

PAPAILLER, Hubert, *La Poésie indigène des Caraïbes: Une prise de conscience des poètes noirs de lange française*. Ann Arbor, Michigan: University Microfilms, 1973.

PIERRE-LOUIS, Ulysse, "Du rayon de nos poètes au rayon des jupes," in *Esquisses littéraires et critiques*. Port-au-Prince: Impr. de l'Etat, 1959, pp. 149–168.

POMPILUS, Pradel, "Les Principales directions de la poésie haïtienne au cours du mouvement indigéniste," *Présence francophone,* 3, automne 1971, pp. 29–40.

RAMIRE, Alain, "Idéologie et subversion chez les poètes de *La Ronde,*" *Nouvelle Optique,* 5, jan.–mars 1972, pp. 143–161.

ROGMANN, Horst J., *Die Thematik der Negerdichtung in spanischer, französischer und portugiesischer Sprache.* Tübingen: Fotodruck Präzis, 1966.

ROUMAIN, Jacques, "La Poésie, arme de combat," *Cahiers d'Haïti,* 2, 4, nov. 1944., p. 40.

SYLVAIN, Georges, "A travers la poésie haïtienne (published as a preface to his *Confidences et mélancholies* [1900], reprinted in *Conjonction,* 99, août 1965, 99, pp. 5–27).

VALMY-BAYSSE, Jean, *La Poésie française chez les noirs d'Haïti.* Paris: Éd. de la Nouvelle Revue Moderne, 1903.

VERNA, Paul, "La moderna poesia haitiana," *Revista nacional de cultura* 9, 68, mayo–junio 1948, pp. 67–79.

WILLIAMS, Perry A., "The Influence of the Vernacular on 19th Century Haitian Poetry: Les Chansons des Cocottes," *French Language in the Americas,* Bulletin annuel no. 15, Dec. 1972.

VIII. STUDIES ON INDIVIDUAL AUTHORS

Alexandre, Antoine C.

AUGUSTE, Yves, "Chansons nègres," *Haiti–Journal, 18 déc. 1947.*

Alexis, Jacques-Stéphen

AMER, Henri, "L'Espace d'un cillement; Romancero aux étoiles," *La Nouvelle Revue française,* 8, 89, 1 mai 1960, pp. 969–970.

ASSALI, N. Donald, "Le Récit paysan alexien: *Les Arbres musiciens,*" *Présence francophone,* 176, aut. 1978, pp. 109–124.

CASTERA Fils, Georges, "L'Expérience de la nuit et l'expérience du jour dans *Compère Général Soleil,*" *Europe,* 49, 501, jan. 1971, pp. 71–81.

DAMAS, André, "Écrire pour vivre," *Mercure de France,* 338, jan. 1960, pp. 706–708.

DASH, Michael, *Jacques-Stéphen Alexis.* Toronto: Black Images, 1975.

DECIUS, Philippe, "Contes et réalités haïtiennes chez Jacques-Stéphen Alexis," *Europe,* 49, 501, jan. 1971, pp. 49–63.

DEPESTRE, René. "Hablar de Jacques-Stéphen Alexis," *Casa de la Américas,* 13, 74, sept.–oct. 1972, pp. 28–40. French vers: "Parler de Jacques-Stéphen Alexis," in *Pour la révolution pour la poésie.* Montréal: Léméac, 1974, pp. 172–203.

JUIN, Hubert, "Romancero aux étoiles," *Les Lettres françaises*, 11 fév. 1960, 3.

LAMARRE, Joseph M., "Le Militaire dans trois romans haïtiens: *Zoune, Gouverneurs de la rosée, Les Arbres musiciens*," *Présence francophone*, 12, printemps 1976, pp. 131–140.

LAROCHE, Maximilien, "Jacques-Stéphen Alexis," *Dérives*, 12, 1978, pp. 23–26.

LAROCHE, Maximilien, *Le "Romancero aux étoiles" et l'oeuvre romanesque de Jacques-Stéphen Alexis*. Paris: Nathan, 1978.

LORENZON, Gabriella, "Hilaron Hilarius: Histoire d'une prise de conscience," *Présence francophone*, aut. 1978, pp. 125–131.

LYNCH, Barbara S., *The Collision of Cultures in the Novels of M.A. Asturias, J.-Stéphen Alexis and C. Acheve*. Ann Arbor, Michigan: University Microfilms, 1973.

MAGLOIRE SAINT-AUDE, Clément, "Compère Général Soleil," *Optique*, 29, juill. 1956, pp. 81–82.

MANUEL, Robert, *La Lutte des femmes dans les romans de Jacques-Stéphen Alexis*. Port-au-Prince: Deschamps, 1980.

MARTY, Anne, "Le Socialisme dans l'oeuvre de Jacques Roumain et Jacques-Stéphen Alexis," *Conjonction*, 136–137, fév. 1978, pp. 29–42.

MUDIMBE-BOYI, *L'Oeuvre romanesque de Jacques-Stéphen Alexis*. Kinshasa: Lovanium Univ., 1967.

PIERRE-CHARLES, Gérard, "Mort et vie de Jacques Soleil," *Europe*, 49, 501, 1971, pp. 64–70.

RODRIGUEZ, Ileana, "En busca de una expresión antillana: lo real maravilloso en Carpentier y Alexis," *Ideologies and Literature*, 2, 10, Sept.–Oct. 1979, pp. 56–68.

RUFFINELLI, Jorge, "Jacques-Stéphen Alexis: Maravilla y terror en Haiti," *Hispamérica*, 2, 6, abr. 1974, pp. 41–49.

SOUFFRANT, Claude, "Le Fatalisme religieux du paysan haïtien," *Europe*, 49, 501, jan. 1971, pp. 27–41.

SOUFFRANT, Claude, "Marxisme et tiers monde noir chez Jacques Roumain, Jacques-Stéphen Alexis et Léopold Sédar Senghor," *Présence francophone*, 14, print. 1977, pp. 133–147.

SOUFFRANT, Claude, *Une négritude socialiste: Religion et développment chez Jacques Roumain, Jacques-Stéphen Alexis et Langston Hughes*. Paris: L'Harmattan, 1978.

Alexis, Stéphen

AUGUSTE, Yves L., "Du *Nègre masqué* de Stéphen Alexis à *L'Homme invisible* de Ralph Ellison," *Présence africaine*, 101–102, ler et 2ème trim. 1977, pp. 176–187.

BROUARD Carl, "*Le Nègre Masqué*," *Action nationale*, 17 jan. 1934.

BRUTUS, Edner, "Stéphen Alexis," *La Relève*, 2, 10, avril 1934, pp. 14–27.

GRIMARD, Luc, "Stéphen Alexis," *Le Temps*, 24 avril 1940.

LÉGER, Jacques, "*Le Nègre masqué*," *La Relève*, 2, 8, 1 fév. 34, pp. 14–20.

Amboise, Ludovic

GRIMARD, Luc, "*Epanchements*, de M. Ludovic Amboise," *Le Temps*, 6 déc. 1939.

Ardouin, Coriolan

ABELLARD, Charles A., "A la mémoire de Coriolan Ardouin, un grand poète manqué," *Le Nouvelliste*, 1 août 1963.

LESPINASSE, Pierre-Eugène, "Coriolan Ardouin, 1812–1835," *Revue de la ligue de la jeunesse haïtienne*, 1, 2, 20 mars 1916, pp. 68–76.

MARCELIN, Émile, "Coriolan Ardouin," *Le Temps-Revue*, 18 mars 1936.

NAU, Émile, "Coriolan Ardouin, étude critique," *L'Union*, 16 nov. 1837.

NAU, Émile, *Littérature*. Port-au-Prince, 1835. About C. Ardouin, repr. in *Conjonction*, 103, déc. 1966, pp. 14–28.

VERNA, Paul, "Coriolan Ardouin," *Action sociale*, 25 juill. 1948, repr. in *Conjonction*, 16, août 1948, pp. 34–37.

Bélance, René

VERNA, Paul, "René Bélance: *Pour célébrer l'absence*," *Conjonction*, 12, déc. 1947, p. 63.

Bellegarde, Dantès

TROUILLOT, Hénock M., *Dantès Bellegarde, un écrivain d'autrefois*. Port-au-Prince: Impr. Théodore, 1957.

Bergeaud, Émeric

DORSINVILLE, Hénec, "Romans et romanciers haïtiens: *Stella*, par Émeric Bergeaud," *L'Essor*, 15 juin 1914, pp. 611–614.

HOFFMANN, Léon-François, "En marge du premier roman haïtien: *Stella*, d'Émeric Bergeaud," *Conjonction*, 131, nov. 1976, pp. 75–102.

POUILH, Duraciné, "Souvenirs littéraires: Émeric Bergeaud," *La Ronde*, 15 fév. 1901.

VAVAL, Duraciné, "E. Bergeaud, romancier," *La Nouvelle revue*, 1, 12, août 1908.

Bernard, Regnor C.

BRIERRE, Jean-F., "Regnor Bernard: *Nègre,*" *Conjonction,* 10–11, août–oct. 1974, p. 59.

GILBERT, Marcel, "Regnor Bernard, un écho inachevé," *Collectif paroles,* 13, août–sept. 1981, pp. 43–44.

Bonhomme, Arthur

JEANNOT, Yvan, "*L'Ame du lambi,*" *La Relève,* oct. 1937.

WERLEIGH, Christian, "*L'Ame du Lambi,*" *Le Temps-revue,* 13 oct. 1937.

Brierre, Jean-F.

BROUARD, Carl, "Jean Brierre," *La Bataille,* 7 mai 1933.

CAMILLE, Roussan, "*Nous garderons le dieu,*" *Haiti-Journal,* 24 août 1945.

CONSTANT, Richard, "Paroles d'aîné sur *Chansons secrètes,*" *La Relève,* 2, 2, 1 août 1933, pp. 9–14.

J.B., "*Chansons secrètes,*" *La Relève,* 2, 3, 1 sept. 1933, pp. 30–31.

KING, Carolyn J., "Brière's *Découvertes:* The Mural of Mankind," *The Claflin College Review,* 1, ii, 1977, pp. 50–62.

KNIGHT, Vere, "Jean Brierre," *Black Images,* 4, 3–4, Aut.–Winter 1975, pp. 30–43.

LANDO, Simon, "Hommage à Jean Brierre," *Conjonction,* 36, déc. 1951, pp. 33–34.

LUBIN, Maurice A., "Jean F. Brierre and his Work," *Black World,* 22, 3 Jan. 1973, pp. 36–48.

NORTH, Philippe, "*Black Soul,*" *Conjonction,* 9, juin 1947, pp. 31–33.

WILLIAMS, Eric, "Four Poets of the Greater Antilles (Guillén, Roumain, Brierre, Palès)," *Caribbean Quarterly,* 2, 4, 1950, pp. 8–19.

Brouard, Carl

BERROU, frère Raphaël & Pradel Pompilus, *Deux poètes indigénistes: Carl Brouard et Émile Roumer.* Paris: Éd. de l'École, 1974.

BERROU, frère Raphaël, "Les Deux visages de Carl Brouard," *Conjonction,* 101, avril 1966, pp. 5–18.

BRUTUS, Edner, "Carl Brouard, fol du coeur," *La Relève,* 6, 3, sept. 1937, p. 32.

BRUTUS, Edner, "Carl Brouard vu de dos," *La Relève,* 1, 2, 1 août 1932, pp.3–8.

DORSINVILLE, Max, "Carl Brouard," *La Relève,* 6, 3, sept. 1937, pp. 4–6.

DUVALIER, François, "Carl Brouard," *L'Action nationale,* 23 déc. 1935.

GAILLARD, Roger, "La Destinée de Carl Brouard," *Conjonction,* 100, déc. 1965, pp. 29–61. 2nd rev. ed., Port-au-Prince: H. Deschamps, 1966.

JEAN, Eddy A. & Justin O. Fièvre, *Carl Brouard, cet immortel.* Port-au-Prince, 1973.

KNIGHT, Vere, "Carl Brouard," *Black Images,* 4, 3–4, Aut.–Winter 1975, pp. 20–29.

LUBIN, Maurice A., "Carl Brouard," *Présence francophone,* 12, printemps 1976, pp. 141–148.

MARC, Jules A., *Regards sur la littérature haïtienne.* Port-au-Prince: mimeo, 1973.

PAPAILLER, Hubert, "C. Brouard, the Poet of Humble Love," *College Language Association Journal,* 21, 2, Dec. 1977, pp. 312–320.

POMPILUS, Pradel, see BERROU, frère Raphaël, supra.

Brun, Amédée

BELLEGARDE, Dantès, "Amédée Brun," *La Ronde,* 5 juin 1898. (Repr. in *Le Temps,* 16 oct. 1937.)

LHÉRISSON, Justin, *Portaitins, 1ère série.* Port-au-Prince: Impr. H. Ambard, 1894.

Camille, Roussan

AUGUSTE, Yves, "*Assaut à la nuit,*" *Haïti-Journal,* 6 déc. 1947.

LALEAU, Léon, "Pour bienvenir un poète d'envergure," *Le Temps,* 18 jan. 1941.

POSY, Bernard, *Roussan Camille, le poète d'Assaut à la nuit.* Port-au-Prince: Impr. des Antilles, 1962.

Carrié, Pierre

ALEXIS, Stéphen, "Pour accueillir un jeune poète," *Haiti-Journal,* 11 oct. 1945.

CORVINGTON, Serge, "*Crépuscule,*" *Haiti-Journal,* 31 mars 1948.

TROUILLOT, Hénock, "*Crépuscule,*" *Haiti-Journal,* 12 oct. 1948.

Casséus, Maurice

BRUTUS, Edner, "Entre les lignes de *Viejo,*" *La Relève,* 4, 5, nov. 1935, pp. 8–13.

HEURTELOU, Daniel, "Nouvelle fantaisie en la ... mineur," *La Relève,* 1, 5, 1 nov. 1932, pp. 18–34.

JEANNOT, Yvan, "*Viejo,*" *La Relève,* 4, 3, 1 sept. 1935, pp. 24–25.

Chassange, Roland

BRUTUS, Edner, "Roland Chassange," *La Relève,* 3, 9, 1 mars 1935, pp.

20–32.

GRIMARD, Luc, "*Le Tambourin voilé*," *Le Temps-Revue*, 8 avril 1933.

VILLEDROUIN, Luc, "*Le Tambourin voilé*," *Maintenant*, 9 mai 1936.

Chauvet, Marie

A.M., "Marie Chauvet, fille d'Haïti," *Conjonction*, 53, oct. 1954, pp. 52–53.

FABRE, A., "*Amour, colère et folie*," *Les Lilas*, juin 1969.

LACROIX, Colette, "Marie Chauvet, une soif d'absolu," *Bingo*, 231, avril 1972.

LARAQUE, Franck, "Violence et sexualité dans *Colère*," *Présence haïtienne*, sept. 1975, pp. 53–56.

MARTINI, Magda, "*Amour, colère et folie*," *Les Nouvelles littéraires*, 12 sept. 1968.

Chenet, Gérard

ALMEIDA, Fernando d', "Gérard Chenet face à la parole problématique," *L'Afrique littéraire et artistique*, 45, 1977, pp. 48–53.

BONNEAU, Richard, "Un Haïtien puise aux sources africaines: *El Hadj* de G. Chenet," *L'Afrique littéraire et artistique*, 31, 1974, pp. 79–80.

Chevallier, André

HÉDOR, "*Mon petit Kodak*," *Le Nouvelliste*, 9 fév. 1916.

Chevry, Arsène

M.C., "*Areytos* d'Arsène Chevry," *L'Opinion nationale*, 3 déc. 1892.

Christophonte, Prosper

BRUTUS, Edner, "*Rêves et chants*," *La Relève*, fév. 1933.

Cinéas, Jean-Baptiste

BURR-REYNAUD, Frédéric, "*Le Drame de la terre*," *Le Temps*, 9 sept. 1933.

C., "*Le Drame de la terre*," *La Petite revue*, 10, 252, 1–15 oct. 1933, pp. 166–169.

DORSINVILLE, Max. H., "*Le Drame de la terre*," *La Relève*, 2, 3, 1 sept. 1933, pp. 26–30.

FOISSET, Père, "*L'Héritage sacré*," *La Phalange*, 1945.

GEORGES-JACOB, Kléber, "*L'Héritage sacré*," *Haïti-Journal*, 26 mai 1945.

LATAILLADE, Nerva, "En Marge de *Le Drame de la terre*," *Le Temps*, 27 jan. 1940.

LATAILLADE, Nerva, "J.B. Cinéas," *Le Temps*, 10 mai 1939.

LESCOUFLAIR, Jean-Baptiste, "*Le Drame de la terre,*" *Le Temps,* 21 mars 1934.

PRICE-MARS, Jean, "*L'Héritage sacré,*" *Haïti-Journal,* 15 mai 1945.

Coicou, Massillon

ANON., "*St. Vincent de Paule,* drame de M. Coicou," *Le Pacificateur,* 28 juin 1907.

[BERROU], frère Raphaël, "*Impressions,* de Massillon Coicou," *Conjonction,* 105, oct. 1967, pp. 69–73.

BRISSON, Adolphe, "*Poésies nationales* de M. Coicou," *Annales politiques et littéraires,* 12 oct. 1902, p. 236.

DUCASSE, Jules, "*L'Empereur Dessalines,* de M. Coicou," *Le Petit Haïtien,* 1, 7, 22 nov. 1906 & 1, 8, déc. 1906.

LUBIN, Maurice A., "Massillon Coicou: étude biographique," *Conjonction,* 105, oct. 1967, pp. 53–59.

PIERRE-LOUIS, Ulysse, "M. Coicou, le bûcher ardent," in *Esquisses littéraires et critiques.* Port-au-Prince: Imp. de l'Etat, 1959, pp. 149–168.

POMPILUS, Pradel, "Massillon Coicou, poète," *Conjonction,* 105, oct. 1967, pp. 60–68.

Colimon, Marie-Thérèse

ST. VICTOR, Henriette, "*Fils de Misère,*" *Lakansièl,* 3 sept. 1975, p. 29.

Darley, Muriel

BRUTUS, Edner, "*La Famille Émeraude,*" *Le Nouvelliste,* 18 jan. 1944.

Delorme, Demesvar

CONJONCTION, 25, 2, 1970; special issue on Demesvar Delorme. Introduction, selected passages and bibliography by Pradel Pompilus, frère Raphaël [Berrou], and Maurice A. Lubin.

DURAND, Oswald, "Demesvar Delorme," *Revue générale,* 1, 15–16, 21 mai 1898.

ÉLIE, L.-Em., "Demesvar Delorme," *Le Justicier,* 2, 22, 6 juin 1904.

HECTOR, Nathan, "Demesvar Delorme," *Le Petit Haïtien,* 2, 16–19, août–nov. 1907.

JEAN, Eddy-A., "Demesvar Delorme, un théoricien bourgeois," *Quisqueya,* 1, n.d. [1977?], pp. 3–14.

LARAQUE, Maurice, "Demesvar Delorme," *Cahiers d'Haïti,* 2, 7, fév. 1945, pp. 35–39.

LECHAUD, Charles, "Le Roman chez Delorme," *La Ronde,* 1, 1, 5 mai 1898.

LECORPS, Marceau, "Demesvar Delorme," *Les Variétés,* 20 jan. 1905.

SANNON, Pauléus, "Demesvar Delorme," *Le Temps,* 25 & 29 juill. 1938.

TROUILLOT, Ernst, *Demesvar Delorme, le journaliste, le diplomate.* Port-au-Prince: Impr. Théodore, 1958.

TROUILLOT, Hénock, *Demesvar Delorme, ou introduction à une sociologie de la littérature haïtienne.* Port-au-Prince: Impr. des Antilles, 1968.

WERLEIGH, Christian, "Demesvar Delorme," *Le Temps,* 18 jan. 1933.

Denis, Villard (Davertige)

BIBLIOPHILE, "Qui êtes-vous, Villard Denis?," *Conjonction, 92–93, 1964, pp. 5–10.*

Depestre, René

CAILLER, Bernadette, "L'Efficacité poétique du vaudou dans *Un arc–en–ciel pour l'occident chrétien,*" *The French Review,* 53, 1, Oct. 1979, pp. 47–59.

CORTANZE, Gérard de, "La Solitude du poète de fonds, René Depestre," *Le Nouvel Observateur,* 844, 12 jan. 1981.

DASH, Michael, "René Depestre and the Haitian Generation of 1946," *Le Français au Nigéria,* 10, 2, sept. 1975, pp. 24–29.

DAYAN, Joan, "René Depestre and the Symbolism of Poetry and Revolution," *Modern Language Studies,* 10, 1, Winter 1979, pp. 75–81.

DAYAN, Joan, *René Depestre: "A Rainbow for the Christian World."* Amherst, Massachusetts: The University of Massachusetts Press, 1977. (Long introduction and bilingual edition of *Un arc–en–ciel pour l'occident chrétien.*)

DORSAINVILLE, Roger, "*Etincelles,*" *Haïti-Journal,* 25 juill. 1945.

GAILLARD, Roger, "René Depestre: *Gerbes de sang,*" *Conjonction,* 6, déc. 1946, pp. 21–23.

LEINER, Jacqueline, "René Depestre, ou du surréalisme comme moyen d'accès à l'identité haïtienne," *Romanische Forschungen,* 89, 1, 1977, pp. 37–50.

LEVILAIN, Guy Viet, *Cultural Identity, Negritude and Decolonization,* American Institute for Marxist Studies, occasional paper no. 29, New York, 1978. (on Roumain and Depestre.)

MÉTELLUS, Jean, "La Négritude et le vaudou," *La Quinzaine littéraire,* 311, 16–31, oct. 1979, p. 12.

MUDIMBE, Valentin Y., "Un goût de la parole: *Le Journal d'un animal marin* de R. Depestre," *Présence africaine,* 79, 3, 1971, pp. 85–95.

WARNER, Keith, "René Depestre, the not so Terrible *enfant terrible,*"

Black Images, 3, 1, Spring 1974, pp. 46–54.

WYLIE, Hal, "La Réception de René Depestre," *Oeuvres et critiques,* 3, 2 & 4, 1, aut. 1979, pp. 133–141.

WYLIE, Hal, "René Depestre Speaks of Negritude, Cuba, Socialist Writing, Communist Eros and his Most Recent Works," *Gar,* 33, fév. 1979, pp. 18–21.

Desroy, Annie

TARDIEU-FELDMAN GINDINE, Yvette, "Une romancière haïtienne méconnue: Annie Desroy, 1893–1948," *Conjonction,* 124, août 1974, pp. 35–51.

Domingue, Jules

VILMENAY, Thomas, "*Les Deux amours d'Adrien,* de J. Domingue," *Le Moment,* 20 mai 1905.

Dorsinville, Roger

GAILLARD, Roger, "*L'Afrique des rois,*" *Conjonction,* 130, sept. 1976, pp. 73–80.

GOURAIGE, Ghislain, "*Kimby,*" *Lakansièl,* 2, juin 1975, p. 29.

LALEAU, Léon, "Profil de poète," in *Apothéoses.* Port-au-Prince: Deschamps, 1952, pp. 91–99.

Durand, Louis-Henry

LALEAU, Léon, "Des troubles de l'amour au calme de la mort," in *Apothéoses.* Port-au-Prince: Deschamps, 1952, pp. 133–140.

LALEAU, Léon, "*Les Roses Rouges* de M. Louis-Henry Durand," *La Relève,* 5, 10, avril 1937, pp. 20–31.

Durand, Oswald

CARRÉ, René, "D'Homère à O. Durand," *Conjonction,* 33, juin 1951, pp. 42–47.

COBB, Martha K., "French Romanticism in a Haitian Setting: The Poetry of Oswald Durand," *College Language Association Journal,* 16, March 1973, pp. 302–311.

FIGNOLÉ, Jean-Claude, *Oswald Durand.* Port-au-Prince: Impr. des Presses port-au-princiennes, 1968.

GRIMARD, Luc, "Oswald Durand—Un poète complet," *Le Temps,* 28 sept. 1940.

LATAILLADE, Nerva, "Causerie," *Le Temps,* 12 déc. 1934.

LECORPS, Marceau, "Oswald Durand," *Les Variétés,* 2, 12, 25 mai 1906 & 2, 13, 25 juin 1906.

POMPILUS, Pradel, *Oswald Durand.* Port-au-Prince: Impr. des Antilles, 1964.

RICOURT, Volvick, "O. Durand," *Le Temps*, 11, 18, & 25 jan. 1941.

VICTOR, Renè, *"Choucoune,"* ou le destin d'un beau poème. Port-au-Prince: Fardin, 1976.

VILMENAY, Thomas A., "Oswald Durand," *Le Moment*, 2 août 1905.

WERLEIGH, Christian, "Le Prodige d'une vie," *Le Temps*, 19 oct. 1940.

Ethéart, Liautaud

A.G., "Quelques mots sur les *Miscellanées* de L. Ethéart," *La Feuille du Commerce*, 26 juill. 1856.

Fabry, Claude

JEANNOT, Yvan, *"L'Ame du Lambi,"* *La Relève*, 6, 4, oct. 1937, pp. 13–14.

Faubert, Fine

BRUTUS, Edner, "Fine Faubert," *La Relève*, 4, 1–2, juill.–août 1935, pp. 12–24.

Ferry, Alibée

ANON., "Un poète homme d'épée: le général Alibée Fleury," *Le Ralliement*, 1, 19, 21 déc. 1887.

Figaro, Georges-Jacques

DORSAINVILLE, Roger, *"Dialogue avec une ombre,"* *Haïti-Journal*, 25 juill. 1946.

Fleury-Battier, Alcibiade

CHEVRY, Arsène, "A. Fleury-Battier, souvenirs personnels," *Haïti illustrée*, 1, 26, 6 nov. 1890.

VAVAL, Duraciné, *"Sous les bambous,* d'A. Fleury-Battier," *La Nouvelle revue*, 1, 5 jan. 1905.

Fouché, Franck

ETIENNE, Gérard, "Sur la vie et l'oeuvre de Franck Fouché," *Présence francophone*, 16, printemps 1978, pp. 191–200.

Franketienne

BOURAOURI, Hédi, "Ecriture–mitrailleuse et réveil des consciences dans *Les Affres d'un défi*," *Conjonction*, 147, mars 1980, pp. 93–97.

FLEISCHMANN, Ulrich, "Entrevue avec Frankétienne sur son roman *Dézafi*," *Dérives*, 7, 1977.

LAMARRE, Joseph M., "*Dézafi*, le premier roman créole de la littérature haïtienne," *Présence francophone*, 21, aut. 1980, pp. 137–154.

LAROCHE, Maximilien, "*Dézafi* de Frankétienne, un tournant de la littérature haïtienne," *Conjonction*, 131, nov. 1976, pp. 107–119.

MOUTEAUD, Yves, *"Ultravocal* de Frankétienne," *Conjonction,* 119, fév.–mars 1973, pp. 94–95.

Gaillard, Roger

DESCHAMPS, Marguerite, *Clé pour "Charades haïtiennes."* Port-au-Prince, 1974.

Garçon, Jean Dieudonné

PALLISTER, Janis L., "Time, Tense and Tempo in the Poetry of Jean Dieudonné Garçon," *L'Esprit Créateur, 17, 2, Summer 1977, pp. 159–167.*

Garoute, Hamilton

ALEXIS, Jacques-Stéphen, "La Lyre et l'épée, témoignage sur *Jets lucides* d'Hamilton Garoute," *Cahiers d'Haïti,* 3, 3, oct. 1945, pp. 24–27.

Grimard, Luc

MARTIN, Adrien, "Luc Grimard," *Conjonction,* 54, déc. 1954, pp. 7–17.

Guilbaud, Tertulien

ANON., "T. Guilbaud," *Les Variétés,* 1, 4, 20 mars 1905.

CHANCY, Jean-Joseph, "T. Guilbaud," *La Nation,* 7 oct. 1884.

Héraux, Edmond

LHÉRISSON, Justin, *"Fleurs des mornes,* de E. Héraux," *La Jeune Haïti, 24 nov. 1894.*

Hibbert, Fernand

BURR-REYNAUD, Frédéric, *"Les Thazar,* de F. Hibbert," *Le Pacificateur,* 17 jan. 1908.

GAILLARD, Roger, "Sexualité des personnages et érotisme du romancier," *Conjonction,* 122–123, 1974, pp. 41–65.

LAHENS, Yannick Jean-Pierre, "Le Paraître féminin, sa structure, sa stratégie dans le roman de Fernand Hibbert *Les Thazar," Conjonction,* 136–137, fév. 1978, pp. 45–55.

LALEAU, Léon, "Profil d'éducateur," in *Apothéoses.* Port-au-Prince: Deschamps, 1952, pp. 115–121.

LATAILLADE, Nerva, "Masques et visages," *Le Temps,* 10 oct. 1936.

LECORPS, Marceau, *"Séna,* de F. Hibbert," *Les Variétés,* 1, 7, 15 nov. 1934.

MAGLOIRE, Auguste, "Une conférence sur Boyer–Bazelais inspirée du roman *Romulus," Le Temps,* 24, 28 nov. 1934.

NAU, John-Antoine, "Un romancier et un poète haïtien, F. Hibbert et Ch. Moravia," *La Phalange* (Paris), repr. in *Haïti littéraire et sociale,*

5–20, jan. 1913, pp. 649–652.

NAU, John-Antoine, "*Séna,*" *Haïti littéraire et sociale,* 5 août 1912.

POMPILUS, Pradel, "F. Hibbert, J. Lhérisson et A. Innocent, romanciers réalistes," *Conjonction,* 122–123, 1974, pp. 15–18.

SANNON, Pauléus, "Autour d'une vie," *Le Temps,* 16–22, avril 1929.

TARDIEU-FELDMAN GINDINE, Yvette, "De la colonie à l'occupation: les étrangers chez Hibbert," *Conjonction,* 122–123, 1974, pp. 23–38.

TROUILLOT, Ernst, "Le Réalisme de F. Hibbert," *Conjonction,* 103, déc. 1966, pp. 63–67.

VILMENAY, Thomas A., "*Séna,* de F. Hibbert," *Le Moment,* 13 sept. 1905.

Hyppolyte, Dominique

GRIMARD, Luc, "Dominique Hippolyte," *Le Temps,* 13 avril 1940.

VIEUX, Antonio, "*Le Baiser de l'aïeule,* de D. Hyppolite," *La Nouvelle revue,* 1, 10, 1er mars 1926, pp. 195–200.

Innocent, Antoine

PRICE-MARS, Jean, "Antoine Innocent, ethnographe," *Conjonction,* 48, déc. 1953, pp. 37–45.

RÉGULUS, Christian, "*Mimola,* d'A. Innocent," *L'Actualité,* 2 juin 1906.

ROMÉUS, Wilhem, "*Mimola,* ou la voie vaudouesque de l'haïtianité," *Le Nouvelliste,* 26–30, juin 1976.

POMPILUS, Pradel, "F. Hibbert, J. Lhérisson et A. Innocent, romanciers réalistes," *Conjonction,* 122–123, 1974, pp. 15–18.

Janvier, Louis-Joseph

POMPILUS, Pradel, *Louis-Joseph Janvier par lui-même.* Port-au-Prince: Éd. Caraïbes, 1978.

Labuchin, Rassoul

DESCHAMPS, Marguerite, *A la découverte de Rassoul Labuchin.* Port-au-Prince, 1974.

LAROCHE, Maximilien, "La Figure du sujet dans *Le Roi Moko,*" *Conjonction,* 127–128, déc. 1975, pp. 57–74.

Laforest, Edmond

LALEAU, Léon, "Edmond Laforest," *La Relève,* 6, 8–9, fév.–mars 1938.

LIAUTAUD, André, "*Cendre et flammes* d'Edmond Laforest," *La Nouvelle Ronde,* 1, 7, 1 déc. 1925, pp. 134–138.

MORAVIA, Charles, "Edmond Laforest," *La Plume,* 19 oct. 1915.

SYLVAIN, Normil, "Le Souvenir d'Edmond Laforest," *La Revue indigène,* 1, 4, oct. 1927, pp. 172–175.

Laleau, Léon

BERROU, frère Raphaël, "*Le Choc,*" *Conjonction,* 114, 4, 1970, pp. 44–52.

BERROU, frère Raphaël, "Léon Laleau, poète indigéniste," *Le Nouvelliste,* avril 1970.

C., "*Le Choc,*" *La Petit revue,* 9, 237, 1–15 jan. 1933, pp. 292–293 & 9, 238, 1 fév. 1933, pp. 309–310.

CONDÉ, Franck, "*Le Choc,*" *Le Temps,* 5 jan. 1935.

CONJONCTION, 87–88, 1963, special issue on Léon Laleau; articles by J. Price-Mars, J. Fouchard, P. Pompilus, G. Gouraige *et. al.*

CONSTANT, Richard, "Léon Laleau," *La Relève,* 2, 12, juin 1934, pp. 8–12.

DORSAINVILLE, Hénec, "Une cause sans effet," *L'Essor,* août 1916.

FOUCHARD, Jean, "*Le Choc,*" *La Relève,* 1, 2, 1 août 1932, pp. 21–24.

[FOUCHARD, Jean] CHANTECLERC, "*Les Ondes courtes,*" *La Relève,* 1, 10, 1 avril 1930.

RAT, Maurice, "Léon Laleau, Haïtien et poète français," *La Muse française,* 16, 6, 15 juin 1937, pp. 263–264. Repr. in *Conjonction,* 1963, 87–88, 1963.

VERGARA ROBLES, Enrique, "Un roman haïtien: *Le Choc,*" *Le Temps,* 7 déc. 1935.

VIEUX, Antonio, "*A Voix basse* de L. Laleau," *La Nouvelle Ronde,* 1, 3, août 1925, pp. 52–55.

Laraque, Paul

MOREJÓN, Nancy, "Poesia y armas cotidianas de Paul Laraque," *Casa de las Américas,* 117, nov.–dic. 1979, pp. 212–216.

WIENER, Wanda, "Une heure avec Paul Laraque," *Haïti-Observateur,* 16–23 jan. 1979.

Lataillade, Robert

BRUTUS, Edner, "Robert Lataillade intime," *La Relève,* 2, 1, juill. 1933, pp. 27–39.

BRUTUS, Edner, "Robert Lataillade," *La Relève,* 8, 12, juill. 1939, pp. 21–27.

VILLEDROUIN, Robert, "*L'Urne close,*" *Le Temps,* 6 nov. 1935.

Lespès, Anthony

BRUTUS, Edner, "A. Lespès," *La Relève,* 1, 5, 1 nov. 1932, pp. 10–15.

MONTAS, Lucien, "*Les Semences de la colère,*" *Conjonction,* 21, juin 1949, pp. 46–48.

MONTAS, Lucien, "*Les Semences de la colère,*" *Optique,* 13, mars 1955, pp. 23–26.

Lhérisson, Justin

AMER, Michel, "J. Lhérisson, spécifique et subversif," *Lakansièl*, 1, mars 1975, pp. 19–25.

ANON. [E.-A. Jean?], "Justin Lhérisson, peintre de la société haïtienne," *Quisqueya*, 1, n.d. [1977?], pp. 18–24.

CHRISPHONTE, Prosper, *Le Poète de "La Dessalinienne."* Port-au-Prince: Impr. Telhomme, 1941.

COURTOIS, Félix, "J. Lhérisson," *Conjonction*, 122–123, 1974, pp. 75–80.

LAMARRE, Joseph M., "Le Militaire dans trois romans haïtiens, *Zoune, Gouverneurs de la rosée, Les Arbres musiciens,*" *Présence francophone*, 12, printemps 1976, pp. 131–140.

POMPILUS, Pradel, "F. Hibbert, J. Lhérisson et A. Innocent, romanciers réalistes," *Conjonction*, 122–123, 1974, pp. 15–18.

POMPILUS, Pradel, "Permanence de Justin Lhérisson," *Conjonction*, 143, mai 1979, pp. 39–46.

FANFANT, Edgard U., "*Zoune*, de J. Lhérisson," *Le Petit Haïtien*, 1, 8, déc. 1906.

VILMENAY, Thomas A., "*La Famille des Pitite-Caille*, de J. Lhérisson," *Le Moment*, 31 mai 1905.

Liautaud, André

BRUTUS, Edner, "André Liautaud," *La Relève*, 6, 1 déc. 1932, pp. 21–27.

Magloire, Nadine

ST.-VICTOR, Henriette, "*Le Sexe Mythique*," *Lakansièl*, 3, sept. 1975, p. 29.

Magloire Saint-Aude, Clément

BERROU, frère Raphaël, "Magloire St.-Aude," *Conjonction*, 118, juill. 1972, pp. 95–101, & 107–110.

DAUMEC, Gérard, "Magloire St.-Aude," *Optique*, 24, fév. 1956, pp. 51–56.

GLÉMAUD, Marie José, "De l'actualité du texte de Saint-Amand *Essai d'explication de 'Dialogue de mes lampes'*" *Lakansièl*, 3 sept. 1975, pp. 71–84.

JADOTTE, Hérard, "Idéologie, littérature, dépendance," *Nouvelle Optique*, 1, 4, déc. 1971, pp. 71–84.

LAROCHE, Maximilien, "Magloire St.-Aude, l'exilé de l'intérieur," *Présence francophone*, 10, printemps 1975, pp. 49–57.

LUBIN, Maurice A., "Magloire St.-Aude, poète surréaliste," *Présence francophone*, 3, automne 1971, pp. 87–93.

ST.-AMAND, Edris, *Essai d'explication de "Dialogue de mes lampes."* Port-au-Prince: Impr. de l'État, 1942. (2nd ed., Port-au-Prince: Fardin, 1975.)

SMITH, William J., "Deux poètes haïtiens," *Optique*, 1, mars 1954, pp. 26–29.

Marcelin, Émile

RÉGULUS, Christian, "*Médaillons littéraires* d'É. Marcelin," *L'Actualité*, 16 juin 1906.

Marcelin, Frédéric

AYRAUD-DEGEORGE, H., "*Marilisse* de F. Marcelin," *L'Intransigeant*, reprod. in *Le Moment*, 5 sept. 1903.

BRISSON, Adolphe, "*Marilisse* de F. Marcelin," *Les Annales politiques et littéraires*, 27 sept. 1903, reprod. in *Le Moment*, 31 oct. 1903.

BRISSON, Adolphe, "*La Vengeance de Mama* de F. Marcelin," *Les Annales politiques et littéraires*, 3 août 1902.

DAVID, Placide, "F. Marcelin, romancier," *Le Temps*, 9 jan. 1935.

GOURAIGE, Ghislain, *Frédéric Marcelin*, Thèse complémentaire pour le doctorat ès lettres. Paris: Sorbonne, 1954.

GOURAIGE, Ghislain, *Frédéric Marcelin, peintre d'une époque*, M.A. Thesis, Quebec, Univ. Laval, 1948.

LALEAU, Léon, "*Au gré du Souvenir*," *La Relève*, 5, 7, jan. 1937, pp. 15–23.

LALEAU, Léon, "Frédéric Marcelin," in *Apothéoses*. Port-au-Prince: Deschamps, 1952, pp. 103–107.

LECORPS, Marceau, "F. Marcelin," *Les Variétés*, 1, 1–3, 20 oct. 1904–20 jan. 1905.

MARCELIN, Frédéric, *Autour de deux romans*. Paris: Kugelman, 1903.

SÉJOURNÉ, G., "Frédéric Marcelin," *Le Temps*, 9 jan. 1935.

SYLVAIN, Georges, "*Thémistocle-Épaminondas Labasterre* de F. Marcelin," *La Ronde*, 3, 2, 15 oct. 1901, pp. 28–33.

TARDIEU-FELDMAN GINDINE, Yvette, "F. Marcelin, premier romancier féministe de Caraïbes," *Conjonction*, 130, sept. 1976.

Marcelin, Pierre: see Thoby-Marcelin, Philippe

Martineau, Fernand

CAMILLE, Roussan, "A propos de *Résonnances*," *La Relève*, 6, 5, nov. 1937, pp. 23–25.

Mayard, Constantin

LARAQUE, Maurice, *Constantin Mayard*. Port-au-Prince: Impr. Tel-homme, 1944.

Métellus, Jean

AUTRAND, Dominique, "Mes mains pleines de mots," *La Quinzaine littéraire*, 289, 1–15 nov. 1978, p. 5.

Moravia, Charles

ANON., "*La Crète-à-Pierrot* de Ch. Moravia et notre patriotisme," *Le Pacificateur*, 19 avril 1907.

NAU, John-Antoine, "Un romancier et un poète haïtiens, F. Hibbert et Ch. Moravia," *La Phalange* (Paris). Repr. in *Haiti littéraire et sociale*, 5–20 jan. 1913, pp. 649–652.

VILMENAY, Thomas A., "Charles Moravia," *L'Informateur haïtien*, 20 fév.

Morisseau-Leroy, Félix

BÉLANCE, René, "*Natif-Natal*," *Conjonction*, 20, avril 1949, pp. 23–30.

PAUL, Emmanuel C., "Le Message de *Diacoute*," *Optique*, 27 mai 1956, pp. 23–30.

Nau, Ignace

LESPINASSE, Pierre-Eugène, "Ignace Nau," *Revue de la ligue de la jeunesse haïtienne*, 1, 5, 20 juin 1916, pp. 227–238.

MARCELIN, Émile, "Ignace Nau," *Le Temps*, 21 mars 1936.

VERNA, Paul, "Ignace Nau," *Conjonction*, 23 oct. 1949, pp. 35–37.

Neptune, Louis

BALMIR, Lucien, "*Gouttes de fiel*," *Haïti-Journal*, 27 mars 1947.

Numa, Edgard N.

LAVENTURE, Jules, "*Clercina Destiné*," *Lakansièl*, 3, sept. 1975, p. 26.

Papailler, Hubert

ANON., "*Les Laboureurs de la mer*," *Conjonction*, 79–80, fév.–mai 1960, pp. 85–86.

Paret, Timothée

MORPEAU, Louis, "*L'âme vibrante*," *L'Essor*, mars 1914.

Phelps, Anthony

ALANTE-LIMA, Willy, "*Mon Pays que voici*," *Présence africaine*, 71, 3ème trim. 1969, pp. 109–111.

ANON., "*Mémoire en colin-maillard*," *Nigrizia*, 20, Dec. 1978, p. 65.

AUDET, Noël, "*La Bélière caraïbe*," *Le Devoir*, 5 juill. 1980.

BRUNER, Charlotte H., "*La Bélière caraïbe*," *World Literature Today*, 55, 2, Spring 1981, pp. 363–364.

CAILLER, Bernadette, "*Mémoire en colin-maillard*," *World Literature*

Today, 51, 4 Aut. 1977, p. 671.

DARY, Bernard, "*Mon Pays que voici,*" *Jeune Afrique,* 442, 23–29 juin 1969.

FIGNOLÉ, Jean-Claude, "*Pour que vivent les hommes,*" *Le Petit Samedi Soir,* 271, 2–12 jan. 1979.

LACOTE, René, "Anthony Phelps," *Les Lettres françaises,* 19 fév. 1969.

MARTEL, Réginald, "L'angoisse mouvante et l'horreur achevée [*Mémoire en colin-maillard*]," *La Presse,* 19 fév. 1977.

MORA, Edith, "Poésie heureuse," *Les Nouvelles littéraires,* 24 déc. 1964.

RICARD, François, "Qui a donné Guy et Jacques Colin?," *Le Devoir,* 19 mars 1977.

RIOUX, Gilles, "*Points cardinaux,*" *Sept-Jours,* 1, 23, 18 fév. 1967, p. 46.

Pommayrac, Alcibiade

CLAUDE, Jean, "Alcibiade Pommayrac," *Cahiers d'Haïti,* 2, 5, déc. 1944, pp. 36–37.

Pressoir, Charles F.

BOUCHEREAU, Charles, "A propos de *Au rythme des coumbites,*" *Le Temps,* 24 mars 1933.

BRUTUS, Edner, "C.F. Pressoir," *La Relève,* 9, 1 mars 1933, pp. 10–22.

HEURTELOU, Daniel, "Fantasie en ut," *La Relève,* 9, 1 mars 1933, pp. 3–9.

PRESSOIR, Charles F., "Comment j'ai été amené à écrire *Au Rythme des coumbites,*" *Le Temps,* 31 mars, 8, 22, & 29 avril & 6 mai 1933.

Price-Mars, Jean

ANTOINE, Jacques C., *Jean Price-Mars and Haiti.* Washington: Three Continents Press, 1981.

AUGUSTE, Granville Bonaparte, "Appréciations générales sur Price-Mars," in *Témoignages, infra,* pp. 115–123.

BLEMUR, Urbain, "Dr. Price-Mars, sa biographie, sa pensée," in *Témoignages, infra,* pp. 92–98.

BROUARD, Carl, "Un livre de M. Price-Mars," *Le Petit Impartial,* 13 oct. 1928.

BULLETIN DE L'ACADÉMIE DES SCIENCES HUMAINES ET SOCIALES D'HAITI, 4, 1972; special issue on Jean Price-Mars.

CINÉAS, Jean-Baptiste, "Price-Mars," *Le Temps,* 20 nov. 1937.

DAMAS, Léon-G., "Price-Mars, père du Haïtianisme," *Présence africaine,* 32–33, juin–sept. 1960, pp. 166–178.

DEPESTRE, René, "Jean Price-Mars et le mythe de l'Orphée Noir, ou les aventures de la négritude," *L'Homme et la société,* 7, jan.–mars

1968, pp. 171–181. Repr. in *Pour la révolution, pour la poésie.* Montreal: Léméac, 1974.

DORSINVILLE, Roger, "Jean Price-Mars," *L'Afrique littéraire et artistique,* 4, avril 1969, pp. 58–61.

FOUCHARD, Jean, "Mes derniers souvenirs de Jean Price-Mars," *Conjonction,* 132, jan. 1977, pp. 25–28.

GOURAIGE, Ghislain, "Le Dr. Price-Mars, chef d'école et critique littéraire," in *Témoignages, infra,* pp. 53–65.

KENOL, Justin, "Le Dr. Price-Mars au service de la communauté," in *Témoignages, infra,* pp. 80–91.

KNIGHT, Vere, "Jean Price-Mars," *Black Images,* 4, 3–4, Aut.–Winter 1975, pp. 4–19.

MARS, Louis, "Bibliographie de Jean Price-Mars," *Conjonction,* 132, jan. 1977, pp. 30–40.

MATHON, François, "A propos de l'homme de couleur," in *Témoignages, infra,* pp. 68–70.

PAULTRE, Emile, *Essai sur M. Price-Mars,* 2ème éd. avec une étude complémentaire. Port-au-Prince: Éd. des Antilles, 1966.

POMPILUS, Pradel, "Mes rencontres avec Jean Price-Mars," *Conjonction,* 132, jan. 1977, pp. 19–23.

TÉMOIGNAGE SUR LA VIE ET L'OEUVRE DU DR. JEAN PRICE-MARS, 1876-1956. Port-au-Prince: Impr. de l'État, 1956.

TROUILLOT, Ernst, "Notes sur le Dr. Jean Price-Mars, critique littéraire et scientifique," in *Témoignages, supra,* pp. 71–79. Repr. in *Conjonction,* 110, 2, 1969, pp. 8–17.

VIATTE, Auguste, "L'Oeuvre du Dr. Jean Price-Mars dans son cadre mondial," in *Témoignages, supra,* pp. 66–67.

VILLARSON, Emmanuel, "L'Humanisme du Dr. Jean Price-Mars," in *Témoignages, supra,* pp. 99–114.

Ricourt, Volvick

BRUTUS, Edner, "Volvick Ricourt," *La Relève,* 2, 12, 1 juin 1934, pp. 24–33.

Rigaud, Milo

ANON., *"Jésus ou Legba?,"* *Le Temps-Revue,* 15 nov. 1933.

LESCOUFLAIR, A., *"Jésus ou Legba?,"* *Le Temps,* 31 jan. 1934.

Roumain, Jacques

ABURA, Lynette, "Le Réalisme de Jacques Roumain et la critique Lukaçsienne," *He Cri!,* Sept. 1978, pp. 17–20.

ACHIRIGA, Jingiri J., *"Gouverneurs de la rosée,* l'exemple haïtien," in *La*

Révolte des romanciers noirs. Sherbrooke, P.Q.: Naaman, 1973, pp. 119–141.

AIRE, Victor O., "Affinités électives ou imitation: *Gouverneurs de la rosée* et *O pays, mon beau peuple* de Sembene Ousmane," *Présence francophone* 15, aut. 1977, pp. 3–10.

A.L., "*Gouverneurs de la rosée* de J. Roumain," *Encyclopédie de la France et Outre-mer,* mai 1950.

ALEXANDER, Douglas, "Jacques Roumain, poète indigéniste," in *Studies in Language and Literature,* ed. Charles Nelson. Richmond, Kentucky: Kentucky University, 1976.

ALEXIS, Stéphen, "*Gouverneurs de la rosée,* " *Cahiers d'Haïti,* 2, 7, fév. 1945, pp. 23–29.

ANON. [A. Locke?], "Jacques Roumain," *Opportunity,* 13, 5, May 1935, pp. 134–135.

ANON., "Jacques Roumain; sa vie, ses oeuvres," *Idées,* 11, mai–juin 1977.

ANON., "Jacques Roumain et la pensée féodale," *Démocratie nouvelle,* avril–mai 1975.

ANON., "*La Proie et l'Ombre,*" *Le Temps,* 27 oct. 1930.

ARNOLD, Stephen H., "Approaches critiques de *Gouverneurs de la rosée* de Jacques Roumain," *Peuples noirs—Peuples africains,* 12, 1979, pp. 85–107.

BALMIR, Guy-Claude, "Gouverneurs de la rosée," in *Les Littératures d'expression française: Négritude africaine, Négritude caraïbe.* Paris: Éds. de la Francité, 1973, pp. 135–139.

BASTIEN, Rémy, "Jacques Roumain, en el décimo aniversario de su muerte," *Cuadernos americanos,* julio–agosto 1954, pp. 243–251.

BERNABÉ, Jean, "La Diglossie littéraire: le cas de *Gouverneurs de la rosée,*" *Textes, Études et Documents* (C.U.A.G.), 1, mai 1978, pp. 1–16.

BERROU, frère Raphaël, "*Gouverneurs de la rosée,*" *Le Nouveau Monde,* 24 août 1970, 1 & 6.

BLOCH, Adèle, "The Mythological Themes in the Fictional Works of Jacques Roumain," *International Fiction Review,* 2, 2, July 1975, pp. 132–137.

BRIERRE, Jean F., *Nous garderons le dieu.* Port-au-Prince: Deschamps, 1945.

BROUARD, Carl, "*La Montagne ensorcellée,*" *Haïti-Journal,* 25 jan. 1932.

BROUARD, Carl, "*La Proie et l'Ombre,*" *Le Petit Impartial,* 9 sept. 1930.

BRUTUS, Edner, *"Gouverneurs de la rosée,"* *Haïti-Journal,* 11 jan. 1945.

BRUTUS, Edner, "Jacques Roumain," *La Relève,* 2, 4, 1 oct. 1933, pp. 4–16.

CAHIERS D'HAITI, 2, 4, nov. 1944; special number on Jacques Roumain. Articles by A. Métraux, E.D. Charlier, R. Camille, U. Rey, and J. Blanchet.

CAMILLE, Roussan, "Jacques Roumain," *Le Nouvelliste,* 27 oct. 1942.

CARRÉ, Hubert, *"Gouverneurs de la Rosée,"* *Le Nouvelliste,* 6 & 13 janvier 1945.

CINÉAS, Jean-Baptiste, *"La proie et l'ombre,"* *Haïti-Journal,* 3, 7, 9, & 11 octobre 1930.

COBB, Martha K., "Concepts of Blackness in the Poetry of Nicolás Guillén, Jacques Roumain and Langston Hughes," *College Language Association Journal,* 18, 2, Dec. 1974, pp. 262–272.

COBB, Martha K., *Harlem, Haiti, and Havana* [Langston Hughes, Jacques Roumain, and Nicolás Guillén]. Washington, D.C.: Three Continents Press, 1979.

CONTURIE, Christiane, *Comprendre "Gouverneurs de la rosée."* Issy-les-Moulineaux: Les Classifiques africains, 1980.

COOK, Mercer, *"Gouverneurs de la rosée,"* *Books Abroad,* 19, 2, Spring 1945, pp. 154–155.

CUNARD, Nancy, "Three Negro Poets," *Left Review,* Oct. 1937, pp. 529–536.

DASH, J. Michael, *Jacques Roumain: Masters of the Dew,* new ed. of the L. Hughes & M. Cook translation, with an introduction by J.M. Dash. London & Kingston, Jamaica: Heinemann, 1978.

DEPESTRE, René, "Message des *Gouverneurs de la rosée,"* *Les Lettres françaises,* 5 fév. 1948.

DEPESTRE, René, "Le Nègre démasqué," *Le Nouvelliste,* 18 mars 1958.

DIXON, Melvin, "Towards a World Black Literature," *Massachusetts Review,* 18, 4, Winter 1977, pp. 750–769.

DOMINIQUE, Jean, "Délire ou délivrance," *Conjonction,* 125, 1975, pp. 85–100.

DUVALIER, François, *"Le Fantoches,"* *Le Nouvelliste,* 28 déc. 1931.

F.D., *"La Proie et l'ombre,"* *Le Pays,* 23 sept. 1930.

FIGNOLÉ, Jean-Claude, *Sur "Gouverneurs de la rosée."* Port-au-Prince: Fardin, 1975.

FOWLER, Carolyn, *A Knot in the Thread.* Washington, D.C.: Howard University Press, 1980.

FOWLER, Carolyn, "Motif Symbolism in J. Roumain's *Gouverneurs de la rosée,*" *College Language Association Journal,* 18, 1, Sept. 1974, pp. 44–51.

FOWLER, Carolyn, "Poésie et religion dans *Gouverneurs de la rosée,*" *Conjonction,* 148, juill. 1980, pp. 103–112.

GAL, H., "*Gouverneurs de la rosée* de J. Roumain," *Revue des conférences françaises en Orient,* jan. 1948.

GAILLARD, Roger, "Il ya vingt ans mourait Jacques Roumain," *Le Matin,* 18 août 1964.

GAILLARD, Roger, "Le Théâtre: éternelle jeunesse de *Gouverneurs de la rosée,*" *Le Nouvelliste,* 20, juill. 1967.

GAILLARD, Roger, "L'Univers romanesque de Jacques Roumain," *Conjonction,* 98, mai 1965, pp. 5–25; also: Port-au-Prince: H. Deschamps, 1965.

GAPOULE, Louis, "Portrait de J. Roumain," *Le Nouvelliste,* 19 déc. 1941.

GAZARIAN-GAUTHIER, Marie-Lise, "Le Symbolisme religieux dans *Gouverneurs de la rosée,*" *Présence francophone,* 7, automne 1973, pp. 19–23.

GOURAIGE, Ghislain, "La Technique de J. Roumain dans *Gouverneurs de la rosée,*" in *Le Roman contemporain d'expression française,* Actes du colloque de Sherbrooke. Sherbrooke, P.Q.: U. de Sherbrooke, 1971, pp. 218–223.

GRIMARD, Luc, "Deux romans de J. Roumain," *Haïti-Journal,* 24 fév. 1932.

GUILLÉN, Nicolás, "Sobre Jacques Roumain," *Hoy,* 25 mayo 1961. Repr. in *Prosa de Prisa,* vol. II. Havana, Arte y Literatura, 1975, pp. 391–394.

HOFFMANN, Léon-François, "Complexité linguistique et rhétorique dans *Gouverneurs de la rosée,*" *Présence africaine,* 98, 1976, pp. 145–161.

JEAN, Eddy-A., "*Gouverneurs de la rosée*": le texte et ses lectures. New York: Ed. Jacques Soleil, 1981.

JONES, Grahame C., "Narrative Point of View in Jacques Roumain's *Gouverneurs de la rosée,*" *L'Esprit Créateur,* 17, 2, Summer 1977, pp. 115–122.

LAMARRE, Joseph M., "Le Militaire dans trois romans haïtiens: *Zoune, Gouverneurs de la rosée, Les Arbres musiciens,*" *Présence francophone,* 12, printemps 1976, pp. 131–140.

LARAQUE, Maurice, "J. Roumain—En marge des *Gouverneurs de la rosée,*" *Optique,* 18 août 1955, pp. 19–28.

LESPES, Anthony, "Ce qui compte, M. Laraque, c'est l'esprit de sacrifice—*Gouverneurs de la rosée,*" *Haïti-Miroir,* 1, 12–13, 19–25 sept. & 26 sept.–1 oct. 1955.

LESPES, Anthony, "En marge des *Gouverneurs de la rosée,*" *Optique,* 18, août 1955, pp. 19–28.

LESPES, Anthony, "*Gouverneurs de la rosée,*" *Le Nouvelliste,* 19 mars 1945.

LEVILAIN, Guy Viet, *Cultural Identity, Negritude and Decolonization,* American Institute for Marxist Studies, occasional paper no. 29. New York, 1978. (on Roumain and Depestre.)

L.G., "*La Proie et l'ombre,*" *Haïti-Journal,* 24 sept. 1930.

LIGAN, Samson, *Le Thème de la religion dans "Gouverneurs de la rosée."* Talence: Université de Bordeaux III, 1978.

LUCRECE, André, "Le Médievisme de Jacques Roumain," *Textes, Études et Documents* (C.U.A.G.), 1, mai 1978, pp. 17–29.

MAGLOIRE, Hubert, *Actualité de Jacques Roumain.* Montréal, 1975.

MAKOUTA-MBOUKOU, Jean-Pierre, *Jacques Roumain, essai sur la signification spirituelle et religieuse de son oeuvre.* Lille: Atelier de reproduction de thèses, 1979.

MARTY, Anne, "Le Socialisme dans l'oeuvre de Jacques Roumain et Jacques-Stéphen Alexis," *Conjonction,* 136–137, fév. 1978, pp. 29–42.

MORAILLE, Yvon, "Hommage à Jacques Roumain," *Haïti-Journal,* 12 avril 1932.

MORAND, Paul, "*Gouverneurs de la rosée,*" *France-Amérique,* mars 1945.

NWEZEH, E.C., "Jacques Roumain's Position in the Haitian Indigenist Movement: The Example of *Gouverneurs de la rosée,*" *Nigerian Journal of the Humanities,* 2, 1978, pp. 69–76.

ORMEROD, Beverly, "Myth, Rite and Symbol in *Gouverneurs de la rosée,*" *L'Esprit Créateur,* 17, 2, Summer 1977, pp. 123–132.

PAUL, Cauvin L, *Manuel . . . un dieu tombé.* Astoria, N.Y., 1975.

PÉPIN, Ernest, "Proposition pour une lecture de *Gouverneurs de la rosée,*" *Textes, Études et Documents (C.U.A.G.),* 1, mai 1978, pp. 30–42.

PETIT, Antoine G., *Richesse lexicale . . . [de] "Gouverneurs de la rosée,"* n.n., n.d. [Montreal, 1978].

PHELPS, Anthony, "Au coeur du mythe," *Conjonction,* 98, mai 1965, pp. 32–39.

PLANET, Claudie, "*Gouverneurs de la rosée,*" *Europe,* 24, 10, 1 oct. 1946, pp. 102–105.

POMPILUS, Pradel, "De l'élégie à la poésie entrainante," *Conjonction,* 98, mai 1965, pp. 26–31.

RENN, Ludwig, "J. Roumain, sa vie," *Afroamérica,* enero–julio 1945.

SERRES, Michel, "Christ noir," *Critique,* 39, 308, jan. 1973, pp. 3–25.

SIGEL, F., "*Gouverneurs de la rosée* de J. Roumain," *Contact,* jan. 1949.

SOUFFRANT, Claude, "Actualité de Jacques Roumain," *Europe,* 54, 569, sept. 1976, pp. 64–83.

SOUFFRANT, Claude, "Le Fatalisme religieux du paysan haitien," *Europe,* 49, 501, jan. 1971, pp. 27–41.

SOUFFRANT, Claude, *Idéologies religieuses et dévelopment social autour de deux romans haïtiens:* "Gouverneurs de la rosée, *de Jacques Roumain et* "Le Arbres Musiciens" *de J.S. Alexis.* Mémoire E.P.H.E. Paris, 1973.

SOUFFRANT, Claude, "Marxisme et tiers monde noir chez Jacques Roumain, Jacques-Stéphen Alexis et Léopold Sédar Senghor," *Présence francophone,* 14, print. 1977, pp. 133–147.

SOUFFRANT, Claude, *Une négritude socialiste: Religion et développement chez Jacques Roumain, Jacques-Stéphen Alexis et Langston Hughes.* Paris: L'Harmattan, 1978.

TOUMSON, Roger, "Mythe et histoire dans *Gouverneurs de la rosée,*" *Textes, Études et Documents* (C.U.A.G.), 1 mai 1978, pp. 42–64.

TROUILLOT, Hénock, *Dimensions et limites de Jacques Roumain.* Port-au-Prince: Fardin, 1975.

VIEUX, Antonio, "Entre nous, Jacques Roumain," *La Revue indigène,* 1, 3, sept. 1927, pp. 103–110.

VIGNAL, Daniel, "Portrait d'une création littéraire: Manuel dans *Gouverneurs de la rosée* de Jacques Roumain," *Peuples noirs–Peuples africains,* 16, 1979, pp. 39–47.

VILLEDROUIN, Luc, "*La Proie et l'ombre,*" *Maintenant,* 6 fév. 1937.

WILLIAMS, Eric, "Four Poets of the Greater Antilles" (Guillén, Roumain, Brierre, Palés), *Caribbean Quarterly,* 2, 4, 1950, pp. 8–19.

ZUCARRELLI, Guy, "*La Montagne ensorcellée,*" *Le Temps,* 26 août 1932.

Roumer, Émile

BERROU, frère Raphaël and Pradel Pompilus, *Deux poètes indigénistes: Carl Brouard et Émile Roumer.* Paris: Éd. de l'École, 1974.

BERROU, frère Raphaël, "Les Fleurs et les fruits dans la poésie d'Émile Roumer," *Conjonction,* 102, août 1966, pp. 53–56.

BRUTUS, Edner, "Émile Roumer," *La Relève,* 1, 4, 1 oct. 1932, pp. pp. 13–18.

LIATAUD, André, *"Poèmes d'Haïti et de France* de E. Roumer," *La Nouvelle Revue,* 1, 11, 1 avril 1926, pp. 215–220.

SMITH, William J., "Deux poètes haïtiens," *Optique,* 1, mars 1954, pp. 26–29.

VIEUX, Antonio, "Entre nous: Émile Roumer," *La Revue indigène,* 1, 2, août 1927, pp. 54–58.

VILLEDROUIN, Luc, *"Poèmes . . .,"* *Maintenant,* 22 déc. 1936.

Roy, Francis-Joachim

FOURCADE, Jean, *"Les Chiens* de F.-J. Roy," *L'École et la nation,* sept. 1961.

LACOMBE, Lia, *"Les Chiens* de F.-J. Roy," *Les Lettres françaises,* 13 avril 1961.

M.M., *"Les Chiens* de F.J.-Roy," *Le Figaro littéraire,* 15 avril 1961.

PORQUEROI, Elizabeth, *"Les Chiens* de F.-J. Roy," *La Nouvelle revue française,* 1 juill. 1961.

Saint-Amand, Edris

HENRIOT, Émile, *"Bon Dieu Rit,"* *Le Monde* (Paris), 29 oct. 1952.

Saint-Louis, Carlos

VERNA, Paul, "C. Saint-Louis: *Flammes,"* *Conjonction,* 13, fév. 1948, pp. 61–62.

Sampeur, Virginie

BROUARD, Raphaël, "Centenaire de Virgine Sampeur," *Le Temps,* 1 avril 1939.

BRUTUS, Edner, "Virginie Sampeur," *La Relève,* 2, 7, 1 jan. 1934, pp. 20–31.

Sylvain, Georges

BERROU, frère Raphaël, "Georges Sylvain," *Conjonction,* 101, avril 1966, pp. 75–81.

PAILLIERE, Madeleine, *"Confidences et mélancolies* de Georges Sylvain," *Conjonction,* 147, mars 1980, pp. 107–120.

PARMEE, Douglas, "*Cric? Crac!* Fables of La Fontaine in Haitian Créole: A Literary Ethno-socio-linguistic Curiosity," *Nottingham French Studies,* 15, 2, nov. 1976, pp. 12–26.

R.L., "En marge de *Cric? Crac!,"* *La Relève,* 5, 1, juill. 1936, pp. 27–29.

ROMÉUS, Wilhem, *La Fixation maternelle dans "Confidences et mélancolies."* Port-au-Prince: mimeo., 1975.

WILLIAMS, P., *La Fontaine in Haitian Creole: A Study of "Cric? Crac!"* Ann Arbor, Michigan: University Microfilms, 1971.

Thoby, Armand

A.B., "A propos d'un ouvrage de M. Thoby" [*Jacques Bonhomme d'Haïti*], *Les Bigailles,* 14 déc. 1901.

SYLVAIN, Georges, "*Jacques Bonhomme d'Haïti* d'A. Thoby," *La Ronde,* 3, 4, 15 déc. 1901, pp. 58–64.

Thoby-Marcelin, Philippe & Marcelin, Pierre

ANON., "In Memoriam Ph. Thoby-Marcelin," *Présence haïtienne,* 2, sept. 1975, pp. 11–15.

BRUTUS, Edner, "Ph. Thoby-Marcelin," *La Relève,* 1, 3, 1 sept. 1932, pp. 27–32.

DRISKELL, Daniel D. & Douglas Radcliff-Umstead, "La Mort dans le roman afro-haïtien," *Présence francophone,* 11, automne 1975, pp. 119–132.

FOISSET, Père, "*Canapé Vert,*" *La Phalange,* mai 1945. Repr. in *Haïti-Journal,* 14 mai 1945.

KNIGHT, Vere M., "P. Marcelin and Ph. Thoby-Marcelin: Sensationalism or Realism?," *Black Images,* 2, 1, Spring 1973, pp. 30–42.

WILSON, Edmund, "The Marcelins, Novelists of Haiti," *The Nation,* 14 Oct. 1950, pp. 341–344.

Valcin, Mme. Virgile

ANON., "*Cruelle destinée* de V. Valcin," *La Petite revue,* 7, 178, 1 juill. 1930, pp. 108–110.

Vaval, Duraciné

DORSINVILLE, Hénec, "*Stances haïtiennes* de D. Vaval," *L'Essor,* nov. 1912.

LIAUTAUD, André, "*Stances haïtiennes* de D. Vaval," *La Nouvelle Ronde,* 1, 4, 1 sept. 1925, pp. 70–72.

Verne, Marc

BALMIR, Lucien, "*Marie Villarceaux,*" *Haïti-Journal,* 23 juin 1948.

Vieux, Damoclès

FIEVRE, Michel, "Damoclès Vieux: l'écrivain, l'esthéticien, le chantre de l'amour," *Le Temps,* 20 & 24 mai 1939.

LALEAU, Léon, "Le Front contre le stèle," in *Apothéoses.* Port-au-Prince: Deschamps, 1952, pp. 108–114.

LALEAU, Léon, "La Poésie de M. Damoclès Vieux," *La Relève,* 5, 3, sept.–oct. 1936, pp. 32–50.

LASSEGUE, Franck, "*L'Aile captive,*" *L'Essor-Revue,* déc. 1919, pp. 487–489.

VIEUX, Antonio, *"L'Aile captive* de D. Vieux," *La Nouvelle Ronde,* 1, 5, 1 oct. 1925, pp. 94–98.

Y.F., *"Dernières floraisons* de D. Vieux," *Conjonction,* 13 fév. 1948, pp. 62–63.

Vilaire, Etzer

FIGNOLÉ, Jean-Claude, "Défense d'Etzer Vilaire," *Le Nouveau Monde,* 28 déc. 1970.

FIGNOLÉ, Jean-Claude, *E. Vilaire, ce méconnu.* Port-au-Prince, Impr. Centrale, 1970.

FIGNOLÉ, Jean-Claude, "Etzer Vilaire, créateur," *Conjonction,* 116, 2ème trim., 1971, pp. 86–88.

GAILLARD, Roger, *E. Vilaire, témoin de nos malheurs.* Port-au-Prince: Presses nationales d'Haïti, 1972.

GAILLARD, Roger, "Fin du purgatoire pour E. Vilaire?," *Le Nouveau Monde,* déc. 1970.

GÉROME, Pétion, "E. Vilaire," *La Ronde,* 8, 5 avril 1901, pp. 130–134 & 9, 15 mai 1901, pp. 137–142.

GÉROME, Pétion, *"Dix Hommes Noirs,"* *Haïti-Journal,* 27 juill. 1912, pp. 346–347.

GIRAULT, Wiener, "E. Vilaire, le thanatophobe," *Le Nouveau Monde,* 8 jan. 1971.

GROSS, René, "Quelques mots sur un poète haïtien: E. Vilaire," *l'Intransigeant.* Reprod. in *Le Matin,* 2 juin 1922.

LAFOREST, Edmond, *L'Oeuvre poétique de M. Etzer Vilaire.* Jérémie– Port-au-Prince: Impr. du Centenaire, 1907.

LALEAU, Léon, "E. Vilaire," *Conjonction,* 34, août 1951, pp. 29–31.

LATAILLADE, Nerva, "Causerie (prononcée en 1923) sur l'oeuvre de Etzer Vilaire," *Le Temps,* 8 juill. 1933.

L.G., *"Années tendres; Les Poèmes de la mort* de E. Vilaire," *La Nouvelle revue,* 1, 7 & 8, mars & avril 1908.

POMPILUS, Pradel, "E. Vilaire," *Conjonction,* 119, fév.–mars 1973, pp. 73–89.

POMPILUS, Pradel, "Etzer Vilaire corrige Etzer Vilaire," *Conjonction,* 138, mai 1978, pp. 83–94.

PRADEL, Seymour, "Etzer Vilaire," *Haïti littéraire et scientifique,* 5 & 20 juill., 20 août & 20 sept. 1912.

SYLVAIN, Georges, *"Nouveaux poèmes,"* *Haïti littéraire et scientifique,* 5, août 1912.

Vilaire, Jean-Joseph

LE CRITIQUE, "*Aube* de J.-J. Vilaire," *Revue de la ligue de la jeunesse haïtienne*, 1, 2, 20 mars 1916, pp. 97–100.

VIEUX, Antonio, "*Aube* de J.-J. Vilaire," *La Nouvelle Ronde*, 1, 6, 1 nov. 1925, pp. 110–114.

Werleigh, Christian

BRIERRE, Jean-F., "*Le Palmiste dans l'ouragan*," *Le Temps*, 12 août 1933.

LATAILLADE, Nerva, "*Le Palmiste dans l'ouragan*," *Le Temps*, 4 mai 1935.

Place of Publication of Periodicals Mentioned in the Bibliography

Action nationale, L'	Port-au-Prince
Action sociale, L'	Port-au-Prince
Actualité, L'	Port-au-Prince
African Literature Today	London
Afrique littéraire et artistique, L'	Paris
Afroamérica	Mexico City
¡Ahora!	Santo Domingo
Americas	Washington, D.C.
Annales politiques et littéraires, Les	Paris
Annali	Feltre, Italy
Antares	Baden-Baden
Bataille, La	Port-au-Prince
BIM	Chirstchurch, Barbados
Bingo	Dakar
Black Images	Toronto
Black Orpheus	Ibadan
Black World	Washington, D.C.
Books Abroad	Norman, Okla.
Bulletin de l'académie des sciences humaines et sociales d'haiti	Port-au-Prince
Cahiers d'Haïti	Port-au-Prince
Caribbean Quarterly	Mona, Jamaica
Caribbean Review	Miami
Caribbean Studies	Rio Pedras, P.R.
Casa de las Américas	Havana
Claflin College Review	Orangeburg, S.C.
Collectif Paroles	La Salle, P.Q.
Conférences historiques, Les	Port-au-Prince
Comparative Literatures Studies	Champaign, Ill.
Congo-Afrique	Kinshasa
Conjonction	Port-au-Prince
Contact	Paris
Crisol, El	Mexico City
Critique	Paris
Cuadernos Americanos	Mexico City
Culture française	Paris
Démocratie nouvelle	Brooklyn, N.Y.
Dérives	Montreal
Devoir, Le	Montreal
École et la nation, L'	Paris
Encyclopédie de la France et outremer	Paris

Esprit créateur, L'	Lawrence, Kans.
Essor, L'	Port-au-Prince
Études littéraires	Quebec
Europe	Paris
Feuille du commerce, La	Port-au-Prince
Figaro, Le	Paris
Figaro littéraire, Le	Paris
Français au Nigeria, Le	Benin City
France-Amérique	New York
Francofonia	Bologna
French Review, The	Champaign, Ill.
Gar	Austin, Tex.
Haïti illustrée	Port-au-Prince
Haïti-Journal	Port-au-Prince
Haïti littéraire et scientifique	Port-au-Prince
Haïti littéraire et sociale	Port-au-Prince
Haïti-Observateur	New York
He Cri	Nairobi
Hispanamérica	College Park, Md.
Homme et la société, L'	Paris
Hoy	Havana
Idées	Jamaica, N.Y.
Ideologies and Literatures	Minneapolis
Informateur haïtien, L'	Port-au-Prince
International Fiction Review	Fredericton, N.B.
Intransigeant, L'	Paris
Jeune Afrique	Paris
Jeune Haïti, La	Port-au-Prince
Journal of Interamerican Studies	Beverly Hills, Cal.
Journal of Negro History	Washington, D.C.
Justicier, Le	Port-au-Prince
Lakansièl	Brooklyn, N.Y.
Left Review, The	London
Lettres françaises, Les	Paris
Lilas, Les	Paris
Maintenant (Montreal)	Montreal
Maintenant	Port-au-Prince
Massachusetts Review	Amherst, Mass.
Matin, Le	Port-au-Prince
Mercure de France, Le	Paris
Modern Language Studies	Kingston, R.I.
Monde, Le (Paris)	Paris
Monde, Le	Port-au-Prince
Moment, Le	Port-au-Prince

Muse française, La	Paris
Nation, La	Port-au-Prince
Nation, The	New York
Neuren Sprache, Die	Frankfurt-am-Main
Ngam	Yaoundé
Nigerian Journal of the Humanities	Benin City
Nigrizia	Verona
Notre librairie	Paris
Nottingham French Studies	Nottingham, Great Britain
Nouveau Monde, Le	Port-au-Prince
Nouvel Observateur, Le	Paris
Nouvelle Optique	Montreal
Nouvelle Revue, La	Cap-Haïtien
Nouvelle Revue des deux-mondes, La	Paris
Nouvelle Revue française, La	Paris
Nouvelle Ronde, La	Port-au-Prince
Nouvelles littéraires, Les	Paris
Nouvelliste, Le	Port-au-Prince
Oeuvres et critiques	Paris
Opinion nationale, L'	Port-au-Prince
Opportunity	New York
Optique	Port-au-Prince
Pacificateur, Le	Port-au-Prince
Panamerican Magazine	New Orleans
Panorama	Port-au-Prince
Pays, Le	Port-au-Prince
Petit Haïtien, Le	Cap-Haïtien
Petit Impartial, Le	Port-au-Prince
Petit Samedi soir, Le	Port-au-Prince
Petite Revue, La	Port-au-Prince
Peuples noirs. Peuples africains	Paris
Phalange, La	Paris
Phalange, La (Port-au-Prince)	Port-au-Prince
Phylon	Atlanta
Plume, La	Port-au-Prince
Poetry	Chicago
Présence africaine	Paris
Présence francophone	Sherbrooke, P.Q.
Présence haïtienne	New York
Presse, La	Montreal
Projection	Port-au-Prince
Quinzaine littéraire, La	Paris
Quisqueya	Paris
Race	London

Ralliement, Le	Port-au-Prince
Relève, La	Port-au-Prince
Revista Nacional de Cultura	Caracas
Revista de la Universidad Nacional de Córdoba	Córdoba, Argentina
Revue de l'Amérique latine	Paris
Revue des conférences françaises	Paris
Revue contemporaine	Paris
Revue des deux-mondes, La	Paris
Revue générale, La	Port-au-Prince
Revue d'histoire, de géographie et de géologie, La	Port-au-Prince
Revue indigène, La	Port-au-Prince
Revue de la ligue de la jeunesse haïtienne	Port-au-Prince
Revue de littérature comparée	Paris
Revue de l'université laurentienne	Sudbury, Ont.
Romanische Forschungen	Erlangen, West Germany
Rond-Point	Port-au-Prince
Ronde, La	Port-au-Prince
Savacou	London and Kingston
Sèl	Brooklyn, N.Y.
Sept-Jours	Montreal
Studies in Language and Literature	Richmond, Kent.
Temps, Le (Paris)	Paris
Temps, Le	Port-au-Prince
Temps-Revue, Le	Port-au-Prince
Textes, études et documents	Fort-de-France, Martinique
Thesaurus	Bogota
Tomorrow	New York
Union, L'	Port-au-Prince
Variétés, Les	Cap-Haïtien
Vie des peuples, La	Paris
World Literature Today	Norman, Okla.
World Theatre	Brussels

BIBLIOGRAPHY OF WORKS
MENTIONED IN TEXT

ALEXIS, Jacques-Stéphen, *Les Arbres musiciens.* Paris: Gallimard, 1957.

ALEXIS, Jacques-Stéphen, *Compère Général Soleil.* Paris: Gallimard, 1955.

ALEXIS, Jacques-Stéphen, "Du réalisme merveilleux des Haïtiens," *Présence africaine,* 8, 10, juin-nov. 1956, pp. 245–271.

ALEXIS, Jacques-Stéphen, *L'Espace d'un cillement.* Paris: Gallimard, 1959.

ALEXIS, Jacques-Stéphen, *Romancero aux étoiles.* Paris: Gallimard, 1960.

ALEXIS, Stéphen, *Le Nègre masqué.* Port-au-Prince: L'État, 1933.

ANON., editorial in *Le Justicier,* 5 déc. 1903.

ANON., editorial in *Le Phare,* 20 jan. 1831.

ANON., editorial in *Le Temps,* 7 oct. 1932.

ANON., "Louis-Joseph Janvier," *Courrier d'Haïti,* 31 mars 1888.

ANON., review of Seabrook (q.v.), *La Petite Revue,* 1 juill. 1930.

ARCHIN-LAY, Luce, "France et Haïti," *Haïti littéraire et sociale,* 20 avr. 1905.

AUBIER, Dominique and Miguel Tuñon de Lara, *Espagne.* Paris: Seuil, 1956.

BARIDON, Sivio F. and Raymond Philoctète, *Poésie vivante d'Haïti.* Paris: Lettres nouvelles–M. Nadeau, 1978.

BEDFORD-JONES, Henry, *Drums of Dambala,* New York, Covici— Friede, 1932.

BELLEGARDE, Dantès, article in *La Ronde,* 5 oct. 1898.

BELLEGARDE, Dantès, *Pour une Haïti heureuse,* 2 vols. Port-au-Prince: Chéraquit, 1927 & 1929.

BERGEAUD, Émeric, *Stella.* Paris: Dentu, 1859.

BONTEMPS, Arna, see HUGHES, Langston

BORNO, C., article in *La Feuille du commerce,* 22 juin 1861.

BRIERRE, Jean-F., *Black Soul.* Havana: Lex, 1947.

BRIERRE, Jean-F., *Province.* Port-au-Prince: Deschamps, 1935.

BROUARD, Carl, "L'Art au service du peuple," *Les Griots,* 2, oct. 1938.

BROUARD, Carl, *Pages retrouvées.* Port-au-Prince: Panorama, 1963.

BRUN, Amédée, *Deux amours.* Port-au-Prince: Vve Chenèt, 1895.

BURR-REYNAUD, Frédéric, review of J.-B. Cinéas' *Le Drame de la terre, Le Temps,* 9 sep. 1933.

CASSÉUS, Maurice, *Mambo.* Port-au-Prince: Séminaire adventiste, 1950.

CASSÉUS, Maurice, *Viejo.* Port-au-Prince: Éd. de "La Presse," 1935.

CÉLESTIN-MÉGIE, Emile, *L'Anmou pa gin baryè.* Port-au-Prince: Fardin, 1975.

CÉSAIRE, Aimé, *Cahier d'un retour au pays natal.* New York: Brentano's, 1947.

CHARLES, Jean-Claude, *Sainte dérive des cochons.* Montreal: Nouvelle Optique, 1977.

CHARMANT, Rodolphe, *La Vie incroyable d'Alcius.* Port-au-Prince: Soc. d'Éd. et de Lib., 1946.

CHAUDENSON, Robert, *Les Créoles français.* Paris: Nathan, 1979.

CHAUVET, Marie, *Amour, Colère et Folie.* Paris: Gallimard, 1968.

CHAUVET, Marie, *La Danse sur le volcan.* Paris: Plon, 1957.

CHAUVET, Marie, *Fille d'Haïti.* Paris: Fasquelle, 1954.

CHAUVET, Marie, *Fonds des nègres.* Port-au-Prince: Deschamps, 1961.

CHENET, Edmond, *Proverbes créoles.* Port-au-Prince: Chenet, n.d.

CHENET, Jean-Baptiste, *Etudes poétiques.* Paris: Impr. Dupont, 1846.

CHEVALLIER, André, "Li blanc!" in *Mon petit kodack.* Port-au-Prince Chenet, 1916.

CINÉAS, Jean-Baptiste, *Le Choc en retour.* Port-au-Prince: Deschamps, 1948.

CINÉAS, Jean-Baptiste, *L'Héritage sacré.* Port-au-Prince: Deschamps, 1945.

CLAGUE, Christopher K., see ROTBERG, Robert I.

COICOU, Massillon, *La Noire,* serialized unfinished novel in *Le Soir,* nov. 1905.

COICOU, Massillon, *Poésies nationales.* Paris: Impr. Goupil & Jourdan, 1892.

COLIMON, Marie-Thérèse, *Le Chant des sirènes.* Port-au-Prince, Éd. du soleil, 1979.

COMHAIRE-SYLVAIN, Suzanne, *Le Créole haïtien.* Wetteren: Impr. de Meester, 1936.

COURTOIS, Félix, *Scènes de la vie port-au-princienne.* Port-au-Prince: Antilles, 1975.

CRAIGE, John Houston, *Black Bagdad.* New York: Minton, Balch, 1933.

CRAIGE, John Houston, *Cannibal Cousins.* New York: Minton, Balch, 1934.

DAVID, Odnell, "Le Créole, langue nationale," *Panorama,* 6, août 1955, pp. 221–226.

DAVIS, Beale, *The Goat Without Horns.* New York: Brentano's, 1925.

DAVIS, H.P., *Black Democracy—The Story of Haiti,* 2nd rev. ed. New York: Biblo & Tanner, 1967. (1st ed., 1928.)

DEJEAN, Yves, *Dilemme en Haïti.* New York: Connaissance d'Haïti, 1975.

DELORME, Demesvar, *Francesca.* Paris: Dentu, 1873.

DELORME, Demesvar, *Réflexions diverses sur Haïti.* Paris: Dentu, 1873.

DÉITA, *Les Désespérés.* Port-au-Prince: Théodore, 1964.

DEPESTRE, René, *Gerbe de sang.* Port-au-Prince: L'État, 1946.

DEPESTRE, René, *Poète à Cuba.* Paris: Oswald, 1976.

DEPESTRE, René. *Pour la révolution, pour la poésie.* Montreal: Léméac, 1974.

DEPESTRE, René, *A Rainbow for the Christian West.* Translated with an Introduction by Joan Dayan, Amherst: The University of Massachusetts Press, 1977. (Translation of his *Un arc-en-ciel pour l'occident chrétien.* Paris: Présence africaine, 1967.)

DESPEIGNES, Jacquelin M., *Nouveau regard.* Sherbrooke, P.Q.: Impr. Paulines, 1975.

DESROY, Annie, *Le Joug.* Port-au-Prince: Impr. Modèle, 1934.

DEREN, Maya, *Divine Horsemen.* New York: Thamers & Hurson, 1953.

DEVIEUX-DEHOUX, Liliane, *L'Amour oui, la mort, non.* Sherbrooke, P.Q.: Naaman, 1976.

DOHRMAN, Richard, *The Cross of Baron Samedi.* Boston: Houghton Mifflin, 1958.

DORSINVILLE, Roger, *Lettre aux hommes clairs.* Port-au-Prince: L'État, 1946.

DUNHAM, Katherine, *The Danses of Haiti,* bi-lingual Spanish/English edition. Mexico: Acta Anthropologica, 1947.

DUPOUX, Antoine, *Fleurs des bouges.* Port-au-Prince: Telhomme, 1940.

ÉLIE, Louis, *Remarques sur le vaudoux,* typescript in Saint Louis de Gonzague collection, n.d. (ca. 1945).

ÉTIENNE, Gérard, *Le Nègre crucifié.* Montreal: Éd. Francophones, 1974.

FAINE, Jules, *Philologie créole.* Port-au-Prince: L'État, 1936.

FANFANT, Edgard, review of J. Lhérisson's *Zoune . . .,* *Le Petit Haïtien,* déc. 1906.

FAUBERT, Pierre, *Ogé.* Paris: Maillet-Schmitz, 1856.

FIRMIN, Anténor, *De l'égalité des races.* Paris: Cotillon, 1885.

FIRMIN, Anténor, *M. Roosevelt . . . et la République d'Haïti.* Paris: Pichon & Durand, 1905.

FLEISCHMANN, Ulrich, *Ideologie und Wirklichkeit in der Literatur*

Haitis. Berlin: Colloquium, 1969.

FLEURY-BATTIER, Alcibiade, "Le Vrai Ouanga," *La Revue Express*, 26 août 1891.

FOUCHARD, Jean, *Trois discours*. Port-au-Prince: L'État, 1962.

FRANKÉTIENNE, *Dezafi*. Port-au-Prince: Fardin, 1975.

FRANKÉTIENNE, *Mur à crever*. Port-au-Prince: Presses port-au-princiennes, 1968.

FRANKÉTIENNE, *Pèlin tèt*. Port-au-Prince: Presses port-au-princiennes, 1978.

FRANKÉTIENNE, *Troufoban*. Port-au-Prince: Presses port-au-princiennes, 1978.

GAILLARD, Roger, *Charades haïtiennes*. Port-au-Prince: Éd. de l'an 2000, 1972.

GARRET, Naomi M., *The Renaissance of Haitian Poetry*. Paris: Présence africaine, 1963.

GINDINE TARDIEU FELDMAN, Yvette, "Images of the American in Haitian Literature During the Occupation," *Caribbean Studies*, 14, 3, Oct. 1974, pp. 37–52.

G.L., article in *Le Temps*, 12 juin 1937.

GOURAIGE, Ghislain, *La Diaspora d'Haïti et l'Afrique*. Sherbrooke, P.Q.: Naaman, 1974.

GRANIER de CASSAGNAC, Adolphe, *Voyage aux Antilles*, 2 vols. Paris: Les Imprimeurs réunis, 1844.

GREENE, Graham, *The Comedians*. London: Bodley Head, 1966.

HALL, Robert A., *Haitian Creole*. Philadelphia: American Folklore Society, 1953.

HECTOR, N., "Demesvar Delorme," *Le Petit Haïtien*, août–nov. 1907.

HERSKOVITS, Melville J., *Life in a Haitian Valley*. New York & London: A. Knopf, 1937.

HIBBERT, Fernand, *Le Manuscrit de mon ami*. Port-au-Prince: Chéraquit, 1923.

HIBBERT, Fernand, *Séna*. Port-au-Prince: L'Abeille, 1905.

HIBBERT, Fernand, *Les Simulacres*. Port-au-Prince: Chéraquit, 1923.

HIBBERT, Fernand, *Les Thazar*. Port-au-Prince: L'Abeille, 1907.

HUGHES, Langston and Arna Bontemps, *Popo and Fifina*. New York: McMillan, 1932.

HUGO, Victor, *Bug-Jargal*. Paris: Canel, 1826.

HURSTON, Zora Neale, *Tell My Horse*. Philadelphia & New York: Lippincott, 1938.

HYPPOLITE, Michelson-P., *Le Devenir du créole haïtien*. Port-au-Prince:

L'État, 1952.

HYPPOLITE, Michelson-P., *Phonétique historique haïtienne.* Port-au-Prince: Fardin, 1978.

JAMES, C.L.R., *The Black Jacobins,* 2nd rev. ed. New York: Random House, 1963. (1st ed., 1938.)

JANVIER, Louis-Joseph, *L'Egalité des races.* Paris: Rougier, 1884.

JANVIER, Louis-Joseph, "La République d'Haïti et ses détracteurs," in Jules Auguste et al., *Les Détracteurs de la race noire et de la République d'Haïti.* Paris: Marpon & Flammarion, 1882.

JÉRÉMIE, Cadet, *L'Effort.* Port-au-Prince: L'Abeille, 1905.

JOHNSON, James Weldon, four articles on the U.S. occupation of Haiti in the August and September 1920 issues of *The Nation.*

LABELLE, Micheline, *Idéologie de couleur et classes sociales en Haïti.* Montreal: Presses Universitaires de Montréal, 1978.

LAFLEUR, P., article in *L'Oeil,* 23 juill. 1885.

LAFONTANT, Delorme, *Célie.* Port-au-Prince: Telhomme, 1939.

LALEAU, Léon, *Le Choc.* Port-au-Prince: Impr. de "La Presse," 1932.

LALEAU, Léon, *Musique nègre.* Port-au-Prince: L'État, 1931.

LAMMING, George, *In the Castle of my Skin.* New York: McGraw Hill, 1953.

LAROCHE, Maximilien, "Panorama de la littérature créole," in Yves Dubé, ed., *L'Haïtien.* Montreal: Éd. Ste Marie, 1968, pp. 84–94.

LE SAGE, Aimard, *L'Amant idéal.* Port-au-Prince: Chéraquit, 1926.

LEYBURN, James G., *The Haitian People.* New Haven: Yale University Press, 1941.

LHÉRISSON, Justin, *La Famille des Pitite-Caille.* Port-au-Prince: Héraux, 1905.

LISET, Léon, "Intoxication," *L'Eclaireur,* 26 mars 1913.

LOFFICIAL, Frantz, *Créole français: une fausse querelle.* La Salle: Collectif Paroles, 1979.

LOUYS, Pierre, *Aphrodite.* Paris: Mercure de France, 1896.

LUBIN, Maurice A., *Poésies haïtiennes.* Rio de Janeiro: Casa do estudante do Brasil, 1956.

LUBIN, Maurice A., see SAINT-LOUIS, Carlos.

LUNDAHL, Mats, *Peasants and Poverty: A Study of Haiti.* New York: St. Martin's, 1979.

MAGLOIRE, Auguste, *Étude sur le tempérament haïtien.* Port-au-Prince: Impr. du "Matin," 1908.

MAGLOIRE, Nadine, *Le Mal de vivre.* Port-au-Prince: Verseau, 1968.

MAGLOIRE SAINT-AUDE, Clément, *Parias.* Port-au-Prince: L'État, 1949.

MANIGAT, Leslie, *Ethnicité, nationalisme et politique.* New York: Connaissance d'Haïti, 1975.

MARCELIN, Frédéric, *Au gré du souvenir.* Paris: Challamel, 1913.

MARCELIN, Frédéric, *Autour de deux romans.* Paris: Kugelmann, 1903.

MARCELIN, Frédéric, *Bric-à-brac.* Paris: Kugelmann, 1910.

MARCELIN, Frédéric, *Thémistocle-Epaninondas Labasterre.* Paris: Ollendorf, 1901.

MARCELIN, Frédéric, *La Vengeance de Mama.* Paris: Ollendorf, 1902.

MARCELIN, Pierre, see THOBY-MARCELIN, Philippe.

MASSONI, Pierre, *Haïti, reine des Antilles.* Paris: Nlls éd. latines, 1955.

MATHON, Alix, *Le Drapeau en berne.* Port-au-Prince: no ed., 1974.

MAXIMILIEN, Louis, *Le Vodou haïtien.* Port-au-Prince: L'État, (1945?)

MERCIER, Louis, article in *Le Temps,* 29 août 1936.

MÉTRAUX, Alfred, *Haïti: la terre, les hommes et les dieux.* Neuchâtel: La Baconnière, 1957.

MÉTRAUX, Alfred, *Voodoo in Haiti.* Translated by Hugo Charteris, New York, Schocken Books, 1972. (Translation of his *Le Vaudou haïtien.* Paris: Gallimard, 1958.)

MONTAGUE, Ludwell L., *Haiti and the United States, 1714–1938.* Durham: Duke University Press, 1940.

MORAL, Paul, *Le Paysan Haïtien.* Paris: Maisonneuve et Larose, 1961.

MOREAU DE SAINT-MÉRY, Médéric, *Description . . . de la partie française de l'île Saint-Domingue,* new rev. ed., 3 vols. Paris: Soc. de l'histoire des colonies françaises, 1958. (1st ed., 1793.)

MORISSEAU-LEROY, Félix, *Antigone en créole.* Pétion-Ville: Culture, 1953.

MORISSEAU-LEROY, Félix, *Diacoute II.* Montreal: Nouvelle Optique, 1972.

MORISSEAU-LEROY, Félix, *Récolte.* Port-au-Prince: Éd. Haïtiennes, 1946.

MORISSEAU-LEROY, Félix, *Roua Kréon.* Dakar: Jadin Kreyol, 1978.

MORPEAU, Louis, *Anthologie d'un siècle de poésie haïtienne.* Paris: Bossard, 1925.

NAIPAUL, Vidiadhar S., *A House for Mr. Biswas.* New York: McGraw-Hill, 1961.

NAU, Ignace, "Isalina," *Revue des colonies,* juill.–sep. 1836.

NICHOLLS, David, *From Dessalines to Duvalier: Race, Colour and National Independence in Haiti.* London: Cambridge University Press, 1979.

NUMA, Nono, *Jénéral Rodrig.* Port-au-Prince: Bon Nouvèl, 1975.

PHELPS, Anthony, *Mémoire en colin-maillard.* Montreal: Nouvelle Optique, 1976.

PHILOCTETE, Raymond, see BARIDON, Silvio F.

PHILOCTETE, René, *Le Huitième jour.* Port-au-Prince: Éd. de l'an 2000, 1973.

PIERRE-JACQUES, Charles, "La Question scolaire en Haïti," *Collectif Paroles,* 8, sep.–nov. 1980, pp. 18–20.

POMPILUS, Pradel, *La Langue française en Haïti.* Paris: Inst. des Htes Ét. de l'Am. latine, 1961.

POMPILUS, Pradel, *Manuel illustré d'histoire de la littérature haïtienne.* Port-au-Prince: Deschamps, 1961.

PRESSOIR, Charles F., *Débats sur la culture et le folklore.* Port-au-Prince: L'État, 1947.

PRICE, Hannibal, *De la réhabilitation de la race noire par la République d'Haïti.* Port-au-Prince: Verrollot, 1900.

PRICE-MARS, Jean, *Ainsi parla l'oncle.* Paris: Impr. de Compiègne, 1928.

RIGAUD, Milo, *Jésus ou Legba?* Poitiers: Amis de la poésie, 1933.

ROTBERG, Robert I. & Christopher K. Clague, *Haiti, The Politics of Squalor.* Boston: Houghton Mifflin, 1971.

ROUMAIN, Jacques, *Analyse schématique du Parti Communiste Haïtien.* Port-au-Prince: Vve Valcin, 1934.

ROUMAIN, Jacques, *Bois d'ébène.* Port-au-Prince: Deschamps, 1945.

ROUMAIN, Jacques, *Les Fantoches.* Port-au-Prince: L'État, 1931.

ROUMAIN, Jacques, "Griefs de l'homme noir," in S.E. le Cardinal Verdier, ed.: *L'Homme de couleur.* Paris: Plon, 1939.

ROUMAIN, Jacques, *Masters of the Dew.* Translated by Langston Hughes & Mercer Cook. New York: Reynal & Hitchcock, 1947. (Translation of his *Gouverneurs de la rosée.* Port-au-Prince: L'État, 1944.)

ROUMAIN, Jacques, *La Montagne ensorcelée.* Port-au-Prince: Chassaing, 1931.

ROUMAIN, Jacques, "Le Peuple et l'élite," *Le Petit impartial,* 22 fév. 1928.

ROUZIER, Sémextan, *Dictionnaire géographique d'Haïti,* 2 vols. Paris: Impr. Blot, 1894.

ST.-JOHN, Sir Spencer, *Hayti, or the Black Republic,* 2nd ed. London: Smith, 1889. (1st ed., 1884.)

SAINT-LOUIS, Carlos & Maurice A. Lubin, *Panorama de la poésie haïtienne.* Port-au-Prince: Deschamps, 1950.

SAINT-LOUIS, René A., *La Présociologie haïtienne.* Montreal: Léméac, 1970.

SEABROOK, William B., *The Magic Island.* New York: The Literary Guild of America, 1929.

"SENTINELLE," article in *L'Opinion nationale,* 4 fév. 1893.

SHAPIRO, Norman R., ed., *Negritude—Black Poetry from Africa and the Caribbean.* New York: October House, 1970.

SMITH, Don, *Haitian Vendetta.* New York: Award Books, 1973.

STEEDMAN, Mabel, *Unknown to the World: Haiti.* London: Hurst & Blackett, 1939.

SYLVAIN, Georges, *Cric? Crac!* Paris: Ateliers haïtiens, 1901.

SYLVAIN, Normil G., "Manifeste," *La Revue indigène,* juill. 1927.

TAFT, Edna, *A Puritan in Voodooland.* Philadelphia: Penn Publ. Co., 1938.

THOBY, Armand, *Jacques Bonhomme d'Haïti.* Port-au-Prince: Smith, 1901.

THOBY-MARCELIN, Philippe & Pierre Marcelin, *Le Bête de Musseau.* New York: Éd. de la Maison française, 1946.

THOBY-MARCELIN, Philippe, *A Fonds perdu.* Paris: Seghers, 1953.

THOBY-MARCELIN, Philippe & Pierre Marcelin, *Tous les hommes sont fous.* Montreal: Nouvelle Optique, 1980.

TROUILLOT, Hénock, *Chair, sang et trahison.* Port-au-Prince: Pierre-Noël, 1977.

TROUILLOT, Michel Rolph, *Ti dife boule sou Istoua Ayiti.* Brooklyn: Lakansièl, 1977.

TUÑON DE LARA, Miguel, see AUBIER, Dominique.

UNDERWOOD, Edna W., *The Poets of Haiti, 1782–1934.* Portland, Maine: The Mosher Press, 1934.

UNITED NATIONS, *Mission to Haiti.* Lake Success, 1949.

VALCIN, Virginie, *La Blanche Négresse.* Port-au-Prince: Valcin, 1934.

VALCIN, Yvon, "Pour une promotion de la littérature nationale," *Rond Point,* 1, juill. 1962, pp. 14–17.

VALDMAN, Albert, *Le Créole.* Paris: Klincksieck, 1978.

VASTEY, Pompée Valentin, baron de, *An Essay on the Causes of the Revolution . . .* Translated by W.H.M.B., Exeter: Western Luminary Office, 1823. (Translation of his *Essai sur les causes de la révolution . . .* Sans-Souci: Impr. Royale, 1819.)

VASTEY, Pompée Valentin, baron de, *Political Remarks on Some French Works . . .* Translated for *The Pamphleteer,* London, 1818. (Translation of his *Réflexions politiques sur quelques ouvrages . . .*

Cap Henry: Impr. du Roi, 1817.)

VAVAL, Duraciné, *Histoire de la littérature haïtienne, ou l'âme noire.* Port-au-Prince: Héraux, 1933.

VERNET, E.L., *Les Pires Ennemis d'Haïti.* Port-au-Prince: Vve Valcin, 1937.

VIATTE, Auguste, *Histoire littéraire de l'Amérique française.* Quebec: Presses de l'Université Laval & Paris: PUF, 1954.

VIGNY, Alfred de, *Chatterton.* Paris: Souverain, 1835.

VILAIRE, Jean-Joseph, *Entre maîtres et esclaves.* Port-au-Prince: Telhomme, 1943.

VILLIERS, Gérard de, *Requiem pour tonton macoutes.* Paris: Plon, 1971.

WILSON, Edmund, *Red, Black, Blond, and Olive.* New York: Oxford University Press, 1956.

INDEX

A

Acaau, Jean-Jacques: 59
Alaux, Gustave d': 14
Alexis, Jacques-Stéphen: 10, 25-27, 38, 45, 46, 65, 79, 81, 82, 84, 119, 120
Alexis, Stèphen: 61, 76, 79, 81
Anon. (*La Feuille du commerce*): 44
Anon. (*Le Justicier*): 37
Anon. (*La Petite Revue*): 38
Anon. (*Le Temps*): 44
Archin-Lay, Luce: 75
Ardouin, Coriolan: 90
Aubier, Dominique: 108 (n.)

B

Baridon, Silvio: 17, 98, 103, 105, 108
Bedford-Jones, Henry: 9
Bélance, René: 83
Bellegarde, Dantès: 10, 36
Bergeaud, Émeric: 17, 51, 60, 69, 70, 77, 109-122
Bernard, Regnor C.: 105
Blot, Pétrus: 105
Bonaparte, Louis-Napoléon: 118 (n.)
Bonaparte, Napoléon: 5, 16, 78
Bontemps, Arna: 80
Borno, Camille: 36
Bourand, Étienne: 104
Boyer, Jean-Pierre: 117
Brierre, Jean-F.: 17, 23, 27, 57, 79, 83, 119
Brouard, Carl: 17, 25, 92, 95, 97, 102
Brown, John: 70, 79
Brun, Amédée: 52, 96
Burr-Reynaud, Frédéric: 42

C

Caperton, William B.: 73
Capoix: 121
Carpentier, Alejo: 27, 122

Casséus, Maurice: 24, 25, 58, 78, 79, 84
Célestin-Mégie, Émile: 41
Césaire, Aimé: 17, 51, 81, 122
Charles, Jean-Claude: 17, 85
Charmant, Rodolphe: 24
Charteris, Hugo: 9
Chaudenson, Robert: 31 (n.)
Chauvet, Henri: 100
Chauvet, Marie: 21, 25-27, 52, 57, 65, 79, 83, 119
Chenèt, Edmond: 40
Chenèt, Gérard: 27
Chenèt, Jean-Baptiste: 53
Chevallier, André: 57
Cinéas, Jean-Baptiste: 14, 24, 25, 43, 57, 64, 82, 119
Clairvaux: 121
Coicou, Massillon: 40, 52, 73
Colimon, Marie-Thérèse: 84, 85
Comhaire-Sylvain, Suzanne: 31 (n.)
Cook, Mercer: 15, 21 (n.), 42 (n.), 45 (n.)
Corneille, Pierre: 26
Courtois, Félix: 16, 79
Craige, John H.: 8, 82

D

David, Odnell: 33
Davis, Beale: 9
Davis, Harold P.: 6
Dayan, Joan: 100
Dejean, Yves: 31 (n.)
Delorme, Demesvar: 13, 37, 71, 74
Denis, Lorimer: 103
Dentu, Edmond: 111
Depestre, René: 17, 27, 38, 46, 56, 98-100, 106, 108
Deren, Maya: 107 (n.)
Despeignes, Jacquelin M.: 61
Desroy, Annie: 76, 77
Dessalines, Jean-Jacques: 6, 51, 53, 54, 75, 116, 117
Devieux-Dehoux, Liliane: 83
Dohrman, Richard: 9
Doret, Frédéric: 40
Dorsinville, Roger: 27, 61, 83
Dubé, Yves: 41 (n.)
Dumesle, Hérard: 51
Dunham, Katherine: 82
Dupoux, Antoine: 17
Durand, Oswald: 40, 98, 99, 102, 103
Duvalier, François: 7, 24, 61, 65
Duvalier, Jean-Claude: 24

E

Élie, Louis: 9
Estimé, Dumarsais: 24, 61 (n.), 62
Étheart, Liautaud: 92
Étienne, Gérard: 27, 83

F

Faine, Jules: 31 (n.)
Fanfant, Edgard: 42
Faubert, Pierre: 51, 60, 70, 71, 90, 93, 94
Firmin, Anténor: 63, 71-73
Fleischmann, Ulrich: 63
Fleury-Battier, Alcibiade: 87, 92, 101, 102
Fouchard, Jean: 38
Fouché, Franck: 27, 40, 83, 101
Fowler, Carolyn: 78
Frankétienne: 26, 40, 41, 83, 86
Franklin, Benjamin: 73

G

Gaillard, Roger: 74, 84
Garret, Naomi: 90, 92, 95, 99, 103
Gindine, Yvette: 75, 76
G.L.: 77
Glenville, Peter: 7
Gouraige, Ghislain: 14
Granier de Cassagnac, Adolphe: 36
Greene, Graham: 7
Grimard, Luc: 94, 103
Guilbaud, Tertulien: 70
Guillard, Mercédès: 63

H

Hall, Robert A.: 31 (n.)
Hector, N.: 37
Henry-Christophe: 51, 112, 117, 121
Herskovits, Melville J.: 57, 82
Hibbert, Fernand: 18, 19, 21-24, 43, 74, 119, 120
Hippolyte, Dominique: 92-94, 103, 106
Holder, Geoffrey: 9
Hughes, Langston: 15, 21 (n.), 42 (n.), 45 (n.), 80
Hugo, Victor: 8, 118 (n.), 122
Hurston, Zora Neale: 80
Hyppolite, Michelson P.: 32, 33

J

James, C.L.R.: 6
Janvier, Louis-Joseph: 37, 63
Jérémie, Cadet: 61
Johnson, Andrew: 71
Johnson, James Weldon: 80

K

Kleist, Heinrich von: 122

L

Labelle, Micheline: 101 (n.)
Lafleur, Pierre: 37
Lafontant, Delorme: 63
Laforest, Edmond: 38, 70, 91
Laleau, Léon: 17, 62, 91, 107
Lamartine, Alphonse de: 122
Lamming, George: 45
Laroche, Maximilien: 41 (n.)
Lataillade, Nerva: 106
Leclerc, Charles: 112, 115, 117, 119
Le Sage, Aimard: 63
Lescot, Élie: 24, 65
Leyburn, James G.: 82
Lhérisson, Justin: 19, 22-24, 42, 52, 61, 119, 120
Liset, Léon: 90
Lofficial, Frantz: 31 (n.)
Louhis, Léon: 94, 95
Louverture, Louis Duplessis: 90, 96
Louys, Pierre: 97
Lubin, Maurice A.: 70, 90-108

M

Magloire, Auguste: 36
Magloire, Nadine: 18, 43, 58
Magloire, Paul: 24, 61 (n.)
Magloire-Saint-Aude, Clément: 23, 42, 91
Makandal: 51
Mangonès, Victor: 95
Manigat, Leslie F.: 60 (n.)
Maran, René: 81
Marcelin, Frédéric: 19-24, 53, 62, 72-74, 119, 120
Marcelin, Philippe Thoby: See Thoby-Marcelin, Philippe

Marcelin, Pierre: See Thoby-Marcelin, Philippe & Pierre Marcelin
Massoni, Pierre: 6
Mathon, Alix: 54, 79
Maulèar-Monton: 40
Maurepas: 121
Maximilien, Louis: 21
Mayard, Constantin: 104
Mellon, William L.: 82
Ménos, Solon: 102
Mercier, Louis: 53
Métraux, Alfred: 9, 32, 107 (n.)
Michelet, Jules: 62
Milscent, Jules Solime: 89
Mistral, Frédéric: 64
Montague, Ludwell L.: 69
Moravia, Charles: 95
Moreau de Saint-Méry, Médéric: 8
Morisseau-Leroy, Félix: 26, 27, 40, 72, 80, 83
Morpeau, Louis: 95, 97-99, 102
Mussolini, Benito: 55

N

Naipaul, V.S.: 45
Napoleon I: See Bonaparte
Nau, Ignace: 41, 63
Neptune, Louis: 97
Nicholls, David: 60 (n.)
Numa, Nono: 26

P

Péralte, Charlemagne: 38
Peters, De Witt: 82
Pétion, Alexandre: 51, 112, 117
Phelps, Anthony: 17, 27, 83, 103, 119
Philoctète, Raymond: 17, 98, 103, 105, 108
Philoctète, René: 13, 103
Pierre-Jacques, Charles: 35
Pierre-Louis, Ulysse: 107
Piquion, René: 80
Pompilus, Pradel: 45, 113
Pradel, Seymour: 104
Pressoir, Charles-Fernand: 32, 96, 107
Price, Hannibal: 55
Price-Mars, Jean: 16, 38, 64, 77, 80, 118

R

Rhodes, Peter: 52

Rigaud, Andrè: 112, 114, 117, 119
Rigaud, Milo: 78
Rivet, Paul: 20
Rochambeau, Donatien: 112, 117, 119
Roumain, Jacques: 10, 15, 17, 20, 21, 23-25, 38, 42, 45, 56, 57, 59, 64, 78-82, 119, 120
Roumer, Émile: 99, 102, 105
Rouzier, Semextan: 37
Roy, Francis-Joachim: 27, 45, 83

S

St.-John, Spencer: 8, 36
St.-Louis, Carlos: 70, 90-108
Saint-Louis, Renè A.: 59, 60
Sartre, Jean-Paul: 25
Savain, Pétion: 120
Seabrook, William B.: 8, 38, 82
Séjour-Magloire, Francis: 83
"Sentinelle": 55
Shapiro, Norman: 98
Sixto, Maurice: 86
Smith, Don: 9
Sonthonax, Léger Félicité: 112, 117, 119
Soulouque, Faustin: 111, 118
Steedman, Mabel: 6
Streicher, Julius: 54
Sylvain, Georges: 36, 40
Sylvain, Normil G.: 35, 36, 105

T

Taft, Edna: 8, 54
Thènor, Auguste: 97
Thoby, Armand: 14
Thoby-Marcelin, Eva: 26
Thoby-Marcelin, Philippe: 65, 95
Thoby-Marcelin, Philippe & Pierre Marcelin: 10, 24-26, 38, 52
Tirolien, Guy: 81
Toussaint-Louverture: 51, 70, 112, 114, 117, 119, 120
Trouillot, Hénock: 64
Trouillot, Michel R.: 33
Tuñòn de Lara, Manuel: 108 (n.)

U

Underwood, Edna W.: 94 (n.), 104
United Nations: 7

V

Valcin, Virginie: 77
Valcin, Yvon: 13
Valdman, Albert: 31 (n.)
Vastey, Pompée Valentin, baron de: 51,
    54, 55, 61
Vaval, Duraciné: 41 (n.), 106
Vernet, E. Louis: 65
Viatte, Auguste: 90
Vieux, Damoclès: 90, 96
Vieux, Isnardin: 102
Vigny, Alfred de: 113
Vilaire, Jean-Joseph: 52
Villiers, Gérard de: 8
Vincent, Sténio: 24
Voegeli, Alfred: 82

W

Washington, George: 73
Wilson, Edmund: 10, 15, 26
Wordsworth, William: 122
Wright, Frances: 69

Z

Zola, Émile: 64

Liberalism with Honor

Liberalism
with Honor

Sharon R. Krause

HARVARD UNIVERSITY PRESS

Cambridge, Massachusetts

London, England

2002

Library of Congress Cataloging-in-Publication Data

Krause, Sharon R.
  Liberalism with honor / Sharon R. Krause.
    p.   cm.
  Includes bibliographical references and index.
  ISBN 0-674-00756-5 (alk. paper)
  1. Liberalism.   2. Honor.   3. Liberalism—United States.
  4. Honor—United States.   I. Title.

  JC574.U6 K73 2002
  320.51'3'0973—dc21   2001039701

For my parents,
with gratitude and admiration

CONTENTS

Preface   ix

1   Liberal Inspirations   1

    Political Agency and the Need for Inspiration   8
    Excavating Honor   21

2   Honor and the Defense of Liberty in the Old Regime   32

    The Place of Honor in the Old Regime   34
    Honor's High Ambitions   43
    Reverence and Reflexivity   47
    The Partiality of Honor   57
    Recognition and Resistance   61

3   Honor and Democracy in America   67

    The Conflict between Honor and Democracy   71
    Honor and Self-Interest Well Understood   78
    "A Little of Their Greatness"   85

4   The Love of Fame and the Southern Gentleman   97

    Honor and the Love of Fame at the Founding   100
    Slavery and the Southern Gentleman   120

5   Honor and Democratic Reform   132

    Lincoln's Principled Ambition   132
    Frederick Douglass: The Soul of Honor   144

Honor and Self-Sovereignty: Elizabeth Cady Stanton and
Susan B. Anthony   *159*
Honor in the Civil Rights Movement   *168*

6   Conclusion: Pluralism, Agency, and Varieties of
Democratic Honor   *181*

Notes   *193*

Bibliography   *247*

Index   *265*

PREFACE

Behind every book of political theory stands a *summum malum,* the one thing in political life its author most fears or despises. This book is animated by a fear of majority tyranny, a temptation to which otherwise decent democratic peoples have a long history of occasionally yielding. Anyone who has ever been on the outside of the majority's opinion, identity, or way of life has felt the fragility of what James Madison called the "parchment barriers" that protect individual liberties in constitutional democracies, and has sensed (if only as the passing of a shadow) the possibility of majority tyranny. There are many ways to approach the problem of majority tyranny as a political theorist; in my case this concern has led to an interest in political agency, because it is agency that generates the possibility of resistance to majorities that go bad. As used in this study, "individual agency" refers to the capacity for intentional, self-initiated action. It goes beyond the act itself to the moral psychology that stands behind the act. Agency implies an awareness of oneself *as* agent, a confidence in one's ability to act, rather than simply react, and to shape, not merely endure, events and the circumstances of one's life. The theme of agency has been relatively unexplored by political theorists in recent years, particularly the sources of agency, or the forms of motivation that support it. Honor is one such source.

What honor is and how it inspires individual agency is the subject of this book. Americans today are ambivalent about the possibility of agency. On the one hand, we celebrate and strive to accommodate the individual power of choice, and hence agency. Never before in the history of humankind have so many apparent choices been on offer in matters ranging from health plans, retirement accounts, and frozen dinners to religion, work, and love. Recent advances in science and technology, which are poised to put the power to engineer life itself into human hands, seem to make us the masters of even more than our own destinies. On the other hand, we have been educated by a generation of theorists about the power of our circumstances to construct our identities and determine our actions. Race, class, and gender are sometimes given all the credit for what we do or fail to do. Add to these factors the impersonal forces of a global economy and the "iron triangle" of interest-group politics, and the capacity for individual agency appears to be little more than a chimera. We are of two minds when it comes to the question of agency, torn between the promise of limitless choice and the seemingly inexorable power of circumstance.

It may even be that we speak the language of choice so emphatically today precisely because we feel so constrained—as a hopeful assertion of the truth rather than an accurate reflection of our experience. The special "bills of rights" that have proliferated in recent years (patients', victims', parents', children's, now even air travelers') speak more to a feeling of powerlessness and the need for protection from forces beyond one's control than to new freedoms. Our lost faith in individual agency is reflected, too, in the nature of our lawsuits. That one can spill hot coffee in one's lap and successfully sue for damages the fast food franchise where it was purchased is an indication of the degree to which we do not recognize individual responsibility because we do not fully believe in individual agency. The treatment of tobacco companies (nobody's heroes) also demonstrates our collective ambivalence in this regard. We are reluctant to regulate the tobacco industry or ban the sale of its products because doing so would infringe on individual choice, and so agency. And yet we sue the same companies for the consequences of the free and informed choices of individuals who smoke. By denying the responsibility of the smokers in such cases, we implicitly deny their power of agency. Smokers, we seem to say, are pawns rather than agents in their own life histories; not they but the tobacco companies are the masters of their destinies. We refuse to regulate because we do not wish to limit our power of agency; we sue because we do not believe in our power of agency. This is the mark of our ambivalence. We are not entirely convinced that we are agents and yet we very much wish to be free.

So this is a book about honor but it is also a book about individual agency. It joins a familiar effort now under way in political theory to invigorate the civic sources of liberal democracy, but it brings a new purpose and new resources to this effort. Unlike previous contributions, the book joins the debate not primarily to improve the morals of American citizens or make American democracy more participatory as an end in it-self, but rather for the sake of revitalizing individual agency. To realize this purpose the book introduces a new resource (or newly recalls us to an old resource) in the form of honor. Recent efforts to identify sources of civic renewal for American democracy, or motivational supports for liberalism in general, have centered on obligations to others. Whether in the form of civic virtue, liberal virtues, the Rawlsian sense of justice, or Scanlon's "agreement motive," these supports all emphasize what we owe to others or to the polity as a whole. Such obligations are important, but they are not the only ones—or even the main ones—that motivate risky and difficult actions in defense of individual liberty. And because obligations to others require altruism, they are always at odds with the self-interest that predominates in modern liberal societies. By contrast, honor rests on the sense of duty to oneself. Since it never renounces self-concern, honor does not require altruism and consequently has a natu-ral (if partial) affinity with the liberal way of life. Yet while honor is self-serving, it is not limited to the lowest forms of self-interest. Honor rises above the natural limits on human action imposed by the motive of ego-istic interest. As a result, it can animate riskier and more difficult ac-tions, even actions that involve the risk of life. Honor is more reliable than altruistic obligations to others and braver than self-interest. This combination of qualities makes honor a powerful source of individual agency especially in cases where the risks of action are high and its bene-fits uncertain, as when one rises to defend individual liberties against encroaching political power or the threat of majority tyranny. Yet for all its potential as a source of civic renewal in American politics, honor has been almost entirely overlooked by contemporary political theorists.

One reason for this neglect is honor's aristocratic associations. The language of honor smacks of privilege and exclusion, fixed social roles and frivolous duels. It seems obsolete today, a part of a world that was renounced at the end of the eighteenth century and undone by the Rights of Man. There is no denying the antipathies between honor and modern democracy, but the old-regime trappings of honor are not the whole of it. Honor also embodies deep and enduring features of individ-ual agency. It is only partly rooted in the social and political conventions that change from one regime to another. The French Revolution did not annihilate the possibility of honor, because it did not fundamentally change human nature. And because political power, as Madison said, has an ineradicable tendency to encroach, the need for occasional acts of resistance to encroaching power in defense of individual liberties will never go out of style. The French Revolution did not make such resistance obsolete. Honor is needed by modern democracy and it is available to modern democracy, albeit in modified form.

The modifications to honor in the new regime leave intact key features of honor as a quality of character, not least the sense of duty to oneself that is such a powerful source of agency. Moreover, while most of the time liberal democracy can get by with good citizens, occasionally it needs great ones. The heroic qualities at the heart of honor answer to this need: high and principled ambition, courage, pride, and the powerful desires for self-respect and public distinction. This combination of qualities is not the special attribute of a single social class, but neither is it commonly held. It marks out a natural aristocracy consisting of the few individuals who, when pressed, will rise to defend their principles and their liberties despite the risks. By highlighting honor, this book calls attention to a neglected but important motivation and thus offers a corrective to the present partiality of political theory in the area of moral psychology. The book brings the issue of agency to the fore, exploring the structure and the sources of individual agency and urging further study. And if it succeeds in moving the study of agency closer to the center of political theory, the book will have accomplished one final goal, which is to shine the light of philosophy on a dark corner of contemporary American public life and thereby bring new clarity to what has come to be a matter of deep, even debilitating, confusion.

Many thanks are due to the teachers, colleagues, friends, family, foundations, and institutions that have supported the research and writing of this book. First mention must be made of Harvey Mansfield, who introduced me to the study of political philosophy. His inspiration, guidance, questions, disagreements, and generosity embody what is best in a liberal education, and in a friend. Michael Sandel and Peter Berkowitz also provided invaluable direction and support as teachers and advisors. Several friends and colleagues read portions of the manuscript in various stages and offered helpful commentary and conversation, including Barbara Allen, Ben Berger, Peter Cannavo, Paul Carrese, David Carrithers, Robert Eden, Jill Frank, Istvan Hont, David Kim, Steve Lenzner, Don Moon, Peter Myers, Paul Rahe, Nancy Schwartz, and Delba Winthrop. I am especially grateful to Michael Mosher and Andy Sabl, who read the whole manuscript and offered incisive and knowledgeable criticism. At Harvard University Press, I thank Michael Aronson for his sage editorial advice and Elizabeth Gilbert for her careful and informed editing. The book would never have materialized without the unfailing backing of my family, especially my partner, Tayhas, whose love and loyalty and adventurous heart make everything seem possible.

The project was supported from beginning to end by grants from the Mellon Foundation, the Kennedy Foundation for Research in France, Harvard University, the Earhart Foundation, Wellesley College, and the John M. Olin Foundation. My thanks go also to Wesleyan University, which administered the Olin Foundation Faculty Fellowship that supported the completion of the book, and to Harvard University, which arranged leave time for that purpose. An earlier draft of Chapter 2 appeared as "The Politics of Distinction and Disobedience: Honor and the Defense of Liberty in Montesquieu," *Polity,* 31, no. 3 (Spring 1999): 469–499. I am grateful to the editor of that journal for permission to use the article here in revised form.

Liberalism with Honor

1

Liberal Inspirations

Why do men and women sometimes risk their necks to defend their liberties? One thinks first of soldiers who defend the collective liberty against foreign enemies, but in liberal democracies individual liberties sometimes need defense as well, and from internal aggressors rather than external ones—think of Martin Luther King, Jr.'s defense of civil rights for blacks, for example, or Elizabeth Cady Stanton's defense of women's suffrage. For all its advantages, democracy is distinctly vulnerable to the problem of majority tyranny. Hence democratic peoples must attend to the defense of individual liberties within the polity even as they protect the collective liberty from foreign enemies. Both types of defense rest on strong exertions of individual agency, the capacity for intentional, self-initiated action. What sustains this capacity for agency in soldiers and activists such as King and Stanton? What inspires the spirited defense of liberty, especially when the risks are high and the benefits uncertain?

The spirited defense of liberty once was explained as a point of honor, as when the first Americans pledged to defend their independence with "our Lives, our Fortunes, and our sacred Honor."[1] But we rarely speak of honor today. The language of honor went out of fashion with the French Revolution, along with powdered wigs and silk hose with breeches. These days honor seems quaint and obsolete, even frivolous, and it makes us vaguely suspicious.[2] Honor has always received mixed reviews, of course, arousing admiration, envy, and contempt all at once, with the result that those receiving honors today are forever in danger of being run out of town tomorrow.[3] And modern democrats even more than others have reason to distrust honor, because the distinctions it draws seem to run afoul of democratic equality.

Honor is a multifaceted phenomenon that includes (a) *public honors* in the form of external recognition; (b) *codes of honor;* and (c) honor as a *quality of character,* the ambitious desire to live up to one's code and to be publicly recognized for doing so. In spite of our contemporary distrust, the various facets of honor still play a role in American democracy, even capturing center stage from time to time. "Honoring F.D.R." is how one newspaper headline described the recent dedication of a new presidential memorial, for example. Similarly, we have a postal stamp that "honors" Rosa Parks, and the parents of schoolchildren who make the honor roll sometimes brag about it by displaying bumper stickers on the rear fenders of their cars: "My Child Is an Honor Student at Central Junior High School." The practice of building monuments, awarding prizes, and displaying bumper stickers in recognition of special achievements is not unfamiliar to us. Public honors reward excellence. They are pleasant for their (living) recipients and they are good for the rest of us, who thereby are shown a high standard and given an incentive to pursue it. And public honors seek to win us over to the high standards they reward by a policy of attraction rather than coercion; they make difficult achievements desirable but not mandatory. Public honors are *inspiring* in the literal sense that they arouse the spiritedness in us, stirring up the ambitious desires that drive extraordinary efforts. In this sense, public honors offer a truly liberal form of education: they teach us without commanding us.

Yet if public honors please our liberal attachment to freedom, they are less friendly to our democratic love of equality. Public honors are always distributed unequally. Not every parent is entitled to display an honor-roll bumper sticker on the rear fender of the family car; not all presidents are endowed with monuments. Most of the time, most of us accept distributive inequalities like these. We know that equalizing public honors would result in either coercion or insignificance. Either we would need to force everyone to meet standards that are higher than most people could or would choose to meet, or we would need to lower the standards to a level that would make their achievement automatic for everyone. Yet if public honors were automatic they would have as much appeal, and as little to teach us, as our social security numbers. Public honors can inspire us only if they are distributed unequally.

Public honors in the form of external recognition are not the only familiar form of honor today, either. We have other uses for the word, as when the occasional college exam is administered on the basis of an "honor code." The honor code is an obligation, not an award, and it articulates a rule of conduct. In the context of a college exam, adhering to the honor code means resisting the temptation to cheat. This usage also implies a quality of character: the student who adheres to the honor code has an honorable character, or she possesses the quality that we call honor. In contrast to public honors, honor as a quality of character is an internal phenomenon. One can be true to the code without receiving public recognition for it. In fact, the honor code typically is invoked to restrain us from temptations when no authority is present to supervise, or recognize, our actions. After all, no honor code is needed for exams that are overseen by official proctors who check identity cards, keep time, and watch for wandering eyes. Instead, the honor code is called upon when an exam is to be taken without supervision, when the student must oversee herself. She is responsible for ensuring that *she* takes the test rather than hiring someone else to take it for her, that she stays within the time limit, that she refrains from looking up the answers in her textbook, and so on. The honorable student adheres to the honor code out of self-respect, not from fear of reprisals or the promise of public approval. She owes it to herself to live up to the code; to do otherwise would be to let herself down. Her reward is personal gratification, the pleasure of having resisted the allures of the ring of Gyges.

The student who resists such temptations for the sake of her self-respect displays a special kind of independence. She shows herself to be in command of herself and not commanded by her lowest impulses, or the opinions of others, or fear. Her independence is the mark of individual agency, the power to act rather than merely to be acted upon. It calls to mind Kant's notion of autonomy, but it is not the same as autonomy, partly because one who abides by the honor code accepts its standard ("Don't cheat") as given. She submits her will to the authority of a standard that is external to her will, and so she is not the author of the code that guides her as Kantian autonomy requires. Yet because of the cloak of invisibility under which her action takes place, she herself must enforce the standard. She must be her own authority figure rather than depending on someone else to supervise her into right action. Honor as a quality of character implies self-command.

If honor in this form bears a (limited) resemblance to autonomy, it also looks something like virtue. Like virtue, honor is in part a quality of character and a form of excellence. And honor motivates the honorable student to adhere to the honor code because of the pleasure of self-respect that it produces. The idea that there is a pleasure (self-respect) that is higher than the pleasure of an unjustly high grade recalls Aristotle's account of the hierarchy of happiness in the *Nicomachean Ethics*.[4] Virtuous actions produce a kind of pleasure in us, Aristotle says, one that is more complete and more noble than the pleasures of the body, albeit less perfect than the pleasure of contemplation. The pleasures produced by virtue make it desirable and so motivate us to act, and to act well. Like virtue, and unlike Kantian autonomy, honor is desirable in the sense that it rewards us with a form of pleasure, and it uses our desire for pleasure as a way of motivating our action. The pleasures produced by honor, like those of virtue, rise above the pleasures produced by the satisfaction of the appetites. It is because of the promise of pleasures that stand above the appetites that honor can sometimes forsake simple self-interest to pursue principled ends.

The resemblance between honor and virtue makes one wonder why we speak of the honor code rather than the "virtue code." The idea of a virtue code is almost nonsensical, however, for a code articulates general rules of conduct whereas a virtue refers to a particular excellence of character. On this basis we distinguish ancient "virtue-centered" theories of moral and political obligation from modern "rule-governed" ones.[5] A rule is a command or a general obligation imposed from the outside; an excellence of character is a particular right desire within. The form of honor implied by the honor code does not fit easily into either category because it draws on both. Honor is both a quality of character and rule-governed. It is the quality of character that makes one wish to live up to certain rules of conduct, a particular desire to uphold a general obligation. And whereas rules tell us what to do, virtues articulate ways of being. It is true that virtuous ways of being also issue in action. Honor and virtue converge in their emphasis on action and agency. Yet to be virtuous one should study how the best person meets a variety of particular situations, rather than follow a fixed set of general prescriptions. To be an honorable student, by contrast, one need only adhere to the general tenets of the code, which apply universally, or at least to all students. Consequently, there is no mean with respect to following the honor code. Honor has a categorical quality: either you follow the rules or you are a cheater. And the rules apply in the same way to everyone who takes the exam, unlike a virtue, where the mean that constitutes the virtue is in some measure relative to the individual and the circumstances.[6] Looking up the answers in the textbook is a violation of the honor code under any circumstances. Honor is more than a virtue because it combines a quality of character, a particular right desire, with general rules of conduct, and consequently cannot be collapsed simply into the category of virtue.[7]

The form of honor that is at stake in the honor code is grounded in an obligation to oneself rather than a duty to others, which distinguishes it from contemporary conceptions of civic virtue. The civic virtue that political theorists sometimes invoke today emphasizes citizens' duties to one another and the political community, rather than to themselves. Civic virtue conceived in this way means putting oneself aside for the sake of the whole, sacrificing one's individual interest to the common good, or at least identifying one's interests with the common good. By contrast, one abides by the honor code not primarily for the sake of others but for one's own sake: one owes it to oneself to take the test fairly, to meet the challenge and master it. And whereas a failure of civic virtue does harm to others and to the whole, one fails *oneself* when one violates the honor code. Cheaters may inflate the curve and this could disadvantage other test-takers, but the real harm that comes from violating the honor code comes to the cheaters themselves, who then must live with themselves without grounds for respecting themselves. It is true that the honorable student may suffer a real loss if her honest performance yields a lower grade than what she could have had by cheating. Yet the sacrifice she makes in this case is not for the sake of others. Instead, she sacrifices what she considers to be a lower good so that she may win a higher one. It is her own good that she has in mind, and despite the loss of the higher grade the honorable student feels herself to be a winner in the end because of the good of self-respect she gains. On the whole, it is good for everyone if everyone abides by the honor code, but the intention that lies behind obedience to the code is not the good of others or the common good but one's own good, the good of self-respect. Even though the honor code implies a common standard and serves a common purpose, the motivation that drives it is self-serving and its direct aim is individualistic, the personal desire for self-respect.[8]

To be sure, there are other forms of virtue that do not involve the collectivism of contemporary civic virtue but center instead on duties to oneself. The Aristotelian virtue of magnanimity is one example, which is defined as "complete virtue" directed toward oneself.[9] The magnanimous man cultivates the moral virtues for his own sake, because he sees that being magnanimous is a more complete and so more desirable way of living. He owes it to himself. We admire him for the completeness of his character because in him we see all forms of moral excellence shine forth. By contrast, we admire the honorable student not for the completeness of her character so much as for her strength of character; not because she displays all the virtues but because she demonstrates self-command. She will not be overcome by the impulse to cheat, whatever the consequences, because she will not be the slave even of her own interests. The student who lives up to the honor code prefers her principles to her interests, or lets her interests be guided by her principles. She acts, rather than simply reacting to the pressures of her circumstance. She may not be generous or temperate or friendly or witty or truthful or munificent or virtuous in any other respect, but she is her own mover. Being honorable, in contrast to being magnanimous, results in self-mastery rather than the perfection of the soul.

Honor does presuppose a certain teleology, if only a partial one. It implies distinctions between higher and lower, especially the distinction between living free through the power of self-command, or the exercise of individual agency, and acting as the instrument of someone else's will, or one's own necessities, or the impersonal forces of circumstance. There is something intrinsically admirable in the ambitious desire to live up to a principled code of conduct, in seeking self-respect on principled grounds, in aiming to fulfill what one takes to be an important duty to oneself. Honor as a quality of character engages more of the complex capacities that distinguish human beings from other creatures than does, say, the unreflective pursuit of appetite. The capacity for honor is among the things that distinguish human beings from the rest of nature, and individual acts of honor distinguish a few human beings from the rest of us. Of course, the capacity for evil is also distinctively human. It, too, engages complex capacities unknown to the lower animals. Malice is more fully human than careless disregard. To say that one action is "more fully human" than another, then, is to give only an incomplete account of its moral worth. The goodness and justice of any particular form of honor necessarily depend on the moral content of its codes. But when its codes are good and just, honor is more than good and just: it is also noble. This is the sense in which the teleology that honor entails is only partial. Honor presupposes that self-command is better than its opposite, but it does not presuppose comprehensive knowledge of the human good or the perfection of the soul. The teleology of honor places self-command above subservience but it does not itself define the ends toward which the self-commanding agent aims. Perhaps because honor is not a mark of perfection, we pay our respects to honorable individuals (as when we visit the Lincoln Memorial or the Washington Monument) but we do not pray to them. Similarly, "honorable mention" is worth noting but is not the highest prize; and when one's team makes it into postseason play one can say that it made an honorable showing even if it did not go all the way. Insofar as honor supports individual agency without promising or requiring the perfection of the soul, it is compatible with liberal forms, purposes, and character.

The substantive content of particular codes of honor may not always contain principles that are compatible with liberalism, however. Honor can serve illiberal as well as liberal ideals, as the case of honor and slavery in the American South explored in Chapter 4 suggests. More generally, to say that honor is compatible with liberal purposes and liberal characters is not to say that liberal thinkers have always treated honor warmly. Early liberals (and quasi-liberals) such as Hobbes and Locke saw the love of honor as a contributor to the ills of humanity's natural condition, on the grounds that it may make persons quixotically idealistic and even warlike. The desire to be a hero may turn into a desire to slay dragons, or to search perpetually for (and even invent) opportunities for heroism. It is not only democrats, then, who have had occasion to object to honor. Yet as we shall see, moderate forms of honor guided by liberal codes not only are compatible with both liberalism and democracy, but have an irreplaceable role to play in liberal-democratic politics.

If we rarely speak of honor today, and then only with some discomfort, we have reason to reconsider it, because individual agency in the United States is in need of liberal inspirations. Despite our present prosperity, there is a widespread sense today that Americans are losing control of the forces that govern their lives.[10] Our beleaguered sense of agency cuts across the familiar cleavages of race, class, and gender. The inner-city poor may feel especially disenfranchised, but they are not the only ones to feel disempowered. In the face of a globalizing economy, big-money politics, escalating environmental crises, entrenched racial tensions and disparities, pervasive gender inequities, and the alarming deterioration of public education, the suburban middle class, too, seems to regard itself as subject to forces that elude its grasp. Rich or poor, white or black, male or female, today we are all, it seems, victims of our circumstances.

Or rather, it *seems* to us that we are the victims of our circumstances. We have lost faith in ourselves as the agents of our destinies. Perhaps this partly accounts for the dramatic rise of communities of faith in the United States in the last generation, especially fundamentalist religious denominations.[11] The rise of faith-based communities reflects, at least in part, a lost faith in individual agency and an effort to recover it through spiritual resources. To replenish the faith in our capacity for agency that is the precondition of constitutional democracy and individual liberty, we need new inspiration. And we ought not rely only on religious inspiration, which, particularly when it is fundamentalist in origin, may threaten the toleration, diversity, and individual liberty that are the cornerstones of liberal democracy. To restore faith in the strong capacity for agency that supports liberal democracy in America, Americans need liberal inspirations.

Political Agency and the Need for Inspiration

A strong capacity for agency is important to liberal democracy because, as James Madison said, political power is "of an encroaching nature."[12] The American founders agreed with Montesquieu that "every man who has any power tends to abuse it. He goes until he finds some limits."[13] Today we have Watergate, the Iran-Contra affair, Whitewater, independent counsels, and congressional ethics committees to remind us of this ineradicable feature of political power. And the problem of encroaching power is even more complex in modern liberal democracies than it was for the old regimes that Montesquieu knew. For in liberal democracies, Madison said, "it is necessary not only to guard the society against the oppression of its rulers, but also to guard one part of the society against the injustice of the other part."[14] The specter of majority tyranny always haunts governments that are based on the principle of popular sovereignty. Along with overreaching executives and unscrupulous legislators, then, we must be on our guard against such developments as Jim Crow laws or Colorado's Amendment Two targeting homosexuals, efforts by one part of the society to restrict the individual liberties of another part. In the United States, a Constitution of separate powers, federalism, and the Bill of Rights all set formal limits on the will of majorities and the powers of government. Yet the formal limits specified by our Constitution are only "parchment barriers"[15] without the springs of individual agency that set them in motion: American liberties need spirited guardians.

Formal liberties, then, can be effective only where there is a will to use and defend them. But what is the character of this will? What motivates the spirited defense of individual liberties, especially in the face of obvious risks and indeterminate benefits? This question has been largely neglected in political theory in recent years, as efforts to specify the meaning of justice and political legitimacy have taken center stage. To the extent that political theorists do attend to the question of motivations today, they divide between the proponents of rational choice theory, who emphasize the motive of self-interest, and those who defend some form of obligations to others. The latter group admits of significant diversity.[16] It includes the communitarians and civic republicans who recommend civic virtue as well as the liberals who invoke "liberal virtues," or the Rawlsian "sense of justice," or Scanlon's "agreement motive." On the civic-republican view, it is a love of the common good or a sense of civic duty that moves citizens to act in politics.[17] Thus to ensure that individuals obey good laws and resist bad laws, it is necessary to cultivate the virtues of citizenship. This means that government must engage in the formation of citizen character. Statecraft is soulcraft, or at the very least statecraft is "selfcraft."[18] One problem with communitarian and civic-republican theories of virtue, as has frequently been noted, is that they run the risk of submerging particular identities in a collective identity and may require the state to play a strongly formative role in the cultivation of virtue. This can threaten the diversity and the individual liberty that are the hallmarks of liberal democracy. And while civic virtue accounts for the shared habits, common identity, and collective vision that support participatory democracy, the collectivism of civic virtue does not easily accommodate individual ambition or support the spirited defense of individual liberties when they contravene the collective (or majority) will.

In an effort to avoid the risks of communitarian and civic-republican virtue, a few liberal theorists have offered their own accounts of "liberal virtues."[19] Liberal virtues are qualities of character that sustain a minimal level of civility in pluralistic societies and support the institutional procedures of liberal government. Toleration often is mentioned in this regard, along with self-restraint and respect for persons. These liberal virtues largely do avoid the problems of exclusion and coercion that attend communitarian and civic-republican conceptions of virtue. Yet important as they are for liberal-democratic government, these liberal virtues also are incomplete. Toleration and self-restraint cannot explain what Rosa Parks did, for example; they do not account for the motivations that animate risky and unusually ambitious forms of action. They are not robust enough to explain great exertions of individual agency.

Despite the differences between them, and leaving aside the particular problems attendant on each one, civic-republican and liberal virtues are alike in being obligations to others. In this respect, the liberal sense of justice and the agreement motive are no different. John Rawls defines the sense of justice as "the willingness . . . to act in relation to others on terms that they also can publicly endorse."[20] The agreement motive likewise moves us to carry out "what we owe to others," which is to live together with them on terms that no one could reasonably reject.[21] These motives are troubled in their own ways by problems of exclusivity and reliability,[22] but the main point for present purposes is that the liberal sense of justice and the agreement motive are obligations to others, and they share their other-regarding orientation with civic-republican and liberal virtues as they are commonly conceived. No sensible person would deny the importance of obligations to others in liberal democracy or any other regime. The sense of duty to others provides a crucial corrective to the potential narrowness and egoism of self-interest, qualities that can make living together difficult or render impossible the large-scale collective projects that political life often requires. Yet the obligations to others implicit in the sense of justice and the agreement motive rest on a measure of altruism that is at odds with the self-centered ethos of modern liberalism.[23] And altruism is notoriously unreliable in politics. In the impersonal arena of the public sphere, where the "others" whom we owe are mainly strangers, the particular bonds of love, friendship, solidarity, and the like, which sustain altruism in other arenas, are largely unavailable. Outside these particular relations of care, what we owe to others tends to have, on the whole, a weaker pull than what we owe (or think we owe) to ourselves. Altruism is perfectly possible, to be sure; most of us have some firsthand experience of it. But altruism is undependable. This familiar fact is one reason for the modern rejection of political systems that require altruism to sustain them, a rejection that unites such otherwise diverse moderns as Machiavelli, Hobbes, Montesquieu, Kant, and Madison.

The conflict between self-interest and the sense of obligation to others has fueled an increasingly polarized debate within political theory between the "realist" proponents of rational choice theory, who seek to explain action on the basis of self-interest alone, and the communitarians, civic republicans, and liberals who emphasize the importance of various duties to others. The strict division of motivations between self-interest and duties to others is a familiar feature of contemporary thought but it is not a particularly productive one. Too often today, our thinking on matters of moral psychology is confined within the limits of these dichotomous categories: interests are what we do for ourselves, it is thought, whereas obligations are what we owe to others. Yet what we do for ourselves ought not be limited to our interests, and what we owe to others does not exhaust our obligations. The contemporary dichotomy leaves out a whole class of motives based on the sense of duty to oneself, of which honor is one. And while honor sometimes requires the sacrifice of certain interests, as a duty to oneself it never renounces self-concern. Thus it does not rest on altruism, which makes it friendly to the liberal way of life. At the same time, honor can animate actions that self-interest, at least conventionally conceived, never would allow, including actions that put one's life in jeopardy in the name of principled ends. It is more reliable than altruism but also spirited and courageous, which makes it a powerful source of individual agency.

The incompleteness of contemporary political theory on the subject of moral psychology is not limited to the neglect of obligations to oneself. Also missing is an acknowledgment of liberal democracy's need for heroic qualities of character—if only on occasion and only in a few. The motives most frequently mentioned by political theorists today rest on qualities that are held to be (if only by the theorists who recommend them) common. Civic virtue, liberal virtues, the sense of justice, and the agreement motive are egalitarian, even though they rely on altruism. They are demanding because they conflict with self-interest, but they are equally demanding and demanding in the same way for all of us. Exceptional qualities and extraordinary efforts are not thought to be required; one need not be a hero to have civic virtue or a sense of justice. These obligations represent societywide ideals, and the regimes they serve can only operate successfully if they motivate all citizens on a regular basis, or at least most citizens most of the time. Consequently, in a well-or-dered civic republic there is nothing distinctive about a virtuous citizen, and nothing exceptional in a Rawlsian liberal democracy about citizens with a sense of justice. Such citizens are no more and no less than what one would expect.

Even in well-ordered polities, however, the encroaching nature of po-litical power means that things sometimes can go wrong. Moreover, American liberal democracy is a hybrid regime, which holds in balance the potentially conflicting principles and practices of individual liberty and popular sovereignty. The balance is not exactly precarious because it has the backing of a written and revered Constitution, but neither is it perfectly impervious to assault. When things go wrong, as they some-times will, and individual liberties come under threat, something more than what is usually expected of citizens may be required of them, or of some of them. In these moments, extraordinary exertions of individual agency may be called for. So even though liberal democracy normally can get by with good or even mediocre citizens, on occasion it needs great ones. The particular combination of qualities intrinsic to honor support heroic action: high and principled ambition, courage, pride, and the desires for self-respect and public esteem. It is neither necessary nor possible for this combination of qualities to be universally held. And however much it needs great citizens, liberal democracy does not need every citizen to be great; indeed, an abundance of heroic types could only be a mixed blessing to any polity.[24] Moreover, while most Ameri-cans are decent folks, few of us could match the shining examples of a Lincoln, or a Washington, or a Frederick Douglass, or an Elizabeth Cady Stanton. Such exceptional citizens protect and serve our liberties, and they also vindicate our faith in individual agency. We ordinary citizens are reminded by the examples they provide that we, too, are more than the victims of our circumstances. If most of us never will fully realize the extraordinary capacity for agency such individuals exemplify, neverthe-less we can aim in that direction. They inspire us to reach for the exer-cise of agency that too often seems to elude us, and in so reaching we may become more fully the agents of our destinies and defenders of our liberties than we otherwise would be.[25] In this respect, honor can inform the lives of all democratic citizens, but unlike some other qualities (such as egalitarian civic virtue, for instance) honor is not a characteristic that is likely to be held in equal measure by all citizens, even though in modern democracies it is open to all.

The qualities inherent in honor that sometimes animate great exertions of agency are irreducibly aristocratic if only in the sense that they are not commonly held, although anyone may hold them and in democratic societies all of us can reach for them. Liberal democracy's occasional need for great citizens is one reason to resist the myth that "modern man" can do without aristocratic honor, at least honor that is aristocratic in this sense. It is a common belief that in the wake of the French Revolution the newly minted modern man traded his honor for the universal status of democratic dignity and never looked back.[26] No one can deny that the modern period ushered in changes in how we conceive of human identities. Whereas premodern cultures and polities identified the individual with his or her social role and institutional status, modern politics regards the "solitary self," devoid of roles and status, as the ultimate ground of personal identity, at least in the political context.[27] "Modern man is Don Quixote on his deathbed, denuded of the multicolored banners that previously enveloped the self and senses," as one interpreter writes.[28] Honor in the old regime was in large part an expression of external status, of one's place in the fixed hierarchy of traditional society, and one's sense of honor was constitutively tied to the particular social role that one inherited. By contrast, individuals in the modern world are not identified with any social roles in particular, especially not hereditary roles. At least we are not, in principle, politically identified with such roles. Social roles and the expectations that go with them continue to exert a powerful influence on individuals today. But most of our roles are chosen rather than inherited, and our political status is independent of all of them, based instead on the ideal of intrinsic human dignity, which applies universally to all persons and establishes a rudimentary equality between them. Because the modern ideal abstracts from (at least in principle) the socially imposed roles and norms that gave content to honor in the old regime, this ideal and the new conditions it serves are said to have led "to the liquidation of honor altogether."[29] The only place for honor is thought to be the now repudiated world of "intact, stable institutions where individuals possess certain attachments between their identities and the institutional roles that society assigns them."[30]

It is true that the role of honor is more circumscribed in modern democracies than it was before the French Revolution. Honor is not *the* spring of modern democracy as it was in the Old World—the passion, as Montesquieu said, that made all the parts of the body politic move. In the new regime, honor competes with a range of other motives, some of which are more consistently supported by democratic institutions and practices than is honor. But the fact that honor is more rare today does not diminish its importance, since even rare instances of honor can have wide and lasting effects. And there should be nothing mysterious in the fact that liberal democracy sometimes leans on motives that it does not regularize. More to the point, the myth of honor's obsolescence is based on an incomplete understanding of what honor is. It reflects a mistake to which Tocqueville drew attention in *Democracy in America,* which is to confuse one type of honor (old-regime or feudal honor) with the whole of it, not seeing the variability of honor, its capacity to adapt and to serve different regimes and the personal identities they inculcate. The modern abandonment of hereditary social roles and fixed, hierarchical status liquidates one form of honor but it does not entail the wholesale disintegration of honor. The sources of personal identity have changed, and they now include the ideal of democratic dignity, but honor in the modern world partially incorporates this change and is by no means wholly undone by it.

The reason that honor can incorporate changes in personal identity is that honor has roots in human nature that run deeper. There is more to human nature than personal identity, including the capacities for courage, pride, high and principled ambition, the sense of duty to oneself, and the desires for self-respect and public distinction. These capacities, which are central features of honor as a quality of character, survive changes in the cultural factors that help shape personal identities. Honor as a quality of character is partly conventional because it interacts with conventional aspects of personal identity, but honor also rests on features of human nature that are more than merely conventional. Far from destroying honor, the personal identity of modern man denuded of social roles and institutional positions supports its own form of honor, as the American founders emphatically asserted. In fact, the founders regarded the fixed social roles and political inequalities associated with the old regime as affronts to what they called "the honor of the human race."[31] They associated honor directly with the dignity of the individual and the democratic self-rule it justified. The American system, they said, "vindicates the honor of the human race"[32]—not by upholding standards attached to some particular social role but by demonstrating the human power of self-determination, which is a universal phenomenon. The American experiment vindicates the honor of the human race by showing that there is more to humankind than its circumstances and its conventional identities. In the process, it demonstrates that there is more to honor than institutional roles and social status.

The fact that honor is more than roles and status, that as a quality of character it engages fundamental human capacities, distinguishes honor from the ideal of intrinsic dignity that is said to have replaced it. Charles Taylor describes this ideal as "the modern notion of dignity, now used in a universalist and egalitarian sense, where we talk of the inherent 'dignity of human beings,' " the underlying premise of which is that "everyone shares in it."[33] This ideal is the founding principle of the United Nations' Universal Declaration of Human Rights, for instance.[34] Dignity in this sense is a given, not an achievement. It is a fixed status that attaches to all persons. Everyone has dignity and has it in the same measure inherently, which means independently of one's particular conditions and actions. Dignity conceived in this way is impossible to lose. One need not do anything distinctive to keep or claim one's dignity; indeed, one need not act at all, for there is no necessary connection between dignity as an intrinsic status and action. Brave or timid, ambitious or lethargic, awake or even asleep, one is in possession of one's intrinsic worth as a human being, or one's equal dignity.

It should be clear from this description that honor as a quality of character and the ideal of intrinsic dignity are fundamentally different sorts of phenomena, and that comparing them is akin to comparing apples and tennis racquets. The assertion of honor's obsolescence is based in part on the faulty premise that a quality of character can be exchanged for and replaced by an ideal of fixed status. The mistake is understandable, because besides being a quality of character the term honor also can refer to public honors, which are tied to status and so are on a par with the ideal of dignity as a form of status, and because in the old regime the external aspects of honor as status had a tendency to predominate over honor as a quality of character. Although the mistake is understandable, however, it is misleading. Dignity cannot simply replace honor because the two are not equivalent terms; there is a remainder between them comprising the courage, pride, high and principled ambition, and the rest that constitute honor as a quality of character.

The idea of inherent dignity provides a valuable justification for equal political rights and universal human rights as well as a standard for assessing the legitimacy of the laws and public policies of particular governments. As such it is irreplaceable, and in liberal democracies the standard set by democratic dignity should never be forgotten. Yet sometimes this standard must be surpassed, if only because the defense of the principle of equal dignity itself occasionally requires unusually spirited forms of action. After all, even if one's intrinsic dignity can never be lost, it may not always be respected. The intrinsic dignity of humankind sometimes must be vindicated, and for its vindication the universal ideal of intrinsic dignity relies on the presence of qualities of character that are more than merely intrinsic and not at all universal. The ideal of intrinsic human dignity is impotent to bring about its own vindication because of the fact that no necessary connection exists between intrinsic dignity and individual agency. The ideal of dignity is a normative standard, not a motivation, or a quality of character, or a source of agency. And the acts of dignity that rise to defend the ideal have more in common with honor as a quality of character than with the ideal of intrinsic dignity itself.

The need to go beyond the standard set by the principle of equal dignity is reflected in another common usage of the word dignity today. Today we can distinguish "dignified" actions and persons from "undignified" ones. We may characterize someone whom we admire as a person of "great dignity." Dignity in this sense is neither universal nor equal. It may be lost or forfeited and it admits of degrees. It is a mark of distinction, not something that inheres intrinsically in everyone. When the word dignity is used in this way it is a democratic euphemism for honor, because it is tied to exceptional action, high achievement, and extraordinary character. To be a man or woman of great dignity one must do something, or many things, to distinguish oneself, and so dignity in this form must be earned. Similarly, we sometimes speak admiringly of the "sense of dignity" that inspires great acts. King's "Letter from Birmingham City Jail" refers to such a sense of dignity as an important motivation for black civil rights activists.[35] But the sense of dignity is not something that is distributed equally, even if dignity in principle adheres equally in us. The sense of dignity goes beyond and rises above intrinsic dignity as a universal status. Some people have a stronger sense of dignity than others, as their different actions attest. Few of us could match the strong sense of dignity that inspired Rosa Parks to hold her seat on the bus, for example. The sense of dignity is not democratic but aristocratic in precisely the way that honor as a quality of character is aristocratic. It is uncommon, even extraordinary, rather than automatic, and so it belongs only to a few, even if it may be achieved by anyone. Thus while all are entitled to have their equal dignity respected, not everyone is entitled to be called "dignified," and not everyone possesses the strong sense of dignity that can inspire risky action. The ideal of intrinsic dignity cannot replace honor because there are features of honor that democratic dignity cannot capture and that liberal democrats should not neglect. Indeed, the democratic ideal of intrinsic dignity could not long survive without the aristocratic sense of dignity, or the quality of honor, that rises to defend it when necessary.

The use of democratic euphemisms to mark aristocratic qualities does a disservice to American democracy. The democratic ideal of intrinsic dignity has an important place in our regime, to be sure, and the language of dignity is perfectly legitimate when applied to this ideal. Too often, however, the language of equal dignity is unreflectively extended to qualities of character (such as the sense of dignity) that are anything but equal. When this happens, the extraordinary character of these qualities is obscured from view. This results in the vague but misguided impression that because in principle we all enjoy the equal status of intrinsic dignity we also intrinsically possess—and so can be relied upon automatically to enact—the extraordinary qualities of character needed to support the principle. The language of honor is better suited to these qualities because it reminds us that the democratic ideal of intrinsic dignity is not self-activating but leans on aristocratic (in the sense of uncommon) supports.

Democratic euphemisms can make remarkable qualities appear to be undistinctive, but they also can make us think that undistinctive or common qualities are the only ones available to us. Calling honor what it is rather than employing democratic euphemisms makes us aware of the aristocratic qualities or capacities in ourselves that have survived the rise of modern man.[36] If the French Revolution vanquished the old order, it did not fundamentally alter human nature. Even the old order itself, while largely undone, was not entirely eradicated. At least since Tocqueville, historians have found vestiges of the old regime in the political societies that survived its overthrow. Indeed, some of the central features of modern liberal democracy—including individual rights, the voluntary associations of civil society, and the separation of powers—have been traced to aristocratic origins.[37] The boundary line between the Old World and the New is more permeable than sometimes is thought. This is true partly because some of the foundations of modern democracy rest on the remains of aristocratic society but also because of the enduring quality of certain aspects of human nature. To the extent that we obscure our own aristocratic capacities and liberal democracy's aristocratic elements, we deny ourselves potentially powerful sources of individual agency and withhold crucial support for individual liberties.

Rawls's idea of "self-esteem" provides an example of this danger. Rawls notes that individuals must have a high opinion of themselves to be forceful agents, and he acknowledges that those who think too little of themselves are easily subjugated in politics. Without self-respect, he says, nothing would seem worth doing and men and women would lack the will to act.[38] Citizens need self-respect in order "to care about their basic liberties and opportunities" and to use and defend their liberties.[39] For this reason, Rawls includes the social bases of self-respect, what he calls "self-esteem," among the primary goods of distributive justice. Self-esteem is the most important primary good, Rawls says, because it enables individuals to make use of other goods.[40] Thus self-esteem is a good to be distributed, according to Rawls, and in a just society it will be distributed equally. Self-esteem even can be guaranteed, he maintains, if only the principles of justice are executed properly. Indeed, "by arranging inequalities for reciprocal advantage and by abstaining from the exploitation of the contingencies of nature and social circumstance within a framework of equal liberty, persons . . . insure their self-esteem."[41] Rawls's concept of self-esteem democratizes the proud self-respect internal to honor by making it equally applicable to all. Self-esteem even can be guaranteed to all as a matter of equal distribution because all that matters for self-esteem is that one's endeavors be "confirmed" by one's associates. The absolute level of one's achievements is irrelevant. All that is needed for self-esteem is the appreciation of others, who are obliged (in a just society) to provide it.

Yet the disjunction between the concept of desert and the sense of one's own value undermines the power of self-esteem as a source of political agency, however unwittingly, especially when it comes to risky and difficult forms of action. In practice, one gains confidence in proportion to the gains one makes in mastering some skill or situation; one's confidence increases with one's abilities. By disconnecting abilities from self-esteem, Rawls makes self-confidence into an assertion rather than an achievement. You might be able to muster a measure of confidence simply by asserting it or having it asserted for you by others, independently of any real abilities or achievements. But surely this would be a false confidence, liable to get you in over your head and apt to crumple under the pressure of the first real challenge. The confidence needed to sustain risky and difficult action in defense of individual liberties (think of what Martin Luther King, Jr., did, for example) cannot be spun from air or from good intentions. Risks like these rest on confidence that is equal to the challenge because it is girded by the experience of achievement. Self-respect cannot simply be asserted or distributed; it must be won, at least if it is to withstand challenge in the toughest cases and so to support strong exertions of individual agency. Moreover, if one can be made to esteem oneself regardless of what one does, what incentive do we have for taking the risks and making the efforts that the defense of liberty sometimes, if not always, requires? Self-respect, which is a necessary condition of agency, cannot be guaranteed without undercutting agency. We must have enough self-respect to have the desire for self-respect, but not so much that we no longer need to reach for it. Rawls means to support agency by democratizing self-respect in the form of equal "self-esteem," but in fact he undercuts agency.

If the democratic ideal of intrinsic dignity and the democratic distribution of self-esteem cannot replace honor, neither can the practice of reciprocal recognition that sometimes is said to have supplanted it. It is the inequalities of recognition entailed by honor that make it objectionable from the standpoint of modern democracy.[42] According to Taylor, for example, these inequalities run counter to the principle of intrinsic dignity, and therefore honor in democratic societies must be replaced with the reciprocal recognition that accompanies "the politics of equal dignity."[43] Yet Taylor's presumption that reciprocal recognition can stand in for honor, like his argument for dignity, is based on an incomplete characterization of honor. He sees only honor's external dimension, its quest for distinction, and does not acknowledge the internal dimension, honor as the quality of character that makes one wish to live up to principled codes of conduct. Or rather, Taylor collapses the two dimensions of honor together, much as Rousseau did, casting honor simply as the quality of character that makes one wish to be recognized. But honor means more than this. The honorable person wants to be the kind of person who lives up to her code of conduct. She also may wish to be *seen* as the kind of person who lives up to her code, but her concern with appearances does not diminish her allegiance to a set of independent principles and the inner desire for self-respect.

Much as Taylor's characterization of honor misses its internal dimension, so too does his recommended replacement. Recognition is not a quality of character, after all. The only basis of recognition, as Taylor construes it, is public opinion or the state, since in order to have recognition one need only—and one must—be recognized by others. It is true that public honors can inspire honorable actions and so support honorable characters. But honorable actions (abiding by the honor code on a take-home exam, for instance) sometimes can go unrecognized and still be honorable, whereas it is always impossible to be recognized without being seen and appreciated. The problem with substituting Taylor's concept of recognition for honor is that it depends too much on public opinion and on political authority. By contrast, honor's attachment to codes of conduct and principled self-respect gives it a measure of independence. One can defend one's principles and thereby respect oneself even when one is unpopular, or officially unrecognized. This makes honor a more powerful source of individual agency, especially for the members of the marginalized and minority groups with whom Taylor himself is most concerned, those persons who are least likely to be on the winning end of public opinion and the political authorities that distribute recognition.

Democratic alternatives to honor, such as recognition, or self-esteem, or the ideal of intrinsic dignity, cannot replace honor as a source of individual agency. Indeed, they may contribute to the dispiriting of agency by detaching self-respect from achievement and dignity from action, and by making self-respect and dignity too dependent on public opinion and the state. Liberal citizens must be able to stand up against public opinion and political authorities on occasion. The reputed obsolescence of honor therefore is something of a myth. There is some truth in it, as old-regime honor has indeed been eclipsed; and in some respects this is a very good thing. But the enduring features of honor as a quality of character that support individual agency are not obsolete. The nature and sources of agency in modern life are more complex than contemporary political theory allows. Only by coming to terms with the mix of aristocratic and democratic elements in the soul of "modern man" can political theory hope to restore the lost faith in individual agency that characterizes contemporary democratic life. Political theory is not responsible for the beleaguered sense of agency that pervades America today, but the remedies it offers are incomplete because its understanding of agency is limited. The concept of honor challenges us to think more expansively about agency and to probe more deeply into the moral psychology that animates it.

Excavating Honor

In this book I explore the meaning of honor and its power to inspire individual agency in the context of liberal constitutional government. The study is philosophical in nature. Others have examined honor empirically using the tools of modern sociology and anthropology.[44] Their work demonstrates the variability of honor to which Tocqueville alluded and identifies examples of honor in societies far removed from old-regime Europe, its most common association for us today. Honor also has been documented by historians, who show both shifts and continuities in honor in different countries and periods.[45] In approaching honor from the standpoint of political philosophy, I treat it not as an artifact of particular cultures and eras but as a lens through which to view fundamental features of human nature and politics, particularly the nature and sources of individual agency. The results of this philosophical investigation should in principle be consistent with the findings in other domains of study, but it does not aim to reproduce them all.

My analysis draws primarily on sources from modern philosophy and politics, and considers honor mainly in the context of liberal constitutional government. The project is animated by the troubled condition of individual agency in American liberal democracy today, and in seeking philosophical resources to meet this condition, it looks relatively close to home in notions of honor that are explicitly tied to liberal or modern democratic purposes and institutions. Montesquieu's concept of honor, with which the analysis begins, establishes direct connections between honor and the idea of a separation of powers in government, the notion of ambition counteracting ambition, civil disobedience, and the defense of individual liberty. Similarly, Tocqueville's defense of aristocratic qualities of character is intended to serve the regime of modern democracy. There is, of course, a rich ancient literature on the theme of honor as well, to which I occasionally refer but which I do not examine at length. My work does not aim to provide a comprehensive catalogue of the various treatments of honor in the history of philosophy as a whole, but rather to illuminate the particular relationship between honor and liberalism.

If the study looks for honor in sources that are relatively close to home, it does not look for them only at home. We do see some manifestations of honor in American public life today and hear the occasional reference to it, and I have argued that despite being modern and democratic we carry the possibility of honor within us. Yet to get a clear picture of honor and its connections to individual agency, one must look beyond contemporary American democracy. The reason is that honor in the United States today very often operates undercover, draped in the language of democratic dignity and obscured by its service to democratic freedoms. Unlike the *honnêtes hommes* of the old regime, honorable Americans who rise to defend individual liberties against encroaching power are more likely to make reference to their human dignity than their personal honor, and they rarely claim superior positions or special distinctions. For the most part, they want for their fellows what they claim for themselves, and their goals are in this sense egalitarian rather than exclusionary.[46] Yet their very actions distinguish them from the rest of us and attest to the superiority that they will not claim. The exceptional qualities of character that drive them to defend their dignity (and by extension ours, too) make them in this respect more than merely equal to the rest of us, and these qualities are closer to honor than to any other single motive.

The concealment of honor today is more habitual than intentional. Montesquieu once remarked that "man, that flexible being . . . adapts himself in society to the thoughts and impressions of others," with the result that he "is equally capable of knowing his own nature when it is shown to him and of losing even the feeling of it when it is withdrawn (*dérobe*) from him."[47] We have lost the feeling of the aristocratic elements in our nature. And not only that, we have so fully embraced the dichotomy between self-interest and self-sacrifice that we have forgotten how to see in ourselves and in others the motives that join personal ambition with principled higher purpose. Part of the aim of this study is to unmask these elements, to reveal honor in its contemporary manifestations, to peel away the concealing layers of democratic euphemisms and so to illuminate the aristocratic foundations and mixed motives frequently implicit in individual agency, which we rely on but no longer see. Yet precisely because of our tendency to conceal from ourselves the instances of honor nearest to hand, it is necessary to begin our exploration of honor at some remove.

We turn first to Montesquieu, who understood the strong sense of agency that supports risky action in defense of liberty. Although he was not in favor of revolution or even sudden reform, he thought that spirited resistance to the abuse of power was crucial for individual liberty, and he saw honor as the spring of such resistance.[48] Chapter 2 explains Montesquieu's idea of honor, showing how the ambitious but principled desire for distinction motivates disobedience to encroaching political power. This analysis serves as a point of departure for the study of honor and liberalism more generally. Four features of honor as a quality of character are elaborated: its high ambition, the balance of reverence and reflexivity, partiality, and the mix of recognition and resistance. The substantive content of codes of honor may vary from one political society to another, as do systems for distributing public honors. The formal features of honor as a quality of character elaborated here are more enduring, however. These aspects of honor remain relatively constant in different contexts. They also illuminate the nature and conditions of political agency in a more general sense.

Honor as Montesquieu presents it is a "human passion"—a desire, not a cognition. Yet honor is not limited to the lowest forms of desire, for while honor is self-serving, it is more than simply self-interest; it is a desire, but more than an appetite. With the concept of honor, Montesquieu meant to restore the higher desires that made ancient virtue such a powerful form of motivation and a rich resource for human agency. But he meant to restore this motivational force without the metaphysical presuppositions or teleological ends of ancient virtue, of which he was both philosophically skeptical and politically suspicious. Therefore in contrast to Plato and Aristotle, Montesquieu approved of "false honor," or

honor detached from moral virtue, at least in the regime of constitutional monarchy. In this context, he thought, the ambitious quest for
distinction, pride, and the desire for self-respect could serve liberty by
motivating the tumults between crown and nobility that limit political
power. As an institutional matter, his concept of honor is intended to
have instrumental value even if it lacks moral worth. To emphasize this
point, Montesquieu draws attention to the unsavory aspects of "false
honor," which can easily degenerate into the "vanities" of the courtier
class. But when he describes the individual resistance of the Viscount of
Orte to the abusive power of his king, an early example of conscientious
objection, Montesquieu clearly means for us to admire honor for its
moral content as well as for its instrumental value. An ambiguity about
the relationship between honor and moral virtue runs throughout Montesquieu's analysis because this ambiguity is endemic to honor itself, as
we shall see. Honor is tied to virtue but it is not identical to virtue.

Chapter 3 explores honor through the lens of Tocqueville's *Democracy
in America*. Tocqueville shows the consequences of democracy that generate its resistance to honor, but he also shows why democracy needs
honor and where in American society supports for honor may be found.
To support individual liberty against the twin dangers of majority tyranny and "mild" despotism, Tocqueville seeks to inspire in the democratic character qualities associated with aristocratic mores and tied to
old-regime honor. Courage, pride, high and principled ambition, the desires for distinction and self-respect, the sense of duty to oneself, and the
love of liberty as an end in itself all prove to be crucial supports for democratic freedom on Tocqueville's account. Today Tocqueville's interest in
these qualities tends to be neglected in favor of the more egalitarian and
collectivist aspects of his civic virtue.[49] Yet Tocqueville's portrait of democracy in America points to the unavoidable conclusion that the aristocratic qualities tied to honor are at least as important to democratic
freedom as the egalitarian and collectivist civic virtues that are so widely
championed in our day. The spirit of individual resistance, not simply
participation or fraternity, is the core of liberty for Tocqueville.[50] To sustain it, something more than civic virtue is needed, qualities closely associated with traditional honor.[51] And while Tocqueville emphasized
that the relationship between honor and democracy in America was far
from harmonious, he did identify a specifically American form of honor,
and he made it clear that a range of qualities associated with traditional

honor could be found in the United States, even if they were not the predominant motives of the new regime.

Many of the traditionally aristocratic qualities associated with honor that Tocqueville championed have in fact helped to sustain democracy in America from the beginning, as Chapters 4 and 5 demonstrate. Chapter 4 examines the meaning and role of honor in the United States at the time of the founding, and then explores the nature of honor in the antebellum South. The founders invoked the concept of honor in the Declaration of Independence, as we have noted, and the word was not infrequently on their tongues. Tocqueville in 1830 identified more honor in the first generation of Americans than in subsequent ones.[52] We shall look for honor first where he found it, in the words and deeds of men such as Washington, Jefferson, Madison, Hamilton, and John Adams, and consider how they viewed honor and what role they accorded it in their own actions. We also consider honor's close cousin, the love of fame, which Hamilton called "the ruling passion of the noblest minds." The love of fame is another democratic euphemism for honor, or a partial euphemism. It means to capture the high ambitions and the quest for distinction that are such powerful engines of political agency without raising the specter of entrenched hierarchy or the external trappings of Old World nobility. *The Federalist* is consulted for evidence of the founders' views on the institutional role that honor and its cousin fame were intended to play in the new American system.

Whereas the honor of the founding generation was explicitly tied to the principles of liberty and equality articulated by the Declaration of Independence, honor in the antebellum South was based on a rejection of these principles. Southern honor more closely resembles the feudal honor of the old regime with its ascriptive social status, entrenched hierarchy, emphasis on lineage and blood ties, dueling, and the exercise of mastery over others as a condition of self-command. It also was deeply implicated in the institution of chattel slavery. In examining this form of honor we see honor's darkest side and some of its gravest dangers. In particular, southern honor shows what can happen when honor as a quality of character serves codes of honor that are deeply unjust and when it is combined with unchecked power. Southern honor makes it clear that honor is not always admirable or just, nor necessarily liberal.

Perhaps because of its associations with the old regime and the military, honor has politically conservative, even reactionary, connotations today. Chapter 5 reveals the limits of these familiar associations. Even the honor of the founders was more innovative than reactionary. Indeed, honor in the founding generation was more than merely innovative; it was revolutionary, and revolutionary in the largest sense of the term, as it served to defend an entirely new form of political order "never before seen among societies of men," as *The Federalist* said. From the very first, though not exclusively so, American honor has been invoked in defense of reform and progress, and it should not be surrendered to political reactionaries. Honor in the United States also illustrates a more general shift away from the exclusive association between honor and military valor (or physical prowess) toward a new relationship between honor and political courage, or the courage of conviction, often resulting in reform. We shall examine honor's contributions to democratic reform in the United States by considering several American reformers who exemplify key features of honor, including Abraham Lincoln and Frederick Douglass, Elizabeth Cady Stanton and Susan B. Anthony, and Martin Luther King, Jr.

Honor as it emerges in these pages is tied to what Elizabeth Cady Stanton called "self-sovereignty," the proud assertion of one's capacity to rule oneself rather than acquiesce to external rule, whether it be the rule of another person, an overreaching political authority, one's own unreflective appetites, or even the impersonal forces of nature and history. Honor here issues in political activism, reform, conscientious objection, and civil disobedience—the distant progeny of Montesquieu's rebellious nobles and Tocqueville's independent aristocrats. Those with honor above all refuse to believe that they are the victims of their circumstances. Honor is somewhat boastful in this respect, as it depends on circumstances, or fortune, more than might first appear. Extraordinary exertions of agency in defense of liberty emerge mainly in moments of crisis, for instance, and so depend on fortune to call them forth and provide a field of opportunity.[53] And because honor involves public recognition, it depends in some measure (though not entirely) on the cooperation of one's peers and the fortuitous recollections of posterity.[54] Moreover, honor requires equipment, which is why Montesquieu emphasized the importance of the nobility's structural and economic independence from the crown. I concentrate on the moral psychology of honor, but political and sociological factors affect honor (and individual agency) as well. American honor relies on equipment in the form of civil and political rights, liberal political institutions, access to education, social recognition, and the opportunity to rise. There is a circle here but not a vicious circle. Honor as a quality of character and the conditions that make it possible are reciprocally reinforcing. Yet honor's need for equipment reveals that its proud assertion of self-command is somewhat overstated. Honor rests on a boastful self-forgetting of its own conditions and an exaggeration of its independence from the power of circumstance. Still, the boastful exaggeration of human independence is an honorable response to the real power of circumstance, because it makes resistance—therefore agency, and ultimately self-government and individual liberty—conceivable.

The examples offered here by no means exhaust the instances of honor in the United States, but they illuminate some of its variety and many of its continuities, and they show honor to be a potentially powerful spring of political agency even for modern democratic citizens. Great acts of honor in the United States resemble the actions of Montesquieu's *honnêtes hommes* and Tocqueville's liberty-loving aristocrats in some respects but they differ in others, and they admit of significant diversity even among themselves. One difference between American honor and its old-regime predecessors has to do with the character of its codes. The principles of liberty and equality articulated by the Declaration have formed the core of one common code of honor in the United States. In contrast to honor codes in the *ancien régime,* this one is based on universal principles of abstract right rather than concrete rules governing particular spheres of conduct, and it is attached to a shared national political identity rather than sited in the extrapolitical intermediary associations of honor in the old regime. This is not the only form of American honor, but it is an important one. Other, more partial forms of honor tied to more particular codes can be found in the many intermediary associations of American civil society, as Chapter 6 shows, but the form of honor tied to the American Declaration has been particularly important to democratic reform in the United States, and it provides a point of special focus for the study. This form of honor itself admits of some variation. For example, although the Declaration provided a common code of conduct for most of the Americans considered in Chapters 4 and 5, the self-proclaimed honor of the planter class in the antebellum South was based on an explicit renunciation of the Declaration's principles. Democratic reformers of the mid-nineteenth century also challenged the meaning of the American code, not by denying its principles but by asserting that the Declaration's promise of liberty and equality should apply not only to propertied white males but also to black men and all women. Such challenges represent shifts in the meaning of honor in the United States even as they reflect underlying continuities. They also show that despite being tied to a shared code, honor not infrequently struggles against the prevailing moral consensus or certain elements of it; indeed, honor's power as a source of democratic reform grows directly out of such struggles.

The new honor and the old honor also differ in that while American honor engages aristocratic qualities of character, it is not tied to political inequalities or an hereditary social order as was honor in the old regime. In the United States, public honors must be won rather than inherited, and when one wins public honors one is not thereby entitled to an extra vote or a political office. Democratic forms of honor coexist with political equality and a rough equality of opportunity in society.[55] This difference in how public honors are distributed affects honor as a quality of character by emphasizing individual action and conscience over status, and these features rise to prominence in American honor as compared with honor in the old regime. This difference is accentuated when public esteem is especially unreliable, as among the members of marginalized groups, with the result that the conscience-related aspects of honor, especially the sense of duty to oneself and the desire for self-respect, predominate among the women and black reformers examined in these pages.

Despite the differences, key features of honor as a quality of character remain relatively constant, both with respect to the transition from the old regime to the new one and with respect to changes within the American polity. First, honor consistently combines personal ambition with principled codes of conduct. The substance of the codes may vary, but a defining feature of honor is that the ambitious desire for distinction is limited, directed, and elevated by reverence for a set of principles that are independent of will or appetite. Yet although honor is a principled motive, it cannot be equated simply with the exercise of impartial reason. Codes of honor may be subjected to the scrutiny of impartial reason, but honor itself is never truly impartial because it always remains attached both to personal distinction and to a particular set of principles. And however universal the principles contained in one's code,

honor as a quality of character retains an irreducible partiality in the further sense that it regards the defense of one's principles as a condition of
one's own self-respect. The partial desire for self-respect reflects the un-
dying self-concern at the heart of honor, which distinguishes honor
from altruism, however general its codes may be.

A second constant feature of honor is the element of courage, especially courageous resistance to encroaching power. In Montesquieu, this
aspect of honor was associated primarily with the nobility's defense of its
political prerogatives against the crown. Tocqueville's account of modern democracy draws explicitly on the legacy of honor in this respect,
emphasizing the need for the aristocratic or heroic courage associated
with honor to defend democratic rights against the tyranny of majority
opinion and the specter of mild despotism. American honor preserves
the pride that is a remnant of the old nobility's sense of self-importance,
which supports courage. Pride tends to be understated in democratic
honor, cloaked in the frequently humble beginnings and egalitarian purposes of America's honorable citizens, and mitigated by the "decent regard" for the opinions of their fellows that they commonly express. If
the demeanor of honorable Americans tends to be more self-effacing
than that of the *honnête homme,* however, their actions nevertheless reflect the "high opinion of oneself and of humanity" that Tocqueville
thought so important to the preservation of democratic liberties. Although no longer the exclusive prerogative of a fixed social caste, honor
still belongs only to a few, the natural aristocracy of individuals who can
summon extraordinary courage in defense of principle when the moment of crisis comes.

The third feature of honor that remains constant is its emphasis on
the sense of duty to oneself. Honorable actions are understood in terms
of duties or obligations rather than interests, although there are important connections between honor and interest. Both are self-regarding, for
instance, and both give priority to individual concerns and individual
judgment. They are alike in that neither one pursues the general will or
the collective good directly. But there are important differences, too. The
sense of honor is in certain respects categorical, rather than merely instrumental. There are some things that the honorable person simply
will not do—or must do—as a matter of principle, whatever the consequences may be. By contrast, however expansively the motive of interest
may be construed, it always remains unambiguously instrumentalist. Al-

though there are dimensions of honor that may be construed in instrumental terms, such as the desire for the self-respect and public recognition that come from living up to one's code, these aspects of honor are inseparable from the noninstrumental, categorical sense that living up to one's code is something one *must* do. And this points to another important difference between honor and interest, which is that unlike interest, honor intrinsically entails an attachment to principle. Interests may be connected to principles, but they need not be, whereas honor without principle would not be honor.

Still, honor (like interest) is always concerned more with what one owes to oneself than with what one owes to others, which is why it resists the altruism implicit in so many contemporary theories of obligation. And unlike conscience or integrity, to which it bears a family resemblance, honor retains a distinctly public persona: it is guided by public codes of conduct (not merely internal standards of right), seeks public recognition, and is especially oriented to public action. It is true that as honor becomes more democratic in the transition from the old regime to the new one, the relative weight accorded its internal and external dimensions shifts. More generally, the democratization of honor with its attendant emphasis on conscience brings honor closer to integrity and to moral virtue, especially the instances of honor that embody political courage or the courage of conviction. Yet even here honor cannot be simply equated with virtue. Honor remains distinct partly because, in contrast to virtue, honor is tied to general rules of conduct, partly because it never fully transcends personal ambition and the concern with external public distinction and partly because it does not imply the perfection of the soul.

The forms of American honor identified here combine aspects of the old and the new regimes. They transcend the great divide introduced by the revolution that spawned "modern man." Or they partly transcend this divide. American honor is *American,* and in this sense particular and different from old-regime honor, but American honor still is *honor* and therefore remains consistent and identifiable in key respects. Honor as it is conceived in the chapters that follow also transcends the partisan divide between Left and Right in contemporary American politics. Because it both requires equipment and calls forth heroic qualities, the concept of honor helps us to conceive political agency in ways that avoid what one commentator has called the "great weakness of the Right—its failure to believe that institutional or social conditions really affect our choices and life chances—and the analogous failure of the Left to imagine how people living under conditions of great adversity and oppression can nevertheless create a space of freedom within which they act to change their lives."[56] Honor unsettles the expectations of both the Left and the Right. It is transpartisan in the manner of Tocqueville, who sought to infuse modern democracy with certain aristocratic qualities—not for the purpose of undoing democracy but for the sake of sustaining it. Honor reminds us of the aristocratic capacities in ourselves that have survived the advent of modern man and calls us to confront liberal democracy's need for them. It transcends another divide as well, which is the contemporary dichotomy between self-interest and self-sacrifice. Honor is especially instructive for us today because of the way it connects personal ambition to principled higher purpose, making right action desirable. It thus brings into view a wider class of motives that add depth and complexity to current thinking on matters of moral psychology and political agency. But if the concept of honor offered here transcends many divides, it nevertheless remains partial as an account of agency. Honor does not claim to provide a comprehensive solution to the dispirited sense of agency that pervades the United States today. It cannot replace motivations such as self-interest, civic virtue, solidarity, faith, friendship, love, or any of the many other sources of human agency. Honor cannot replace them but it can add to them. And what it adds is important both philosophically and politically because it recalls us to aspects of ourselves and our polity that we have forgotten or ceased to understand, qualities on which our liberties cannot help but depend.

2

Honor and the Defense of Liberty in the Old Regime

Honor's association with the old regime has seemed to many to disqualify it from the democratic politics of the New World. Yet if the French Revolution largely vanquished the old order, it did not change human nature or reverse the encroaching nature of political power. Montesquieu's concept of honor, which found its home in the constitutional monarchy of eighteenth-century France, remains illuminating today because the fundamental nature of agency, like that of power, has not changed. It is true that real differences exist between the old regime and the new despite the continuities between them, and honor has not remained unaffected by its new surroundings. But the continuities are significant, and they are less familiar to us than the differences. The modern democratic regime—and with it the modern democratic soul—has come to be defined almost entirely in opposition to its prerevolutionary forebears, a practice that has overlooked, and eventually concealed, what one writer calls "its vestigial aristocratic features."[1] These aristocratic features are important resources for modern democracy, so important in fact that democracy cannot hope to sustain itself without recourse to them. Like individual rights, the intermediary bodies of civil society, and the separation of powers, honor is a part of liberal democracy's aristocratic inheritance that it cannot do without.

This chapter explains Montesquieu's idea of honor, showing how the ambitious desire for distinction motivates principled disobedience to encroaching political power. His understanding of honor is consistent with the tripartite scheme elaborated in Chapter 1, which includes public honors, codes of honor, and honor as a quality of character. Although

Montesquieu was not in favor of revolution or even sudden reform,[2] he thought that spirited resistance to the abuse of power was crucial for individual liberty, and he saw honor as the spring of such resistance. For this reason, honor in Montesquieu has been called "openly rebellious toward authority,"[3] a form of "regulated disobedience,"[4] "interference,"[5] and even "anarchy."[6] Montesquieu's man of honor distinguishes himself though his disobedience, and the politics of distinction and disobedience that characterizes moderate monarchies divides political power and therefore limits it. To limit power is, for Montesquieu, the essence of liberty and the best protection for individual security. What one interpreter has called Montesquieu's "vacillating attitude toward honor" reflects its morally ambiguous character, for even the most shining examples of honor display mixed motives.[7] If honor in Montesquieu sometimes seems similar to the magnanimity of the Aristotelian gentleman,[8] at other times it appears to be nothing more than "having someone to look down on."[9] This complexity makes honor difficult to categorize. It cannot be reduced to self-interest, even self-interest well understood, partly because honor may motivate the sacrifice of one's most fundamental interest, life itself, and partly because of the principled and categorical quality of honor. At the same time, honor in Montesquieu should not be confused with contemporary civic virtue, because if honor sometimes involves personal sacrifice, it does not aim directly for the common good, as civic virtue does. In contrast to civic virtue—and like interest—honor is primarily self-serving. Moreover, on Montesquieu's account honor's function is not so much to motivate political participation as an end in itself as to arouse resistance to the abuse of power.

Little sustained, systematic attention has been given to the concept of honor in Montesquieu.[10] In part, this neglect reflects the difficulty of categorizing honor on the basis of present typologies. In part, too, it is a sign of democratic discomfort with what appears to be an aristocratic concept. Thus honor has been overshadowed by Montesquieu's remarks on republican virtue, because they seem to contain the precursor to Rousseau's idea of the general will, and so to speak more directly to today's democratic citizens. Yet on Montesquieu's account, it is honor, not republican virtue, that checks encroaching political power and thereby serves individual liberty. Because of the way in which honor divides political power, even supports a nascent form of separate powers, the concept of honor is more significant for Montesquieu's liberalism as a whole than prior scholarship has acknowledged. Honor reflects both his conviction that the institutions of limited government need lively defense and his reluctance to assign this task to virtue.

Following a brief account of how honor fits into Montesquieu's typology of regimes, four features of honor as a quality of character are elaborated: high ambition, the balance of reverence and reflexivity, partiality, and the mix of recognition and resistance. The substantive content of codes of honor may vary from one political society to another, as do systems for distributing public honors or recognition. The formal features of honor as a quality of character elaborated here are more enduring. These aspects of honor remain relatively constant in different contexts. They also illuminate the nature and conditions of political agency more generally, especially the strong exertions of agency that support individual liberty in the face of obvious risks and indeterminate benefits.[11]

The Place of Honor in the Old Regime

Montesquieu's typology of regimes identifies three species of government, each with its own "nature" and "principle."[12] The nature of a government is "that which makes it what it is, and its principle that which makes it act. The one is its particular structure and the other the human passions that make it move" (III.1). The nature of a republic is popular sovereignty and its principle is what Montesquieu calls "political virtue"; despotism is the rule of one on the basis of arbitrary will and its principle is fear; monarchy is the rule of one according to fixed established laws and its principle is honor. Each of the three regimes exists only as a "totality," as the unity between its nature and its principle.[13] Despotism, for example, cannot be sustained unless the people are made to fear the ruler, because fearless individuals capable of "esteeming" themselves very highly "would be in a condition to make revolutions." Therefore, fear must beat down everyone's courage, and extinguish self-respect and even the slightest feeling of ambition (III.9). Without the support of fear, the "passion that makes it move," the institutional apparatus of despotism would give way. Similarly, a republic cannot survive without what Montesquieu calls political virtue. In the absence of a monarch or a despot, a people must do for themselves what a strong central authority otherwise would force them to do. In particular, they must restrain themselves from harming others by loving equality and the laws, and they must defend the interests of the state (through military service, for example) by subordinating their individual interests to the common good (V.3). The constant preference for the public interest over one's own, and even the "renunciation of oneself," is the essence of republican virtue for Montesquieu (IV.5). Without this, the institutions of republican government collapse; its nature dissolves without its principle.

It is worth pausing to consider Montesquieu's treatment of republican virtue because it prepares the way for his concept of honor and helps to clarify it. Montesquieu distinguishes what he calls the political virtue of ancient republics from moral virtue in a foreword to the book: "For an understanding of the first four books of this work, one must observe that what I call virtue in a republic is love of the homeland. . . . It is not at all a moral virtue or a Christian virtue" (Author's foreword). He reiterates the distinction periodically throughout the early sections of *The Spirit of the Laws* (III.5n, IV.5, V.2,4). The point needed emphasis because most of his readers would indeed have identified the unspecified term "virtue" with both moral and Christian virtue.[14] In part, Montesquieu's distinction is meant to emphasize the instrumental rather than the comprehensive quality of political virtue as he uses the term. In part, too, it is intended to defuse hostility toward his general critique of virtue.[15] As it happened, his critique of what he calls political virtue was interpreted by many readers, including the *nouvelles ecclésiastiques,* as a thinly veiled attack on moral and Christian virtue. The clerics were not altogether wrong in their interpretation of the critique. In other places, Montesquieu clearly identifies political virtue with Christian virtue, as when he illustrates "what virtue is in the political state" by describing the self-sacrifice of Christian monks (V.2). Passages such as this one suggest that his ecclesiastical critics were on to something, and more recent commentary has supported their suspicions.[16] For Montesquieu, the effectual truth of all virtue, whether of the political, moral, intellectual, or religious variety, is self-renunciation, the forgetfulness of the worldly goods and the particular desires of the individual as an embodied being.[17] He criticized virtue to illuminate the dangers of any regime based on self-renunciation, thus continuing a line of attack on classical and Christian political philosophy initiated by his "realist" forebears, Machiavelli and Hobbes. His political teaching is a good deal more moderate than that of either one, but for him the path to political moderation must begin from and never forsake a realistic assessment of human nature.

Montesquieu's portrait of virtue as self-renunciation departs markedly from ancient accounts, of course.[18] According to Aristotle, political, moral, and intellectual virtue were forms of self-fulfillment, not self-renunciation. Virtue brought about happiness, and the good man had a desire for virtue. Citizens had good reason to make the personal sacrifices that political virtue required of them because these sacrifices opened the door to their own higher well-being. One gave up lower goods for the sake of higher ones. In a similar way, good Christians turn their backs on all that belongs to this world for the sake of the more perfect pleasures of the next world (XXIV.11).[19] In both cases, the required detachment from the particular concerns of the individual as an embodied being is justified by rewards that are above the body. When Montesquieu identifies political virtue (and implicitly all virtue) with self-renunciation simply, he suggests that no such rewards await, or justify, the sacrifices of republican citizens or persons of virtue more generally. His position in this regard is based on two considerations. The first is his genuine skepticism about the adequacy of ancient teleology. On the Greek account, it was the realization of the human telos through virtue that transformed the self-renunciation virtue required into the self-fulfillment it promised. If this teleology were inadequate or even questionable, as Montesquieu suspected, the promised self-fulfillment would prove baseless, and self-renunciation would be all that remained to virtue.

The second reason for identifying virtue with self-renunciation involves a historical rather than a metaphysical consideration. The modern world is distinguished from the ancient world by the fact of plurality in moral and political standards of conduct, according to Montesquieu. He draws attention to the modern condition of plurality in a passage on political virtue, saying that "today we receive three different or contrary educations: that of our fathers, that of our schoolmasters, and that of the world," and he contrasts this modern plurality with the unity that characterized ancient life (IV.4). Elsewhere he remarks that "there are three tribunes that are almost never in accord: that of the laws, that of honor, and that of religion."[20] Montesquieu accepts this plurality as an irremediable fact of modern life, due largely to the spread of Christianity together with the rise of modern commerce. There is reason to believe that he approves of it, as well, on the grounds that a plurality of normative standards, like the division of political powers, tends to encourage moderation.[21] The historical fact of pluralism is a second reason why virtue in general appears to the modern subject as simple self-renunciation, however, as pluralism undercuts the teleological assumptions that transform virtue's self-renunciation into self-fulfillment.[22]

Instead of aspiring to the higher ends posited by Greek teleology, the republican virtue that Montesquieu describes aims at general ends.[23] Self-renunciation is understood as the sacrifice of one's particular self to the common "self" of the political community, rather than as the sacrifice of what is lower to what is higher in one's soul.[24] Yet from the standpoint of early liberalism, a standpoint that Montesquieu here adopts, the sacrifices of the republican citizen, the Christian monk, and the ancient philosopher appear to be equally empty. From this perspective, it is the particular, embodied self that matters, at least in politics.[25] And from this point of view, the common denominator of the virtues of the philosopher, the Christian, and the republican citizen is obedience to rule (even if it is self-rule) that mortifies the particular interests of the embodied self. Because it renounces particular interests, this obedience is rendered devoid of the ends that justify it: all their virtue is in vain.[26] In fact, their virtues are worse than vain; they are positively dangerous because they give rise to extremism. In the chapter entitled "What virtue is in the political state," the passage that most dramatically brings political virtue together with Christian virtue, Montesquieu remarks on the extremism of both:

> The less we can satisfy our particular passions, the more we give ourselves up to passions for general ones. Why do monks love their order so much? It is exactly due to the same thing that makes their order intolerable to them. Their rule deprives them of all the things upon which ordinary passions rest; there remains, therefore, this passion for the very rule that afflicts them. The more austere it is, that is, the more it cuts out their inclinations, the more strength it gives to those that remain. (V.2)[27]

If Montesquieu's identification of virtue with simple self-renunciation departs from ancient and Christian conceptions of virtue, it is meant to articulate a deeper truth about the effect of these forms of virtue, which is the same despite their different aspirations. All result in the suppression of human particularity and private desires. For the modern subject, they are felt as a painful denial of self, because of the skepticism of modern scientific reason and the plurality of modern standards of right, which make questionable the goods that once eased the pain of virtue. And the political effect of the self-denial that virtue requires is extremism, which leads to immoderate government and the insecurity of persons.

The concept of honor, which resembles virtue in being a quality of character, a form of motivation, and a source of individual agency, is intended to meet the new conditions of modern politics. Montesquieu's argument for honor largely accepts Hobbes's denial of a single *summum bonum*, at least as a political matter. It also rejects the moral and physical harshness of ancient life, which Montesquieu thinks had to give way to a "more agreeable way of living" in the modern period. Under the new conditions of skepticism and plurality, and in light of the new expectation of comfort, "one felt that there had to be other mores" (VII.4). Honor is based not on self-renunciation but on self-love (*l'amour propre*), ambition, and the desire to distinguish oneself. It reflects the self-centered quality of modern mores, and it is meant to serve a liberal, or limited, regime rather than a salvific one, and yet it engages fundamental features of human nature. Honor does presuppose a certain teleology, it is true, but the teleology it presupposes is a partial one. Honor as a quality of character is compatible with a range of conceptions of the good and a variety of moral and political standards of right. The teleology of honor places self-command above subservience but it does not in itself define the ends toward which the self-commanding agent aims. Moreover, because honor is experienced as being less harsh than virtue, and because it is tied to a modern constitutional order, Montesquieu regards it as more moderate in its effects than what he calls virtue. The concept of honor allows Montesquieu to discuss character—the sources of individual agency and forms of motivation that serve liberal political institutions—in a more nuanced way than earlier liberals had done, while largely steering clear of the comprehensive teleology of the Greeks and the Christians. Because he aims above all for moderation in politics (XXIX.1), he wants to avoid the oppression of the particular interests and private desires that virtue (at least to the modern mind) had come to imply, and the zealous fervor that tends to accompany it.

Honor finds its home in the government of constitutional monarchy, on Montesquieu's account, where it serves the division of power that is central to this regime. The structure of monarchy includes the "intermediary bodies" that stand between the king and his subjects. They mediate the flow of political power and check the exercise of authority, for "in order to form a moderate government, one must combine powers, regulate them, temper them, make them act; give, that is to say, a ballast to one to put it in a position to resist another" (V.14). By mediating the will of the sovereign, the intermediary bodies support the rule of law, because without limits on sovereign authority, nothing can be fixed and there is no fundamental law. The intermediary bodies include the lords, clergy, nobility, and towns. Each is a power recognized as "independent" that "checks (*arrête*) arbitrary power" (II.4). The intermediary bodies provide alternative sites of authority from which the king's use of power can be contested.[28] Of these bodies, Montesquieu emphasizes the role of the nobility, saying that "the nobility enters in some fashion into the essence of monarchy, of which the fundamental maxim is: no monarch, no nobility; no nobility, no monarch. Rather one has a despot" (II.4).[29]

Lawyers, administrators, and military men, the nobility were charged with carrying out the will of the sovereign. As members of the *parlements* they adjudicated and administered his laws, as mayors of local villages they minded his subjects and collected his taxes, and as soldiers they commanded his armies and oversaw his conquests.[30] Although the nobility was charged with taking care of the king's business, this charge gave them the power to interfere in the king's business, and the legislative and judicial prerogatives of the nobility had the status of constitutional rights.[31] In theory the courts had only to receive, record, transmit, and enforce the sovereign's directives, but in practice the *parlements* prided themselves on the right to delay registration of a questionable law while they presented their objections to the king and awaited his response.[32] This right of remonstrance was supplemented with other forms of "interference" by the nobility at the level of local adjudication, administration, and enforcement. All were further enhanced by the ability to arouse public support for such interference.[33] Every delegation of authority resulted in a potential pocket of resistance so that "just as the sea, which seems to want to cover the whole earth, is checked by the grasses and the smallest bits of gravel on the shore, so monarchs, whose power seems boundless, are checked by the slightest obstacles" (II.4). As Montesquieu presents it in *The Spirit of the Laws*, honor is the "spring" (*ressort*) that animates the perpetual tumults between the nobility and the crown, tumults that serve liberty by dividing power.

It is worth noting that Montesquieu's discussion of the nobility elides an important division within this category.[34] There had long been tensions, even hostilities, between the nobility of the sword consisting of soldiers (*noblesse d'épée*), and the nobility of the robe comprising magistrates and the members of the administrative *parlements* (*noblesse de robe*).[35] The former traced its lineage to the medieval warriors whose role it had been to defend the realm against external aggression.[36] The members of the latter group were relative newcomers to high society, beneficiaries of an expanding and increasingly complex state apparatus. Although the *noblesse d'épée* traditionally had claimed greater prestige, by Montesquieu's day the status of the robe was comparable, and on some accounts even superior.[37] Nor was the robe the mere instrument of the king, despite the fact that its ranks were populated by political appointees. On the contrary, its ideology aimed at limiting the power of the crown.[38] The debates in French constitutional theory of the first half of the eighteenth century, to which Montesquieu contributes at the end of *The Spirit of the Laws,* often played the two classes of nobility against each other, however. From Montesquieu's point of view, such skirmishes could only increase the power of the crown by dividing its most potent opposition. This is one reason why he runs the two groups together in his discussion of honor, and why he has been called the reconciler of the feudal and magistral traditions within the nobility.[39]

Montesquieu's elision of the two classes of nobility also reflects a more general historical trend. The boundaries between the two branches of the French nobility had already begun to be transgressed by the sixteenth century.[40] At that time, the *noblesse d'épée* was deprived of a good part of its military efficacy as the result of technological innovations in warfare and greater political stability, and many nobles began to turn to activities other than fighting.[41] The establishment of universities, the expansion of the state, and ultimately the advent of court life and salon society opened up new fields of endeavor for them. These changes had consequences for the meaning of honor. Feudal honor had been rooted in the acts of conquest and the martial practices of the Frankish warriors who invaded Roman Gaul. To be "noble" was "to count among one's ancestors no one who had been subjected to slavery."[42] Where war was an everyday matter and slavery often the result of conquest, the physical strength that enabled one to remain free from servitude was highly prized. For this reason, the medieval knight was associated above all with the display of physical strength, what one commentator calls "the strength of a splendid animal."[43] His honor was identified almost exclusively with his strength and his external goods, especially his fief.[44] In the following centuries, however, honor was increasingly internalized. The emphasis on physical qualities and external goods gradually gave way to a new understanding of honor as an internal quality of character, although it remained closely associated with the battlefield.[45] Honor came to mean valor rather than simple strength.

Still later, as the *noblesse d'épée* was invaded by and integrated with the *noblesse de robe,* the internal qualities associated with honor underwent further change. In particular, the assimilation of the martial and administrative classes within the nobility tended to demilitarize noble mores. As the power and prestige of the robe increased, the ideals of violent mastery and physical prowess associated with the sword were eclipsed by new notions of honorable conduct. Courage continued to be central to honor, but it was combined with qualities suited to the new nobility represented by the peaceful administrator, the moderate judge, the country gentleman, and the *honnête homme.*[46] This shift was part of a larger movement that one commentator has called a "revolution" in the "political values and practices" of the nobility in the seventeenth and eighteenth centuries.[47]

The rise of the robe class suggested a novel separation between political power and military might, since the new administrators held effective political control but did not fight.[48] These civil servants were men of letters, law, and politics, not war, and the nonmilitary ideal that they embodied was more in keeping with the standards being championed by Enlightenment humanists.[49] The humanist emphasis on letters challenged the military basis of noble rank.[50] And although *les lettres* had originally been scorned by the high nobility for its "feminizing" effects, the new orientation eventually displaced the warrior ethos as the primary outlook of the nobility in the eighteenth century.[51] This displacement was never perfectly complete or fully conscious, to be sure.[52] The old warrior honor was not so much abandoned by the nobility as extended and transformed. Although courage remained a constant feature of honor, it assumed new forms that went beyond martial valor.

Montesquieu's concept of honor reflects these historical shifts. It exemplifies the modern domestication of honor in which the martial valor of medieval soldiers was infused with qualities specific to the new administrative class of the *noblesse de robe.* He notes the connection between honor and soldiering, but his idea of honor also includes the moderation of the judicious administrator, the restraint of the equitable judge, and even the gentle manners and fine speech of the *courtiers*. His *honnêtes hommes* are more men of society and politics than warriors. They have courage, as we shall see, but it is civilized and directed by the rule of law, and moderated by the security of an established constitutional regime. Their courage also is political rather than merely physical, as manifested in the parliamentary acts of remonstrance and the individual acts of civil disobedience that check encroaching political power and protect individual liberty.

Moreover, honor in Montesquieu serves the defense of principle, not simply self-defense or the defense of territory, as the honor of medieval soldiers had done. This innovation to feudal honor was begun before Montesquieu by the Christian church. When the church appropriated the feudal virtues of the medieval nobility, it effected an important shift in the meaning of honor. Instead of using his strength and courage in the service of personal protection or gain, the Christian knight was expected to "defend Holy Church, particularly against the infidel. He will protect the widow, the orphan, and the poor."[53] Instead of defending himself or his lord, the man of honor henceforth would defend *the right*. Yet while Montesquieu's man of honor glories in defending a cause, rather than simply his person and property, the code of the *honnête homme* is secular, not religious; it is grounded in social practices and customs, and in a political tradition with constitutional standing. In fact, Montesquieu points out that codes of honor in modern monarchies sometimes oppose the "tribune" of religion.[54] Moreover, the codes of honor that Montesquieu has in mind do not constitute universal standards of right, as does the Christian creed. Eighteenth-century codes of honor provided concrete rules of conduct regulating specific spheres of activity and particular categories of persons. The connection between honor and principles of right that are both secular and universal came later. The American founders, who pledged their "sacred Honour" to defend the universal principles of liberty and equality, exemplify this modern development, as we shall see. Montesquieu's concept of honor, in which honor as a quality of character is tied to established rules of conduct rather than simply physical prowess, points in this direction but remains more limited in its scope.

So although honor in Montesquieu has roots in the martial valor of feudal warriors and the piety of Christian knights, it also departs from these roots in important ways. The class of honorable men now includes not just soldiers but administrators and judges. And those with honor pursue glory not simply through conquest but through the defense of principles, and not by defending religious principles but by defending traditional codes of right action, political principles (such as the division of power and the rule of law), and constitutional rights (such as the parliamentary right of remonstrance). Because honor sets in motion the division of political power that moderates government and protects individual liberty, it is indispensable to monarchy, just as virtue is indispensable to republican government and fear to despotism. Without honor, the differentiated structure of monarchy would dissolve into the perfect unity of the unopposed will of the sovereign.

Honor's High Ambitions

The heart of honor in Montesquieu is principled desire, or ambition (*l'ambition*), defined as "the desire to do great things."[55] Insofar as ambition subverts equality, and therefore unity, it "is pernicious in a republic" (III.7), Montesquieu says; and because it is fearless, the spread of ambition would be catastrophic for a despot. Yet ambition "has good effects in monarchy" (III.7) because of its enlivening influence on the intermediary bodies. Those with honor are more contentious than bipartisan, but this contentiousness serves to divide and so to limit political power. In moderate monarchies, the ambitions of the nobles counteract the ambitions of the king, which is good for individual liberty. Yet as everyone knows, ambition can be low-minded and petty, and countless commentators have faulted Montesquieu for his defense of it.[56] Indeed, honor frequently is interpreted as nothing more than "ambition in idleness, baseness in pride, the desire to enrich oneself without work, aversion to truth, flattery, treachery, [and] perfidy" (III.5). Readers who take this account of "the wretched character of courtiers" (III.5) as the sum total of honor have missed a great deal, however.[57] Montesquieu is nothing if not realistic, and he makes no attempt to sweeten honor. The petty vanities of the courtiers are indeed its not-so-distant relations. Yet honor is a complex quality of character, not least because it includes ambition without being limited to the lowest forms of ambition, such as that of the courtiers.

The story of the Viscount of Orte displays the higher ambitions of honor and its complexity:

> After Saint Bartholomew's Day, Charles IX having written to all the governors to massacre the Huguenots, the Viscount of Orte, who was in command at Bayonne, wrote to the king, "Sire, I have found among the inhabitants and the warriors only good citizens, brave soldiers, and no executioner; thus, they and I beg Your Majesty to use our arms and our lives for things that can be done (*choses faisables*)." This great and generous courage regarded an act of cowardice as an impossible thing. (IV.2)[58]

Orte's disobedience parallels the "interference" of the *parlements*, although it is more spectacular. Why did he do it? Not from self-interest or civic virtue or solidarity, and not because he applied the principle of "universalizibility," as we say today. Instead the story of Orte's courage must be understood together with Montesquieu's definition of honor as a form of personal ambition and even the prejudice (*prejugé*) of each person and each condition for himself and his own (III.6). Orte refused the king's command because he thought too much of himself to undertake such brutality. He expects more of himself than to kill innocents just because someone told him to do so, even his king. He is, so to speak, better than that; he would not stoop so low. He owes it to himself to uphold his code of honor because this is what distinguishes him from those who are simply the instruments of someone else's will, and he is proud that he is more than just that.

Honor is a mixed motive, and the courage of Orte is not altogether different from the vanities of the courtly air. What distinguishes Orte from the courtiers is not that his motives are purer than theirs, in the sense of being more altruistic or more universal, for he thinks of himself no less than they do. If anything, Orte thinks more of himself. It is his high opinion of himself that turns his desire for distinction to this brave act of resistance rather than obsequious social climbing, which is the vocation of the courtiers. The courtiers are obsequious because although they think only of themselves, they think too little of themselves, and so they freely debase themselves. They are ambitious and yet they will put up with anything.

And so Orte's "great and generous courage" reflects his ambition to be someone special. After all, it is no small thing to refuse a king. This ambition is an unusual (for us) mix of partiality and higher purpose. The mixed quality of honor explains why Montesquieu says that with honor, "one does not judge the actions of men as good but as fine, not as just but as great; not as reasonable but as extraordinary" (IV.2). What Orte did was "fine" *(belle)* in the sense of being beautiful or admirable. It exceeded average expectations. Honor is something to live *up* to because it is above average. It is wonderful to see, like a beautiful painting, because it reminds us that there is more to being human than getting by.[59] So honor is an excellence that "elevate[s] the heart" (IV.3), but honor, Montesquieu says, is not the same as virtue. Thus honor yields "fine" actions but not necessarily "good" ones. For "in order to be a good man *(homme de bien),* it is necessary to have the intention of being one and to love the state less for oneself than for itself" (III.6). The good man or woman has a pure and selfless heart, and does the right thing for the right reason. But that is not Orte, who acted for himself. If he did the Huguenots a good turn, their welfare was not his sole intention. Orte treated the Huguenots not only as ends in themselves but also as the means to his own self-respect and even his distinction. Their plight was his opportunity and he made the most of it.[60] Thus one must judge Orte's courage not as good but as fine.

If honor is not necessarily "good" neither is it intrinsically "just."[61] Contemporary accounts of honor very often treat it as a subset of justice, but Montesquieu emphatically distinguishes them.[62] With honor, one judges actions "not as just but as great," for "the virtues we are shown here are always less what one owes others than what one owes oneself; they are not so much what calls us to our fellow citizens as what distinguishes us from them" (IV.2). What one owes others is the province of justice; what one owes oneself is the province of honor. By emphasizing this distinction, Montesquieu reminds us that they do not always coincide. Justice and honor may conflict. What I owe to myself may very well come at the expense of what I owe to you. Nor does Montesquieu provide a clear rank ordering of the two. Moreover, except under despotism, where there are no fixed laws, one usually can act in a just fashion simply by following the law. So except where the laws are nonexistent or very bad, it is possible to be just without making much effort. By contrast, honor calls forth a certain "greatness of soul" (V.12) because it cannot be had so easily. Indeed, "the things that honor prohibits are more rigorously prohibited when the laws do not concur in proscribing them, and those things that honor demands are more strongly demanded when the laws do not ask for them" (IV.2). Honorable people such as Orte ask more of themselves than what is minimally required by the laws.[63] Risk is involved in honor, self-assertion, and the willingness to undertake something difficult. So honor is an effort even if it is not exactly self-sacrifice.

Finally, one judges honorable actions "not as reasonable but as extraordinary" because they interrupt the ordinary processes and resist the constraints that condition our expectations. In this regard, honor resembles Hannah Arendt's concept of "action," although there are important differences as well. Action, on Arendt's account, means asserting one's capacity for what she calls "natality," or new beginnings, against the "automatic" processes of nature and civilization.[64] Arendt's actions are "interruptions of some natural series of events, of some automatic process, in whose context they constitute the wholly unexpected."[65] They manifest humankind's "sheer capacity to begin," a strong exertion of agency, because they imply a departure from the given. Honor in Montesquieu is not as creative or "authentic" as Arendt's concept of action, because it is tied to hereditary social codes and fixed laws. But like "action," honor cannot be made routine. It is true that Orte's disobedience is in line with, even demanded by, the laws of honor contained in his code. Yet if the laws of honor can be known in advance, individual acts of honor are more difficult to predict. Honor cannot be "reckoned on" with the same assurance that Hobbes attributed to the need for self-preservation, for example, because individual acts of honor are so "extraordinary" in this sense. Honorable actions are risky, and so call for a greater measure of intention, and therefore agency, than does the automatic response to bodily needs on which Hobbes reckoned. Honor is not radically spontaneous in the sense that it does not produce arbitrary actions. Individual acts of honor are not arbitrary because the codes that guide them are well established, but they are unpredictable because they are so extraordinary.

So honor is ambitious and assertive, and it aims high. It cannot be denied that honor in Montesquieu begins in rank or that it depends partly on public recognition and the distribution of public honors. But the story of Orte demonstrates that for Montesquieu honor does not end with either rank or public recognition. The fact that Montesquieu associates honor with ambition emphasizes the active quality of honor.[66]

Honor as a quality of character requires an act of individual self-assertion that goes beyond rank and recognition, and sometimes even against the authorities that establish rank and distribute recognition. Indeed, the fact that honor cannot be provided by the authorities gives it the independence needed to resist them when necessary. The self-assertion that honor in Montesquieu requires is not the open-ended striving that one finds in a competitive society, but rather the striving to prove worthy of one's appointed station. Honor holds that "when we have once been placed in a rank, we should do or suffer nothing that might show that we hold ourselves inferior to the rank itself" (IV.2). Yet this is not a passive affair, for it may demand actions that are, as Montesquieu says, *belles, grandes,* and *extraordinaires.* Moreover, those with honor have high opinions of themselves, which means that they have much to live up to, which makes them willing to undertake risky actions. This explains why the quest for distinction is central to honor. Would Orte have stood up to the king if he could have esteemed himself either way? If doing something exceptional had not been necessary to his sense of self-respect, would he have gone to the trouble? Would he have bothered to risk his life? If we can respect ourselves regardless of what we do, why make the effort that the defense of liberty occasionally requires? In a "well-ordered society," it is true, great acts of resistance to political authority in defense of individual liberties are not often called for. But the rare instances in which they are called for can make all the difference.[67] The loss of high ambition risks a politics in which, as Tocqueville warned, "each day the appearance of the body social may become more tranquil and less aspiring *(haute)*"—even toward liberty.[68] The high ambitions of honor stand in the way of such acquiescence.

Reverence and Reflexivity

In a moderate monarchy, those with honor distinguish themselves by defending their constitutional liberties and the principles of right contained in their codes of honor.[69] Honor is not mere "self-expression" but rather "has its supreme rules" *(ses règles suprêmes)* (IV.2). The codes that give honor its rules, and thus its constraints, cannot be derived from divine will, or natural law, or reason itself. But they are not merely willful creations, either. Instead, codes of honor are grounded in social and political roles, in institutions that have histories, and in collective traditions with constitutional standing. They are not freely chosen on an individual basis but neither are they handed down by God or nature. Their authority comes from the weight of tradition, and so they rest on the conventional reverence that the members of a society hold for their institutions, traditions, and principles. Codes of honor must be revered in order to provide strong grounds for contesting the abuse of power. After all, who would risk life and limb in defense of principles that could be discarded at will? This explains why Montesquieu says of Orte that he regarded a cowardly action as an "impossible thing." Killing innocents was not only unsavory for Orte, or undignified, but *impossible*.[70] This is how seriously Orte took his code of honor, how he revered his principles. The categorical quality of honor is tied to the reverence the honorable person holds for his or her code. Somewhat paradoxically, then, a measure of reverence fuels honor as a source of resistance to violations of political right.

Honor's need for reverence distinguishes it from Machiavelli's *virtù*, but there are similarities, as well.[71] Like both the "great men" of Machiavelli's *Discourses* and his "new prince," Montesquieu's *honnêtes hommes* seek glory. And as in Machiavelli, the individual pursuit of glory indirectly produces public benefits. In republican governments, according to Machiavelli, the glory-seeking of princely types contributes to their "tumults" with the people and to "the good effects" that they engender.[72] In a principality, the pursuit of glory by a single individual leads to the consolidation of power and thus to political stability. Montesquieu wants to divide power, not consolidate it, but the pursuit of honor supplies the defect of better motives in a way that parallels the pursuit of glory in Machiavelli, since with honor each person works for the common good, believing he works for his individual purposes (III.7). The nobility's prideful defense of its prerogatives serves the liberty of all by checking the perpetually encroaching power of the sovereign.

Although honor yields general benefits, those with honor sometimes distinguish themselves at the expense of particular others, if only because, as Montesquieu says, "one excessively great man renders others small" (IV.2). Even aside from the social inequalities that accompanied honor in the old regime, honor is intrinsically inegalitarian in the sense that those with honor stand out from the rest of us and thereby command our respect.[73] Honorable persons show up their fellows. Occasionally, they may even make use of their fellows. For this reason, the concept of honor has been called Machiavellian, "in the morally pejorative sense in which Montesquieu understood it."[74] Even though Montesquieu seems sincerely to see in honor a "more noble" motive than immediate interest, nevertheless one must admit that the "velvet gloves" of the gentleman sometimes may "conceal claws."[75] Still, honor does not engender the great acts of terror that made "Machiavellianism" a pejorative term for Montesquieu. Honor impresses and sometimes stings, but it does not "stupefy" others the way that Cesare Borgia's bisection of Remirro d'Orco did, because it does not terrify them.[76]

Honor is less fearsome than *virtù* because it is more moderate. The example of Orte is striking in this regard. As a soldier, Orte initially makes us think of the honor of the medieval knight, with its thirst for military glory and the ambition to conquer and to subjugate. But Orte's ambition does not consist in conquest and subjugation. Indeed, he refuses even to take the battlefield against the Huguenots, much less subdue them. Even his disobedience is moderate, for while he resists his king's command, Orte does not attempt to unseat him. His honor issues in an act of conscientious objection, not a regicide.[77] Orte's disobedience is counterbalanced by respect for the king's authority, which is what makes it civil. Montesquieu maintains that while "there is nothing in monarchy that the laws, religion, and honor prescribe so much as obedience to the wills of the prince," nevertheless "this honor dictates to us that the prince should never prescribe an action that dishonors us because it would render us incapable of serving him" (IV.2). The fact that honor supports both obedience to the crown and (when necessary) principled disobedience makes it resemble "a force that repels without ceasing all bodies from the center and a force of gravity that brings them back to it" (III.7).[78] Honor preserves the balance of power that sustains moderate monarchies by maintaining a balance of obedience and disobedience to sovereign authority. Respect for the authority of the crown makes honor's disobedience civil rather than a simple act of anarchy. At the same time, it is only because the honorable man also reveres his code of honor that he is willing to take the risks that civil disobedience entails. Honor thus brings courage together with moderation, as the merging of the manners of the *noblesse d'épée* and the *noblesse de robe* also suggests.

Honor is further distinguished from the virtue of Machiavelli's "new prince" by being tied to particular social codes, political traditions, and a constitutional order. Killing innocents is something that the Viscount of

Orte simply will not do because his code of honor forbids it. By contrast, there is nothing, in principle, that the new prince will not do. He will do anything because there is no standard above him to limit him.[79] His virtue is his self-assertion; he is a self-made man. This quality of being self-made explains the *newness* of the new prince and his virtue. He should found his own principality, rather than inheriting one, and he must establish new modes and orders rather than binding himself to the old standards.[80] The new virtue of the new prince is unbounded because of its newness. But honor is old and limited by its past. It depends on the old modes and orders, and this dependence constrains and directs its ambitions. Unlike *virtù*, then, honor has an inheritance consisting of traditional, customary codes of conduct. This means that honor leans on reverence, even though it sometimes leads to political resistance. Indeed, honor's reverence for its codes supports its resistance to encroaching political power.

If honor's history is a constraint from the point of view of *virtù*, however, it is a liberation when seen from the standpoint of Aristotelian magnanimity. Aristotle defined magnanimity as complete virtue directed toward oneself, and distinguished it from complete virtue in relation to another person, which he called justice.[81] Montesquieu's distinction between honor and virtue parallels Aristotle's distinction between magnanimity and justice. Like Aristotelian magnanimity, honor is concerned with what one owes to oneself; like Aristotelian justice, what Montesquieu calls political virtue is concerned with obligations to others (IV.2). The honorable person is like the magnanimous one "who, being worthy of great things, requires of himself that he be worthy of them."[82] And much as the honorable person "aims for superiority" (V.4) and demands preferences and distinctions (III.7), so the magnanimous one "wishes to be superior" and expects to be recognized as such.[83] Thus Aristotle's magnanimous man was concerned with public honors most of all.[84]

Yet Aristotle emphasized that a magnanimous man should be a "good" man, for honor was the prize of virtue, and it was "bestowed only on good men."[85] Magnanimity without both nobility and goodness was impossible.[86] By contrast, Montesquieu maintains that those with honor are not necessarily *good*, as we have seen, for one judges honorable actions not as good but as fine. While the magnanimous man must do the right thing for the right reason,[87] it is enough for Montesquieu's man of honor to do the right thing, even if his reasons are not, morally speaking, the right ones. The honorable man's reasons for doing great things may not be morally pure, for "mores are never as pure in monarchies as in republican governments" (IV.2). The morally mixed character of honor does not mean that anything goes, however. Even though the honorable person's reasons for doing great things may not be morally pure, honor as a quality of character is guided by established codes of honor rather than by arbitrary will. If honor does not require a city of angels, then, neither would it be possible for a race of devils.

The morally mixed character of honor partly explains why Montesquieu sometimes refers to modern monarchical honor as "false honor": "It is true that, philosophically speaking, it is a false honor that drives all the parts of the state; but this false honor is as useful to the public as true honor would be to the individuals who could have it" (III.7). "Philosophically speaking," honor is "false" because it does not presuppose perfect virtue and does not aim directly at the common good.[88] Honor in Montesquieu is not, in contrast to Aristotelian magnanimity, the "crown" of all the moral virtues. This point emphasizes Montesquieu's distinction between honor and virtue, a distinction that puzzled readers in his own day as much as in our own.[89] After all, if honor is admitted to be a form of excellence that "elevates the heart," why not call it a virtue? And how can a quality of character that requires virtues such as courage and moderation nevertheless fail to be a virtue itself? The term virtue can be employed without conveying moral value, of course, as when it is used to mean efficacy in fulfilling some function.[90] Virtue in this sense is related to virtuosity or technical skill, and it has no intrinsic moral value. Montesquieu's concept of honor clearly is a "virtue" in this limited sense, insofar as honor is instrumental to the regime of monarchy. As the "spring" of monarchical government, Montesquieu says, honor "makes all the parts of the body politic move," and it preserves the balance of power and the rule of law that distinguish monarchy from despotism.

Yet Montesquieu makes it clear that honor has more than merely instrumental value, which indicates that honor cannot be contained within the category of virtue as virtuosity. He describes honorable actions as "great," "fine," and "extraordinary," for example, and his reference to the "great and generous courage" of Orte clearly carries moral weight. Elsewhere Montesquieu contrasts honor with the debasement of subjects under despotic government who act "only out of hope for the conveniences of life" or else from fear (V.17–18). By contrast, monarchy, the regime of honor, gives each subject, "so to speak, a larger space" in which "he can exercise those virtues that give the soul not independence but greatness" (V.12). Finally, Montesquieu's remarks on the corruption of honor indicate indirectly the moral worth of honor in its noncorrupt forms. Honor is corrupted "when *honor* has been placed in contradiction to *honors* and when one can be at the same time covered with infamy and with dignities" (VIII.7).[91] As an example, Montesquieu cites the triumphal ornaments given to informers in the reign of Tiberius, which, he says, "so demeaned these honors that those who merited them disdained them" (VIII.7, n. 10). For these reasons, it is not sufficient to characterize honor as mere virtuosity. Yet honor does not presuppose moral purity or perfection. And to complicate matters further, honor in contrast to virtue is more than merely a quality of character. Honor as a quality of character is also constitutively tied to codes of honor and public honors. To act from a sense of honor involves following rules and seeking distinction, neither of which is intrinsic to moral virtue per se. This explains why the common classificatory division between virtue-centered and rule-governed theories of right action cannot comprehend honor, which contains elements of both. Honor is tied to virtue but remains distinct from it.[92] Honor is more than virtuosity (although it is that, too) because it draws on some true virtues and may yield others, but it neither requires nor produces complete virtue. And it is constitutively tied to general rules and public recognition, which have no part in virtue traditionally conceived.

The differences between honor and Aristotelian magnanimity reflect Montesquieu's reluctance to endorse in any simple way the idea of nature as a standard. Like everything else under the sun, Aristotelian magnanimity had its place in the natural order. It was important that the magnanimous man also be a good man[93] because political recognition should reflect natural deserts,[94] and this was important because the political order should be commensurate with the natural order.[95] By contrast, honor is embedded in a social and historical order, not a natural one; in traditions and constitutions rather than cosmology. To be sure, the ambition, courage, and attachment to principle that give rise to honor as a quality of character have roots in human nature. Honor as a quality of character has a natural basis, but honor as a whole is underdetermined by its natural basis because the content of its codes is not specified by nature. Montesquieu denies that nature determines human ends directly and that it can be a definitive guide for politics. It is true that he opposes despotism, like slavery, on the grounds that they are bad for "human nature" (VIII.8, XV.13).[96] To the extent that human nature has a role in political standards, however, it is one that is mediated by the "spirit" of the laws of particular societies; by the climate and conditions of a country; by the customs, manners, and religion of the inhabitants; and by their political histories (I.3). Montesquieu does not fully exclude nature from political standards, but neither does he believe that absolute, universal standards of political right are given to human beings fully formed by nature, or that such standards can be taken directly from an analysis of human nature. Montesquieu's skepticism in this regard marks another point of convergence with earlier liberals. Like Hobbes and Locke, Montesquieu thought that the nature of the highest goods was impossible for human beings (even the best human beings) to know with any certainty.[97] This skepticism leads Montesquieu, as it led Hobbes and Locke, to defend political orders that aim for individual liberty rather than the perfection of the soul, which would require certain knowledge of the nature of the highest goods. In contrast to magnanimity, then, honor has a history. The social codes and political constitutions that underwrite it change over time. And they are human constructs, rather than natural endowments or commands of God.[98]

These considerations illuminate the two sides of honor as a historical phenomenon. On the one hand, the historicity of honor limits it by setting constraints on what one can honorably do. These constraints, grounded in the weight of tradition, distinguish honor from Machiavelli's *virtù* and from mere willfulness. On the other hand, the historicity of honor frees it from what Montesquieu regarded as the determinism of ancient metaphysics.[99] Even though the Viscount of Orte did not personally choose his code of honor, this code was the product of a long series of collective human choices rather than a dictate of nature or command of God.[100] And so the historicity of honor is simultaneously a constraint and a freedom. Consequently, honor is both a limit on agency and a source of agency, and reverence for its codes makes both its power and its limits possible.

If honor rests on reverence, however, it is far from simple obedience. After all, Orte risked his life to oppose the command of his king, not obey it. Most of the time today a soldier's disobedience to the chain of command is grounds for a dishonorable discharge, not a mark of honor. This fact makes the story of Orte all the more striking as an example of honor. It disrupts our conventional association between honor and obedience, for Orte distinguishes himself by his disobedience.[101] By contrast, obedience is central to the motive that Montesquieu calls "political virtue," which requires that one's particular self be made to obey the common self of the political community. Honor works with our particular inclinations, or at least with some of them, and so cannot be reduced to obedience, even in effect. Similarly, because honor "is favored by the passions and favors them in turn" (IV.5), it does not require a heavy-handed education.[102] The principal education of honor is not in the public institutions where children are instructed. Instead, Montesquieu says that "the world is the school of what is called honor, the universal master that ought everywhere to guide us" (IV.2). The world is the school of honor because the world is a stage for the rivalries and the achievements that inspire (rather than coerce) the ambition to do the "great things" that bring self-respect and public recognition. The particular associations and roles that one inhabits from the time one enters the world shape the standards that guide one's ambition, and provide the recognition that rewards it. By contrast, "in republican government . . . the whole power of education is needed" because the obedience that political virtue demands, its self-renunciation, "is always a very painful thing" (IV.5). For the same reason, virtue needs the continual support of censors. Thus the Spartans were "always correcting or always corrected, always instructing and being instructed" (XIX.16). Virtue needs supervision and enforcement (V.19), whereas honor cannot be enforced because it cannot be forced. For while "it is easy to regulate by law what one owes others, it is difficult to include in them all that one owes to oneself" (VII.10). Honor "attracts rather than orders" in the words of one interpreter,[103] and this makes it "impressive," for honor can motivate difficult and risky actions that otherwise would require force (III.7).

While virtue can be habitual and even half-forgotten, honor is always aware of itself, for better or worse. Virtue can be forgotten when one is sufficiently habituated to it to act automatically. And political virtue, as Montesquieu construes it, is by definition self-forgetting because it gives priority to purposes other than one's own. But the world, the school of honor, "teaches man never to forget himself," as one commentator puts it.[104] Honor is always aware of itself because it is always self-regarding and because it is never automatic, since honor interrupts the automatic processes and resists the necessities that constrain us. Those with honor are self-regarding and self-aware *agents*. This self-awareness, or the reflexive character of honor, can be seen in its claim to be the "arbiter" (*l'arbitre*) of its obligations:

> Honor prescribes nothing more to the nobility than serving the prince in war. In effect, this is the most distinguished profession because its hazards, successes, and even misfortunes lead to greatness. But, in imposing this law, honor wants to be the arbiter; and if it finds itself offended (*choqué*) it requires or permits one to retire to one's home. (IV.2)

Orte's "great and generous courage" was the result of an arbitration over which he was the presiding judge. He regarded his situation, his orders, and his code of conduct, and he adjudicated the conflict between them (IV.2). The claim to arbitrate one's obligations opens up a field of action not available to those whose material interests constitute their only legitimate source of agency. For whereas we are moved by our interests, as arbiters we move ourselves. Indeed, honor rests upon some conception of human autonomy, albeit not Kant's conception of autonomy. Orte's disobedience reflects an awareness of himself as arbiter but not as legislator: he judges and he executes but he does not *legislate* the laws of honor. These laws are given to him rather than legislated by him, which separates honor from autonomy in the Kantian sense. But for Montesquieu, as for Kant, liberty is possible only if there is more to the self than its material interests and more to action than either a response to necessity or an obedience to command.

Honor's claim to be an arbiter does not make it intrinsically arbitrary, but it does open the door to this possibility. Montesquieu sometimes refers to honor as "eccentric (*bizarre*)," saying that honor "makes the virtues only what it wants and as it wants them: on its own, it places rules on all that which is prescribed to us; it extends or limits our duties according to its fancy (*fantaisie*), whether they have their source in religion, politics, or morality" (IV.2). Yet the eccentricity of honor (leaving aside the special case of its corrupt forms) should not be understood as arbitrary caprice. Honor is eccentric from the standpoint of the king, who cannot control it and whose laws do not define its codes. But Montesquieu emphasizes that honor has "its supreme rules, and education is obliged to conform itself to them," which means that honor is embodied in publicly known, shared, and socially regulated codes of conduct (IV.2). Honor is not intrinsically arbitrary and capricious, then, but it is independent of the will of the prince as well as the standards of religion, and to some extent those of morality as well. It is precisely the "eccentricity" of honor in this sense that makes it an effective source of the resistance that checks encroaching political power.[105] Thus "in monarchical and moderate states, power is limited by that which is its spring; I mean honor, which reigns, like a monarch, over the prince and the people" and "from that there result necessary modifications of obedience" (III.10).

Still, if honor is not intrinsically arbitrary it can become excessively reflexive, which may be dangerous for political liberty. The responsibility for arbitrating one's obligations may be pushed to the point of license rather than balanced with a measure of reverence for those obligations, and so may issue in acts of arbitrary willfulness. In other words, the activity of arbitrating one's obligations may undermine their power to guide and to limit individual ambition. After all, if Orte can disobey the king, why not also disobey his own code of honor? There is a paradox at the heart of honor, for it presses conflicting demands upon us. It brings together reverence and reflexivity because it requires both, but it does not dissolve the tension between them. This paradox reveals a fundamental tension within human agency more generally. If one's reverence is too complete, then one's actions are nothing more than obedience and so not free. But with perfect reflexivity, or radical autonomy, one has no good reason to act in one way rather than another, and then it is difficult to distinguish one's choices from mere willfulness or simple impulse. In other words, there is a point at which radical choice fades into non-choice.[106] The unchosen attachments, identities, and obligations that constrain our choices also give us reason to choose one course of action over another. In this sense, they support our capacity for choice and thus for agency. The paradox of honor as both reverent and reflexive captures this deep feature of individual agency. By preserving the tension rather than dissolving it, the concept of honor helps us see why a theory of agency that privileges one at the cost of the other is bound to be incomplete. It reminds us that even the self-determination of the modern subject rests on reverence of one sort or another. Honor balances choice with limits on choice. Our limits make our choices meaningful and effective, and if these limits are not to be coerced from the outside (by God or nature or king), they will need to be revered from the inside.

The Partiality of Honor

Honor does not require an abstraction from human partiality but instead makes public use of it. There are two aspects to the partiality of honor in Montesquieu. First, honor is grounded in particular social and political identities that yield specific standpoints and obligations. Honor does not take a universal view. It is not an altogether subjective view, because honor is tied to general codes of conduct that extend its scope beyond the particular case and give it wider bearing than individual interest can achieve. Yet honor always is a view from somewhere.[107] And even though honor is self-serving rather than collectivist in its aims, its beginnings are corporate in character, not individualistic. The substantive content of one's code of honor in Montesquieu grows out of one's condition or membership in a particular social body, so that the same action that would dishonor a noble might have no significance if done by a commoner. Thus honor is "the prejudice" not simply of "each person" but also of "each condition" (III.6). The collective dimension of honor is significant for its role in checking the crown. Individual acts of honorable disobedience carry weight because they draw on the existing recognition and independent authority of the particular intermediary bodies to which individual nobles belong. Thus when an Orte defends his honor against the command of his king, he is more than a solitary man facing off against the state; he is a member of a recognized body exercising a legitimate political prerogative. His association with the traditional authority and prestige of this larger body both makes possible his honorable disobedience and makes it effective as a check on the crown. These conditions constitute part of the equipment of honor. Yet the group identities that support honor are not comprehensive. Honor rests on the multiple shared identities of the "intermediary bodies" of monarchical society, not on the single shared identity of the political community as a whole, and so honor cannot "be linked with a unified vision of society enforced from the center," as one interpreter puts it.[108] The shared but partial identities and social ties that sustain the intermediary bodies of monarchy are crucial to honor.

Honor also is partial in the sense of being based on affective attachments rather than on a form of reason that abstracts from such attachments.[109] Those with honor defend their codes on the basis of an attachment to them as much as a reasoned assessment, which helps explain why Montesquieu calls honor the "prejudice" of each person and each condition (III.6). Honor is a prejudice because it prejudges the worth of one's principles and one's claim to distinction, rather than arising directly from rational scrutiny of them. The honorable person is self-confident without being particularly self-examining, and perhaps even self-confident *because* not so very self-examining. This is not meant to be a criticism of honor, as the effectiveness of honor in motivating risky action is tied to its partiality in this second sense, which engages the desiring part of the human psyche. Nor does the partiality of honor mean that it is without rational foundations altogether. It only means that rational scrutiny is not the basis of this form of agency, or of political agency in general. So even though Orte did not scrutinize the foundations of his code of honor, Montesquieu does. In his presentation of French constitutional history in Books XXVIII, XXX, and XXXI of *The Spirit of the Laws,* for example, Montesquieu examines the history of the codes of honor of the French nobility, and he evaluates them as to their reasonableness.[110] In fact, *The Spirit of the Laws* as a whole is a study of the reasons for different codes of conduct the world over. But the rational scrutiny of the principles that underlie honor is Montesquieu's job, not Orte's. Or at least, it is not Orte's job *in the moment.* In the moment of crisis, Orte's attachments, not his reason, make him act. And this is true even though what he is attached to in this case is an established code of conduct, not something purely private or subjective. Honor itself is not strictly cognitive, but it is bound by codes the rationality of which can be cognitively evaluated. Soldiers should fight fair, for example; they should fight each other, not civilians; they should not kill innocents; and so on. These codes distinguish honor from motivations such as ethnic nationalism, in which the foundation of one's allegiance is blood ties and not anything that is even open to rational scrutiny or justification.

Still, honor is incomplete in the sense that it needs the direction—and sometimes the correction—of impartial reason. In this respect, honor calls to mind *thymos.* Like *thymos,* which Aristotle called the capacity of the soul by which we feel affection,[111] honor shares in reason even though it is not simply reducible to reason. On Aristotle's account, it was spirited attachments that moved those who guarded the city to defend it bravely. And not only the defense of the city but also the capacity for ruling and the capacity for political freedom stemmed from *thymos.*[112] In a similar way, the partiality of honor, its spirited attachments to its principles, makes it effective as a guardian of individual liberties. Yet honor is incomplete because of its partiality. Without the critical reflections of impartial reason (and the fixed and fundamental laws of constitutional government), honor may find itself defending unreasonable codes, even unjust ones. Honor needs reason, but even when honor is guided by reason it cannot be simply reduced to reason.

Montesquieu's idea is to channel and direct human partiality rather than suppress it. Efforts to suppress partiality usually fail because it tends to come out anyway, and when suppressed, it comes out in uncontrolled and extreme ways. Repression breeds zealotry, as Montesquieu's description of Christian monks and virtuous republicans illustrates (V.2). There is nothing that a religious zealot will not do for God, and nothing that a virtuous republican will not do for the sake of his homeland. Similarly, Montesquieu remarks in passing that "speculative sciences" render men "savage (*sauvage*)" (IV.8). Contemporary usage of the term *sauvage* carried the meaning of ferocious (*féroce*) as well as uncultivated and shy (*farouche*).[113] The suppression of human partiality whether by virtue or by reason leads to extremism and so makes for immoderate and unstable politics. Moreover, it is difficult to suppress partiality without forcing the issue, which means relying on fear, which is despotism.[114] The partial attachments and desires that inspire action can be moderated more effectively by being channeled and directed than by being suppressed. Montesquieu's concept of honor channels them by tying individual ambition to established codes of honor and by arranging political institutions in such a way that particular ambitions check and balance one another.

Montesquieu can resist the temptation to suppress partiality because of his conviction that liberty is possible without perfect unity. This conviction explains much of the difference between Hobbes's scorn for pride and Montesquieu's defense of honor. Honor resembles pride, which Hobbes defined as the breach of the precept that "every man acknowledge others for his equal by nature."[115] Honor is more principled than Hobbesian pride, because it is tied to established codes of conduct, but like pride honor is a form of personal ambition, a preference for oneself the nature of which is to seek distinction (III.7). Like pride, too, honor sometimes ignores the dictates of narrow self-interest. But whereas honor in Montesquieu serves liberty, Hobbes thinks that pride undermines liberty because it threatens political stability. Pride is a threat to the sovereign because prideful subjects think too much of themselves and consequently forget the constraints that the necessity of self-preservation imposes upon them, in particular the constraint of perfect obedience. For "the laws of nature . . . of themselves, without the terror of some power to cause them to be observed, are contrary to our natural passions, that carry us to partiality, pride, revenge, and the like." There is, therefore, no "peace without subjection."[116] Hobbes hates pride because he thinks that the consequence of pride is the division of power, and he thinks that divisions of power destroy the authority that makes individuals secure. For Montesquieu, too, the consequence of honor is the division of power, but he believes that the division of power is not the enemy of liberty but its best guarantee.

Rousseau also was troubled by the partiality of honor. He thought the desire for distinction a form of enslavement. It divided the individual from himself and from his fellows by making him dependent on the opinions of others. The *honnête homme* was a dissembler for whom "to be and to appear became two entirely different things."[117] In other words, *amour-propre* fractured the original unity of the human being and the unity of humankind because honor inexorably seeks honorers, and the "ardor to have ourselves talked about . . . this frenzy to distinguish ourselves almost always keeps us outside ourselves" and in conflict with others.[118] Montesquieu does not distinguish between *amour-propre* (what Rousseau disdained as vanity) and *amour de soi* (what Rousseau accepted as authentic love of self) because he thinks that being self-divided can be a source of liberty and not only a form of subjugation.[119] Montesquieu does not conceive of the human being as originally whole, and so does not regard the divisions of self that one finds in civil society as a loss.[120] He does not resist the divided self any more than he resists divided authority in politics, and for him the two are related.

There *are* some perfectly complete, undivided characters in *The Spirit of the Laws,* to be sure. The first is the despot, whose unlimited will is subject to nobody's opinion. His authority rests on force, not public recognition. In relation to him, everyone else "is nothing" (VI.2) and so there is no one whom he must please. He is not divided from himself because he is the only one who matters. Nor is he self-divided by being an "arbiter" of conflicting obligations, although he may suffer from conflicting appetites, as the character of Usbek in Montesquieu's *Persian Letters* illustrates. The despot's personal will is the source of all obligations, and consequently "he does not have to deliberate, to doubt, or to reason;

he has only to want" (IV.3). The government of despotism, too, displays perfect unity; it is uniform throughout because it is unopposed from within, much like the despot himself (V.14). The second complete character in *The Spirit of the Laws* is the virtuous republican. His wholeness is artificial, as it rests on the "renunciation" of himself as a particular being. He is not tormented by a division between his public and his private selves because he has relinquished his private self, but he is made complete only by extinguishing his particular passions. Because virtuous republicans sacrifice their individual interests to the common good, there is no dissembling among them, no conflict between what I want and what I want you to think that I want. There is no conflict because there is no "I" that is separate from the "we."[121] And just as there is no private self among virtuous republicans so there is no private sphere in a good republic as Montesquieu understands it, for everything is public there.[122] The republican regime is as much a whole as the despotic one; both are perfect unities undifferentiated from within. There is too little partiality here for Montesquieu, who resists undifferentiated politics populated by undivided selves. For him, perfect unity is indistinguishable from perfect subjection.[123] As a general rule, he says, "whenever we see everyone tranquil in a state that calls itself a republic, we can be sure that liberty does not exist there."[124] The partiality of honor supports the division of power in a differentiated and divisive, and therefore limited, regime.

Recognition and Resistance

Although honor as a quality of character is distinct from public honors in the form of recognition and distinction, the two are closely linked. Montesquieu's concept of honor leans on public honors because the honorable person desires public recognition. One can imagine that Orte might have done what he did this time even if, this time, nobody happened to be watching. But probably he would not do this kind of thing regularly if no one ever were to watch. Being seen is important to honor. Those with honor want to be the kinds of persons who live up to their principles *and* they want to be *seen* as the kinds of persons who live up to their principles. Their ambition has these two sides to it, an internal and an external dimension.[125] The public dimension of honor provides a measure of accountability. With honor, one respects oneself with reference to a standard; but at the same time, the visibility of honor means that other people can judge, by the same standard, whether one is right to respect oneself.[126] Honor is not an altogether subjective condition, both because it is tied to established codes of conduct and because it is in principle visible, even if not every instance of honor is in fact seen.

The fact that honor takes public opinion seriously rather than disdaining it also makes honor political. The political concern with appearances and public acceptance is tied to the this-worldly character of honor. The worldliness of honor moderates it and provides further protection against the potential zealotry of what Montesquieu calls virtue. Honor is not prone to the extremism that comes from locating one's ends in another life. Similarly, if honor has been offended, "it requires or permits one to retire to one's home" (IV.2)—not to fight a holy war. Honor has no zeal for proselytizing; the honorable person does not wish to save the world but only to be able to face himself in the mirror and look his fellows in the eye without shame or regret. Honor is more a civil disobedient, or a conscientious objector, than a missionary.[127] Its attachment to public opinion moderates its actions; honor does not require the consent of others, but it leans on their goodwill. Of course the desire for recognition is no guarantee of moderation. One has only to think of the violence engendered by the struggle for recognition in Hegel's master-slave dialectic.[128] More generally, history does not lack examples of immoderate glory-seekers whose hunger for public acclaim led them to extremism and brought ruin on their countries.[129] Then, too, the desire to win approval may tempt one to abandon one's code if it is unpopular, which could lead to unprincipled and immoderate action. If the interest in public recognition is no guarantee of moderation, however, neither are the limits it provides insignificant. Nor is it possible to fully dispel the dangers that arise from strong exertions of agency without also dissolving agency itself, which would be devastating for liberty.

Although honor leans on public recognition, it cannot be reduced to recognition. The fact that one's honor is tied to one's code and to self-respect gives honor a measure of independence from recognition, or public opinion. Orte's principles will always be there for him to defend even when no one is looking. His code of honor gives him a consistent standard to live up to, and so a consistent foundation for his self-respect, whatever anybody else may think of him, even when nobody recognizes him. These features of honor distinguish it from contemporary "recognition," the sole basis of which is public opinion. To have recognition, one need only be recognized by others, but one *must* be recognized by them. The problem with substituting recognition for honor is that you cannot be recognized if everybody, or the majority, does not like you or your class or your tribe. But you can honorably defend your principles (and thereby respect yourself) even when you are unpopular. The recognition recommended by some contemporary political theorists is a gift, not a quality of character, whose main players are "beneficiaries," not agents.[130] And this is a dangerous thing to rely on, especially when the times are against you and your liberty is at stake. Honor's attachment to its codes gives it standards to live up to and so implies a concept of desert that lends it protection from the vagaries of public opinion and political power.[131]

The disjunction between honor and recognition is important to sustain honor's capacity for political resistance. As we have seen, resistance is an essential feature of honor despite Montesquieu's reputation as a conservative thinker. He did not favor revolution or even aggressive reform, but the idea of resistance to overreaching political power is central to his understanding of political liberty and moderate government. Both Orte's disobedience and the "interference" of the *parlements* exemplify this element of resistance. The division of moral authority and the balance of political powers partly explains how honor's need for recognition can be reconciled with its capacity for resistance. In modern monarchies, as we have seen, there are three tribunes that are almost never in accord: that of the laws, that of honor, and that of religion.[132] This competition between authorities may tend to undercut reverence for any one of them, much as the capacity for reflexivity does. A society of multiple and conflicting authorities could never sustain forms of motivation that were based on a pure and comprehensive reverence for any set of standards. Yet honor does not presuppose pure reverence. Pure reverence would be simple obedience, which would not be conducive to individual liberty. Indeed, the unity of authority that characterized ancient republics was partly responsible for the extreme and obedient self-renunciation of republican virtue and was implicated in the immoderate tendencies of republican government. Important as it is to individual agency, reverence, like virtue, has need of limits, and should be taken in moderation. The multiplicity of moral authorities, the division of political power, and the plural sites of recognition in modern monarchical society moderate reverence. Orte's reverence for his particular code of honor leads him to resist the encroaching power of the king, and if he distinguishes himself in the eyes of his peers, perhaps this is sufficient. He can resist the king's command because he does not need the king's recognition, since he receives recognition from other sources and looks to the authority of other "tribunes."[133] As long as the sources of recognition and moral authority are not consolidated into a single set of hands, then honor, which rests on recognition, also can animate political resistance.

Honor is above all a form of personal ambition, but one that is guided and constrained by established codes of conduct. By promising the pleasures of self-respect and public renown, honor makes the defense of its codes and its obligations desirable. Its high ambitions make honor difficult to subjugate and inspire resistance to the abuse of power. Honor reveres the codes that direct and elevate its ambitions, and this reverence both limits and fuels honor. Reverence fuels honor by giving it something to take seriously. Yet honor also claims to be the arbiter of its obligations and therefore to stand above them. This reflexivity makes it possible for honor to resist political authority but also invites resistance to honor's own codes and so threatens the reverence that fuels it. Finally, much as honor balances reverence and reflexivity, so too does it mix recognition with resistance. Together, the fragmentation of political obligation and the attachment to principle explain how honor, which depends on recognition, does not therefore end in subjection. Honor must be seen, but not necessarily by everyone and not only by those in power. Plural sites of recognition and divided sources of moral and political obligation are good for honor as they are good for liberty.

The substantive content of honor is variable.[134] Codes of honor vary from one society to the next, and even within a society codes of honor may be multiple. Orte's military code of honor, for instance, was substantially different from the code that guided Montesquieu himself as a judge and parliamentarian. As Montesquieu presents it, there is no one comprehensive and universal code of honor. Honor as a quality of character is compatible with a variety of codes of honor. What is not compatible with honor is the rejection of principled action or the denial of human agency.[135] The features of honor as a quality of character elaborated here illuminate important aspects of political agency in general and suggest that the significance of honor extends beyond the particular context of constitutional monarchy. The high ambitions of honor remind us that elevated and principled expectations of oneself are crucial to strong exertions of individual agency, and that the desire for distinction can be a powerful source of motivation. Honor's balance of reverence and reflexivity illuminates the productive power of this tension for individual agency, and it suggests that a theory of agency that privileges one at the cost of the other is bound to be incomplete. The partiality of honor emphasizes the effectiveness of mixed motives and self-concern in inspiring political action and supporting political obligations, as against the purity of forms of reason that abstract from partial attachments and the self-renunciation of civic virtue and other forms of altruism. Finally, the mix of recognition and resistance that honor entails suggests that recognition on its own is an insufficient foundation for agency and that the division of political power and moral authority is good for both individual agency and political liberty.

Montesquieu's concept of honor faces a fundamental dilemma, however. On his account, honor can support the balance of power that sustains individual liberty only in the context of a relatively entrenched social order. The nobility's spirited resistance to the crown is possible because it has an independent base of power, authority, prestige, and wealth. Honor requires equipment as well as an ambitious character. The equipment of honor, on Montesquieu's account, includes titles, wealth, political office, established prerogatives, and especially land, because one cannot separate "the dignity of the noble from that of his fief" (V.9). And the independence of the nobility is sustainable only if it is hereditary, as the principle of heredity is needed to protect the nobility from being captured by the crown (V.9). The prerogatives of the nobility must also be exclusive, Montesquieu continues, and must not transfer to the people "unless one wants to attack *(choque)* the principle of the government, unless one wants to diminish the force of the nobility and the force of the people" (V.9). Indeed, the nobility should regard it as the "sovereign infamy to share power with the people" (VIII.9). Although the nobility's "demand for preferences and distinctions" (III.7) can degenerate into empty vanity (VIII.7), Montesquieu sees these social distinctions and political prerogatives as crucial to maintaining the balance of power that protects liberty.

At the same time, however, Montesquieu defends what appears to be a contrary position. He suggests that an inflexible social order is antithetical to political liberty, as "the laws that order each to remain in his profession and to pass it down to his children are and can be useful only in despotic states, where no one can or ought to have rivals" (XX.22). "The political world," and especially a regime of political liberty, "is sustained by the inner desire and restlessness that each one has for leaving the place where he has been put."[136] Suppressing this natural restlessness is despotic. Moreover, restlessness can be used to good effect if it is harnessed and channeled in such a way as to fuel the rivalries between political powers. This is one reason why Montesquieu advocates venality, the practice of buying offices (V.19). Venality supports the rise of the ambitious and the industrious and so puts political influence into the hands of individuals who are, if not necessarily wiser or more virtuous than others, at least more assertive and therefore more likely to enliven the rivalries between political powers that sustain liberty. A hereditary nobility tends toward "ignorance," "inattention," and "scorn for civil government," which undercuts its effectiveness as a rival to the king (II.4). And the royal appointment of posts or selection by the courtier class gives political prerogatives to persons who are more likely to flatter the king than to offer principled resistance (V.19). An overly fixed social order thus works against the separation of powers because it suppresses rivalries and the personal ambitions that sustain them and prevents persons of "merit" from coming to the fore.[137] Thus the fixity of ranks and orders needed to protect the nobility from manipulative monarchs also invites its degradation and with it the enervation of honor. The implication is that for honor to operate effectively, the social and political orders must be democratized in the sense of providing more equality of opportunity. Only when the prerogatives that give individuals leverage in contesting political power are open to ambition and merit rather than closed by lineage can honor reliably animate the tumults between political powers that protect liberty. Paradoxically, old-regime honor needs but cannot tolerate a fixed social order. It simultaneously requires and resists democratization.

3

Honor and Democracy in America

The suggestion that honor must escape the entrenched inequalities of the old regime to preserve itself is unexpected, as honor today most often is associated with these very conditions. The contemporary associations are not altogether wrong, since as much as honor needs a regime of opportunity and mobility, these conditions may also undercut it. Alexis de Tocqueville's analysis of democracy in America brings honor's dilemma to the fore and provides a foundation for our investigation of honor's status in modern democratic regimes.[1] Tocqueville shows the consequences of democracy that generate its resistance to honor, but he also shows why democracy needs honor and where in American society honor might be found. To support individual liberty against the twin dangers of majority tyranny and "mild" despotism, Tocqueville seeks to inspire in the democratic character qualities associated with aristocratic mores and tied to old-regime honor. Courage, pride, high and principled ambition, the desires for distinction and self-respect, the sense of duty to oneself, and the love of liberty as an end in itself all prove to be crucial supports for democratic freedom on Tocqueville's account.

Today Tocqueville's interest in these qualities is largely neglected in favor of the more egalitarian and collectivist aspects of democratic civic virtue that are emphasized by his contemporary interpreters.[2] Tocqueville himself tends to confound the collectivist, egalitarian elements of civic virtue with the more "heroic" qualities tied to honor, an obfuscation that is in keeping with his explicit intention to address modern democracy in friendly terms.[3] Yet he recommended participation and civic virtue for the liberal purposes of restraining the power of public opinion,

67

the force of majority tyranny, and the trend toward centralization.[4] Not simply participation or fraternity, but individual resistance to majority tyranny and mild despotism is the core of liberty for Tocqueville.[5] And to sustain such resistance, something more than civic virtue is needed, qualities more closely associated with traditional honor.[6]

Tocqueville provides a natural point of transition between the study of honor in Montesquieu and the study of honor in America because he was a student—and an admirer—of both. Tocqueville's debts to Montesquieu are well known.[7] Montesquieu was one of three thinkers (along with Rousseau and Pascal) whose work Tocqueville claimed to read every day.[8] When *Democracy in America* first appeared in 1835, one reader declared that "nothing like it has appeared since Montesquieu."[9] Comments like this one reflect the two thinkers' common commitment to study politics and society from what has been called a "socio-political" perspective.[10] In part, too, the family resemblance comes from the comparative nature of both approaches. Tocqueville's range was narrower than that of Montesquieu, but like his predecessor, Tocqueville sought to illuminate fundamental features of modern political life through a comparative analysis of different existing regimes rather than to postulate a single best regime. Both Montesquieu and Tocqueville were interested in the interaction between the institutional mechanisms of liberty and the character of citizens, but in neither case did the interest in citizen character undermine the commitment to liberal institutions and the end of individual liberty. Both also disputed the common identification of liberty with democracy. Montesquieu emphatically distinguished the two in *The Spirit of the Laws,* saying that while liberty was often identified with the democratic form of political order, in fact democratic regimes as much as any others could violate individual liberties.[11] Tocqueville, too, sought to counter this common confusion, a task that would occupy him all his life.[12]

Tocqueville's two major works document the causes and the consequences of the "great social revolution" then under way across Europe, the revolution for modern democracy. He claimed to have seen in America "the image of democracy itself . . . its penchants, character, prejudices, and passions; I wanted to become acquainted with it so as at least to know what we might have to fear or hope from it" (I, Introduction, p. 12).[13] Democracy in America and democracy in France differed in important respects, but the dangers posed by democracy were universal, according to Tocqueville.[14] It is because the logic of democracy transcends any one regime that he can speak so frequently of French democracy in *Democracy in America*.[15] For the same reason, Tocqueville's preface to *The Old Regime* identifies its subject, which is the connection between equality and despotism in France, with what he had written twenty years before in *Democracy in America*.[16] Although democratic regimes may differ as to particulars, they share common qualities and characteristic dangers.

The dangers Tocqueville most feared in democracy were majority tyranny and mild despotism. He found the idea of majority tyranny in *The Federalist,* but he gave it a richer formulation by elaborating its social as well as its political dimension. Majority tyranny can arise as a political phenomenon when the popular branch of government overreaches its constitutional authority in its relations with the other branches. It can also be a social phenomenon, consisting in public opinion mobilized against the liberties of members of minority groups.[17] The social and political dimensions of majority tyranny tend to run together in practice, because political democracy by its nature gives institutional form to the power of public opinion.[18] "Mild" despotism, which is a form of paternalism, results from an overly centralized administration and from the quiescence of a populace that gives priority to its material interests over its political liberties. Not intolerant majorities but withdrawn and passive individuals are its main causes.[19] It represents a new type of despotism, one that Tocqueville thinks is "particularly to be feared in democratic ages" (II.4.7, p. 328; II.2.4, p. 109). The new despotism is mild *(doux)* rather than harsh, based on degradation instead of torment (II.4.6, p. 323). It is mild because its absolute power results from the voluntary submission of the populace, who accede to the extension of political power in hopes of receiving security and material comforts. And it exercises its power mildly insofar as it makes good on the promise to provide the material benefits sought by citizens, controlling them through the satisfaction of their appetites and the force of public opinion rather than through harsh laws and violent punishments. Like traditional despotism, however, the new mild despotism leads to the unlimited power of the state and the loss of individual liberties.[20] Despite differences in emphasis, the dangers of majority tyranny and mild despotism reflect the same underlying logic of modern democracy, according to Tocqueville, which tends to promote equality at the expense of liberty and to throw off formal limits on political power, risking a new form of despotism that renders individual liberties insecure even as it accommodates the democratic ideal of popular sovereignty and the material interests of the majority.[21] And as we shall see, the twin dangers of democracy have a common set of solutions.[22]

Tocqueville seeks to illuminate the dangers of the new order so as to protect against them. Understanding democracy makes it possible to "instruct" it, to "rekindle" its "beliefs, purify its mores *(moeurs)*, regulate its movements" (I, Introduction, p. 5), and so to enable democratic polities to sustain themselves and the liberties of their citizens. By educating modern democrats about themselves and their way of life Tocqueville means to support the capacity for political liberty in the form of both collective self-government and individual agency.[23] He hoped to counter the perception, prevalent in his day as in ours, that individuals and political societies were simply the products of impersonal forces. He attributed this perception to "democratic historians," who denied "the particular action *(l'action particulière)* of individuals," which made it seem as though "the world is moved without a driving force *(moteur)* to be discovered." The result was that "one is tempted to believe that this movement is not voluntary and that societies obey without knowing it a force that dominates them." While Tocqueville acknowledged that "general causes" had an impact on societies and individuals, he denied that such forces were wholly determinative or entirely irresistible (II.1.20, pp. 90–91). The belief that they were irresistible was "dangerous" because it led to acquiescence and the abdication of responsibility, and served to "strike down *(abattre)* the souls" of citizens (ibid., p. 92), a development that would undermine democratic freedoms. Tocqueville's two major works represent a rejection of the idea of a "certain destiny that all efforts cannot change" (ibid., p. 91). The faith in human agency, even if exaggerated, was a necessary precondition of action in defense of political liberty, in his view. By educating democracy, Tocqueville meant to enlighten modern democrats about both the impersonal forces that influenced democracy *and* the possibilities for resisting and directing these forces.[24]

As much as Tocqueville wanted to protect democracy from itself, however, he had no interest in returning to the old world of the *ancien régime,* a world that he regarded as both imperfect (I.2.7, p. 261) and dead (I, Introduction, pp. 4, 11).[25] Although modern democracy uncon-

sciously retained vestiges of the past,[26] Tocqueville regarded the new ruling principle of equality as "an accomplished fact or one that is ready to
be accomplished" (ibid., p. 11). Therefore his proposed solutions to the
dangers of democratic despotism are democratic solutions, and modern
democratic solutions in particular. To the extent that they draw on modern democracy's aristocratic heritage, it is by drawing out what is implicit in or compatible with democratic institutions and character, rather
than by rejecting them in favor of a return to the old regime. Tocqueville
was convinced that modern democracies could remain free only by in-
corporating certain features of aristocratic society. This is one reason
why he dubbed himself a "new species of liberal."[27] The liberals of his
day defined themselves by their strict opposition to all aspects of the old
regime. Tocqueville thought that modern democratic societies had to
find democratic equivalents for the intermediary bodies of the old regime, for religion, and for the spirited courage, high ambitions, pride,
and love of liberty traditionally associated with aristocratic honor.[28]
American democracy met the need for intermediary bodies with its
plethora of voluntary associations, and for religion with its many and
enthusiastic Protestant sects. Finding democratic equivalents for honor
proved somewhat more difficult, however, if no less necessary. Tocqueville did identify a specifically American form of honor, and he made it
clear that a range of qualities associated with traditional honor could be
found in the United States, but he emphasized that the relationship between honor and democracy in America was far from harmonious.

The Conflict between Honor and Democracy

Although the tensions between honor and democracy surface periodically throughout *Democracy in America,* Tocqueville addresses them
directly in a chapter entitled "Of Honor in the United States and Democratic Societies" (II.3.18). Here Tocqueville defines honor as: (a) "esteem, glory, or reputation *(considération)*"; and (b) "those rules by which
one obtains such esteem, glory, and reputation" (II.3.8, p. 238, n. 1).
This definition highlights two of the three dimensions of honor explored
in Chapter 2: public honors and codes of honor. Before showing how
democratic society transforms these two aspects of honor nearly to the
point of eradicating them, Tocqueville suggests a measure of compatibil-
ity between them. He points out that the traditional honor of feudal so-

ciety is "only one of its forms." Honor may not be as prominent in democracy as it was in aristocratic societies or in the constitutional monarchy that Montesquieu described, but "honor is found in democratic centuries as well as in aristocratic times" (II.3.8, p. 245). Those who think that honor is inextricably tied to feudalism have mistaken one instance of honor for the whole of it, and so "have given a generic name to what [is] only a species" (ibid.). Traditional feudal honor has been mistaken for honor per se largely because of the prominence accorded to honor in the old regime. Honor displays "a different physiognomy" *(une autre physionomie)* in the new regime because the specific content of the rules by which the regime accords esteem, glory, and reputation are different (ibid.). Yet despite these differences, Tocqueville says, every society has some notion of honor because "every time men assemble in a particular society, an honor is established among them right away, that is to say, a collection of opinions proper to them concerning what should be praised or blamed" (ibid., pp. 242–243).

Tocqueville even identifies an "American honor." The United States, being a trading nation, naturally honors those "peaceable virtues that tend to give a regular appearance in the body social and that favor business" (ibid., p. 243). Americans place their honor in being chaste because "the inner order of the family [is] so necessary to success in business" (ibid., pp. 244–245). At the same time, commercial and industrial enterprises could not thrive without "audacious enterprise" and "commercial boldness" (ibid., p. 244). Thus Americans "look with favor on, and honor, audacity in the matter of industry," viewing the love of wealth as a "noble and estimable ambition" (ibid.). Work itself is another point of honor. Tocqueville describes meeting some "rich persons, youths, enemies by temperament of all painful effort who were forced to take up a profession" because "public opinion imperiously forbade" idleness (ibid., p. 245). Chastity, commercial daring, and work win esteem in the America that Tocqueville describes because all are "necessary for the maintenance and the prosperity of the American association" (ibid.). To the extent that honor consists in public recognition and the standards that guide it, one will find honor in most any society.[29] Public honors and codes of honor have instrumental value for political society, and any regime will honor the behaviors that promote the realization of its ends. Honor has more than merely instrumental value in Tocqueville's view, but the fact that honor does have instrumental value means that its "physiognomy" varies. Every regime can be expected to have honor, but in a form useful to itself.

Having shown the existence of democratic honor, however, Tocqueville goes on to elaborate conflicts between democracy and honor that weaken honor as an influence on individual action. The first difficulty is that honor's injunctions are "less numerous" in democracies than in aristocratic societies. Codes of honor, which provide the basis for judging whether an action is to be praised or blamed, "are less numerous among a people that is not at all divided into castes" (ibid., p. 246). Honor's prescriptions are fewer in democracies than in aristocratic societies because the same set of prescriptions applies to everyone. In fact, if group distinctions were ever to be fully eradicated in a given society, honor would "be limited to a small number of precepts" that would "stray less and less from the moral laws adopted by the community of humanity in general" (ibid.). Yet to the extent that codes of honor move toward universal moral standards applicable to humanity in general, honor loses its particularism, and its distinctive character is overwhelmed by a more generalized humanitarianism.

Rules of honor are also "less clear" in democracy (ibid.). In the old regime, Tocqueville says, "the generations followed each other *en vain*" and "ideas scarcely varied more than conditions" (ibid.). Those who belonged to the same caste "had the same objects in view and saw things from the same point of view" (ibid.). Consequently, honor had a "clear and precise form," with codes of honor being "complete and detailed" and giving "a fixed and always visible rule for human actions" (ibid., p. 247). By contrast, in modern democratic regimes "where all the citizens are mobile, where society, being modified every day, changes its opinions with changing needs," the meaning attached to the word "honor" proves difficult to fix with precision (ibid., p. 246). Democratic honor "is necessarily less powerful" because it is less clearly defined, "for it is difficult to apply with certainty and firmness a law that is imperfectly known" (ibid., p. 247). The strength and prominence of honor in the old regime owed a great deal to the power of tradition and the fixity of the social order there, even if, paradoxically, a stagnant social order also tends to corrupt honor.

Another reason for the relative weakness of honor in democracy is the obscurity of individuals in mass society. Among aristocratic peoples, "all ranks differ," and consequently "no one can either hope or fear that he will not be seen." No one can, by his obscurity, escape praise or blame (ibid., p. 248). When equality of conditions prevails, persons "are mixed together in the same crowd" (ibid.). The result is that individuals tend to become similar and can "no longer be distinguished from one another by any characteristic traits" (ibid., p. 249). Ironically, the equal recognition that comes with social and political equality tends to make individuals invisible instead of equally distinguished. Andy Warhol's facetious observation that everyone in America gets fifteen minutes of fame speaks both to the overwhelming obscurity in which modern democratic lives are lived (fifteen minutes of personal distinction in a whole lifetime) and to the undistinctive quality of democratic fame (since everyone gets it). The obscurity, even invisibility, of individuals in democratic societies keeps them from obeying honor's rules closely, because obscurity interferes with the public regulation of praise and blame. Where individuals emerge into public view only to fade away again into the crowd of their equally undistinguished fellows, "public opinion has no grip; its object disappears each instance and escapes it" (ibid., p. 248). The invisibility of individuals in democratic societies undercuts honor and makes for looser adherence to its prescriptions. For all these reasons, Tocqueville concludes at the end of the chapter that honor is ineluctably tied to inequality of conditions (ibid., pp. 248–249, 247). Although democratic forms of honor exist, they are not likely to have the same power and predominance as honor in aristocratic societies.

The chapter of *Democracy in America* devoted explicitly to honor by no means exhausts the subject, for Tocqueville employs a narrow definition of honor there, one that is limited to its two external dimensions, public honors and codes of honor. Throughout the work, however, there are indications that honor as a quality of character also conflicts with the character of modern democrats. In particular, honor is at odds with democratic individualism and materialism. Individualism is "a recent expression that a new idea has given birth to," one that Tocqueville claims "our fathers" did not know (II.2.2, p. 105). It differs from "egoism," which is "a passionate and exaggerated love of self," by being "reflective and peaceable" instead of based on "blind instinct" and "depraved feeling" (ibid.). Beyond that, the egoist is concerned only with himself, whereas Tocqueville's idea of individualism involves a somewhat wider sphere of concern. Yet with individualism, "one takes an interest only in those who are nearest" (ibid., p. 106). In modern democracies, Tocqueville says, each citizen tends to "isolate himself from the mass of his fellows and retire to a small arena with his family and friends," thus abandoning "the greater society" (ibid., p. 105). The isolation of the modern democrat is made possible by the democratization of the social structure, which liberates individuals from earlier relations of corporate attachment, family lineage, and dependence on superiors. Tocqueville sees the value of this liberation, but he is also convinced that individualism disempowers modern democrats. Individuals are weaker when standing alone than when acting together, and this weakness is exacerbated in modern democracies by an increase in the power of government. As a result, "the sometimes oppressive but often conserving force of a small number of citizens has been succeeded by the weakness of all" (I, Introduction, p. 8). And when individuals "are very weak, but the state . . . is very strong" (II.1.12, p. 58), it becomes difficult to defend individual freedoms from encroaching political power (II.1.3, p. 53). Individualism undermines honor by eroding social attachments, especially attachments to the intermediary bodies that stand between the household and the state, undercutting the individual sense of efficacy in the process and disabling the capacity for individual agency. The loss of the strong assertions of agency associated with traditional honor is a serious problem for modern democracy, according to Tocqueville. A central purpose of his project, as one commentator notes, is to recover the activist quality and function of the old nobility but without its special privileges, or to preserve honor as a quality of character while democratizing its conditions.[30]

Another consequence of individualism is that "each man is narrowly withdrawn in himself, and claims to judge the world from there" (II.1.1, p. 12). Because of the social mobility that prevails in modern democracies, "men who live in such a society can no longer base their beliefs on the opinions of the class to which they belong, for, so to speak, there are no longer any classes," or at least the classes are "composed of such changing elements" that they wield little influence as groups over individual beliefs (ibid.). Nor do individuals wield much influence over one another. Where all are considered equals, Tocqueville maintains, none "perceive among them any signs of greatness or an incontestable superiority," and so all "are continually brought back to their own reason as the most visible and nearest source of truth" (ibid., p. 12). The authority of tradition also is rejected by modern democrats, according to Tocque-

ville. The American tendency to take "old beliefs as providing information but not a rule" reflects a more general orientation (II.3.8, p. 202),
according to which democracy typically "destroys or obscures almost all
former social conventions," which consequently have little authority
over individual judgment (ibid., p. 205).[31] This can be a good thing,
Tocqueville thinks, but when taken to the extreme the result is not the
independence of mind he admires from the old aristocracy, but rather a
form of subjectivism that leads away from independence and invites the
tyranny of public opinion instead. Ironically, when individuals consider
themselves equals and therefore are not inclined "to believe blindly in a
certain man or a certain class, . . . the disposition to believe the mass
grows, and it is more and more public opinion that runs the world"
(II.1.2, p. 18). Having rejected other sources of authority, men and
women fluctuate between the extremes of subjective judgment and "an
almost unlimited confidence in the judgment of the public" (ibid.).
Consequently, public opinion comes to have an unprecedented power in
modern democracies, which threatens to confine "the action of individual reason within limits so narrow that it does not suit the grandeur and
the happiness of the human species" (ibid., p. 19).

Tocqueville speaks with a kind of aristocratic disdain of America's
democratic conformists, saying, "I know of no other country in which,
speaking generally, there is less independence of mind and true freedom
of discussion than in America" (I.2.7, p. 267). This dependence on public opinion exacerbates the democratic vulnerability to majority tyranny,
which operates by means of "an immense pressure of the mind of all
upon the intelligence of each," imposing the ideas of the majority and
causing them to "penetrate the souls" of individuals (II.1.2, p. 18), thus
inducing each "to not think at all" (ibid., p. 19). For this reason, Tocqueville worries that democracy "might restrict the intellectual freedom that
the democratic social state favors," and in so doing "discover only a new
face of servitude" (ibid.). Individualism produces swings between the
extremes of idiosyncratic subjectivism and slavish conformity.[32]

Both extremes undercut honor as a quality of character, which rests
on a moderate mix of reverence and reflexivity, as we have seen. Tocqueville's discussion of democratic individualism thus points to another
conflict between honor and democracy. Honor presupposes a measure of
reverence for the collective and conventional codes that guide it. When
individuals reject virtually all sources of authority that are external to

their own minds, honor loses its capacity to elevate, direct, and constrain personal ambition. If honor presupposes a measure of reverence for the authority of established codes, however, it also requires a capacity for critical reflection and may issue in resistance to authority. Tocqueville himself associates honor with resistance to the dictates of public opinion, saying that there is more diversity of opinion where aristocratic mores prevail (I.2.7, p. 267) and more instances of independent action as opposed to conformism (II.4.7, p. 329).[33] A measure of reverence for the authority of principles external to one's will can provide a powerful basis for resisting the pressures of public opinion. The aristocratic *honnête homme* could muster the courage to resist the command of his king when it violated his code of honor precisely because of his reverence for the authority of his code. By denying the authority of such independent standards, modern democrats unwittingly disable their own wills and undercut the capacity for political agency. Thus Tocqueville suggests that one may widen the sphere of independent action by constraining the individualism that rejects the authority of external standards, because this individualism leads ultimately to conformity.[34] Honor's reverence for its codes supports strong exertions of individual agency, and so independence, but democratic individualism tends to undermine honor.

Still another reason for the tension between honor and modern democracy is the materialism that pervades the character of democratic citizens. In the United States, "cupidity is always breathless, and the human mind, distracted at every moment from pleasures of the imagination and works of intelligence, is driven by the pursuit of wealth" (II.1.9, p. 41). In fact, the motives "that stir Americans most profoundly are commercial" ones (I.2.9, p. 298). Love of money predominates because virtually everyone participates in the commercial economy and so adopts the habits of mind and heart that commerce engenders. Moreover, money really is important for modern democrats, who cannot rely on family lineage, title, or a hereditary fief to secure their positions in society (II.3.17, p. 236). Only money will provide such security, and democrats, unlike aristocrats, must obtain their money for themselves. To live and to secure their positions, democrats must concern themselves with acquiring money, and from this unavoidable concern with money they naturally develop the habit of loving it. Democrats love money "not because their souls are smaller" by nature but because their conditions are equal and their positions insecure (ibid.). For these reasons, material self-interest is the predominant motive in modern democracies, and the predominance of materialism further weakens the prospects for honor as a quality of character. It is true that Americans honor commercial ambition and that Tocqueville sometimes identifies American honor with commercial ambition. On this point, Tocqueville differs from Montesquieu, for whom the idea of "commercial honor" would have been a contradiction in terms.[35] Yet the materialism of commercial ambition remains at odds with the aristocratic qualities that Tocqueville associates with traditional honor and recommends to modern democrats, as we shall see. Commercial honor cannot on its own provide what the defense of liberty sometimes requires.

Honor and Self-Interest Well Understood

American democracy leans heavily on the motive that Tocqueville calls "the doctrine of self-interest well understood" (*l'interêt bien entendu*). This motive is not new, he tells us, but "it is among the Americans of our time that it has been universally accepted." Self-interest well understood refers to the view that "the interest of each is to be good." An "enlightened self-love" leads Americans "to aid one another and disposes them to sacrifice voluntarily for the good of the State a part of their time and their wealth" (II.2.8, p. 128). This doctrine combats narrow egoism by encouraging individuals to think beyond their private interests, but it does not ask them to forget their private interests or to abandon calculating, consequentialist reasoning for the sake of a more categorical sense of duty. Instead, self-interest well understood ties the private interests of each to the interests of others and to the shared interests of the community as a whole, thus preserving the motivational force of individual interest while broadening its objectives. Because it does not ask citizens to abandon their private interests, the doctrine "accommodates itself marvelously to the weaknesses of men and so easily obtains a great empire" (ibid., p. 129). In addition to being attainable, the doctrine is accessible: "it is within the range of all intellects" and consequently "each one knows it easily and holds on to it without difficulty" (ibid.). The motive of self-interest well understood does not require special exertions of either heart or mind. Consequently, "it does not seek to attain great objects; but it attains without too much effort those for which it aims" (ibid., p. 128). Because it is attainable and accessible, it is reliable, and Tocqueville recommends the doctrine as "the most appropriate to the needs of men in our time" (ibid., p. 129).

Self-interest well understood may seem to be sufficient to sustain democracy in America. It oils the springs of citizenship by giving individuals a reason to participate in political associations and by leading them to the broader standpoint of overlapping interests. At the same time, because citizens remain closely attuned to their interests, they tend to keep a close eye on government to "prevent their representatives from deviating from a certain general line that their interests mark out" (I.2.6, p. 243). Thus self-interest well understood can make citizens vigilant keepers of their elected representatives. If it can foster participation and vigilance, the doctrine may also support the exercise of the rights that sustain individual liberties. Insofar as political rights protect interests, individuals who act from the doctrine of self-interest well understood will have reason to be "jealous of their rights" (ibid.) and so to resist encroachments on these rights and respect the rights of others. In fact, Tocqueville indicates that the doctrine is not merely adequate to its task but also intrinsically worthy. For example, the "love of well-being," while "more vulgar," also is a "less dangerous passion" than "ambition for power" (I.1.8, p. 165). Similarly, it is more orderly and less "turbulent" than honor, which brings "splendor" *(l'éclat)* but often "trouble" as well (I.2.6, p. 243). Self-interest well understood produces "regulated, temperate, moderate, careful, and self-controlled citizens," and if it stops "some men from rising far above the common level of humanity" it restrains many others from falling below that level. Overall, Tocqueville maintains, the doctrine of self-interest well understood "elevates the species" (II.2.8, p. 129). In some instances it can even give rise to an admirable courage, as when American traders brave the dangers of the seas in search of profits (I.2.10, p. 420) or American pioneers risk grisly deaths to seek their fortunes on the western frontier (I.2.9, pp. 293–294). Tocqueville sees "a sort of heroism" in such ambitions and in the commercial honor of American democrats (I.2.10, p. 421), a heroism that is connected to the experience of individual striving and the ideal of self-mastery as against the limits imposed by nature. The American does not "perceive any limit that nature can have placed on the efforts of man; to his eyes something that does not exist is only something that has not yet been attempted" (ibid., p. 422). This is the positive side of democracy's tendency to regard the past as providing "information" but not a "rule." It is consistent with Tocqueville's emphasis on the need to reject the idea of a "fixed destiny" as a precondition for the possibility of political liberty. Then, too, innovations sometimes improve the human condition, and the American democrat's identity as an innovator implies the possibility (if not the certainty) of "elevating" humankind.[36]

Yet if the doctrine of self-interest well understood can support the regular operations of democratic government and even promote a kind of heroism, it nevertheless remains "incomplete" *(imparfaite)* as a spring of democratic freedom (II.2.8, p. 129). Self-interest, even when it is well understood, cannot on its own protect a democratic populace from the threats of majority tyranny and mild despotism. The sense of weakness that arises from individualism causes citizens of democratic regimes to turn to the state for support and protection (II.4.3, p. 301). Tocqueville describes this dependence as it arose in France after (and even before) the Revolution, saying that "no one imagined he could succeed in any important affair unless the state got involved. Farmers themselves, a people ordinarily rebellious toward rules, have been brought to believe that if agriculture is not perfect, the fault is principally that of the government, which gives them neither enough advice nor enough assistance."[37] In troubled times, farmers blame the government for providing insufficient advice and assistance because in other times government has provided too much advice and assistance. They do not suspect that "under the protector could be hidden a master."[38] Americans are more resistant to this delusion than Europeans, according to Tocqueville, as they have retained a relatively decentralized administrative structure, which encourages greater self-sufficiency on the part of citizens. Yet however resistant they may be, Americans are not altogether invulnerable to the logic of democracy, which tends toward increasing centralization. As democrats, they, too, are "singularly" open to "the establishment of a despotism" (II.4.6, p. 322).[39]

The doctrine of self-interest well understood is "incomplete" because it can mitigate but not eradicate this tendency. A centralized authority frequently can provide material comforts with greater efficiency than otherwise would be possible, and the desire for material comfort and security may lead citizens to support the expansion of such an authority rather than to resist it. Moreover, citizens whose main motive is the advancement of their material interests tend to favor the maintenance of public order, which protects their property and secures their comforts, over the exercise of freedom. Tocqueville believes that "public peace is a great good," but he is also convinced that "it is through good order that all peoples have arrived at tyranny" (II.3.14, pp. 147–148). When people "who have a passion for material pleasures" see that agitation in favor of liberty threatens their prosperity, he says, they tend to "throw out liberty at the first disorder" (ibid., p. 147). And once a tyrant (or a faction) assumes the role of protector-master in a state in which political and administrative power has been centralized, "he finds the way to all usurpations is open." As long as "he sees to it for some time that material interests prosper, he can easily get away with everything else" (ibid.). Material self-interest turns out to be an insufficient barrier to such encroachments. In the form of the desire to save or increase one's property, it even can be an inducement to acquiesce. Materialism, even a "decent materialism" (*matérialisme honnête*), may "weaken and silently slacken the springs of action" (II.3.11, p. 139).[40]

To be sure, the doctrine of self-interest well understood is not limited in its objectives to material ends. It can also help people identify their nonmaterial interests, such as the interest in liberty, and can "lead them to appreciate its [liberty's] utility for producing goods such as wealth and power."[41] The problem with this motive, however, is that it remains mired in utility. Ultimately, Tocqueville insists, liberty can be maintained only if it is valued as an end in itself.[42] The only real and durable basis for freedom is not commercial ambition or self-interest well understood but the love of liberty as an end in itself, what one commentator calls "the dignity of the human soul refusing to serve either demagogy or caesarism."[43] The doctrine of self-interest well understood reconfigures the category of interest, expanding it beyond the confines of narrow egoism and elevating it above mere materialism, but what it cannot do is produce nonconsequentialist reasoning and noninstrumental action. Yet this is precisely what Tocqueville has in mind when he refers to the love of liberty as an end in itself, which is needed (if only on occasion) to supplement self-interest well understood for the protection of individual liberty. Tocqueville thus makes clear the incompleteness of self-interest well understood, and with it commercial honor, even though he regards them as basically laudatory motives. Self-interest is respectable, important, even necessary for modern democracy, but it is insufficient. His remarks in this regard highlight again the distinction between interest and honor. While one always has a certain interest in acting honorably, insofar as doing so brings about the desirable ends of self-respect and public recognition, honor (like the love of liberty as an end in itself) has intrinsic, not merely instrumental, value. It takes the form of an imperative along the lines of Luther's "Here I stand; I can do no other." This imperative has a categorical quality, albeit not in the strict Kantian sense, since one's code of honor may not be universalizable. Honor is categorical in the sense that it imposes obligations that are not subject to the contingencies of a utility calculus. And one need not accept Kant's rationalist conceptions of moral duty and the person to see the powerful connection between principled, noninstrumental imperatives and individual agency.

If Tocqueville recognizes the insufficiency of self-interest, however, he is equally clear-eyed about the potential failings of traditional honor. Tocqueville faults aristocracy for the lack of "true sympathy" to be found among persons there (II.3.1, p. 172). Indeed, "humanity and gentleness" have no part in traditional aristocratic mores (II.3.18, p. 240), and consequently "aristocracies often undertake very tyrannical and inhuman actions" (II.1.10, p. 49).[44] Inequality of conditions means that among an aristocratic people each caste has a separate existence, with the result that "the men who compose [each caste] do not resemble the others and have difficulty thinking and feeling that they are part of a single humanity." As a result, "they cannot well understand what others suffer" (II.3.1, pp. 171–172). Tocqueville cites as an example the letters of Madame de Sévigné, a noblewoman who in 1675 witnessed the brutal suppression of a local revolt among the lower classes. After describing to her daughter the punishment dealt one of the ringleaders, which included breaking on the wheel followed by quartering and the exposure of his limbs at the four corners of the town, her letter goes on to report cheerfully on the recent visit of a Mme. de Tarente, who "was here yesterday in the woods in charming weather" (ibid., p. 173). Tocqueville maintains that Mme. de Sévigné was not a selfish or barbarous person, as she was "passionately fond of her children and showed herself very sensitive to the sorrows of her friends." She likewise treated her vassals and servants "with kindness and indulgence" (ibid., p. 174). What Mme. de Sévigné lacked was a generalizable sense of sympathy, which "is possible only between similar persons" or those who believe themselves to be similar (ibid., p. 172).

To be sure, a nobleman might "believe that his duty and his honor constrained him to defend, at the peril of his own life, those who lived on his land" (ibid.). Yet this obligation arose from a sense of distinction, not identification. The local landowner owed protection to his dependents, not his equals. He owed it *because* they were his dependents and hence because they were different instead of similar, and different in the sense of being less able than himself. By the same token, Tocqueville attributes the cruelties practiced by the lower classes on the nobility during the periodic revolts that arose in feudal times to the absence of a sense of common humanity or "general compassion" (ibid., pp. 172–173). The moral particularism of aristocratic mores, including traditional honor, could be harmful even when it was not ill intentioned. It made for a hard society, too immune to suffering and too willing to abide injustice. This is a serious failing of honor, one that was illustrated in the American context by the insensitivity and injustice of southern slaveholding society, as we shall see. It suggests that honor is no replacement for the political institutions of a just regime and the democratic mores that support them. It must only ever be a supplement, and it may not always be a harmonious supplement, but in liberal societies it will always be a necessary one. In contrast to the distinctions associated with honor, the equality of conditions in democracy renders persons more alike and (perhaps more important) makes them believe in their similarity. When ranks are equal, Tocqueville says, the individual citizen "can judge in a moment the feelings of all others; he casts a rapid glance at himself, and that suffices . . . It makes no difference if strangers or enemies are in question; his imagination places him right away in their place." Social and political equality therefore soften mores and tend to make citizens more "gentle" (ibid., p. 174).

Yet as obligations become more general in scope they tend to be more loosely obeyed.[45] Equality of conditions makes individuals unwilling to inflict pointless suffering, but also may render them unwilling to sacrifice for one another. In democratic ages, Tocqueville says, "men show a general compassion for all the members of the human species" (ibid.) but do not have strong attachments between them (II.3.2, p. 176). Typically, they take pleasure in relieving the pains of another if they can do so without much nuisance to themselves (II.3.1, p. 174). This general but detached compassion "renders their habitual relations easier" (II.3.2, p. 176), but it may not accomplish much in moments of extraordinary need and risk. In this respect, it resembles self-interest well understood. Self-interest, like "general compassion," can keep things running smoothly in the ordinary course of affairs so long as no serious conflicts emerge and persons can get along without much bother. When something goes wrong, however, and citizens *are* asked to trouble themselves, something more than general compassion and self-interest well understood will be called for. As one commentator puts it, "the doctrine of self-interest rightly understood is suitable for men where no deadly peril, domestic or foreign, threatens it. It could not inspire the Gettysburg Address."[46] More forceful motives are occasionally needed, even in well-ordered democracies.[47]

Perhaps because Tocqueville recognizes the inevitability of such extraordinary cases, he thinks it important that democratic societies incorporate some elements of aristocratic mores alongside the motives of general compassion and self-interest well understood, particularly for the sake of defending individual liberties against encroaching power, whether in the form of tyrannical majorities or centralized government. For this reason he hopes to inspire in modern democrats some of the qualities of character associated with traditional honor. He warns his contemporaries to "beware how we despise our ancestors; we have no right to do so. Would to God that we could recover, even with their prejudices and their defects, a little of their greatness."[48] Tocqueville does not reject democracy because of its characteristic dangers, but he calls democrats to transcend democracy in certain respects for the sake of defending it. Democracy must transcend itself by endowing citizens "with some of the interests that make nobles act in aristocratic lands" (II.3.26, p. 290). Tocqueville also recommends several structural features of the old regime, such as vigorous intermediary associations and individual rights, as we shall see, but character is important, as well. Qualities of character associated with aristocratic honor are needed to counter the "habit and passion for well-being" (ibid.) that leads to "a degrading form of servitude"[49] and opens the door to democratic despotism. The call for honor by no means renders democratic mores unnecessary, however. Tocqueville does not mean to imply that democratic norms should simply be replaced by aristocratic ones; honor should supplement, not eradicate, self-interest and compassion. His recommendation to modern democrats points to a regime that integrates democratic equality in politics and society, as well as democratic mores, with features of aristocratic society, including qualities of character associated with traditional honor.

"A Little of Their Greatness"

Throughout both *Democracy in America* and *The Old Regime,* Tocqueville indicates that some aspects of honor can persist in the new regime, if not as the dominant motive of most modern democrats then as the occasional assertion of an exceptional few.[50] Yet these qualities are no less important for being rare. While Tocqueville associates them with the "aristocratic spirit," he rarely calls them honor. The reason for resisting an explicit association with honor may be partly rhetorical. In his day, as in our own, the language of honor was greeted with suspicion, largely because of its anti-egalitarian and premodern connotations. Tocqueville tells us directly in *Democracy in America* that anyone who wishes to be heard by modern democrats must appear to be a friend of modern democracy (II.4.7, p. 328). It would be risky to point out democracy's need for something it regards as an enemy, and so Tocqueville recommends honor in friendly terms, speaking more often of "dignity" than honor per se.[51] Yet if the term dignity sounds more democratic than honor, in Tocqueville's hands its substance remains aristocratic.

Tocqueville may avoid the language of honor for other reasons as well. He genuinely has no intention of imposing aristocratic forms on democratic peoples (II.4.7, p. 328; II.4.8, p. 338).[52] In recommending some aspects of honor as a quality of character, he does not mean to advocate a restoration of traditional feudal honor. Instead of simply reinstating the old honor, which was in any case only one species of it, he means to show how honor in some form can be combined with democratic conditions and institutions. Yet precisely how this combination might materialize is an open question for Tocqueville. Here as elsewhere in *Democracy,* he is describing a phenomenon that is still unfolding in history. This uncertainty may help to explain why he treats different aspects of aristocratic honor in piecemeal fashion in the new democratic context. Whatever the reasons, however, this piecemeal treatment of key features of honor opens the door to a richly nuanced account of the moral psychology that sustains political liberty in modern democracy. By separating the fundamental features of honor as a quality of character, which remain relatively constant, from the external dimensions of honor, which

vary, Tocqueville makes it possible for us to conceive honor in a democratic context, severed from the social conditions of inequality and immobility associated with feudal aristocracy and constitutional monarchy.

Toward the end of *Democracy in America,* Tocqueville remarks that
"far from believing that it is necessary to recommend humility to our
contemporaries, I would like an effort to be made to give them a more
vast idea of themselves and of their species; humility is not at all healthy
for them; what they most lack in my view is pride" (II.3.19, p. 255).
Pride was a central component of the aristocratic honor that "gave an
extraordinary force to acts of individual resistance" in the old regime
(I.2.9, p. 328). Those who "dared in isolation to resist the pressure of
public authority" were "men who . . . held a high idea of their individual
value" (ibid.). Pride, the high idea of one's individual worth, is a spring
of action, particularly the risky and difficult actions that instrumental
reason would not be likely to recommend. By contrast, Tocqueville worried that the democratic fear of pride, as one commentator notes, had
"dried up all the strong passions without which all sense of purpose and
all will to action was lost."[53] Tocqueville told a friend in 1841 that the
passions "give birth to strength, and strength, wherever it is met with,
appears to advantage in the midst of the universal weakness which sur-
rounds us. Everyone I see is weak-spirited, trembling at the least agitation of the human heart and talking only of the perils with which the
passions threaten us . . . We no longer know how to desire, to love, or to
hate. Doubt and philanthropy make us incapable of action."[54]

Pride is at odds with democracy insofar as it implies a sense of personal distinction and runs counter to the passion for equality that characterizes the virtuous democrat. Humility, not pride, appears to democrats to be the proper demeanor for their kind, at least in their relations
with one another, as Tocqueville reports.[55] Yet humility plunges individuals into the "common obscurity" of the undistinguished crowd that is
characteristic of democratic society and thereby loosens the springs of
action (ibid.). The humble man sees himself as nothing special, and he
neither claims anything special for himself nor asks anything special of
himself. The problem with humility, according to Tocqueville, is that the
democratic citizen on occasion must ask something special of himself.
The courage and energy required to resist majority tyranny, to take a
principled stand against public opinion, or to object to the violation of
individual liberties represent extraordinary exertions of individual char-

acter and will. A citizen who asks nothing special of himself because he sees himself as nothing special is not likely to meet this challenge. Yet without at least a few citizens able to meet the challenge when it arises, democratic freedoms are bound to be tenuous.

Although pride is not itself a virtue, pride is the helpmate of virtue. Those with pride would be mortified to be chintzy with a tip, or to endure an affront, or to take more than their share. Thus pride can support generosity, courage, and justice. Our pride makes us believe that we are worth troubling about and so moves us to take the trouble to do the right thing. By contrast, humility tempts us to turn the other cheek when affronted, which is not always a bad thing, but in politics turning the other cheek can be devastating to liberty. Humility may also tempt us to deliver less than we owe (to others and ourselves) if it convinces us that there is nothing in our actions that is worth noticing. Pride tightens the springs of action by making us believe that what we do is worth remarking on and that we ourselves are sufficiently remarkable as to be worthy of the effort the actions require. Thus pride is tied to self-respect. Aristocratic honor, which inspired resistance to arbitrary rule in the old regime, also nourished self-respect, or "pride of self."[56] In the new regime, as one student of Tocqueville notes, "the greatest contribution aristocratic pride could make . . . was to show how self-respect in a society of equals required self-government."[57] Pride cuts against the grain of democratic love of equality. Yet it is crucial to the defense of democratic liberties because it tightens the springs of agency that modern democrats, according to Tocqueville, are always in danger of forsaking.[58]

Pride is also connected to what Tocqueville calls "great ambitions *(grandes ambitions)*." While virtually everyone in the United States has ambition, Tocqueville says, almost no one has any great ambitions (II.3.19, p. 250). By removing the artificial obstacles to individual ambition imposed by the fixed hierarchies of aristocratic societies, democracy permits citizens to realize their ambitions to an unprecedented degree. The increased opportunity to realize ambition promotes its spread, as "the desire to raise oneself is born in every heart at the same time, and each man wants to leave his place. Ambition is a universal feeling" (ibid., p. 251). At the same time, however, the equality of conditions that makes ambition widespread lowers its aims. The reason is that everyone, as we have seen, must work to live, which leads to a constant occupation with obtaining material necessities and comforts. Few have the luxury to concern themselves with greater objectives. Even if they should gain this luxury through their material success, the habit of aiming low is likely to persist, having been long ingrained. Consequently the objects of democratic ambition tend to remain within the "fairly narrow limits" of material prosperity (ibid.), and "one scarcely encounters an ambition that is proportionate, moderate, and vast" (ibid., p. 254). The low ambitions to which self-interested individuals may incline makes them sitting ducks for prospective tyrants and democratic factions, however. "I tremble, I confess," Tocqueville says, "that [democratic citizens] may permit themselves to be so fully possessed by a cowardly love of present pleasures that . . . they may prefer to follow feebly the course of their destiny rather than make a sudden energetic effort as needed to set things right" (II.3.21, p. 269).

The fact that the individual citizen "scorns himself to the point that he thinks he is born only for the enjoyment of vulgar pleasures" is an example of insufficient pride producing insufficiently great ambitions. Such a person "voluntarily holds himself to mediocre desires without daring to face any high enterprises; he scarcely imagines them" (II.3.19, p. 255). Of course, great ambitions can be volatile, particularly in democracies, where the same equality of conditions that makes ambition "a universal feeling" and generally orients it to material prosperity also undercuts the traditional obstacles to its extreme expressions.[59] As a result, when ambitious men have seized power, they think they can "dare to do anything" (ibid., p. 254).[60] For this reason, Tocqueville agrees on the need to control ambition (ibid.). Yet it would be equally dangerous to liberty, he thinks, to attempt "to impoverish" ambition "or confine it beyond reason" (ibid.). To confine ambition too narrowly would be to undercut individual agency. Tocqueville's "new species" of liberalism is driven by ambitions that sometimes rise above material interest, and consequently it is a liberalism that brings individual agency to the fore, both as an end in itself and as a means to political liberty.

Yet Tocqueville accepts the warning by earlier liberals about the drawbacks of ambition. The solution he recommends is not to eradicate ambition but to guide it by means of principled codes of conduct. Although democratic individualism tends to work against reverence for such codes, Tocqueville insists that this tendency is not inexorable. The legalistic spirit of American lawyers and judges counters individualism, for example. It protects the established laws and generates respect for law in general (I.2.8, pp. 274–288).[61] The institutional independence of the judiciary, with its relative insulation from the pressures of popular will, means that judges tend to be more attached than the general populace to the established principles that shape the American legal and political tradition. Lawyers form a "quasi-aristocracy,"[62] in the words of one interpreter, because of their "respect [for] the law and old things" as against the democratic "fascination with novelty."[63] Jurists display principled ambition, even a kind of honor, and they teach it to others. The popular jury system, too, educates citizens to revere the laws and the legal traditions of the regime and to think in principled terms rather than simply instrumentally.[64] Such principled ambitions draw on the power of self-concern to motivate action, but they extend the motivating force of self-concern to wider and loftier objectives than interest on its own can inspire. Neither self-interest nor generalized compassion can match the power of such ambitions in motivating difficult and risky actions.[65] For this reason, Tocqueville recommends that the leaders of modern democratic societies seek to elevate and direct the ambitions of citizens, rather than neutralizing ambition by means of compassion or replacing ambition with interest, especially material interest.

Besides pride and *grandes ambitions,* Tocqueville recommends that modern democrats cultivate the love of liberty as an end in itself, another quality that he associates with aristocratic mores and traditional honor. The love of liberty points to the capacity for higher, nonmaterial ends and to the individual dignity that comes from self-mastery. The capacity for nonmaterial ends is a defining feature of the human being, according to Tocqueville. Religion and family life provide important sources of nonmaterial goods, but liberty is the key. Although liberty frequently does yield material benefits, those who value liberty only for the sake of such benefits never preserve it for long.[66] Moreover, love of liberty cannot be inspired by the passion for material advantages because the material advantages that liberty procures "often are obscured."[67] Indeed, the defense of liberty may call for the sacrifice of material advantages. Therefore modern democrats must love liberty not simply as a means to material benefits but also as an end in itself. This unconditional love of freedom is necessary to the individual's capacity to be free, as "he who seeks in freedom anything but freedom itself is made to serve."[68] What has always attracted "certain men" to liberty is "its own charm, independent of its benefits, it is the pleasure of being able to speak, to act, to breathe without restraint, under the sole government of God and the laws."[69] This "sublime taste" (goût sublime) cannot be analyzed, according to Tocqueville, and it is not universal. It has a place "in great hearts that God has prepared to receive it; it fills them, it enflames them."[70]

Although Tocqueville associates the taste for freedom with the noble class of the old regime,[71] he makes it clear that this association is not a necessary one. The taste for freedom is possible outside the particular context of European aristocracy. It is a naturally occurring quality in human beings, or in some human beings, and it can be inspired in others by exposure to the judicial system, participation in intermediary bodies, the possession of individual rights, and religion. Like honor, it concerns what one owes to oneself rather than what one owes to others.[72] It is fundamentally self-serving rather than other-regarding, although one who loves freedom and defends it may benefit others indirectly. The unconditional love of freedom need not be universally held to have positive effects on democratic society as a whole.[73] Periodic acts of resistance by a liberty-loving few can benefit all by checking encroaching power. Unlike the motives of self-interest and compassion, which Tocqueville thinks operate on a continuous societywide basis in American democracy, the love of liberty that supplements them may manifest itself sporadically and still have widespread effects. Pride, great ambitions, and the love of liberty all have aristocratic implications for Tocqueville. They are qualities of character that he connects with aristocratic honor, but they are not limited to the context of European aristocracy. To the extent that they can be found on occasion in democratic societies, they suggest the possibility of new democratic forms of honor, a partial and intermittent aristocratic spirit within modern democracy.

Democratic civil and political associations are important sources of this unfolding honor. These associations are the equivalents of the intermediary bodies that Montesquieu thought crucial to moderate monarchies and that Tocqueville identified with aristocracy. To attempt to found democratic liberties on aristocratic privilege would be a mistake, in Tocqueville's view, but this does not prevent the creation and development of institutional supports for liberty that recover some of the power of aristocratic privilege.[74] In aristocracies "the people are always sheltered from the excesses of despotism because one always finds organized forces ready to resist a despot" (I.1.5, p. 96). The democratic replacements for these forces are the "secondary bodies formed temporarily of plain citizens" that assume administrative and political functions (II.4.7, p. 329). These secondary bodies supplement the constitutional separation of powers. They include associations such as townships, cities, and counties as well as political parties and all manner of voluntary civil associations (I.11.4, p. 194). Although they consist of ordinary citizens, Tocqueville calls these bodies "aristocratic" because they establish countervailing sites of authority from which the central authority (both government and public opinion) can be contested, and so they serve to divide and balance political power much like the functions entrusted to the nobility in the old regime (II.4.7, p. 330).[75] They introduce "the greatest political advantages of an aristocracy," which means the limitation of power, without aristocracy's "injustices and dangers" (ibid.).

In addition to this structural function, associations encourage certain salutary qualities of character in citizens. Participation in civil and political associations encourages individuals to think beyond the narrow confines of their private interests and to take an interest in the affairs of larger bodies, ultimately even an interest in "the destiny of the whole state" (I.2.4, p. 111). Participating in the decisions that affect daily life and the projects that provide for common needs gives those who make the effort a sense of their own efficacy. By associating, individuals make themselves stronger and more capable of self-defense against encroaching power. Intermediary associations thus mitigate the weakness and passivity of citizens in a society of equal conditions, where individualism and isolation are the norm. Associational life teaches us as much about what we owe to ourselves as about what we owe to others, however. As much as communality and solidarity, it fosters the pride, high ambitions, desires for distinction and self-respect, and energetic self-assertion that are central features of honor.[76] In American democracy, secondary associations democratize these qualities by permitting all citizens to reach for them, but the qualities themselves retain an aristocratic character—precisely because it is necessary to reach for them and because not everyone will be willing or able to do so.

By uniting persons on a smaller scale, for example, associations make the individual visible again. The New England township provides an arena in which citizens can distinguish themselves and so stand out from the undistinguished crowd of mass society. It is in the township that "the desire for esteem, the pursuit of substantial interests, the taste for power and attention are concentrated" (I.1.5, p. 66). By providing an arena for distinction, associations give citizens an incentive to make the effort to pursue what Tocqueville calls *grandes ambitions,* even if only a few are likely to do so. Associations thus excite the pride of a few. And by putting the great ambitions of a few on public display, associations give the rest of us reason for pride, too. We ordinary citizens may never match the extraordinary actions of our great citizens, but by taking pride in them we may be brought to a "higher opinion" of ourselves and humanity, as Tocqueville hoped, and so be inspired to reach higher in defense of our liberties than otherwise would be the case. Thus associational life mitigates the democratic tendency to make individuals invisible and loosen the springs of action, a tendency that erodes honor in democracy. Even as the greater visibility of individuals in associations encourages the quest for distinction, however, visibility also moderates this quest. The passions for esteem, distinction, and power, "which so often trouble society," change their character "when they can be exercised as though on the domestic foyer and in a sense in the bosom of the family" (ibid.). Visibility simultaneously enlivens individuals and makes them accountable, fostering both energy and moderation.

In addition to associations, Tocqueville points to individual rights as sources of the aristocratic qualities that democracy needs. He views rights themselves as vestiges of aristocratic privilege (II.4.4, p. 306), omitting all mention of liberal theory in this regard.[77] Aristocratic privileges secured certain persons a voice in government and provided protections for individual action in the private sphere. Metaphorically speaking, one might say that rights resemble fiefs, territory within which an individual is entitled to exercise command. Yet whereas the feudal noble was *"un chef, un juge, un capitaine,"* whose command included his family and his vassals or the inhabitants of the district, the democrat's command is both broader and more limited.[78] As a participant in democratic government, he shares in ruling all citizens; outside this context, the democrat's rights permit him to command only himself. But much like aristocratic privilege, democratic rights facilitate individual agency.[79] They give persons the power and the authority to assert themselves in the public sphere. By reminding us of the aristocratic origin of rights, Tocqueville calls us back to the connection between rights and individual agency, to the idea of rights as the conditions of self-command, personal responsibility, and honor.[80]

Tocqueville's idea of rights emphasizes the capacity for individual self-mastery and not only the satisfaction of needs. This explains why he refers to rights as "nothing but the idea of virtue introduced into the world of politics" (I.2.6, p. 248). Tocqueville identifies the idea of rights with the idea of virtue because rights, like virtues, are conditions of self-mastery and individual agency.[81] Rights make the virtue of self-command possible, and democratic rights extend the conditions of the virtue of self-command to all citizens. Rights, like virtues, save individuals from servility and redeem them from their subjection to others, to circumstances, and to their own unreflective impulses. By supporting self-command, rights sustain individual dignity. They also transform the meaning of obedience. Guided by the idea of rights, Tocqueville says, each one can show himself "independent without arrogance and subjected without baseness. The man who obeys violence bows and debases himself; but when he submits himself to the recognized right of a fellow to command him, he elevates himself in a certain way above the very one who commands him" (ibid.). He rises above the giver of commands because by recognizing the other man's right to command him, he himself authorizes it. In so doing, the one who receives the command makes himself the author of the command, thus preserving, or asserting, his dignity. In a regime of rights, individuals can be obedient without being servile; they can keep their dignity—and assert their honor—even while being ruled.[82] The love of liberty as an end in itself therefore finds expression in the commitment to the democratic rights that sustain honorable self-command.[83]

Another potential source of honor in democratic societies is religion, because religion elevates individual ambitions beyond the level of material desire.[84] Religion "places the object of man's desires beyond and outside the goods of the earth" and thereby counters the democratic tendency "to open immeasurably one's soul to the love of material pleasures" (II.1.5, p. 29). Too great a fixation on material comforts makes individuals vulnerable to any tyrant who is a good provider.[85] Insofar as religious belief endows the individual with higher aspirations it can support honor, and Tocqueville approves of it, especially in democracy. "It is particularly in times of democracy," he says, "that it is important to make spiritual opinions reign" (II.2.15, p. 152) so as to counteract the fact that "democracy disposes men to believe that everything is only matter" (ibid., p. 151). Materialism enervates citizens and undercuts individual agency. By contrast, "everything that elevates, enlarges, and expands the soul renders it more capable of succeeding" (II.2.16, p. 154) and so strengthens the individual's capacity for agency and thus for liberty. To the extent that religion counters materialism, it can support honor, and because modern democratic society contains few such counters to materialism, the connection between honor and religion may be closer in this context than it was in the old regime.

If religion can elevate ambition, it also sets limits on ambition by establishing mores and codes of conduct. These limits can be good for individual agency, which is supported by principled limits and direction. "When there is no longer any authority in the matter of religion or politics," Tocqueville points out, "men are soon frightened at the aspect of this limitless independence . . . As everything is on the move in the world of the intellect, they want the material order at least to be firm and stable" (II.1.5, p. 29). Not being able to turn back to their old beliefs, "they give themselves over to a master" (ibid.). Radical subjectivism thus may lead to tyranny. For this reason, Tocqueville doubts "whether man can ever support at the same time a complete religious independence and entire political liberty" (ibid.). Tocqueville identifies the same dynamic at work in the phenomenon of democratic public opinion, where the individualism that prevails in democratic societies leads citizens to subject themselves to the master of public opinion for want of more principled guidance. By fostering mores, religion can provide limits and direction for individual ambition and so support honor and individual agency (I.1.2, p. 43).[86] Religion, which guards mores, balances the democratic individualism that tends to erode mores.

In discussing religion, Tocqueville makes it clear that American democracy has strong customs and deeply ingrained, widely held mores. Indeed, the American example shows that "laws and above all mores can permit a democratic people to remain free" (I.2.9, p. 329).[87] In fact, in the United States Tocqueville finds an "extreme regularity of habits and great rigidity of mores (moeurs)" (II.1.19, p. 88; II.3.11, p. 212). Although democracy's spirit of individualism is the "most dangerous enemy" of religion, nevertheless American democracy is strongly religious (I.1.5, p. 34). In modern democratic societies, then, there are forces that tend to erode customary codes of conduct but there are other forces, such as religion, mores, and the judicial system, that support such codes. Consequently, democratic codes of conduct, which elevate and constrain individual ambition, and which are so central to honor, may not be impossible to sustain. The democratic religion, mores, and social customs to which Tocqueville draws our attention in these passages are important sources of the aristocratic qualities of character that he thinks necessary to the defense of liberty.[88] Together with civil and political associations and individual rights, religion and mores support the possibility of democratic forms of honor.

Although Tocqueville's analysis of modern democracy illuminates the conflicts between democracy and honor, it also shows modern democracy's need for qualities of character traditionally associated with honor and suggests sources of such qualities in the United States. His aim is not to replace democratic mores with aristocratic ones but to infuse democracy with the aspects of honor that are most compatible with egalitarian political and social conditions.[89] He means for the sense of honor to be combined with equality before the law and to coexist (however conflictually) with the self-interest that predominates in modern democratic motives.[90] He avoids attaching the label of honor to the aristocratic qualities of character he defends, partly for prudential reasons and partly because the combination of qualities he has in view is still unfolding before his eyes, much like the new regime itself. Tocqueville's tendency to confound honor with civic virtue leads many readers to overlook the importance of honor in his analysis and to focus instead on the egalitarian qualities of communalism and solidarity, which seem to be friendlier to democracy. The aristocratic qualities of character that Tocqueville thinks necessary to the defense of democratic liberties cannot be comprehended under the rubric of civic virtue alone, however. These qualities do not aim exclusively at the collective interest but involve a quest for individual distinction, a desire for individual self-respect, and a defense of individual rights—conceivably even against the common good. They rest on a prideful sense of what one owes to oneself rather than what one owes to one's fellows. While they reflect high ambitions, however, they do not constitute an excessively self-sacrificing form of virtue. As in Montesquieu, the aspects of honor that Tocqueville suggests to us build on the power of self-concern even though they are not limited to the lowest and narrowest forms of self-interest.

Despite the real tensions between modern democracy and the aristocratic qualities associated with honor, Tocqueville insists that such qualities are available to modern democrats, even if they are not the predominant motives of the new regime. Equality of conditions ensures that
honor is not a societywide ideal in democratic societies, but equality
does not make occasional instances of honor impossible. Intermediary
associations, individual rights, the judiciary, and religion are potential
sources and supports for democratic honor. Democracy's tendency to
undercut the conditions of honor, and individual agency more generally,
therefore is real but not invincible. Tocqueville repeatedly warned
against the false doctrine of a "certain destiny that all efforts cannot
change" (II.1.20, p. 91), and countered this "doctrine of fatality" with
the view that "in order to become master of his fate and to govern his fellows a man need only master himself" (ibid., p. 92). This idea exagger-
ates the truth somewhat, but Tocqueville regarded it as particularly edi-
fying "in the present epoch," when his contemporaries were in danger of
losing faith in themselves as agents. In our epoch, too, one finds the
widespread sense in America that we are governed, even determined, by
our circumstances rather than by ourselves. As much as we prize our
freedom, we tend to have more faith in the power of what Tocqueville
called "impersonal forces" than in the capacity for individual agency.
The qualities of character that both Montesquieu and Tocqueville associated with honor are as crucial to sustaining individual agency in modern
democracies as they were in the old regime. By supporting strong exertions of individual agency, these qualities give rise to self-determining
individuals and self-governing citizens. The place to look for them is not
so much in the regular operations of democratic government or the daily
activities of ordinary citizens but in the occasional, extraordinary instances in which individuals undertake risky and difficult actions in defense of their principles and their liberties.

4

The Love of Fame and the Southern Gentleman

Perhaps the most interesting aspect of the story of honor in the United States is that there is a story to tell at all. It is one marked by ambivalence, which results from the inevitable tensions between honor and democracy. Yet honor has been a guardian of American democracy from its inception, when the American revolutionaries signed the Declaration of Independence at Philadelphia and pledged "for the support of this Declaration . . . our Lives, our Fortunes and our sacred Honor." To be sure, liberty in the United States has leaned on many motives besides honor, and there are other motives on which it has leaned more regularly. Yet if honor has not been the most common support of American democracy, it has been one of the most important. Perhaps honor's most distinctive contribution has been to set in motion great acts of courage in defense of liberty at defining moments in American history, first at the founding and then later at crucial turning points in which America was called back to its founding principles, often in ways that transformed the nation and redirected its course. Consequently, democratic suspicions of honor in the United States have long been accompanied by a recognition of honor's political importance and an uneasy admiration for the few in whose actions it shines forth.

This chapter and the one that follows examine several manifestations of honor in the American political tradition, including honor at the founding, honor in the antebellum South, honor in the leadership of Lincoln and the early black reformers and women activists who were his contemporaries, and finally honor in the black civil rights movement of the mid-twentieth century. In the United States, principles of liberty and

97

equality articulated by the Declaration of Independence have to a significant degree formed the core of a common code of honor. The examples considered here, with the exception of the southern gentleman, are united by an attachment to this American code. They do not exhaust the instances of honor in the United States, but they illuminate some of its variety and many of its continuities, and they show honor to be a potentially powerful spring of political agency, even for modern democratic citizens. An attentive student of American history and contemporary public life will find many less celebrated examples of honor in the smaller acts of principled ambition and courage that serve to check the abuse of power in its many guises in both the public and the private spheres. Indeed, besides the common political code of honor articulated by the American founding documents, a great variety of more particular codes of honor can be found among the many voluntary associations and intermediary bodies of American civil society. In contrast to civic virtue, which implies homogeneity, honor can have many faces, even within a single society. Part of what makes it compatible with liberal politics is precisely this ability to accommodate pluralism. The intermediary bodies of American civil society and the forms of honor found there offer a corrective to the democratic potential (even within democratic honor) toward homogeneity. They reproduce in democratic form an important feature of Montesquieu's moderate monarchies, with their social and moral complexity and the many intermediary avenues for the assertion of plural standards of honor. These more particular and more varied exertions of honor will be discussed in Chapter 6; for the present we shall consider only honor writ large, that strand of public honor that takes the American creed for its code.

Great acts of honor in the United States resemble the actions of Montesquieu's *honnêtes hommes* and Tocqueville's liberty-loving aristocrats in some respects, but they differ in others and they admit of significant diversity even among themselves. Tocqueville called attention to the variability of honor, as we have seen, emphasizing that the feudal honor associated with the *ancien régime* was only one instance of honor rather than the whole of it. And Montesquieu suggested the possibility of multiple codes of honor even within old-regime France. Unlike honor in the old regime, however, public honors in the United States are not tied to political inequalities or a hereditary social order. Public honors must be won rather than inherited. Equally important, when one wins public honors one is not thereby entitled to an extra vote or a political office. This difference in how public honors are distributed affects honor as a quality of character by emphasizing individual action and conscience over status. Individual action and conscience were a part of honor even in the old regime, but in the democratic context they rise to the fore. This difference in the distribution of public honors also brings honor closer to the ideal of democratic dignity, although the two remain distinct. Insofar as they inhabit a modern democratic regime, American forms of honor presuppose the principle of the intrinsic dignity of all human beings. As a consequence, honorable Americans more often act to demonstrate or assert their dignity than to claim superiority.

Another difference is that the American code contained in the nation's founding documents is based on universal principles of abstract right, rather than concrete rules governing particular spheres of conduct, as in the old regime. And while the American code has been widely revered by Americans on the whole, important exceptions exist. The self-proclaimed honor of the planter class in the antebellum South, for instance, was based on an explicit renunciation of the Declaration's principles. In examining southern honor we shall see the dangers that arise when honor as a quality of character serves codes of conduct that are unjust and when it operates in conjunction with unchecked power. Political reformers of the mid-nineteenth century also challenged the meaning of the American code of honor—not by denying its principles but by asserting that the Declaration's promise of liberty and equality should apply more widely. Such challenges represent shifts in the meaning of honor in the United States even as they reflect underlying continuities. Thus the substantive content of American honor differs from that of honor in the old regime and American honor is itself a variegated phenomenon.

Despite the differences, however, certain features of honor as a quality of character remain relatively constant, both with respect to the transition from the old regime to the new one and with respect to transitions within the American polity. The first is that honor combines personal ambition with principled codes of conduct. The substance of the codes may vary, but a defining feature of honor is that the ambitious desire for distinction is limited, directed, and elevated by reverence for a set of principles that are independent of will or appetite. A second constant feature of honor is its emphasis on the sense of duty to oneself, which is distinguished from both self-interest and obligations to others. The third feature of honor that remains constant in the American cases is the element of courage, specifically courageous resistance to encroaching power. In Montesquieu, this aspect of honor was associated primarily with the nobility's defense of its political prerogatives against the crown. Noble resistance to encroaching power came in the form of both institutional checks on the monarch (as in acts of remonstrance by the *parlements*) and individual acts of disobedience (such as Orte's refusal to carry out his king's command to kill innocent Huguenots). Tocqueville's account of modern democracy draws explicitly on the legacy of honor in this respect, emphasizing the need for the "aristocratic" courage associated with honor to defend democratic rights against the tyranny of majority opinion and the specter of "mild" despotism. Courageous resistance is a feature of American honor, as well. And American honor remains aristocratic in spirit despite its democratic conditions. Although no longer the exclusive prerogative of a fixed social caste, it still belongs only to a few, the "natural aristocracy," whose rolls anyone of merit can join, composed of those individuals who can summon extraordinary courage in defense of principle when the moment of crisis comes. Here too pride is an important spring of courage. American honor preserves the pride that is a remnant of the old nobility's sense of self-importance. If the demeanor of honorable Americans tends to be more self-effacing than that of the *honnête homme,* their actions nevertheless reflect the "high opinion of oneself and of humanity" that Tocqueville thought so important to the preservation of democratic liberties.

Honor and the Love of Fame at the Founding

As we saw in the last chapter, Tocqueville criticized the Americans he met in 1830 for their lack of *grandes ambitions,* saying that while he had found "many men of ambition in the United States," he had seen "few of great ambitions."[1] He regarded this as a potential problem for American democracy. Indeed, he thought it important "to rouse ambition" to higher objectives and to cultivate a greater measure of pride in modern democracies.[2] Only by "giving [individuals] a higher idea of themselves and of humanity," he thought, could their modest ambitions for comfort and security be made more expansive and turned to loftier aims, including the love of liberty. Yet if he was disappointed in this respect with

Jacksonian America, Tocqueville was more sanguine when he reflected on the founding generation. The Constitutional Convention, he remarked, "included the men of greatest intelligence and noblest character ever to have appeared in the New World."[3] The ambitions of these men were *grandes* in both scope (their accomplishments would affect large numbers of people over many generations, perhaps indefinitely) and quality (they served the noble principles of liberty and equality and the high purpose of self-government "by reflection and choice").

Such admiring views of the founders came under attack early in the twentieth century by Progressive historians beginning with Charles Beard. Beard's 1913 book, *An Economic Interpretation of the Constitution of the United States,* argued that economic interest was the determining motive in the American founding and his view set the terms of the debate for several generations to come.[4] The economic interpretation has since been challenged by various works showing the important role of ideas as independent variables in the American Revolution and founding, ideas that cut across economic cleavages and so cannot be explained strictly on the basis of economic interests.[5] Implicit in the "ideological origins" thesis, however, was the assumption that those who rose to defend the principles of republican liberty at the peril of their property and prestige, not to mention their lives, were acting in a spirit of sacrifice far removed from self-serving concerns. This assumption, in turn, has been disputed by Douglas Adair, whose *Fame and the Founding Fathers* sought to dispel the dichotomy between self-interest and selfless devotion to the common good that characterized the then prevailing theories of human motivation.[6]

On Adair's account, the founders were "passionately selfish and self-interested men," but their notions of interest were not limited to narrow, material concerns. They were moved in particular by the love of fame, which Alexander Hamilton called "the ruling passion of the noblest minds," a passion that according to Adair "transmuted the leaden desire for self-aggrandizement and personal reward into a golden concern for public service and the promotion of the commonwealth as the means to gain glory."[7] Adair's interpretation recalls portraits of the founders from before the advent of Progressive historiography, not least that drawn by Lincoln. In a speech to the Young Men's Lyceum of Springfield, Illinois, in 1838 Lincoln reflected on the founding and the motives that supported the creation of American government "in its original form":

Through that period, it was felt by all, to be an undecided experiment; now, it is understood to be a successful one. Then, all that sought celebrity and fame, and distinction expected to find themselves in the success of that experiment. Their all was staked upon it:—their destiny was inseparably linked with it. Their ambition aspired to display before an admiring world, a practical demonstration of the truth of a proposition, which had hitherto been considered, at best not better, than problematic; namely, the capability of a people to govern themselves. If they succeeded, they were to be immortalized; their names were to be transferred to counties and cities, and rivers and mountains; and to be revered and sung, and toasted through all time. If they failed, they were to be called knaves and fools, and fanatics for a fleeting hour; then to sink and be forgotten. They succeeded. The experiment is successful; and thousands have won their deathless names in making it so.[8]

Adair's account of fame and the founding echoes Lincoln's vivid portrait. In more recent years, Adair's thesis has been revived and explored with new interest by political theorists and historians.[9] In part, this renewed interest reflects the fact that contemporary political theory still clings to the same "simple, two-fold schema" of human motivation that Adair found untenable in 1965 and sought to correct.[10] Today, too, we tend to conceive human motivation in terms of a dichotomy between self-interest and self-sacrifice. The renewed attention to the love of fame is driven by a dawning recognition that neither self-interest nor self-sacrifice (or even the simple sum of the two) adequately comprehends the complexity of the motives required to sustain a liberal-democratic polity.

Hamilton insisted that the love of fame was "a very strong, and perhaps the strongest, incentive for public service,"[11] and that it could "prompt a man to plan and undertake extensive and arduous enterprises for the public benefit," thus transcending the simple dichotomy between self-interest and self-sacrifice.[12] For Hamilton and his fellows, as Adair put it, the love of fame became "a spur and a goad" that urged some of them "to act with a nobleness and a greatness that their earlier careers had hardly hinted at."[13] The love of fame was by no means the sole motive of men like Hamilton, Washington, Adams, Jefferson, and Madison; it was combined with a nascent patriotism and with a genuine desire to serve the public good, but such men were not, in Adair's words, "entirely disinterested."[14] And while the common run of material interests was not unknown to them, the personal interests that they sought to serve were by no means limited to material gain. George Washington, for example, is known to have been "passionate for distinction" and ambitious for public honors.[15] If he did not especially "contrive to be emulated," as one pair of commentators has noted, he did exhibit "both a tremendous thirst for glory and a sometimes painful sensitivity about his reputation."[16] Thomas Jefferson championed the public value of personal pride because he thought that a prideful concern with fame provided a powerful incentive for public service.[17] Statesmen, he said, answer the call of duty on the basis of naturally self-serving motives, such as a "laudable" ambition, pride in eminence of character, desire for esteem, and the hope of remembrance.[18] John Adams also regarded "the passion for distinction" as the crucial means to "attract the talented into public service and induce them to sacrifice temporary, private, material advantages for the common good."[19] On the basis of this conviction, Adams as vice president in 1789 even sought to establish "grand titles" for the "leading magistrates and legislators of the new republic." The idea of fancy titles went too far for most of his contemporaries, however, as it called to mind the hereditary hierarchy of the *ancien régime,* and Adams was widely ridiculed for the suggestion.[20] Nevertheless, there was general agreement about the need "to regulate" rather than "eradicate" the self-serving passion for distinction so that it could be "gratified, encouraged, and arranged on the side of virtue."[21] Even James Madison "was not indifferent to memory or fame," although his personal desire for distinction was less "flamboyant" than that of Hamilton.[22] Madison, too, hoped to win the admiration of "the wise and good among posterity," and expressed some regret that in his own day "more ample materials were not before the world of the part which he took in promoting the union."[23] For the founders, the love of fame pointed to a moderate mean between self-denying altruism, which was too lofty to be reliable and could become excessively harsh, and egoistic self-interest, which was too narrow to support risky and difficult public purposes.[24]

The love of fame is not the same thing as honor, but the two are closely related, especially in democratic regimes. They are especially close in democracies, because here honor, like fame, must be earned. In the old regime, the nobility could in practice claim public honors without doing anything honorable, even without doing anything at all. Montesquieu, who considered individual action and conscience to be crucial components of honor, criticized this tendency, and emphasized the danger of detaching honor as a quality of character from public honors as recognition, a corruption to which he thought monarchies prone.[25] To win fame in a democratic context, it is always necessary to do something. And when fame is defined (as Hamilton defined it) as "the esteem of the discerning,"[26] winning fame requires doing something especially worthy. In democratic regimes, honor, too, must be won because public honors are no longer underwritten by hereditary entitlements.[27] The constitutional prohibition on hereditary titles in the United States thus reverses the former predominance of public honors, bringing to the fore honor as a quality of character. Public honors continue to be a part of honor conceived as a whole in the democratic context, but they operate primarily as incentives for exertions of honorable character rather than as entitlements that can be claimed independently of character, as in the old regime. Democratic honor thus resembles the love of fame in being what Adair called "a dynamic element in the historical process; it rejects the static complacent urge in the human heart to merely *be* and invites a strenuous effort to *become*—to become a person and a force in history larger than the ordinary."[28] Both motives encourage "a man to make history, to leave the mark of his deeds and his ideals on the world . . . to refuse to be the victim of events and to become an 'event-making' personality."[29] It should therefore come as no surprise that the first Americans pledged to defend the Declaration of Independence with their "sacred Honor." That document voiced their collective refusal to simply accede to "the course of human events," or acquiesce to "an absolute Tyranny." And for support in asserting themselves as agents of history rather than its pawns, the American revolutionaries invoked their honor.

The invocation of "our sacred Honor" in defense of American independence also reveals that honor need not be "inevitably conservative," "reactionary," or linked to the status quo, as often is thought.[30] The closing words of the Declaration demonstrate that honor can be positively revolutionary in the sense that it may be deployed in defense of new modes and orders. And the new political order that the American revolutionaries fought to assert and that the founders later established was not simply new to them but was *wholly* new, a type of government never before seen "among societies of men"[31] for which "a precedent could not be discovered."[32] In *Federalist* 14, Madison refers to the proposed government as "a novelty in the political world" that "has never yet had a place in the theories of the wildest projectors," and he calls "the numerous innovations displayed on the American theater, in favor of private rights and public happiness . . . the glory of the people of America." It is true that the ambitions of the founders were guided by the established principle of natural rights. Honor *is* intrinsically conservative in the limited sense that it always seeks to conserve the principles that guide it. But the conserving character of honor in this respect should not be confused with political conservatism. By conserving the ideal of natural rights, the first Americans brought about a political revolution and then revolutionized the very nature of republican politics.

Both honor and fame raised a quandary for the founders concerning the question of desert, however.[33] The ambitious quest for distinction can produce actions that are "memorable because of their superlative wickedness or their vice,"[34] and public honors may be accorded individuals whose actions stand out in the popular imagination without being particularly noble. The opinion of the founding generation was that if one's only objective was to be honored or win fame simply as an end in itself, then the honor one received was not deserved.[35] Thus Washington, for example, sought to act honorably as well as to be honored, and he struggled within himself to preserve the priority of the former.[36] When he decided to accept his election to the presidency in 1789 after having promised to give up public life at the end of the war, he worried about being seen as "inconsistent" and "ambitious":

> [W]ould there not even be some apparent foundation for the two former charges? Now justice to myself and tranquillity of conscience require that I should act a part, if not above imputation, at least capable of vindication. Nor will you conceive me to be too solicitous for reputation. Though I prize, as I ought, the good opinion of my fellow citizens; yet, if I know myself, I would not seek or retain popularity at the expense of one social duty or moral virtue.[37]

The founders were not as willing as Montesquieu had been to approve "false honor," at least for themselves.[38] Hamilton likewise distinguished the love of fame from what he called simple ambition. As he understood it, the love of fame included an attachment to principle, whereas simple ambition was not guided by anything independent of individual interest or will. It was on this basis that Hamilton compared the character of Thomas Jefferson with that of Aaron Burr. While both were "men of extreme ambition, . . . he regarded Jefferson as the clear superior because his ambition was governed by principle, whereas Burr was totally without principle."[39] Hamilton connected fame to principle so closely that in a letter to a friend, he wrote that he hoped posterity would remember that "Mr. Burr has never appeared solicitous for *fame*, & that great ambition unchecked by principle, or the love of glory, is an unruly tyrant which can never keep long in a course which good men will approve . . . Ambition without principle never was long under the guidance of good sense."[40]

Like Hamilton's emphasis on principle, Washington's reference to conscience points to the irreducible duality of honor as a quality that looks both outward and inward. Honor as a quality of character includes not only the desire for public esteem but also the ambition to live up to one's code (and the desire for the self-respect that comes from doing so). Those with honor seek to live up to their codes and to be publicly recognized for doing so; the fact that they wish for the latter outcome should not be thought to undermine the validity of the former ambition. At the same time, however, the balance between honor's internal and external dimensions is dynamic rather than static, and therefore potentially unstable. As a result, "honor in the sense of repute and fame . . . regularly threaten[s] to become the defining purpose and goal of the honorable man's life," usurping the attachment to principle and the desire for self-respect.[41] It is difficult to know for sure what finally moves the person of honor in any given instance: has the passion for distinction slipped into a position of dominance or is the commitment to principle holding sway? As one commentator points out, this uncertainty leaves the question of "what moves the very noblest hearts in tantalizing ambiguity— an ambiguity that is not uncommon among men of honor."[42] Yet the mixed quality that makes honor an "ambiguous" motive—the fact that it looks both inward and outward—is also a source of its forcefulness in motivating risky action. To "purify" honor would be to undermine its energy and dynamism, which result from the admittedly precarious balance that defines it.

Washington's desire to do "justice to myself" also emphasizes the sense of duty to oneself that is central to honor as a quality of character. It refers to a motive that transcends the contemporary categories of liberal justice and communitarian civic virtue as much as it resists the usual meaning of interest.[43] As one commentator puts it, honor is "connected to higher principles that the honorable man seeks for selfish reasons."[44] Washington owed it to himself to live up to his code, embodied in the Declaration and the Constitution, which he held to be "sacredly obligatory on all" Americans.[45] To fail to live up to these principles would have been to let himself down and so to treat himself unjustly, and although it might also have brought harm to others, Washington tells us that he was distinctly (albeit not exclusively) concerned with doing justice to himself. Washington's sense of honor, then, went beyond the desire for public honors to include the desire to be worthy of public honors, and he conceived this inner dimension of honor as a duty to himself and a condition of his own self-respect.[46] In this, his motive was neither fully disinterested nor entirely selfish.[47]

The connection between honor and natural rights in the founding generation marks an important departure from traditional forms of honor. Democratic honor frequently (although not always) is tied to universal principles of right rather than to concrete codes of conduct applicable only to a particular group.[48] Montesquieu emphasized that honor in traditional monarchies had "its supreme rules" and that those with honor would regard it as "an impossible thing" to violate their codes, even at the command of a king. Yet the content of such codes was relatively narrow in scope in that it applied to some groups but not others and governed specific realms of activity. And honor in the old regime was infused with inherited family and class loyalties, which contributed to its narrow scope. By contrast, the principles so "revered" by the American founders, which elevated and constrained their personal ambitions, were the universal principles of liberty and equality, and their sense of honor was largely (albeit not entirely) independent of family attachments and inherited class status.[49] To the extent that the Declaration of Independence comprised a code of honor for these first Americans, honor in the founding period embodies the universalism that Tocqueville predicted of honor in democratic societies: "The prescriptions of honor will . . . always be less numerous among a people not divided into castes than among any other. If ever there come to be nations in which it is hard to discover a trace of class distinctions, honor will then be limited to a few precepts, and these precepts will draw continually closer to the moral laws accepted by humanity in general."[50] The universalistic orientation of American honor as codified in the nation's founding documents reflects its democratic surroundings, which by eradicating castes give general scope to the codes that guide conduct. The sense of honor supports a standard of what is right in general rather than what is right for the inhabitant of a particular social role.

This shift partly accounts for the fact that the founders were somewhat less willing than Montesquieu had been to accept false honor. Democratic honor—especially honor writ large—converges more closely with moral virtue than did Montesquieu's concept of honor. Nevertheless this greater convergence does not amount to a simple identification. Despite being tied to a more universal code, honor as a quality of character retains the powerful partiality of self-concern as a motivating force of action.[51] With honor, living up to one's code is conceived as a precondition for one's self-respect, whether the code is narrow and infused with familial loyalty or tied to the universal ideals of natural rights. However universal the code, one retains a particular attachment to it. Thus the power of partiality in motivating action is preserved even in the most egalitarian, universalist manifestations of honor, a fact that Tocqueville overlooked. As we saw in the last chapter, Tocqueville regarded democratic honor as generally weaker because of the universalism of its codes. He thought that partial attachments were more powerful motives than abstract principles, and he questioned whether honor could survive over time in the absence of the "dissimilarities and inequalities among men" that give rise to more partial codes.[52]

The multiplicity of motives among the founding generation indicate that Tocqueville was right to think that honor would not monopolize citizens' motives in the new regime, as it may once have monopolized the motives of certain groups in earlier orders. Honor is not *the* spring of American liberty in the way that it was the spring of traditional monarchy on Montesquieu's account. Honor is exceptional in liberal democracies in the sense that it occurs relatively infrequently, at least in its more outstanding forms. Hamilton, for example, considered it a rare thing to find the love of fame and sacred honor of the American revolutionaries, the "enthusiasm for liberty, that makes human nature rise above itself, in acts of bravery and heroism."[53] In ordinary times, he thought, "a more sober calculation of interests or . . . the gratification of more immediate passions" would predominate. But while ordinary times make up the bulk of any nation's history, as one commentator has remarked, "no political community can long endure and none can confront a great crisis requiring sacrifice and bloodshed" unless at least some citizens are on occasion "animated by something transcending the narrow, prosaic con-

cern" with self-interest.[54] If democratic honor was admittedly an exceptional phenomenon rather than a societywide ideal even in the founding
generation, it has nonetheless proved to be more resilient than Tocqueville's comments in the preceding passage would predict. Without being
the dominant ideal of American politics, it has emerged periodically
among a few to play a defining role in the regime.

The presence of principles at the heart of both honor and the love of
fame may seem to imply that the ostensibly affective components of
these motives ultimately are dominated by reason. Thus Washington is
said to have acted "not so much from passion as from principle, not so
much from a desire to win honor as from a desire to be worthy of the
greatest honor."[55] Yet the sharp divide between passion and principle
(and between desire and worthiness) obscures what is perhaps the most
distinctive feature of honor, which is the fact that it cannot be reduced to
either one. Washington's desire to be worthy of the highest honors did
not make him unconcerned with actually receiving them. In this respect,
the shift from the simple desire for public honors to the principled desire to be publicly recognized for living up to one's code points in the direction of Kant's hierarchical ordering of desert over happiness, but it
does not go all the way to the finish line. Even in its noblest forms,
honor remains "heteronomous" in Kantian terms, because it never fully
turns away from public recognition and never entirely transcends affective attachments to one's principles and one's self-respect. Washington's
desire to be worthy of the highest honor does not represent a simple triumph of principle over passion so much as an interaction of principles
with passions, in which reason guides and directs but never fully transcends the desiring part of the psyche.

The partiality of honor is one reason why honor should never be
thought to represent a complete picture of moral or political motivation, much less a comprehensive characterization of the soul. Any polity
needs leaders who are adept at exercising impartial reason and so rising
above their attachments in matters of justice, law, and public policy. Average citizens need the capacity for impartial reason, as well, not least to
assess the validity of their codes of conduct and to judge whether they
themselves are worthy of their self-respect and whatever public distinction they may have won. Reason is a crucial component of political
agency; without it, one's movements could only be reactions to impulse,
appetite, or external force, and could not rise to the level of intentional,

self-initiated action. But the perfect triumph of impartial reason over the affective dimensions of the soul would not be conducive to strong exertions of political agency, either, because it would risk undermining the springs of action. It would transform the individual from a citizen into a philosopher, from a spirited defender of liberty to a student of it. "[R]eason is the guide of life," as John Adams put it, but "the senses, the imagination and the affections are the springs of activity. Reason holds the helm, but passions are the gales."[56]

The interactive relationship between principles and passions suggests that even when honor is guided by principled codes of conduct, its thymotic element is never fully tamed by reason. The founders read Plutarch's *Lives* and took to heart its lessons about the intrinsic unruliness of honor. Individuals who are extremely ambitious for distinction, such as an Alcibiades or a Coriolanus, can be difficult for the political community to accommodate even if they are necessary for its survival.[57] Plutarch gave the founders as many reasons to be wary of honor as to admire it, and, as one historian remarks, they were fully "cognizant of the dangers . . . attendant on the quest for honor."[58] Thus Hamilton in *Federalist* 70 notes the need to secure liberty "against the enterprises of ambition" even as he defends the necessity of an energetic executive, saying that "[e]very man the least conversant in Roman history knows how often that republic was obliged to take refuge . . . against the intrigues of ambitious individuals who aspired to tyranny."

Yet it would be a mistake simply to reduce honor to the appetite for power, as Hobbes did. Washington's decision to resign the presidency at the end of his second term is a case in point. Had he wanted a third term he surely would have won it.[59] Jefferson remarked to James Monroe in the summer of 1796, in reference to Washington, that "one man outweighs them all in influence over the people. Republicanism must lie on its oars, resign the vessel to its pilot, and themselves to the course he thinks best for them."[60] As it turned out, Washington voluntarily returned the vessel to its oarsmen, thus prioritizing the principle of republicanism over the accumulation of political power as an end in itself. To his contemporaries as to subsequent generations, Washington's resignation of office was a mark of his honor, not an exception to it.[61] Jefferson himself believed that the spirited resistance to encroaching power required for democracy to flourish presupposed the desire to rule over oneself but not necessarily the desire to dominate others.[62] Spiritedness, he thought, could thrive only by the exercise of power and responsibility, and so he championed political participation, but in the new American system the exercise of political power and responsibility did not imply (indeed, it denied) the subjection of others.[63] One might think of Montesquieu's Orte in this regard, as well. Orte's purpose in disobeying his king was to make himself an obstacle to the abuse of power, not to increase his own power. Of course, if he had never acquired any power he would not then have been in a position to make himself an effective obstacle to its abuse. But his refusal to massacre innocent Huguenots was not a ploy for more power. The Hobbesian appetite for power does not comprehend either Orte's honorable disobedience or Washington's honorable resignation.

Still, one cannot deny honor's potential for unruliness. Hamilton, after all, died in a duel trying to defend his honor. Precisely because honor "glories in scorning life," as Montesquieu said, it does not recognize the natural limits on action imposed by self-interest in the usual sense. One might be tempted to prefer Locke's right of resistance to the motive of honor for this reason. According to Locke, the inalienable right of resistance serves as a constant threat to political sovereigns who may be tempted to trespass against the life, liberty, or property of their subjects.[64] But while the people always possess the right to resist, Locke maintains that they will rarely do so because of the risks involved. They know that resistance is likely to bring them "ruine and perdition."[65] Thus the threat of popular rebellion moderates encroaching rulers while the threat of ruin moderates self-interested rebels. There is much to recommend this balance, but there are flaws in it, as well. In particular, the self-interest that restrains the populace from undertaking acts of opposition may weaken the springs of individual agency. Self-interest restrains as much as it incites resistance to encroaching power. Especially in the face of a political sovereign who holds the power of life and death over his subjects, self-interest may as easily lead to fearful submission as to forceful defiance. Moreover, as Tocqueville pointed out, self-interest may not be sufficient to motivate resistance to the encroaching power of a commodious despot, or one who accommodates the appetites of his subjects even as he restricts their liberties. Even with the right of resistance, liberty in the long run cannot be maintained without motives that rise above self-interest, if only on occasion and only in a few. And no polity can enjoy the benefits of the spirited defense of liberty without having spirited guardians in its midst. If such persons are unruly on occasion, the risks they pose to their fellows and to the regime are as nothing compared with the risks engendered by a regime that has succeeded in taming them entirely.

The importance of honor and the love of fame as personal motives of the founders illustrates one way that honor has played a role in the American political tradition. But what role, if any, did the founders accord honor in the system of government they established? On the one hand, they were convinced that neither "moral" nor "religious" motives on their own could reliably control human actions in politics.[66] The American system would protect liberty with the help of an institutional separation of powers supported by a program of checks and balances. On the other hand, even though this institutional apparatus would significantly reduce reliance on the character of citizens and their representatives, it would not make liberty altogether independent of character. As Madison told the Virginia Ratifying Convention in 1788, "if there be not . . . virtue among us . . . [n]o theoretical checks, no system of government, can render us secure."[67] On another occasion, he argued that "the partitions and internal checks of power" established by the Constitution "are neither the sole nor the chief palladium of constitutional liberty. The people, who are the authors of this blessing, must also be its guardians. Their eyes must be ever ready to mark, their voice to pronounce, and their arm to repel or repair aggressions on the authority of their constitutions."[68] The "great security against a gradual concentration of the several powers," he says in *Federalist* 51, consists in combining "the necessary constitutional means" for each branch to resist the encroaching power of the others with the most effective "personal motives" for such resistance. In other words, constitutional checks and balances are impotent without the spring of personal motives, and the motives that Madison has in mind here cannot be equated simply with self-interest.

The founders were not inattentive to the motive of self-interest, to be sure. *Federalist* 10 makes much of the "different interests and parties" arising from "the possession of different degrees and kinds of property," such as "a landed interest, a manufacturing interest, a mercantile interest, a moneyed interest," and "many lesser interests." But while the people's representatives must attend to the interests of their constituents, the representatives themselves are not to be ruled by the motive of material interest. The founders did not conceive the quest for personal gain as the main currency of the new system. Instead, *The Federalist* presupposes what one commentator has called "the honorable determination to be more than . . . producers and consumers."[69] Hamilton emphasized this point in *Federalist* 76, saying, "The supposition of universal venality in human nature is little less an error in political reasoning than the supposition of universal rectitude. The institution of delegated power implies that there is a portion of virtue and honor among mankind, which may be a reasonable foundation of confidence. And experience justifies the theory."

Hamilton's remarks on the importance of virtue and honor come as part of a discussion of the president's power to nominate ambassadors and other public ministers. They address the objection that the president, "by the influence of the power of nomination, may secure the complaisance of the Senate to his views."[70] To meet the objection, Hamilton invokes the "integrity of the Senate," which he says is a "guard against the danger of executive influence upon the legislative body."[71] The character of senators is not the only guard against executive encroachment, but it is a crucial one. Hamilton calls attention to England on this point, where the reputed "venality of the British House of Commons" was said by many to jeopardize the independence of the legislative power and so to threaten the separation of powers. He maintains that in fact the English Commons has more virtue in it than is often thought, that there is "a large proportion of the body which consists of independent and public-spirited men," and that these men are usually able "to control the inclinations of the monarch" and so to sustain the separation between the legislative and executive powers.[72] So, too, he says, Americans have reason for confidence "in the probity of the Senate."[73] On this basis, Americans may rest satisfied that while "the executive might occasionally influence some individuals in the Senate, yet the supposition that he could in general purchase the integrity of the whole body would be forced and improbable."[74] Thus while Hamilton denies that the separation of powers is in fact in danger in England or likely to be so in America, he acknowledges that without "a portion of virtue and honor" in the people's representatives, the separation of powers would indeed be vulnerable. After all, if the Senate were to abandon "probity" entirely and give its votes for personal gain to the president in matters of appointment, this particular constitutional means of separating the executive and legislative powers would be seriously eroded. *The Federalist* accepts the proposition that character is a necessary (albeit not a sufficient) support for the constitutional separation of powers.

The mechanism of representation helps to incorporate the requisite portion of virtue and honor into the system.[75] Large republics make the most of the mechanism in this respect because by enlarging the field of potential candidates while retaining a limit on the number of available offices, they increase the probability of "fit characters" being elected, or "men who possess the most attractive merit and the most diffusive and established characters."[76] Fit characters have "the wisdom to discern the true interests of their country" and a special measure of "patriotism and love of justice,"[77] but they also have "honor" and a love of fame.[78] And while their wisdom, patriotism, and sense of justice equip them to represent the interests of their constituents and the polity as a whole, it is their honor and their love of fame that provide effective resistance to encroaching power. When Madison says in *Federalist* 51 that "ambition must be made to counteract ambition" and that "the interest of the man must be connected with the constitutional rights of the place," he has in mind the "pride and vanity" that attach each representative to the form of government that "favors his pretensions and gives him a share in its honors and distinctions."[79] Because the personal standing of each representative is tied to the perceived integrity of his branch of government in relation to the others, each representative has a personal motive to stand and defend the larger body against its rivals. For example, if the president in negotiating a treaty with a foreign power should pervert the instructions or contravene the views of the Senate, Hamilton says, there will arise "a disposition in that body to punish the abuse of their confidence or to vindicate their own authority. We may thus far count on their pride, if not upon their virtue."[80] It is important to note that the ambition *The Federalist* incorporates is defensive; it is turned from an attempt to rule over others to a defense of rights, institutional prerogatives, and liberty itself. In this respect it resembles the ambition of Montesquieu's intermediary bodies and Tocqueville's liberty-loving aristocrats.[81] The president himself is encouraged to restrain his inclination to encroach on the Senate (through his power of appointment, for example) by an "exact regard to reputation."[82] His virtue is buttressed by the "danger to his own reputation . . . from betraying a spirit of favoritism" in proposing appointments, a concern that "could not fail to operate as a barrier" against the temptation to overreach his legitimate authority.[83] More generally, the "unity" of executive power means that the president cannot easily hide from the prying eyes of public opinion and, provided that he is interested in his reputation and in the distinction of retaining office, the fact that he serves alone will provide "security" for the Republic by restricting him from pernicious encroachments on the other branches.[84] What one commentator calls "the human pride in being distinctive"[85] and another calls "honorable self-assertion"[86] is crucial to the separation of powers. The American system constitutionalizes the tumults that produce this balance of power more explicitly than Montesquieu's system of moderate monarchy did, and it democratizes the motive that enlivens them by opening it to the people's elected representatives rather than largely restricting it to a hereditary nobility.

The importance of both "disinterested wisdom" or "justice," in Madison's words, and the prideful love of fame may explain why Hamilton bothered to distinguish virtue from honor in speaking about the qualities of character presupposed by the new system. The virtue of "fit characters," which permits the calm sentiments of the community to prevail, serves the right representation of the people. Honor serves the limitation of power by motivating the spirited defense of the particular prerogatives of each branch against encroachments by the other branches.[87] So while a portion of virtue in the people's representatives serves the democratic principle of popular sovereignty, their honor serves the liberal principle of limited power. If virtue and honor deserve to be distinguished, however, they may also be mutually supportive. The ambitions of elected representatives help sustain the fidelity of representatives to their constituents and to the polity as a whole, since "whatever hopes or projects might be entertained by a few aspiring characters," elected officials are bound to find infamy rather than glory in projects that are "subversive of the authority of the people."[88] Similarly, "those who represent the dignity of their country in the eyes of other nations will be particularly sensible to every prospect of public danger, or of a dishonorable stagnation in public affairs."[89] In this respect, the separation of powers with its system of checks and balances is more than a mechanism for securing liberty; without cultivating character directly, the system "calls it forth."[90] It transforms ambition from narrow interest to higher and broader concerns, as representatives are forced to seek the common interest (including the shared interest in separated powers) to win fame for themselves. Moreover, "to the extent that it succeeds in eliciting a simulacrum of virtue from the nation's highest officials," as one historian has said, the system "educates the general public in the most effectual way: by the shining examples it holds up for emulation."[91]

The theme of resistance to encroaching power associated with honor in Montesquieu and with aristocratic character in Tocqueville was elaborated by the founders in a wide range of contexts. Washington, for instance, praised education for "teaching the people to know and value their rights: to discern and provide against invasions of them," and for "uniting a speedy but temperate vigilance against encroachments, with an inviolable respect to the laws."[92] The mix of "vigilance against encroachments" and "inviolable respect to the laws" reminds us of the civility of honorable disobedience as Montesquieu presented it. Citizens of liberal-democratic regimes must be as jealous of their rights as the old nobility was jealous of its prerogatives. And yet they also must revere the laws, much as the nobility was obliged to revere the king. Madison, too, emphasized that "it is proper to take alarm at the first experiment on our liberties," and held "this prudent jealousy to be the first duty of Citizens, and one of the noblest characteristics of the late Revolution."[93] For Jefferson, civic virtue itself included a spirit of opposition to encroaching power as much as law-abidingness.[94] The capacity for resistance and the courage to resist made human nature "rise above itself," as Hamilton said, illuminating the potential for high-heartedness in the human species, or the "honor of the human race."[95]

For the most part, the founders did not regard politics or political freedom as the highest human end, but they did see the honor of the human race, or human dignity, as tied to the capacity for self-governance.[96] The Federalist treats society's choice of government as a point of honor,[97] referring to "men's honorable wish to choose for themselves."[98] For the founders, a government that protected individual liberties without also establishing popular sovereignty would be much better than despotism, but such a government would not be nearly as noble as the one they had invented. The American system, which combines popular sovereignty with individual liberties, pays respect to the sovereign dignity of humankind both inside politics (popular sovereignty allows the individual to act, or participate, in the public sphere, even if indirectly) and outside politics (in the form of liberties that protect individual action in the private sphere). In this respect, it is a more complete expression of human dignity than even the most moderate of the old regimes, and so more "noble" than any other government "on the face of the globe," as Madison put it in *Federalist* 14. The American system honors the capacity for agency that is distinctive to humankind. It also elicits honor, which, by motivating resistance to encroaching power, supports individual self-command and collective self-government. Madison's remarks in this regard call attention to the link between honor and choice, and, perhaps surprisingly, imply a special affinity between honor and democracy.

The resistance to encroaching political power associated with honor and with the dignity of individual and collective self-rule has a parallel in the refusal to acquiesce to the external power of circumstance. The American system claims to have been established "from reflection and choice" rather than "accident and force."[99] It "vindicates the honor of the human race" by showing that the accidents and forces of the natural world do not determine the character of a people, its degree of prosperity, or the nature of its political order. This assertion is a response to the "profound philosophers" of the day who had "attributed to [Europe's] inhabitants a physical superiority and . . . gravely asserted that all animals, and with them the human species, degenerate in America— that even dogs cease to bark after having breathed awhile in our atmosphere."[100] The beauty and nobility of the American Constitution give the lie to the thesis of American degeneracy without simply asserting American superiority. The American experiment becomes "interesting to the world," as one interpreter puts it, because it shows that the principal cause in human affairs in general is a political decision rather than prepolitical factors such as physical environment or race.[101] The primacy of political decision demonstrates the human power of self-determination, which is a universal phenomenon not limited to the citizens of the United States. Thus American government vindicates the honor of the whole human race, not just the honor of Americans.

These considerations call to mind Tocqueville's remarks on the "democratic historians" of his day who emphasized the role of "impersonal forces" in human societies, denying the "particular action of individuals" and giving the impression that societies merely "obey without knowing it a force that dominates them."[102] Tocqueville denied the idea that politics was determined by a "blind fatality,"[103] as we saw in the last chapter, and he regarded the dissemination of this thesis as an extremely dangerous development for modern democracy. The belief in blind fatality undermines individual agency and "strike[s] down the souls" of citi-zens,[104] making them passive and pliable in the face of encroaching power. The American experiment elevates the souls of those who take part in it, and provides a counterexample for the downcast souls of those who have come to believe that blind fatalities govern their lives. It vindi-cates the honor of the human race by showing that there is more to hu-mankind than its circumstances. By proving the honor of a few, it proves the potential honor of all. Thus the American system as a whole embod-ies honor as resistance to tyranny, both the tyranny of despots and the tyranny of nature and circumstance. It pridefully asserts the dignity, even the nobility, of humankind in the form of individual and collective self-rule. This is a somewhat boastful assertion, for no one fully resists the power of nature or circumstance, and even the honorable few who rise up against tyrants may come out on the losing end in a direct con-frontation with them. One might wonder whether this boastfulness is a good thing. Perhaps, following Marx, we should dress down such brag-garts in the name of unmasking the true power of historical forces as against human agency. Yet the boastful exaggeration of human indepen-dence is an honorable response to the real powers of nature, circum-stance, and tyrants because it makes resistance conceivable. In this re-spect, it may be a necessary condition of whatever power of agency is possible for us.

In his first inaugural address, Jefferson called Americans "too high-minded to endure the degradations" of European tyrannies.[105] Pride is the helpmate of many virtues, but a special ally of honor. One thinks of Orte's proud refusal to undertake actions that he believed to be beneath him. In the old regime, the nobleman's idea that some actions were be-neath him was accompanied by the conviction that some persons, too, were beneath him. This explains why traditional honor has been criti-cized as "nothing more than having someone to look down on."[106] In the democratic context, by contrast, honor preserves a prideful disdain of certain types of action without disdaining any fixed class of persons. To the extent that the honorable person looks down on others, it is those persons who engage in what he or she considers to be degrading actions, such as slavish acquiescence to tyrants. Thus Gouverneur Morris in 1800 exhorted Americans to the "high, haughty, generous and noble Spirit which prizes Glory more than wealth and holds Honor dearer than Life," and which "despis[es] whatever is little and mean whether in Character Council or Conduct . . . dreading Shame and Dishonor as the greatest Evil, esteeming Fame and Glory above all Things human."[107] Democratic honor scorns "all low and vulgar Considerations," but not low-born or uncultivated *persons*.[108] Indeed, as *Federalist* 11 suggests, the existence of a ruling class affronts the honor of the human race.[109] Still, the pride inherent in honor gives it an aristocratic cast, as it presupposes distinctions of quality among actions and, by extension, among the persons who undertake them. Even when honor occurs in a democratic context devoid of a fixed class structure, is guided by principles that emphasize the freedom and equality of all, and serves to promote such principles and to resist encroaching power, the proud distinctiveness of honorable persons is difficult to ignore.

The pride associated with honor poses problems in the democratic context. Americans, as one commentator notes, "do not consider themselves the inferiors of anyone, an attitude that leads to individual well-being and social robustness, but also to a certain prickliness regarding others' claims to superiority, even where they might be justified."[110] Even in the absence of explicit claims to superiority, democrats can be sensitive about actions that simply demonstrate one's superiority. As Montesquieu said, "one exceptionally great man renders others small."[111] Americans' prickliness about pride and distinction has many merits and is itself in keeping with the practice of honorable resistance to encroaching power, but it poses challenges for democratic leadership, as "finding a way in which political leadership can be exercised," even on the opposition, is a tricky business "in a society like America, where egalitarianism creates sensitivity about any claims to precedence" or acts of precedence.[112] Democrats with honor therefore must avoid as much as possible the appearance of pride, even as their actions embody it. Yet American democracy is not simply hostile to distinction. Anyone who has visited the Lincoln Memorial recently, or viewed the exhibition devoted to Martin Luther King, Jr., in the rooms below it, knows that there are a few distinguished Americans whom we average Americans love to love. And one regularly hears from civic and religious leaders that the United States needs more heroes—or "role models," the democratic euphemism for heroes. For all our prickliness about superiority in others, there is a powerful and elevating pleasure that comes from admiring individuals who have done outstanding things. The gift of something fine to live up to (which is very different from the forced cultivation of virtue) is a precious gift indeed, for democratic peoples as much as for any others.

No one has ever understood the value of this gift better than George

Washington did. His voluntary resignation of the presidency endowed the United States with a model for the peaceful transition of power and the priority of constitutional democracy over the cult of personality. The sense of honor on display in this decision was admired and emulated by his contemporaries. It combined high ambitions and a desire for distinction with a firm commitment to republican principles and a sense of duty to himself as well as to his country. Washington and his fellow founders considered the sense of honor to be a crucial support for republican government. Honor was invoked in the Declaration on behalf of the collective liberty and newly announced political sovereignty of the United States. It was understood to motivate spirited resistance to encroaching power, both by elected officials within the government and by individual citizens from the outside. It was seen as a unique spur to risky and arduous undertakings on behalf of the public, which self-interest alone could not inspire and civic virtue could not be relied upon to inspire. Because it was potentially unruly and because it was always prideful, the founders did not place unrestrained confidence in honor, however. In the next section, we shall see some of the dangers inherent in honor that made the founders ambivalent about it.

Slavery and the Southern Gentleman

Southern honor was everything the founders feared. It was more pretentious than principled, and the principles it did serve were reactionary, not republican. It asserted itself through mastery of others rather than simply through democratic self-command, and it provoked ridiculous displays of volatility ending not infrequently in individual deaths and ultimately in the breakdown of the Republic. Yet for all that, honor in the antebellum South is an important part of the story of American honor.

The southern plantation economy and social structure that reached its peak between 1800 and 1860 was the closest thing to the Old World way of life ever seen in the United States. The planter class of the American South consciously identified itself as the landed aristocracy of the new Republic.[113] Plantation owners ruled over family members and their black slaves in a manner that resembled that of the feudal lords of early modern Europe. Social hierarchy, with its accompanying entitlements and exclusions, played a more visible role in the southern than in the northern states. This had much to do with the presence of large landholders and the relative dearth of the industry and small-scale independent farming that had produced a larger proportion of persons of moderate means in the North. The more entrenched social hierarchy in the South also resulted from the institution of chattel slavery and the very visible distinction between free whites and black slaves. Then, too, southerners were generally slower to relinquish the traditional understanding of moral identity as a function of social status, a view that justified disparate treatment of differently placed persons.[114] Southern whites did not entirely reject the idea of natural rights that severs individual moral status from social position, or at least they did not reject it for themselves. The antebellum South was democratic in many respects, which was always one of its cruel ironies. Indeed, (white) popular sovereignty was embraced there in a more direct and unmediated fashion than it was in the northern states.[115] Southern honor itself was partly democratic insofar as honors or entitlements had to be "fairly won in competition for public favor."[116] For whites, "honor was not an exclusive commodity to which bluebloods had sole access or claim,"[117] and consequently "those belonging to the circle of honor were much greater in number than in any other traditional society. Democracy, that is white democracy, made that possible."[118] But while southern honor was more egalitarian in some respects than honor in the old regime, it nevertheless presupposed a rigid racial hierarchy such that public honors were universally denied to blacks, and honor as a quality of character was thought by whites to be antithetical to the moral status of blacks as slaves.[119] The honor of whites was largely defined in explicit opposition to the dishonor associated with black slave status. In this respect, southern honor was parasitic on the degradations generated by institutional slavery; it was on the backs of their black slaves that southern gentlemen made themselves "honorable."

Like honor among the founders, southern honor combined the sense of duty to oneself and the desire for self-respect with the quest for public recognition. It was grounded in "a sense of personal worth,"[120] what Tocqueville called "the high opinion" of oneself that makes certain actions and ways of life appear to be beneath one. This is the quality that Jefferson claimed for Americans when he called them "too high-minded to endure the degradations" of European tyrannies. For southerners, as for the founders, the sense of personal worth was understood to be contingent upon one's resoluteness in living up to a set of principles, or "the laws of honor."[121] To fail in this regard would be to let oneself down, to violate what Washington called "justice to myself." Southern honor also involved public recognition, of course. As a young student at South Carolina College wrote in 1828, "Honor is that principle of nature which teaches us to respect ourselves, in order that we may gain the respect of others."[122] This remark suggests a certain priority for self-respect as against public recognition. Yet in practice southern honor had a tendency to degenerate to the mere desire for external public recognition. Honor is always vulnerable in this respect, but it is especially vulnerable in societies where established inequalities and a fixed hierarchy entitle certain groups to public honors and exclude other groups from them. When certain persons can rely on receiving public esteem simply for being who they are, the internal dimension of honor withers from disuse and its external trappings rise to predominance. This is true regardless of the specific content (and merit) of the codes involved. Whatever the content of the codes, the internal dimensions of honor tend to rise to predominance in the absence of a fixed social hierarchy that allocates public esteem and status independently of character-based merit. By the same token, when persons are required to earn the respect of their fellows through their actions, the external trappings of honor are forced into a secondary position; they follow honorable actions (actions deemed honorable on the basis of their adherence to some principled standard) and therefore are dependent upon them. This fact explains why honor as a quality of character is in some respects better served by democracy than by the more fixed order of the old regime.

Society in the antebellum South was a hybrid between the old European order and the new democracy. Partly because the fixed racial hierarchy was such a defining feature of the regime (southern planters themselves maintained that their whole way of life rested on the institution of slavery) and partly because of the presence of a landed gentry class, southern honor was marked by a significant measure of entitlement. Certain persons, such as all whites as against all blacks and all large landholders as against the propertyless, expected and received a measure of public honor and esteem simply for being who they were.[123] This system of entitlement led to a "stress upon external, public factors in establishing personal worth," as opposed to principled self-respect.[124] At least in the American South, "[t]he individual dependent on honor [had to] have respect from others as the prime means for respecting himself."[125]

At the same time, however, honor among whites was not simply conferred by personal status but was also partly competitive and open to a fairly wide circle so that "southern yeomen, no less than rich planters, found meaning in honor's demands."[126] The combination of obvious (and extreme) distinctions in status, on the one hand, and open competition for nonhereditary marks of status, on the other, made southern honor excessively outward looking in its orientation.

The South's hybrid character as both Old World and new regime thus exacerbated a characteristic corruption of honor. Southern society was highly "rank conscious," for example, more so than in the North, and men in slaveholding states, according to one historian, were particularly "prone to designate status by titles."[127] State militia rankings were particularly popular marks of distinction. The rankings were "especially coveted by those whose property holdings might not otherwise have provided them with status."[128] The officer corps in the state militias was democratically elected, but once a title had been won it became a lifetime possession. As a consequence, it was not uncommon for men to gain an elective title and then promptly resign the post, as one Virginia officer complained, who was disappointed in the many men who seemed to "care so little about" the duties associated with their stations.[129] But once a colonel, always a colonel. The high rate of dueling in the antebellum South also reflects the intense competition for external marks of honor that characterized this hybrid society. In the old regime, dueling had been a means for settling disputes that arose between members of the established nobility. Commoners did not duel. In the American South, dueling became a means to demonstrate status in the sense of laying claim to it.[130] Men fought duels to prove their status, not because they believed their status required it of them. A challenge to duel frequently was welcomed as "a reception into the world of gentlemen,"[131] and the use of the duel as a stepping stone to a higher station in life led to a remarkably high rate of dueling. As one historian reports, the duel flourished in the American South as "nowhere else in the civilized world, attended by the greatest ferocity and the highest proportion of fatalities."[132] Here "men called each other out for trifles which would never have been noticed in any other part of the world."[133] The reason for their exaggerated sensitivity was a desire to prove themselves as proud—and therefore "as delicately sensitive in recognizing an insult"—as any "peer of England or nobleman of France."[134] "We are all *parvenus,* pretenders, or snobs," admitted William J. Grayson in the 1850s.[135] We shall have more to say about the duel presently, but for now note that in the South it functioned less as a venue for displaying internal qualities of character and more as means of attaining external status. In this respect, it was in keeping with the tendency of southerners to emphasize the external dimensions of honor more than the internal ones.

The emphasis on external marks of status distinguished southern honor from its northern variants of the same period, which tended to emphasize honor's internal aspects, particularly conscience[136] and what one historian terms "individualistic dignity."[137] Another difference between the two was the "primacy northerners gave national honor over community and even family honor."[138] In the southern political setting, "family heritage and local loyalties were exceedingly important," and political parties were shaped less by "ideological differences" than by "the county's neighborhood structure and ties of kinship."[139] As a result, "pride of family and loyalty to friends" played a defining role in local elections, where "obligations of blood, past favors, present indebtedness, and other commitments cemented political allegiances."[140] In this context, the codes of conduct that guided individual ambition and provided standards for awarding public honors were more akin to the particular rules of conduct that characterized honor in the old regime than to the abstract principles of right embodied in the Declaration of Independence. Honor in the South was an "ethic of the small-scale community where loyalties remained personal and intense."[141] One's honor often was tied directly to the ideal of family protectiveness. When the Civil War began, as one historian reports, "Samuel David Sanders of Georgia mused about Confederate enlistment, 'I would be disgraced if I staid at home, and unworthy of my revolutionary ancestors.' "[142] In a similar vein, William Yancey, senator from Alabama, remarked in 1860 to the Democratic convention in Charleston that "ours is the honor at stake—the honor of children, the honor of families, the lives, perhaps, of all."[143] In general, the "fear of reproach for failing to fulfill one's duty to serve family and community at war was so great that antebellum southern whites, like earlier peoples, questioned the value of peace in submission."[144] In direct contrast to the honor of men such as Washington, Hamilton, Jefferson, and Madison, southern honor was based upon "faithfulness to a particular place and people and their past, not upon some abstract idea such as 'democracy' or 'freedom.' "[145]

In keeping with its emphasis on external marks of distinction and the more concrete quality of its codes, southern honor also was closely bound up with physical prowess.[146] As we saw in Chapter 2, this was an important feature of medieval and early modern notions of honor. In unstable, continuously warring societies, brute strength was highly prized both as a condition of personal independence and as an instrument of collective security. The rise of the nation-state, which gradually established internal peace and security from foreign attack, diluted the connection between physical prowess and honor. External qualities such as strength were gradually replaced by internal qualities that brought courage together with conscience. The concern for collective security never became obsolete, of course, and consequently honor has always retained a connection to martial valor. Polities cannot help but honor the qualities needed to defend their borders. Yet increasingly, the physical strength and martial valor of soldiers was accompanied by another type of honor, one that emphasized political courage, or the courage of conviction, and that motivated spirited resistance to encroachments on individual liberties within the regime itself. George Washington exemplified both types of honor, martial valor on the battlefield as well as courage and ambition in defending abstract principles as an elected official. Perhaps his greatest act of honor—the resignation of the presidency—was far from being a simple act of physical prowess. The historical shift from martial to constitutional regimes makes honor more political in character, or introduces a new type of honor in the form of political courage.

In addition to the historical shift from martial to constitutional regimes, modern technology contributed to loosening the tie between honor and physical prowess. Jefferson observed in 1813 in a letter to John Adams that "the invention of gunpowder had rendered 'bodily strength . . . but an auxiliary ground of distinction.' "[147] Modern honor is increasingly detached from physical prowess and increasingly puts courage and ambition in service to abstract principles and political action rather than feats of bodily strength. These changes, among others, contribute to making honor increasingly accessible to women, a theme we shall address in the next chapter. The southern emphasis on physical prowess as a component of honor reflects its reactionary character, the fact that honor in the antebellum South was in some respects closer to feudal honor than to the honor of the founders.[148] This emphasis also helps explain the prevalence in the South of the duel, which, though typically fought with guns, was thought to provide a stage for the display of physical prowess. Both the emphasis on external displays of status and the concrete rather than principled character of honor's codes, including the centrality of physical prowess, exacerbated the potential for superficiality and unruliness implicit in honor. These features of southern honor contributed to making it divisive and even deadly, as the high mortality rate associated with southern duels indicates.

To the extent that southern honor was tied to any abstract principles at all, it was based on an explicit rejection of the principle of natural rights articulated by the Declaration. Alexander Stephens, the recently appointed vice president of the new Confederacy, told a convention of his fellow Georgians in March of 1861:

> The prevailing ideas entertained by [Jefferson] and most of the leading statesmen at the time of the formation of the old constitution, were that the enslavement of the African was in violation of the laws of nature; that it was wrong in *principle*, socially, morally, and politically . . . Those ideas, however, were fundamentally wrong. They rested upon the assumption of the equality of the races. This was an error. It was a sandy foundation, and the government built upon it fell when "the storm came and the wind blew."
>
> Our new government is founded upon exactly the opposite idea; its foundations are laid, its cornerstone rests upon the great truth, that the Negro is not equal to the white man; that slavery—subordination to the superior race—is his natural and normal condition.[149]

By the time of the Civil War, then, southern honor had coalesced around the defining ideology of a slaveholding society. As one historian reflects, "what had been in 1788 an entrenched interest occasioning shame and considerable embarrassment nearly everywhere had become for many by 1861 a matter of principle and honor to be defended to the death."[150] All across Dixie, "proslavery apologists disparaged the Declaration of Independence and the idea of human equality as 'a self-evident lie' " and "trumpeted Negro bondage as a great and glorious good."[151] An Alabama newspaper exclaimed, "Free society! We sicken of the name! What is it but a conglomeration of greasy mechanics, filthy operatives, small-fisted farmers, and moonstruck theorists?"[152] As the war approached, and then as it progressed, the content of the southern code of honor increasingly came to be defined in explicit opposition to the ideal of natural rights. Southern honor thus became—indeed always was—the spirited guardian of a distinctly illiberal regime.

This case makes it clear that honor is not always admirable, because it may serve deeply unjust principles. In this respect, of course, honor resembles many other human motives, including self-interest, civic virtue, solidarity, faith, friendship, love, and patriotism, all of which may go wrong or be used to ill effect. Even the contemporary liberal sense of justice and the agreement motive, which may seem to avoid this danger, can serve to reinforce existing inequities and exclusions in societies in which justice is imperfectly realized. Thus the fact that honor sometimes can go wrong, even very wrong, does not distinguish it from other motives without which political life would be impossible. But it does indicate that honor is incomplete as an account of moral and political agency in a good regime. Any liberal form of honor presupposes the background condition of a basically (if not perfectly) just society ordered by liberal institutions and committed to the principles of liberty and equality for all. Similarly, liberal forms of honor must coexist with impartial reason so that the moral content of codes of honor can be critically evaluated. Without liberal institutions, justice, and reason, honor may well go bad. In the antebellum South, the institution of chattel slavery meant that the background conditions of honor were not only illiberal but even despotic.

In addition to the institutional injustice of slavery, southern honor was permitted too wide an influence in activities, such as judging, that should have been governed by other norms. All too frequently in the southern courts, impartial reason gave way to honor as "a medium or filter through which specific cases were . . . decided."[153] The law "was intimately connected with family honor, serving as the court of last resort in kinfolk disputes, sometimes including charges of murder," and decisions were made "less by abstract principles than by the contingencies of the hour—as perceived locally."[154] The system took customary codes of honor rather than abstract principles of justice as the guideposts for juridical decision making, and permitted the partial desire to preserve the honor of families and communities to triumph over impartial reason. In doing so, it put honor in a position that honor never should have and gave it a breadth of influence that no liberal society should permit. The result was the "whimsicality of Southern justice."[155] Honor's role in the courtroom should at most be limited to motivating judges and jurors to uphold the norms of impartial judgment and lawyers to abide by fair procedures. Thus southern honor was abhorrent partly because it served unworthy principles and an unjust regime—and in the hands of slaveholders it motivated the defense of their unlimited power—and partly because it was given too wide a sphere of influence.

Although "honor existed before, during, and after slavery in the Southern region," as one historian notes, over time "white man's honor and black man's slavery became in the public mind of the South practically indistinguishable."[156] Why was this the case? We have already seen that the idea of mastery is in a certain sense central to honor as a quality of character. Honor counters the "blind fatalities" that sometimes seem to govern our lives with strong exertions of individual agency. By motivating spirited resistance to the tyranny of despots and the tyranny of nature and circumstance, it pridefully asserts the capacity for human agency as against external forces. In the courage to risk one's life in defense of one's principles, honor masters the all-too-human fear of death and the more mundane pull of the desire for comfortable self-preservation. For the American founders, the claim to internal and external mastery was associated with individual and collective self-rule. In the southern case, however, the claim of mastery was tied to the actual rule of masters over slaves. Southern honor forces us to consider whether this is a necessary connection. Does honor itself presuppose slavery or is the connection between southern honor and slavery merely incidental?

The connection is more than merely incidental but it is by no means necessary. It is more than incidental because the idea of ruling over others has deep roots in the tradition of honor. Medieval knights commanded their soldiers and feudal barons ruled their fiefs, and in both cases having power over others was a condition of honor. Property and local rule were crucial components of the equipment of honor because only by commanding a sizable territory and population could the members of the nobility act effectively to check the power of the crown, thus preventing the exercise of unlimited power over everyone. Their effectiveness came from the fact that, in a pinch, they could raise a fighting force against the king. Later, the constitutional prerogatives of the lords, clergy, nobility, and towns provided these bodies with the equipment they needed to function as effective "obstacles" to the "boundless power of a monarch."[157] These prerogatives included rights of local rule and titles to control certain domains of public activity (such as the lords' control over the seigneurial courts). In the shift from the old regime to modern democracy, the special prerogatives of the privileged bodies were replaced by the individual rights of citizens.[158] Individual rights operate in parallel fashion insofar as they establish the conditions of independence on the basis of which citizens can legitimately and effectively resist encroaching political power. Rights establish protected spheres of activity (such as religion, speech, and property holding) within which individuals are, so to speak, masters of their domains and so rulers of themselves. They also establish the conditions for sharing in the exercise of political power, or collective rule. Yet democratic rights preserve the element of ruling without producing subjugation. In liberal democracy, honor presupposes the powers of individual and collective self-rule established by the civil and political rights of citizens, but it does not entail mastery over others. At least when the equipment of individual rights and constitutional government is at hand, one need not command others in order to be in sufficient command of oneself to act honorably. And even independently of this equipment, honor can in principle be detached from rule over others. The lowliest enlisted man can die on the battlefield as honorably as the most celebrated general, for example, a fact that is recognized in the United States by the Congressional Medal of Honor, which rewards such actions. The founders proved that honor is not intrinsically tied to subjection when they vindicated the honor of the human race by establishing a regime of democratic self-rule.

Nevertheless, the traditional associations between honor and ruling over others were exploited by southern slaveholders as part of a white ethos of justification. Slaveholders appealed to a conception of liberty as the prerogative of policing one's own domain that was reminiscent of feudal society.[159] Their emphasis on the principle of states' rights was rooted in this appeal and attached to the ideal of honor. States' rights were thought to be a precondition of honor because if federal authority were permitted to encroach on local domains, local whites could not exercise the mastery they regarded as central to their honor. Southern planters maintained that northern attacks on the "peculiar institution" would dishonor them, not only by undercutting their public marks of distinction but also by making it difficult or impossible for them to be honorable men, since the eradication of the slave-based economy would destroy what they considered to be the conditions of their rule. Thus

several historians have argued that for many white southerners secession was a matter of honor as much as economic interest.[160] Certainly
the planter class, which was most closely associated with honor, is also
thought to have "masterminded secession and fomented the war."[161]

The southern system tied the honor of some to the enslavement of
others in another way, as well. The slaveholder's constant proximity to
his slaves, who obviously were not in command of their domains or
their circumstances or even their own persons, seems to have enhanced
by comparison his own sense of mastery, and his pride. Honor has always defined itself in opposition to the metaphorical "slavishness" of appetite and political acquiescence. The insults that most frequently led
to duels among southerners were ones that implied a slavish character, such as lying.[162] Gift giving and even gambling, which were both
popular among men of honor, were thought to prove a kind of independence from material want, the former through generosity and the latter
through careless disregard of loss.[163] White southerners defined a slave
(metaphorically and otherwise) as one who lacked honor.[164] They "believed that every slave had chosen a life of humiliation over an honorable death. It was precisely this preference for life that marked them as
slaves."[165] The belief seemed to many whites to justify the institution of
slavery, while at the same time it enhanced the southern gentleman's
sense of himself as honorable.

Yet in holding this belief, southern whites contradicted their own convictions about the necessary conditions of honor, such as states' rights,
the possession of property, and external marks of distinction. White
southerners conveniently overlooked the fact that their black slaves possessed none of the basic equipment of honor that they themselves regarded as necessary. The pride implicit in honor tends to conceal its conditions and to make the honorable man believe that he has only himself
to thank for his admirable character. In fact, honor, like human agency
itself, has conditions. This is one reason why modern liberalism attends
so carefully to the procedures and formalities of free government, which
establish the conditions of individual agency and therefore liberty. The
equipment of honor cannot guarantee its exercise, of course. It is also
true that rare individuals may make themselves forceful political agents
or display great acts of honor without much in the way of equipment.
The black slave Frederick Douglass was such a man, as we shall see in
the next chapter. What he described as his "glorious resurrection from

the tomb of slavery to the heaven of freedom"[166] came precisely, as one historian has noted, "by assuming the posture of a southern man of honor—asserting his willingness to die in defending himself against an insult to his character and body."[167] But Douglass assumed the posture of a man of honor without the benefit of property, prestige, status, rights, or even the ownership of his person. Acts of honor in the absence of the conditions of honor are especially glorious, even if they tend to be less celebrated. In general, however, honor leans on the support of its equipment.

The connection between slavery and southern honor is neither merely incidental nor intrinsically necessary. More generally, the shameful aspects of southern honor—its insistence on mastery over others as opposed to self-mastery and democratic leadership, the prevalence of ridiculous but deadly duels, its emphasis on empty displays of status, its defense of despotic power and unjust political institutions—could have been avoided, but they do reflect dangers that are always implicit in honor. The potential dangers of honor partly can be avoided by establishing political liberties and the institutions of a just polity that prohibit despotism in all its guises, and by keeping honor in its place. By the same token, the defense of political liberties and just institutions, as well as resistance to encroaching power, is likely to prove impossible without honor in some form. If honor must be made to keep its place, it must also *assert* its place if the conditions of its own exercise are to be preserved. There is an irreducibly reciprocal relation between the institutions of a liberal order and the motivational "springs" that set them in motion, including the spring of honor, as Montesquieu, Tocqueville, and the American founders all knew. Southern honor was abhorrent because the principles it served and the institutions it supported were so deeply flawed. It marked a turn backward, an appropriation of some of the worst aspects of the old regime made even worse by the despotic practice of chattel slavery. In the next chapter we consider several cases in which honor turned America back in a different sense—not to the old regime but to its own founding principles—and in doing so moved the nation forward to the fuller realization of its promise of liberty and equality for all.

5

Honor and Democratic Reform

The reactionary honor of the antebellum South is an important part of the story of honor in the United States, but it is by no means representative of honor in the American tradition as a whole. Even the honor of the founders was more innovative than reactionary. Indeed, honor in the founding generation was more than innovative; it was revolutionary, and revolutionary in the largest sense of the term in its defense of an entirely new form of political order "never before seen among societies of men." From the very first, though not exclusively so, American honor has been invoked in defense of reform and progress. This chapter explores honor in connection with democratic reform in the United States by examining several American reformers who exemplify key features of honor, including Abraham Lincoln and Frederick Douglass, Elizabeth Cady Stanton and Susan B. Anthony, and Martin Luther King, Jr. For all those considered in this chapter, qualities of character traditionally associated with honor provided a powerful spring of individual agency and a potent force for political reform. All demonstrate the distinctive combination of qualities that characterizes honor: high ambition, pride, courage in defense of principle, the quest for distinction and self-respect, and the sense of duty to oneself. Yet in each case, these aristocratic qualities served democratic liberties and democratic reform.

Lincoln's Principled Ambition

Perhaps because of his martyrdom, it is difficult for many Americans today to think of Abraham Lincoln as a personally ambitious man.[1] Yet

Lincoln's ambition was well known to his associates. He liked "to take center stage,"[2] and his friends generally regarded him as "one of the most ambitious men" they had ever seen, "with an aspiration for high station in life that burned in him like a furnace."[3] His "intense, unsleeping ambition" was clear to all who knew him.[4] "Even before he left home," as one historian puts it, "Lincoln had been trying hard to raise himself from his inherited station in life and to improve his standing in the world."[5] He not only wished to advance up the social ladder but also sought public recognition and distinction.[6] He referred to this quest in his first political platform in 1832, saying that he had no ambition "so great as that of being truly esteemed of my fellow men."[7] He taught himself the law and at age twenty-five won a seat in the Illinois state legislature, soon becoming a leader of the state Whig Party, an "indefatigable party campaigner," and a regular candidate for public office.[8] Orville Browning, who knew the young Lincoln, described him as "always a most ambitious man," who sought "to fit himself properly for what he considered some important predestined labor or work."[9] "Even in his early days," Browning recalled, Lincoln "had a strong conviction that he was born for better things than seemed likely or even possible," and he believed "that he was destined for something nobler than he was for the time engaged in."[10] Lincoln himself, in a fit of melancholy in the winter of 1840–41, told a friend that he almost would not mind dying except that he had not yet accomplished anything "to make any human being remember that he had lived."[11]

Yet if Lincoln was hungry for public honors he also sought to be worthy of them, much in the manner of George Washington. Thus he wished to be esteemed "by rendering myself worthy of esteem."[12] He was a man not merely of many ambitions but also of high ambitions, in whom the desire for distinction was guided by principled codes of conduct.[13] Lincoln maintained that the guiding principles of his ambitions were contained in the Declaration of Independence. Natural rights were not the only ideals to which he was attached. He also promoted the value of economic growth through internal improvements, for instance, and supported the Whig Party for its economic policies even when its opposition to the spread of slavery, let alone slavery itself, seemed weak and pragmatic at best. But natural rights were the guiding (if not the exclusive) lights of his ambition. In a speech at Independence Hall in Philadelphia in February of 1861, he told those assembled that "all my political warfare has been in favor of the teachings coming forth from [this] sacred hall. May my right hand forget its cunning and my tongue cleave to the roof of my mouth, if ever I prove false to those teachings."[14] The next day he told another audience gathered in the same place that "all the political sentiments I entertain have been drawn, so far as I have been able to draw them, from the sentiments which originated, and were given to the world from the hall in which we stand. I have never had a feeling politically that did not spring from the sentiments embodied in the Declaration of Independence."[15] He regarded the principles of natural rights articulated by the Declaration as the highest political truths.[16] They alone made possible the "form, and substance of government, whose leading object is, to elevate the condition of men—to lift artificial weights from all shoulders—to clear the paths of laudable pursuit for all—to afford all, an unfettered start, and a fair chance, in the race of life."[17] The Declaration guaranteed Americans "the right to rise"[18] and stood as a model for "the liberty party throughout the world."[19] What one writer has called Lincoln's "deep personal reverence for the Declaration"[20] guided his personal ambitions and served as a powerful source of agency. So while he "never professed indifference to the honors of official station," as he said in an 1858 speech, Lincoln emphasized that for him the "republican cause [was] a higher aim than that of mere office" and he claimed to have a higher regard for his principles than for his fame.[21]

After the passage of the Kansas-Nebraska Act in 1854, which legalized the expansion of slavery into new territories, Lincoln remarked that "[t]he spirit of seventy-six and the spirit of Nebraska are utter antagonisms," and he bemoaned the fact that "the former is being rapidly displaced by the latter." In response, he called for a return to first principles: "Our republican robe is soiled, and trailed in the dust. Let us repurify it. Let us turn and wash it white, in the spirit, if not the blood, of the Revolution . . . Let us re-adopt the Declaration of Independence, and with it, the practices, and policy, which harmonize with it."[22] His remarks reverberate in this regard with the high ambitions of the founders, which Lincoln had described so vividly in 1838 when he spoke of "their ambition . . . to display before an admiring world, a practical demonstration of the truth of a proposition . . . namely, the capability of a people to govern themselves" and their desire to be "immortalized . . . revered and sung, toasted through all time" for this accomplishment.[23]

Lincoln, too, sought fame and influence, and like the founders his ambition was wedded to his principles. When he signed the Emancipation Proclamation on January 1, 1863, he paused to note, "If my name ever goes into history it will be for this act,"[24] a comment that reveals the marriage of principle and personal ambition that drove him.[25] In signing the Proclamation, he was putting into effect principles that he had defended publicly for decades, but he was also leaving the mark of his deeds and his ideals on the world and asserting himself as what Adair called "a force in history larger than the ordinary."[26]

Lincoln's example shows how personal ambition can serve general principles of political right by bringing them out of the parlors of good people and into the halls of political power where they can influence law and public policy directly. This aspect of honor calls to mind John F. Kennedy's *Profiles in Courage*. Toward the end of the book Kennedy reflects that "the acts of courage described in this book would be more inspiring and would shine more with the traditional luster of hero-worship if we assumed that each man forgot wholly about himself in his dedication to higher principles." Yet he finds (quoting John Adams) that this would be too much to hope for, since "it is not true, in fact, that any people ever existed who love the public better than themselves." Kennedy continues:

> If this be true, what then caused the statesmen mentioned in the preceding pages to act as they did? It was not because they "loved the public better than themselves." On the contrary it was precisely because they did *love themselves*—because each one's need to maintain his own respect for himself was more important to him than his popularity with others—because his desire to win or maintain a reputation for integrity and courage was stronger than his desire to maintain his office."[27]

Sound principles of political right ride into the public sphere and rise to predominance there on the backs of the personal ambitions of individuals. If citizens were angels, no such intermediary as personal ambition would be necessary. Until the day when citizens become angels, however, liberal democracy will rely on intermediaries such as honor, which engage personal ambition, pride, the desire for self-respect, and the quest for public distinction to attach us to our principles and move us to better politics.

Although he had a vision of the "better angels of our nature," Lincoln himself was no angel. He was not above using "cunning and stealth" to advance his political aims, as one historian reports.[28] Lincoln once responded to a complaint about the low methods employed by his fellow Whigs in the Harrison presidential campaign of 1840 by saying, "We must fight the devil with fire; we must beat the Democrats, or the country will be ruined."[29] He is known to have resorted "to underhanded methods when writing for newspapers, where his identity was hidden from public view."[30] Enemies accused him of double-dealing, manipulation, and ruthlessness.[31] Some noted a tendency toward cruelty, especially in his early years, when he "could be cutting and scornful" in inflicting "pain and humiliation" on political opponents.[32] Even William Herndon, Lincoln's law partner and later his biographer, noted defects in Lincoln's character. Herndon "affirmed his partner's basic honesty and that he was 'justly and rightfully entitled to the appellation, Honest Abe,' but he also pointed out in a public lecture that Lincoln 'was not always—to all persons & at all times *absolutely* Honest.' "[33] Albert Bledsoe, an estranged friend of Lincoln's from the days of the Harrison campaign, once said that Lincoln was "honest and truthful in all the ordinary affairs of life" but was "no stickler for truth in contests before the people for political office and power. On the contrary, he entertained the opinion, that 'all is fair in politics.' It was one of his favorite maxims, that 'we must fight the devil with fire'; that is, with his own weapons."[34] If Lincoln "could not be bought or bribed," he was no saint.[35] His honor elevated his ambitions by attaching them to a principled code of political right, but honor did not purify his motives.

Honor can be noble when it serves reasonable principles and a just regime, as we have seen, but honor is never pure. Nor does honor presuppose comprehensive moral virtue, although it can be combined with virtue. One who combined honor with virtue would be both great and good, much as Aristotle's magnanimous man, whose honor was the "ornament" of all the moral virtues. But the important lesson that Montesquieu taught, and that Lincoln illustrates, is that honor can support political agency and serve a liberal-democratic regime without presupposing moral perfection. Even when honor is not accompanied by all the moral virtues, it can be a powerful spring of individual action, especially the risky and difficult actions that check encroaching political power in a modern constitutional regime. A person who had both honor and virtue would be more praiseworthy than one who had only honor, in view of having a more perfect soul, but the perfection of souls is not a prerequisite for the protection of individual liberties. Imperfect men such as Lincoln can be spirited defenders of liberty, and it may even be the case that some of their imperfections make them especially effective in this respect. One whose soul is so fully perfected as to transcend partial ambition entirely would make an ideal philosopher or priest but perhaps not such a great liberal citizen or democratic leader, at least in a world in which ambitious persons still outnumber angels.

Lincoln's honor took shape as the political courage of a statesman and reformer rather than as the martial valor of a soldier. Although he has been described as a "warrior for the American dream,"[36] and although he led the United States through what may have been its most terrible military conflict, he himself was a man not of war but of law and politics. One historian has documented the period in which Lincoln, who had been a fighter in his youth, traded physical courage for political courage. His decision "to give up fighting" in the years 1828–1831 coincided with a shift in his political allegiance from Jacksonian Democrat to Whig, a move that alienated neighbors and family.[37] From this time forward, Lincoln regarded "the courage required to take . . . a stand" on political issues, even "political dissent" itself, "if it were done fearlessly and well," as a mark of "honor."[38] Surely his greatest mark of honor was his fortitude and resolve in leading the country through what he called the "fiery trial" of civil war to preserve the viability of the only nation in the world "dedicated to the proposition" that all persons are created equal. In this, he risked everything in defense of principle, redeemed American liberty, and glorified his own name. He also changed the United States fundamentally by enhancing the power and prestige of the federal government and by eradicating slavery and setting the United States on a path (albeit not without reversals) toward the progressive fulfillment of its promise of liberty and equality for all. Lincoln's honor led to political reform, and to democratic reform at that.[39]

Not surprisingly, however, Lincoln characterized himself as a conservator of the American experiment and a preserver of American principles rather than an innovator. His efforts to conserve the principles of the Declaration resulted in political reform in part because the principles as he interpreted them were intrinsically progressive. The Declaration, he said in an 1857 speech on the Dred Scott decision, "contemplated the progressive improvement in the condition of all men everywhere."[40] He insisted that when the founders declared that "all men are created equal" they meant *all* men, black as well as white. They did not mean to assert, he said, "the obvious untruth, that all were then actually enjoying that equality, nor yet, that they were about to confer it immediately upon them. In fact, they had no such power to confer such a boon. They meant simply to declare the *right,* so that the *enforcement* of it might follow as fast as circumstances should permit."[41] Lincoln denied that the founders' concessions to slavery invalidated the universalism of their declared principles of natural rights. He was convinced that they had temporarily accepted the institution of slavery where it existed as a matter of necessity, believing this the only course to constitutional ratification and therefore to the establishment of a polity the founding principles of which would eventually make slavery untenable.[42] He thought that these principles, together with prohibitions initiated by the founders against the expansion of slavery into new territories and against the slave trade, were intended to eradicate slavery gradually without so alienating the slave states as to make union untenable and the experiment in free government impossible.

Lincoln believed that Americans' dedication to the principles of free government would eventually shift public opinion and make the theoretically "inalienable" rights articulated by the Declaration practically enforceable for blacks as well as for whites. The assertion that "all men are created equal," in his view, "was placed in the Declaration . . . for future use."[43] It was the key to doors that were at the time of the founding still locked but that were intended by the founders to be opened later. This is the sense in which Lincoln calls the Declaration "progressive": "They [the founders] meant to set up a standard maxim for free society, which should be familiar to all, and revered by all; constantly looked to, constantly labored for, and even though never perfectly attained, constantly approximated, and thereby constantly spreading and deepening its influence, and augmenting the happiness and value of life to all people of all colors everywhere."[44] The standard established by the Declaration should constantly "spread" and "deepen" its influence over the course of time, unfolding progressively so that the principle of liberty and equality for all might come to be understood as applicable to a wider class of persons, thus "augmenting the happiness" of "all people of all colors." The Declaration was intrinsically reformist insofar as it would push the nation forward and upward by promising universal liberty and equality for all, thereby inviting the reforms required to fulfill its promise.[45]

The powerful potential for reform implicit in the Declaration presupposes the people's reverence for the principles it codifies, however. Lincoln emphasized that the document should be "revered by all" so that it could be "constantly approximated," even if never perfectly attained. These remarks call to mind the importance for honor of reverence for one's codes and the balance between reverence and reflexivity discussed in Chapter 2. Even when honor issues in political opposition, it cannot survive without a measure of reverence for its codes, because with honor one's ambitions are guided and constrained by principles. By giving us something to take seriously, reverence for a principled code of conduct gives us reason to act even when the risks are high and the benefits are uncertain. The importance of reverence in sustaining honor sometimes has been taken as proof that honor must be reactionary. If honor rests on reverence, it is thought, honor must be intrinsically antithetical to reform. But Lincoln's honor shows us that reverence for the right codes can be a powerful engine of reform. It also suggests that while reflexivity in the form of critical reflection and rational deliberation must have a central place in any liberal-democratic polity, to theorize reflexivity as the whole of politics would be to risk disabling as much as liberating political agency.

If Lincoln displayed the courage of his convictions by sometimes taking principled stands against prevailing public opinion and by resolutely defending his principles in the face of armed conflict, he also exemplified the moderation that is a feature of honor at its best. He knew the value of moderation in persons of high ambition and extraordinary courage. Like the founders, he saw that ambitious types could be unruly. When "men of ambition and talents" arise, he said, they "naturally seek the gratification of their ruling passion."[46] Yet such persons typically cannot be gratified "in supporting and maintaining an edifice that has been erected by others":

Many great and good men sufficiently qualified for any task they should undertake, may ever be found, whose ambition would aspire to nothing beyond a seat in Congress, a gubernatorial or a presidential chair; *but such belong not to the family of the lion, or the tribe of the eagle.* What! Think you that these places would satisfy an Alexander, a Cae-

sar, or a Napoleon? Never! Towering genius disdains a beaten path . . .
It thirsts and burns for distinction; and, if possible, it will have it,
whether at the expense of emancipating slaves, or enslaving freemen.[47]

These remarks were made twenty-five years before Lincoln himself
emancipated the slaves of the American South. No doubt he was too
modest in his demeanor ever to have claimed for himself the status of
"towering genius." Yet it is difficult to deny in retrospect that he belonged "to the family of the lion, or the tribe of the eagle." If he did not
exactly "disdain" the beaten path, neither did he stick to it. He revered
the Declaration, a document written by others, and he loved America, a
polity erected by others, but he was not content simply to "maintain the
edifice." Instead, he was determined to remake it. Lincoln, too, was a
founder; in calling Americans back to their first principles, he effectively
refounded the regime.[48] In the process, he settled two issues that had
plagued it from its first founding: the contradiction posed by slavery in a
republican regime and the question of the ultimate priority of state versus federal power.

Lincoln's expansion of federal authority also grew out of his commitment to the principles articulated by the Declaration of Independence. A
strong central government was a necessary condition for the success of
the American experiment, in his view, and he had long been a defender
of national unity and federal power.[49] Secession challenged the viability
of the federal government, and with it the viability of the American experiment and popular government everywhere.[50] It was Lincoln's commitment to conserve the principles of popular government that led him
into the war, but waging it resulted in reform and led to "changes more
fundamental and profound than either side had expected when the conflict began."[51] Viewed simply as an exercise of executive authority, Lincoln's Emancipation Proclamation, as one historian notes, was "the most
revolutionary measure ever to come from an American President up to
that time" and an "unprecedented use of federal military power against a
state institution."[52] In the words of another historian, Lincoln "presided
over the most dramatic expansion of presidential power to date. Without asking for Congress's approval, Lincoln mobilized troops, waged
war, suppressed newspapers, and emancipated slaves."[53] In the name of
necessity, he suspended the writ of habeas corpus "and authorized army
commanders to declare martial law in various areas behind the lines and

to try civilians in military courts without juries."[54] He enforced the confiscation of enemy property, as well. The suspension of civil liberties and the unprecedented assertions of executive initiative independent of congressional approval moved some to chastise him as a dictator.[55] Chief Justice Roger B. Taney himself accused Lincoln of "usurping power."[56]

Lincoln did not use the power he asserted for personal aggrandizement, however. He sought and won congressional sanction after the fact for the broad emergency powers he asserted in the early months of the war.[57] He gave public justifications for his actions, including the suspension of habeas corpus, in addresses to Congress and in open letters to citizens.[58] When the presidential election of 1864 arrived with "Union fortunes still uncertain, some men urged Lincoln to cancel the contest lest it result in the victory of antiwar Democrats who would sell out the Union cause."[59] He refused on the grounds that "[w]e cannot have free government without elections; and if the rebellion could force us to forego, or postpone a national election, it might fairly claim to have already conquered us."[60] Lincoln's refusal to suspend the election demonstrates that personal aggrandizement was not his objective. His personal ambition had principled limits; his honor knew moderation even as it gave rise to unprecedented acts of boldness and extraordinary exertions of political agency. This moderation calls to mind Washington's resignation of the presidency. Both acts show that honor is not simply reducible to the limitless quest for power.

Perhaps because he was aware of the potential damage that "lions" and "eagles" like himself could cause, however, Lincoln went out of his way to demonstrate a decent respect for the opinions of his fellows. Even his strongest statements against slavery, in which he forcefully asserted that the Declaration's inalienable rights applied equally to blacks, were tempered by protestations that he did not seek to promote racial equality in all areas. In a speech on the Dred Scott decision, for instance, he attacked "that counterfeit logic which concludes that, because I do not want a black woman for a *slave* I must necessarily want her for a *wife*. I need not have her for either, I can just leave her alone. In some respects she certainly is not my equal."[61] He consistently denied that he favored social or even political equality for the races, much less integration. For years he proposed colonization to "transfer the African to his native clime."[62] By the standards of our own day, many of Lincoln's remarks on race seem bigoted, and he surely was not without prejudice.[63]

But without excusing them, such remarks must be read with an eye to the times. Lincoln's political opponents played mercilessly on the racial prejudices and fears of white Americans, for instance, and he was forever defending himself against others' distorted presentations of his position.[64] When he defended colonization for blacks it was at least in part because he knew that "without a promise of colonization, . . . most northern whites would never accept emancipation." Northern whites feared that emancipation would result in local labor markets' being overwhelmed by newly freed blacks looking for work.[65] Lincoln finally abandoned the colonization plan after issuing the Emancipation Proclamation.[66] He was no advocate of full equality or racial integration, but he was ahead of prevailing opinion on racial matters. Frederick Douglass once said of Lincoln that he was "the first great man that I talked with in the United States freely who in no single instance reminded me of the difference between himself and myself, of the difference of color."[67] Although on other occasions Douglass was more critical of Lincoln,[68] he understood the significance of Lincoln's hedging as well as anyone: "From the genuine abolition view, Mr. Lincoln seemed tardy, cold, dull, and indifferent, but measuring him by the sentiment of his country—a sentiment he was bound as a statesman to consult—he was swift, zealous, radical, and determined."[69]

Other examples of Lincoln's moderation can be mentioned. As much as he hated slavery, for example, until the onset of war he conceded "that bondage was a thoroughly entrenched institution in the southern states, one protected by the U.S. Constitution and a web of national and state laws."[70] He refrained from a direct attack on the institution even through the first year of the war, pushing instead for a "gradual, compensated emancipation program to commence in the loyal border states" on a voluntary basis.[71] When this failed and it became clear that slavery was sustaining the insurrection and that Union forces could not achieve a decisive victory without eradicating slavery entirely, Lincoln decided that an exercise of presidential authority was unavoidable.[72] He defended the Emancipation Proclamation as "an act of justice, warranted by the Constitution, upon military necessity."[73] He exempted from its authority all slaveholding states and parts of states not then in rebellion, because he believed that he had the constitutional authority to override only the laws of rebel states.

Although emancipation was forced on the South, and forced violently, it would be wrong to say that Lincoln himself zealously imposed his principles on others. In defense of his principles, he argued, he exhorted, he shamed, but he did not force. When he resorted to force, it was because he did not believe the Republic could be preserved in any other way, and as president he had a clear duty to preserve it in any way he could. The fact that the necessary means for preserving the Republic coincided with the antislavery principles he had so long defended was a function of fortune. Thus Lincoln exhibited moderation even in the defense of his principles, not merely in his personal ambitions. If his refusal to suspend the 1864 presidential election showed that he would not seek personal aggrandizement at the expense of the public good, his handling of emancipation showed that he would not permit his commitment to the ideal of free government to jeopardize the defense of the only actual, if imperfect, free government then in existence.[74]

No doubt Lincoln's moderation was motivated by prudence as much as anything else. As a candidate, he hardly could have been elected, nor as president been effective, had he been immoderate in expressing his antislavery views. While too much regard for public opinion may lead to slavishness and the abandonment of one's principles, honor's external concern for public recognition can have a moderating influence on one's actions. It could be objected that slavery was such an extreme evil that it called for an extreme response, even that moderation in such cases is its own kind of evil. This objection is a reasonable one, and perhaps it is the most moral view to take. But the best political response is not always the same thing as the best moral response, even though the best political response may be best precisely by virtue of its success in making possible the most moral outcome. In politics, as Montesquieu said, extremism, even for the good, has a way of going bad. A measured regard for the opinions of others tends to encourage moderation, which is a potentially positive aspect of the outward-looking character of honor. The political honor of a man such as Lincoln is likely to be more moderate than the martial honor of a Coriolanus precisely because politics is so deeply immersed in the world of opinions. If they hailed from the same stock of lions and eagles, Lincoln was no Coriolanus. Whether Lincoln's moderation was the product of his political role or his moral character or the constraints of the constitutional government in which he served, it was an important dimension of his honor. Lincoln shows that even extraordinary ambition and uncommon political courage can be combined with moderation, that honor does not inevitably degenerate into unbridled power-seeking or even simple unruliness. He also demonstrates that honor can serve republican principles, and even can support democratic reform.

Lincoln's status as a self-made man has always been much celebrated. To the democratic eye, his humble beginnings make his final stature all the more glorious. They reveal his powerful capacity for individual agency, his ability to rise above and to go beyond his circumstances. He seems to have made himself honorable without having been given any of the traditional equipment of honor, such as wealth or notable lineage. Yet despite not being born into a rich or distinguished family, Lincoln did enjoy at least the conditions necessary for the acquisition of honor's equipment. Perhaps most fundamentally, Lincoln was born as the exclusive owner of his own person. He also had full citizenship rights, both civil and political, including the right to vote and the right to run for office. He could own property and dispose of it according to his wishes. He could hold a job and he could work for pay in any profession he chose, and he had full command of the pay he earned. So if he was not born to power or property, he did possess the rights necessary to acquire both. Similarly, while no one provided him with an education, he was able to educate himself without impedance and without incurring the wrath of his family or the scorn of his society. More than that, he could reasonably expect to enjoy high status and public esteem as the reward for his educational efforts and later for his professional labors at the bar. And for his fine speeches and his deft political maneuvering, he won the admiration of his fellows. All these factors support honor as a quality of character, and in a democratic regime, these conditions and opportunities constitute the equipment of honor. In the next sections, we shall consider several instances of honor among Americans who lacked the equipment of honor because they belonged to politically marginalized groups, notably American blacks and white women.

Frederick Douglass: The Soul of Honor

W. E. B. Du Bois invoked honor as a catalyst for political action in defense of black freedom in the 1906 "Resolutions of the Niagara Movement." He called on American blacks "to sacrifice money, reputation, and life itself on the altar of right" and to "reconsecrate ourselves, our honor, and our property to the final emancipation of the race for whose freedom John Brown died."[75] Du Bois saw honor much as the founders had seen it, as a spring of risky but principled action. He invoked honor for the same purpose that the Declaration had done, to inspire political agency and the spirited defense of liberty. Among Du Bois's predecessors in the tradition of black American reformers, no one exemplifies more aspects of honor than Frederick Douglass, a man whom Booker T. Washington once called "the soul of honor."[76] Douglass was born into bondage in Maryland in 1818, escaped to freedom in New York in 1838, and thereafter became a leader in the antislavery movement, an abolitionist lecturer, author, newspaper editor, and the most famous and admired black figure of his time. Black leaders who came after him were sometimes critical but always revered him for his pride, his high ambitions, his noble demeanor, his attachment to the principles articulated by the Declaration, and above all his courage in defense of liberty. Today he is regarded as the "prototypical black American hero" and a democratic embodiment of "heroic greatness," in which heroism and greatness coexist with the principle of equality.[77]

Resistance to overweening power has been a central theme throughout our analysis, and Douglass is a powerful exemplar of this aspect of honor. His autobiography describes one such act of resistance, which he came to see as the turning point in his life as a slave. In 1834 Douglass was in service to a man named Covey, a "snakish" man who had a penchant for beating his slaves.[78] After one particularly brutal beating, Douglass had resolved "to obey every order, however unreasonable, if it were possible," but "if Mr. Covey should then undertake to beat me, to defend and protect myself to the best of my ability."[79] The next day, Covey attacked him again. Douglass later recounted what happened next:

> I now forgot my roots, and remembered my pledge to *stand up in my own defense* . . . Whence came the daring spirit necessary to grapple with a man who, eight and forty hours before, could, with his slightest word have made me tremble like a leaf in a storm, I do now know; at any rate, *I was resolved to fight,* and, what was better still, I was actually hard at it. The fighting madness had come upon me, and I found my strong fingers firmly attached to the throat of my cowardly tormentor; as heedless of consequences, at the moment, as though we stood as equals before the law . . . "*Are you going to resist,* you scoundrel?" said

he. To which, I returned a polite *"yes sir;"* steadily gazing my interroga-
tor in the eye . . . Covey soon cried out lustily for help; not that I was
obtaining any marked advantage over him, or was injuring him, but
because he was gaining none over me, and was not able, single handed,
to conquer me . . . the cowardly tyrant asked if I "meant to persist in
my resistance." I told him "I *did mean to resist, come what might;"* that I
had been by him treated like a *brute* during the last six months; and
that I should stand it *no longer* . . . Covey at length (two hours had
elapsed) gave up the contest. Letting me go, he said,—puffing and
blowing at a great rate—"now, you scoundrel, go to your work; I would
not have whipped you half so much as I have had you not resisted."
The fact was, *he had not whipped me at all.*[80]

Covey did not lay a hand on Douglass during the six months that Douglass remained in his service. Even under the rule of other masters, Douglass was never again whipped; although "several attempts were made,"
he reports, "they were always unsuccessful."[81] Douglass described the
event as "the turning point in *my life as a slave,*" because, he said, "it rekindled in my breast the smouldering embers of liberty . . . and revived a
sense of my own manhood."[82] The fight "recalled to life my crushed self-
respect and my self-confidence, and inspired me with a renewed determination to be a freeman."[83] He spoke of the event in political terms,
saying, "he only can understand the effect of this combat on my spirit,
who has himself incurred something, hazarded something, in repelling
the unjust and cruel aggressions of a tyrant."[84] It was an act of resistance
not merely to encroaching power but to despotic power, and Douglass
regarded it as a mark of "honor."[85] It was a mark of honor in the sense
that it made him respectable in his own eyes and in the eyes of "human
nature" itself, he said, for "human nature is so constituted, that it cannot
honor a helpless man, although it can *pity* him."[86]

The connection that Douglass draws between honor and human nature reflects a shift in the meaning of honor that was already present in
the founding generation. For Douglass, the honorable act of resistance
vindicates his "manhood," or what he calls his "essential dignity" as a
human being, not his status as a member of some particular social class
or the inhabitant of a specific social role. This reference to human nature
and human dignity rather than to social roles and status is a feature of
democratic honor more generally. What Douglass calls the "essential
dignity of humanity"[87] rests on the power to act, to be one's own mover

and master rather than the instrument of another's will. In this respect, Douglass's use of the term "dignity" is more closely linked to honor than to the contemporary usage of the term, which refers to the intrinsic worth of every human being. Douglass did not deny the ideal of intrinsic dignity; indeed, this ideal forms the basis of his opposition to slavery. Yet he clearly believes that the other kind of human dignity—the dignity that, like honor, must be earned through action—is a prerequisite for "self-respect" and "self-confidence." The ideal of intrinsic human dignity can provide a modicum of self-respect as a simple condition of being human, but Douglass indicates that for him to "recall his crushed self-respect" it was not sufficient for him simply to be; he also had to act. It was the action, not the ideal, that won him self-respect and self-confidence. Whereas before the fight "I was *nothing*," he tells us, afterward "I was a man." It was his resistance that resulted in his redemption, through which he became "a freeman in *fact*" even as he remained "a slave in *form*. When a slave cannot be flogged he is more than half free. He has a domain as broad as his own manly heart to defend."[88] The ideal of intrinsic human dignity as a universal condition of persons could not produce this redemption on its own. The individual action was the key; without it, neither freedom nor self-respect was possible. Without the "signs of power" that issue from the exercise of individual agency, as Douglass sees it, one is "without the essential dignity of humanity." One historian has even described the fight between Douglass and Covey as a "duel," because it called forth the quality of honor in Douglass's character to vindicate his dignity.[89] It was not in fact a duel, but it did have a great deal to do with honor.

As in a duel, Douglass's resistance demonstrates his willingness to risk his life for the sake of his self-respect and for a kind of freedom, which is an important feature of honor as a quality of character. It calls to mind Tocqueville's discussion of the aristocratic love of liberty that motivates defiance in the face of despots and potential despots. The preference for liberty and self-respect over life is at the heart of the traditional opposition between honor and slavery. Douglass himself maintains that slavery can never be overcome so long as one prioritizes life (and material self-interest more generally) over everything else. Thus "[w]hile slaves prefer their lives, with flogging, to instant death, they will always find christians enough, like unto Covey, to accommodate that preference."[90] He himself, he says, would "prefer death to hopeless bondage."[91] Douglass reports that at the time of the Covey incident he had "reached the point, at which I was *not afraid to die.*" It was this spirit, he says, "that made me a freeman in *fact.*"[92] Mastery of the fear of death was a condition of his new freedom and his "essential dignity." Mastering the fear of death has always been a central feature of honor, which is one reason for the traditional association between honor and martial valor. In resisting the seemingly irresistible impulse for self-preservation, the soldier shows himself capable of intentional, self-initiated action, or agency, and so is free. Douglass's resistance to Covey embodies this aspect of honor.[93]

Douglass's spirit of resistance is only a partial embodiment of honor, to be sure. His account of the event demonstrates some central features of honor as a quality of character, but not all of them. He makes no mention of any codes of honor, for example, and he was not at the time concerned with fame. Principled ambition and public honors came later for Douglass, but they did come, and they were important aspects of his evolving sense of honor, as we shall see. In his fight with Covey, however, one sees the courage to resist oppressive power, which is a key feature of honor. With Frederick Douglass the metaphorical opposition between honor and slavery takes a literal turn. In this extreme case, one comprehends the power of honor as a source of individual agency because one sees a nascent sense of honor overcome the terrible weight of human bondage. This nascent honor is the beginning of an overcoming through which Douglass ultimately ceased to be a slave. "After resisting him," Douglass tells us, "I felt as I had never felt before. It was a resurrection from the dark and pestiferous tomb of slavery, to the heaven of comparative freedom."[94] His courage in this instance is physical; later Douglass would demonstrate considerable political courage, as well, but here the emphasis is on his strength, forcefulness, power, and manliness. Indeed, force is the ground of this nascent honor, as Douglass conceives it, since a man "without force" is without the essential dignity of humanity.[95] Such a man will not even be pitied by his fellows for long, Douglass says, "if the signs of power do not arise" in him.[96] In this respect, Douglass's honor as it is manifest in the battle with Covey most resembles the physical prowess of the medieval knight. This should come as no surprise, as the regime that Douglass inhabited, like the warring states of feudalism, was based on brute force, and brute strength was required to oppose it.

Yet even this rudimentary honor was not simply reducible to brute strength or the exercise of physical force. Moderation was also evident in his approach to the fight, at least as Douglass describes it. Although he tells us initially that a "fighting madness had come upon me," he never loses control or gives the appearance of blind rage or an impassioned hunger for vengeance. Instead, he says that "every blow of [Covey's] was parried, though I dealt no blows in turn. I was strictly on the *defensive,* preventing him from injuring me, rather than trying to injure him."[97] In the end, Douglass admits that he took "satisfaction" from having "drawn blood" from Covey, but he then reasserts that "my aim had not been to injure him, but to prevent his injuring me."[98] No doubt Douglass had good reason in his public writings to emphasize that he was not the aggressor in this incident, and he had even better reason at the time of the fight to restrain himself from attacking Covey aggressively. Even so, his evident restraint is significant because it indicates that there was more to his honor, even in its nascent form, than simple brute force or an instinct to dominate. He had a point to make, which was that he refused to be conquered or tyrannized. He used the force necessary to make this point, but no more than was necessary. The use of force, or the conquest of another, was not itself his principal objective. This is consistent with the restraint of an Orte, and the defensive posture of the ambition that the founders placed at the center of the American system.

As we have seen, the identification of honor with brute strength that was typical of the warring societies of medieval Europe dissolved over time with increasing political stability and the rise of constitutional government. Even in Montesquieu, brute strength plays little role in the depiction of honor as it operates to limit political power in constitutional monarchy. Certainly one does not think of the members of the eighteenth-century *parlements*—men of learning and polite society such as Montesquieu himself—as exemplars of physical prowess. Their honor rested on other foundations. Similarly, after Douglass's escape from bondage his honor came to manifest itself in the defense of political principles rather than in the exercise of physical strength. When he lived in the North as a citizen of a constitutional democracy, he displayed his honor, as Lincoln did, in beautiful speeches meant to inspire and persuade instead of in fighting, because he saw that in a constitutional regime one wields influence, proves independence, and wins distinction through speech and legitimate political action rather than through the use of force, as in despotism. This shift in the character of Douglass's honor suggests that the extent to which honor is identified with physical strength and force depends on the extent of stability and civility present in the society.

Douglass's raw courage in fighting Covey contrasts sharply with the pretensions of southern gentlemen, and makes their duels look like vain playacting. He fought the southern honor of the white slave owner, which defined itself in opposition to the perceived characteristics of black slaves, with a nascent honor of his own.[99] If democratic honor is in some respects more natural than traditional forms of honor tied to artificial class status, the nascent honor of a slave such as Douglass may be the most natural honor of all, because the slave lacks virtually all the external (and artificial) supports of honor. The fight with Covey was the "turning point" in his life as a slave, but Douglass had another life as well that was lived after his escape from bondage. In his new life, he became a man of politics and society, a leader, a famous reformer, and an exemplar of honor in its fullest sense, complete with principled codes of conduct and public distinction. His honor in this new life was closer to the political courage of a Lincoln than to the physical force that he himself first associated with honor. Yet his new honor preserved the core elements of defiance and the proud love of liberty exemplified in that earlier act of resistance.

Although his first ten years as an abolitionist in the North were lived by the doctrine of the Garrisonian school, which held that "the Constitution was wholly a pro-slavery document, called for the destruction of the American Union, and opposed the use of the ballot against slavery," he revised his views on these points in the early 1850s.[100] By 1853 he had broken with the Garrisonians and had come to believe in the Union's potential for redemption and in the power of the American founding documents to help bring this about.[101] Thereafter he defended the principles articulated in the Declaration and Constitution until he died in 1895. In an 1857 speech, for instance, he maintained that "[t]he Constitution, as well as the Declaration of Independence, and the sentiments of the founders of the Republic, give us a platform broad enough, and strong enough, to support the most comprehensive plans for the freedom and elevation of all the people of this country, without regard to color, class, or clime."[102] The principles articulated by the Declaration came to constitute the guiding standard of his personal ambitions, articulated in speech after rousing speech and exemplified in his public actions.[103]

In an 1865 address entitled "What the Black Man Wants," he advocated the "immediate, unconditional, and universal enfranchisement of the black man, in every State in the Union," and defended this demand on the basis of the Declaration's principles and promises.[104] Without the right to vote, he said, "[the black man's] liberty is a mockery; without this you might as well almost retain the old name of slavery for his condition; for in fact, if he is not the slave of the individual master, he is the slave of society, and holds his liberty as a privilege, not as a right. He is at the mercy of the mob, and has no means of protecting himself."[105] He appealed to "the American sense of honor" to "see that this war shall not cease until every freedman at the South has the right to vote" in an effort to motivate white citizens to live up to their constitutional principles.[106] On another occasion, he accused white Americans of having "dishonored" the Declaration by "bartering away the eternal principles of right it enunciated."[107] The spirited assertion of individual liberties against what he called "the mob" that denied them reflects the pride and aristocratic love of liberty that Tocqueville thought crucial to defending democratic freedoms against majority tyranny. Too proud to accept "the charge of inferiority" that white America had laid on him,[108] Douglass possessed what Tocqueville called "a higher idea of himself" and his race. Moreover, he was unwilling to exploit the new opportunities he enjoyed as a free man in the North simply to advance his personal interests. Instead, he turned his personal ambition to the promotion of his principles and to social and political reform. In a speech delivered on the Fourth of July in 1862, he spoke of the connection between principles and individual agency, saying that one who abandons "honest principles and high purposes" is bound to be "swept on as if by the power of fate."[109]

In 1866 Douglass was elected by the city of Rochester to serve as its sole delegate to a national convention organized for the purpose of obtaining the sense of the country on the subject of black suffrage. White delegates balked at his election, and what followed was a dramatic display of the political courage that had come to define Douglass's honor. When his train passed through Harrisburg, Pennsylvania, en route to the conference at Philadelphia, several cars filled with representatives from some of the western states were added to the train. Douglass later recalled what happened next:

> When my presence became known to these gentlemen . . . I was duly waited upon by a committee of my brother delegates to represent to me the undesirableness of my attendance upon the National Loyalists'

Convention. . . . [They said] that I must know that there was a very strong and bitter prejudice against my race in the North as well as in the South and the cry of social and political equality would not fail to be raised against the Republican party if I should attend this loyal National convention . . . I listened very attentively to the address, uttering no word during its delivery; but when it was finished, I said to the speaker and the committee, with all the emphasis I could throw into my voice and manner, "Gentlemen, with all respect, you might as well ask me to put a loaded pistol to my head and blow my brains out, as to ask me to keep out of this convention to which I have been duly elected . . . If I am not admitted, the public will ask, 'Where is Douglass? Why is he not seen in the convention?' and you would find that inquiry more difficult to answer than any charge brought against you for favoring political or social equality; but ignoring the question of policy altogether and looking at it as one of right and wrong, I am bound to go into that convention; not to do so would be to contradict the principles and practice of my life."[110]

Booker T. Washington reported that when Douglass arrived at the convention, which was held at Independence Hall, "he was not only snubbed generally, but it was hinted to him that if he attempted to walk in the procession through the streets . . . he would be jeered at, insulted, and perhaps mobbed."[111] Washington emphasized that "it required no little courage to act in the face of these conditions, but Douglass never wavered. He was strong enough not to falter even at the desertion of men whom he had a right to regard as his friends."[112] In the end, Douglass not only attended the convention but went on "to win from this body a resolution in favor of the franchise for his people. He delivered one of those powerful and convincing addresses that he was well able to make when aroused. As a result, he quite captured and controlled the sentiment of the convention in favor of his resolution."[113] In Douglass's new life as a man of affairs and a political reformer, his honor no longer took the form of physical prowess but instead embodied political courage and resolution in defense of principle. As in the fight with Covey, however, his sense of honor gave rise to an uncommon assertion of individual agency and a proud and spirited defense of liberty.

Douglass was a "self-made man . . . in the fullest sense of the word."[114] Washington reports that Douglass came to be "one of the most popular men on the lecture platform, and at a time when . . . illustrious personages . . . gave to the American lyceum its highest distinction," his lectures "showed a wide reading, and a mastery of the art of eloquence."[115] Douglass was "bold, direct, and fearless," and he displayed "prudence and sagacity" as well as "great personal charm," all of which "made him welcome in the councils of his party."[116] In addition to these qualities, he was successful in obtaining influence with important persons and in gaining the political power to push forward his reforms effectively. He established "a wide acquaintance among men in public life," and his "commanding abilities and personal attractiveness to men" made "many persons in and out of Congress . . . willing to follow his leading." Indeed, "no other Negro in this country, at the time, knew political leaders in and out of Congress so intimately."[117] He also was respected by President Lincoln and was received at the White House on several occasions, including Lincoln's second inaugural. Douglass had a way, Washington says, "of getting close to the men in power and of reaching their hearts and enlisting their sympathies for the objects in whose service he was engaged."[118]

A man without ambition could not have achieved the political influence that Douglass achieved, and in the mid-nineteenth century, a black man without extraordinary ambition could not have come close to accomplishing so much. Douglass's ambition was a crucial component of his honor, because it equipped him to advance his principles effectively, to be a strong leader of American blacks and an effective advocate. By the 1860s he was a highly distinguished man of power and standing, considered "one of the great men of the occasion" at any public event he attended.[119] As Washington said later, Douglass's "authority on every matter that concerned the Negro, North or South, was seldom questioned," and "[h]is leadership, up to this time, was not often disputed."[120]

Yet despite his ambition and the fact that he achieved an unprecedented measure of public distinction for a black man, Douglass did not display the same love of fame that was characteristic of the founders, or even Lincoln. After the passage of the thirteenth, fourteenth, and fifteenth amendments, Washington relates, friends urged Douglass to run for Congress from one of the reconstructed states in the South. At the time, Washington says, "there was some curious speculation as to what place Frederick Douglass would take in this larger world of citizenship that he had helped to create. A number of his friends and admirers thought that he had led his people so successfully out of the wilderness of slavery that he should now put himself into a position where he could guide them further in the proper use of the rights and privileges as citizens of the republic."[121] Douglass finally decided against a run for national office on the grounds that "the idea did not entirely square well with my better judgment and sense of propriety. The thought of going to live among a people in order to gain their votes and acquire official honors was repugnant to my sense of self-respect."[122] Later in life he "never regretted that I did not enter the arena of Congressional honors."[123] In Douglass, the balance between the internal and the external dimensions of honor was weighted in favor of the former. He seems to have preferred self-respect to public esteem and not to have sought fame, even the principled fame of an Alexander Hamilton or a George Washington or an Abraham Lincoln. Still, he was no hermit. Despite his apparent lack of interest in public honors, his ambitions had a distinctly public quality. He made a name for himself in the public arena, for example, and he sought public influence. Indeed, despite his protestations to the contrary, some contemporary critics accused him of office-seeking from the 1870s onward, resulting in what they charged was excessive loyalty to the Republican Party and a loss of his earlier radicalism.[124] Whether or not his critics were right in this regard, he clearly cultivated public qualities such as eloquence, erudition, and charm. By distinguishing him personally, these qualities brought distinction to the principles he promoted. If he did not hunger for fame as an end in itself, he nevertheless won it, and he used his fame to advance his cause. Nor was he oblivious to how his fame would affect the success of his cause. He saw himself, and wanted to be seen, as "an example and inspiration to all people, especially blacks."[125] He was, in the words of one historian, a "self-conscious hero."[126]

Perhaps one reason why Douglass did not speak of the love of fame as a personal motive is that as a black man he knew all too well the fickleness of the public opinion that is the source of fame. Once while riding a full train from Boston to New Bedford, he attempted to sit down in an unoccupied seat next to a white man. The man objected and, in a state of agitation, abandoned his seat. A short time later, a Colonel Clifford, who was an acquaintance of Douglass, came over to greet him:

[A]pparently forgetful of his rank, [he] manifested, in greeting me, something of the feeling of an old friend. This demonstration was not lost on the gentleman whose dignity I had, an hour before, most seri-ously offended. Col. Clifford was known to be about the most aristo-cratic gentleman in Bristol county; and it was evidently thought that I must be somebody, else I should not have been thus noticed, by a per-son so distinguished.[127]

Immediately after the two parted, Douglass "found myself surrounded with friends; and among the number, my offended friend stood nearest, and with an apology for his rudeness."[128] Douglass concluded from this incident that the esteem granted blacks by the white public was based on nothing more than "pride and fashion."[129] In the same passage he re-counts that he "once heard a very plain man say, (and he was cross-eyed, and awkwardly flung together in other respects,) that he should be a handsome man when public opinion shall be changed."[130] Fame, dis-tinction, and public honors are a particularly unreliable currency for members of marginalized groups. Even when Douglass won public dis-tinction, as when he was elected delegate to the Loyalists' Convention, it frequently was accompanied by public scorn and even virulent hostility. To some extent, this is always a problem for distinguished individuals in democratic societies, since democratic citizens tend to resent public marks of superiority even when they themselves have freely bestowed them. Yet for members of marginalized groups public distinctions are even more dangerous because they are more fiercely resented. The sug-gestion of superiority in a member of a group thought to be constitu-tionally inferior is frequently perceived as a special affront by those in the majority, especially the ones who harbor doubts about their own standing or abilities. For a man such as Douglass, public honors were not only undependable but also potentially deadly.

Moreover, at least until the eradication of Jim Crow laws in the 1960s American blacks faced institutionalized public degradation, and conse-quently a black youth such as Douglass had little reason to set his sights on public honors. For a slave, the idea of winning the admiration of peo-ples, nations, and posterity through great accomplishments, which the American founders had hoped to do, was too implausible to be a serious motive for action. The implausibility of public honors was thus another reason for Douglass to focus on the internal dimensions of honor, partic-ularly pride and self-respect, instead of external public esteem. These qualities were highly developed in Douglass. On another occasion of train travel, he was compelled to sit for several hours in a portion of the freight car on account of his race. Booker T. Washington later recounted the story:

> A friend went into the freight car to console him and said to him that he hated to see a man of his intelligence in so humiliating a position. "I am ashamed that they have thus degraded you." But Douglass, straightening himself up in his seat, looked the friend in the face and said, "They cannot degrade Frederick Douglass." And so they cannot degrade a single individual who does not want to be degraded.[131]

Douglass's refusal to draw his sense of personal worth from white society's sense of it reflects the predominance he accorded self-respect over public esteem. The claim of self-command implicit in this refusal and in Washington's assertion that "nobody can degrade a big man or a big race" against his will is a boastful claim. However strong in character an individual may be, a lifetime on the losing side of injustice will take its toll. But the boast is a noble one. It calls to mind the founders' claim that the American system "vindicates the honor of humanity" by resisting tyranny, both the tyranny of despots and the tyranny of nature and circumstance. The boastful exaggeration of human independence is an honorable response to the real powers of nature, circumstance, and tyrants, because it makes resistance in the form of individual and collective self-rule conceivable. The noble boast of immunity from the public degradation dealt by a prejudiced majority represents a similarly honorable response to the real power of injustice. It makes conceivable the political agency needed to resist injustice. Of course, to make this resistance possible, equipment and fortune are needed as well. The boastful moral psychology of honor is incomplete on its own, but is a powerful component of political agency. The example of Douglass also shows how pride can be reconciled with democratic equality because it demonstrates that one can be extraordinarily proud without lording it over others. Douglass had a sense of superiority insofar as he knew himself to be superior to the man that white society thought him to be, but this sense of superiority did not relegate anyone else (much less any fixed class of persons) to the status of an inferior. And the political effect of his sense of superiority was to promote greater equality, not perpetuate inequality. The possibility of such a reconciliation between pride and political equality is why Tocqueville was not reluctant to recommend more pride to modern democrats.

The forceful assertion of self-respect in the absence of public esteem, which was a central feature of Douglass's honor, is the mirror opposite of southern honor, in which the external dimension of public esteem had a tendency to dominate. When public esteem is guaranteed to certain classes of persons, as it was in the American South and the old regime, the external dimensions of honor tend to color the whole of it. Conversely, the internal dimensions of honor naturally take precedence when public esteem is especially unreliable. In this respect, honor among the members of marginalized groups accentuates a feature of democratic honor in general, which is the relative predominance of conscience-related aspects of honor, especially the sense of duty to oneself and the desire for self-respect.

Although Douglass placed more value on self-respect than on public honors, he was sufficiently attuned to public opinion to be an effective advocate for his race. His rhetorical grace, his elegant appearance, his "great personal charm," and his ability to influence powerful men all testify to the public or outward-looking dimensions of his character. And while he was, according to Washington, "far more radical than some of the most ardent of his anti-slavery associates," he was careful to account for the opinions (and the fears) of the majority. Thus in defending black enfranchisement "he always declared that political equality was a different thing from social equality. He vigorously protested that the right of suffrage did not mean Negro domination in the slave states, if the best white people would wisely assume the leadership of the blacks."[132] Yet he did not hesitate to accuse President Andrew Johnson directly and publicly of "unsound and prejudicial" opinions or to openly criticize measures before Congress that he thought detrimental to his race.[133] He combined the defense of his principles with an attentiveness (albeit not deference) to the majority opinion that he knew he could not ignore, and the result was a political moderation that had parallels to that of Lincoln. Douglass always was more willing than Lincoln to denounce majority opinion outright, and he was frequently critical of what he took to be Lincoln's excessive reticence in this regard.[134] But like Lincoln's moderation, the comparative moderation of Douglass proved effective in promoting reforms that were more radical than anything the majority on its own would have conceived and more effective than what the radicals on their own could have realized. While Douglass did not associate himself with the love of fame and did not put too much stock in public recognition, then, his sense of honor was sufficiently outward looking to be politic and therefore to be a source of effective political action.

This outward-looking quality also distinguishes honor from personal conscience, which need take no interest in others and easily may become zealous. Douglass was a man of conscience, to be sure, but he was more than simply a man of conscience. Besides being politic, he was guided by the public principles contained in the Declaration of Independence, defended these principles in public actions, and aimed for political reform. Nor does the category of conscience capture the pride and the high ambitions that were characteristic of Douglass, qualities more properly associated with honor. The honor of Douglass differed from honor in Montesquieu, and it was not a perfect balance of principle and public esteem. But perhaps this less-than-perfect balance was more perfectly suited to his circumstances. His honor was a more powerful source of agency because it was less concerned with public honors in a world in which, no matter what he did, he could not reasonably rely on receiving them. If the honor of Frederick Douglass departs in some ways from earlier forms of honor, it nevertheless remains recognizable. Booker T. Washington was not amiss when he called Douglass "the soul of honor." The high and principled ambitions, the pride, the courageous resistance to oppressive power, and the desire for self-respect all capture crucial features of honor as a quality of character and make it an important source of political agency.

Du Bois wrote in 1903 that "there are to-day no truer exponents of the pure human spirit of the Declaration of Independence than the American Negroes." White Americans, running blind in "the dusty desert of dollars and smartness," had become complacent about their liberty, he said. For them, the founding principles had lost their immediacy. Liberty as an end in itself had been obscured by the material prosperity it had made possible. American blacks, by contrast, still retained a "simple faith and reverence" in the promises of the Declaration because they were still reaching to realize these promises. Although denied full inclusion in the American polity, Du Bois argued, blacks were in a way its truest citizens, or truest to its founding spirit. The honor of Frederick Douglass brought this spirit to life in a way that had a profound and lasting impact on America. Douglass was not alone. During the same period, the first wave of feminism in the United States arose to show that there were women, too, who were reaching to realize the promises of the American founding and drawing on their sense of honor to do so.

Honor and Self-Sovereignty: Elizabeth Cady Stanton and Susan B. Anthony

Historically honor has been associated mainly with males, at least the type of honor under consideration here, the high and principled ambition that inspires risky exertions of individual agency in defense of liberty. Politics and the battlefield—the traditional sites of honor—have been male domains until very recently. It should come as no surprise, then, that the qualities of character associated with these practices more often have been seen and celebrated in men than in women. Honor in women traditionally was conceived in terms of chastity, or sexual modesty. Yet it would surely ring false to assert that women are incapable of the high ambitions, courage, defense of principle, desire for distinction, sense of duty to oneself, pride, independence, and self-mastery that are associated with aristocratic honor in its broader sense. Nevertheless, the traditional association between honor and martial valor or physical prowess has seemed to many to render women physiologically unfit for honor as a quality of character. Thus one commentator has classified honor as intrinsically masculine on the grounds that it essentially amounts to the "instinct for killing,"[135] an instinct that he regards as particular to males of the species. The question of biological determinism as it relates to the character and conduct of human males and females is beyond the scope of this project, but it would be incorrect to equate honor with a biological instinct for killing. At least in the modern period, honor has always been thickly overlaid with history and convention, and mediated by reason in the form of principled codes and by society in the form of public honors. Montesquieu's honorable soldier, the Viscount of Orte, displays honor precisely by *refusing* to kill innocent persons, not by mechanically reacting to a biological instinct to kill. Nor did Montesquieu himself limit examples of honor to the valor of soldiers. As we have seen, his *honnêtes hommes* were not primarily men of war but men of society who were refined and civilized—one might even say feminized—by fixed, established laws and eighteenth-century French manners. More generally, a defining feature of honor as a quality of character is the refusal to be determined by biological instincts, such as the instinct for self-preservation. Honor embodies an assertion of self-command as against the command of political despots and the impersonal forces of history, society, and nature itself. One need not endorse the radical postmodern denial of human nature to be skeptical about accounts of honor that reduce it to an expression of biological necessity.

Even the physical courage that Frederick Douglass identified with his honor and his "manhood" in the fight against Covey is not unknown to women.[136] Douglass himself describes the "noble resistance" of a female slave named Nelly who lived on the same plantation as he, an incident not dissimilar to the one that marked his own "resurrection" from slavery to comparative freedom. Nelly was being punished by the plantation overseer for "impudence," a charge that Douglass thought credible on the grounds that "in Nelly there were all the necessary conditions for committing the offense." She was, he says with admiration, "a vigorous and spirited woman, and one of the most likely, on the plantation, to be guilty of impudence."[137] When the overseer began to beat her she screamed and cursed him, and by the time Douglass arrived on the scene "Nelly was sternly resisting." Douglass reports that "there were numerous bloody marks" on the overseer's face as a result of the scuffle, including "the imprints of Nelly's fingers."[138] Although she "nobly resisted," she was "severely whipped."[139] Yet even with her back "covered with blood," she still "was not subdued, for she continued to denounce the overseer, and to call him every vile name. He had bruised her flesh but had left her invincible spirit undaunted."[140] If there was a nascent honor in Douglass's resistance to Covey, there was honor in Nelly's, as well. Consider, too, the case of Martha Dickinson, a female slave being offered for sale on the public auction block, who rebelled against the degrading poking and prodding of a prospective buyer. When the buyer put his hand in her mouth to examine her teeth, as one historian tells it, "she bit his finger to the bone," thus eliciting a brutal beating.[141]

It cannot be denied that in the premodern period, when honor was equated with physical prowess and derived directly from the capacity to prevail over one's enemy in combat, the greater size and physical strength of most males as compared with most females, together with women's isolation in the domestic sphere, established a natural association between honor and masculinity. Yet honor in American democracy has always been associated as much with political courage as with martial valor or physical prowess. And honor can indeed be found among notable women in American history, particularly among the reformers who transcended the limits of the traditionally feminine role to act in the public sphere, as the lives of Elizabeth Cady Stanton and Susan B. Anthony demonstrate. These women displayed the high ambitions, the courageous defense of principle, the desires for distinction and self-respect, and the sense of duty to oneself that make honor such a powerful spring of agency. In addition, they managed to call forth honor from within themselves and to act on it without the promise of public honors, even in the face of strong social disapproval. To be sure, they sought public recognition and personal distinction, but unlike men such as Lincoln, Washington, and Jefferson, their high ambitions were not provoked by the reasonable hope of fame and kindled by the admiration of their contemporaries. Although Lincoln was attacked for the content of his "radical" antislavery position, he was not, after all, scorned for the very act of standing publicly to defend his position. In this respect, the public honor of women (like that of black reformers) is doubly extraordinary as it represents resistance on two fronts—against the encroaching power that denied their rights to liberty and equality and against the tyranny of public opinion that ridiculed them for their very resistance.

If one sees something close to the physical courage of a soldier in Nelly's nascent honor, the honor of women activists such as Elizabeth Cady Stanton and Susan B. Anthony embodies the political courage of great reformers. Stanton once remarked that it was better to "suffer the occasional insults or die outright, than live the life of a *coward,* or never move without a protector. The best protector any woman can have, one that will serve her at all times and in all places, is *courage.*"[142] Stanton and Anthony are the most famous representatives of the nineteenth-century women's rights movement in the United States, and while there were differences of temperament and policy emphasis between them, they were sufficiently alike in respect of honor to treat them together here. Both were women of high ambition and uncommon courage, and both were deeply committed to the American creed. Their ambitions were guided by the principles articulated in the Declaration, and they rose to resist the insufficiently limited power of males in American families, society, and politics so as to claim for women the liberties promised by that document. They sought what Stanton called "self-sovereignty," or the capacity to carve out their own destinies, and they aimed to reach the "highest places of honor" in American society, both to satisfy their own ambitions and to open the door to self-sovereignty for other women. They insisted, much as the founders had, on "their right—and capacity—to change society and affect history," and they claimed to act from the sense of duty to oneself that is a central feature of honor.[143]

No doubt because of the common association between honor and martial valor, both Stanton and Anthony frequently invoked military metaphors and likened themselves to soldiers. When she asked Stanton to write an address for her to deliver to the New York State Teacher's Conference in 1856, Anthony exhorted her friend to "*load my gun,* leaving me only to pull the trigger and let fly the powder and ball."[144] She frequently referred to "fight[ing] our battle for the ballot,"[145] and in 1857, when Stanton had been incapacitated for a time after the birth of her seventh child, Anthony wrote to her saying, "Oh Mrs. Stanton how my soul longs to see you in the great Battle field. When will the time come?"[146] Stanton, too, spoke of the importance of continuously "turning our guns on new strongholds" so that "wherever and whatever any class of women suffer[,] whether in the home, the church, the courts, in the world of work, in the statute books, a voice in their behalf should be heard."[147] Both women invoked the honorable spirit of the founders, calling themselves "the daughters of the revolutionary heroes of '76."[148] By identifying themselves as soldiers, they symbolically laid claim to honor, and the use of military metaphors suggests how risky and difficult they took their project to be. Yet when late in life Anthony advised a young suffragist to "take your stand and hold it; then let come what will, and receive blows like a good soldier," she had in mind political, not physical, courage. "The only fear you need have," she said, "is the fear of not standing by the thing you believe to be right."[149]

The stand they took and held was first publicized in Stanton's "Declaration of Sentiments and Resolutions" at the women's rights convention held at Seneca Falls, New York, in 1848. The document was based on the Declaration of Independence and sought to make its promises apply explicitly to women. In this respect, the form of honor they exemplified is in keeping with the form of American public honor explored in this chapter and the previous one.[150] "We hold these truths to be self-evident," Stanton wrote, "that all men and women are created equal; that they are endowed by their Creator with certain inalienable rights; that among these are life, liberty, and the pursuit of happiness; that to secure these rights governments are instituted, deriving their just powers from the consent of the governed."[151] The Declaration of Sentiments objected to the white American woman's exclusion from the elective franchise, by means of which she was "compelled . . . to submit to laws in the formation of which she had no voice." There were other objections, as well, including the fact that "man" had made the married woman "in the eye of the law, civilly dead" (a reference to the principle of coverture), that man "has taken from her all right in property, even to the wages she earns," that "he closes against her all the avenues to wealth and distinction which he considers most honorable to himself," that "he has denied her the facilities for obtaining a thorough education, all colleges being closed against her," and that "he has monopolized nearly all the profitable employments." Finally, the document asserted that man had "endeavored, in every way that he could, to destroy [woman's] confidence in her own powers, to lessen her self-respect, and to make her willing to lead a dependent and abject life."[152] Together these offenses constituted "a history of repeated injuries and usurpations on the part of man toward woman, having in direct object the establishment of an absolute tyranny over her."[153]

When Stanton and Anthony spoke of male "tyranny," they did not mean to imply that all men were brutes. By "tyranny" they meant essentially the same thing that Frederick Douglass and the founders (and even Montesquieu) had meant by it: arbitrary power. "We do not propose to petition the legislature to make our husbands just, generous and courteous, to seat every man at the head of a cradle, and to clothe every woman in male attire," she told the assembly at Seneca Falls. "None of these points, however important they may be considered by leading men, will be touched on in this convention." Instead, she continued,

> We are assembled to protest against a form of government, existing without the consent of the governed—to declare our right to be free as a man is free, to be represented in the government which we are taxed to support, to [eradicate] such disgraceful laws as give man the power to chastise and imprison his wife, to take the wages she earns, the property which she inherits, and in case of separation, the children of her love; laws which make her the mere dependent on his bounty.[154]

Without equal civil and political rights for women, there was no effective check on the power of individual males over individual females. Under these circumstances, it was only the goodness of their hearts that prevented men from abusing their power. Early suffragists knew that there were many good-hearted men and fair husbands in America, but like Montesquieu, Tocqueville, and the American founders they did not think that good hearts were sufficient checks on political power. "Who ever saw a human being that would not abuse unlimited power?" they asked.[155] They extended the logic of *The Federalist*, which held that if men were angels no external checks on their power would be needed, but since men are not angels effective mechanisms had to be found to limit what they could do to one another. Stanton and Anthony argued that it was not enough to prevent men from dominating one another; they must also be prevented from dominating the women.

The Declaration of Sentiments therefore demanded that women "have immediate admission to all the rights and privileges which belong to them as citizens of the United States."[156] The document explicitly re-called Americans to the nation's founding principles of liberty and equality while reinterpreting the principles so as to include women within their scope.[157] Nearly twenty-five years later, Anthony's "Consti-tutional Argument" took the same approach in appealing to the Declara-tion and the Constitution, and throughout their lives both women invoked the ideal of "inalienable rights," or what Stanton called the "birth-right to self-sovereignty," as the guiding principle of their la-bors.[158] Their aim, Stanton said in 1888, had always been "to establish in the New World a government in which the sound principles of our Constitution and Declaration of Independence may be fully realized, in which there shall be no privileged classes, but equal rights for all."[159]

If principles guided their labors, ambition drove them. Both Stanton and Anthony were extremely ambitious women. Both had sought leader-ship positions in early forums for women's public activities such as the temperance and abolition movements. Participation in such forums gave women, as one historian notes, "a wider field for [their] labors than teaching," virtually the only reputable vocation then open to profession-ally ambitious women, or women whose professional ambitions pointed beyond the domestic sphere.[160] In an 1852 letter to the women's journal *The Lily*, Anthony wrote that "Auxiliary Temperance Societies have been formed in very nearly all the towns I have visited and the women are beginning to feel that they have something to do in the Temperance

Cause—that woman may speak and act in public as well as in the home circle."[161] After being driven out of the New York State Women's Temperance Society in 1853 for promoting their woman suffrage program, however, Stanton and Anthony concentrated their ambitions on women's rights exclusively.[162] Their ambitions were *grandes* in Tocqueville's sense in that they sought to be, like the founders, "agents of history" rather than its "pawns." In particular, they wanted women to demonstrate "their claim to equality in the world of work, in agriculture, manufacturing, mechanics, inventions, the arts and sciences," as Anthony put it, to establish themselves "in education, literature, and politics," and to seize "actual possession of the highest places of honor and emolument, by the industry of their own hands and brains, and by election or appointment."[163] They had the aristocratic pride (although it wore a democratic cloak) to reject the limits imposed by others on their lives and to reach for more on behalf of themselves and their kind, even "the highest places of honor and emolument." To do otherwise would be "distasteful" to the "self-respectful woman," Anthony said.[164]

Stanton and Anthony aimed not only to accomplish much but also to accomplish something lofty: the more perfect realization of America's founding principles. They claimed for women "those rights that are dearer . . . than life itself—rights which have been baptized in blood—and the maintenance of which is even now rocking to their foundations the kingdoms of the Old World."[165] "It is not enough for us," Stanton told the New York State legislature in 1854, "that by your laws we are permitted to live and breathe, to claim the necessaries of life."[166] American women were well fed but not free, and for the sake of freedom Stanton "demand[ed] the full recognition of all our rights as citizens of the Empire State."[167] This is precisely the spirit that Tocqueville had hoped would emerge, if only on occasion, in modern democracy, the "aristocratic" love of liberty that will not rest satisfied with material satisfactions but instead rises to defend liberty as an end in itself. Liberty or "self-sovereignty" was the great ambition of the early suffragists. They laid claim to the heritage of the American Revolution as the "daughters" of the "heroes of '76" because life without liberty was not good enough for them.[168] "With the spirit in bondage," Stanton told the International Council of Women in 1888, "it is the same whether housed in golden cages, with every want supplied, or wandering in the dreary deserts of life."[169] Stanton and Anthony possessed the high ambitions so central to honor; they wanted to rise, and they wanted American women as a whole to rise, and the guideposts of their ambitions were the principles articulated by the Declaration of Independence.

They were, as Jefferson once claimed of Americans in general, "too high-minded to endure the degradations" of anything but self-government. Anthony pointed out in 1872, after being arrested for voting, that "women are taxed without representation, governed without their consent, tried, convicted and punished without a jury of their peers." She noted that these very violations of the "great fundamental principles of . . . free government" had driven "our Revolutionary fathers when they rebelled against King George." "Is all this tyranny any less humiliating and degrading to women under our democratic-republican government today," she demanded, "than it was to men under their aristocratic, monarchical government one hundred years ago?"[170] As a matter of self-respect, she refused to abide such humiliation and degradation. Stanton acknowledged Anthony's suitable pride when she referred to Anthony in her memoirs as "that great-souled woman."[171] Like Anthony, Stanton held that "there can be no true dignity" where there is "subordination to the absolute will of another, no happiness without freedom."[172] It was, she said, "too grossly insulting to the dignity of woman to be longer quietly submitted to."[173]

Stanton encouraged women to have "a proper appreciation of themselves as factors in civilization,"[174] or as Tocqueville would have said, more "pride."[175] "Let [woman] know that her spirit is fitted for as high a sphere as man's," she exhorted at Seneca Falls, "and that her soul requires food as pure and exalted as his."[176] She never denied the intrinsic worth of domestic virtues and practices, including mothering, but she objected to the wholesale confinement of women to the domestic sphere. She regarded it as a duty that every woman should seek to claim the highest sphere for which her spirit was fitted, whatever that might be. It was a matter of being "just to herself," Stanton said.[177] Each woman owed it to herself to live up to the principles of liberty and equality by claiming and exercising the rights these principles justified. Stanton was alive to what George Washington called "justice to myself," and it moved her to undertake bold and courageous action in defense of her principles. Although her proud self-assertion sometimes conveyed an air of superiority, she tried to encourage it in other women, as well, and she did so precisely because she saw its powerful effects on political agency.[178] Stanton and Anthony summoned (middle-class white) American women from the slumber of material sufficiency and sought to awaken them to liberty.

Although they rejected material sufficiency as an end in itself, Stanton and Anthony saw it as a crucial condition for liberty. Anthony was particularly active in defending "pecuniary independence" for women.[179] In speeches she quoted Alexander Hamilton, who "said 100 years ago 'take my right over my subsistence and you possess absolute power over my moral being.' "[180] Property rights together with the right "to control of her own person" and "the ownership of her own earnings," were central components of the early women's rights platform. Stanton told the men in the New York State legislature in 1853 that "you have in your hands the means of self-protection. Not so with us. The law gives to the man the right to all he can get, and to what we get too. The new property law protects what we inherit, but not what we jointly earn."[181] Women, like men, needed the legal and economic basis for what one historian has called "an honorable independence."[182] Stanton and Anthony also championed access to a "complete education," political equality, "credit in the market place, recompense in the world of work, a voice in choosing those who make and administer the law, a choice in the jury before whom they are tried, and in the judge who decides their punishment."[183] Such equipment provided the conditions for agency. Without it, as Anthony said, a woman "is not allowed to control her own circumstances. The pride of every man is that he is free to carve out his own destiny. A woman has no such pride."[184] It was no use, Stanton maintained, to "talk of sheltering woman from the fierce storms of life." The storms of life "beat on her from every point of the compass, just as they do on man," but "with more fatal results, for he has been trained to protect himself, to resist, and to conquer."[185] Like the founders, Stanton and Anthony were reaching for "the honor of the human race," the bold assertion of individual agency and self-rule.

Stanton and Anthony themselves possessed more of the equipment of honor than many of their peers. Both had been born into reform-minded and relatively prosperous families and were better educated than most women of the day. While Anthony never married, Stanton's husband largely tolerated (and frequently supported) her activism. Nevertheless, Stanton periodically faced "painful opposition" from her husband, as well as from her father and friends. In a letter to Anthony in 1855, she reported that she had "passed through a terrible scourging when last at my father's." She continued,

> I never felt more keenly the degradation of my sex. To think that all in me of which my father would have felt a proper pride had I been a man, is deeply mortifying to him because I am a woman. That thought has stung me to a fierce decision—to speak as soon as I can do myself credit. But the pressure on me just now is too great. Henry sides with my friends, who oppose me in all that is dearest to my heart. They are not willing that I should write even on the woman question. But I will both write and speak.[186]

As the mother of seven children, she felt limited in what she could accomplish in the "true associative life" of politics.[187] "How much I do long to be free from housekeeping and children," she confessed to Anthony in 1852, "so as to have some time to read, and think, and write."[188] In another letter, she likened herself to a "caged lioness," pacing "up and down these two chambers of mine . . . watching, bathing, dressing, nursing, and promenading the precious contents of a little crib in the corner of the room."[189] Thirty years later, she reflected back on "those who inaugurated the movement for woman's enfranchisement, who for long years endured the merciless storm of ridicule and persecution, mourned over by friends, ostracized in social life, scandalized by enemies, denounced by the pulpit, scarified and caricatured by the press."[190] Stanton and Anthony never won much in the way of public honors, at least not commensurate with the contributions they made, perhaps because they were not alive for the passage of the nineteenth amendment establishing woman suffrage.[191] The public marginalization of women had the effect of making the internal dimensions of honor especially salient for them, much as it did for Frederick Douglass. Yet despite this shift, key features of honor remain constant in these cases and illuminate the sources and conditions of political agency more generally, especially the extraordinary exertions of agency that rise to the defense of individual liberties in the face of obvious risks and indeterminate benefits.

Honor in the Civil Rights Movement

The same features of honor were on display in the character of Martin Luther King, Jr. King was a complex man of mixed and not always transparent motives, and it would be wrong to say that honor was the sole spring of his action. Even in his public life as a civil rights leader, one can detect a variety of motives, including faith, civic virtue, a sense of justice, and self-interest. But honor played a role, as well, or qualities associated with honor, such as high and principled ambitions, pride, a sense of distinction, courageous resistance to encroaching power, the desire for self-respect, and the sense of duty to oneself. These qualities supported his extraordinary capacity for political agency. King's honor also inspired political agency in others, and the connection between honor and agency was important for the civil rights movement as a whole.

It may seem strange to speak of honor in conjunction with King, who had a reputation for being a humble man. When *Time* magazine published a feature story on him in February of 1957, the reporter characterized King as "personally humble, articulate, and of high educational attainment."[192] These qualities came to define his public persona. In private, too, his demeanor was relatively free of pretension and vanity; he did not put on airs. As one friend recalled, "Martin did not have any of this pompous arrogance that characterize[s] so many people who have high education and also get into a position of leadership and power." Another friend remarked that he found King "completely unaffected by the attention that has come to him in the world. He's always just Martin around anybody . . . there isn't any swagger to his psyche at all."[193] Aside from King's personal manner, to many observers the whole method of nonviolent resistance he defended gave an impression of humble resoluteness, even (as one critic thought) "self-effacement."[194] King was no Alexander Hamilton: pretentious, overtly ambitious, frankly seeking fame. To be sure, an arrogant man who tried to do what King did in the American South in the 1950s and 1960s would have alienated both the black masses he intended to lead and the powerful whites he intended to change, but the political efficacy of his humble demeanor should cast no doubt on its authenticity. King was a man of faith, after all, and no faith is possible without humility. Yet he was a man of extraordinary ambition as well, and his humble demeanor ought not blind us to this ambition and the pride that made it possible.

King's great, even grandiose, effort to recall America to its foundations and simultaneously to radically reform it was anything but humble, after all. In fact, his high ambitions were as visible to those who knew him as his humility. "He has a sense of humility and awe at what has happened to him, but he also has a sense of destiny," remarked a Montgomery friend.[195] King knew the magnitude of the project he had undertaken and, although he had moments of self-doubt and depression, on the whole he had the confidence and even the pride needed to shoulder the burden. He had a sufficiently high opinion of himself to conceive and to carry through *grandes ambitions.* For this reason, one biographer has spoken of the "alternately dominant strains in his personality—grandiosity and common sense."[196] When in 1959 King announced to his congregation in Montgomery that he was moving to Atlanta to continue his work there, he told them, "I can't stop now. History has thrust something upon me which I cannot turn away. I should free you now."[197] King's sense of destiny, his claim to a world-historical mission, implied a powerful sense of distinction, however humble his personal demeanor. The remark consequently has been interpreted by various commentators as "a shrewd combination of high ambition—even hubris—and humility,"[198] and as a "mixture of hubris, grandeur, and historical prevision."[199] What one historian refers to as King's "reluctance to call attention to his own ambition"[200] did not conceal this ambition from his associates, even if it largely has concealed his ambition from posterity.

King was born into Atlanta's black aristocracy, and his family background provided some of the equipment of honor. The King family was "certainly materially successful" and well positioned "in the politics of the community."[201] His maternal grandfather, the Reverend Alfred Daniel Williams, had founded Ebenezer Baptist Church in Atlanta and was "one of the rare people in the black community who was financially secure and independent of whites."[202] Alfred Williams played a leading role in race relations in the city. He was a charter member of the local chapter of the NAACP, for example, and a leader in establishing the city's first secondary school for black children in the 1920s. He was an uncommonly proud man. When a local newspaper denounced black supporters of the school as "dirty and ignorant" protesters, he and several colleagues organized a boycott of the paper that eventually helped drive it out of business.[203] King's father, Martin Luther King, Sr., also was a leader in the community. He, too, was a minister, a founding member of the Atlanta Voters' League, a sponsor of programs for Atlanta youth, and a graduate and trustee of Morehouse College.[204] All these achievements were marks of the highest status in the black community. King, Sr., exuded the aristocratic pride—the high sense of himself—that Tocqueville championed. Because of it, he "periodically surprised" Atlanta whites with his "forthright opposition to racial effrontery," as one encounter with an Atlanta police officer illustrates:

> The arrogant traffic policeman, drawling through a lecture begun with the traditional salutation, "Boy," was instantly reprimanded with Reverend King's impatient correction, "That's a boy," pointing to Mike [MLK, Jr.] sitting beside him, "I'm a man."[205]

On another occasion, a white shoe-store clerk declined to serve King, Sr., and his son unless they moved to the rear of the store. The elder King replied, on the way out the door, "We'll either buy shoes sitting here or we won't buy any shoes at all."[206]

The family position and the proud expectations associated with it were impressed on King as a child. He shared in his family's sense of pride and sought to continue its distinguished place in black society. In his dealings with neighborhood boys, for example, he displayed a sense of "superiority" that motivated him "to suffer the lesser indignity of not fighting a social inferior. There were some youngsters with whom one did not 'go to the grass.' "[207] In his professional life he aimed suitably high. With a bachelor's degree from Morehouse and having been ordained as a minister in the Baptist church, he could have ended his formal education in 1948. Instead he decided to pursue advanced degrees, first a bachelor of divinity degree at Crozer Theological Seminary and then a doctorate in philosophy at Boston University. Although as an adult, he "professed indifference to material things and . . . tried to be like Gandhi," accepting a personal income that was "scarcely commensurate with his labors and prestige," he nevertheless "had a fascination with men of affluence . . . and enjoyed the company of wealthy SCLC benefactors."[208] Likewise, he prized the "more than fifty awards and honorary degrees" that he had won, and made a point of displaying them on the walls of his Atlanta home.[209] He had high expectations of himself, was proud and personally ambitious, and if he did not hunger for wealth he clearly sought prestige and influence.

His pride and high ambitions and the air of distinction they entailed were inspiring to some of his fellows but resented by others. After his victory in the Montgomery bus boycott in 1956, a family friend and admirer wrote to him, "May God continue to bless you that you may reach higher heights. Your future is unlimited . . . There is no position in any church, religious body, University and etc., which you could not fill. I have picked you for three outstanding positions in our race. I will be glad to risk my prophesy on that."[210] On the other side, many in Atlanta's old guard "viewed him as an aggrandizing upstart—and a sanctimonious one at that."[211] Local preachers in Montgomery thought that he "was using the movement to get attention."[212] Members of the NAACP accused him of "laboring under a messiah complex,"[213] and the student leaders of SNCC took to calling him "de Lawd," complaining that he had a tendency to seize "all the publicity and the glory."[214] One organizational head in Montgomery told him reproachfully, "Don't talk with me through no [secretary]. I'm as big as you are, King."[215] As a friend said later, there was "a lot of jealousy of Martin among Negro leaders."[216]

The comments of King's critics should be considered with an eye to the envy that greatness always induces, particularly in democratic polities.[217] Even when they pursue democratic purposes, such as the expansion of liberty and equality, reformers such as Stanton, Anthony, and King distinguish themselves from their peers by their uncommon ambitions and abilities. They illustrate the fact that the very defense of equality in the form of democratic rights sometimes requires ambition, talent, and character that is far superior to the norm. And though democratic reformers do not seek special privileges for themselves (as Montesquieu's *honnête homme* did), their extraordinary actions demonstrate their conviction that they are too good for the conditions in which they find themselves, however common these conditions may be. King's resistance set him apart and was an implicit indictment of the posture of resignation assumed by so many of his fellows. A civil rights worker in southwest Georgia put it this way: "When you ask a man to join you, you are asking for a confession that his life up until now has been lived upside down."[218] This is how even democratic forms of honor are inseparable from pride and distinction. King's reform agenda inescapably implied a critique of black as well as white America. The same was true for early women's rights activists, and it is a common dilemma for democratic reformers in general. When women such as Elizabeth Cady Stanton and Susan B. Anthony stood up to demand the civil and political rights that are the conditions of "self-sovereignty" and so of human dignity, they implicitly called into question the dignity of all the women who had ever acquiesced to the disenfranchisement of their traditional status, even their own mothers and grandmothers. Without having to say so directly, their very actions announced to American women: "The prevailing arrangements are not good enough for us, and they should not be good enough for you either." In this way, pride and the sense of distinction inescapably play a role in the acts of resistance that lead to social and political reform, including reforms for greater equality, and so they frequently engender resentment.

This resentment is one reason why an outward demeanor of humility was so crucial for King. Yet if his critics frequently were driven by resentment, they nevertheless saw something in his character that really was there: his extraordinary ambitions. In fact, King combined personal ambition with principled higher purposes in a way that is much closer to honor than to the humble altruism that American mythology has come to ascribe to him. Like the other exemplars of honor considered in this chapter, King disrupts the contemporary dichotomy between interests and obligations. This dichotomy erroneously forces individuals such as King into the category of self-effacing altruists simply because they display a capacity for great sacrifice in an era in which we have forgotten how to connect sacrifice to personal ambition, or higher purposes to self-concern. Honor, perhaps more than any other quality, combines them.

The principles that guided King's personal ambitions derived from a variety of sources, including the Bible and the civil disobedience doctrines of Gandhi and Thoreau. His "Letter from Birmingham City Jail" quoted Augustine, Aquinas, Martin Buber, Paul Tillich, Martin Luther, John Bunyan, Thomas Jefferson, and T. S. Eliot, and invoked the models of Socrates and Jesus—all to defend the moral legitimacy of civil disobedience to unjust laws. But the letter concluded with a direct appeal to America's founding principles. The civil rights movement was an effort to recall America to its foundations, he said:

> One day the South will know that when these disinherited children of God sat down at lunch counters they were in reality standing up for the best in the American dream and the most sacred values in our Judeo-Christian heritage, and thusly, carrying our whole nation back to those great wells of democracy which were dug deep by the Founding Fathers in the formulation of the Constitution and the Declaration of Independence.[219]

In a speech at the Dexter Baptist Church that initiated the Montgomery bus boycott, King began by saying, "We are here in a general sense because first and foremost, we are American citizens, and we are determined to acquire our citizenship to the fullness of its meaning."[220] "The great glory of American democracy," he said at Montgomery and later at Memphis, "is the right to protest for right."[221] He noted on another occasion that the nation had begun in such protests, and he named the Boston Tea Party and the Revolution itself as examples. He concluded that civil rights protesters were "standing up for the highest and the best in the American tradition."[222] In laying claim to the full liberties of American citizenship, protesters "forced the nation to confront the gap between its professed ideals and the realities of the Jim Crow South," and in doing so brought about a "political rejuvenation or revitalization" of the American polity, a re-creation of "the spirit of the laws."[223] And as with the American founders, Lincoln, Frederick Douglass, and the early suffragists, King's spirited defense of the American code produced not only resistance to encroaching power but substantial political reform.

It is worth emphasizing the point first enunciated by Lincoln, that the American national code of honor as articulated by the Declaration carries within itself the seeds of reform. As a more recent commentator notes, "the language of Natural Rights has been the central subversive strain in American political life."[224] This fact has had important implications for honor in the United States. Because of the intrinsic dynamism of the principles codified in the Declaration, American honor has survived one of the conflicts that Tocqueville identified between honor and democracy, or at least it has survived the conflict better than Tocqueville expected. The conflict is that honor as a quality of character requires consistency in the codes that guide it, which seems to be at odds with the social mobility engendered by democratic societies. The Declaration has provided a common code of honor since the founding, and for many generations it has served as a polestar for great Americans with high ambitions. Yet it has guided, constrained, and elevated individual ambitions without imposing stasis on American society. The dynamism inherent in the principles has accommodated the dynamism of American democracy, thus (somewhat paradoxically) making possible the principled consistency of progressive reforms, which have on the whole brought about a polity in which the gap between our principles and our practices has become increasingly narrow. At the same time, however, the reformist potential of the American principles can only be realized if the principles remain authoritative over successive generations and can only be unleashed by individuals who revere them. Consistency and reverence

open up the possibility of reform. This explains why Lincoln emphasized equally the progressive character of the American creed and the
need for American citizens to revere it.

The willingness to risk one's life in defense of liberty also was a key
characteristic of King, and a quality that permeated the civil rights
movement more generally. The practice of nonviolent civil disobedience
is consistent with the shift from honor as martial valor to honor as political courage, but like the early suffragists, civil rights leaders frequently
invoked military metaphors and so laid claim to the honor such metaphors call to mind. Ralph Abernathy called King the "peaceful warrior,"
for instance, and King himself did "not hesitate to call our movement an
army." "But it was a special army," King said, "with no supplies but its
sincerity, no uniform but its determination, no arsenal except its faith,
no currency but its conscience. It was an army that would move but not
maul."[225] Like the martial valor of a soldier, however, King's political
courage made him willing to risk death. There was faith behind his
courage, to be sure, but there was an honorable pride in it as well. At the
height of the Montgomery bus boycott, King was receiving "thirty to
forty hate letters a day," as well as obscene phone calls (as many as
twenty-five a day), his house had been bombed with his wife and infant
daughter inside, and there were reliable reports of plans to have him as-
sassinated.[226] King admitted he was "scared to death,"[227] but he refused
to curtail his activities. On a brief visit with his parents in Atlanta, his father along with several friends tried to convince him to stay away from
Montgomery until calm could be restored. He declined, saying that it
"would be the height of cowardice for me to stay away. I would rather be
in jail ten years than desert my people now. I have begun the struggle,
and I can't turn back. I have reached the point of no return."[228] As is typical for those with honor, he feared cowardice (and the appearance of
cowardice) more than death. And he not only feared cowardice, but
scorned it: "As much as I deplore violence, there is one evil that is worse
than violence, and that's cowardice."[229] King believed that "no man is
free if he fears death."[230] "If there is any one fear I have conquered," he
told friends late in his life, "it is the fear of death."[231]

As a way of generating honorable resistance, the civil rights movement as a whole tried to cultivate the preference for liberty over life that
Tocqueville associated with aristocratic mores. Before the movement,
southern blacks lived in fear, much like the subjects of despotism de-

scribed in *The Spirit of the Laws.* Life lived under arbitrary power is intrinsically risky, and mass participation in the program of nonviolent civil disobedience was intended to transform the fear this risk inspired by making risk intentional. As one historian notes, "to participate publicly in civil rights demonstrations, even in larger cities, made participants feel distinctly vulnerable to verbal, not to mention physical, abuse from angry whites. But what was different about risking such vulnerability was that it was chosen rather than experienced as fate."[232] Fear could be overcome, even transformed into courage, by being undertaken willfully. Through nonviolent civil disobedience, King said, black Americans "become, for the first time, somebody and they have, for the first time, the courage to be free."[233] Consequently, the willingness to risk one's life is "central to any understanding of what it meant for King (and for many participants in the movement . . .) to become political beings."[234] Participating in nonviolent demonstrations served a function similar to that of the duel insofar as it provided an arena in which one could prove to oneself and to others that one had conquered the fear of death and therefore had become one's own master. As John Lewis put it, "Being involved tended to free you . . . you saw yourself as the free man, as the free agent, able to act."[235] Yet the shift from fear to courage involved "overcoming a whole sense of self organized around fear."[236] The movement as an organizational body helped provide the equipment for this shift. The songs and the sermons, the "freedom schools" and the church committees, served to reorient black Americans toward "habits of free thinking and ideas of how a free society works."[237] Stories of slaves who "refused to back down from their masters and fought them to the death" were told and retold with relish.[238] The result of triumphing over fear and subjection through courage and voluntary risk-taking was a new self-respect, the vindication of the "essential dignity" that Frederick Douglass associated with acts of honor.

Common as they are in politics, instrumental calculations of interest do not provide compelling grounds for such radical risks.[239] For this reason, many historians of the civil rights movement have concluded that the category of interest is not adequate to explain the motives of its participants, at least not without expanding the category of interest to the point of reducing its explanatory power.[240] As one SNCC worker put it, organizing blacks involved "convincing them that being a citizen is worth risking one's life,"[241] and to do this, something more than the satisfaction of self-interest had to be at stake. Self-interest may well be the "driving force of 'normal' American politics," but as it is commonly conceived it cannot explain the important if rare cases in which individuals risk their lives to defend, "revitalize," or reform the existing political order.[242] To motivate unusually forceful exertions of individual agency, the movement emphasized "a sense of self-respect and pride," both central features of honor as a quality of character.[243] In the past, King told a crowd after the victory of the boycott in Montgomery, "we have sat in the back of the buses, and this had indicated a basic lack of self-respect. It shows that we thought of ourselves as less than men."[244] King himself, whether by nature or upbringing or some combination of the two, had an uncommon measure of self-respect for a black man in America at the time, given the many factors that tended to the disparagement of blacks. He and fellow leaders sought to ignite the desire for self-respect in others as a catalyst for individual and collective action. For this reason, going to jail became a badge of honor.[245] This reversed "the traditionally negative connotations of jail" as a "place of shame."[246] Jail is traditionally a place of shame and "dishonor" at least in part because incarceration curtails individual agency and makes citizens into subjects.[247] Jail became a badge of honor for civil rights activists because for them going to jail was a demonstration of agency. It was proof of one's principled ambition and one's courage, and a vindication of one's "human dignity." This badge of honor also provided public recognition, an external reward that complemented the internal prize of self-respect.

The desire for self-respect is a more powerful source of agency than self-interest, at least when it comes to risky and difficult actions in defense of principle, because with self-respect the good one seeks is ensured by what one does and not dependent on what one gets. In other words, the fact that demonstrators could not be sure of satisfying their material interests by boycotting the Montgomery public buses made self-interest (at least in the narrow sense in which it is most usefully conceived) a weak foundation for political action. By contrast, King and other leaders tried to instill the conviction that, whatever the outcome of the boycott, the demonstrators could win the good of self-respect simply by the act of participating.[248] In this way, the desire for self-respect provides a greater basis for independence than does self-interest, the satisfaction of which remains contingent on external factors frequently outside one's control.

In the early stages of the movement, King and other leaders empha-sized the theme of freedom, rather than simply justice, for similar rea-sons. It is true that justice was always a concern for civil rights activists and a subject of frequent reference, as in King's repeated "evocation of the biblical image of 'justice roll[ing] down like waters.' "[249] And in the years after 1964, it came to take an increasingly predominant place in his rhetoric.[250] But at the outset of the movement, the demand for justice only could be "a demand from black people that white people take re-sponsible action."[251] It did not refer to an aspiration on the part of Amer-ican blacks to become more just themselves, since they were not the source of the injustices they faced. For themselves, American blacks as-pired to be more free, as one historian notes, not to be more just.[252] As a rule, demands for justice, like contemporary claims to recognition, de-pend for their satisfaction on what someone else does. They rely on the kindness of strangers, or even enemies. This fact is not a reason to turn away from justice, but it does point up one of the limits of justice. Free-dom, unlike justice, "implies a potential or actual capacity for action."[253] From the standpoint of civil rights activists, justice could only be de-manded and hoped for; freedom could be realized, or could begin to be realized, through one's own action. Freedom could be achieved, or partly achieved, by what one did rather than by depending on what one might get. The rhetoric of freedom thus expressed the honorable aspira-tion for a greater power of agency. To be sure, the accomplishments of the civil rights movement could not help but depend in some measure on the kindness, or justice, of strangers: a tyrant might have had them all shot. The rule of law and the moral conscience of the wider public, which proved itself capable of being persuaded, were crucial to the suc-cess of the movement. In the absence of these circumstances, the honor-able self-assertions of participants would have been fruitless or deadly, or both.[254]

King's objective was for American blacks to be able to "say to our-selves and the world, 'I am somebody. I am a person. I am a man with dignity and honor.' "[255] Dignity, honor, and agency went together and made the spirited defense—or assertion—of liberty possible. King knew that the desire for self-respect, like honor, could "degenerate into self-proving (and self-defeating) macho confrontations with the enemy," which sometimes happened with the black power movement that came to prominence after his death.[256] The doctrine of nonviolent and *civil* disobedience, together with King's rhetorical eloquence in appealing to the common ground of the American code of honor, maintained a powerful moderating influence on the movement as long as he was alive. In this respect, both he and the movement displayed the balance of courage and moderation characteristic of honor at its best. King was attacked by radicals such as Malcolm X for being too conciliatory, and for too fully accepting the American code of honor as the polestar of his political action campaign. Yet much like Lincoln, King's moderation issued in radical accomplishments, ultimately transforming public conscience in the United States, together with American politics, policy, and law.

The qualities associated with honor that one sees in King and in the civil rights movement as a whole—high and principled ambition, pride, the desires for self-respect and public recognition, courageous resistance to encroaching power, the sense of duty to oneself—all represent continuities within American honor. They converge with key features of honor in Montesquieu and with the aristocratic character that Tocqueville described. The honor of King and his fellow activists was not the sole spring of their action, but it was a central component of their uncommon capacity for individual agency and their willingness to take the risks and make the effort that reform required. Honor's contribution to the civil rights movement demonstrates that honor has a place in liberal democracy despite the tensions between them. It may not be a universal motive that operates continuously in liberal-democratic regimes, or even the main motive of "normal" liberal politics. And even in the rare moments in which great acts of honor are called into play, it may not be necessary for all citizens to have honor. Occasional great acts of honor by a few may be sufficient to forestall encroachments on liberties, to recall the nation to its code, and to point the direction to the more complete fulfillment of its constitutive principles.

Not all acts of honor have these extraordinary effects. The preceding pages have highlighted the exemplary honor of some who made it to the center of the national stage and who have since been rewarded in the national pantheon. But surely there have been noble lives lived in obscurity in American history; no doubt such lives are being lived among us today. There are no guarantees that American history will reward the honorable; to expect it to do so would be to place too much faith in public opinion. It would also be to link honor in the United States too categorically to the singular code articulated by the Declaration. As important as this form of honor has been in American history, it is not alone. Much as Montesquieu's disobedient aristocrats engaged multiple and overlapping standards of honor even within the old regime, so American civil society contains the foundations for a variety of more partial forms of honor. The life of intermediary associations—with all its plurality and moral complexity—may generate acts of honor that go unrecognized by the culture at large even as they are rewarded from within the particular associations in which they arise. We shall turn to this theme in the concluding chapter.

The varieties of American honor point to a class of motives that is overlooked in the contemporary study of politics but that is a powerful source of individual agency. These are the motives that combine a proud sense of what one owes to oneself with uncommonly high ambitions. Such motives transcend the dichotomy between self-interest and obligations to others, and they remind us of liberal democracy's occasional need for aristocratic qualities of character. Because politics fundamentally concerns action, the analysis of individual agency constitutes a critical domain of political theory. Yet too often the topic of agency takes a back seat to deliberations about the meaning of justice and the conditions of legitimacy. Political theory is right to be concerned with these normative matters, but to the extent that it permits them to obscure the issue of agency, political theory renders itself unnecessarily partial. The study of honor helps to remedy this incompleteness by bringing the issue of agency to the fore and by elucidating its complex structure and multiple sources.

6

Conclusion: Pluralism, Agency, and Varieties of Democratic Honor

Honor—even democratic honor—is irreducibly aristocratic in the sense that it requires a measure of courage and ambition that not all of us can or do muster, although it need not presuppose a fixed social hierarchy or political inequalities. Being the prerogative of a "natural aristocracy," honor in the United States is more natural than the honor of the old regime. Here honor is less a function of artificially imposed social roles and status and more fully a function of individual action and character. It still includes an element of external public recognition, but increasingly honor is an achievement rather than an entitlement. This explains why democratic honor is more closely tied to virtue than Montesquieu's concept of honor was, although the two remain distinct. And the more honor becomes an achievement, the better it supports individual agency. Ironically, honor may be a more powerful source of agency, even may be more fully itself, in democracy than in the artificially fixed society of the old regime, despite the real tensions between honor and democracy. A central theme of this book has been that modern liberal democracy has an aristocratic inheritance, which includes not only honor but also individual rights, the separation of powers, and the intermediary bodies of civil society, and that liberal democracy cannot long sustain itself without embracing this inheritance.

Although honor is in one sense unavoidably aristocratic, acts of honor are not always extraordinary on the grand scale of those examined in the preceding chapters. In addition to the exemplary acts guided by a common code of honor composed of the principles contained in the Declaration and the Constitution, one sometimes sees instances of

181

honor that are rooted in the various and more partial codes of conduct that regulate the voluntary associations of American civil and political society. These more modest manifestations of democratic honor can also serve to check encroaching power in its many guises. Michael Walzer has argued for the importance of honor in this form. His notion of honor brings its formal features as a quality of character together with the principles of equal opportunity, pluralism, and consent that characterize American politics and contemporary American civil society.

The voluntary associations in which Walzer finds democratic forms of honor are the democratic equivalents of the corporate orders or intermediary bodies of the *ancien régime,* the traditional sites of honor. They are important sources of the shared identities and interconnected communities that support honor. Insofar as these various democratic codes of honor are associated with different associations, they will be (like the identities and communities that support them) plural and partial. They are not simply private, but neither are they universal in scope. Instead they are relative to the particular organizations and social institutions in which they are found, and tied to their particular purposes. To the vocational associations that Walzer emphasizes, one could add political parties, community associations, advocacy groups, and even families. The codes of conduct that regulate these different associations provide principled limits and direction for individual ambitions, and so mitigate the twofold tendency of democratic forms of honor to become either increasingly subjective or increasingly universal. Yet they do so without returning to a fixed, hereditary social order or political inequalities.

Walzer's account of honor also preserves the element of desert. With honor, as he presents it, one respects oneself not just for being (as with Rawlsian self-esteem), or for being accepted (as with Taylor's politics of recognition), but for acting well, in accordance with the established rules of conduct and standards of achievement that constitute one's code of honor. Thus Walzer's notion of honor restores the concept of desert, which Rawls rejects explicitly and Taylor implicitly erodes. Walzer recognizes the moderating influence of the idea of desert, based on standards that are fixed in the sense that they are not simply reducible to expressions of a particular individual will.[1] Without standards that are fixed in this sense, he points out, honor (or esteem, or recognition) "is simply available for tyrannical use. Because I have power, I shall honor so and so. It doesn't matter whom I choose, because no one really deserves to be honored . . . and I don't recognize any intrinsic connection between honor and any particular set of performances."[2] The concept of desert based on fixed standards protects self-respect from the tyranny of public opinion as well as the tyranny of a despot. And if some sense of self-respect is needed for the defense of individual liberties, as Rawls acknowledges it to be, such protection is essential. A strong sense of individual agency is linked inextricably to the idea of desert based on established standards.

Following Tocqueville, recent scholarship in political theory and empirical political science has shown the value of civil society for American citizenship, as we have seen. Voluntary intermediary associations are said to serve the collective liberty by making individuals more participatory. By taking part in the associational life of small organizations, individuals learn to see with a collective vision and develop the habit of working together for common purposes, which prepares them for the challenges of democratic participation. Such associations support democracy by increasing communality; they build reservoirs of "social capital"—shared beliefs and values, trust in one another and in the whole—that fuel large-scale political enterprises. Yet while democracies need social capital and a measure of civic virtue, liberal democracy also needs individual ambition, as Tocqueville knew, despite the fact that ambition may be at odds with the collectivism of civic virtue. And while the resources within civil society for the cultivation of civic virtue have been articulated in recent years, the resources there for inspiring honor have not been explored. Yet they are important. The social attachments, the principled codes of conduct, the standards of achievement, the competition and the public distinction that such associations provide support the high ambitions, the accomplishments, and the self-respect that give rise to strong exertions of individual agency. They create reservoirs not just of the social capital that serves political participation but also of the high expectations, the pride, and what Tocqueville called the *grandes ambitions* that fuel principled action when the risks are high and the benefits uncertain.

The self-serving character of Walzer's democratic honor is in keeping with the other forms of honor examined in these pages. The physician and the trade unionist who stand up to defend their codes, whom Walzer offers as contemporary examples of honor, are concerned to preserve their self-respect. They might also regulate their actions in order to meet additional sets of obligations. The physician may treat her patients compassionately out of a love of humanity or religious commitment, for example, or she may make her best effort because she feels bound by the contractual relations between them. But the idea of honor points to another motivation, based on the sense of obligation to oneself rather than to others or the whole. Similarly, the trade unionist might hold out for a better contract because he is moved by a sense of workers' solidarity, or because he wants to make the world a better place, or because he wants to maximize his individual interest. But when his honor is involved, he also holds out for the sake of his self-respect. It is honor that tells him that "he ought not to lower himself for some personal advantage," but also that "he ought not to sell himself short," and further that "he ought not to endure such-and-such an affront."[3] Walzer's notion of honor thus challenges the familiar dichotomy between interest and obligation according to which interests are what we do for ourselves and obligations are what we owe to others. It recognizes that what we do for ourselves ought not be limited to our interests and that what we do for others does not exhaust our obligations. Walzer sees the potential power of honor as a form of motivation that cannot be reduced to self-interest, or civic virtue, or the sense of justice, a motive that is grounded in a sense of personal obligation, but in an obligation to oneself rather than a duty to others. Honor engages our self-concern, making right action desirable, which makes honor forceful as a form of motivation, but in a way that goes beyond the narrowest forms of interest. And Walzer regards it as an important source of individual agency, even though it is not the only one.

Even the liberal-democratic forms of honor that Walzer describes cannot be distributed equally, however. It is not only the most dramatic instances of honor, exemplified by an Orte or a Lincoln or a Stanton, that are exceptional. The more prosaic and more particular forms of honor that arise within the private and semipublic spheres of civil society also represent exceptions to business as usual. Not every trade unionist rises to resist an exploitative corporate practice as a point of honor; not every physician battles on principle for quality of care against the for-profit heath care industry. Even these forms of honor, which one finds closer to home, cannot be distributed equally because honor as a quality of character must be asserted. As long as one's self-respect is tied to the worthiness of one's actions, honor will never be a matter of simple distribution.

Yet while the difficulty of distributing honor means that not every one will possess it, this difficulty also reinforces the potential power of honor as a source of agency. The power of honor would be radically reduced if it were, as Rawls's self-esteem and Taylor's recognition are conceived to be, goods that one receives from a benevolent authority or a well-intentioned "Other." One's honor does not depend exclusively on the beneficence of political authorities or rely on the kindness of Others. This independence makes it a particularly important resource for the forms of individual agency that issue in resistance to the abuse of powerful authorities, political or otherwise.

Still, so long as honor as a quality of character must be asserted, it never will be had by all, or never will be had equally by all. In this sense, even the more modest expressions of honor found among persons who may never seize the national stage retain something of the aristocratic character of honor's more celebrated exemplars. It is limited in practice to the few who make the effort to achieve it, even though it is open to anyone who does so. Similarly, public honors in the form of awards and prizes can inspire outstanding achievements only if they reward *only* outstanding achievements, rather than all achievements. Yet even though liberal-democratic honor is intrinsically aristocratic in this respect, it need not violate the political expression of the principle of equal dignity. The codes of conduct that regulate the voluntary associations in American civil society do not contest the equality of political rights, after all. We honor Martin Luther King, Jr., with a national holiday and we do so because of his great acts of honor, but if he were alive today he would not thereby be entitled to an extra vote or a political office. Thus the concept of honor need not challenge the ideal of equality as it applies to basic political liberties.

It is worth emphasizing that democratic honor need not be a continuous and societywide ideal in the usual sense. Whether democratic honor is tied to a singular common code or to more partial ones, individual acts of honor are bound to be episodic achievements rather than universally shared habits. The episodic character of honor further distinguishes it from civic virtue and the sense of justice, which as usually conceived govern (or should govern) the actions of most citizens on a continuous basis. By contrast, honor can have great effects on political society as a whole even if instances of it are relatively few and far between. Honorable actions can set precedents, which then may be sustained and even extended without the continuous or universal operation of honor. Honor also may admit of varying degrees of risk and impact. The motives of an honorable trade unionist or physician may resemble those of a King or a Lincoln—pride, principled ambition, the desire for self-respect, the sense of distinction, the quest for public esteem—without matching their intensity, or the universalism of their codes, or the scale of their achievements.

Moreover, codes of honor need not yield comprehensive or universal standards for action, even though there is a form of American honor, described in Chapters 4 and 5, that does take as its code the universal principles of the Declaration. The famous acts of honor considered in those chapters did rely on a common code composed of universal principles. But the more prosaic examples of honor that Walzer describes, which share in the formal features of honor as a quality of character (albeit at a more muted level), are relative to specific spheres of activity and to the various purposes of particular social and political institutions. Because most of us inhabit a variety of roles in a variety of settings today, each of us may be subject to multiple codes of honor. In this sense, honor is not only compatible with the moral complexity of modern pluralistic societies, but friendly to it. Today one lives by different codes in one's various roles as a parent, a friend, and a citizen, for example; and by still other codes as a professor, or a physician, or a carpenter. This plurality marks a difference between modern democratic forms of honor and honor in Montesquieu, but the difference is one of degree, not of kind. Although Montesquieu's *honnête homme* was not himself divided between different codes of honor, Montesquieu acknowledged that codes of honor in the modern world sometimes conflict with other morally binding standards of conduct, not least those of religion. And Montesquieu recognized that the content of codes of honor was variable both across cultures and within any given society. The greater measure of pluralism and fragmentation that characterizes contemporary democratic societies means that conflicts of honor may take place within the individual as well as between persons or across regimes. It also means that any single code of honor is unlikely to regulate one's life as a whole. To make moral sense of one's life as a whole, and to order all of one's various obligations into a single framework (if this is possible), one would need to look beyond honor. Honor is too limited and too plural to provide a comprehensive, unitary standard for moral and political life. And in the democratic context, no code of honor is universally binding, because each code regulates only those who assent to its creed or engage in the sphere of activity it governs.

So honor is limited in the sense of being episodic and relatively rare, rather than continuous and societywide, and also by not being comprehensive or universal. Honor is further limited in the sense that it cannot provide a complete account of political agency or of individual agency more generally. Honor cannot replace motivations such as self-interest, civic virtue, solidarity, faith, friendship, love, or any of the many other sources of human agency. It cannot replace them, but it can add to them. And the very limitedness of honor in this regard reminds us of the irreducible multiplicity of human motivations. We lose richness and depth, not to say accuracy, in our understanding of agency when we attempt a unification theory of motivations, reducing genuine diversity to an artificial unity.

Finally, honor is limited by the fact that it cannot justify its own codes. As we have seen, those with honor defend their principles on the basis of an allegiance to them rather than on the basis of a reasoned assessment. A reasoned assessment of codes of honor is possible but it is not what sets the person of honor in motion. The affective character of honor makes it active rather than contemplative, but it also makes honor incomplete in the sense that it is not self-justifying. Codes of honor may be ill conceived, after all; the honorable person may defend a set of principles that are irrational when viewed from the standpoint of impartial reason, or illegitimate when judged from the perspective of an independent moral or political standard. But every form of human motivation can go wrong. Self-interest, solidarity, virtue, faith, friendship, and the rest all may be ill used. Honor is no more or less risky in this respect than any other form of motivation. Like all our motivations, honor needs the direction of impartial reason. And liberal forms of honor in particular must be tied to liberal principles and combined with liberal political institutions. The political structure matters with respect to the substantive content of honor.

None of its limitations are reasons to reject honor, but the need to justify codes of honor undeniably raises a pressing difficulty for contemporary liberal democrats, perhaps more so than it did under the old regime. To have legitimacy, liberal-democratic forms of honor must be open to argument and revision, and so must be subject to more regular scrutiny than what Montesquieu envisioned. For this reason, the particular balance of reverence and reflexivity that sustained honor under the old regime requires a shift in the new regime. Honor in modern liberal democracy necessarily entails less reverence and more reflexivity, even though it continues to need both. The professional codes of honor that Walzer describes, for example, are open to review by the members of the associations that establish them, but they could not be effective in motivating action and directing ambition if they were not revered. The American Constitution, too, is subject to review and revision, even though much of its power to limit government and overreaching majorities rests on our reverence for it. The consequence of more scrutiny is that the reverence that supports democratic codes of honor is moderated, even diminished, when compared with Orte's veneration for his inherited code.

In the extreme, replacing affective reverence with rational scrutiny can undermine the power to motivate action, since it runs the risk of making citizens into philosophers, trading the life of action for that of contemplation. But liberal democracy would be impossible if citizens did not scrutinize political authorities and deliberate about matters of law and policy. Moreover, scrutiny of political authority is a cornerstone of honorable independence and a central component of the acts of civil disobedience and principled resistance that honor makes possible. And honorable reformers frequently challenge not only political authorities but also key features of the prevailing moral consensus, rather than blindly revering it, even if their claims and their sense of honor typically draw on other components of that consensus. The practice of rational scrutiny can also enhance the power of codes of honor to motivate action insofar as it reassures us of the legitimacy of our allegiances. An honorable American, for example, might defend the right to free speech on the grounds that the American Constitution establishes it. The principle of free speech, one might say, is a part of the American citizen's code of honor. She reveres the Constitution, and her allegiance to it can motivate risky undertakings on its behalf. Her allegiance may be enhanced if she is convinced that the principles it establishes, such as the right to free speech, are rationally justifiable: she loves it because it is *hers,* and she admires it because it is *right,* and her admiration may increase her love. This is what Montesquieu had in mind in the Preface to *The Spirit of the Laws,* when he said that he hoped that his philosophical inquiry would "give everyone new *reasons* for *loving* his duties, his prince, his homeland and his laws."[4] So the rational scrutiny of codes of honor may support honor as a quality of character, but there remains an irreducible tension between the reverence and the reflexivity intrinsic to honor, and the relentless reflexivity of modern democratic life can pose a threat to democratic forms of honor and, ultimately, to individual agency itself. Still, this inescapable tension is endemic to liberty, and the fact that there is a tension between reverence and reflexivity is no reason to conclude that we can do without either one.

While the conflicts between honor and liberal democracy are real, they do not make honor obsolete today. The politics of distinction and disobedience has a role to play in any polity that takes the limitation of power seriously. Contemporary liberalism needs a richer treatment of the motivations that drive political action. The current categories of self-interest and obligations to others are too limited to capture the full complexity of political agency. Honor offers an account of motivations that bridges the gap between self-interest and self-sacrifice, and that has both natural and historical connections to the defense of individual liberties. Honor is not exactly a virtue, but it does some of the work of virtue. It can, as Montesquieu said, inspire the finest actions, risky undertakings that yield great public benefits. Yet honor achieves the effects of virtue without oppressing the particular passions or individual ambition. Indeed, much of the power of honor lies in the fact that it is a mixed motive. As a duty to oneself, it builds on the particular attachments and private desires that make us who we are and move us to act. It channels and directs personal ambitions rather than suppressing them in the name of a comprehensive common good or a universal standpoint. It does not require the state to cultivate character or submerge diverse identities into a homogeneous collective one. And as a *grande ambition,* honor reminds us of the aristocratic capacities in ourselves that have survived the rise of modern man and liberal democracy's need for them.

Today we cannot help but feel that there is more to politics than self-interest, even that interest may be an insufficient spring for liberty, and yet we resist the rule of virtue. And while we see that the principle of autonomy abstracts from the particularities of human identity, we will not trade our choices for our encumbrances and we refuse to let our identities displace our principles as the constituting factor of American politics. All this is more or less as it should be in a liberal democracy. But while these tensions reflect real complexities, they also reveal the limited horizons of political agency as we currently conceive it. Moreover, even democratic authority can overreach itself, giving rise to the danger of majority tyranny. When this happens neither self-interest, nor civic virtue, nor the sense of justice, nor reason itself can always be relied upon to motivate principled opposition. And contemporary alternatives to honor, such as dignity, self-esteem, and recognition, lack its spiritedness and high ambitions. So if we resist some features of honor today because we are democrats, because we are liberal democrats we need some of them. A strong sense of agency is crucial to liberal government, and as long as political power is of an encroaching nature liberalism will have need of honor. Until the day when democracy is no longer vulnerable to overreaching majorities and the abuse of power, Americans occasionally will rely on the honor of the few who stand up to resist encroaching power, men and women willing to risk their necks to defend their liberties.

Notes

Bibliography

Index

NOTES

1. Liberal Inspirations

1. Declaration of Independence.
2. See Peter Berger, "On the Obsolescence of the Concept of Honor," in *Liberalism and Its Critics,* ed. Michael J. Sandel (New York: New York University Press, 1984), 149–158.
3. On the practice of running exceptional individuals out of town, see Aristotle's discussion of the use of ostracism in democracies, in his *Politics,* trans. Carnes Lord (Chicago: University of Chicago Press, 1984), 1284a17–34. For historical accounts of ostracism in Greek democracies, see H. D. F. Kitto, *The Greeks* (Baltimore: Penguin, 1966), 116; and *Aristotle and Xenophon on Democracy and Oligarchy,* trans. with commentary by J. M. Moore (Berkeley: University of California Press, 1975), esp. 241–244.
4. Aristotle, *Nicomachean Ethics,* trans. Hippocrates G. Apostle (Grinnell, Iowa: Peripatetic Press, 1984), 1095b15f.
5. See Charles Larmore, "The Right and the Good," in *The Morals of Modernity* (Cambridge: Cambridge University Press, 1996), 19–40.
6. While " 'the mean,' in the case of the thing itself, [represents] that which lies at equal intervals from the extremes, and this mean is just one thing and is the same for everyone; . . . when related to us, it neither exceeds nor falls short [of what is proper to us], and this is neither just one thing nor the same for everyone." Aristotle, *Nicomachean Ethics,* 1106a32–33. For example, "generosity depends not on the quantity of what is given but on the habit of the giver, and, in giving, this habit takes into account the extent of the substance available." *Nicomachean Ethics,* 1120b8–10.
7. If honor is more than virtue in some respects, one might say that it is less than virtue in others, precisely because honor, unlike virtue, does rely on general rules. Virtue requires no such guidance. Its very essence is self-command, and in this sense it looks more like autonomy than honor does.
8. There is a justice concern that underlies college honor codes, and the justification for such codes is in large part that they prevent unfairness to others. But the justification for the code need not be the same thing that moti-

vates adherence to it. Over and above the collective good of justice, the honor code promotes the individual goods of earned achievement and self-respect, which are crucial to motivating adherence.

9. Aristotle contrasts magnanimity, complete virtue toward oneself, with justice, which is complete virtue toward others. *Nicomachean Ethics,* 1129b27–1130a11. More generally, one might say that all virtue in Aristotle is self-regarding in the sense that it depends on a kind of self-love.

10. Michael J. Sandel, *Democracy's Discontent: America in Search of a Public Philosophy* (Cambridge: Harvard University Press, 1996), 1.

11. On the rise of Christian fundamentalism in the United States, see, for example, Mark A. Shibley, *Resurgent Evangelicalism in the United States* (Columbia: University of South Carolina Press, 1996); Martin A. Bradley et al., *Churches and Church Membership in the United States* (Atlanta: Glenmary Research Center, 1992); Wade Clark Roof and William McKinney, *American Mainline Religion: Its Changing Shape and Future* (New Brunswick, N.J.: Rutgers University Press, 1987); and Robert C. Liebman and Robert Wuthnow, eds., *The New Christian Right* (New York: Aldine, 1983).

12. Alexander Hamilton, James Madison, and John Jay, *The Federalist Papers,* ed. Clinton Rossiter (New York: Mentor, 1961), no. 48.

13. Montesquieu, *The Spirit of the Laws,* bk. XI, chap. 4, in *Oeuvres complètes de Montesquieu,* ed. Roger Caillois (Paris: Pléiade, 1949–1951), vol. II. Translations are my own.

14. *The Federalist,* no. 51.

15. *The Federalist,* no. 48.

16. The former group admits of diversity, too. In particular, disagreement exists among rational choice theorists as to whether or not all action is narrowly egoistic. See Jeffrey Friedman, ed., *The Rational Choice Controversy* (New Haven: Yale University Press, 1996). Those rational choice theorists who attempt to connect interest to higher and broader ends (and thereby to bridge the gap between self-interest and self-sacrifice) have something in common with my study of honor. Dennis Chong, for instance, argues from within a rational choice framework that reputational concerns tied to honor often underlie apparently public-spirited collective action. Chong, *Collective Action and the Civil Rights Movement* (Chicago: University of Chicago Press, 1991), 9. Andrew Sabl, though not a rational choice theorist, also takes a broader view of interest in his *Ruling Passions: Political Offices and Democratic Ethics* (Princeton: Princeton University Press, 2002). More generally, there are important points of convergence between honor and interest, not least of which is that both involve self-concern. Yet there are enough differences between them that it would be a mistake to treat honor simply as a species of interest. This point is developed in the following pages.

17. See, for example, Alasdair MacIntyre, *After Virtue* (Notre Dame, Ind.: University of Notre Dame Press, 1984); Amitai Etzioni, *The Spirit of Community: Rights, Responsibilities, and the Communitarian Agenda* (New York: Crown, 1993); Robert Bellah et al., *Habits of the Heart: Idealism and Commitment in American Public Life* (Berkeley: University of California Press, 1985); George F. Will, *Statecraft as Soulcraft* (New York: Simon and Schuster, 1983); and Michael J. Sandel, *Liberalism and the Limits of Justice* (Cambridge: Cambridge University Press, 1982).

18. Peter Digeser, *Our Politics, Our Selves?* (Princeton: Princeton University Press, 1995).

19. See, for example, Stephen Macedo, *Liberal Virtues: Citizenship, Virtue, and Community in Liberal Constitutionalism* (Oxford: Clarendon Press, 1991); William Galston, *Liberal Purposes: Goods, Virtues, and Diversity in the Liberal State* (Cambridge: Cambridge University Press, 1991); and Peter Berkowitz, *Virtue and the Making of Modern Liberalism* (Princeton: Princeton University Press, 1999).

20. John Rawls, *Political Liberalism* (New York: Columbia University Press, 1993), 19. See also 49–50, note 2: "justice as fairness relies on the kind of motivation Scanlon takes as basic."

21. See T. M. Scanlon, *What We Owe to Each Other* (Cambridge: Harvard University Press, 1998), 156. Brian Barry's liberal theory of justice also relies heavily on the agreement motive. See his *Justice as Impartiality* (New York: Oxford University Press, 1995).

22. For a discussion of the problems of exclusivity and reliability in the agreement motive, see Sharon Krause, "Partial Justice," *Political Theory,* 29, no. 3 (June 2001): 316–336.

23. Contemporary liberal theories of justice do not intend to rely on altruism. They intend to offer procedures that guarantee the motive to do what is right, insofar as the reason a moral proposition is right is held to be identical to the motive for upholding it. Theoretical aspirations aside, however, as a practical matter the agreement motive in its various forms, while it may be effective in many cases of "normal" politics where widespread agreement on the relevant matters does in fact exist, is neither particularly reliable in motivating adherence to the norms of justice in cases of deep disagreement nor effective in supporting adherence to unconventional moral truths. For further discussion of these issues, see Krause, "Partial Justice."

24. See Michael Walzer, *Obligations* (Cambridge: Harvard University Press, 1970), 200.

25. Some no doubt would dispute this characterization. David Garrow, for instance, maintains in his biography of Martin Luther King, Jr., that by idolizing those we honor we fail to see that we could do likewise ourselves. See

David J. Garrow, *Bearing the Cross* (New York: Quill, 1986), 625. For this reason, Garrow seeks to "demythologize" King by showing him to have been an "ordinary" and "average" man. Yet if Garrow's concern is a reasonable and respectable one, the idea that King was an average man and that we all could do likewise is as much a myth as any excessively idolizing portrait could be. It must be possible to be inspired by such persons without being cowed into inaction by excessive idolization of them.

26. Charles Taylor, "The Politics of Recognition," in *Multiculturalism*, ed. Amy Gutmann (Princeton: Princeton University Press, 1994), 27. See also Berger, "On the Obsolescence," 152–154. Berger does speculate, however, that "a rediscovery of honor in the future development of modern society is both empirically plausible and morally desirable."

27. There are, of course, notable exceptions to this rule, as the modern history of political exclusions of women, racial minorities, and the propertyless make clear.

28. Berger, "On the Obsolescence," 152.

29. Ibid.

30. Ibid., 156.

31. On this point see David F. Epstein, *The Political Theory of "The Federalist"* (Chicago: University of Chicago Press, 1984), 121.

32. *The Federalist,* no. 11.

33. Taylor, "The Politics of Recognition," 27.

34. Universal Declaration of Human Rights, (1948) U.N.G.A. Res. 217A (III), 3(1) U.N. GAOR Res. 71, U.N. Doc. A/810 (1948): "Whereas recognition of the inherent dignity and of the equal and inalienable rights of all members of the human family is the foundation of freedom, justice and peace in the world . . ."

35. Martin Luther King, Jr., "Letter from Birmingham City Jail," in *Testament of Hope: The Essential Writings and Speeches of Martin Luther King, Jr.,* ed. James M. Washington (New York: HarperCollins, 1986), 302.

36. The idea that there are aristocratic qualities or capacities in human nature that survive the break between the ancient and modern worlds, that "the old is deeply engraved on our souls and must be taken more seriously," is developed by Andreas A. M. Kinneging, in *Aristocracy, Antiquity, and History* (New Brunswick, N.J.: Transactions, 1997), xi and throughout.

37. Tocqueville, *Democracy in America,* II.4.4. All references to *Democracy in America* are from vol I. of *Oeuvres complètes d'Alexis de Tocqueville,* ed. J. P. Mayer, 13 vols. (Paris: Gallimard, 1951). Translations are my own. For more on liberal democracy's aristocratic inheritance, see David D. Bien, "Old Regime Origins of Democratic Liberty," in *The French Idea of Freedom: The Old Regime and the Declaration of the Rights of 1789,* ed. Dale Van Kley (Stanford: Stanford University Press, 1994).

38. Rawls, *Political Liberalism*, 318.
39. Ibid., 76f. and 318f.
40. John Rawls, *A Theory of Justice* (Cambridge: Harvard University Press, 1971), 440.
41. Ibid., 179.
42. Taylor, "The Politics of Recognition," 27.
43. Ibid., 64f.
44. See, for example, J. G. Peristiany, ed., *Honor and Shame* (Chicago: University of Chicago Press, 1966); Frank Henderson Stewart, *Honor* (Chicago: University of Chicago Press, 1994); and Lyman L. Johnson and Sonya Lipsett-Rivera, *The Faces of Honor: Sex, Shame, and Violence in Colonial Latin America* (Albuquerque: University of New Mexico Press, 1998).
45. Guy Chaussinand-Nogaret, *La nobles au XVIIIe siècle: De la féodalité aux lumières* (Paris: Librairie Hachette, 1976); Jean Meyer, *La noblesse française à l'époque moderne (XVIe–XVIIIe siècle)* (Paris: Presses Universitaires de France, 1991); Léopold Genicot, *La noblesse dans l'Occident médiéval* (London: Variorum Reprints, 1982); Jonathan Dewald, *The European Nobility, 1400–1800* (Cambridge: Cambridge University Press, 1996); M. L. Bush, *Noble Privilege* (Manchester: Manchester University Press, 1983); and Jean-Pierre Labatut, *Les noblesses européennes de la fin du XVe siècle à la fin du XVIIIe siècle* (Paris: Presses Universitaires de France, 1978).
46. See Bruce Miroff, *Icons of Democracy* (Lawrence: University Press of Kansas, 2000), 2.
47. Montesquieu, *The Spirit of the Laws,* Preface.
48. Although Montesquieu did not equate individual liberties with equal political rights, he did conceive of liberty in terms of the personal security of individuals. That is, he did not define liberty as civic participation or collective self-determination, or identify it with the perfection of the soul. Insofar as honor served to divide political power, and so limit it, honor defended individual liberties such as religious liberty, freedom of press, conscience, and private property, and protection from torture and cruel punishment, as well as a division between the public and the private spheres. (For references to liberty as security, see *The Spirit of the Laws*, XI.6, XII.5, XII.12, XII.23, XIII.7, and XIX.6.) In this respect, there is broad consensus among interpreters as to Montesquieu's liberal conception of liberty. See, for example, Norman Hampson, *Will and Circumstance: Montesquieu, Rousseau, and the French Revolution* (London: Duckworth, 1983), 10; Phillip Knee, "La question de l'appartenance: Montesquieu, Rousseau, et la Révolution française," *Canadian Journal of Political Science,* 22, no. 2 (June 1989): 303; and Franklin Ford, *Robe and Sword: The Regrouping of the French Aristocracy after Louis XIV* (Cambridge: Harvard University Press, 1953), 20. Keohane agrees that while Montesquieu "greatly admired the

extraordinary virtue and patriotism that made self-government possible, he did not greatly admire self-government *per se*," because "the exercise of political responsibility is not itself, for Montesquieu, a part of the good life," in Nannerl O. Keohane, *Philosophy and the State in France* (Princeton: Princeton University Press, 1980), 418. See also her "Virtuous Republics and Glorious Monarchies: Two Models in Montesquieu's Political Thought," *Political Studies*, 20, no. 4 (December 1972): 392. Honor serves the defense of individual liberties, even though, for Montesquieu, it does not serve the defense of individual liberties that are equal for all. This is one way in which contemporary liberal-democratic appropriations of honor differ from Montesquieu's concept of honor. The individual liberties that liberal-democratic forms of honor serve are available to all citizens on an equal basis. This issue is discussed below.

49. Tocqueville's interest in the exceptional qualities associated with honor occasionally has been noted but never fully elaborated. See Delba Winthrop, "Rights: A Point of Honor," in *Interpreting Tocqueville's "Democracy in America,"* ed. Ken Masugi (Lanham, Md.: Rowman & Littlefield, 1991); Paul O. Carrese, "Judicial Statesmanship, the Jurisprudence of Individualism, and Tocqueville's Common Law Spirit," *Review of Politics,* 60, no. 3 (Summer 1998): 465–496; Peter Augustine Lawler, *The Restless Mind* (Lanham, Md.: Rowman & Littlefield, 1993); James F. Pontuso, "Tocqueville on Courage," in *Tocqueville's Defense of Human Liberty,* ed. Peter Augustine Lawler and Joseph Alulis (New York: Garland, 1993); and James Ceaser, "Alexis de Tocqueville on Political Science, Political Culture, and the Role of the Intellectual," *American Political Science Review,* 79, no. 3 (September 1985): 656–672.

50. Jean-Claude Lamberti, *Tocqueville and the Two Democracies,* trans. Arthur Goldhammer (Cambridge: Harvard University Press, 1989), 8f.

51. Thus while Lamberti contends that Tocqueville is opposed to traditional feudal honor, he asserts that Tocqueville's work as a whole aims to infuse democracy with aristocratic values. Lamberti, *Tocqueville and the Two Democracies,* 56. On the same point, see Roger Boesche, *The Strange Liberalism of Alexis de Tocqueville* (Ithaca, N.Y.: Cornell University Press, 1987), 172; Joseph Alulis, "The Promise of Democracy and the Problem of Liberty," in *Tocqueville's Defense of Human Liberty,* ed. Lawler and Alulis, 55; and Pontuso, "Tocqueville on Courage," 97.

52. Tocqueville, *Democracy in America,* I.1.8, I.2.7.

53. Peter McNamara, "Alexander Hamilton," in *The Noblest Minds: Fame, Honor, and the American Founding,* ed. Peter McNamara (Lanham, Md.: Rowman & Littlefield, 1999), 157; C. Bradley Thompson, "John Adams and the Quest for Fame," in *The Noblest Minds,* ed. McNamara, 91; and

Paul Rahe, *Republics Ancient and Modern* (Chapel Hill: University of North Carolina Press, 1992), 566.

54. McNamara, "Alexander Hamilton," 151.

55. Or what Tocqueville referred to as "equality of conditions," meaning the absence of a fixed, hereditary hierarchy.

56. Richard H. King, *Civil Rights and the Idea of Freedom* (New York: Oxford University Press, 1992), 124.

2. Honor and the Defense of Liberty in the Old Regime

1. Andreas A. M. Kinneging, *Aristocracy, Antiquity, and History* (New Brunswick, N.J.: Transactions, 1997), esp. 319.

2. "[I]n a time of enlightenment, one trembles even when one does the greatest goods. One feels the old abuses, one sees their correction; but one sees also the abuses of the correction itself. One permits the ill if one fears something worse; one permits the good if one is in doubt about something better" (*The Spirit of the Laws*, Preface).

3. Michael A. Mosher, "The Particulars of a Universal Politics: Hegel's Adaptation of Montesquieu's Typology," *American Political Science Review,* 78, no. 1 (March 1984): 180; Corrado Rosso, *Montesquieu moraliste* (Bordeaux: Ducros, 1971), 100; and David Carrithers, "Montesquieu's Philosophy of History," *Journal of the History of Ideas,* 47, no. 1 (1986): 76.

4. Louis Althusser, *Politics and History: Montesquieu, Rousseau, Marx,* trans. Ben Brewster (London: Verso, 1982), 80; Mark Hulliung, *Montesquieu and the Old Regime* (Berkeley: University of California Press, 1976), 179; Lawrence M. Levin, *The Political Doctrine of Montesquieu's Esprit des Lois: Its Classical Background* (New York: Columbia University Press, 1936), 104.

5. Ford, *Robe and Sword,* 20.

6. Rosso, *Montesquieu moraliste,* 100.

7. Levin, *The Political Doctrine,* 103f. On the difficulty of determining whether or not Montesquieu approves of honor, see also Paul Vernière, *Montesquieu et L'esprit de lois ou la raison impure* (Paris: Société d'Édition d'Enseignement Supérieur, 1977), 68.

8. Anne M. Cohler, *Montesquieu's Comparative Politics and the Spirit of American Constitutionalism* (Lawrence: University Press of Kansas, 1988), 91.

9. Hulliung, *Montesquieu and the Old Regime,* 30.

10. Honor is mentioned by nearly everyone who has written on Montesquieu, but for the most part briefly and in passing. An exception is Michael Mosher, who treats Montesquieu's concept of honor as interesting in its own right, in "The Judgmental Gaze of European Women: Gender, Sexuality, and the Critique of Republican Rule," *Political Theory,* 22, no. 1 (Feb-

ruary 1994), esp. 38–40, and in his "Monarchy's Paradox: Honor in the Face of Sovereign Power," chapter 4 in *Montesquieu's Science of Politics,* ed. David W. Carrithers, Michael Mosher, and Paul A. Rahe (Lanham, Md.: Rowman & Littlefield, 2001).

11. The term "agency" is not Montesquieu's own, but it captures the sense of the human capacity to act rather than merely to react to external forces, a capacity that Montesquieu regarded as foundational for liberty and as the admirable antithesis to despotism. Even as he elaborates the complex conditions (social, cultural, economic, geographic, and so on) that constrain human action, Montesquieu insists that "man . . . must direct himself *(il faut qu'il se conduise)*" (*The Spirit of the Laws,* I.1). He rejects the efforts of some of his predecessors and contemporaries to explain human action in terms of the laws of causality that govern the material world: "A great genius [Spinoza] has promised me that I will die like an insect. He is looking to flatter me with the idea that I am only a modification of matter. He employs a geometrical order and some reasons that are said to be very strong, and that I have found very obscure, to elevate my soul *(l'âme)* to the dignity of my body, and, in place of the immense space that my spirit *(l'esprit)* embraces, he gives me to my material body alone and to a space of four or five feet in the universe." Montesquieu refers to this effort to subsume human behavior under a mechanistic-materialist framework an attempt "to destroy liberty in me" *(détruire en moi la liberté).* (Montesquieu, *Mes pensées,* in *Oeuvres complètes,* ed. Roger Caillois [Paris: Gallimard, 1949–51], vol. I, no. 615[1266], 1138.) Human actions cannot be explained on the basis of the same causal relations that determine the flights of "insects," because human beings, Montesquieu says, possess *l'âme* and *l'esprit.* It is because of *l'âme* and *l'esprit* that "the intelligent world . . . unlike the physical world, . . . does not follow its laws constantly." Although "particular intelligent beings are limited by their nature and are consequently subject to error" (*The Spirit of the Laws,* I.1), the indeterminacy of human behavior does not result from errors alone. For even if human beings were perfectly rational, their actions would not be perfectly predictable, since "it is in their nature to act by themselves" (I.1). Because we have the capacity for what today is called agency, human action is underdetermined.

The use of contemporary terms such as "agency" to explicate texts from earlier periods can run the risk of overlaying and thus distorting the text's own meaning with our contemporary associations and prejudices. Therefore the employment of such terms must be done with care. Yet their use, if accurate and careful, can illuminate texts in important ways. Here the term agency is useful because it provides a focus for examining issues of moral psychology, motivation, and action. The book presupposes that some features of human agency are consistent across time and culture, and that for this reason it is possible to learn about human agency from philosophers who lived long ago, such as Montesquieu. Where other contemporary terms are used as tools in the analysis of older texts, as for example with the terms "reflexivity" and "recognition," care is taken to explain the ideas these terms comprehend in the language of the original texts themselves. The use of terms such as "agency," "reflexivity," and "recognition" to clarify texts written in earlier eras has well-respected precedents, such as (among others) Charles Taylor, *Sources of the Self* (Cambridge: Harvard University Press, 1989); Alexander Nehemas, *Nietzsche: Life as Literature* (Cambridge: Harvard University Press, 1985); and Seyla Benhabib, *Critique, Norm, and Utopia* (New York: Columbia University Press, 1986).

12. Montesquieu, *The Spirit of the Laws*, III.1. Montesquieu actually enumerates four types of government, insofar as he notes that a republic can be either democratic or aristocratic (II.4). Although he distinguishes the two, he gives pride of place to the democratic form of republicanism, saying that "the more an aristocracy approaches democracy, the more perfect it will be" (II.3). Throughout the analysis, democratic republicanism is treated as the exemplary form, and self-renouncing democratic viture, rather than aristocratic "moderation," is treated as the defining principle of republicanism in general (as, for example, in V.2). Hereafter references to *The Spirit of the Laws* will be inserted parenthetically into the text with roman numerals indicating book and arabic numerals indicating chapter.

13. Althusser, *Montesquieu, Rousseau, Marx*, 46.

14. Andrew J. Lynch, "Montesquieu and the Ecclesiastical Critics of *L'esprit des lois*," *Journal of the History of Ideas*, 38, no. 3 (July–September 1977): 490.

15. Montesquieu wrote with both religious and political censors in mind. In his *Pensées*, he complains about "the censors whom princes have established, who direct all pens" (no. 1456[1525], 1342). Indeed, he says, "since the discovery of the printing press, there is no longer any true history. The princes used not to be attentive, and the police did not concern themselves about [books]. Today, all books are submitted to the inquisition of this police, which has established rules of discretion. To violate them is an offense. One has learned from this that princes are offended by what one says about them. In other times, they did not concern themselves with it; one then spoke the truth" (*Mes pensées*, no. 1455[1462], 1342). He had good reason to worry about offending the king and the Church, as much because he wanted his book to be read as out of fear for his safety. Still, safety was a concern. There is evidence that friends advised him not to publish *The Spirit of the Laws*, fearing repercussions (George Saintsbury,

French Literature and Its Masters [New York: Alfred A. Knopf, 1946], 88). When he did publish it in 1748, Voltaire already had been incarcerated, and Diderot would be imprisoned the following year at Vincennes (see Solange Fricaud, "Pour qui est écrit *L'esprit des lois?"* in Joel Askenazi et al., *Analyses et réflexions sur Montesquieu* [Paris: Edition Marketing, 1987], 181). Montesquieu took the precautions of publishing his book anonymously, and in Geneva rather than France, but even so, he was reprimanded by the Sorbonne for his "disparagement" of the crown, and the book was placed on the *Index* of works proscribed by the Church (Kingsley Martin, *French Liberal Thought in the Eighteenth Century* [London: Turnstile Press, 1954], 167). Today we tend to expect and reward transparency in writing, and are suspicious of anything else, but Montesquieu did not expect to be so rewarded, and he wrote accordingly.

16. Rosso, for example, concludes that "Montesquieu's distinction between political and moral virtue never has convinced anyone." Rosso, *Montesquieu moraliste,* 119. On the same point, see Pierre Manent, *The City of Man,* trans. Marc A. LePain (Princeton: Princeton University Press, 1998), esp. 21–28; and Harvey C. Mansfield, Jr., *Taming the Prince* (Baltimore: Johns Hopkins University Press, 1993), 225ff.

17. Mansfield, *Taming the Prince,* 224–225.

18. For an account of how Montesquieu's republican virtue differs from political virtue in Aristotle, see Thomas Pangle, *Montesquieu's Philosophy of Liberalism: A Commentary on "The Spirit of the Laws"* (Chicago: University of Chicago Press, 1973), esp. 56–65.

19. Ostensibly, Montesquieu is speaking of Muslims in this passage, but he means it to apply to Christians as well, for he makes the same point explicitly about Christians in XXIV.19, saying that the "Christian religion . . . makes us hope for a state that we believe in, not a state that we feel or that we know; everything, including the resurrection of the body, leads us to spiritual ideas." The following chapter, XXIV.20, which he calls a "continuation of the same subject," returns again to the Persians. With respect to turning one's back on this world for the sake of the next, Montesquieu clearly regards Islam and Christianity as interchangeable.

20. Montesquieu, *Mes pensées,* no. 1905(51), 1458.

21. The pluralism that Montesquieu defended was more modest than the one that predominates in the United States today, but it is significant nonetheless. For further discussion of how Montesquieu's moderate monarchy sustained an "internally differentiated society, which tended by its very differentiation to block claims to cultural hegemony," see Mosher, "The Judgmental Gaze," esp. 39.

22. Along similar lines, Mansfield points out that virtue that is merely politi-

cal, or politically instrumental, cannot say what is the end of virtue—"to promote the self, or mortify it?" Mansfield, *Taming the Prince,* 226.

23. Ibid., 224–225.

24. In this, Montesquieu foreshadows Rousseau's concept of the "general will," although he does not share Rousseau's unbridled enthusiasm for it. A number of commentators have recognized the seed of the "general will" in Montesquieu's account of republican virtue. See, for example, Judith Shklar, "General Will" in *Dictionary of the History of Ideas,* ed. Philip P. Wiener (New York: Scribner, 1973–74), II, 275; and Pangle, *Montesquieu's Philosophy of Liberalism,* 57.

25. This is not to say that early liberalism regarded the worldly, particular concerns of the body, especially the interest in self-preservation, as the only or the highest ends of the human being, but rather that early liberalism regarded the worldly, particular concerns of the body as the only legitimate ends of politics. For a nuanced account of the ends of politics in Locke, one that presents a somewhat different view, see Peter C. Myers, *Our Only Star and Compass: Locke and the Struggle for Political Rationality* (Lanham, Md.: Rowman & Littlefield, 1998).

26. Manent, *The City of Man,* 27, and see 28–36.

27. For a discussion of how this passage anticipates Nietzsche's idea of "slave morality," see Richard Myers, "Christianity and Politics in Montesquieu's *Greatness and Decline of the Romans,*" *Interpretation,* 17, no. 2 (Winter 1989–90): 223–238.

28. See Ford, *Robe and Sword,* 7. For an account of how the nobility stood between the king and the populace, see Gabriel Loirette, "Montesquieu et le problème, en France, du bon gouvernement," in *Actes du congrès Montesquieu réuni à Bordeaux du 23 au 26 mai 1955 pour comémorer la deuxième centenair de la mort de Montesquieu* (Bordeaux: Impriméries Delmas, 1956), 219–239.

29. Although Montesquieu includes the clergy among the intermediary bodies, he does not emphasize its role here. He regards religion as a crucial check on sovereign power: "One will abandon one's father, one will even kill him, if the prince orders it, but one will not drink wine if the prince wants it and orders it. The laws of religion are of a superior precept, because they are given to the prince as to the subjects" (*The Spirit of the Laws,* III.10). He also criticizes "a great state in Europe" (England) for "constantly striking down" the "ecclesiastical jurisdiction" as well as that of the nobility (*The Spirit of the Laws,* II.4). Yet here he emphasizes the role of the nobility, and keeps quiet about the role of the clergy. Perhaps he believes that the ecclesiastical jurisdiction is less in need of support in France than that of the nobility. It is also true that there were tensions between the

clergy and the nobility. A common cause of remonstrance in the French *parlements* of the late seventeenth and early eighteenth centuries was concern over intrusions into secular political authority by the "Court of Rome." See Emmanuel Michel, *Biographie du parlement de Metz* (Metz: Nouvian, 1853). For further discussion of the causes of remonstrance in the *parlements,* see William Doyle, *The Parlement of Bordeaux and the End of the Old Regime, 1771–1790* (New York: St. Martin's Press, 1974); Rebecca Kingston, *Montesquieu and the Parlement of Bordeaux* (Geneva: Librairie Droz, 1996); Ford, *Robe and Sword,* esp. 87–89; and Pierre Barrière, *Un grand provincial: Charles-Louis de Secondat, baron de La Brède et de Montesquieu* (Bordeaux: Delmas, 1946), 119–130. Another explanation for why Montesquieu emphasizes the role of the nobility and not that of the clergy is that he does not want to establish the divine authority that stands behind the clergy as a part of the constitution of monarchy.

30. For further discussion of the privileges, prerogatives, and duties of the French nobility up to the eighteenth century, see, for example, Chaussinand-Nogaret, *La noblesse au XVIIIe siècle;* Meyer, *La noblesse française;* Léopold Genicot, *La noblesse dans l'Occident médiéval;* Dewald, *The European Nobility;* Bien, "Old Regime Origins of Democratic Liberty"; Bush, *Noble Privilege;* Labatut, *Les noblesses européennes;* and Kinneging, *Aristocracy, Antiquity, and History,* esp. 50–55.

31. There was a sizable literature in the early eighteenth century on the constitutional standing of the French nobility and the status of their legislative and judicial rights. Books XXVIII and XXX–XXXI of *The Spirit of the Laws* contain Montesquieu's contribution to these debates. For further discussion, see Keith Michael Baker, *The Old Regime and The French Revolution* (Chicago: University of Chicago Press, 1987); Iris Cox, *Montesquieu and the History of French Laws* (Oxford: Voltaire Foundation, 1983); Martin, *French Liberal Thought;* and Ford, *Robe and Sword.*

32. Ford, *Robe and Sword,* 80. And note *The Spirit of the Laws,* V.10: "The bodies that are the depository of the laws never obey better than when they act slowly and bring into the affairs of the prince the reflectiveness that one can scarcely expect given the lack of enlightenment in the court about the laws of the state and the haste of the prince's councillors . . . What would have become of the finest monarchy in the world if the magistrates, by their slowness, their complaints, by their prayers, had not checked the course of even the virtues of its kings."

33. Ford, *Robe and Sword,* 80.

34. For an extensive treatment of the two classes of nobility and Montesquieu's treatment of them, see Ford, *Robe and Sword;* and Baker, *The Old Regime.*

35. Montesquieu himself was a member of the latter class, and held the office of *président* of the *parlement* of Bordeaux from 1716 to 1726.

36. As a class, the nobility had its origins in the tripartite medieval order in which the clergy would pray for the realm, the third estate would produce for the realm, and the nobility would protect the realm. Kinneging, *Aristocracy, Antiquity, and History*, 44; and see Dewald, *The European Nobility*, 15.

37. Kinneging, *Aristocracy, Antiquity, and History*, 41; Dewald, *The European Nobility*, 35; Labatut, *Les noblesses européennes*, 108.

38. Labatut, *Les noblesses européennes*, 108f.

39. Ford, *Robe and Sword*, 222.

40. Labatut, *Les noblesses européennes*, 15f.; Dewald, *The European Nobility*, 36.

41. Meyer, *La noblesse française*, 22; Dewald, *The European Nobility*, 15f., 143f.

42. Marc Bloch, *Feudal Society*, trans. L. A. Manyon (Chicago: University of Chicago Press, 1961), II, 286.

43. Ibid., II, 293.

44. Robert A. Nye, *Masculinity and Male Codes of Honor in Modern France* (New York: Oxford University Press, 1993), 16; Stewart, *Honor*, 35.

45. Stewart, *Honor*, 35, 39, 41, 46; Nye, *Masculinity and Male Codes*, 16.

46. See Dewald, *The European Nobility*, 109.

47. Ibid.

48. Ibid., 39f.; Kinneging, *Aristocracy, Antiquity, and History*, 77.

49. Dewald, *The European Nobility*, 40.

50. Ibid., 151, 153.

51. Kinneging, *Aristocracy, Antiquity, and History*, 69, 57.

52. Ibid., 85.

53. Bloch, *Feudal Society*, II, 318.

54. Montesquieu, *Mes pensées*, no. 1905(51), 1458.

55. Ibid., no. 549(30), 1060.

56. See, for example, Condorcet, in Destutt de Tracy, *Commentary and Review of Montesquieu's "The Spirit of the Laws,"* trans. Thomas Jefferson (New York: Burt Franklin, 1969), 286f.; and G. W. F. Hegel, *Philosophy of Right*, trans. T. M. Knox (Oxford: Oxford University Press, 1967), 178.

57. For example, Judith Shklar thinks that Montesquieu simply "deplores" honor. See Judith Shklar, *Ordinary Vices* (Cambridge: Harvard University Press, 1984), 219. Similarly, Hulliung argues that for Montesquieu honor "withers before virtue" in *Montesquieu and the Old Regime*, 29.

58. The viscount of Orte was Adrien d'Aspremont, vicomte d'Orthe, gouverneur de Bayonne.

59. For a discussion of the aesthetic dimension of honor, see Edwin Dargan,

The Aesthetic Doctrine of Montesquieu (Baltimore: J. H. Furst Co., 1907). For an interesting treatment of the "theatricality" of honor in Montesquieu, see E. J. Hundert and Paul Nelles, "Liberty and Theatrical Space in Montesquieu's Political Theory: The Poetics of Public Life in '*The Persian Letters*,' " *Political Theory*, 17, no. 2 (May 1989): 223–246.

60. This points to a potential danger of honor, which is that those who seek it may be tempted to engage in unnecessary battles, or even to "save" unwitting beneficiaries who might otherwise have acted more prosaically for themselves. There is a kind of moral aggrandizement that parallels military glory, which may tempt undesirable and immoderate forms of action. In the democratic context, this temptation may pose an even greater danger than the ambition for power, which honor also may excite. This consideration is closely connected to Hobbes's and Locke's reservations about honor mentioned in Chapter 1.

61. Although it may be either good or just, or both. The point is that honor is not simply a subset of either "the good" or "the just." It is also worth noting that Montesquieu's effort to distinguish honor from justice is not meant to suggest that justice is irrelevant to monarchical government. Indeed, Montesquieu argues that the administration of justice in a monarchy must be scrupulous (VI.1). But honor cannot be reduced to a form of justice.

62. See, for example, Rawls, *A Theory of Justice*, especially 178f., 440ff. and 544ff.; and Michael Walzer, *Spheres of Justice* (New York: Basic Books, 1983), chap. 11.

63. People such as Orte may be few in number. Montesquieu is somewhat ambiguous about exactly what portion of the population is motivated by honor in monarchy. On the one hand, he says that honor "reigns, like a monarch, over the prince and the people," (III.10) and that honor "makes all the parts of the body politic move" (III.7). On the other hand, he draws attention to "the wretched character of courtiers" (III.5), which contrasts strongly with the great and generous courage of Orte, and in discussing punishments in monarchy, he remarks that it is in "the spirit of monarchy" that "the noble loses his honor and his power to speak at court while the villein, who has no honor, is punished in his body" (VI.10). One way to reconcile these apparently conflicting stands is to recall the distinction between public honors as awards or marks of public recognition, and honor as an individual quality of character. A societywide system of public recognition that distinguishes between different categories of persons on the basis of their status, and that requires everyone to participate in the system in the sense of recognizing and *honoring* these distinctions, could be said to "reign over the prince and the people"—even if individual acts of honor

such as Orte's are few and far between. For surely Montesquieu's description of Orte, while it is intended to illustrate the essence of honor as a quality of character, is not meant to depict a universal characteristic of monarchical subjects. Honorable actions, Montesquieu says, are "extraordinary" (IV.2).

64. "Human life, placed on the earth, is surrounded by automatic processes— by the natural processes of the earth, which, in turn, are surrounded by cosmic processes, and we ourselves are driven by similar forces insofar as we too are a part of organic nature. Our political life, moreover, . . . also takes place in the midst of processes which we call historical and which tend to become as automatic as natural or cosmic processes, although they were started by men." Hannah Arendt, *The Human Condition* (Chicago: University of Chicago Press, 1958), 168f.

65. Ibid.

66. Montesquieu distinguishes *honor* (the quality of character) from *honors* (public distinctions) in *The Spirit of the Laws,* VIII.7. Thus Meyer emphasizes that honor in the old regime had an active dimension in view of its being a quality of character as well as the passive one of public esteem (Meyer, *La noblesse française,* 22). Peristiany also notes that one who never risked anything could not be said to have honor, on the old regime definition of it, precisely because honor as a quality of character could not be gained through passive obedience to social regulations or from mere heredity. Even when honorable status was inherited with the family name, it had to be asserted to be vindicated. See Peristiany, "Introduction," in *Honor and Shame,* 10–11.

67. It is true that the acts of resistance that Montesquieu associates with honor are not revolutionary. Indeed, one might say that the resistance prompted by honor on Montesquieu's account is better characterized as forms of *inaction* than as activism. Thus Montesquieu says that "if honor has been offended it requires or permits one to retire to one's home" (IV.2). Yet some forms of political inaction can be powerfully activist in effect. Montesquieu capitalizes on this fact, which allows him to defend forms of (in)action that have the effect of checking the overbearing power of the monarch without appearing to attack him. An example is his assertion that the *parlements* "never obey better than when they go slowly and bring into the affairs of the prince the reflectiveness that one can scarcely expect given the lack of enlightenment in the court . . ." (V.10). The *parlements* never obey better than when they resist. And one way they resist is by doing "nothing."

68. Tocqueville, *Democracy in America,* II.3.19.

69. Honor presupposes an institutional division of power, even as it supports

such a division. The destruction of the intermediary bodies devastates honor because it puts all power into the hands of the sovereign and makes everyone dependent upon him. In the absence of independent sites of authority, the nobles direct their ambitions to social climbing within the court rather than to the defense of their social codes and constitutional prerogatives. Under these conditions, honor turns from the prideful defense of principle to unprincipled self-promotion. Montesquieu's scornful description of the vanities of courtiers in *The Spirit of the Laws*, III.5, should be understood as a criticism of the tendency of the French monarch to undermine the powers of the intermediary bodies rather than as a criticism of the concept of honor itself. These considerations also emphasize that while honor is necessary for the defense of liberty in monarchy, it is not sufficient for liberty. Montesquieu's definition of monarchy combines an account of the institutional structure that "makes it what it is," together with the "human passion" that "makes it move" (III.1). Neither the nature of monarchical government nor its principle on its own can sustain monarchy. Without honor, the formal division of power (especially the limits on the power of the king) fails; without a formal division of power, the rule of fixed and fundamental laws, and an independent base of authority for the nobility in particular, honor deteriorates into the petty vanities of the courtly air. Both the nature and the principle of monarchy are necessary to sustain liberty; neither one is sufficient on its own.

70. Thus Pitt-Rivers points out that the old-regime belief that one's honor was "sacred" demonstrates that the commitments involved were more than conditional. Julian Pitt-Rivers, "Honor and Social Status," in Peristiany, *Honor and Shame*, 34.

71. For treatments of Montesquieu's debt to, and departures from, Machiavelli, see Robert Shackleton, "Montesquieu and Machiavelli: A Reappraisal," *Comparative Literature Studies*, 1, no. 1 (1964): 1–13; Marc Duconseil, *Machiavel et Montesquieu: Recherche sur un principle* d'autorité (Paris: Les Éditions Denoël, 1943); Maurice Joly, *Dialogue aux enfers entre Machiavel et Montesquieu, ou, La politique de Machiavel au XIXe siècle* (Brussells: Imprimerie de A. Mertens et Fils, 1864); and A. Bertière, "Montesquieu, lecteur de Machiavel," *Actes du congrès*, 141–158.

72. Niccolò Machiavelli, *Discourses on Livy*, trans. Harvey C. Mansfield and Nathan Tarcov (Chicago: University of Chicago Press, 1996), I.4.

73. Kinneging, *Aristocracy, Antiquity, and History*, 152.

74. Rosso, *Montesquieu moraliste*, 100. For evidence of Montesquieu's disapproval of Machiavelli, see *Mes pensées*, no. 1573(207), 1380, in which after calling the Spanish conquistadors "les Machiavélistes" for their treatment of Indians, he remarks, "But the crime loses nothing of its blackhearted-

ness by the utility that one draws out from it. It is true that one always judges actions by their success; but this judgment of men is itself a deplorable abuse in morality." Similarly, in *The Spirit of the Laws,* XXI.20, he says that the rise of commerce has established alternative sites of wealth and power from which the authority of kings can be contested, and consequently, "one has begun to be cured of Machiavellianism, and one will continue to be cured of it. There must be more moderation in councils."

75. Rosso, *Montesquieu moraliste,* 101.

76. Machiavelli, *The Prince,* trans. Harvey C. Mansfield, Jr. (Chicago: University of Chicago Press, 1985), chap. VII.

77. Similarly, Montesquieu conceives the "interference" of the *parlements* as aimed to limit the king's power, not to establish a monopoly on political power for the nobility.

78. Mosher makes this point in "Monarchy's Paradox," 205f. He also emphasizes there that this is a tenuous balance, and he presses the important point that honor's disobedience, however civil, is never immune from becoming anarchical.

79. It is true that Machiavelli's princely types are limited by their own necessities and by their knowledge of these necessities. Still, such limits no doubt were small comfort to Remirro d'Orco.

80. Machiavelli, *Prince,* chap. VI.

81. Magnanimity is "greatness in every virtue." Aristotle, *Nicomachean Ethics,* 1124a. Justice is defined at 1129b.

82. Ibid., 1123b.

83. Ibid., 1124b, 1123b–1124a.

84. Ibid., 1124a.

85. Ibid., 1123b.

86. Ibid., 1124a. Aristide Tessitore agrees that while Aristotelian magnanimity is related to honor, it should be distinguished from honor, saying that "greatness, not honor, is the measure of the magnanimous person . . . [for] although magnanimous persons also exhibit the proper attitude toward honors, this proves to be the result of their primary attachment to nobility and goodness." See his *Reading Aristotle's Ethics* (Albany: SUNY Press, 1996), esp. 28–35.

87. Aristotle, *Nicomachean Ethics,* 1106b.

88. Kinneging emphasizes that Montesquieu calls honor "false" on the grounds that it does not aim at the common good. Kinneging, *Aristocracy, Antiquity, and History,* 288.

89. Pitt-Rivers, "Honor and Social Status," 36. See also Kinneging, who calls the distinction "idiosyncratic." Kinneging, *Aristocracy, Antiquity, and History,* 20.

90. As Peter Berkowitz emphasizes in *Virtue and the Making of Modern Liberalism*, 8f.

91. Emphasis added.

92. Kinneging, *Aristocracy, Antiquity, and History*, 149. Kinneging's remark here refers less to Montesquieu himself than to other old-regime thinkers and to the Romans, whom they so admired. Both groups wavered on whether or not honor made men act virtuously and ultimately concluded that honor and virtue were linked but not identical (150). Kinneging contrasts this position to that of Montesquieu, who in his view established a more complete break between honor and virtue than either his predecessors or his contemporaries had done, believing that honor without virtue need not be harmful and even could be salutary (150).

93. Aristotle, *Nicomachean Ethics*, 1124a.

94. Ibid., 1123b.

95. The political order should be commensurate with the natural order, even if it is not always so in practice. In the best regime, which is the final standard for all regimes (*Nicomachean Ethics*, 1135a5–6), the good man and the good citizen are the same (*Politics*, 1288a137–38). Similarly, it is conceivable that the content of magnanimity could vary somewhat from one society to another, but only as instances of imperfection. Ultimately, the standard of magnanimity, like the standard of every virtue, is given by the nature of the absolutely best man. Variations that depart from that standard may be good, but they are not the best, according to Aristotle.

96. On this point, see Michael Zuckert, "Natural Law, Natural Rights, and Classical Liberalism: On Montesquieu's Critique of Hobbes," *Social Philosophy and Policy*, 18, no. 1 (2001): 247.

97. See *Mes pensées*, no. 2063(1154), 1537: "[W]hen one says that there is not at all an absolute quality, that does not mean that there is nothing at all but that . . . our spirit cannot determine them."

98. That Montesquieu resisted the idea of a single, universal standard of right derived directly from nature is the most widely accepted interpretation of his view, and the one most supported by the evidence that his words provide. See, for example, Robert Shackleton, *Montesquieu: A Critical Biography* (London: Oxford University Press, 1961), 250ff.; Georges Benrekassa, *Montesquieu: La liberté et l'histoire* (Paris: Librairie Générale Française, 1987), 175; Cohler, *Montesquieu's Comparative Politics*, 48; Jean Ehrard, "Presentation" in *Politique de Montesquieu* (Paris: Armand Colin, 1965), 10f.; Simone Goyard-Fabre, *La philosophie du droit de Montesquieu* (Paris: Librairie C. Klincksieck, 1973), 54; Robert Alun Jones, "Ambivalent Cartesians: Durkheim, Montesquieu and Method," *American Journal of Sociology*, 100, no. 1 (July 1994): 13, 29f.; Emile Durkheim, *Montesquieu and Rousseau: Forerunners of Sociology*, trans. Ralph Manheim (Ann Arbor:

University of Michigan Press, 1966); Knee, "La question de l'appartenance"; and Mosher, "The Particulars of a Universal Politics." A notable
exception to this interpretation is Mark Waddicor, who characterizes Montesquieu as a natural law theorist in *Montesquieu and the Philosophy of Natural Law* (The Hague: Martinus Nijhoff, 1970).

99. Montesquieu criticized ancient philosophy for not seeing that "[t]he terms
beautiful, good, noble, great, perfect are attributes of objects which are
relative to the beings who consider them" (*Mes pensées,* no. 2062[410],
1537).

100. It is questionable how far Aristotle himself regarded standards of conduct
in politics as "dictates of nature." His ambiguous discussion of justice in
Nicomachean Ethics, Book V, for example, suggests that the meaning of jus-
tice is not simply given by nature, but that human judgment and choice
contribute as well. On the ambiguity of justice in Aristotle, see Martha
Nussbaum, *Aristotle's De Motu Animalium* (Princeton: Princeton University
Press, 1985); Bernard Yack, "Natural Right and Aristotle's Understanding
of Justice," in *Political Theory,* 18, no. 2 (May 1990): 216–237; and Delba
Winthrop, "Aristotle and Theories of Justice," *American Political Science
Review,* 72 (1978): 1208. For present purposes, it is enough to say that
Montesquieu's criticism of ancient philosophy suggests that he interpreted
Aristotle as believing that political standards are simply given, but he may
have misconstrued Aristotle.

101. In this regard, Levin contrasts honor in Montesquieu to honor in Plato,
saying that while Plato's honorable man is obedient, honor in Montesquieu
rests on disobedience. Levin, *The Political Doctrine,* 104.

102. See also *The Spirit of the Laws,* III.10: Honor resembles "natural feelings,"
such as "respect for a father, tenderness for one's children and women, . . .
or the state of one's health."

103. Rosso, *Montesquieu moraliste,* 102.

104. Althusser, *Montesquieu, Rousseau, Marx,* 62.

105. On the relation between honor's eccentricity and its independence, see
Mosher, "Monarchy's Paradox," 205f., 211–217.

106. See Charles Taylor's discussion of the way in which "radical choice . . .
fades into non-choice" in "What is Human Agency?" in *Human Agency and
Language* (Cambridge: Cambridge University Press, 1985), esp. 28–35.

107. And never a "view from nowhere," as in Thomas Nagel, *The View from Nowhere* (Oxford: Oxford University Press, 1986).

108. Mosher, "Judgmental Gaze," 39.

109. Reflecting on honor in general, Stewart remarks that the "sense" of honor
is an "attachment" to certain standards of conduct, which is distinct from
an "understanding" of such standards. Stewart, *Honor,* 47.

110. What he found was mixed. On the one hand, history showed that some os-

tensibly irrational practices, such as proof by single combat, had "a certain reason founded in experience." On the other hand, he said, "One will be astonished to see that our fathers . . . made the honor, fortune, and life of citizens depend on things that were less under the jurisdiction of reason than that of chance" (*The Spirit of the Laws,* XXVIII.17).

111. Aristotle, *Politics,* 1327b41.

112. Ibid., 1328a6–7.

113. R. Richelet, ed., *Dictionnaire François* (Geneva: Jean Herman Widerhold, 1680), 350; and see *The Spirit of the Laws,* trans. Anne M. Cohler, Basia Carolyn Miller, and Harold Samuel Stone (Cambridge: Cambridge University Press, 1989), 41, translators' note j.

114. For an elaboration of Montesquieu's view of Christian virtue as despotic, see Cohler, *Montesquieu's Comparative Politics,* 35–44; Diana J. Schaub, *Erotic Liberalism: Women and Revolution in Montesquieu's "Persian Letters"* (Lanham, Md.: Rowman & Littlefield, 1995), 71–72, 145–147.

115. Hobbes, *Leviathan,* ed. Edwin Curley (Indianapolis: Hackett, 1994), chap. 15.

116. Ibid., chap. 17.

117. Jean-Jacques Rousseau, "Discourse on Inequality," in *The First and Second Discourses,* trans. Victor Gourevitch (New York: Harper & Row, 1986), 180.

118. Ibid., 195.

119. See Montesquieu, *Considerations on the Causes of the Greatness of the Romans and their Decline,* trans. David Lowenthal (New York: Free Press, 1965), 116, translator's note d.

120. According to Montesquieu's brief depiction of the state of nature, human beings do not first perceive themselves to be complete, or whole, but rather weak, inferior, and needy; and among their first desires is the "desire to live in society" (*The Spirit of the Laws,* I.2). Shklar agrees that Montesquieu does not resent the modern divided self. Shklar, *Montesquieu,* 76.

121. As Mosher puts it, for Montesquieu "a republican community is organized to express a unified point of view, and hence it is vulnerable to the tyranny of a hegemonic culture." Mosher, "Judgmental Gaze," 38.

122. "Those who want to make similar [that is, republican] institutions will establish the community of goods of Plato's *Republic.*" Montesquieu, *The Spirit of the Laws,* IV.6.

123. "As the principle of despotic government is fear, its end is tranquility; but this is not a peace, it is the silence of the towns that the enemy is about to occupy." (*The Spirit of the Laws,* V.14.) Isaiah Berlin remarks that, according to Montesquieu, "only those societies are free that are in a state of agi-

tation . . . and unstable." Isaiah Berlin, *Against the Current* (New York: Viking Press, 1980), 158. On the same point, see Shklar, *Montesquieu*, 59; and David Carrithers, "Introduction" to *The Spirit of the Laws* (Berkeley: University of California Press, 1977), 15; Cohler, *Montesquieu's Comparative Politics*, 83; and Keohane, *Philosophy and the State in France*, 398.

124. Montesquieu, *Romans*, chap. 9.

125. On this point, see Stewart, who argues that honor in the fullest sense includes both internal and external aspects, although it is possible to have one without the other in any given case. Stewart, *Honor*, 12f., 15, 18. Pitt-Rivers agrees that honor involves not only external ideals but also the internalization of these ideals, and that it combines value in the eyes of others with value in one's own eyes. Pitt-Rivers, "Honor and Social Status," 21–22.

126. Walzer, *Spheres of Justice*, 274.

127. Missionaries can be civil disobedients and conscientious objectors, too. The distinction here goes to the different orientations of those who are primarily concerned to preserve their self-respect and those whose express purpose is to save the souls of others.

128. G. W. F. Hegel, *Phenomenology of Spirit*, trans. A. V. Miller (Oxford: Oxford University Press, 1977), 111–119.

129. Walzer drives this point home in his *Obligations*, 200. See also Kinneging, *Aristocracy, Antiquity, and History*, 154.

130. The term "beneficiaries" is Taylor's, in "The Politics of Recognition," 70.

131. On the importance of attaching honor to a standard of desert, see Walzer, *Spheres of Justice*, 262.

132. Montesquieu, *Mes pensées*, no. 1905(51), 1458.

133. It is true that titles of nobility could only be dispensed by kings. Yet once a title was granted, it had the status of property and, like property, was hereditary. This status made titles, and the offices to which they gave access, independent of the need for the king's continuing favor and the favors of future kings. A desire to preserve the independent standing of the nobility explains Montesquieu's defense of hereditary titles and private property. It also explains why he supported the sale of offices, at least in monarchies. Offices granted by commission were to be served at the pleasure of the king, whereas offices that were sold possessed established standing as private property, which "render[ed] the orders of the state more permanent," and shored up the power of the intermediary bodies (*The Spirit of the Laws*, V.19). On Montesquieu's defense of venality, see Peter Gay, *The Enlightenment: An Interpretation* (New York: Alfred A. Knopf, 1969), II, 469; and Ford, *Robe and Sword*, 123.

134. On the substantive variability of honor in the old regime, see Mosher,

"Judgmental Gaze," 39: "Honor had no substantive content; it could not be linked with a unified vision of society enforced from the center. Because each resistant group's honor required an audience, each group created its own. New definitions of honor proliferated through every rank and condition of society. This created a more highly differentiated social order. It was not held together by a unified vision of itself, except in a procedural sense. Every group had evolved internally its own standards of honor, which were only loosely linked with each other."

135. Walzer, *Obligations,* 196.

136. Montesquieu, *Mes pensées,* no. 69(5), 993.

137. For a discussion of merit and membership in the nobility in eighteenth-century France, see, for example, Jean Egret, *Louis XV et l'opposition parlementaire, 1715–1774* (Paris: Armand Colin, 1970); Cox, *Montesquieu and the History of French Laws,* 167; William Doyle, *The Parlement of Bordeaux and the End of the Old Regime, 1771–1790* (New York: St. Martin's, 1974); and Ford, *Robe and Sword,* 117–119.

In a similar vein, Schaub points out that Montesquieu calls attention to "the moral bankruptcy of the nobility" in *Persian Letters* (no. 74), where "we make the acquaintance of a 'grand seigneur' of the realm—'who took snuff with such haughtiness, who blew his nose so pitilessly and spat so phlegmatically, and who caressed his dogs in a manner so offensive to mankind.' Montesquieu dwells on the physical repulsiveness of this 'little man,' the manner of whose expectorations shows a lack of even the merest civility towards his fellows. Whereas he holds himself superior (and indifferent) to the rest of mankind, he stoops low indeed in his unseemly attachment to his pets. We may speak figuratively of the 'bestiality' of the nobility when their social standing is no longer accompanied by any real human excellence." Schaub, *Erotic Liberalism,* 124. This assessment is consistent with Montesquieu's comments on the corruption of honor in *The Spirit of the Laws,* VIII.7.

3. Honor and Democracy in America

1. One commentator has found the seeds of Tocqueville's account of American democratic character in Montesquieu's treatment of the English in Book XIX, chapter 27, of *The Spirit of the Laws.* See Cohler, *Montesquieu's Comparative Politics,* 181–182. While Cohler is right to note the connection between Montesquieu's statement of the individualism inherent in modern commercial societies and Tocqueville's analysis of America, it should be emphasized that Tocqueville and Montesquieu differed somewhat in their interpretations of England. In particular, Tocqueville classi-

fied the English regime as "aristocratic," a term that he used to describe all nondemocratic societies, including the monarchy of prerevolutionary France. He regarded the English nobility as particularly strong when compared with those of other European societies, and believed that the aristocratic character of this nobility defined English society as a whole. Indeed, he once remarked that "the English character is nothing other than the aristocratic character" (*Oeuvres complètes,* vol. V, I, 191). By contrast, Montesquieu saw England as more democratic socially (and potentially more democratic politically as well) than Tocqueville did. To Montesquieu's eyes, the English commercial republic was a novelty rather than an example of traditional order. And far from believing the English character to be a model of the aristocratic mores of the old regime, he portrayed it as a hitherto unseen combination of "fear, hatred, envy, jealousy," isolation, subjectivism, and unprincipled ambition (XIX.27). For further analysis of Tocqueville's views on England, see Max Beloff, "Tocqueville et l'Angleterre," in *Alexis de Tocqueville: Livre du centenaire, 1859–1959* (Paris: Éditions du Centre National de la Recherche Scientifique, 1960), 87–100; François Furet, "Naissance d'un paradigme: Tocqueville et le voyage en Amérique (1825–1831)," *Annales, Économies, Sociétés, Civilisations,* 39, no. 2 (March–April 1984): 228f., 233–237; Lamberti, *Tocqueville and the Two Democracies,* 15; André Jardin, *Alexis de Tocqueville, 1835–1859* (Paris: Hachette, 1984), 190–192; Georges Lefebvre, "A propos de Tocqueville," *Annales historique de la Révolution française* 27 (1955): 316; Seymour Drescher, *Tocqueville and England* (Cambridge: Harvard University Press, 1964), esp. 20f., 32, 208; and François Furet, *Interpreting the French Revolution,* trans. Elborg Forster (Cambridge: Cambridge University Press, 1981), 133.

2. Sung Ho Kim notes the tendency of contemporary civic republicans and those he calls "right-Tocquevillians" to emphasize the egalitarian, collectivist aspects of Tocqueville's associational life as against "the cultivation of defiant individual autonomy" that Kim finds in Max Weber's account of civil society. Sung Ho Kim, " 'In Affirming Them, He Affirms Himself': Max Weber's Politics of Civil Society," *Political Theory,* 28, no. 2 (April 2000): 220. Kim's distinction is an important one, but it can be found in Tocqueville as well as in Weber. Examples of contemporary theorists who emphasize the communalist aspects of Tocqueville's account of associational life include Robert Bellah et al., *Habits of the Heart* (Berkeley: University of California Press, 1985); Robert Putnam, "Bowling Alone: America's Declining Social Capital," *Journal of Democracy,* 6 (January 1995): 65–78; Mary Ann Glendon and David Blankenhorn, eds., *Seedbeds of Virtue: Sources of Competence, Character, and Citizenship in American Society*

(Lanham, Md.: Madison Books, 1995); Sandel, *Democracy's Discontent,*
esp. 314, 420, 347; Francis Fukuyama, *Trust: The Social Virtues and the
Creation of Prosperity* (London: Penguin, 1996); and Jean Bethke Elshtain,
Democracy on Trial (New York: Basic Books, 1995).

3. Tocqueville, *Democracy in America,* vol. II, pt. 4, chap. 7, p. 328. Hereafter
references to *Democracy in America* will be inserted parenthetically in the
text, with roman numerals indicating volume, followed by arabic numerals indicating part and chapter, and finally the page number in the
Gallimard edition.

   Robert P. Kraynak discusses Tocqueville's tendency to confound civic
and heroic virtues in "Tocqueville's Constitutionalism," *American Political
Science Review,* 81, no. 4 (December 1987): 1175–1195. Tocqueville regarded the ancient democracies as being in fact aristocracies (II.1.15),
which helps explain why he mixes the different types of virtue appropriate
to each. Lawler calls attention to this point in *The Restless Mind,* 133.
Other possible explanations are considered below.

4. As one commentator puts it, Tocqueville "did not value the act of participation [simply] as a means towards a closer fraternity, a tighter-knit communal feeling, a stronger subordination of the individual to communal life
and the communal mind." Jack Lively, *The Social and Political Thought of
Alexis de Tocqueville* (Oxford: Clarendon, 1965), 114.

5. Lamberti, *Tocqueville and the Two Democracies,* 8f.

6. Thus while Lamberti contends that Tocqueville is opposed to traditional
feudal honor, he asserts that Tocqueville's work as a whole aims to infuse
democracy with aristocratic values. Ibid., 56. On the same point, see
Boesche, *The Strange Liberalism,* 172; Alulis, "The Promise of Democracy
and the Problem of Liberty," 55; and Pontuso, "Tocqueville on Courage,"
97.

7. For discussion of Tocqueville as Montesquieu's successor, see Raymond
Aron, *Main Currents in Sociological Thought* (New York: Transaction,
1998), I, esp. 243–245, 262–263, 237–302; Daniel J. Mahoney, "Tocqueville and Socialism," in *Tocqueville's Defense of Human Liberty,* ed. Lawler
and Alulis, 180; Harvey Mansfield and Delba Winthrop, "Introduction"
to *Democracy in America* (Chicago: University of Chicago Press, 2000),
xxxiv–xxxvi; Melvin Richter, "The Uses of Theory: Tocqueville's Adaptation of Montesquieu," *Essays in Theory and History,* ed. Melvin Richter
(Cambridge: Harvard University Press, 1970); and Lamberti, *Tocqueville
and the Two Democracies,* esp. 14, 18f., 41, 88, 180, 239, 242.

8. Tocqueville, *Oeuvres complètes,* vol. XII, I, p. 148. Quoted in Lamberti,
Tocqueville and the Two Democracies, 5.

9. Quoted in J. P. Mayer, *Alexis de Tocqueville,* trans. M. M. Bozman and C.
Hahn (New York: Viking, 1940), 36.

10. François Furet, "Tocqueville est-il un historien de la Révolution française?" *Annales Économies, Sociétés, Civilisations* 25, no. 2 (March–April 1970): 435. On the same point, see Larry Siedentop, *Tocqueville* (Oxford: Oxford University Press, 1994), 12.

11. Montesquieu, *The Spirit of the Laws,* XI.2.

12. Lively, *The Social and Political Thought,* 19.

13. Tocqueville told J. S. Mill in 1836 that "America was only the frame, my picture was Democracy." Alexis de Tocqueville, *Memoirs, Letters, and Remains of Alexis de Tocqueville,* 2 vols. (Boston: Ticknor and Fields, 1862), II, 38. Quoted in James W. Ceaser, *Liberal Democracy and Political Science* (Baltimore: Johns Hopkins University Press, 1990), 26n1. On the same point, see Furet, "Naissance d'un paradigme," 228.

14. First among the differences between the United States and France was the fact that the former was born into a condition of rough social equality. It did not have a long history of hereditary aristocracy that had to be overthrown in order for democracy to take hold, as in France. In addition, the decentralized quality of political administration, the strong influence of religion on mores, and fortuitous circumstances, such as the absence of hostile neighbors and the abundance of natural resources, gave democracy in America a distinctive hue and helped to protect it from its own excesses.

15. Seymour Drescher notes the abundance of references to France in *Democracy in America,* pointing out that discussion of American democracy per se occupies only 20 percent of volume II and only 2 percent of its final part. Drescher, "More than America: Comparison and Synthesis in *Democracy in America,"* in *Reconsidering Tocqueville's "Democracy in America,"* ed. Abraham S. Eisenstadt (New Brunswick, N.J.: Rutgers University Press, 1988), 79–80.

16. Tocqueville, *La ancien régime et la Révolution* (3 vols.), vol. I, Preface, p. 75 (xxviii). All references to *La ancien régime* are from *Oeuvres complètes,* vol. II. Translations are my own. References are given with roman numerals indicating volume, followed by arabic numerals indicating chapter, and finally the page number in the Gallimard edition.

17. For a discussion of the two forms of majority tyranny, see Jardin, *Alexis de Tocqueville,* 208.

18. Lively, *The Social and Political Thought,* 107. Tocqueville gives two examples of majority tyranny in the United States. The first involves a Baltimore newspaper that voiced strong opposition to the War of 1812, a war that was popular in Baltimore at the time. In response, enraged members of the public assembled, "broke the presses, and attacked the house of the editors" (*Democracy in America,* I.2.7, p. 263, n. 4). After the editors and journalists involved were jailed, the mob broke into the prison, killed one journalist, and left the others for dead. The responsible parties were later

brought before a jury and acquitted. Tocqueville's second example of "the excesses to which the despotism of the majority may lead" involves Pennsylvania restrictions on black suffrage. Although state law permitted blacks to vote, few exercised this right because they feared maltreatment by local whites. In this case, the law lacked force because the majority took informal action to thwart it as a result of "the strongest prejudice against Negroes" (ibid.). The source of majority tyranny ultimately lies outside the laws, in the principle of popular sovereignty that legitimates the laws and defines a democratic regime. And because the power of public opinion operates in large part informally outside the laws, the legal separation of powers and a system of institutional checks and balances can go only so far in constraining its force. Thus Tocqueville regarded the *Federalist's* solution to majority tyranny as insufficient. See Paul Bastid, "Tocqueville et la doctrine constitutionnelle," in *Alexis de Tocqueville: Livre du centenaire, 1859–1959,* 46; and Siedentop, *Tocqueville,* 62.

19. Jardin, *Alexis de Tocqueville,* 258.
20. The nature of the relationship between the two dangers diagnosed by Tocqueville has been the subject of extensive discussion. See Seymour Drescher, "Tocqueville's Two Democracies," *Journal of the History of Ideas,* 25, no. 2 (1964): 201–216; Arthur Schlesinger, Jr., "Individualism and Apathy in Tocqueville's *Democracy in America,*" in *Reconsidering Tocqueville's Democracy in America,* ed. Eisenstadt, 101; Melvin Richter, "Tocqueville, Napoleon, and Bonapartism," in *Reconsidering Tocqueville's "Democracy in America,*" ed. Eisenstadt, 118; Lamberti, *Tocqueville and the Two Democracies,* 123, 232–238; Max Lerner, "Introduction" to *Democracy in America* (New York: Fontana, 1968), 91; James T. Schleifer, *The Making of Tocqueville's Democracy in America* (Chapel Hill: University of North Carolina Press, 1980), 285; Furet, "Naissance d'un paradigme," 225–239; Lawler, *The Restless Mind,* 133; Mansfield and Winthrop, "Introduction"; and Kraynak, "Tocqueville's Constitutionalism," 1180. The two dangers of modern democracy appear to be opposed, since majority tyranny seems to represent an excessive energy in the populace and mild despotism a debilitating passivity. To some extent, Tocqueville treated them separately, emphasizing majority tyranny in the first volume of *Democracy* and mild despotism in the second volume. The two volumes were published five years apart, in 1835 and 1840, and Tocqueville told friends that his understanding of both democracy and America had deepened in the intervening years. Perhaps the most significant shift from volume I to volume II is the recognition that threats to individual liberty in modern democracy may come from individuals themselves who acquiesce to—even invite—increasingly unlimited political power for the sake of the material comforts it

can secure (Lively, *The Social and Political Thought,* 15). The problem is not simply that power is of an encroaching nature, but that human nature may have reason to find such encroachment desirable.

21. The two volumes of *Democracy* thus share a common central theme, which is the question of how to maintain liberty (both individual and collective) in a modern democratic polity. See Jardin, *Alexis de Tocqueville,* 257.

22. Mansfield and Winthrop, "Introduction," liii, lxxi.

23. For discussion of Tocqueville's project as an effort to foster the capacity for agency, see Boesche, *The Strange Liberalism,* 117; Michael Hereth, *Alexis de Tocqueville: Threats to Freedom in Democracy,* trans. George Bogardus (Durham: Duke University Press, 1986), 181; Pontuso, "Tocqueville on Courage," 99, 106; and Kraynak, "Tocqueville's Constitutionalism," 1179f. Tocqueville's idea of political liberty is more democratic than Montesquieu's, and hence more participatory. It includes the "positive liberty" of political participation as well as the "negative liberty" to be free from unwarranted government intrusion. See Lamberti, *Tocqueville and the Two Democracies,* 60, 187.

24. On Tocqueville's resistance to the idea of inevitability in human affairs, see Pierre Birnbaum, *Sociologie de Tocqueville* (Paris: Presses Universitaires de France, 1970), esp. 17f.; Marvin Zetterbaum, *Tocqueville and the Problem of Democracy* (Stanford: Stanford University Press, 1967), 4–16; Pierre Manent, *Tocqueville and the Nature of Democracy,* trans. John Waggoner (Princeton: Princeton University Press, 1996), 26; Lamberti, *Tocqueville and the Two Democracies,* 38, 102; Albert Salomon, "Tocqueville's Philosophy of Freedom," *Review of Politics,* 1, no. 4 (October 1939): 410; Ceaser, "Alexis de Tocqueville on Political Science," 660f.; Lively, *The Social and Political Thought,* 8f.; and Carrese, "Judicial Statesmanship," 485. Boesche regards Tocqueville as ambivalent on this point, in *The Strange Liberalism,* 69.

25. Lamberti, "Two Ways of Conceiving the Republic," in *Interpreting Tocqueville's Democracy in America,* ed. Masugi, 11; Lamberti, *Tocqueville and the Two Democracies,* 33; Boesche, *The Strange Liberalism,* 51; Alulis, "The Promise of Democracy and the Problem of Liberty," 38, 42f., 54; and Jardin, *Alexis de Tocqueville,* 243.

26. Tocqueville, *L'ancien régime,* I.Preface, p. 69.

27. Quoted in Salomon, "Tocqueville's Philosophy of Freedom," 403. Emphasis added. For discussion of the liberal milieu in France in the early nineteenth century, see R. Pierre Marcel, *Essai politique sur Alexis de Tocqueville* (Paris: Félix Alcan, 1910), 1–54. Tocqueville meant to distinguish himself from natural rights theorists such as Hobbes and Locke, utilitarians such as Bentham and James Mill, and such notable liberals of his own day as

Benjamin Constant and Madame de Staël. In contrast with these others, Tocqueville (like Montesquieu) believed that a liberal constitution and individual rights were necessary but not sufficient conditions for individual liberty. Salomon, "Tocqueville's Philosophy of Freedom," 403. On the same point, see Eugène d'Eichthal, *Alexis de Tocqueville et la démocratie libérale* (Paris: Librairie Nouvelle, 1897), 131; Lively, *The Social and Political Thought*, 127; and Siedentop, *Tocqueville*, 67. In part, this conviction reflected Tocqueville's more comprehensive understanding of the nature of encroaching power.

28. Ceaser makes a similar point in "Alexis de Tocqueville on Political Science," 668.

29. Peristiany also maintains that honor is a universal aspect of social classification. Peristiany, "Introduction" to *Honor and Shame*, 11.

30. Hereth, *Alexis de Tocqueville: Threats to Freedom*, 18.

31. On this point, see Robert N. Bellah, "The Quest for the Self: Individualism, Morality, Politics," in *Interpreting Tocqueville's "Democracy in America,"* ed. Masugi, 332f., 338; and Manent, *Tocqueville and the Nature of Democracy*, 59.

32. Thus Manent notes that modern democrats, according to Tocqueville, tend to recognize only two legitimate sources of action: the personal will and the general will. See Manent, *Tocqueville and the Nature of Democracy*, 10.

33. For further discussion of this point, see ibid., 38.

34. On the need to balance intellectual authorities and independent thought, see Boesche, *The Strange Liberalism*, 142f., 152; Lamberti, *Tocqueville and the Two Democracies*, 168; and Kraynak, "Tocqueville's Constitutionalism," 1180.

35. Thus Montesquieu favored laws in monarchies prohibiting members of the nobility from taking part in commerce, saying that to adopt laws in France engaging the nobles to carry on commerce would be to "destroy the nobility" without being of any use to commerce. Montesquieu, *The Spirit of the Laws*, XX.22.

36. Along these lines, Pontuso points out that not all democratic qualities lead to the loss of courage. See his "Tocqueville on Courage," 106.

37. Tocqueville, *L'ancien régime*, II.6, pp. 135–136.

38. Ibid., p. 136.

39. Tocqueville also notes that "what most repulses" him in America (*qui me répugne le plus*) "is the paucity of guarantees that one finds against tyranny" (I.2.7, p. 263).

40. For discussion of how materialism disables individual agency, see Lamberti, "Two Ways of Conceiving the Republic," 17; Edward C. Banfield,

"The Illiberal Tocqueville," in *Interpreting Tocqueville's "Democracy in America,"* ed. Masugi, 250; Boesche, *The Strange Liberalism,* 86ff., 158; Kraynak, "Montesquieu's Constitutionalism," 1183; Hereth, *Alexis de Tocqueville: Threats to Freedom,* 22. Schlesinger objects to Tocqueville's argument here, saying that "civic apathy is even more marked in nations that seek to abolish the acquisitive impulse than it is in capitalist nations." Schlesinger, "Individualism and Apathy in Tocqueville's *Democracy,*" 99. Schlesinger's point is well taken, but Tocqueville's concerns about the effects that materialism may have on individual agency do not point to the eradication of commerce or the acquisitive impulse. Tocqueville means to encourage supplemental motives that rise above mere materialism, but he does not mean for such motives to replace commercial ambition or the pursuit of self-interest well understood.

41. Tocqueville, *L'ancien régime,* III.3, p. 217. On this point, see Ceaser, "Alexis de Tocqueville and Political Science," 670.

42. Tocqueville, *L'ancien régime,* III.3, p. 217.

43. Eichthal, *Alexis de Tocqueville et la démocratie libérale,* 131. See also Lively, *The Social and Political Thought,* 14.

44. On this point, see Jardin, *Alexis de Tocqueville,* 243; and Salomon, "Tocqueville's Philosophy of Freedom," 416.

45. Pontuso emphasizes Tocqueville's commitment to restoring "the stature of devotion to the particular," albeit to particular objects that extend beyond the narrowest forms of material self-interest. He quotes Tocqueville's personal correspondence on this point, in which Tocqueville explained that "Man has been created by God (I do not know why) in such a way that the larger the object of his love the less directly attached he is to it. His heart needs particular passions; he needs limited objects for his affections to keep these firm and enduring." Tocqueville, *The European Revolution and Correspondence with Gobineau,* ed. and trans. John Lukacs (Gloucester, Mass.: Peter Smith, 1968), 167. Quoted in Pontuso, "Tocqueville on Courage," 107. On the same point, see also Manent, *Tocqueville and the Nature of Democracy,* 73.

46. Manent, *Tocqueville and the Nature of Democracy,* 123.

47. On the need for modern democrats occasionally to go beyond the civic duty that sustains the regular operations of government, see Pontuso, "Tocqueville on Courage," 103.

48. Tocqueville, *L'ancien régime,* II.11, p. 176.

49. Ibid.

50. On this point, see Hereth, *Alexis de Tocqueville: Threats to Freedom,* 23.

51. As Kraynak puts it, virtue "must speak the language of democracy." Kraynak, "Tocqueville's Constitutionalism," 1182. Lamberti also draws at-

tention to Tocqueville's "prudent self-censorship," in *Tocqueville and the Two Democracies*, 34.

52. Delba Winthrop, "Rights: A Point of Honor," in *Interpreting Tocqueville's "Democracy in America,"* ed. Masugi, 423.

53. Lively, *The Social and Political Thought*, 102.

54. Letter to Ampère (10 August 1841) in *Oeuvres et correspondance inédits*, ed. Gustave de Beaumont (Paris, 1861), ii, 116–117. Quoted in Lively, *The Social and Political Thought*, 102.

55. One might say that the dogma of the sovereignty of the people generalizes personal pride to the nation or even the species. Democratic peoples retain their pride vis-à-vis other peoples, but among themselves Tocqueville worries that they have too fully adopted the mantle of humility.

56. Tocqueville, *L'ancien régime*, II.11, pp. 176–177. Pride can bridge the gap between civic duty and self-interest, as Kraynak points out in "Tocqueville's Constitutionalism," 1186.

57. Siedentop, *Tocqueville*, 95.

58. Lively, *The Social and Political Thought*, 103. Cohler also notes that part of Tocqueville's solution to the ills of modern democracy is to enlarge the souls of modern democrats by means of pride. Cohler, *Montesquieu's Comparative Politics*, 188. On the same point, see Lawler, *The Restless Mind*, 137f.

59. See Pontuso, "Tocqueville on Courage," 102.

60. For further discussion of the dangers of ambition in democracy, see Lamberti, *Tocqueville and the Two Democracies*, 205f.

61. On this point, see Carrese, "Judicial Statesmanship," 482, 483, 486, 490; Jardin, *Alexis de Tocqueville*, 209; and George Wilson Pierson, "Le 'second voyage' de Tocqueville en Amérique," in *Alexis de Tocqueville: Livre du centenaire*, 78.

62. Siedentop, *Tocqueville*, 62.

63. Ceaser, "Alexis de Tocqueville and Political Science," 665.

64. Carrese, "Judicial Statesmanship," 484; and Siedentop, *Tocqueville*, 63.

65. Tocqueville's emphasis on great ambitions, which are self-serving but not reducible to the narrowest forms of egoism, suggests that those commentators who fault him for dichotomizing self-interest and "noble virtue" are off the mark. See, for example, Banfield, "The Illiberal Tocqueville," 251, and Schlesinger, "Individualism and Apathy in Tocqueville's *Democracy*," 105f. In fact, Tocqueville's defense of the aristocratic qualities associated with honor, such as high ambition, indicates that he saw the importance of linking self-concern to generalized compassion or civic virtue.

66. Tocqueville, *L'ancien régime*, III.3, p. 217.

67. Ibid.

68. Ibid.
69. Ibid.
70. Ibid.
71. Ibid., II.11, p. 176.
72. Manent, *Tocqueville and the Nature of Democracy,* 119.
73. Ibid., 118; Lawler, *The Restless Mind,* 136.
74. Eichthal, *Alexis de Tocqueville,* 123f.
75. Thus they are "aristocratic" only in a political sense, as they do not fix individuals in a certain place within a social hierarchy. See Manent, *Tocqueville and the Nature of Democracy,* 15.
76. See Pontuso, "Tocqueville on Courage," 103; and Mansfield and Winthrop, "Introduction," liv.
77. Winthrop, "Rights: A Point of Honor," 395; and Lawler, *The Restless Mind,* 135. See also Bien, "Old Regime Origins of Democratic Liberty," esp. 25, 50, 70.
78. The characterization of the feudal noble is Genicot's. Genicot, *La noblesse dans l'Occident médiéval,* 55.
79. Thus Lefebvre points also to the aristocratic origin of liberty itself in Tocqueville. Lefebvre, "A propos de Tocqueville," 316.
80. Winthrop, "Rights: A Point of Honor," 398.
81. Kinneging points out that for the ancients the choice between virtue and vice was a choice between mastery and slavery. Kinneging, *Aristocracy, Antiquity, and History,* 145.
82. Winthrop, "Rights: A Point of Honor," 397.
83. This commitment to rights is a point of honor because it cannot be explained on the basis of self-interest alone. See Winthrop, "Rights: A Point of Honor," 418, 422.
84. For further discussion of Tocqueville's views on religion, see Françoise Mélonio, "La religion selon Tocqueville: Ordre moral ou esprit de liberté?" *Études,* 360, no. 1 (January–June 1984): 73–89; William A. Galston, "Tocqueville on Liberalism and Religion," *Social Research,* 54, no. 3 (Autumn 1987): 499–518; Catherine Zuckert, "Not by Preaching: Tocqueville on the Role of Religion in American Democracy," *Review of Politics,* 43, no. 2 (April 1981): 259–280; Lawler, *The Restless Mind;* and Joshua Mitchell, *The Fragility of Freedom: Tocqueville on Religion, Democracy, and the American Future* (Chicago: University of Chicago Press, 1995); and Lively, *The Social and Political Thought,* chap. 6.
85. Of course, it is also true that excessive otherworldliness can lead to despotism by making citizens insufficiently vigilant in politics. On this point, see Lamberti, *Tocqueville and the Two Democracies,* 159.
86. Manent discusses democracy's special need for religion, in *Tocqueville and*

the Nature of Democracy, 85f., 87, 95f. On the same point, see Lawler, *The Restless Mind,* 133 and chap. 8.

87. Manent, *Tocqueville and the Nature of Democracy,* 26; Winthrop, "Rights: A Point of Honor," 92.

88. Zetterbaum points out that self-interest can support civic virtue and the bourgeois virtues but cannot go beyond them. For this, religion, rights, and associations are required. Zetterbaum, *Tocqueville and the Problem of Democracy,* 106f., 109.

89. Lawler, *The Restless Mind,* 132.

90. Lefebvre, "A propos de Tocqueville," 317.

4. The Love of Fame and the Southern Gentleman

1. Tocqueville, *Democracy in America,* II.3.18.

2. Ibid., II.3.19.

3. Ibid., I.1.8; see also I.2.7.

4. Charles Beard, *An Economic Interpretation of the Constitution of the United States* (1913; New York: Free Press, 1986).

5. See, for example, Bernard Bailyn, *The Ideological Origins of the American Revolution* (Cambridge: Harvard University Press, 1967); Gordon S. Wood, *The Creation of the American Republic, 1776–1787* (Chapel Hill: University of North Carolina Press, 1969); and Lance Banning, *The Jeffersonian Persuasion: Evolution of a Party Ideology* (Ithaca, N.Y.: Cornell University Press, 1978). More recently, Michael Sandel's argument that the founding generation was committed to a political economy of virtue presupposes that economic interests were subordinate to political convictions about good government instead of themselves determining the nature of the government. See his *Democracy's Discontent,* esp. chap. 5.

6. Douglas Adair, *Fame and the Founding Fathers* (New York: Norton, 1974). For further discussion on this point, see James W. Ceasar's incisive opening paragraphs in his "Fame and *The Federalist,*" in *The Noblest Minds,* ed. McNamara, 187–188.

7. Adair, *Fame and the Founding Fathers,* 24.

8. Lincoln, "Address to the Young Men's Lyceum of Springfield, Illinois," in *Abraham Lincoln: Speeches and Writings, 1832–1858* (New York: Library of America, 1989), 33–34.

9. See, for example, the essays in McNamara, *The Noblest Minds.*

10. This is Ceasar's phrasing, in "Fame and *The Federalist,*" 187.

11. *The Federalist,* no. 72. For further discussion of Hamilton and the love of fame, see Peter McNamara, "Alexander Hamilton, the Love of Fame, and Modern Democratic Statesmanship," in *The Noblest Minds,* ed. McNamara.

12. *The Federalist,* no. 72.
13. Adair, "Fame and the Founding Fathers," 8.
14. Ibid.
15. Richard Brookhiser, *Founding Father* (New York: Free Press, 1996), 116.
16. Lorraine Smith Pangle and Thomas L. Pangle, "George Washington and the Life of Honor," in *The Noblest Minds,* ed. McNamara, 59, 61.
17. Jean Yarbrough, *American Virtues: Thomas Jefferson on the Character of a Free People* (Lawrence: University Press of Kansas, 1998), 105.
18. Quoted in ibid., 148.
19. Paul A. Rahe, *Republics Ancient and Modern* (Chapel Hill: University of North Carolina Press, 1992), 716.
20. Ibid.
21. Ibid.
22. Lance Banning, "James Madison: Memory, Service, and Fame," in *The Noblest Minds,* ed. McNamara, 135.
23. Ibid., 135, 134.
24. Washington, for example, was a reader and admirer of Plutarch's *Lives,* but he thought the virtues of the ancients too severe and potentially inhumane. See Brookhiser, *Founding Father,* 125–126. Jefferson, too, warned against virtues that too fully suppressed self-interest. Yarbrough, *American Virtues,* 104.
25. Montesquieu, *The Spirit of the Laws,* VIII.7.
26. *The Papers of Alexander Hamilton,* ed. Harold Syrett, 27 vols. (New York: Columbia University Press, 1961–87), 17:366, 11 November 1794. Quoted in McNamara, "Alexander Hamilton," 149.
27. Adair neglects this point. He makes the mistake of identifying all honor with feudal honor. Additionally, in treating honor he discusses only public honors, never honor as a quality of character. In fact, honor conceived as a whole is closer to Adair's definition of "fame" than he realizes. Both motivate individuals to strive to carry out exceptional deeds that are guided by principles and admired by "the discerning."
28. Adair, "Fame and the Founding Fathers," 11.
29. Ibid.
30. Ibid., 10.
31. *The Federalist,* no. 1.
32. *The Federalist,* no. 14.
33. Pangle and Pangle, "George Washington," 61.
34. Adair, "Fame and the Founding Fathers," 11.
35. Pangle and Pangle, "George Washington," 61.
36. See Lorraine Smith Pangle and Thomas L. Pangle, *The Learning of Liberty: The Educational Ideas of the American Founders* (Lawrence: University Press of Kansas, 1993), esp. 244f.

37. George Washington to Henry Lee, 22 September 1788, in *The Writings of George Washington from the Original Manuscript Sources*, ed. John C. Fitzpatrick, 39 vols. (Washington, D.C.: U.S. Government Printing Office, 1931–40), 30:97–98. Quoted in Pangle and Pangle, "George Washington," 62.

38. Pangle and Pangle, *The Learning of Liberty*, 14, 243.

39. McNamara, "Alexander Hamilton," 151.

40. Hamilton, letter to Bayard, 16 January 1801, in *Papers*, 25:323. Quoted in McNamara, "Alexander Hamilton," 151. Emphasis added.

41. Thomas L. Pangle, "Classical and Modern Liberal Understandings of Honor," in *The Noblest Minds*, ed. McNamara, 210.

42. Ibid.

43. It is true that if one's self-respect is conceived to be contingent upon acting honorably, one could be said to have an "interest" in honor, as we have seen, but the category of interest as normally construed leaves out so much of what is central to honor (its principled codes, for instance, and the noninstrumental conviction that one's self-respect must be tied to one's code) that it is neither correct nor particularly illuminating to classify honor simply as a species of interest. More generally, while it makes good sense to expand the category of interest beyond the overly narrow, materialist construction associated with traditional utilitarianism, there are also limits to the explanatory power of an excessively broad conception of interest. If the category of interest included every conceivable human objective, its explanatory power vis-à-vis human action would be much reduced. This point is elaborated by Richard King in *Civil Rights and the Idea of Freedom*, 66–69.

44. C. Bradley Thompson, "John Adams and the Quest for Fame," in *The Noblest Minds*, ed. McNamara, 78.

45. Washington, Farewell Address, 19 September 1796. Quoted in William J. Bennett, *Our Sacred Honor* (New York: Simon and Schuster, 1997), 91.

46. Thompson says the same about Adams in "John Adams," 77f. This emphasis on the sense of duty to oneself calls into question Pangle's assertion that true honor is "unselfish" and "public-spirited" in an altruistic way, and that it requires "the few unselfish and public-spirited men of honor to expend their lives in the role of servants to the predominantly selfish or privately interested many." Pangle, "The Classical and Modern Liberal Understandings of Honor," 209. The "puzzle" that Pangle points to as a central (and problematic) feature of honor, which is the question of how those whom he calls the "best" (meaning public-spirited) could be for the sake of those he refers to as the "lower" (meaning self-interested), is at least partially resolved by the sense of duty to oneself and the good of self-re-

spect that honor engenders. Those with honor are not so much for the sake of their less admirable peers but for the sake of themselves and their principles. They benefit others, but indirectly. They do what they do, as Montesquieu said, because they owe it to themselves to do so, not because they see themselves as the "servants" of others.

47. Pangle and Pangle, *The Learning of Liberty,* 248. They go on to say that by providing an example of how to care for the self in the deepest possible way, Washington gave his country the "greatest gift."

48. Democratic forms of honor also may be tied to more particular codes, as Chapter 6 shows. Chapters 4 and 5 highlight one form of honor that has been important in the American political tradition, but it is not the only type of honor present in American democracy.

49. Bennett, *Our Sacred Honor,* 26.

50. Tocqueville, *Democracy in America,* II.3.18.

51. An example of how partial self-concern can be employed to serve general principles is given by Michael Ignatieff's description of the modern "warrior's honor" (Michael Ignatieff, *The Warrior's Honor: Ethnic War and the Modern Conscience* [New York: Henry Holt, 1997]). The Geneva Convention of 1864 sought to universalize the content of traditional military codes of honor by setting a standard of conduct applicable to soldiers in all cases, regardless of the particular identities of their enemies. It promoted the idea that practices such as the indiscriminate slaughter of civilians or the murder and torture of prisoners were always "beneath a soldier's dignity" (116). By contrast, the content of traditional warrior codes was "sharply particularist" in that their protections covered only certain classes of persons. The protections established by the chivalric code applied only to Christians, for example; a warrior could behave without restraint toward infidels (117). Yet while the content of the modern code reflects a new aspiration to universalism, the motive that sustains it draws on the traditional partiality of the soldier's honorable desire for dignity and self-respect. The motive for adhering to the universal code remains rooted in a form of partiality, even self-concern, the feeling that one could not live with oneself if one failed to live up to one's code. The connection between self-respect and general principles can be extended beyond the battlefield to modern civilian life, as well, according to Ignatieff. The fact that "to think well of oneself in this century, it is necessary to believe in moral universals" (55) illustrates the way in which the desire for self-respect ("to think well of oneself") is a natural intermediary between our powerful partiality for ourselves and the universalism of modern standards of moral and political right.

52. Tocqueville, *Democracy in America,* II.3.18.

53. Hamilton, "Farmer Refuted," 23 February 1775, *Papers,* 1:156. Quoted in McNamara, "Alexander Hamilton," 153.

54. Rahe, *Republics,* 772

55. Pangle and Pangle, "George Washington," 63.

56. John Adams, *Discourses on Davila* (New York: DeCapo Press, 1973), no. 6, 41.

57. On this point, see Paul A. Rahe, "Fame, Founders, and the Idea of Founding," in *The Noblest Minds,* ed. McNamara, 11.

58. Ibid.

59. Brookhiser, *Founding Father,* 100.

60. Quoted in Stanley Elkins and Eric McKitrick, *The Age of Federalism* (New York: Oxford University Press, 1993), 448.

61. Brookhiser, *Founding Father,* 103.

62. See Yarbrough, *American Virtues,* 104, 114.

63. Ibid., 150f.

64. John Locke, *Second Treatise of Government,* in *Two Treatises of Government,* ed. Peter Laslett (Cambridge: Cambridge University Press, 1960), chap. XIX.

65. Ibid.

66. *The Federalist,* no. 10.

67. Madison, Address to the Virginia Ratifying Convention, 20 June 1788, in *The Debates in the Several State Conventions,* ed. Jonathan Elliot (Philadelphia, 1876), III, 536–537. Quoted in Banning, "James Madison: Memory, Service, Fame."

68. Madison, "Government of the United States," *National Gazette,* 4 February 1792, in *Papers of James Madison,* ed. William T. Hutchinson et al. (Chicago: University of Chicago Press and Charlottesville: University Press of Virginia, 1962–77), 14:218. Quoted in Banning, "James Madison: Memory, Service, Fame." Banning maintains that Madison "believed that his and others' honor was at stake in the commitment to prepare a Bill of Rights," in ibid., 130.

69. David F. Epstein, *The Political Theory of "The Federalist"* (Chicago: University of Chicago Press, 1984), 192.

70. *The Federalist,* no. 76.

71. Ibid.

72. Ibid.

73. Ibid.

74. Ibid.

75. *The Federalist,* no. 10.

76. Ibid.

77. Ibid.

78. *The Federalist,* no. 72.

79. *The Federalist,* no. 57. The "private interests" mentioned in *Federalist* 51 that act as "sentinels" over "the public rights," and so "supply the defects of better motives," are interests in distinction, reputation, and fame, not material gain. After all, as a recent commentator has noted, one who acts exclusively on the basis of material self-interest "is more likely to be a free rider than an ambitious man. He will let someone else do the work, take the risk, and suffer the indignity of running for office. And, in fact, if the system of ambition counteracting itself works, no personal gains in office can be hoped for." See Harvey C. Mansfield, Jr., *America's Constitutional Soul* (Baltimore: Johns Hopkins University Press, 1991), 214.

80. *The Federalist,* no. 66. Here Hamilton seems to accept something like what Montesquieu called "false honor," the prideful defense of prerogative not strictly equated with virtue.

81. On this point, see William Kristol, "Ambition and the Separation of Powers," in *Saving the Revolution,* ed. Charles R. Kesler (New York: Free Press, 1987), 123. An example of this defensive ambition can be seen in Senator Robert Byrd's spirited resistance to the line-item veto. In a series of fourteen addresses to the Senate in 1993, Byrd exhorted his colleagues to recognize the importance of an independent legislature, "free of domination by an all-powerful executive." See Robert C. Byrd, *The Senate of the Roman Republic: Addresses on the History of Roman Constitutionalism* (Washington, D.C.: U.S. Government Printing Office, 1995), 41. Byrd asserted his own "reverence" for the American Constitution and reminded senators of their "solemn oath to protect and defend the delicate constitutional structure" (11, 15, 59). Byrd's speeches were modern acts of remonstrance, efforts to obstruct encroaching power, in particular the expansion of executive power (89–90, 169, 172).

82. *The Federalist,* no. 76.

83. Ibid.

84. *The Federalist,* no. 70.

85. Kristol, "Ambition and the Separation of Powers," 123.

86. Epstein, *The Political Theory of "The Federalist,"* 124, 125.

87. Rahe, *Republics,* p. 601.

88. *The Federalist,* no. 57.

89. *The Federalist,* no. 59. See Rahe, *Republics,* 600.

90. Mansfield, *America's Constitutional Soul,* 215; Rahe, *Republics,* 601.

91. Rahe, *Republics,* 601.

92. Washington, "First Annual Message to Congress," 8 January 1790, in *A Compilation of the Messages and Papers of the Presidents, 1789–1897,* ed. James D. Richardson (Washington, D.C., 1896), I:66. Quoted in Rahe, *Republics,* 713.

93. Madison, Memorial and Remonstrance against Religious Assessments, 20

June 1785, in *Papers of James Madison,* VIII:300. Quoted in Rahe, *Republics,* 721.

94. Yarbrough, *American Virtues,* 104, 114, 156.
95. *The Federalist,* no. 11.
96. Rahe, *Republics,* 571.
97. Epstein, *The Political Theory of "The Federalist,"* 15.
98. *The Federalist,* no. 12. Similarly, *Federalist* no. 42 holds that it would "dishonor" Americans simply to appropriate England's system of laws instead of choosing and establishing their own. For further discussion, see Epstein, *The Political Theory of "The Federalist,"* 16.
99. *The Federalist,* no. 1.
100. *The Federalist,* no. 11.
101. Ceaser, "Fame and *The Federalist,*" 200.
102. Tocqueville, *Democracy in America,* II.1.20.
103. Ibid.
104. Ibid.
105. Jefferson, First Inaugural Address, 4 March 1801. Quoted in Bennett, *Our Sacred Honor,* 347.
106. Hulliung, *Montesquieu and the Old Regime,* 30.
107. Gouverneur Morris, "I am an American," speech, 1800. Quoted in Bennett, *Our Sacred Honor,* 86.
108. Ibid.
109. Epstein, *The Political Theory of "The Federalist,"* 121.
110. Steven Forde, "Ben Franklin, Hero," in *The Noblest Minds,* ed. McNamara, 49.
111. Montesquieu, *The Spirit of the Laws,* IV.2.
112. Forde, "Ben Franklin, Hero," 49.
113. William Oliver Stevens, *Pistols at Ten Paces: The Story of the Code of Honor in America* (Boston: Houghton Mifflin, 1940), 31.
114. Bertram Wyatt-Brown, *Yankee Saints and Southern Sinners* (Baton Rouge: Louisiana State Press, 1985), 8f.
115. Bertram Wyatt-Brown, *Southern Honor: Ethics and Behavior in the Old South* (Oxford: Oxford University Press, 1982), 439.
116. Wyatt-Brown, *Yankee Saints,* 9.
117. Ibid., 203.
118. Wyatt-Brown, *Southern Honor,* 61.
119. It is worth noting here that in view of the racial hierarchy, the American South before the Civil War was more rigidly hierarchical even than eighteenth-century France.
120. Wyatt-Brown, *Yankee Saints,* 186, and *Southern Honor,* 14.
121. Wyatt-Brown, *Southern Honor,* 113.

122. Quoted in ibid., 103.
123. Ibid., 66.
124. Ibid., 46.
125. Ibid., 186.
126. Ibid., xv.
127. Ibid., 354.
128. Ibid., 355.
129. Ibid., 354.
130. Ibid., 355.
131. Ibid.
132. Stevens, *Pistols at Ten Paces*, 7. Stevens adds later that "the mortality record of the code of honor in Europe did not compare with that in the United States, where meetings on the field were always conducted with deadly weapons," 272.
133. Ibid., 272.
134. Ibid., 31.
135. Quoted in Wyatt-Brown, *Southern Honor*, 355.
136. Wyatt-Brown, *Southern Honor*, 126f.
137. Wyatt-Brown, *Yankee Saints*, 189.
138. Ibid., 192. On the same point, see James M. McPherson, *For Causes and Comrades: Why Men Fought in the Civil War* (Oxford: Oxford University Press, 1997), 24.
139. Wyatt-Brown, *Yankee Saints*, 194.
140. Ibid., 195.
141. Ibid., 202.
142. Quoted in Wyatt-Brown, *Southern Honor*, 35.
143. Ibid., 39.
144. Wyatt-Brown, *Southern Honor*, 40.
145. Ibid., 112.
146. Ibid., 31f.
147. Jefferson, letter to John Adams, 28 October 1813, in *The Adams-Jefferson Letters*, ed. Lester J. Cappon (Chapel Hill, 1959), II:387–392. Quoted in Rahe, *Republics*, 702.
148. Although some of the founders were southern slave owners, the ownership of slaves was quite obviously at odds with the universal principles of liberty and equality on which their expressed public sense of honor was founded. Some of them, such as Jefferson, seem to have felt the contradiction keenly. The difference between the founders who owned slaves and the southern gentleman of the antebellum years is that the latter explicitly conceived black slavery as a positive good and considered it to be an integral component of his own honor. By contrast, owning slaves was a viola-

tion of the founders' honor, rather than a vindication of it. Some of them chose to live with the violation, but such cases demonstrate the fallibility of human nature, not an intrinsic failing of honor. In general, honor is a more reliable motive than altruistic self-sacrifice, but its moral worth cannot be guaranteed, as this chapter argues. And even those who display a noble honor on some occasions may fail to live up to their codes on other occasions.

149. Alexander Stephens, The Cornerstone Speech, 21 March 1861, in Henry Cleveland, *Alexander H. Stephens in Public and Private* (Philadelphia, 1866), 717–729. Quoted in Rahe, *Republics,* 766f.

150. Rahe, *Republics,* 767.

151. Stephen B. Oates, *Abraham Lincoln: The Man behind the Myths* (New York: Harper & Row, 1984), 68.

152. Quoted in ibid., 69.

153. Wyatt-Brown, *Southern Honor,* 364.

154. Ibid., 363f.

155. Ibid., 364.

156. Ibid., 16.

157. Montesquieu, *The Spirit of the Laws,* II.4.

158. Wyatt-Brown points out that the "rights of Englishmen" originally were understood as *honors.* See his *Southern Honor,* 70f. See also Tocqueville, *Democracy in America,* II.4.4; Winthrop, "Rights: A Point of Honor," 395; and Bien, "Old Regime Origins," 25, 50, 70.

159. Wyatt-Brown, *Southern Honor,* 371.

160. Ibid., 5, 113; Wyatt-Brown, *Yankee Saints,* esp. chap. 7, "Honor and Secession"; Rahe, *Republics,* 767.

161. Oates, *Abraham Lincoln,* 97.

162. Kenneth S. Greenberg, *Honor and Slavery* (Princeton: Princeton University Press, 1996), 62.

163. Ibid., 65f., 137, 142.

164. Ibid., xiii.

165. Ibid., 98.

166. Quoted in ibid., 36.

167. Greenberg, *Honor and Slavery,* 36.

5. Honor and Democratic Reform

1. Michael Burlingame has remarked that "to think of Lincoln as an ambitious man is, for some, as difficult as it was for respectable Victorians to think of their parents as sexual beings." See his *The Inner World of Abraham Lincoln* (Urbana: University of Illinois Press, 1994), 236.

2. Douglas L. Wilson, *Honor's Voice* (New York: Knopf, 1998), 109.

3. Oates, *Abraham Lincoln,* 51.

4. Don E. Fehrenbacher, *Prelude to Greatness: Lincoln in the 1850's* (Stanford: Stanford University Press, 1962), 24f. Lincoln's law partner, William Herndon, described him as "inordinately ambitious," "a man totally swallowed up in his ambitions," and even as "the most ambitious man in the world." Quoted in Burlingame, *The Inner World,* 236. Burlingame provides ample evidence of Lincoln's ambition, but has a tendency to psychologize it, arguing that Lincoln's ambition resulted from an emotionally damaging boyhood (see especially 255). The present analysis is less concerned with the causes of Lincoln's ambition than with its political effects and its effects on Lincoln's capacity for individual agency. For further discussion of Lincoln's ambition, see Harry V. Jaffa, *Crisis of the House Divided* (Garden City, N.Y.: Doubleday, 1959), 9; Mark Neely, *The Last Best Hope of Earth* (Cambridge: Harvard University Press, 1993), 17; and David Herbert Donald, *Lincoln* (New York: Touchstone, 1995), 162.

5. Wilson, *Honor's Voice,* 124.

6. Ibid., 293.

7. Quoted in Oates, *Abraham Lincoln,* 40. Despite the fact that Lincoln's humble beginnings have been much celebrated by later generations, he himself "felt embarrassed about his log-cabin origins and never liked to talk about them," as Oates tells us. "He seldom discussed his parents either and became permanently estranged from his father, who was all but illiterate. In truth, Lincoln had considerable hostility for his father's intellectual limitations, once remarking that Thomas 'never did more in the way of writing than to bunglingly sign his own name.' When his father died in a nearby Illinois county in 1851, Lincoln did not attend the funeral." Stephen B. Oates, *Our Fiery Trial* (Amherst: University of Massachusetts Press, 1979), 64.

8. Oates, *Abraham Lincoln,* 51.

9. Wilson, *Honor's Voice,* 308.

10. Quoted in ibid.

11. Wilson, *Honor's Voice,* 309. For further discussion of Lincoln's many-sided ambition, see Burlingame, *The Inner World,* esp. 236–267.

12. Oates, *Abraham Lincoln,* 40.

13. On this point, see Burlingame, who maintains that Lincoln was ambitious, but not at the expense of his principles. *The Inner World,* 236. For further discussion of the principled nature of Lincoln's ambition, see Lord Charnwood, *Abraham Lincoln* (Garden City, N.Y.: Garden City Pub. Co., 1938), 123; and James M. McPherson, *Abraham Lincoln and the Second American Revolution* (New York: Oxford University Press, 1990), 126.

14. Abraham Lincoln, *Speeches and Writings, 1859–1865,* ed. Don E. Fehren-bacher (New York: Library of America, 1989), 212.

15. Ibid., 213.

16. Oates, *Abraham Lincoln,* 59.

17. Lincoln, "Message to Congress, 4 July 1861," in *Speeches and Writings, 1859–1865,* 259.

18. Oates, *Abraham Lincoln,* 59f.

19. Ibid., 60.

20. Ibid.

21. Burlingame, *The Inner World,* 245, 246, 247.

22. Lincoln, "Speech on the Kansas-Nebraska Act," in *Speeches and Writings, 1832–1858,* ed. Don E. Fehrenbacher (New York: Library of America, 1989), 340.

23. Lincoln, "Address to the Young Men's Lyceum of Springfield, Illinois," in *Speeches and Writings, 1832–1858,* 34.

24. Quoted in Oates, *With Malice toward None,* 35.

25. On this point, see Charnwood, *Abraham Lincoln,* 118, 126; and Fehren-bacher, *Prelude to Greatness,* 22, 25.

26. Adair, *Fame and the Founding Fathers,* 11.

27. John F. Kennedy, *Profiles in Courage* (New York: Harper & Row, 1964), 250–251.

28. Wilson, *Honor's Voice,* 205.

29. Quoted in ibid., 203.

30. Wilson, *Honor's Voice,* 301.

31. Ibid., 314f. See also Philip B. Kunhardt, Jr., et al., *The American President* (New York: Riverhead Books, 1999), 105. Kunhardt quotes a colleague of Lincoln's who said that Lincoln "handled men remotely," like "pieces on a chessboard."

32. Burlingame, *The Inner World,* 148. See also Carl Sandburg, *Abraham Lincoln: The Prairie Years,* 2 vols. (New York: Harcourt Brace, 1926), 1:392; and Benjamin P. Thomas, *Abraham Lincoln: A Biography* (New York: Alfred A. Knopf, 1952), 84, both cited in Burlingame, 148. Lincoln was particu-larly adept at mimicking accents, mannerisms, gestures, and physical de-fects, according to Burlingame, 149.

33. Quoted in Wilson, *Honor's Voice,* 315.

34. Ibid., 315f.

35. Wilson, *Honor's Voice,* 315.

36. Oates, *Abraham Lincoln,* 126.

37. Wilson, *Honor's Voice,* 296f.

38. Ibid., 297.

39. Thus he has been called "the foremost political spokesman in America for the liberating impulse of the age." Oates, *Abraham Lincoln,* xii.

40. Lincoln, "Speech on the Dred Scott Decision," in *Speeches and Writings, 1832–1858,* 400.

41. Ibid., 398.

42. Lincoln, "Speech on the Kansas-Nebraska Act," in *Speeches and Writings, 1832–1858,* 337f.

43. Lincoln, "Speech on the Dred Scott Decision," in *Speeches and Writings, 1832–1858,* 398f.

44. Ibid., 398.

45. For further discussion of Lincoln's progressive interpretation of the Declaration, see Jaffa, *Crisis of the House Divided,* 315–321.

46. Lincoln, "Address to the Young Men's Lyceum," 1:34.

47. Ibid.

48. See McPherson, *Abraham Lincoln and the Second American Founding.*

49. Oates, *Abraham Lincoln,* 60. Since early in his political career, he had advocated "a national bank, internal improvements financed by the federal government, federal subsidies to help the states build their own canals, turnpikes, and railroads, and state banks whose task was to ensure financial growth and stability." In general, he regarded it as "the legitimate object of government . . . to do for the people what needs to be done, but which they can not, by individual effort, do at all, or do so well, for themselves." Lincoln, *Collected Works,* ed. Roy P. Basler et al., 9 vols. (New Brunswick, N.J., 1953–55), 2:220–221. Quoted in Oates, *Abraham Lincoln,* 60.

50. In a special message to Congress on July 4, 1861, Lincoln described the Civil War, which had begun at Fort Sumter on April 12 of that year, in world-historical terms: "It presents to the whole family of man, the question, whether a constitutional republic, or a democracy—a government of the people, by the same people—can, or cannot, maintain its territorial integrity, against its own domestic foes . . . It forces us to ask: 'Is there, in all republics, this inherent, and fatal weakness?' 'Must a government, of necessity, be too *strong* for the liberties of its own people, or too *weak* to maintain its own existence?' " Lincoln, "Message to Congress in Special Session," in *Speeches and Writings, 1859–1865,* 250.

51. Oates, *Abraham Lincoln,* 111. On the same point, see McPherson, who maintains that Lincoln effected a true revolution in American political life, in *Abraham Lincoln and the Second American Revolution,* 24, 42. Fehrenbacher, in contrast, sees Lincoln as neither a conservative nor a radical but a combination of both, a statesman who "favored slow, firm progress toward a revolutionary goal," in *Prelude to Greatness,* 148.

52. Oates, *Abraham Lincoln,* 111.

53. Kunhardt, *The American President,* 348.

54. Oates, *Abraham Lincoln,* 121.

55. Kunhardt, *The American President*, 348.
56. Oates, *Abraham Lincoln*, 122.
57. Ibid., 121.
58. See, for example, Lincoln's special message to Congress in *Speeches and Writings, 1859–1865*, 246–261. For further discussion of Lincoln's efforts to justify his actions, see Oates, *Abraham Lincoln*, 122–123.
59. Oates, *Abraham Lincoln*, 125.
60. Quoted in ibid.
61. Lincoln, "Speech on the Dred Scott Decision," 1:398.
62. Ibid., 1:402.
63. For this reason, the legend of Lincoln as the Great Emancipator has been challenged by what Oates calls "a counterlegend" of Lincoln "as a bigot, as a white racist who championed segregation, opposed civil and political rights for black people, wanted them all thrown out of the country." Oates, *Our Fiery Trial*, 61.
64. Indeed, Lincoln lost his 1858 Senate race to Stephen Douglas largely because "his controversial views on slavery and the Negro . . . were too advanced for his neighbors" in Illinois (Oates, *Abraham Lincoln*, 74). See also McPherson for a discussion of the political reasons why Lincoln took a relatively conservative position on slavery in 1861, in *Abraham Lincoln and the Second American Revolution*, 31.
65. Oates, *Abraham Lincoln*, 101, 113f.
66. Ibid., 113.
67. Quoted in ibid., 118.
68. See, for example, the speech entitled "The Slaveholders' Rebellion" (July 4, 1862) in *Frederick Douglass: Selected Speeches and Writings*, ed. Philip S. Foner (Chicago: Lawrence Hill, 1999), 501–503, 506; and "Oration in Memory of Abraham Lincoln" (April 14, 1876) in *The Life and Writing of Frederick Douglass*, ed. Philip S. Foner (New York: International, 1975), 4:309–319.
69. Ibid.
70. Oates, *Abraham Lincoln*, 62.
71. Ibid., 101.
72. Ibid., 104.
73. Lincoln, "Final Emancipation Proclamation," in *Speeches and Writings, 1859–1865*, 425; and see his letter to John A. McClernand, 8 January 1863, in *Speeches and Writings, 1859–1865*, 428. On this point, see Neely, *The Last Best Hope*, 95.
74. One sees the same type of moderation in Lincoln's reluctance to offer "resistance" to the authority of the Supreme Court over what he considered to be its "erroneous" decision in the Dred Scott case (Lincoln, "Speech on the Dred Scott Decision," 393). He emphasized the importance of "obedience

to, and respect for the judicial department of government" (392) even as he denied that the decision "established a settled doctrine for the country" and attacked it point by point (393). He clearly meant to influence the Court in the direction of a future reversal and to influence public opinion, as well, but he meant to effect his influence in a civil fashion.

75. W. E. B. Du Bois, "Resolutions of the Niagara Movement," in *African-American Social and Political Thought*, ed. Howard Brotz (New Brunswick, N.J.: Transactions, 1995), 539.

76. Booker T. Washington, "Early Problems of Freedom," in *African-American Social and Political Thought*, ed. Brotz, 388f.

77. Waldo E. Martin, Jr., *The Mind of Frederick Douglass* (Chapel Hill: University of North Carolina Press, 1984), 253, 277.

78. Frederick Douglass, *My Bondage and My Freedom* (New York: Dover, 1969), 251.

79. Ibid., 241.

80. Ibid., 241–246. Emphasis in the original. Douglass surmises that Covey refrained from punishing him later or turning him over to the authorities out of fear for his own reputation. To do so would have been to admit that he had been unable to control one of his slaves. See ibid., 248.

81. Ibid., 247.

82. Ibid., 246.

83. Ibid., 246f.

84. Ibid., 247.

85. Ibid.

86. Ibid. Emphasis in the original.

87. Douglass, *My Bondage,* 247.

88. Ibid.

89. Kenneth S. Greenberg, *Honor and Slavery* (Princeton: Princeton University Press, 1996), 35f.

90. Douglass, *My Bondage,* 247.

91. Frederick Douglass, *Narrative of the Life of Frederick Douglass* (New York: Dolphin, 1963), 86.

92. Douglass, *My Bondage,* 247.

93. When Douglass suggests that slaves will always be slaves as long as they are afraid to die, one could think him callous or guilty of "blaming the victim," as we say today. One might think it preferable to draw attention to the shamefulness of the slave owner or the ignominy of a society that forces upon any human being the desperate choice between slavery and death. How many of us, if confronted with such a choice, would be high-hearted enough to take the latter course, even if death by resistance were indeed to make us "free in fact," as Douglass maintained it would do? To instruct the oppressed that they ought to prefer a noble death over an

undignified life is no solution to the problem of injustice. A complete solution to the problem of injustice, if it could be achieved, would mean eradicating the necessity of such a choice entirely. Even a partial solution, or a piecemeal attack on injustice, would have to attend as much to the motives of those in power as to those of the oppressed. And no theory of justice would be feasible if it required perfect fearlessness in the face of death. Such a theory would be so ill suited to human nature as to be unjust itself. Yet if Douglass's remarks in this regard do not contribute much to a theory of justice, his example does help us to understand individual agency, which is the primary object of this inquiry. For liberal societies, the meaning of justice and the sources of individual agency are related concerns, but they mark out two distinct terrains.

94. Douglass, *My Bondage,* 247.

95. Ibid., 246f.

96. Ibid., 247.

97. Ibid., 242.

98. Ibid., 246.

99. In connection with Frederick Douglass, Leonard Harris has emphasized that "honor as a quality of character and public honors need not go together." Slave owners, Harris points out, "had honor as status but not necessarily as a quality," while a "slave could be honorable without public honors." Leonard Harris, "Honor and Insurrection," in *Frederick Douglass: A Critical Reader,* ed. Bill E. Lawson and Frank M. Kirkland (Oxford: Blackwell, 1999), 235.

100. Philip S. Foner, "Introduction" to Douglass, *My Bondage,* x. For more on Frederick Douglass's relation to and break with the Garrisonian school, see David E. Schrader, "Natural Law in the Constitutional Thought of Frederick Douglass" in *Frederick Douglass: A Critical Reader,* ed. Lawson and Kirkland, p. 86; Charles W. Mills, "Whose Fourth of July? Frederick Douglass and 'Original Intent,' " in *Frederick Douglass: A Critical Reader,* ed. Lawson and Kirkland, 104; Diana Schaub, "Frederick Douglass's Constitution," in *The American Experiment: Essays on the Theory and Practice of Liberty,* ed. Peter Augustine Lawler and Robert Martin Schaefer (Lanham, Md.: Rowman & Littlefield, 1994); and Herbert Storing, "Frederick Douglass," in *American Political Thought,* ed. Morton Frisch and Richard Stevens (Itasca, Ill.: F. E. Peacock, 1983).

101. For a discussion of Douglass's conversion from Garrisonianism, see David W. Blight, *Frederick Douglass' Civil War: Keeping Faith in Jubilee* (Baton Rouge: Louisiana State University Press, 1989), 32f.

102. Frederick Douglass, "Speech on the Dred Scott Decision," in *African-American Social and Political Thought,* ed. Brotz, 253.

103. Kelly Miller maintains that Frederick Douglass's conduct was actuated by the principles found in the Declaration and the Constitution. Kelly Miller, "Radicals and Conservatives" in *Critical Essays on Frederick Douglass,* ed. William L. Andrews (Boston: G. K. Hall, 1991), 36.

104. Frederick Douglass, "What the Black Man Wants," in *African-American Social and Political Thought,* ed. Brotz, 278.

105. Ibid.

106. Ibid., 282.

107. Douglass, "The Slaveholders' Rebellion," 500.

108. Douglass, "What the Black Man Wants," 281.

109. Douglass, "The Slaveholders' Rebellion," 499–500.

110. Washington, "Early Problems of Freedom," 393.

111. Ibid., 394.

112. Ibid.

113. Ibid., 395.

114. Ibid., 388. Douglass's famous, most widely delivered speech, entitled "Self-Made Men," indicates a very *grand* (in Tocqueville's sense) self-conception on his part as being not only the exemplary black man or even American, but even the exemplary human being. Frederick Douglass, "Self-Made Men," in *The Frederick Douglass Papers,* ed. John W. Blassingame (New Haven: Yale University Press, 1979–92), vol. 5.

115. Washington, "Early Problems of Freedom," 388.

116. Ibid.

117. Ibid.

118. Ibid.

119. Ibid., 395.

120. Ibid., 388.

121. Ibid., 395.

122. Quoted in ibid., 395f.

123. Washington, "Early Problems of Freedom," 396.

124. See Wilson Moses, "Where Honor Is Due: Frederick Douglass as Representative Black Man," *Prospects,* 17 (1992): 177–189.

125. Martin, *The Mind of Frederick Douglass,* 253.

126. Ibid., 272.

127. Douglass, *My Bondage,* 404.

128. Ibid., 404f.

129. Ibid., 405.

130. Ibid.

131. Booker T. Washington, "On Making Our Race Life Count in the Life of the Nation," in *African-American Social and Political Thought,* ed. Brotz, 382.

132. Washington, "Early Problems of Freedom," 389.

133. Ibid., 390, 392.

134. See, for example, Douglass's 1876 address on the occasion of the unveiling of the Freedmen's Monument. For further discussion on this point, see Storing, "Frederick Douglass."

135. Stevens, *Pistols at Ten Paces*, 1.

136. Although Douglass often links manhood specifically with being male, the self-respect and honor it entails are achievements that come "from wrenching oneself away from enslavement and by implication from biological creation altogether. The struggle . . . puts literal [that is, biological] survival at risk in the name of self-respect and honor." R. King, *Civil Rights and the Idea of Freedom*, 79. King also discusses the "confrontational model of freedom," tied to the sense of honor, in relation to black women in the civil rights movement, 79–81.

137. Douglass, *My Bondage*, 92.

138. Ibid., 93.

139. Ibid., 95.

140. Ibid.

141. Greenberg, *Honor and Slavery*, 39.

142. Elizabeth Cady Stanton, "Address to the Woman's Convention, Held at Akron, Ohio, May 25, 1851," reprinted in *The Female Experience: An American Documentary*, ed. Gerda Lerner (Indianapolis: Bobbs-Merrill, 1977), 416. Emphasis in original.

143. Ellen Carol DuBois, ed., *Elizabeth Cady Stanton, Susan B. Anthony: Correspondence, Writings, Speeches* (New York: Schocken, 1981), "Introduction," xiii.

144. Susan B. Anthony, letter to Elizabeth Cady Stanton, 5 June 1856, in *Correspondence, Writings, Speeches*, ed. DuBois, 62.

145. Susan B. Anthony, "Constitutional Argument," in *Correspondence, Writings, Speeches*, ed. DuBois, 165.

146. Anthony, letter to Stanton, 29 September 1857, in *Correspondence, Writings, Speeches*, ed. DuBois, 67.

147. Elizabeth Cady Stanton, "Address to the Founding Convention of the National American Woman Suffrage Association," February 1890, in *Correspondence, Writings, Speeches*, ed. DuBois, 226.

148. Elizabeth Cady Stanton, "Address to the Legislature of New York on Women's Rights," 14 February 1854, in *Correspondence, Writings, Speeches*, ed. DuBois, 44.

149. Quoted in Anna Howard Shaw, "The Passing of Aunt Susan," in *Correspondence, Writings, Speeches*, ed. DuBois, 260.

150. Not all honorable women in American history have shared this particular form of honor or tied their ambitions to this set of principles. For some,

the sense of honor has been tied to more traditional, specifically feminine codes of conduct and spheres of activity.

151. Elizabeth Cady Stanton, Lucretia Mott, et al., "Declaration of Sentiments and Resolutions," in *From Many, One: Readings in American Political and Social Thought*, ed. Richard C. Sinopoli (Washington, D.C.: Georgetown University Press, 1997), 119.

152. Ibid., 120.

153. Ibid., 119.

154. Elizabeth Cady Stanton, "Address Delivered at Seneca Falls," in *Correspondence, Writings, Speeches*, ed. DuBois, 31.

155. Stanton, "Address to the Legislature of New York on Women's Rights," 49.

156. Stanton, "Declaration of Sentiments," 120.

157. Thus Miroff notes that Stanton simultaneously subverted and fulfilled traditional American values. Miroff, *Icons of Democracy*, 126.

158. Stanton, "Address to the Legislature of New York on Women's Rights," 46; and Elizabeth Cady Stanton, "The Solitude of Self," in *Correspondence, Writings, Speeches*, ed. DuBois, 247.

159. Elizabeth Cady Stanton, "Address of Welcome to the International Council of Women," in *Correspondence, Writings, Speeches*, ed. DuBois, 215.

160. DuBois, "Introduction," 16.

161. Anthony, letter to *The Lily*, 26 August 1852, in *Correspondence, Writings, Speeches*, ed. DuBois, 40. See also DuBois, "Introduction," 16f., 21.

162. DuBois, "Introduction," 17.

163. Anthony, "Homes of Single Women," in *Correspondence, Writings, Speeches*, ed. DuBois, 148.

164. Ibid.

165. Stanton, "Address Delivered at Seneca Falls," 33.

166. Stanton, "Address to the Legislature of New York on Women's Rights," 45.

167. Ibid.

168. Ibid., 44. See also Miroff, who emphasizes that the objective of legal reform for Stanton went beyond women's interests to freedom and dignity as ends in themselves. Miroff, *Icons of Democracy*, 133.

169. Stanton, "Address of Welcome to the International Council of Women," 210.

170. Anthony, "Constitutional Argument," 163.

171. Elizabeth Cady Stanton, *Eighty Years and More: Reminiscences, 1815–1897* (New York: T. Fischer Unwin, 1898), 187.

172. Stanton, "Address Delivered at Seneca Falls," 34.

173. Ibid., 32.

174. Stanton, "Address of Welcome to the International Council of Women," 209.

175. Elizabeth Griffin notes that Stanton's "most remarkable trait was her self-confidence." Elizabeth Griffin, *In Her Own Right* (New York: Oxford University Press, 1984), xiv.

176. Stanton, "Address Delivered at Seneca Falls," 3. In *The Woman's Bible,* Stanton characterized Eve as a woman of "lofty ambition," driven by "the highest strivings of the human heart." Elizabeth Cady Stanton, *The Woman's Bible* (Boston: Northeastern University Press, 1993), 24–25. And like Lincoln and the American founders, she defended the passion for distinction as a worthy motive for political life. See Miroff, *Icons of Democracy,* 148–149. Her autobiography was self-consciously constructed as "heroic," as Griffin shows, and she thought of herself in historic and heroic terms, fully expecting to be remembered by history. Griffin, *In Her Own Right,* xvii, xix.

177. Stanton, "Address Delivered at Seneca Falls," 29.

178. On Stanton's proud air of superiority, see Miroff, *Icons of Democracy,* 155.

179. Susan B. Anthony, "Suffrage and the Working Woman," in *Correspondence, Writings, Speeches,* ed. DuBois, 139.

180. Ibid., 139, 140.

181. Elizabeth Cady Stanton, "Appeal for the Maine Law," in *Correspondence, Writings, Speeches,* ed. DuBois, 42.

182. DuBois, "Introduction" to part 2, *Correspondence, Writings, Speeches,* ed. DuBois, 99.

183. Stanton, "The Solitude of Self," 249.

184. Anthony, "Suffrage and the Working Woman," 140.

185. Stanton, "The Solitude of Self," 251.

186. Stanton, letter to Anthony, 10 September 1855, in *Correspondence, Writings, Speeches,* ed. DuBois, 58, 59.

187. Stanton, letter to Anthony, 20 June 1853, in *Correspondence, Writings, Speeches,* ed. DuBois, 56.

188. Stanton, letter to Anthony, 2 April 1852, in *Correspondence, Writings, Speeches,* ed. DuBois, 55.

189. Stanton, letter to Anthony, 10 June 1856, in *Correspondence, Writings, Speeches,* ed. DuBois, 63.

190. Stanton, "Address of Welcome to the International Council of Women," 211.

191. Stanton died in 1902 and Anthony in 1906; the nineteenth amendment was passed in 1920.

192. *Time,* 18 February 1957. Quoted in Stephen B. Oates, *Let the Trumpet Sound: A Life of Martin Luther King, Jr.* (New York: Harper Perennial, 1994), 115.

193. Quoted in Oates, *Trumpet,* 280.

194. David L. Lewis, *King: A Critical Biography* (New York: Praeger, 1970), x.
195. Quoted in Oates, *Trumpet,* 127.
196. Lewis, *King,* 60.
197. Quoted in R. King, *Civil Rights and the Idea of Freedom,* 92.
198. Ibid., 93.
199. Lewis, *King,* 109. Miroff also refers to King's "opposing tendencies—to grandiosity and humility." Miroff, *Icons of Democracy,* 308, 314.
200. R. King, *Civil Rights and the Idea of Freedom,* 93.
201. Lewis, *King,* 8.
202. Ibid., 4, 5.
203. Ibid., 5.
204. Ibid. Richard Lischer emphasizes the high social status of the clergy in the black community. A black preacher, he says, especially in the South, was akin to a "king in a private kingdom," and a special place in the social hierarchy was reserved for the preacher's son. Richard Lischer, *The Preacher King* (New York: Oxford University Press, 1995), 25.
205. Lewis, *King,* 7.
206. Ibid.
207. Ibid., 14.
208. Oates, *Trumpet,* 149.
209. Ibid.
210. Williams Holmes Borders, letter to King, 19 December 1956, in Martin Luther King, Jr., Collection, Mugar Memorial Library, Boston University. Quoted in Oates, *Trumpet,* 104.
211. Oates, *Trumpet,* 150.
212. Ibid., 85.
213. Ibid., 157.
214. Ibid., 308, 352. David Garrow reports that some thought King "took too many bows and enjoyed them," and that he tended to forget that the movement was a collective effort. Garrow, *Bearing the Cross,* 89.
215. Quoted in Oates, *Trumpet,* 127.
216. Oates, *Trumpet,* 127.
217. This envy is not an altogether bad thing, as it may spark a healthy skepticism of political authorities, which is central to the spirit of honorable independence that sustains individual liberties. And as Miroff emphasizes, political leaders idolized by the public sometimes have undermined the possibilities for democratic participation. Indeed, excessive idolization of democratic leaders may itself engender passivity on the part of citizens. See Miroff, *Icons of Democracy,* x, 1; and Chapter 1, note 25 above.
218. Quoted in R. King, *Civil Rights and the Idea of Freedom,* 51.
219. M. King, "Letter from Birmingham City Jail," 302.

220. Quoted in Oates, *Trumpet*, 70.
221. Quoted in R. King, *Civil Rights and the Idea of Freedom*, 103.
222. Quoted in Oates, *Trumpet*, 167.
223. R. King, *Civil Rights and the Idea of Freedom*, 202, 203.
224. Daniel Rodgers, *Contested Truths: Keywords in American Politics since Independence* (New York: Basic Books, 1987), 78. Quoted in R. King, *Civil Rights and the Idea of Freedom*, 30.
225. Martin Luther King, Jr., *Why We Can't Wait* (New York: Harper and Row, 1964), 59.
226. Oates, *Trumpet*, 87.
227. Ibid.
228. Quoted in ibid., 93.
229. Quoted in ibid., 282.
230. Quoted in R. King, *Civil Rights and the Idea of Freedom*, 93.
231. Quoted in Oates, *Trumpet*, 455. Garrow reports that King once remarked, "Once you become dedicated to a cause, personal security is not the goal. It is greater than that." Garrow, *Bearing the Cross*, 84.
232. R. King, *Civil Rights and the Idea of Freedom*, 47.
233. Quoted in ibid., 124.
234. R. King, *Civil Rights and the Idea of Freedom*, 93.
235. Quoted in ibid., 57.
236. R. King, *Civil Rights and the Idea of Freedom*, 50.
237. Ibid., 56, 57.
238. Ibid., 51.
239. Harris, "Honor and Insurrection," 238.
240. See, for example, Pat Watters and Reese Cleghorn, *Climbing Jacob's Ladder* (New York: Harcourt, Brace and World, 1967); Pat Watters, *Down to Now* (New York: Pantheon, 1971); David Garrow, *Protest at Selma* (New Haven: Yale University Press, 1978); and Charles Hamilton and Stokely Carmichael, *Black Power* (New York: Vintage, 1967); all cited in R. King, *Civil Rights and the Idea of Freedom*, 6.
241. Quoted in R. King, *Civil Rights and the Idea of Freedom*, 47.
242. R. King, *Civil Rights and the Idea of Freedom*, 66, 69.
243. Ibid., 14.
244. Quoted in Oates, *Trumpet*, 104.
245. Oates, *Trumpet*, 209, 218; and R. King, *Civil Rights and the Idea of Freedom*, 43.
246. R. King, *Civil Rights and the Idea of Freedom*, 43.
247. Ibid.
248. This is not to deny that they felt terrible after failed demonstrations. Nev-

ertheless, Miroff draws attention to the redemptive power of democratic action and its connection to the sense of dignity in *Icons of Democracy,* xv.

249. R. King, *Civil Rights and the Idea of Freedom,* 15.

250. Garrow, *Bearing the Cross,* 430.

251. R. King, *Civil Rights and the Idea of Freedom,* 15.

252. Ibid.

253. Ibid.

254. And despite the limits of justice as a source of agency, standards of justice matter a great deal as a check on the content of honor codes and the proliferation of honor claims.

255. Quoted in Oates, *Trumpet,* 424.

256. R. King, Civil Rights and the Idea of Freedom, 119, 155–157.

6. Conclusion

1. Thus by "fixed standards" I do not refer to standards that are timeless or fixed forever in history. Codes of honor are fixed not in the sense of being absolutely unchanging but in the sense of being more than merely the expression of individual will.

2. Walzer, *Spheres of Justice,* 262.

3. Ibid., 274f.

4. Montesquieu, *The Spirit of the Laws,* Preface. Emphasis added.

BIBLIOGRAPHY

Works by Montesquieu

Montesquieu, Charles-Louis de Secondat baron de la Brède et de. *Considerations on the Causes of the Greatness of the Romans and Their Decline.* Translated by David Lowenthal. New York: Free Press, 1965.

———— *De l'esprit des lois.* In vol. II of *Oeuvres complètes,* edited by Roger Caillois, 2 vols. Paris: Gallimard, "Bibliothèque de la Pléiade," 1949–51.

———— *Mes pensées.* In vol. I of *Oeuvres complètes,* edited by Roger Caillois, 2 vols. Paris: Gallimard, "Bibliothèque de la Pléiade," 1949–51.

———— *Persian Letters.* Translated by George R. Healy. Indianapolis: Bobbs-Merrill, 1964.

———— *The Spirit of the Laws.* Translated by Anne M. Cohler, Basia Carolyn Miller, and Harold Samuel Stone. Cambridge: Cambridge University Press, 1989.

Works about Montesquieu

Althusser, Louis. *Politics and History: Montesquieu, Rousseau, Marx.* Translated by Ben Brewster. London: Verso, 1982.

Baker, Keith Michael. *Inventing the French Revolution.* Cambridge: Cambridge University Press, 1990.

———— *The Old Regime and the French Revolution.* Chicago: University of Chicago Press, 1987.

Barrière, Pierre. *Un grand provincial: Charles-Louis de Secondat, baron de La Brède et de Montesquieu.* Bordeaux: Delmas, 1946.

Baum, John Alan. *Montesquieu and Social Theory.* Oxford: Pergamon, 1979.

Behdad, Ali. "The Eroticized Orient: Images of the Harem in Montesquieu and His Precursors." *Stanford French Review,* 13, nos. 2–3 (Fall–Winter 1989): 109–126.

Benrekassa, Georges. "Kant, la question du droit et Montesquieu." In *Lectures de Montesquieu,* edited by Edgar Mass, 11–23. Naples: Liguoir Editore, 1993.

———— *Montesquieu: La liberté et l'histoire*. Paris: Librairie Générale Française, 1987.

Berlin, Isaiah. "Montesquieu." In *Against the Current*. New York: Viking Press, 1980.

Bertière, A. "Montesquieu, lecteur de Machiavel." *Actes du congrès Montesquieu réuni à Bordeaux du 23 au 26 mai 1955 pour comémorer la deuxième centenair de la mort de Montesquieu*, 141–158. Bordeaux: Impriméries Delmas, 1956.

Beyer, Charles Jacques. "Montesquieu et l'esprit Cartésien." *Actes du congrès Montesquieu réuni à Bordeaux du 23 au 26 mai 1955 pour comémorer la deuxième centenair de la mort de Montesquieu*, 159–173. Bordeaux: Impriméries Delmas, 1956.

Bianchi, Lorenzo. "Nécessité de la religion et de la tolérance chez Montesquieu." In *Lectures de Montesquieu*, edited by Edgar Mass, 25–40. Naples: Liguoir Editore, 1993.

Boesche, Roger. "Fearing Monarchs and Merchants: Montesquieu's Two Theories of Despotism." *Western Political Quarterly*, 43, no. 4 (December 1990): 741–762.

Callot, Emile. *La philosophie de la vie au XVIIIe siècle*. Paris: Éditions Marcel Rivière, 1965.

Carcassone, E. "La Chine dans *L'esprit des lois*." In *Revue d'histoire littéraire de la France*, 193–205. Paris: Librairie Armand Colin, 1924.

———— *Montesquieu et le problème de la constitution française au XVIIIe siècle*. Paris: Les Presses Universitaires, 1926.

Carrese, Paul. "Montesquieu's Moderate Constitutionalism." Paper presented at the annual meeting of the American Political Science Association, Atlanta, Georgia, 1999.

Carrithers, David. "Introduction" to *The Spirit of the Laws*. Berkeley: University of California Press, 1977.

———— "Montesquieu's Philosophy of History." *Journal of the History of Ideas*, 47, no. 1 (1986): 61–80.

———— "Montesquieu's Philosophy of Punishment." *History of Political Thought*, 19, no. 2 (Summer 1998): 213–240.

———— "Not So Virtuous Republics: Montesquieu, Venice, and the Theory of Aristocratic Republicanism." *Journal of the History of Ideas*, 52, no. 2 (June 1991): 245–268.

Chevallier, J. J. "Montesquieu ou le libéralisme aristocratique." *Revue Internationale de la Philosophie*, 9 (1955): 330–345.

Cohler, Anne M. *Montesquieu's Comparative Politics and the Spirit of American Constitutionalism*. Lawrence: University Press of Kansas, 1988.

Conroy, Peter V., Jr. *Montesquieu Revisited*. New York: Twayne Publishers, 1992.

Cotta, A. "L'idée de parti dans la philosophie politique de Montesquieu." *Actes du congrès Montesquieu réuni à Bordeaux du 23 au 26 mai 1955 pour comémorer la deuxième centenair de la mort de Montesquieu,* 257–263. Bordeaux: Imприméries Delmas, 1956.

Courtney, C. P. *Montesquieu and Burke.* Oxford: Basil Blackwell, 1963.

———. "Montesquieu and Revolution." In *Lectures de Montesquieu,* edited by Edgar Mass, 41–62. Naples: Liguoir Editore, 1993.

Cox, Iris. *Montesquieu and the History of French Laws.* Oxford: Voltaire Foundation, 1983.

Dalat, Jean. *Montesquieu magistrat.* Paris: Minard, 1971.

Dargan, Edwin. *The Aesthetic Doctrine of Montesquieu.* Baltimore: J. H. Furst Co., 1907.

Dedieu, J. *Montesquieu et la tradition politique anglaise en France.* New York: Burt Franklin, 1909.

Desgraves, Louis. *Montesquieu.* Paris: Maxarine, 1986.

de Tracy, Destutt. *A Commentary and Review of Montesquieu's "Spirit of the Laws."* Translated by Thomas Jefferson. New York: Burt Franklin, 1969.

Devletoglou, Nicos. *Montesquieu and the Wealth of Nations.* Athens: Constantinides and Mihalos, 1963.

Dodds, Muriel. *Les recits de voyages: Sources de L'esprit des lois de Montesquieu.* Paris: Les Presses Modernes, 1929.

Doyle, William. *The Parlement of Bordeaux and the End of the Old Regime, 1771–1790.* New York: St. Martin's Press, 1974.

Duconseil, Marc. *Machiavel et Montesquieu: Recherche sur un principle d'autorité.* Paris: Les Éditions Denoël, 1943.

Durkheim, Emile. *Montesquieu and Rousseau: Forerunners of Sociology.* Translated by Ralph Manheim. Ann Arbor: University of Michigan Press, 1960.

Egret, Jean. *Louis XV et l'opposition parlementaire, 1715–1774.* Paris: Armand Colin, 1970.

Ehrard, Jean. "Presentation." In *Politique de Montesquieu.* Edited by Jean Ehrard. Paris: Armand Colin, 1965.

Eisenmann, Charles. "*L'esprit des lois* et la séparation des pouvoirs." *Cahiers de philosophie politique.* Reims: Université de Reims, 1985.

Faguet, Emile. *La politique comparée de Montesquieu, Rousseau, et Voltaire.* Paris: Société Française d'Imprimerie et de Librairie, 1902.

Fletcher, F. T. H. *Montesquieu and English Politics.* London: Edward Arnold, 1939.

Ford, Franklin. *Robe and Sword: The Regrouping of the French Aristocracy after Louis XIV.* Cambridge: Harvard University Press, 1953.

Fricaud, Solange. "Pour qui est écrit *L'esprit des lois?*" In *Analyses et réflexions sur Montesquieu,* edited by Joel Askenazi et al., 180–188. Paris: Edition Marketing, 1987.

Furet, François. "Révolution française et tradition jacobine." In *The French Rev-*

olution and the Creation of Modern Political Culture, vol. 2, 329–339. Oxford: Pergamon, 1988.

Gay, Peter. *The Enlightenment: An Interpretation.* Vol. 2. New York: Alfred A. Knopf, 1969.

Gilbert, Alan. " 'Internal Restlessness': Individuality and Community in Montesquieu." *Political Theory,* 22, no. 1 (February 1994): 45–70.

Goyard-Fabre, Simone. *Montesquieu: La nature, les lois, la liberté.* Paris: Presses Universitaires de France, 1993.

———— *Montesquieu adversaire de Hobbes.* Paris: Lettres Modernes, 1980.

———— *La philosophie du droit de Montesquieu.* Paris: Librairie C. Klincksieck, 1973.

Granpre Molière, Jean Jacques. *Theorie de la constitution anglaise Montesquieu.* Leyde: Presse Universitaire, 1972.

Green, F. C. *Eighteenth-Century France.* London: J. M. Dent & Sons, 1929.

Grosrichard, *Structure du sérail: La fiction du despotisme asiatique dans l'occident classique.* Paris: Éditions du Seuil, 1979.

Gwyn, W. B. *The Meaning of the Separation of Powers.* The Hague: Nijhoff, 1965.

Hampson, Norman. *Will and Circumstance: Montesquieu, Rousseau and the French Revolution.* London: Duckworth, 1983.

Hearnshaw, F. J. C. *The Social and Political Ideas of Some Great French Thinkers of the Age of Reason.* New York: Barnes and Noble, 1931.

Hirschman, Albert O. *The Passions and the Interests.* Princeton: Princeton University Press, 1977.

Hulliung, Mark. *Montesquieu and the Old Regime.* Berkeley: University of California Press, 1976.

Hundert, E. J., and Paul Nelles. "Liberty and Theatrical Space in Montesquieu's Political Theory: The Poetics of Public Life in *'The Persian Letters.'* " *Political Theory* 17, no. 2 (May 1989): 223–246.

Ilbert, Courtenay. *Montesquieu.* Oxford: Clarendon Press, 1904.

Joly, Maurice. *Dialogue aux enfers entre Machiavel et Montesquieu, ou, La politique de Machiavel au XIXe siècle.* Brussells: Imprimerie de A. Mertens et Fils, 1864.

Jones, Robert Alun. "Ambivalent Cartesians: Durkheim, Montesquieu and Method." *American Journal of Sociology,* 100, no. 1 (July 1994): 1–39.

Kassem, Badreddine. *Décadence et absolutisme dans l'oeuvre de Montesquieu.* Paris: Librairie Minard, 1960.

Keohane, Nannerl O. *Philosophy and the State in France.* Princeton: Princeton University Press, 1980.

———— "Virtuous Republics and Glorious Monarchies: Two Models in Montesquieu's Political Thought." *Political Studies,* 20, no. 4 (December 1972): 383–396.

Kessler, Sanford. "Religion and Liberalism in Montesquieu's *Persian Letters*." *Polity,* 15 (Spring 1983): 380–396.

Kingston, Rebecca. *Montesquieu and the Parlement of Bordeaux.* Geneva: Librairie Droz, 1996.

Knee, Philip. "La question de l'appartenance: Montesquieu, Rousseau, et la Révolution française." *Canadian Journal of Political Science,* 22, no. 2 (June 1989): 285–311.

Koebner, R. "Despot and Despotism: Vicissitudes of a Political Term." *Journal of the Warburg and Courtauld Institutes,* 14 nos. 1–2 (1951): 275–302.

Kra, Pauline. "Montesquieu and Women." In *French Women and the Age of Enlightenment,* edited by Samia Spencer. Bloomington: Indiana University Press, 1984.

Krause, Sharon. "Despotism in *The Spirit of Laws*." In *Montesquieu's Science of Politics,* edited by David Carrithers, Michael Mosher, and Paul Rahe. Lanham, Md.: Rowman & Littlefield, 2001.

Larrère, Catherine. "Les typologies des gouvernments chez Montesquieu." *Études sur le XVLLLe siècle.* Clermont, 1979.

Levin, Lawrence M. *The Political Doctrine of Montesquieu's Esprit des Lois: Its Classical Background.* New York: Columbia University Press, 1936.

Loirette, Gabriel. "Montesquieu et le problème, en France, du bon gouvernement." *Actes du congrès Montesquieu réuni à Bordeaux du 23 au 26 mai 1955 pour comémorer la deuxième centenair de la mort de Montesquieu,* 219–239. Bordeaux: Impriméries Delmas, 1956.

Lowenthal, David. "Introduction" to Montesquieu, *Considerations on the Causes of the Greatness of the Romans and Their Decline.* New York: Free Press, 1965.

Lynch, Andrew J. "Montesquieu and the Ecclesiastical Critics of *L'esprit des lois*." *Journal of the History of Ideas,* 38, no. 3 (July–September 1977): 487–500.

Manent, Pierre. *The City of Man.* Translated by Marc A. LePain. Princeton: Princeton University Press, 1998.

——— "Montesquieu and the Modern Experience." *Government and Opposition,* 29, no. 3 (Summer 1994): 378–391.

Mansfield, Harvey C., Jr. *Taming the Prince: The Ambivalence of Modern Executive Power.* Baltimore: Johns Hopkins University Press, 1989.

Martin, Kingsley. *French Liberal Thought in the Eighteenth Century.* London: Turnstile Press, 1984.

Mason, Sheila M. *Montesquieu's Idea of Justice.* The Hague: Martinus Nijhoff, 1975.

Mathiez, A. "La place de Montesquieu dans l'histoire des doctrines politiques du XVIIIe siècle." In *Annales historiques de la Révolution française,* vol. 7, 97–112. Paris: Dawson-France, 1930.

McLelland, Jane. "Metaphor in Montesquieu's Theoretical Writings." *Studies on Voltaire and the Eighteenth Century,* 199 (1981): 205–224.

Merry, Henry J. *Montesquieu's System of Natural Government.* West Lafayette, Ind.: Purdue Research Foundation, 1970.

Michel, Emmanuel. *Biographie du parlement de Metz.* Metz: Nouvian, 1853.

Mosher, Michael A. "The Judgmental Gaze of European Women: Gender, Sexuality, and the Critique of Republican Rule." *Political Theory,* 22, no. 1 (February 1994): 25–44.

———— "Monarchy's Paradox: Honor in the Face of Sovereign Power." In *Montesquieu's Science of Politics,* edited by David Carrithers, Michael Mosher, and Paul Rahe. Lanham, Md.: Rowman & Littlefield, 2001.

———— "The Particulars of a Universal Politics: Hegel's Adaptation of Montesquieu's Typology." *American Political Science Review,* 78, no. 1 (March 1984): 179–188.

Myers, Richard. "Christianity and Politics in Montesquieu's *Greatness and Decline of the Romans.*" *Interpretation,* 17, no. 2 (Winter 1989–90): 223–238.

Neumann, Franz. "Montesquieu." Introduction to *The Spirit of the Laws.* New York: Hafner Press, 1949.

Oake, Roger B. "Montesquieu's Analysis of Roman History." *Journal of the History of Ideas,* 16 (1955): 44–59.

Pangle, Thomas L. *Montesquieu's Philosophy of Liberalism: A Commentary on "The Spirit of the Laws."* Chicago: University of Chicago Press, 1973.

Plamenatz, John. *Man and Society.* Vol. 1. New York: McGraw-Hill, 1963.

Rahe, Paul. "Forms of Government: Structure, Principle, Object, and Aim." In *Montesquieu's Science of Politics,* edited by David Carrithers, Michael Mosher, and Paul Rahe. Lanham, Md.: Rowman & Littlefield, 2001.

———— *Republics Ancient and Modern.* Chapel Hill: University of North Carolina Press, 1992.

Richter, Melvin. "Montesquieu's Comparative Analysis of Europe and Asia: Intended and Unintended Consequences." In *L'Europe de Montesquieu: Actes du Colloque de Genes (26–29 mai 1993) organisé par la Société Montesquieu, la Societa italiana di studi sul secolo XVIII, l'Istituto italiano per gli studi filosofici, et le Centro di Studi sull'Eta Moderna,* réunis par Alberto Postigliola et Maria Grazia Battaro Paulumbo. Naples: Liguori Editore, 1995; Oxford: Voltaire Foundation, 1995.

———— *The Political Theory of Montesquieu.* Cambridge: Cambridge University Press, 1977.

Riley, Patrick. *The General Will before Rousseau.* Princeton: Princeton University Press, 1986.

Rosso, Corrado. *Montesquieu moraliste.* Bordeaux: Ducros, 1971.

Sainte-Beuve, Charles-Augustin. *Portraits of the Eighteenth Century: Historic and*

Literary. Vol. 1. Translated by Katherine P. Wormeley. New York: G. P. Putnam's Sons, 1905.

Saintsbury, George. *French Literature and Its Masters.* Edited by Huntington Cairns. New York: Alfred A. Knopf, 1946.

Schaub, Diana. *Erotic Liberalism: Women and Revolution in Montesquieu's "Persian Letters."* Lanham, Md.: Rowman & Littlefield, 1995.

Shackleton, Robert. "Asia as Seen by the French Enlightenment." In *Essays on Montesqueiu and on the Enlightenment,* edited by David Gilson and Martin Smith. Oxford: Voltaire Foundation, 1988.

———— *Montesquieu: A Critical Biography.* London: Oxford University Press, 1961.

———— "Montesquieu and Machiavelli: A Reappraisal." *Comparative Literature Studies,* 1, no. 1 (1964): 1–13.

———— "Les mots 'despote' et 'despotisme.' " In *Essays on Montesquieu and on the Enlightenment,* edited by David Gilson and Martin Smith. Oxford: Voltaire Foundation, 1988.

Shklar, Judith. "General Will." In *Dictionary of the History of Ideas,* edited by Philip P. Wiener, vol. II, 275. New York: Scribner, 1973–74.

———— *Montesquieu.* Oxford: Oxford University Press, 1987.

———— *Ordinary Vices.* Cambridge: Harvard University Press, 1984.

Sorel, Albert. *Montesquieu.* Translated by Melville B. Anderson and Edward Playfair Anderson. Chicago: A. C. McClurg & Co., 1888.

Spitz, David. "Montesquieu's Theory of Freedom." In *Essays in the Liberal Idea of Freedom.* Tucson: University of Arizona Press, 1964.

Starobinski, Jean. *Montesquieu.* Paris: Seuil, 1994.

Venturi, Franco. "Oriental Despotism." *Journal of the History of Ideas,* 24, no. 1 (January–March 1963): 133–142.

Vernière, Paul. *Montesquieu et L'esprit des lois ou la raison impure.* Paris: Société d'Édition d'Enseignement Supérieur, 1977.

———— *Spinoza et la pensée française.* Paris: Presses Universitaires de France, 1954.

Vile, M. J. C. *Constitutionalism and the Separation of Powers.* Oxford: Clarendon Press, 1967.

Vlachos, G. C. *La politique de Montesquieu.* Paris: Éditions Montchretien, 1974.

Volpilhac-Auger, Catherine. *Tacite et Montesquieu.* Oxford: Oxford University Press, 1985.

Waddicor, Mark. *Montesquieu and the Philosophy of Natural Law.* The Hague: Martinus Nijhoff, 1970.

Wade, Ira. *The Clandestine Organization and Diffusion of Philosophic Ideas in France from 1700 to 1750.* Princeton: Princeton University Press, 1938.

Weil, Françoise. "Montesquieu et le despotisme." *Actes du congrès Montesquieu réuni à Bordeaux du 23 au 26 mai 1955 pour comémorer la deuxième centen-air de la mort de Montesquieu,* 191–215. Bordeaux: Impriméries Delmas, 1956.

Wood, Neal. "The Value of Asocial Sociability: Contributions of Machiavelli, Sidney, and Montesquieu." In *Machiavelli and the Nature of Political Thought,* edited by Martin Fleisher. New York: Atheneum, 1972.

Young, David. "Montesquieu's View of Despotism and His Use of Travel Litera-ture." *Review of Politics,* 40, no. 3 (1978): 392–405.

Zuckert, Michael. "Natural Law, Natural Rights, and Classical Liberalism: On Montesquieu's Critique of Hobbes." *Social Philosophy and Policy,* 18, no. 1 (2001): 227–251.

Works by Tocqueville

Tocqueville, Alexis de. *L'ancien régime et la révolution* (3 vols.). In vol. II of *Oeuvres complètes d'Alexis de Tocqueville,* edited by J. P. Mayer, 13 vols. Paris: Gallimard, 1951.

——— *La démocratie en Amérique* (2 vols.). In vol. I of *Oeuvres complètes d'Alexis de Tocqueville,* edited by J. P. Mayer, 13 vols. Paris: Gallimard, 1951.

Works about Tocqueville

Aron, Raymond. *Main Currents in Sociological Thought.* New York: Transaction, 1998.

Banfield, Edward C. "The Illiberal Tocqueville," In *Interpreting Tocqueville's "De-mocracy in America,"* edited by Ken Masugi. Lanham, Md.: Rowman & Lit-tlefield, 1991.

Bastid, Paul. "Tocqueville et la doctrine constitutionelle." In *Alexis de Tocque-ville: Livre du centenaire, 1859–1959.* Paris: Éditions du Centre National de la Recherche Scientifique, 1960.

Beloff, Max. "Tocqueville et l'Angleterre." In *Alexis de Tocqueville: Livre du centenaire, 1859–1959.* Paris: Éditions du Centre National de la Recherche Scientifique, 1960.

Birnbaum, Pierre. *Sociologie de Tocqueville.* Paris: Presses Universitaires de France, 1970.

Boesche, Roger. *The Strange Liberalism of Alexis de Tocqueville.* Ithaca, N.Y.: Cor-nell University Press, 1987.

Carrese, Paul O. "Judicial Statesmanship, the Jurisprudence of Individualism, and Tocqueville's Common Law Spirit." *Review of Politics,* 60, no. 3 (Sum-mer 1998): 465–496.

Ceaser, James. "Alexis de Tocqueville on Political Science, Political Culture, and the Role of the Intellectual." *American Political Science Review,* 79, no. 3 (September 1985): 656–672.

———— *Liberal Democracy and Political Science.* Baltimore: Johns Hopkins University Press, 1990.

———— "Political Science, Political Culture, and the Role of the Intellectual." In *Interpreting Tocqueville's "Democracy in America,"* edited by Ken Masugi. Lanham, Md.: Rowman & Littlefield, 1991.

Drescher, Seymour. *Dilemmas of Democracy: Tocqueville and Modernization.* Pittsburgh: University of Pittsburgh Press, 1968.

———— "Tocqueville's Two Democracies." *Journal of the History of Ideas,* 25, no. 2 (1964): 201–216.

———— "More than America: Comparison and Synthesis in *Democracy in America.*" In *Reconsidering Tocqueville's "Democracy in America,"* edited by Abraham S. Eisenstadt. New Brunswick, N.J.: Rutgers University Press, 1988.

———— *Tocqueville and England.* Cambridge: Harvard University Press, 1964.

Eichthal, Eugène de. *Alexis de Tocqueville et la démocratie libérale.* Paris: Librairie Nouvelle, 1897.

Furet, François. *Interpreting the French Revolution.* Translated by Elborg Forster. Cambridge: Cambridge University Press, 1981.

———— "Naissance d'un paradigme: Tocqueville et le voyage en Amérique (1825–1831)." *Annales Économies, Sociétés, Civilisations,* 39, no. 2 (March–April 1984): 225–239.

———— "Tocqueville est-il un historien de la Révolution française?" *Annales Économies, Sociétés, Civilisations,* 25, no. 2 (March–April 1970): 434–450.

Galston, William A. "Tocqueville on Liberalism and Religion." *Social Research,* 54, no. 3 (Autumn 1987): 499–518.

Hereth, Michael. *Alexis de Tocqueville: Threats to Freedom in Democracy.* Translated by George Bogardus. Durham: Duke University Press, 1986.

Jardin, André. *Alexis de Tocqueville, 1825–1859.* Paris: Hachette, 1984.

Kim, Sung Ho. " 'In Affirming Them, He Affirms Himself': Max Weber's Politics of Civil Society." *Political Theory,* 28, no. 2 (April 2000).

Kraynak, Robert P. "Tocqueville's Constitutionalism." *American Political Science Review,* 81, no. 4 (December 1987): 1175–1195.

Lamberti, Jean-Claude. *Tocqueville and the Two Democracies.* Translated by Arthur Goldhammer. Cambridge: Harvard University Press, 1989.

———— "Two Ways of Conceiving the Republic." In *Interpreting Tocqueville's "Democracy in America,"* edited by Ken Masugi. Lanham, Md.: Rowman & Littlefield, 1991.

Lawler, Peter Augustine. *The Restless Mind.* Lanham, Md.: Rowman & Littlefield, 1993.

Lawler, Peter Augustine, and Joseph Alulis, eds. *Tocqueville's Defense of Human Liberty*. New York: Garland, 1993.

Lefebvre, Georges. "A propos de Tocqueville." *Annales historiques de la Révolution française*, 27 (1955): 313–323.

Lively, Jack. *The Social and Political Thought of Alexis de Tocqueville*. Oxford: Clarendon, 1965.

Mahoney, Daniel J. "Tocqueville and Socialism." In *Tocqueville's Defense of Human Liberty*, edited by Peter Augustine Lawler and Joseph Alulis. New York: Garland, 1993.

Manent, Pierre. *Tocqueville and the Nature of Democracy*. Translated by John Waggoner. Princeton: Princeton University Press, 1996.

Mansfield, Harvey, and Delba Winthrop. "Introduction" to *Democracy in America*. Chicago: University of Chicago Press, 2000.

Marcel, R. Pierre. *Essai politique sur Alexis de Tocqueville*. Paris: Félix Alcan, 1910.

Mayer, J. P. *Alexis de Tocqueville*. Translated by M. M. Bozman and C. Hahn. New York: Viking, 1940.

Mélonio, Françoise. "La religion selon Tocquville: Ordre moral ou esprit de liberté?" *Études*, 360, no. 1 (January–June 1984): 73–89.

Mitchell, Joshua. *The Fragility of Freedom: Tocqueville on Religion, Democracy, and the American Future*. Chicago: University of Chicago Press, 1995.

Pierson, George Wilson. "Le 'second voyage' de Tocqueville en Amérique." In *Alexis de Tocqueville: Livre du centenaire, 1859–1959*, 71–85. Paris: Éditions du Centre National de la Recherche Scientifique, 1960.

Richter, Melvin. "The Uses of Theory: Tocqueville's Adaptation of Montesquieu." In *Essays in Theory and History*, edited by Melvin Richter. Cambridge: Harvard University Press, 1970.

Salomon, Albert. "Tocqueville's Philosophy of Freedom." *Review of Politics*, 1, no. 4 (October 1939): 400–431.

Schleifer, James T. *The Making of Tocqueville's "Democracy in America."* Chapel Hill: University of North Carolina Press, 1980.

Schlesinger, Arthur. "Individualism and Apathy in Tocqueville's *Democracy in America*." In *Reconsidering Tocqueville's "Democracy in America,"* edited by Abraham S. Eisenstadt. New Brunswick, N.J.: Rutgers University Press, 1988.

Siedentop, Larry. *Tocqueville*. Oxford: Oxford University Press, 1994.

Winthrop, Delba. "Rights: A Point of Honor." In *Interpreting Tocqueville's "Democracy in America,"* edited by Ken Masugi. Lanham, Md.: Rowman & Littlefield, 1991.

Zetterbaum, Marvin. *Tocqueville and the Problem of Democracy*. Stanford: Stanford University Press, 1967.

Zuckert, Catherine. "Not by Preaching: Tocqueville on the Role of Religion in American Democracy." *Review of Politics*, 43, no. 2 (April 1981): 259–280.

Other Works Cited

Adair, Douglass. *Fame and the Founding Fathers.* New York: Norton, 1974.

Adams, John. *Discourses on Davila.* New York: DeCapo Press, 1973.

Andrews, William L. *Critical Essays on Frederick Douglass.* Boston: G. K. Hall, 1991.

Arendt, Hannah. *The Human Condition.* Chicago: University of Chicago Press, 1958.

Aristotle. *Nicomachean Ethics.* Translated by Hippocrates G. Apostle. Grinnell, Iowa: Peripatetic Press, 1984.

———— *The Politics.* Translated by Carnes Lord. Chicago: University of Chicago Press, 1984.

Augustine. *City of God.* Translated by Henry Bettenson. New York: Penguin, 1984.

Bailyn, Bernard. *The Ideological Origins of the American Revolution.* Cambridge: Harvard University Press, 1967.

Banning, Lance. "James Madison: Memory, Service, and Fame." In *The Noblest Minds: Fame, Honor, and the American Founding,* edited by Peter McNamara. Lanham, Md.: Rowman & Littlefield, 1999.

———— *The Jeffersonian Persuasion: Evolution of a Party Ideology.* Ithaca, N.Y.: Cornell University Press, 1978.

Barry, Brian. *Justice as Impartiality.* New York: Oxford University Press, 1995.

Bayle, Pierre. *Various Thoughts on the Occasion of a Comet.* Translated by Robert C. Bartlett. Albany: SUNY Press, 1997.

Beard, Charles. *An Economic Interpretation of the Constitution of the United States.* New York: Free Press, 1986.

Beiner, Ronald, ed. *Theorizing Citizenship.* Albany: SUNY Press, 1995.

Bellah, Robert, et al. *Habits of the Heart: Idealism and Commitment in American Public Life.* Berkeley: University of California Press, 1985.

Benhabib, Seyla. *Critique, Norm, and Utopia.* New York: Columbia University Press, 1986.

Bennett, William J. *Our Sacred Honor.* New York: Simon and Schuster, 1997.

Berger, Peter. "On the Obsolescence of the Concept of Honor." In *Liberalism and Its Critics,* edited by Michael J. Sandel. New York: New York University Press, 1984.

Berkowitz, Peter. *Virtue and the Making of Modern Liberalism.* Princeton: Princeton University Press, 1999.

Bien, David. "Old Regime Origins of Democratic Liberty." In *The French Idea of Freedom: The Old Regime and the Declaration of the Rights of 1789,* edited by Dale Van Kley. Stanford: Stanford University Press, 1994.

Blight, David W. *Frederick Douglass' Civil War: Keeping Faith in Jubilee.* Baton Rouge: Louisiana State University Press, 1989.

Bloch, Marc. *Feudal Society.* 2 vols. Translated by L. A. Manyon. Chicago: University of Chicago Press, 1961.

Bradley, Martin, et al. *Churches and Church Membership in the United States.* Atlanta: Glenmary Research Center, 1992.

Brookhiser, Richard. *Founding Father.* New York: Free Press, 1996.

Brotz, Howard, ed. *African-American Social and Political Thought.* New Brunswick, N.J.: Transactions, 1995.

Burlingame, Michael. *The Inner World of Abraham Lincoln.* Urbana: University of Illinois Press, 1994.

Bush, M. L. *Noble Privilege.* Manchester: Manchester University Press, 1983.

Byrd, Robert C. *The Senate of the Roman Republic: Addresses on the History of Roman Constitutionalism.* Washington, D.C.: U.S. Government Printing Office, 1995.

Ceaser, James W. "Fame and the Federalist." In *The Noblest Minds: Fame, Honor, and the American Founding,* edited by Peter McNamara. Lanham, Md.: Rowman & Littlefield, 1999.

Charnwood, Lord. *Abraham Lincoln.* Garden City, N.Y.: Garden City Pub. Co., 1938.

Chaussinand-Nogaret, Guy. *La noblesse au XVIIIe siècle: De la féodalité aux lumières.* Paris: Librairie Hachette, 1976.

Chong, Dennis. *Collective Action and the Civil Rights Movement.* Chicago: University of Chicago Press, 1991.

Dewald, Jonathan. *The European Nobility, 1400–1800.* Cambridge: Cambridge University Press, 1996.

Digeser, Peter. *Our Politics, Our Selves?* Princeton: Princeton University Press, 1995.

Donald, David Herbert. *Lincoln.* New York: Touchstone, 1995.

Douglass, Frederick. *Frederick Douglass: Selected Speeches and Writings.* Edited by Philip S. Foner. Chicago: Lawrence Hill, 1999.

———— *The Frederick Douglass Papers.* Edited by John Blassingame. New Haven: Yale University Press, 1979–1992.

———— *The Life and Writing of Frederick Douglass.* Edited by Philip S. Foner. New York: International, 1975.

———— *My Bondage and My Freedom.* New York: Dover, 1969.

———— *Narrative of the Life of Frederick Douglass.* New York: Dolphin, 1963.

DuBois, Ellen Carol. *Elizabeth Cady Stanton, Susan B. Anthony: Correspondence, Writings, Speeches.* New York: Schocken, 1981.

Du Bois, W. E. B. *The Souls of Black Folk.* New York: Bantam, 1989.

Elshtain, Jean. *Democracy on Trial.* New York: Basic Books, 1995.

Epstein, David F. *The Political Theory of "The Federalist."* Chicago: University of Chicago Press, 1984.

Etzioni, Amitai. *The Spirit of Community: Rights, Responsibilities, and the Communitarian Agenda.* New York: Crown, 1993.

Fehrenbacher, Don E. *Prelude to Greatness: Lincoln in the 1850's.* Stanford: Stanford University Press, 1962.

Friedman, Jeffrey, ed. *The Rational Choice Controversy.* New Haven: Yale University Press, 1996.

Fukuyama, Francis. *Trust: The Social Virtues and the Creation of Prosperity.* London: Penguin, 1996.

Galston, William. *Liberal Purposes: Goods, Virtues, and Diversity in the Liberal State.* Cambridge: Cambridge University Press, 1991.

Garrow, David J. *Bearing the Cross.* New York: Quill, 1986.

Genicot, Léopold. *La noblesse dans l'Occident médiéval.* London: Variorum Reprints, 1982.

Glendon, Mary Ann, and David Blankenhorn, eds. *Seedbeds of Virtue: Sources of Competence, Character, and Citizenship in American Society.* Lanham, Md.: Madison Books, 1995.

Greenberg, Kenneth S. *Masters and Statesmen.* Baltimore: Johns Hopkins University Press, 1985.

———— *Honor and Slavery.* Princeton: Princeton University Press, 1996.

Griffin, Elizabeth. *In Her Own Right.* New York: Oxford University Press, 1984.

Hamilton, Alexander, James Madison, and John Jay. *The Federalist Papers.* Edited by Clinton Rossiter. New York: Mentor, 1961.

Hegel, G. W. F. *Philosophy of Right.* Translated by T. M. Knox. Oxford: Oxford University Press, 1967.

Hobbes, Thomas. *Leviathan.* Edited by Edwin Curley. Indianapolis: Hackett, 1994.

Ignatieff, Michael. *The Warrior's Honor: Ethnic War and the Modern Conscience.* New York: Henry Holt, 1997.

Jaffa, Harry V. *Crisis of the House Divided.* Garden City, N.Y.: Doubleday, 1959.

Johnson, Lyman L., and Sonya Lipsett-Rivera. *The Faces of Honor: Sex, Shame, and Violence in Colonial Latin America.* Albuquerque: University of New Mexico Press, 1998.

Kennedy, John F. *Profiles in Courage.* New York: Harper & Row, 1964.

Kesler, Charles R., ed. *Saving the Revolution.* New York: Free Press, 1987.

King, Martin Luther, Jr. *Testament of Hope: The Essential Writings and Speeches of Martin Luther King, Jr.* Edited by James M. Washington. New York: Harper-Collins, 1986.

———— *Why We Can't Wait.* New York: Harper & Row, 1964.

King, Richard H. *Civil Rights and the Idea of Freedom.* New York: Oxford University Press, 1992.

Kinneging, Andreas A. M. *Aristocracy, Antiquity, and History.* New Brunswick, N.J.: Transactions, 1997.

Kitto, H. D. F. *The Greeks.* Baltimore: Penguin, 1966.

Krause, Sharon. "Partial Justice." *Political Theory* 29, no. 3 (June 2001): 316–336.

Kristol, William. "Ambition and the Separation of Powers." In *Saving the Revolution,* edited by Charles Kesler. New York: Free Press, 1987.

Kunhardt, Philip B., et al. *The American President.* New York: Riverhead Books, 1999.

Labatut, Jean-Pierre. *Les noblesses européennes de la fin du XVe siècle à la fin du XVIIIe siècle.* Paris: Presses Universitaires de France, 1978.

Larmore, Charles. *The Morals of Modernity.* Cambridge: Cambridge University Press, 1996.

Lawson, Bill E., and Frank M. Kirkland, eds. *Frederick Douglass: A Critical Reader.* Oxford: Blackwell, 1999.

Lerner, Gerda, ed. *The Female Experience: An American Documentary.* Indianapolis: Bobbs-Merrill, 1977.

Lewis, David L. *King: A Critical Biography.* New York: Praeger, 1970.

Liebman, Robert C., and Robert Wuthnow, eds. *The New Christian Right.* New York: Aldine, 1983.

Lincoln, Abraham. *Abraham Lincoln: Speeches and Writings, 1832–1858.* Edited by Don E. Fehrenbacher. New York: Library of America, 1989.

——— *Speeches and Writings, 1859–1865.* Edited by Don E. Fehrenbacher. New York: Library of America, 1989.

Lischer, Richard. *The Preacher King.* New York: Oxford University Press, 1995.

Locke, John. *Two Treatises of Government.* Edited by Peter Laslett. Cambridge: Cambridge University Press, 1960.

Macedo, Stephen. *Liberal Virtues: Citizenship, Virtue, and Community in Liberal Constitutionalism.* Oxford: Clarendon Press, 1991.

Machiavelli, Niccolò. *Discourses on Livy.* Translated by Harvey C. Mansfield, Jr., and Nathan Tarcov. Chicago: University of Chicago Press, 1996.

——— *The Prince.* Translated by Harvey C. Mansfield, Jr. Chicago: University of Chicago Press, 1985.

MacIntyre, Alasdair. *After Virtue.* Notre Dame: University of Notre Dame Press, 1984.

Mansfield, Harvey C., Jr. *America's Constitutional Soul.* Baltimore: Johns Hopkins University Press, 1991.

Martin, Waldo E., Jr. *The Mind of Frederick Douglass.* Chapel Hill: University of North Carolina Press, 1984.

McNamara, Peter, ed. *The Noblest Minds: Fame, Honor, and the American Founding.* Lanham, Md.: Rowman & Littlefield, 1999.

McPherson, James M. *Abraham Lincoln and the Second American Revolution.* New York: Oxford University Press, 1990.

——— *For Causes and Comrades: Why Men Fought in the Civil War.* New York: Oxford University Press, 1997.

Meyer, Jean. *La noblesse française à l'époque moderne (XVIe–XVIIIe siècle).* Paris: Presses Universitaires de France, 1991.

Mills, Charles W. "Whose Fourth of July? Frederick Douglass and 'Original Intent.' " In *Frederick Douglass: A Critical Reader,* edited by Bill E. Lawson and Frank M. Kirkland. Oxford: Blackwell Publishers, 1999.

Miroff, Bruce. *Icons of Democracy.* Lawrence: University Press of Kansas, 2000.

Moore, J. M., trans. *Aristotle and Xenophon on Democracy and Oligarchy.* Berkeley: University of California Press, 1975.

Moses, William. "Where Honor Is Due: Frederick Douglass as Representative Black Man." *Prospects,* 17 (1992): 177–189.

Myers, Peter C. *Our Only Star and Compass: Locke and the Struggle for Political Rationality.* Lanham, Md.: Rowman & Littlefield, 1998.

Nagel, Thomas. *The View from Nowhere.* Oxford: Oxford University Press, 1986.

Neely, Mark. *The Last Best Hope of Earth.* Cambridge: Harvard University Press, 1993.

Nehemas, Alexander. *Nietzsche: Life as Literature.* Cambridge: Harvard University Press, 1985.

Nussbaum, Martha. *Aristotle's De Motu Animalium.* Princeton: Princeton University Press, 1985.

Nye, Robert A. *Masculinity and Male Codes of Honor in Modern France.* New York: Oxford University Press, 1993.

Oates, Stephen B. *Abraham Lincoln: The Man behind the Myths.* New York: Harper & Row, 1984.

——— *Let the Trumpet Sound: A Life of Martin Luther King, Jr.* New York: HarperPerennial, 1994.

——— *Our Fiery Trial.* Amherst: University of Massachusetts Press, 1979.

——— *With Malice toward None: A Life of Abraham Lincoln.* New York: HarperPerennial, 1994.

Pangle, Lorraine Smith, and Thomas L. Pangle. *The Learning of Liberty: The Educational Ideas of the American Founders.* Lawrence: University Press of Kansas, 1993.

——— "George Washington and the Life of Honor." In *The Noblest Minds: Fame, Honor, and the American Founding,* edited by Peter McNamara. Lanham, Md.: Rowman & Littlefield, 1999.

Pangle, Thomas L. "The Political Psychology of Religion in Plato's *Laws.*" *American Political Science Review,* 70, no. 4 (December 1976): 1059–1077.

——— "Classical and Modern Liberal Understandings of Honor." In *The No-*

blest Minds: Fame, Honor, and the American Founding, edited by Peter McNamara. Lanham, Md.: Rowman & Littlefield, 1999.

Peristiany, J. G. Honor and Shame. Chicago: University of Chicago Press, 1966.

Pitkin, Hanna. "Justice: On Relating Private and Public," Political Theory, 9, no. 3 (August 1981): 327–352.

Plato. Republic. Translated by Allan Bloom. New York: Basic Books, 1968.

Plutarch. Lives of the Noble Greeks and Romans. Translated by John Dryden. New York: Modern Library, 1932.

Putnam, Robert. "Bowling Alone: America's Declining Social Capital." Journal of Democracy, 6 (January 1995): 65–78.

Rahe, Paul A. "Famous Founders and the Idea of Founding." In The Noblest Minds: Fame, Honor, and the American Founding, edited by Peter McNamara. Lanham, Md.: Rowman & Littlefield, 1999.

——— Republics Ancient and Modern. Chapel Hill: University of North Carolina Press, 1992.

Rawls, John. A Theory of Justice. Cambridge: Harvard University Press, 1971.

——— Political Liberalism. New York: Columbia University Press, 1993.

Richelet, R., ed. Dictionnaire François. Geneva: Jean Herman Widerhold, 1680.

Roof, Wade Clark, and William McKinney. American Mainline Religion: Its Changing Shape and Future. New Brunswick, N.J.: Rutgers University Press, 1987.

Rousseau, Jean-Jacques. The First and Second Discourses. Translated by Victor Gourevitch. New York: Harper & Row, 1986.

Sabl, Andrew. Ruling Passions: Political Offices and Democratic Ethics. Princeton: Princeton University Press, 2002.

Sandel, Michael J. Democracy's Discontent: America in Search of a Public Philosophy. Cambridge: Harvard University Press, 1996.

——— Liberalism and the Limits of Justice. Cambridge: Cambridge University Press, 1982.

Scanlon, T. M. What We Owe to Each Other. Cambridge: Harvard University Press, 1998.

Schaub, Diana. "Frederick Douglass's Constitution." In The American Experiment: Essays on the Theory and Practice of Liberty, edited by Peter Augustine Lawler and Robert Martin Schaefer. Lanham, Md.: Rowman & Littlefield, 1994.

Schrader, David E. "Natural Law in the Constitutional Thought of Frederick Douglas." In Frederick Douglass: A Critical Reader, edited by Bill E. Lawson and Frank M. Kirkland. Oxford: Blackwell Publishers, 1999.

Shibley, Mark A. Resurgent Evangelicalism in the United States. Columbia: University of South Carolina Press, 1996.

Sinopoli, Richard C., ed. *From Many One: Readings in American Political and Social Thought.* Washington, D.C.: Georgetown University Press, 1997.

Stanton, Elizabeth Cady. *Eighty Years and More: Reminiscences, 1815–1897.* New York: T. Fischer Unwin, 1898.

―――― *The Woman's Bible.* Boston: Northeastern University Press, 1993.

Stevens, William Oliver. *Pistols at Ten Paces: The Story of the Code of Honor in America.* Boston: Houghton Mifflin, 1940.

Stewart, Frank Henderson. *Honor.* Chicago: University of Chicago Press, 1994.

Storing, Herbert. "Frederick Douglass." In *American Political Thought,* edited by Morton Frisch and Richard Stevens. Itasca, Ill.: F. E. Peacock, 1983.

Taylor, Charles. "The Politics of Recognition." In *Multiculturalism,* edited by Amy Gutmann. Princeton: Princeton University Press, 1994.

―――― *Sources of the Self.* Cambridge: Harvard University Press, 1989.

―――― "What Is Human Agency?" In *Human Agency and Language.* Cambridge: Cambridge University Press, 1985.

Tessitore, Aristide. *Reading Aristotle's Ethics.* Albany: SUNY Press, 1996.

Thompson, C. Bradley. "John Adams and the Quest for Fame." In *The Noblest Minds: Fame, Honor, and the American Founding,* edited by Peter McNamara. Lanham, Md.: Rowman & Littlefield, 1999.

Van Kley, Dale. *The French Idea of Freedom: The Old Regime and the Declaration of the Rights of 1789.* Stanford: Stanford University Press, 1994.

Walzer, Michael. *Obligations.* Cambridge: Harvard University Press, 1970.

―――― *Spheres of Justice.* New York: Basic Books, 1983.

Watters, Pat. *Down to Now.* New York: Pantheon, 1971.

White, Leonard. *The Federalist.* New York: Macmillan, 1948.

Will, George F. *Statecraft as Soulcraft.* New York: Simon and Schuster, 1983.

Wilson, Douglas L. *Honor's Voice.* New York: Knopf, 1998.

Winthrop, Delba. "Aristotle and Theories of Justice." *American Political Science Review,* 72 (1978): 1201–1216.

Wood, Gordon S. *The Creation of the American Republic, 1776–1787.* Chapel Hill: University of North Carolina Press, 1969.

Wyatt-Brown, Bertram. *Southern Honor: Ethics and Behavior in the Old South.* Oxford: Oxford University Press, 1982.

―――― *Yankee Saints and Southern Sinners.* Baton Rouge: Louisiana State University Press, 1985.

Yack, Bernard. "Natural Right and Aristotle's Understanding of Justice." *Political Theory,* 18, no. 2 (May 1990): 216–237.

Yarbrough, Jean. *American Virtues: Thomas Jefferson on the Character of a Free People.* Lawrence: University Press of Kansas, 1998.

Index

Adair, Douglas, 101–102, 104, 105
Adams, John, 25, 102, 103, 110, 125
Advocacy groups, 182
Agency: and the teleology of honor, 6–7, 38, 64, 136; and self-respect versus self-esteem, 9; extraordinary exertions of, 12, 177; contrasted with the ideal of intrinsic dignity, 16, 147–148; and importance of principles, 20, 82, 151; and recognition, 20, 65; limits of current thinking on, 23, 31, 180, 189; tied to ambition and distinction, 25, 65, 158, 177; external conditions of, 27, 130–131, 167; and "action" in Arendt, 46; tied to reverence and reflexivity, 53, 55–56, 65; dangers of, 62; and political liberty in Tocqueville, 70; versus "impersonal forces," 70, 96, 117–118, 128, 156, 160; and individualism in Tocqueville, 75; and pride, 87, 167; and associational life in Tocqueville, 92; and materialism, 94; and self-interest in Locke's right of resistance, 111; and self-government in *The Federalist,* 117–118; honor as incomplete account of, 127; and honor in Du Bois, 145; and fear, 176
Altruism, 10, 11, 29, 30, 44, 103
Ambition: as a component of honor, 14, 24, 43–47, 67, 133, 169, 179; ambition counteracting ambition, 22, 24, 43, 48, 59, 114; tied to principled higher purposes, 23, 28, 31, 64, 99, 145, 158, 161, 173; as engine of agency, 25, 32, 64; as self-concern, 38, 59; ambition to subjugate, 49; great ambitions in Tocqueville, 87–89, 92, 100, 101, 189; and religion in Tocqueville, 94; tied to common interest in *The Federalist,* 115–116; of early suffragists, 164–166; conflict with civic virtue, 183

American founders, 8, 14, 25, 26, 42, 100–120, 131, 134, 138, 139, 153, 167, 174
Amour-propre and *amour de soi,* 38, 60
Anthony, Susan B., 159–168. *See also* Stanton, Elizabeth Cady
Arendt, Hannah, 46
Aristocracy: and aristocratic sources of liberalism, 17, 21, 22–23, 28, 31, 32, 71, 75, 84, 85, 90–92, 95, 100, 129, 132, 181, 189; in the old regime, 24, 26, 39–43, 48, 65, 82, 100, 116, 118, 128–129; and natural aristocracy of honorable individuals, 29, 90, 100, 181, 185
Aristotle, 6, 23, 33, 36, 50–51, 52, 58, 136
Autonomy, 3, 4, 55, 56

Beard, Charles, 101
Burr, Aaron, 105–106

Chastity and honor, 72, 159
Civic republicanism. *See* Communitarianism and civic republicanism
Civic virtue. *See* Virtue
Civil disobedience and conscientious objection, 22, 24, 26, 32, 49, 57, 116, 173, 175, 188
Civil rights movement, 171–179
Civil society, 27, 180, 182, 183, 184
Civil War, 124, 126, 137
Codes of honor: as structural feature of honor, 2, 32; and the honor code, 3–6; as source of independence from public opinion and political authorities, 20, 62–63, 106; variance of, 23, 64; illiberal, unjust codes, 25, 127, 131; in old regime contrasted with American codes, 27, 42, 99, 107–108, 124; and Declaration of Independence as a common code in United

Codes of honor (*continued*)
States, 27, 98, 107, 139, 174, 180; and multiplicity of particular codes in United States, 27, 98, 180, 183, 185; subject to scrutiny of reason, 28, 109; as a basis for self-respect, 30, 47; as general rules of conduct, 30; eighteenth-century codes contrasted with Christian creed, 42; social-historical foundations of, 47–48, 56; reverence for, 47–50, 56, 64, 76, 139, 174–175, 188; as limit on and guide of action, 49–50, 51, 64, 88, 106, 109; in democracy, 73; in antebellum South, 121–122, 124, 126–127
Commercial honor, 72, 78, 79, 81
Communitarianism and civic republicanism, 9. *See also* Virtue
Compassion, 82, 83–84, 90
Conscience, 28, 30, 99, 103, 106, 124, 125, 158
Constitution, 12, 107, 112, 142, 150, 164, 181, 188
"Constitutional Argument," 164
Constitutional government, 8, 21, 38, 42, 59, 115, 120, 127, 129, 131, 136, 149, 187
Corruptions of honor, 52, 66, 104, 123
Courage, 24, 29, 41–42, 44–45, 51, 67, 97, 100, 132, 145; and political courage, 26, 125, 137, 148, 149–150, 160–161, 175–176

Declaration of Human Rights. *See* United Nations Universal Declaration of Human Rights
Declaration of Independence: honor in, 1, 97, 104, 120, 145; as American code of honor, 25, 27, 98, 107, 174, 180, 181, 186; and universal principles of right, 99, 124; and reform, 104; and assertion of honorable self-rule, 104, 120; rejection of, in the antebellum South, 126; and Lincoln's ambition, 133–134, 137–139, 140, 141; and Frederick Douglass, 150–151; and Du Bois, 158; and ambition of suffragists, 161, 162, 164, 166
Declaration of Sentiments (Stanton), 162–163, 164
Democracy, modern: dangers of, 1, 68–70; tensions with honor, 67, 73–78, 86, 95,

96; logic of, 69–70, 80; greater justice in, 82–83
Democratic leadership, 119
Democratic self-rule and honor, 15, 27, 96, 110–111, 116, 117, 120, 128, 129, 156, 167
Desert: in regard to honor and fame, 63, 105, 109; and self-respect, 101, 109, 182–183
Desire, as source of agency, 4, 23, 31, 58
Despotism: mild despotism, 24, 67, 69–70, 80, 100; in Montesquieu, 34, 43, 59, 60, 84
Dichotomization of self-interest and self-sacrifice, 11, 23, 31, 102, 135, 173, 180, 184, 189
Dignity, 13, 15, 16, 19, 20, 22, 85, 93, 99, 116–117, 146–147, 148, 172, 176, 178
Distinction, public: desire for, as component of honor, 14, 23, 30, 47, 59, 67, 132; as mark of achievement, 16; desire for, as motive for political resistance, 32; desire for, as form of self-concern, 38; and voluntary associations as sites for, 92; contra collectivism, 95; and the American founders, 97–112; desire for, balanced with principles, 106, 109; worthiness of, 109, 183; desire for, exaggerated in antebellum South, 123, 125; basis of, in public opinion, 155; resentment of, 155, 172–173; desire for, in suffragists, 161; desire for, in Martin Luther King, Jr., 171
Diversity, 9. *See also* Pluralism
Domestic virtues and honor, 166
Douglass, Frederick, 12, 26, 130–131, 132, 142, 145–158, 168, 174; and resistance to slavery, 145–150; courage of, 148, 151–152; moderation of, 149, 157; and principled ambition of, 150–153; pride of, 151, 156, 158; and political leadership of, 152–154, 157; and the love of fame, 153–158
Dred Scott decision, 137
Du Bois, W. E. B., 144–145, 158
Duels, 25, 111, 123–124, 125, 131, 147, 150
Duty: to oneself, xi, 5, 11, 14, 24, 29, 30, 45, 54, 67, 90, 95, 99–100, 121, 132, 161, 162, 169, 179, 184, 189; to others, 10

Eccentricity of honor, 55–56
Education of honor, 2, 54

Emancipation Proclamation (1863), 135, 140, 142

Equality, and honor, 28, 73–74, 75, 84, 86, 95, 96, 103, 115, 119, 121, 122, 123, 150, 156, 182, 185

Equipment of honor, 26–27, 57, 65, 128–129, 130–131, 144, 156, 170

Extremism, 38, 59, 62, 63, 143, 167–168

Fame, love of, 25, 74, 101–106, 108, 112, 115, 148, 153, 154, 157, 161

Families, 182

Fear, 34; of death, 128, 147–148, 175–176

Federalist Papers, 26, 104, 110, 112–117

Feudalism. *See* Old regime

Freedom schools, 176

French Revolution, xi–xii, 1, 13, 14, 17, 32

Gambling and gift giving, 130

General will, 29, 33, 37; and public interest, 35

Hamilton, Alexander, 25, 102, 103, 104, 105, 106, 108, 110, 111, 113, 114, 115, 116, 124, 154

Hegel, G. W. F., 62

Heroic action, xii, 7, 12, 67, 80, 108, 119, 135, 154

Hierarchy, 13, 25, 74, 98, 115, 157, 181; entrenched in old regime, 65, 66, 82; in antebellum South, 120–121, 122

Hobbes, Thomas, 7, 11, 35, 38, 46, 53, 59–60, 110, 111

Honnête homme, 22, 27, 29, 41, 42, 48, 60, 77, 98, 100, 159, 186

Honor: obsolescence of, xi, 1, 14, 15, 20–21; definition of, 2, 23, 71; of human race, 15, 116–118, 156, 167; empirical studies of, 21; false honor, 23, 24, 51, 105, 108; history and, 53, 159; volatility of, 79, 110–112, 120, 126, 139–140, 143, 178; limits of, 109

Human nature. *See* Nature: human

Human rights. *See* United Nations Universal Declaration of Human Rights

Humility, 86, 87

Identity, 14

Illiberal forms of honor, 7, 25, 127, 131

Impersonal forces, and effects on individual agency, 70, 96, 117–118, 128, 156, 160

Independence of mind, 76, 94

Individualism, 74–77, 80, 94

Instrumental reasoning contrasted with honor, 29–30, 81–82, 88, 176–177

Instrumental value of honor, 51, 72

Intermediary associations: in modern democracy, 18, 27, 71, 75, 84, 90–92, 95, 98, 114, 180, 181, 182, 183, 185; in the old regime, 27, 32, 38–39, 57

Jail, as a badge of honor, 177

Jefferson, Thomas, 25, 102, 103, 105, 110, 116, 118, 121, 124, 125, 126, 161, 173

Judiciary, American, 88–89, 90

Justice: and honor, 6–7, 25, 45, 50, 109, 114, 115, 127, 136; to oneself, 106–107, 122, 166; and freedom in the civil rights movement, 178

Kansas-Nebraska Act (1854), 134

Kant, Immanuel, 3, 4, 11, 55, 82, 109

Kennedy, John F., 135

King, Martin Luther, Jr., 1, 16, 19, 26, 119, 132, 168–179, 185, 186; humble persona of, 169; pride of, 169–170, 172; background of, 170–171; resentment toward, 171–177; principles of, 173–174; courage of, 175–176; self-respect and, 176–177; moderation of, 178–179

Law, rule of. *See* Constitutional government

Liberal democracy, 7, 10, 12, 13, 18, 21, 32, 108, 135, 146, 181, 183

Liberty: and individual liberties, 9, 12, 22, 27, 33, 47, 58, 68, 86, 116, 125, 131, 136, 189; love of, 67, 81, 89–90, 93, 100, 108, 147–148, 150, 165, 175–176

Lincoln, Abraham: 12, 126, 101–102, 119, 132, 144, 153, 154, 161, 174, 179, 184, 186; principled ambition of, 132–136, 141; courage of, 137; moderation of, 139–144; prejudice of, 141–142; self-made status of, 144

Locke, John, 7, 11, 53, 111

Machiavelli, 11, 35, 48–49, 50

Madison, James, ix, xi, 8, 11, 25, 102, 103, 104, 112, 114, 115, 124

Magnanimity, 33, 50–51, 52, 136

Majority tyranny, ix, xi, 1, 8, 24, 67, 68, 69–70, 76, 80, 84, 86, 190

Martial valor, 26, 41, 42–43, 125, 137, 159, 162, 175

Marx, Karl, 118

Masculinity and honor, 159, 160

Mastery, and honor, 25, 79, 93, 120, 128, 129, 130, 147, 148

Materialism, 77–78, 80–81, 88, 93–94, 101–102, 165

Moderation, 92, 120, 139–144

Modern man, 13, 14, 30

Monarchy in Montesquieu, 38, 43, 49, 52, 56, 98, 107, 108

Montesquieu, Charles-Louis de Secondat, Baron de la Brède and de: on the abuse of power, 8; on altruism, 11; idea of honor, 14, 21–24, 32–66, 103, 107, 111, 136, 159, 188; on political resistance of nobility, 26, 100, 111, 114, 116; and the *honnête homme,* 27, 98, 159, 186; approval of false honor of, 51–52, 105, 108, 181; influence on Tocqueville, 68; and the multiplicity of honor codes, 98, 180, 186; on extremism, 143

Montgomery bus boycott, 171, 173, 177

Moral goodness, 6–7, 50

Moral psychology, 11, 21, 26, 31, 85

Mores, 84, 94–95

Motivations, 9, 14, 16, 31, 38, 58, 102, 108, 127, 176–177, 180, 187, 189

Nature: human, 14, 18, 21, 52–53, 146; as a limit, contested by honor, 26, 79, 118, 156, 160; as a standard, 48, 52–53

Nobility, in old regime. *See* Aristocracy

Noble action, 7

Normative political theory, 9, 180

Obedience, 53–54, 63

Obligation, rule-governed versus virtue-centered, 4. *See also* Duty

Old regime, 14, 18, 25, 27, 30, 32, 70, 98, 103, 107, 120, 122, 123, 128, 180

Orte, Vicomte d', 44–45, 46, 48, 49, 50, 53, 54, 57, 61, 63, 100, 111, 159, 184, 188

Parks, Rosa, 2, 10, 17

Parlements, 39, 63

Partiality, 28, 34, 45, 57–61, 65, 108, 109, 173, 189

Passions, 14, 23, 34, 86, 109, 110, 189

Physical prowess and honor, 26, 40–41, 125, 126, 148, 160

Planter class of the antebellum South, 27, 99, 120, 130

Pluralism, 36, 37, 63, 64, 98, 182, 186

Plurality of forms of honor, 38, 72, 98, 180, 182, 186–187

Plutarch, 110

Political participation, 33, 67, 79, 111, 116, 183

Political parties, 182

Political reform and honor, 26, 27, 104–105, 132–180

Political resistance. *See* Resistance

Power: encroaching nature of, 8, 190; love of, 110–111, 144

Prejudice, 44, 57–58

Pride: and democratic honor, 29, 100; scorn of Hobbes for, contrasted with Montesquieu, 59–60; and agency in Tocqueville, 86–88; and self-respect, 87; and virtue, 87, 118; and great ambitions, 92; and the American founders, 103, 114, 118–119; and Douglass, 156; and suffragists, 166–167; and Martin Luther King, Jr., 170, 171, 172–173

Principles, as key feature of honor. *See* Codes of honor

Public opinion: as basis for self-respect, 20, 154; decent regard for, 62, 142, 143; power of, 67, 76, 86, 161, 183

Rank, 46–47, 123

Rational choice theory, 9, 11

Rawls, John, 18–19, 182, 185; and the sense of justice, xi, 9, 10, 11, 185

Reactionary quality of honor disputed, 104–105, 132, 139

Reason, 58–59, 109, 127; as reflexivity, 55–56, 63, 64, 139; limits of, 58, 110, 188; and the justification of honor codes, 58–59, 187–188; and agency, 109–110, 188–189

Recognition, 19–20, 23, 26, 27, 30, 46, 47, 54, 61–64, 104, 121, 122, 156, 157–158, 179, 185, 186

Reform. *See* Political reform and honor

Religion, 8, 71, 88, 90, 93–95
Representation, 114, 115
Republican government in Montesquieu, 34, 54
Resistance: necessity of in liberal democracy, ix, 1, 8–9, 190; in Montesquieu, 23, 33, 56, 100, 116, 125; to powers of nature, circumstance, and tyranny, 27, 118, 156; and democratic reform, 28, 100, 116; honor as a source of, 47; and recognition, 61–64; and disjunction between honor and recognition, 63; tied to reverence and reflexivity, 64, 188; in Tocqueville, 68, 86, 90; and insufficiency of self-interest as a motive for, 111; and right of resistance in Locke, 111; and the American founders, 116; of Douglass to slavery, 145–150; of the slave Nelly, 160; of suffragists, 161; of Martin Luther King, Jr., 169, 174, 179
Reverence, 23, 28, 63, 64, 116, 139, 158, 174–175; and reflexivity, 23, 34, 47–56, 65, 76–77, 188–189
Right and Left in American politics, 25, 30–31, 104–105
Rights, x, 18, 27, 32, 79, 90, 92–93, 95, 116, 129, 144, 163–164, 181; natural rights, 105, 107, 108, 126–127, 133, 174
Roles. *See* Social roles
Rousseau, Jean-Jacques, 20, 60

Scanlon, T. M., and agreement motive, xi, 9, 10, 11
Security, 81
Self-esteem, 18–19, 20, 185
Self-interest: contrasted with honor, xi, 29–30, 33, 44, 55, 59, 90, 95, 108, 111, 112–113; and rational choice theory, 9; opposed to obligations to others, 11, 23, 95, 101; self-interest well understood, 33, 78–82, 84; insufficiency of, as a source of agency, 111, 176, 177
Self-respect, 14, 18–19, 20, 24, 30, 54, 67, 87, 107, 108, 132, 147, 154, 155, 156, 157, 158, 161, 166, 169, 176, 177, 179, 183, 186
Self-sacrifice, 34–35, 63
Self-sovereignty, 26, 159, 161–162, 164, 172
Seneca Falls Women's Rights Convention (1848), 162

Separation of powers, 9, 18, 22, 32, 33, 38, 39, 49, 60, 65, 66, 112, 113–114, 115, 181
Sévigné, Madame de, 82
Skepticism, 23, 36, 37, 53
Slavery, 25, 83, 120–121, 126, 127, 128–131, 137–138, 140, 142, 143, 148, 150
Social capital, 183
Social mobility and effects on honor, 73, 75, 174
Social roles, 13–14, 15, 181
Southern honor, 25, 99, 120–131; contrasted with Northern honor, 124
Stanton, Elizabeth Cady, 1, 12, 26, 132, 159–168, 172, 184; and courage of, 160–162; and principles of, 161, 162–164; and ambition of, 161, 164–166; and pride of, 166–167
States' rights, 129–130
Status, 13, 14, 15, 25, 28, 121, 123, 131, 144, 181
Student Nonviolent Coordinating Committee (SNCC), 172, 176

Taylor, Charles, 15, 19–20, 182, 185
Teleology: of honor, 6–7, 38; of ancients, 23, 36, 37
Thymos, 58, 110
Tocqueville, Alexis de: and the variability of honor, 14, 72; and aristocratic sources of liberalism, 18, 31; and honor in American democracy, 24–25, 67–96, 107, 108, 109, 174; and political resistance of the nobility, 26, 27, 98, 114, 116; and the need for high ambitions, 47, 100, 86–90, 121, 165, 166, 175; and "impersonal forces," 70, 117; and self-interest well understood, 78–85; and love of liberty, 89–90; and associations, 90, 92, 183; and rights, 92–93; and religion, 94–95
Tradition, 46–47, 49–50, 52, 53, 75–76, 88

Uniformity, 61
United Nations Universal Declaration of Human Rights, 15, 16
Unity, 59, 60–61, 63
Universalism, 15, 17, 27, 28, 42, 44, 57, 73, 82, 83–84, 99, 107, 108, 182, 186, 187
Usbek, 60
Utility, 81

Virtue: contrasted with honor, 4–5, 24, 30, 45, 50–52, 108; ancient moral virtue, 6, 23; liberal virtues, 9, 10, 11; civic virtue, 9, 11, 13, 24, 33, 44, 67, 68, 95, 98, 106, 116, 120, 183, 185; political virtue in Montesquieu, 33, 34, 35–38, 54, 61, 63; Christian virtue in Montesquieu, 35–38; virtue and rights in Tocqueville, 93; virtue and *The Federalist,* 112–116
Vocational associations and honor, 182
Voluntary associations. *See* Intermediary associations

Walzer, Michael, 182–184, 186
Washington, Booker T., 145, 152, 153, 156, 158
Washington, George, 12, 25, 102, 103, 105, 106, 107, 110, 116, 119–120, 124, 125, 133, 154, 161, 166
Women and honor, 159–161
Women's rights, 162–164, 166
Work and honor, 72